Introduction to Criminology

Sixth Edition

Hugh D. Barlow
Southern Illinois University, Edwardsville

HarperCollins*CollegePublishers*

To the memory of my father,
Bill Barlow

Acquisitions Editor: Alan McClare
Project Coordination and Text Design: York Production Services
Cover Design: Kay Petronio
Production/Manufacturing: Michael Weinstein/Paula Keller
Compositor: York Production Services
Printer and Binder: R.R. Donnelley & Sons Company
Cover Printer: The Lehigh Press, Inc.

Library of Congress Cataloging-in-Publication Data

Barlow, Hugh D.
    Introduction to criminology / Hugh D. Barlow.—6th ed.
        p.   cm.
    Includes bibliographical references and index.

    ISBN 0-673-52265-2
    1. Criminology.   2. Criminal justice, Administration of.
    I. Title.
HV6025.B29, 1993   92-34178
    364'.0973—dc20   CIP
92 93 94 95   9 8 7 6 5 4 3 2 1

Brief Contents

CONTENTS

PART

II   Doing Crime   85

3   Murder and Assault   87

7 Occupational Crime   219

8 Organized Crime   265

17   General Theories of Crime   569

Preface

My goal in writing the original edition of *Introduction to Criminology* was to make a difficult subject accessible to beginning students without glossing over its complexities and controversies. Furthermore, I felt that contemporary texts did a poor job of illustrating how history and societal reactions help shape the criminal activities of our times, and vice versa. It seemed to me that the students were also being short-changed on the very thing that interested them most—what actually goes on when people do crime. The original edition sought to correct these deficiencies.

Over the years each edition has retained the emphasis on history, societal reactions, and the doing of crime, yet each revision has incorporated substantial amounts of new information. Colleagues who have continued to teach from this text over the years have expected each edition to be a comprehensive, up-to-date, and well-referenced introduction to the field that is also interesting and challenging to students.

The sixth edition maintains the strengths of the previous editions but also incorporates a significant change in organization, one that I believe students especially will appreciate. The chapters discussing criminological theories in detail have been moved to the back of the book. This change is not meant to demean theory—in fact quite the opposite. It is now my belief, based on feedback from instructors and students, that the lessons of theory are best learned after students have had an opportunity to learn about the crime scene and the methods of criminological research; only then can they appreciate how theories are applied to particular crime problems—murder, say, or sneak theft, or punishment. At the very least, readers have a better understanding of what it is that criminological theories are trying to explain.

The discussion of theory has in fact been expanded in this edition. An entirely new chapter (17) has been added that discusses recent attempts to construct a general theory of crime. Periodically since the 1960s there have been claims that criminological theory is engulfed in darkness—plenty of heat, certainly, but no new light. Suddenly, it seems, along come important contributions to the century-long search for a general theory of crime, the first published in 1985, the most recent in 1990. Chapter 17 discusses the contributions of Wilson and Herrnstein; Cohen and Machalek; Braithwaite, Katz, and Gottfredson and Hirschi. There may be new light after all.

A second change in the organization of material for this edition concerns public policy issues. These are now incorporated in an expanded Chapter 1.

Ideology, law, and politics breathe life into the idea of crime, and students are now invited to consider how this works at the outset of their journey rather than at the end.

Other significant changes in the sixth edition include new sections on research methods (Chapter 2), disaggregation (Chapter 3), transnational crime (Chapter 7), asset forfeiture (Chapter 9), styles of policing (Chapter 10), and intermediate penalties (Chapter 11). This edition also includes expanded and updated discussions of female criminality and gender issues, sociobiological perspectives, robbery violence, inequality and crime, enterprise structures in crime, computer crime, and issues pertaining to race.

Descriptive data have been updated wherever possible, and I have made extensive use of graphs and charts in this edition, many showing trends. As in prior editions, boxed inserts are used to highlight special information, controversial issues, or excerpts from interesting new research. New to this edition is a list of recommended readings at the end of each chapter. The list is composed mainly of books containing in-depth discussions of issues raised in each chapter. I do not necessarily agree with the authors' ideology or conclusions, however.

I have many people to thank for helping me make this a better book. Over the years, numerous colleagues and students have been a source of inspiration and insight. I am especially grateful for the encouragement and counsel I have received from colleagues who have used the text in their courses, particularly Dr. Christine Rasche. I am also grateful for the many critical comments from criminologists who reviewed the fifth edition and thus helped me prepare the sixth: George Caffrey, Southern Connecticut State University; Donald E. Davis, North Hennepin Community College; David James Dodd, Montclair State College; Paul Hahn, Xavier University; Rodney J. Henningsen, Sam Houston State University; Jack Katz, University of California, Los Angeles; A. Javier Trevino, Marquette University; Gennaro F. Vito, University of Louisville. These scholars certainly bear no responsibility for any errors or omissions.

Faculty, staff, and students in the Department of Sociology and Social Work at Southern Illinois University at Edwardsville have shown patience and understanding as their chair juggled teaching and administrative duties with the periods of intensive work that this revision entailed. Special thanks go to graduate assistants Molly Drebes and Bill McKirgen for their help in preparing new material, and to my secretary, Dolores Schafer, for assistance with the test bank and especially for putting up with me when the various deadlines approached.

This edition would not have come about without the support and encouragement of my editor at HarperCollins, Alan McClare, and without the diligence of Angie Gladfelter, who coordinated the project at York Production Services. My wife, Lynne, and my children, Colin, Chelsea, Alison, and Melissa overlooked the many hours I stole from them. This edition is also dedicated to them.

Hugh D. Barlow
Edwardsville

Part I

Studying Crime

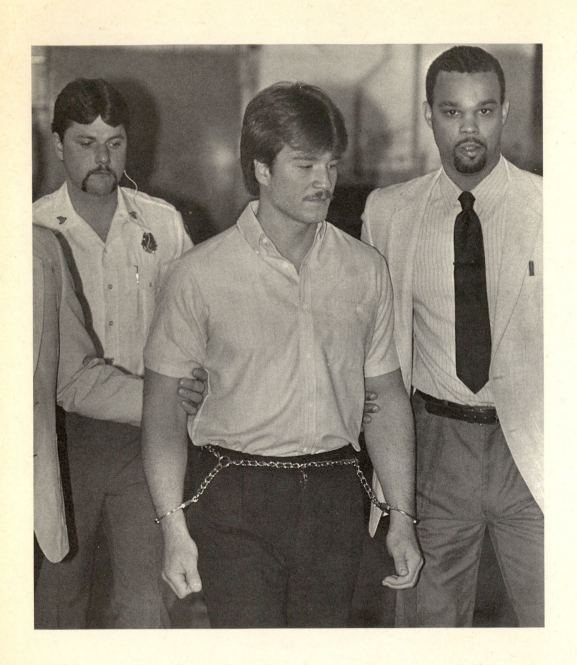

Chapter 1

Crime and Criminality

Open almost any newspaper and you will find at least one article about crime. However, big city papers do not bother to report petty thefts and vandalism, or even most robberies, assaults, and burglaries, while small town papers often make them headline news. Big city newspapers seldom give front page coverage even to rape or murder unless there is a sensational angle to it. Even the sensational stories do not stay on the front page for long. They are largely forgotten by the time the cases come to trial and sentencing.

If newspapers were the sole source of information about crime and criminals, the picture would be highly distorted. The media weigh the information they receive according to its newsworthiness and then report it selectively. The resulting "reality" is far from the truth. The reality of crime reported by the press is one of exceptionally violent, exceptionally greedy, or exceptionally corrupt people picking on exceptionally vulnerable victims. The image portrayed on TV or on movie screens is even more distorted. The crimes are sensational, and the criminals are brought to justice because of exceptionally talented police, exceptionally tenacious lawyers, or exceptionally wily private eyes (see Lichter and Lichter, 1983).

Crime

Criminologists try to uncover the true story of crime. The lessons revealed are sometimes painful. As you read through the next 17 chapters, you will learn that the most likely victims of crime are the people who can least afford it; you will learn that crime is like a huge iceberg of which only the tip is reported by the police (and even less by the media); you will learn that most criminals are not punished for most of their crimes, and that many criminals are never caught. You will learn that the most likely place where women and children are assaulted is the home, and the numbers are staggering—as many as two million women and two million children are abused by other family members in the United States each year. You will learn that American jails and prisons are full of young males, almost half of them black, and most of them from city neighborhoods where unemployment, overcrowding, and physical deterioration are commonplace. You will learn that even though the costs of corporate crime far exceed those of robbery, burglary, and auto theft combined, white-collar criminals are less likely than others to be arrested and prosecuted, and, if convicted, less likely to go to jail or prison.

The picture is bleak, but more so if you are African-American. Although the risk of being a victim of most street crimes has remained relatively stable or even declined during the past 15 years (see Figure 1.1), the risks are not borne equally: Blacks have higher rates of victimization than whites for rape, robbery, aggravated assault, burglary, and motor vehicle theft (see Figure 1.2).

Fear of Crime

Many Americans fear crime. Public opinion surveys show that over 40 percent of those polled are afraid to walk alone at night in their own

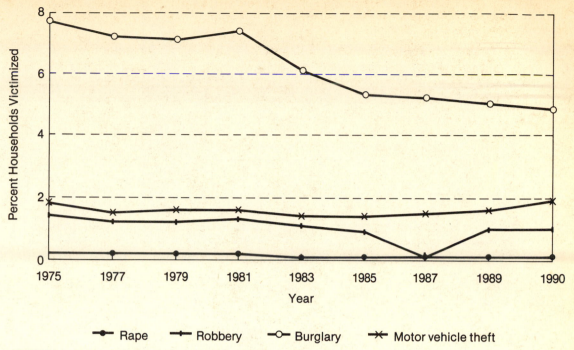

FIGURE 1.1   **Household Victimization by Type of Crime,**
1975–1990. *Source:* Compiled from Bureau of Justice Statistics (1991a). *Crime and the Nation's Households, 1990.* Washington, D.C.: U.S. Department of Justice.

neighborhoods (see Maguire and Flanagan, 1991:184–185). Ten percent feel that their own homes are not secure against crime.

Although there has been a national downward trend in fear of crime, for some populations fear still appears to be a major problem. For example, women are three times more likely than men to indicate that their neighborhoods are unsafe at night. Fear of crime is affecting school children: Twenty-two percent of a national sample said they were afraid of being physically attacked while at school. There were virtually no differences by sex or race, although inner-city school children are most likely to be afraid (Bastion and Taylor, 1991:10; Maguire and Flanagan, 1991:184–185). People living in inner-city slums like Harlem show the effects of fear in ways that would be unimaginable in middle-class neighborhoods.

> In any Harlem building, . . . every door has at least three locks on it. Nobody opens a door without first finding out who's there. . . . If you live in Harlem, USA, you don't park your automobile two blocks from your apartment house because that gives potential muggers an opportunity to get a fix on you. You'd better find a parking space within a block of your house, because if you have to walk two blocks you're not going to make it. (Claude Brown, cited in Moore and Trojanowicz, 1988:2)

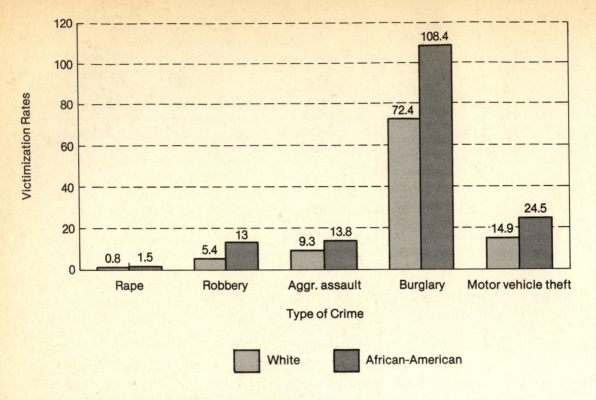

**FIGURE 1.2   Victimization Rates by Race for Selected Crimes,
1979–1986.** Rate is the number of households victimized by crime for
every 10,000 households. *Source:* Compiled from Bureau of Justice Statistics
(1990a). *Black Victims.* Washington, D.C.: U.S. Department of Justice.

Conventional wisdom holds that the people most afraid of crime are the
ones who have been personally victimized by it. While this is true to some
extent, the relationship between experiencing crime and fearing crime is not
simple. Elderly women, for example, are most afraid yet least often victimized, and young men are least afraid yet most often victimized (Skogan and
Maxfield, 1981). Those who have experienced crime themselves are no more
likely to be afraid than people who have merely heard about other people's
victimization. In fact, Skogan (1986) discovered that actual criminal victimization is less important as a cause of fear than the physical and social
environments in which people live.

Moore and Trojanowicz (1988:3–4) argue that reversing conventional
wisdom might actually lead to crime reduction: "[I]nstead of controlling
victimization to control fear, we would manage fear to reduce victimization."
This argument nicely illustrates how the discoveries of criminology challenge
conventional images of crime while also suggesting ways to reduce criminal
victimization.

Fear of crime results in emotional and behavioral changes: People feel anxious, isolated, and vulnerable, and they cannot enjoy simple things like a trip to the grocery store. Fear of crime also results in massive expenditures on private security (estimated at more than $50 billion annually. It contributes to an erosion of community life by causing people to withdraw into their homes, to reduce patronage of local businesses and organizations, and to move away. Moore and Trojanowicz (1988:4) illustrate how fear of crime may even displace crime onto others.

> For example, when individuals retreat behind closed doors and shuttered windows, they make their own homes safer. But they make the streets more dangerous, for there are fewer people watching and intervening on the streets. Or, when individuals invest in burglar alarms or private security guards rather than spending more on public police forces, they make themselves safer, but leave others worse off because crime is deflected onto others.

Moore and Trojanowicz believe that crime victimization can be reduced if fear can be channeled into programs that strengthen community ties. As one step in this direction they propose closer contacts between citizens and the police centered around the police neighborhood foot patrol. Their ideas need considerable investigation and are not without critics (see Chapter 10). However, their work illustrates what some criminologists are doing to uncover the facts about crime, including how people experience and respond to it.

Criminology

Research on fear and crime illustrates one of the reasons criminology is an important field of study. Most crime harms people directly, and all crime harms in some way, if only through increased taxation to pay people to fight it. Other reasons can also motivate people to study crime. It may sound trite, but people are fascinated by crime and that makes it a worthwhile subject. There is also a substantial public interest in knowing why and how certain behaviors are singled out as crimes or certain people as criminals. Arrest, detention, and punishment are repressive actions that the state sanctions; they are not merely responses to crime, but also part of the crime problem. If police saturate a neighborhood, people are affected both there and elsewhere. If authorities ignore a category of crimes, people are affected. Crime is important to study because it raises fundamental questions about civil liberties and the power of the state. Finally, criminal behavior merits study precisely because it *is* behavior—what criminological studies reveal may be important in understanding human behavior in general.

The remaining sections of this chapter discuss some of the important concepts and ideas that define the subject matter of criminology. What is crime? Who is the criminal? Where does law come in? What is the connection between crime and public policy?

The Meaning of the Term "Crime"

The legal or legalistic definition of crime is a departure point for considering the subject matter of criminology. The definition simply states: *Crime is a human act that violates the criminal law.*

This definition has two important components. First, crime involves *behavior:* Someone has to perform some act. Second, this behavior is identified in terms of a body of substantive *law*. According to that law, a number of specific criteria must normally be met for an act to be considered a crime and the perpetrator a criminal. First, there must be *conduct*, or *actus reus* (mere thoughts, no matter how terrible, are not crimes). Second, the conduct must constitute a *social harm*; that is, the conduct must be injurious to the state (or "the people"). Third, the conduct must be *prohibited by law*. Fourth, the conduct must be performed *voluntarily*. Fifth, the conduct usually must be performed *intentionally* (the issue here is criminal intent, expressed in the concept of *mens rea*, meaning guilty mind); however, unintentional acts of negligence or omission may qualify as crimes in some cases. Sixth, the harm must be *causally related* to the conduct; that is, the act must produce the harm. Finally, the conduct must be *punishable by law* (in fact, the punishment must be specified in advance of the conduct).

Many years ago, Thorsten Sellin (1938) argued for a more universally applicable definition that would encompass any violation of what he calls "conduct norms." Sellin believed that the legal criteria used in legal definitions of crime are at best artificial and arbitrary and at worst ignore other actions that conflict with the "general social interest." In Sellin's view, criminologists should study all conduct that violates group norms.

Other critics have pointed out that many harmful acts are not considered crimes in law. Should criminology study them? Jeffrey Reiman (1984) lists a variety of acts and conditions that are analogous to crime in terms of their consequences, for example, loss of life, physical injury, or property loss.

> The workplace, the medical profession, the air we breathe, and the poverty we refuse to rectify lead to more human suffering, far more death and disability, and take more dollars from our pockets than the murders, aggravated assaults, and thefts reported annually by the FBI. (Reiman, 1984:75)

A quite different approach is taken by Gottfredson and Hirschi (1990), although they, too, believe that the subject matter of criminology should not be restricted to legal categories of crime. They believe that many acts are analogous to common crimes, from smoking cigarettes and eating between meals to gambling and speeding. Just like robbery, murder, rape, employee theft, and drug use, these acts are easy to commit, require little or no planning or skill, and are exciting, risky, or thrilling. Needless to say, this conceptualization of crime couldn't be more at odds with Reiman's. Suffice it to say that how criminologists define crime determines how they study it and the sorts of questions they ask. Definitions also shape the theories that are developed to explain crime, as Chapters 13–17 will show.

The Labeling Perspective: Crime as Status   The so-called labeling, or societal reactions, perspective argues that crimes are distinguished from other acts precisely because they have been defined as crimes by people whose reactions matter. The social significance of a given act is in the reactions it calls forth.

The idea that crimes are identifiable in terms of the reactions to them is not new. Emile Durkheim ([1893]1964a:70), one of the fathers of sociology, noted that a crime is "every act which, in any degree whatever, invokes against its author the characteristic reaction we term punishment." Speaking on the more general topic of deviance, Howard Becker (1963:9) has observed that

> . . . deviance is *not* a quality of the act the person commits, but rather a consequence of the application by others of rules and sanctions to an 'offender.' The deviant is one to whom the label has been successfully applied; deviant behavior is behavior that people so label.

Pursuing this reasoning, what makes behavior distinctive is the kinds of reactions it calls forth. The distinctive aspect of criminal behavior is that the behavior in question has been labeled crime (Hartjen, 1974:5–8).

When labeled as crime, behavior is transformed into criminal behavior, and the actor may be transformed into a criminal. This transformation is called *criminalization*. The opposite process—when the label *criminal* is removed from an action, event, or person—is called *decriminalization*. For those who favor the *labeling perspective*, as it is often called, why and how the transformation occurs is crucial to an understanding of crime. In their view, how people perceive the actions of others, and what they do about it, should be central issues in criminology.

The acquisition of criminal status is rarely determined solely by what a person does, and sometimes people escape criminal labeling despite doing criminal or delinquent things (see Tannenbaum, 1938). This is illustrated in a classic study of criminal labeling by William Chambliss (1973). Chambliss followed the experiences of two small-town juvenile gangs whose members were students at "Hannibal High." The youths regularly broke the law. However, only the members of one gang, the "Roughnecks," were considered delinquent by officials and repeatedly arrested. The other gang, called by Chambliss the "Saints," largely escaped criminalization, and no members were ever arrested. Why the difference?

According to Chambliss, four factors played an important role in the differential response, and all related to the class position of the gang members—the Roughnecks came from lower-class families, and the Saints came from "respectable" upper middle-class families.

First, the Roughnecks were more visible. Unlike the Saints, whose members had access to cars and could escape the local community, the Roughnecks had little choice but to hang out under the surveillance of neighbors and local authorities.

Second, the outward demeanor of the Saints deceived parents and officials. Around authority figures they wore masks of courtesy and obedience, and if accused of misbehavior they were apologetic. The Roughnecks, on the other hand, made no pretense at penitence when accused, and they made no effort to hide their hostile feelings. They were commonly rude to passersby, and they engaged in disturbances and fights, which the Saints avoided. In short, the Roughnecks misbehaved openly and showed little regard for social customs or the feelings of others; the Saints largely kept their misbehavior hidden. (For more on hostile and unpenitent demeanor as an affront to authority, see Black, 1980.)

Third, in responding to the gangs' misbehavior, authorities and community members displayed bias that favored the Saints. The Saints were characterized as typical adolescents who were merely sowing their wild oats as normal boys do.

Fourth, in defining the Roughnecks as boys who get into trouble, the community reinforced the "deviance" of gang members and helped produce a self-fulfilling prophecy: Deviant self-images promoted further deviance, and Roughnecks found themselves seeking out, and being sought by, friends with similar self-images. As time went by the escalating delinquency of the Roughnecks was matched and reinforced by escalating community disapproval and punishment. The Saints, in the meantime, remained respectable in the eyes of the community, although in fact they continued to maintain a high level of delinquency. Chambliss concludes his analysis as follows:

> Selective perception and labeling—finding, processing and punishing some kinds of criminality and not others—means that visible, poor, nonmobile, outspoken, undiplomatic "tough" kids will be noticed, whether their actions are seriously delinquent or not. Other kids, who have established a reputation for being bright (even though underachieving), disciplined and involved in respectable activities, who are mobile and monied, will be invisible when they deviate from sanctioned activities. They'll sow their wild oats—perhaps even wider and thicker than their lower-class cohorts—but they won't be noticed. (Chambliss 1973:31)

Aaron Cicourel's (1968) study of juvenile justice in two California cities confirms the downward skew of delinquency labeling (for more recent literature, see Brooks, 1989). Cicourel found that most official delinquents came from semiskilled and unskilled backgrounds, especially those recommended for prosecution and detention. Cicourel shows that these decisions are routine constructions influenced by what officials perceive to be the "real" causes of delinquency (e.g., disorganized families, a defiant attitude) and by the need to "get the job done." In addition, in the less likely event that a child from a middle- or upper-class family is caught up in the enforcement net, the family's greater resources are also mobilized routinely to reduce the likelihood that their child's homelife will be tagged as "bad," thus explaining the delinquency and warranting the child's removal from the home.

The labeling perspective views crime as status rather than as behavior. Viewed in this way, crime actually has five distinct meanings. The five levels of meaning depend on which stage in the legal process is being considered.

When youths congregate in public places to have fun they are not necessarily doing anything that is delinquent or criminal. However, the characteristics of people and places may have more to do with criminal labeling than actual behavior.

Legislatures and other agencies, whose job it is to *create* legal definitions of behavior, provide formulations of criminal law. These formulations identify acts that violate them and that therefore are crimes. But those who *enforce* the criminal law also define crime. In 1923, Roscoe Pound advocated the study of *law in action*; he recognized that many laws on the books are never enforced. The act of arrest applies the crime label; persons who are not arrested escape the imposition of the crime label at this and any subsequent stages. In the *prosecution* and *conviction* stages, specific interpretations of conduct are again made within the framework of criminal law. The personal and social consequences of labeling at these stages are different from those at earlier stages. Finally, the fifth stage is when *punishment* is meted out. Conduct reaching this stage may be said to constitute crime at all levels of meaning.

Bearing these points in mind, an alternative definition of crime can be stated: *Crime is a label that is attached to behavior and events by those who create and administer the criminal law.*

It is important to stress that the creation of criminal labels is often noncontroversial (see Braithwaite, 1989a:38–42). In other words, there is general agreement among members of society that certain acts should be designated as crimes. This agreement or consensus even extends to attitudes toward the relative seriousness of crimes.

In the early 1960s, for example, Thorsten Sellin and Marvin Wolfgang (1964) asked samples of judges, police officers, and university students to rate the seriousness of 141 offenses. They found much agreement. A later survey of adults in Baltimore (Rossi et al., 1974) again found much consensus on a similar list of illegal acts. This study, however, did find a prominent difference between white and black respondents: Blacks rated violence among family and friends lower in seriousness than did whites. Thus, although there may be general agreement on crime seriousness, subgroups of the population may not share the general attitude toward particular crimes.

These findings have been confirmed by a more recent study (Wolfgang et al., 1985). A total of 204 crimes were rated by a national sample of 60,000 respondents (though no one person rated more than 25 offenses). Some of the specific crimes and their seriousness scores are shown in Box 1.1. Overall, there was broad consensus. Violent crimes were rated as more serious than property offenses, and drug dealing was taken very seriously. The study showed also that people evaluate crimes according to their consequences for the victims, and, not surprisingly, respondents who had been victims of crime tended to assign higher seriousness scores than did others. Whites tended generally to assign higher scores than did minority groups (for comments on these studies, see Miethe, 1982; Cullen, et al., 1985).

Criminals

The preceding section has defined crime, but who is the "criminal"? From the standpoint of criminal law, a criminal is an individual who is legally capable of conduct that violates the law and who can be shown to have actually and intentionally engaged in that conduct. If it cannot be demonstrated that the person committed the illegal act, that he or she was capable of committing it—for example, by meeting requirements of age and mental condition—and that the act was intentional (or the result of negligence), then the person is not legally a criminal. Box 1.2 shows some of the defenses against criminal charges. Emphasizing the legalistic view, Tappan (1947) suggests that "only those are criminal who have been adjudicated as such by the courts."

A definition of the criminal more in keeping with the labeling perspective would stress that those suspected of violating the law are treated in a special way. Arrest, prosecution, conviction, and punishment are each status-conferring actions that single out certain people as criminals (whether or not they truly are). Accordingly, a criminal can be defined as *a person whose behavior has been labeled a crime by those who create and administer the criminal law.*

The criminal label can be applied at different stages in the legal process, from the point at which criminal conduct is created in law to the point at which punishment ends. In addition, the label often stays with people long after they have paid their "debt" to society. Criminal labels stigmatize. When friends or associates know a person has been arrested and they react punitively because of this knowledge, then that person's social identity essentially becomes that of a criminal.

You may be wondering: Why emphasize the activities of those who enforce the law when surely people are criminals because of something *they* do, not because of something the enforcers do? From a legalistic perspective this is true. However, from a social constructivist position it is inadequate because it underemphasizes the social dimension of human existence. It fails to take into account the extent to which the ideas and actions of other people give meaning to an individual's behavior. The idea of the "criminal" is created by people; criminality is imputed to another's behavior and sometimes merely to another's appearance. That person's behavior is not criminal until others say it is by their words and deeds. On its own, the physical act that a person performs is only that, a physical act. Even its meaning to the actor depends on how others react to it.

To summarize, individuals are defined partly by what they do and partly by what others do to them. People are criminal not simply because they break the law, but because those who make official judgments about their behavior decide to treat them as criminal and act on that decision. Discretion is involved in applying the criminal label, and power and social position influence how and to whom discretionary judgments are applied. People who are young, black, poor, less well educated, or live in the inner-city slums are more susceptible than others to being labeled criminal. The police concentrate their energies in areas of towns and cities where such people are likely to be found. Another reason is that legal agencies make decisions and exercise power as a political process. Low-status people are generally excluded from that process and are in effect without voice in the creation and enforcement of criminal law. As relatively powerless members of society, they are more susceptible to actions that identify their behavior as "deviant."

Whereas the legalistic perspective takes law and the process of criminalization largely for granted, the labeling perspective runs the risk of ignoring the content of criminal activities and events, that is, the what, who, and why of crime. This text tries to strike a balance between the two perspectives by exploring crime as both behavior and status. How and why people commit crimes are no less important questions than how and why authorities react to events and people as criminal.

Victims

Victims are arguably the forgotten people in the crime scene. The primary reason is historical: The development of modern criminal law and the

Box 1.1 ■ Seriousness Scores from the National Survey of Crime Severity

Highest Scores

72.1 A person plants a bomb in a public building. The bomb explodes and 20 people are killed.

52.8 A man forcibly rapes a woman. As a result of physical injuries, she dies.

47.8 A parent beats his young child with his fists. As a result, the child dies.

43.2 A person robs a victim at gunpoint. The victim struggles and is shot to death.

39.2 A man stabs his wife. As a result, she dies.

39.1 A factory knowingly gets rid of its waste in a way that pollutes the water supply of a city. As a result, 20 people die.

35.7 A person stabs a victim to death.

35.6 A person intentionally injures a victim. As a result, the victim dies.

33.8 A person runs a narcotics ring.

33.0 A person plants a bomb in a public building. The bomb explodes and one person is injured but no medical treatment is required.

32.7 An armed person skyjacks an airplane and holds the crew and passengers hostage until a ransom is paid.

30.0 A man forcibly rapes a woman. Her physical injuries require hospitalization.

27.9 A woman stabs her husband. As a result, he dies.

Lowest Scores

0.2 A person under 16 years old plays hooky from school.

0.3 A person is a vagrant. That is, he has no home and no visible means of support.

0.5 A person takes part in a dice game in an alley.

0.6 A person trespasses in the backyard of a private home.

0.7 A person under 16 years old breaks a curfew law by being out on the street after the hour permitted by law.

0.8 A person is drunk in public.

0.8 A person knowingly trespasses in a railroad yard.

0.8 A person under 16 years old runs away from home.

0.9 A person under 16 years old is reported to police by his parents as an offender because they are unable to control him.

1.1 A person under 16 years old illegally has a bottle of wine.

corresponding decline of primitive law (discussed in the next section) left victims no formal role in the criminal process. The word *victim* does not even appear in many statute books. In modern criminal law the victim is the state, not the individual actually injured by a crime.

A secondary reason relates to the orientation of science and public policy in criminal matters, which has traditionally focused on how to explain and deal with the behavior of criminals. Little attention has been paid to victims, and when they are brought in it is either as contributing causes of crime

Some Other Scores

1.3 Two persons willingly engage in a homosexual act.

1.4 A person has some marijuana for his own use.

1.6 A person breaks into a parking meter and steals $10 worth of nickels.

1.6 A person is a customer in a house of prostitution.

2.1 A person engages in prostitution.

2.2 A person steals $10 worth of merchandise from the counter of a department store.

3.1 A person breaks into a home and steals $100.

3.6 A person knowingly passes a bad check.

6.2 An employee embezzles $1,000 from his employer.

6.7 A person, using force, robs a victim of $10. The victim is hurt and requires treatment by a doctor, but not hospitalization.

7.4 A person illegally gets monthly welfare checks.

7.9 A teenage boy beats his father with his fists. The father requires hospitalization.

9.0 A person, armed with a lead pipe, robs a victim of $1,000. No physical harm occurs.

9.2 Several large companies illegally fix the retail prices of their products.

10.3 A person operates a store where he knowingly sells stolen property.

10.5 A person smuggles marijuana into the country for sale.

12.0 A police officer takes a bribe not to interfere with an illegal gambling operation.

13.9 A legislator takes a bribe from a company to vote for a law favoring the company.

14.6 A person, using force, robs a victim of $10. The victim is hurt and requires hospitalization.

16.4 A person attempts to kill a victim with a gun. The gun misfires, and the victim escapes injury.

17.7 An employer orders one of his employees to commit a crime.

18.3 A man beats his wife with his fists. She requires hospitalization.

20.6 A person sells heroin to others for resale.

21.7 A person pays another person to commit a serious crime.

Source: Marvin E. Wolfgang, Robert M. Figlio, Paul E. Tracy, and Simon I. Singer (1985). *The National Survey of Crime Severity*. Washington, D.C.: U.S. Department of Justice, pp. vi–x.

(especially common in discussions of assault, rape, and murder), in debates over whether some crimes are victimless (consensual sex offenses and drug use, for example), or as people who can help "nail" the offender.

But this picture has been changing dramatically in recent years. An international effort is under way to study the victimizing effects of crime (and other social ills) and to bring the real victim back into the picture. Much of this effort has been directed at changing criminal justice policy and practice to accommodate a more active role for victims who for years have been "twice

Box 1.2 ■ Defenses Against Criminal Charges

Self-Defense. Use of force is deemed justifiable when one can establish that one feared for one's life, could not reasonably escape the situation, and was not the initiator of aggressive actions. The belief that one must use deadly force to prevent harm to self need only be *reasonable* given the circumstances.

Necessity. Illegal acts commited against third parties in the belief that doing so will prevent harm to others or avoid a greater evil.

Defense of Property. Most states allow a person to use force to prevent the commission of a felony, to arrest a person who has committed a felony involving property, or to prevent forcible entry into one's residence. However, *deadly* force may not generally be used unless the property owner reasonably fears for his or her life.

Time Limitations. Statutes of limitation exist for most offenses (an exception being murder), and they specify for different offenses a time limit during which criminal responsibility lasts. A person accused after the time limit runs out is no longer held criminally responsible.

Duress. Duress is a defense *if* the defendant, through no personal fault, is put in fear for his or her life or the life of another. Most states require that the threat seem of greater magnitude than the crime itself.

Absence of Intent by Mistake. Absence of intent is a defense when, for example, someone mistakenly believes he or she is the owner of a piece of property and removes it for his or her own use.

Entrapment. Entrapment is a defense if it is shown that a law enforcement agent posing as a participant in a crime convinced the defendant to commit the crime when he or she would not normally have done so.

Involuntary Act. An example of this defense is a person doing injury to another while sleep-walking, hypnotized, or in a state of near unconsciousness.

Involuntary Intoxication. A person who is intoxicated or drugged at the hands of another without permission or by trick or deceit will normally not be held criminally responsible for any offense committed while intoxicated or drugged.

victimized," first by the criminal, and then by the very system to which they have turned for help. Treated as nonentities, victims have been shuffled around, kept in the dark, had their property taken and not returned; worse still, they have been subjected to abuse and ridicule in court.

The impact of crime on victims can be devastating. Horror stories abound about victims who were horribly mutilated, killed, driven insane, or made

Victim Consent. A defense of consent may be accepted when the victim of a crime in fact gave consent to it voluntarily. This defense is rarely used and surfaces mostly in sex-related cases.

Alibi. An alibi is a witness-supported defense based on the claim that the defendant was not present at the scene of the crime during the time it was carried out.

Insanity. Insanity is a defense when it can be shown that the defendant lacks the mental capacity for criminal responsibility or suffers from a mental illness that renders the defendant insane or of unsound mind. Four prevalent tests for insanity are:

1. *The "Wild Beast" Test.* To claim innocence under this rule, the defendant must have been acting more or less like a "raving maniac," to have had no more knowledge of what he or she was doing than a wild beast.
2. *The McNaghten Rule.* It must be competently shown that the defendant did not know what he or she was doing or did not know that it was wrong.
3. *Irresistible Impulse Test.* This adds an element of mental impulse to the traditional McNaghten Rule; defendants may be declared innocent if irresistible impulses render them incapable of controlling their behavior.
4. *Severe Mental Disease.* In federal courts, defendant, as a result of severe mental disease or defect, was unable to appreciate the nature and quality of the wrongfulness of his or her acts.

Accident. Accident is a defense when there is not such negligence in the commission or omission of an act that defendant could be held criminally culpable. An example would be death caused when a pedestrian falls in the path of a car that could not stop in time. The driver would not be held criminally responsible unless other damaging factors (intoxication, driving recklessly) were present.

Further details on these defenses may be found in the following sources: Gary N. Holten and Melvin E. Jones (1982). *The System of Criminal Justice*, 2nd ed. Boston: Little, Brown; Norval Morris (1988). *Insanity Defense*, NIJ Reports. Washington, D.C.: U.S. Department of Justice.

penniless by crime. Every time a sensational murder comes to light—Jeffrey Dahmer's atrocities, the "Son of Sam" killings, the Tylenol murders, the Gacy killings, the "Manson family" murders—our sympathies go out to the families and friends of the victims. But on a much more mundane level, millions of crime victims—many not even realizing they are victims—suffer unsensationally and find that few seem to care about their plight. Estimates of losses, damage, and personal injuries suffered by victims of theft, burglary, and unarmed robbery show the magnitude of the problem nationwide. Of 32,799,325 victimizations in 1980, only 7 percent did not result in property loss, damage, or personal injury (Harland, 1981:7).

A variety of constructive responses are now being directed to the needs of crime victims. Some of these responses seek to reduce the probability of victimization and in that sense are part of crime prevention efforts. Neighborhood crime watch programs and "Operation Identification" are examples. Other responses seek to improve the treatment of victims by the judicial process, and others seek to redress the grievance occasioned by crime.

The 1984 Victims of Crime Act helps victims in the criminal process. Among its provisions are the collection of fines, penalties, and other assessments from those convicted of federal crimes for distribution to states for improved victim/witness services. Other legislative efforts around the country will help keep victims in the foreground, at least for a while. The heart of these legislative initiatives consists of specification of victim rights, including the right to be informed of, present at, and heard during criminal proceedings.

In 1986 the state of Maryland passed a statute authorizing that a Victim Impact Statement (VIS) be compiled in all felony cases prior to sentencing (see Reid, 1989:495–496). The report must list identification of the victim; economic losses resulting from the crime; physical injuries, including seriousness and permanence; any change in the victim's welfare or familial relationships; requests by the victim or victim's physician for psychological services; and any other information pertinent to the crime reflecting its impact on the victim. In *Payne* v. *Tennessee* (1991), the U.S. Supreme Court ruled 6 to 3 that the VIS is constitutional.

There is evidence that victims feel better about criminal justice proceedings if they are present when crucial decisions are made. However, victims' contacts with police and counsel may *lessen* their opinions of the accused (Hagan, 1982a). This may explain some of the dissatisfaction that many victims express with the sentencing actions of judges (Forst and Hernon, 1985). For their part, judges show less inclination than either prosecutors or police to use victims as a direct source of information about the harm to victims resulting from crime (Forst and Hernon, 1985). Victims who seek justice may find that participation in the process does not necessarily ease their frustration with the outcome.

Social Control and Law

Crime and law are intertwined. As a type of law, criminal law is generally regarded as a relatively recent development. Although no specific date of origin can be identified, criminal law in the Western world developed 2000 years ago from already existing systems of law and began to take shape in the later years of the Roman Empire. In considering the development of criminal law, an examination of the nature of law in general is desirable.

In any social group, efforts are made to ensure that members behave predictably and in accordance with the expectations and evaluations of others. These efforts are at the heart of social control, and their success is thought to be indispensable to orderly group life. It is difficult to imagine how group life could endure if members simply acted impulsively or in continued violation of the expectations of others.

Social control may be informal or formal: It may appear in facial expressions, gestures, gossip, or ostracism. It may consist largely of unwritten rules passed on by word of mouth or by example. Or it may take the form of written rules backed by force. Sometimes conformity is promoted through the use of rewards (positive sanctions), and sometimes through the use of penalties (negative sanctions). The effect of all these measures may be to create a sense of guilt and shame, which becomes an internal control.

Law is a type of social control. It is an example of formal social control, described here by F. James Davis (1962:43):

> Formal social control is characterized by (1) explicit rules of conduct, (2) planned use of sanctions to support the rules, and (3) designated officials to interpret and enforce the rules, and often to make them.

A classic definition of law was written by German sociologist Max Weber (1954:2):

> An order will be called *law* if it is externally guaranteed by the probability that coercion (physical or psychological), to bring about conformity or avenge violation, will be applied by a *staff* of people holding themselves specially ready for that purpose.

Weber contends that law has three essential features that, taken together, distinguish it from other normative orders such as custom and convention. First, regardless of whether an individual wants to obey rules or does so out of habit, pressures to conform must be external, in the form of actions or threats of action by others. Second, these external actions or threats involve coercion or force. Third, those who carry out the coercive threats are persons whose formal role is enforcing the law. When this staff or administrative body is part of an agency of political authority, Weber defines it as "state" law.

Customs are rules *of* conduct that people follow "without thinking," or as Weber put it, with "unreflective imitation." There is no sense of "oughtness," or obligation, about them. On the other hand, conventions are rules *for* conduct, and they do involve a question of obligation. Pressures to conform are brought to bear on rule breakers, and these usually involve some form of disapproval. However, unlike law, a conventional order "lacks specialized personnel for the implementation of coercive power" (Weber, 1954:27).

Some scholars take issue with two major points raised by Weber. First, by emphasizing coercion Weber ignored other factors that influence people to conform to obligatory rules. For example, people may obey laws because they feel it is simply right to do so. Weber appears to have been quite aware of this issue. People, he said, obey laws for a variety of reasons—sometimes because of an emotional commitment to them, sometimes through fear of disapproval, sometimes because it is in their interests to do so, and sometimes simply out of habit. Many laws are obeyed because citizens feel it is their duty to obey them, and this feeling seems to articulate a special kind of obligation that is built into authority relations. But Weber makes it clear that the question of *why* people obey obligatory rules is irrelevant to a definition of law.

The second objection is over the special staff. Some critics claim that Weber's definition unnecessarily restricts use of the term *law* when making cross-cultural and historical comparisons. Rather than use the word *staff*, which implies an organized administrative apparatus that may not exist in certain nonliterate and primitive societies, some suggest using a less restrictive term. Jack P. Gibbs (1966:29) offers "special status"; E. Adamson Hoebel (1954:28) mentions persons possessing "a socially recognized privilege."

Origins and Development of Criminal Law

Much of what is known about the origins and development of criminal law has come through the efforts of legal historians and cultural anthropologists. Classic historical works such as *Ancient Law* by Sir Henry Sumner Maine (1905) and *The Growth of Criminal Law in Ancient Greece* by George Calhoun (1927) provide important interpretative accounts of early law. Twentieth-century anthropologists have added to the store of knowledge through their studies of primitive societies. Works by A. R. Radcliffe-Brown (1948), Bronislaw Malinowski (1926), E. Adamson Hoebel (1941), and E. E. Evans-Pritchard (1940) are among the best-known studies.

The Decline of Primitive Law It is generally agreed that "primitive law"—the system of rules and obligations in preliterate and semiliterate societies—represents the foundation on which modern legal systems were built. Primitive law contains three important features: (1) Acts that injured or wronged others were considered "private wrongs"; that is, injuries to particular individuals rather than the group or tribe as a whole. (Exceptions to this were acts deemed harmful to the entire community; for example, aiding an enemy or witchcraft.) (2) The injured party or family typically took personal action against the wrongdoer, a kind of self-help justice. (3) This self-help justice usually amounted to retaliation in kind. Blood feuds were not uncommon under this system of primitive justice.

Strongly entrenched customs and traditions, the relative autonomy of the family, homogeneity of the population and its activities, and other features of primitive life were undermined as technological progress and a growing division of labor moved society toward the modern era. Growing differences in wealth, prestige, and power were consolidated in new patterns of authority and decision making. The rise of chieftains and kings set the stage for the centralization of political authority, the establishment of territorial domain, and the emergence of sovereign authority and the civil state. The handling of disputes slowly moved out of the hands of the family and into the hands of sovereign and state. The creation of legal rules became the prerogative of central authority.

These changes did not happen overnight. Today's criminal law is a product of centuries of change. The earliest known code of written law dates back to the twenty-first century B.C. This is the code of Ur-Nammu, the Sumerian king who founded the Third Dynasty of Ur. The famous Code of Hammurabi was discovered in 1901 in Susa, near the Persian Gulf. This code dates from around 1750 B.C. Other ancient codes of law include the Twelve Tables of Rome, the Mosaic code, the laws of ancient Greece, and the laws of Tacitus. All these codes show strong ties with the self-help justice typical of more primitive eras. As Maine (1905:341–342) notes, early penal law was primarily the law of torts (or private wrongs). The Twelve Tables treated theft, assault, and violent robbery as *delicta* (private wrongs), along with trespass, libel, and slander. The person, not the state or the public, was the injured party.

The maturing legal systems of ancient Greece and Rome moved steadily toward the formulation of offenses against the state (public wrongs, or *crimena*) and the establishment of machinery for administration and enforcement. According to Maine, the legislative establishment of permanent criminal tribunals around the first century B.C. represented a crucial step in the emergence of true criminal law.

One of the most interesting features of these early codes is the number of activities they cover. The Code of Hammurabi is particularly wide ranging. The laws covered such diverse areas as kidnapping, unsolved crimes, price fixing, rights of military personnel, the sale of liquor, marriage and the family, inheritance, and slavery (Gordon, 1957). The contents of these early codes suggest three observations: (1) some laws articulate long-established customs and traditions and can be thought of as formal restatements of existing mores; (2) some laws reflect efforts to regulate and coordinate increasingly complex social relations and activities; and (3) some laws articulate prevailing moral standards and show close ties to religion.

Mala Prohibita and Mala in Se   In the minds of some people, law is based on moral beliefs, and criminal codes are a sort of catalog of sins. But others have argued that there is much in criminal codes that bears no obvious connection with ethics or morality (see Smith and Pollack, 1975). In what sense, for example, are laws prohibiting certain forms of drug use or certain kinds of business activities matters of sin?

Laws were once indistinguishable from the general code governing social conduct. As primitive societies became more complex, law and justice were identified as concepts that regulated the moral aspects of social conduct. Even the extensive legal codes of Greece and Rome fused morality with law. In some languages (Hungarian, for example) the word for *crime* means not only an act that is illegal but also one that is evil or sinful (Schafer, 1969). In time, criminal codes expanded and laws were passed to regulate activities in business, politics, the family, social services, and even people's intimate

At the top of an ancient pillar (c. 1760 B.C.) is the image of Hammurabi, King of Babylonia, confronting the Sun God. Hammurabi authored one of the most extensive of the early legal codes.

private lives. The connection between law and morality became less clear, and people categorized crimes as *mala prohibita*—meaning evil because they are forbidden—or *mala in se*—meaning evil in themselves. *Mala prohibita* crimes include drug offenses, traffic violations, and embezzlement; examples of *mala in se* crimes, acts that are inherently evil, include incest, murder, arson, and robbery.

Interests and the Development of Law   Studies of the history of criminal law have documented the role that *interests* play in the creation, content, and enforcement of legal rules. Interests are simply the things that people value, and different people sometimes value different things.

One of the first systematic discussions of interests in the formulation of law was by Roscoe Pound. According to Pound (1943:39), law helps to adjust and harmonize conflicting individual and group interests.

> Looked at functionally, the law is an attempt to satisfy, to reconcile, to harmonize, to adjust these overlapping and often conflicting claims and demands, either through securing them directly and immediately, or through securing certain individual interests, or through delimitations or compromises of individual interests, so as to give effect to the greatest total of interests, or to the interests that weigh the most in our civilization, with the least sacrifice of the scheme of interests as a whole.

The functionalist/interest theory of sociological jurisprudence offered by Pound has been attacked for its emphasis on compromise and harmony and for its suggestion that there will be consensus where important social interests are concerned. Some scholars believe a conflict perspective better reflects the real workings of societal institutions. According to Richard Quinney (1970:35),

> society is characterized by diversity, conflict, coercion, and change, rather than by consensus and stability. Second, law is a *result* of the operation of interests, rather than an instrument that functions outside of particular interests. Though law may control interests, it is in the first place created by interests. Third, law incorporates the interests of specific persons and groups; it is seldom the product of the whole society. Law is made by men, representing special interests, who have the power to translate their interests into public policy. Unlike the pluralistic conception of politics, law does not represent a compromise of the diverse interests in society, but supports some interests at the expense of others.

Historically, those low in status or power have been labeled criminals most often and punished most severely for their crimes. Early legal codes specified different reactions according to distinctions of status. The most powerful were the most privileged. Conflict and power help explain why some activities are not crimes. This is especially evident in matters relating to business and government but also applies to laws regarding sexual assault. Still today, women and poor people find it hard to protect their interests through law.

This last point can be illustrated by a controversy over the conflicting interests of a multinational corporation and Third World mothers. Some years ago the Nestlé Company launched an international campaign to promote its infant formula. Ads proclaiming "Give your baby love and Lactogen" were used to promote the product in less developed countries, where families are typically large. However, the promotion discouraged mothers from breast feeding and encouraged practices that were more expensive, irreversible, and, because of contaminated water supplies, potentially harmful. Many babies became ill, and some died. But Nestlé had committed no crime, nor were any sanctions imposed on the company. In effect, the law both here and abroad protected the company, and had it not been for publicity surrounding the efforts of social activists in England and America, the company doubtless would have continued its legal but ultimately victimizing practices (see Post and Baer, 1978).

John Hagan (1982b) argues that the advantages enjoyed by corporations in matters of crime also extend to situations in which corporations are the victims of crime. He concludes: "The form and content of criminal justice in modern capitalistic societies supports and legitimates the use of criminal law for the protection of corporate property against individuals. That is . . . the modern criminal justice system better serves corporate than individual interests" (p. 1019). These issues are examined in detail in Chapter 7, but you will come across them from time to time throughout the text.

Anglo-American Criminal Law   Criminal law in the United States draws mainly from Greek, Mosaic, and Roman law via English law. The common law of England can be traced to the reign of Henry II (1154–1189). For centuries English law had been a system of tribal justice, the primitive law of private wrongs and self-help retaliation. As feudalism took hold in the eighth and ninth centuries, Anglo-Saxon society underwent important changes. The family lost its autonomy; kings and kingdoms emerged; and the blood feud was replaced by a system of material compensation (usually money), directed by individuals with special status—by king, lord, or bishop. Equally important, political unification was underway, as territorial acquisitions by the new kings transformed a patchwork of small kin-dominated domains into fewer, larger kingdoms. With the Norman conquest of 1066, complete political unification was but a short step away.

The Normans centralized their administrative machinery, including that of law. During the reign of Henry II, new legal procedures emerged, including a court of "common law." Those with complaints against others could bring them to traveling courts, and justice dispensed there became a body of precedent to guide future judgments. During this period certain acts were identified as offenses against king and country ("Breaches of the King's Peace"), and these are the bones of modern criminal law.

The Puritans brought English criminal law to the New World. Over the next 400 years English common law was slowly "Americanized."

The rules embodied in American criminal law come from four sources: (1) federal and state constitutions; (2) decisions by courts (common law or case law), including decisions of precedent and Supreme Court rulings; (3) administrative regulations—those policy decisions employed by agencies on the federal, state, and local levels as they carry out their legal duties; and (4) statutory enactments by legislatures.

Procedural rules govern the way we officially handle matters of criminal law. They are applicable at all stages of the legal process. They govern the different groups handling offenses and offenders—the police, the prosecution and defense, the courts, and those who administer punishment. They shape the administration of criminal justice and help determine whether given acts and individuals will be officially identified as criminal, how offenders will be "processed," and what will happen to them if they are found guilty of a crime. Procedural aspects of criminal law are vital to the study of crime, criminals, and legal sanctions. They set the tone for the process of criminalization and

Each year state legislatures enact new criminal laws or modify existing ones. Inevitably, political agendas and special interests come into play in the process of creating crimes and prescribing penalties.

provide insights into criminal law in action. Together with the substance of criminal prohibitions, procedural rules reflect and reinforce public policy and the ideology that underlies it. The following section deals with the important topic of public policy.

Crime and Public Policy

Public policy impinges on all aspects of the crime scene. Its impact begins with official decisions about what and whom to identify as criminal, and continues through all phases of the criminal process.

Many things shape public policy, whether on crime or anything else. The attitudes, beliefs, ideas, and assumptions about crime of people with power and influence comprise the ideological underpinnings of policy and shape the positions taken on specific issues. The particular ideology underlying public policy is not always obvious, but it is there nonetheless and actual policy decisions cannot be divorced from it. As Walter Miller has observed, "ideology is the permanent hidden agenda of criminal justice" (1973:142).

The same ideology is not, of course, shared by everyone, nor does a particular ideology necessarily retain its influence over time. Policies will change as time passes. Different assumptions and beliefs about criminal matters have achieved prominence at different times. The underlying ideology sometimes stimulates policy changes and sometimes reinforces existing policies. Whether or not a particular ideology influences policy depends on many things, and most important are the power and influence of those subscribing to it.

There have been few attempts to identify and classify beliefs and assumptions about crime. Walter Miller (1973) offers one of the most detailed statements on major ideological positions. He analyzed public statements on criminal matters made by a variety of Americans, including novelists, sociologists, journalists, government officials, lawyers, police, clergy, historians, and labor leaders. Though one does not hear so much these days from the radical left, the distinctions that Miller presents provide a useful starting point in thinking about ideology and public policy on crime.

Miller placed the different ideological positions he was able to identify on a one-dimensional scale:

	Leftist			Centrist			Rightist		
5	4	3	2	1	0	1	2	3	4	5
	radical							conservative		

The most extreme ideological positions were given the value 5. More moderate ones ranged between the extreme left and extreme right positions. The ideological position left 3 is more leftist than position left 1 but less leftist than position left 5. Each ideological position Miller identified concerns a specific crime issue and is made up of assumptions and beliefs about that issue.

For example, left 5 opinions on the causes of crime include assertions that the behavior called crime by the ruling elite "is an inevitable product of a fundamentally corrupt and unjust society. True crime is the behavior of those who perpetuate, control, and profit from an exploitative and brutalizing system . . ." (Miller, 1973:155).

In contrast, right 5 views on the causes of crime include assertions that "crime and violence are a direct product of a massive conspiracy by highly organized and well-financed radical forces deliberately seeking to overthrow the society . . . [through an] . . . unrelenting attack on the fundamental moral values of the society. . . ." (Miller, 1973:156).

More moderate views are reflected in left 3 and right 3 positions. Left 3 views place the responsibility for crime on the shoulders of public officials who allocate "pitifully inadequate resources to criminal justice agencies" and on the shoulders of "damaging social conditions:" poverty, urban collapse, lack of jobs and educational opportunities, and race/ethnic segregation (Miller, 1973:156–157).

Right 3 views include this sort of statement: "The root cause of crime is a massive erosion of the fundamental values which traditionally have served to deter criminality, and a concomitant flouting of the established authority which has traditionally served to constrain it. The most extreme manifestations of this phenomenon are found among . . . the young, minorities, and the poor" (Miller, 1973:157).

When Miller looked at people's views about the proper ways to deal with criminals and the proper operating policies of criminal justice agencies he found differences that were consistent with differences relating to the causes of crime. More radical opinions stressed the brutalizing and militaristic strategies of government crime control, while more conservative views stressed the dangerousness of offenders and the need for swift, certain, and severe punishment.

Left 1 and right 1 opinions show that the moderate left and right converge on policy matters: moderate liberals stress a holistic approach to crime in which the criminal justice apparatus is coordinated with other agencies that serve the general welfare of the community, and where the role of the federal government is to finance and oversee reform of the criminal justice system. Moderate conservatives also stress system reform, but put more emphasis on increasing criminal justice efficiency through modern management and information processing techniques.

Miller observes that there are convergences and divergences, consistencies and inconsistencies, among and within the various ideological positions. He also notes that although the statements might reflect the gist of someone's ideology, that person is unlikely to feel comfortable with all statements exactly as phrased. But most interesting is Miller's (1973:148) observation that both left and right can be reduced to basic governing principles or values and that few Americans would quarrel with them, since they are "intrinsic aspects of our national ideals":

> For the right, the paramount value is order—an ordered society based on a pervasive and binding morality—and the paramount danger is disorder—social, moral and political. For the left, the paramount value is justice—a just society based on a fair and equitable distribution of power, wealth, prestige, and privilege—and the paramount evil is injustice—the concentration of valued social resources in the hands of a privileged minority. . . .

> Stripped of the passion of ideological conflict, the issue between the two sides could be viewed as a disagreement over the relative priority of two valuable conditions: whether *order with justice,* or *justice with order* should be the guiding principle of the criminal justice enterprise.

The expectation that ideology influences public policy is based on the assumption that views or theories about an issue largely determine how people deal with it. In the last hundred years or so, public policy on criminal matters has indeed incorporated competing crime strategies. Two "ideal type" models of organized reactions to crime and criminals have been identified. One rests heavily on order with justice, the other on justice with order. Although neither model exactly reproduces the real world, both are drawn from criminal justice in action and emphasize what are thought to be fundamental divergences in assumptions and beliefs about the correct way to deal with criminals. The models were first suggested by Herbert L. Packer (1964, 1968), who calls them the *crime control model* and the *due process model.*

Order with Justice: The Crime Control Model

According to Packer (1968:158), the ideology underlying the crime control model emphasizes repression of criminal behavior as the most important function of the criminal process:

> The failure of law enforcement to bring criminal conduct under tight control is viewed as leading to the breakdown of public order and thence to the disappearance of an important condition of human freedom. If the laws go unenforced—which is to say, if it is perceived that there is a high percentage of failure to apprehend and convict in the criminal process—a general disregard for legal controls tends to develop. The law-abiding citizen then becomes the victim of all sorts of unjustifiable invasions of his interests. His security of person and property is sharply diminished, and, therefore, so is his liberty to function as a member of society. The claim ultimately is that the criminal process is a positive guarantor of social freedom.

To support this ideology the crime control model pays the most attention to the capacity of the criminal justice system to catch, prosecute, convict, and dispose of a high proportion of criminal offenders. With its emphasis on a high rate of apprehension and conviction, and given limited resources, the crime control model places a premium on speed and finality. Speed is enhanced when cases can be processed informally and when procedure is uniform or standardized; finality is secured when the occasions for challenge are minimized. To ensure that challenges are kept to a minimum, those who work in criminal justice presume that the apprehended are in fact guilty. This places heavy emphasis on the quality of administrative fact finding and the coordination of agency tasks and role responsibilities. Success is gauged by how expeditiously nonoffenders are screened out of the process and whether offenders are passed through to final disposition. Packer likens the crime control model to a conveyer belt, down which flows an endless stream of cases processed by workers who perform routine tasks.

Justice with Order: The Due Process Model

Whereas the crime control model resembles an assembly line, Packer (1968:163) visualizes the due process model as an obstacle course: "Each of its successive stages is designed to present formidable obstacles to carrying the accused any further along in the process."

The due process model sees the crime control function as subordinate to ideals of justice. This model emphasizes ensuring that the facts about the accused are subjected to formal scrutiny; ensuring that the accused is afforded an impartial hearing under adversary procedures; ensuring that coercive and stigmatizing powers are not abused by those in an official position to exercise them; maintaining the presumption of innocence until guilt is legally proven; ensuring that all defendants are given equal protection under the law, including the chance to defend themselves adequately; and ensuring that suspects and convicted offenders are accorded the kind of treatment that supports their dignity and autonomy as human beings. The emphasis, then, is on justice first.

The First Priority Is Order

American public policy on crime is dominated by the ideology and practices of the crime control model. Through the years there has been a proliferation of public and private police forces whose primary goal is the detection and apprehension of criminals and the defense of order. There have been continued efforts to create and enforce laws dealing with moral questions and essentially private behavior. There have been increasing efforts to unite and coordinate crime control at the federal, state, and local levels. There has been a growing emphasis on informality in the criminal process, best exemplified in the extensive use of plea bargaining. There have been continued efforts to promote efficiency, productivity, and professionalism in the activities and personnel of law enforcement agencies. There have been, conversely, a paucity of judicial decisions supporting due process values and few serious efforts to organize and fund programs to ensure equal protection under the law and to guarantee the dignity and autonomy of either victims or offenders.

Important congressional support for the crime control model came in 1968 when Congress passed the Omnibus Crime Control and Safe Streets Act. Under Title 1 of the act, Congress established the Law Enforcement Assistance Administration (LEAA) under the Department of Justice. Through this move, Congress extended federal involvement in the enforcement activities of state and local governments, and helped establish what were to become the primary crime strategies throughout the nation. Although the Constitution specifically places the major responsibility for criminal matters in the hands of the states, the federal government was able to assume considerable power and influence in such matters.

To help the LEAA carry out its mandate, Congress allocated just over $60 million for operation in 1969. Over the next few years, the LEAA was one of the fast growing federal agencies; its annual budget quickly reached half a billion dollars (in 1971), then climbed to over $800 million, and by 1976 it stood at $1.015 billion (U.S. Department of Justice, 1976:42).

As a result of numerous criticisms of agency practices during the 1970s, however, Congress voted the LEAA only $486 million for 1980 and then scrapped the agency altogether. The Justice System Improvement Act of 1979 established as its successor agency the Office of Justice Assistance, Research and Statistics (OJARS). Its budget for fiscal 1981 was $144,397,000 and, after a couple of leaner years, grew to $197.3 million in 1984 (McGarrell and Flanagan, 1985:25). In 1984, Congress created the Office of Justice Programs (OJP) as successor to OJARS, and the OJP budget for 1990 was $762 million

(Maguire and Flanagan, 1991:15). The 1980s thus saw a complete swing of the pendulum, and President Bush vowed to continue the onslaught on crime through even more largesse now that the Cold War is over.

Most of the federal money goes to police agencies. In 1988, for example, just under half of all federal expenditures on criminal justice went to police protection (Maguire and Flanagan, 1991:2). Funds are used to purchase new and sophisticated police equipment (from weapons and ammunition to vehicles, computers, and bulletproof clothing); to train officers and to reorganize police departments; to finance management training programs and operations research; to fund scientific and technological research; and to plan future policy throughout the various levels of the legal process.

Henry Pontell (1984:51–55) shows that state expenditures mirror the federal outlays on crime control. In California, for example, police budgets increased 126 percent between 1968 and 1974, compared with only a 50 percent increase for the courts, which also suffered a *decrease* in percapita personnel. Pontell warns that this sort of funding policy gives rise to a "structural imbalance" in the criminal justice system, reducing the capacity of certain agencies to sanction violators and thereby undermining the crime control capacity of the system as a whole (1984:35).

Information Systems   The development of sophisticated systems to handle information about crime has been one of the federal government's major contributions to crime control. Most of these systems center on computers, and all have been designed with one central aim—to improve detection, apprehension, and conviction rates.

Today computers are a fact of life in America. Few, if any, of us have escaped them. The value of computers in law enforcement was recognized early in their development, but the high cost of running them put them beyond the reach of most agencies. But the federal government could afford them, and the FBI was one of the first agencies to put them to use. Today the FBI's National Crime Information Center (NCIC) is hooked up to teleprinters in most of the nation's law-enforcement agencies (see Box 1.4). Computers, and the electronic technology that goes with them, now provide immediate access to millions of bits of information about crime, suspects, and offenders, and this information can be stored, manipulated, retrieved, and passed on at a moment's notice.

Privatization

One of the most interesting trends in recent years has been the growth of private sector involvement with the criminal justice system (see Figure 1.3). This involvement goes in two directions: (1) Private individuals and organizations are doing work traditionally thought of as the responsibility of governments; and (2) criminal justice personnel employed by the government are working for the private sector.

The first type of involvement is often referred to as *privatization*. It is controversial, and its benefits are by no means established. Most controversial

Aggressive federal strategies to improve police efficiency in the detection and apprehension of criminals have funneled millions of dollars into information processing techniques. Today, many patrolling officers have direct access to the computer at police headquarters.

is the use of private sector organizations to finance, build, run, and essentially control entire law-enforcement operations. The typical setting for this type of privatization is in corrections. In 1988, there were 13 private jails and prisons operating in nine states, providing 1910 prison beds (Bureau of Justice Statistics, 1988a:119). Not many, but the ideas is catching on.

The financial opportunities associated with privatization are substantial for two reasons. First, there are a lot of criminals and no signs that this will change soon; somebody has to pay for the system that catches and processes them and this makes criminal justice big business. Second, the technology of law enforcement is becoming more specialized and sophisticated; this creates openings for all kinds of expensive experts and services. Even academic criminologists get in on the act (see Gitchoff, 1988).

Financial considerations also dominate the other side of the coin, that is, when uniformed police officers and other justice personnel go to work in the private sector. Grocery, department, and discount store chains in many states now employ off-duty uniformed police officers who moonlight as store security. Although they are working for a private company, they often wear local or county police uniforms and even park their official patrol cars outside. Moonlighting provides the officer with an extra paycheck and the store with relatively cheap well-trained, well-recognized protection. The extent of moonlighting is unknown, but in both Seattle, Washington, and

Box 1.4 ■ Criminal Justice "Hot" Files

The computerized files of the Federal Bureau of Investigation's National Crime Information Center (NCIC) held almost 8 million records of wanted or missing persons and stolen property as of August 1986.

Among law enforcement officials, these files are commonly called "hot files," and the information in them is perhaps the most heavily used type of criminal justice information.

As of September, 1985, law enforcement officers in the United States and Canada were querying the NCIC system more than 400,000 times a day—54 percent were about wanted or missing persons and 42 percent were about stolen vehicles or license plates.

On August 1, 1986, the hot files included records concerning

■ more than 2.1 million stolen securities
■ 2 million stolen or recovered guns
■ 1.4 million stolen articles
■ 1.2 million stolen vehicles
■ 616,000 stolen license plates
■ 249,000 wanted persons
■ 53,000 missing persons (mostly juveniles)
■ 26,000 stolen boats
■ 1,300 unidentified persons
■ 253 Canadian warrants

Source: Bureau of Justice Statistics (1988b). *BJS Data Report, 1987.* Washington, D.C.: U.S. Department of Justice, p. 74.

Colorado Springs, Colorado, around half of the sworn officers had applied for permits to moonlight according to one investigation (Reiss, 1988).

Privatization and moonlighting raise many questions. Some are practical—about costs, efficiency, performance, danger, control—while others are ethical—about conflicts of interest, for example, or fraud, extortion, and bribery. None of these issues has yet been resolved. But another concern has been expressed by Stanley Cohen (1985—summarized in Barlow, 1987). Essentially, the argument is that the boundary between public and private control systems is blurring and therefore both the state's role as validator of its laws and the delicate balance between control and freedom are threatened. Cohen sees an ever widening net of control.

But all may not be bad. Cohen believes it possible that net widening can do both good and justice (Barlow, 1987:439):

"Good" comes in the forms of rape crisis centers, counseling programs, and shelters for battered women; the teaching of techniques for survival; the providing of talk, friendship, and intimacy . . . and the creation of more opportunities. "Justice" comes in the form of emphasizing less severe sen-

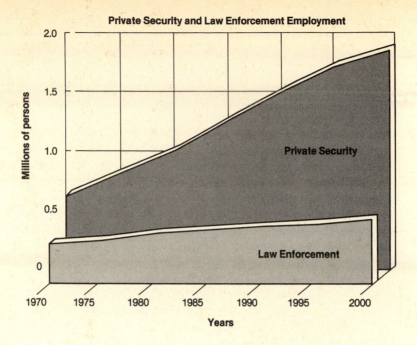

Private Security and Law Enforcement Employment

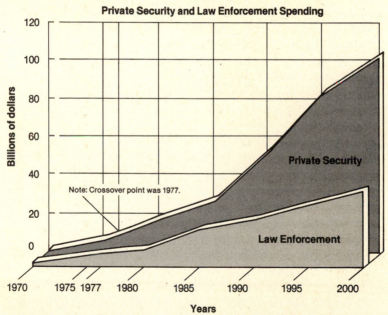

Private Security and Law Enforcement Spending

Note: Crossover point was 1977.

FIGURE 1.3   Involvement of the Private Sector with the Criminal Justice System. *Source:* National Institute of Justice (1991b). *Research in Brief.* Washington, D.C.: U.S. Department of Justice, p. 3.

tences for middle-range offenses; providing genuine alternatives to imprisonment for offenders who otherwise would have been released. . . .

Public Policy and Criminal Stereotypes

President Johnson, in calling for a war on crime, and Congress, in passing the Omnibus Crime Control and Safe Streets Act, drew attention only to certain crimes and certain criminals. Despite using such broad expressions as "lawlessness in America," they considered the real crime problem to be the overt threats to public order and prevailing institutions represented in street crimes—muggings, forcible rapes, burglaries, assaults, and armed robberies—and the activities of junkies and dope pushers, militant activists, and other so-called radicals. Except for the last two groups, the bulk of those identified as the real threat to law and order are lower-class individuals living mostly in the poverty areas of the nation's cities. Nineteenth-century officials dubbed such persons "the dangerous classes."

Because current crime policies show no evidence of changing focus, people have no incentive to alter their long-held stereotypes of the criminal. On the contrary, current policies merely reinforce these stereotypes. Americans are encouraged to view the streets as the unsafe turf of the criminal class. They are encouraged to distrust less well-off neighbors and to demand speedy and harsh disposition of criminal offenses. The destruction of an entire city block in Philadelphia in 1985 when police dropped a bomb on religious deviants is testimony to the link between stereotypical images of the dangerous class and crime control policy.

The targets of crime policy often feel oppressed by the authorities and see their own illegal actions as political crimes (Allen, 1974:75–76). They feel oppressed because they lack political power and believe their "crimes" are legitimate reactions to this political condition. Crime control policy further alienates and aggravates the disadvantaged segments of society when they realize that middle-class criminality escapes the serious attention of the state. With all of the money spent on projects and programs dealing with drugs, burglary, robbery, and street crimes generally, the government has little left over to spend on policing the middle class even if it wanted to.

This is not to say that street crimes should receive no attention or even that they should receive less attention than they do. The issue is how much and what kind of attention they receive relative to other forms of criminality. The relative lack of attention authorities give to occupational crime is hard to justify when one considers its impact on society (see Chapter 7). This inattention reinforces prevailing stereotypes about the middle-class criminal. For when middle-class offenders are apprehended, unusual as that is, the view seems to be that they must be ill or disturbed, since real criminals do not come from this class:

> The middle-class offender does not *need* to steal and is, therefore, in a different category from the working-class offender who is assumed to *need* to

steal and must, therefore, be prevented by the threat of prosecution. . . . Underlying the attitudes expressed by the police, the prosecution, and the magistrates and judges is the belief that the wealthy do not need to commit crimes, especially crimes of theft, so that if they do it is because of physical ill health, mental illness, or evil influence. (Chapman, 1968:72–75)

Since existing policies play down the detection, apprehension, and harsh punishment of occupational criminals, they confirm the belief that only the rare middle-class person turns to crime. People are encouraged to continue thinking that crime is a lower-class phenomenon.

An extreme version of this view is presented in Jeffrey Reiman's 1979 book, *The Rich Get Richer and the Poor Get Prison*. Reiman believes that the criminal justice system has failed to reduce crime and protect society precisely because that failure "serves the interests of the rich and powerful in America." How can that be? Reiman asserts that this failure performs an ideological service by funneling discontent toward those depicted as responsible for rising crime—the poor, the black, the lower classes—and away from the rich and powerful. At the same time, the system focuses on individual wrongdoing rather than on the institutions that make up social order, thus "implicitly conveying the message that the social conditions in which crime occurred are not responsible for the crime." If social conditions are not responsible for crime, then cries for fundamental change in the social order are without substance; the "radical" threat can be resisted by a united middle class urging continuation of prevailing policies.

Due Process

Justice with order has been a poor competitor of crime control, yet significant enough for some people to assert that criminals are being "mollycoddled" and that the hands of the police and courts are tied. These comments are usually directed at those seeking due process for criminal defendants or advocating increased use of probation, pretrial release, therapy, or community-based corrections.

The doctrine of *due process of law* originated with the signing of Magna Carta in 1215. This document set out the terms of an agreement between King John and English barons. It was a charter of liberties and rights designed by the barons to counteract the threat that the state would abuse its coercive powers in dealing with them. The king promised that "no man shall be arrested, or imprisoned, or disseized [deprived of his lands], or outlawed, or exiled, or in any way molested; nor will we proceed against him unless by the lawful judgment of his peers or by the law of the land" (Cole, 1975:105).

In America, the legal document outlining due process of law is the Constitution, particularly the Fourth, Fifth, Sixth, Eighth, and Fourteenth amendments. The essential provisions of these amendments are:

[*Fourth Amendment*] The right of the people to be secure in their persons, houses, papers, and effects, against unreasonable searches and seizures, shall not be violated, and no Warrants shall issue, but upon probable cause, supported by Oath or affirmation, and particularly describing the place to be searched, and the persons or things to be seized.

[*Fifth Amendment*] No person shall . . . be subject for the same offence to be twice put in jeopardy of life or limb; nor shall be compelled in any criminal case to be a witness against himself, nor be deprived of life, liberty, or property, without due process of law. . . .

[*Sixth Amendment*] In all criminal prosecutions, the accused shall enjoy the right to a speedy and public trial, by an impartial jury . . . ; to be confronted with the witnesses against him; to have compulsory process for obtaining Witnesses in his favor, and to have the assistance of counsel for his defence.

[*Eighth Amendment*] Excessive bail shall not be required, nor excessive fines imposed, nor cruel and unusual punishments inflicted.

[*Fourteenth Amendment*] . . . No State shall make or enforce any law which shall abridge the privileges or immunities of citizens of the United States; nor shall any State deprive any person of life, liberty, or property, without due process of law; nor deny to any person within its jurisdiction the equal protection of the laws.

The U.S. Supreme Court and Due Process   The U.S. Supreme Court has the responsibility to rule on constitutional matters. It reacts to requests for rulings on constitutional questions rather than initiating them, and so its decisions are always set against a backdrop of legal controversy. Also, its rulings are not fixed; it may rule one way and later rule another way on the same question. This fact explains why basic policy questions often return again and again for rulings by the Court. It also explains why the composition of the Court is such an important issue, and why, when a President makes a new appointment, the ratification process in Congress is often so heated: whoever is appointed could shift the direction of Court rulings.

Rulings that advance due process values have been relatively rare in the history of the Court. Should a number of such rulings come from any particular Court, the Court is honored with the reputation of being "liberal" or "radical." The court under Chief Justice Earl Warren was so honored.

Landmark due process rulings include *Weeks* v. *United States* (1914), in which the court established the "exclusionary rule," arguing that evidence obtained illegally by the police must be excluded from subsequent criminal proceedings. In *Rochin* v. *California* (1952) the Court ruled that the sanctity of a person's body is inviolate and that attempts to remove evidence from it for a conviction (in this case, narcotics pumped from a suspect's stomach were used to convict him) constitute illegal search and seizure. In *Mapp* v. *Ohio* (1961) the Court ruled that neither state nor federal courts can accept evidence obtained in violation of the constitutional requirements of reasonable search and seizure. In *Gideon* v. *Wainwright* (1963) the Court ruled that any indigent defendant should be allowed free legal counsel. In *Escobedo* v. *Illinois* (1964), *Gideon* was extended to include right to counsel at the time of interrogation. In *Miranda* v. *Arizona* (1966), the Court ruled that upon arrest, the police must

The United States Supreme Court in 1992. Seated from left: John Paul Stevens, Byron White, Chief Justice William H. Renquist, Harry A. Blackmun, Sandra Day O'Connor; Standing from left: David Souter, Antonin Scalia, Anthony M. Kennedy, Clarence Thomas.

notify suspects of their rights during interrogation, their right to counsel, and the possible uses of evidence obtained during interrogation. In *Katz* v. *United States* (1967) the Court ruled that a court order is required to use electronic surveillance. In *Duncan* v. *Louisiana* (1968) the Court reaffirmed the right to a jury trial regardless of the legal seriousness of the offense. In *Witherspoon* v. *Illinois* (1968) the Court reaffirmed that the jury must be impartial. *Chimel* v. *California* (1969) restricted the physical vicinity subject to search without a warrant to that within the "immediate control" (reach) of a suspect.

Many of these significant due process decisions came out of the last few years of the Warren Court. However, the Warren Court's last major decision, *Terry* v. *Ohio* (1968), was a break with its earlier due process rulings. In this decision, eight justices agreed (Justice William O. Douglas dissented) that a police officer may frisk a suspect when the officer "observes unusual conduct which leads him reasonably to conclude in the light of his experience that criminal activity may be afoot and that the persons with whom he is dealing may be armed and presently dangerous."

However, in Justice Douglas's opinion, there was no "probable cause" to believe that a crime was being committed, had been committed, or was about to be committed in the case under consideration. With this decision the Supreme Court began chipping away at due process safeguards. The trend continued throughout the seventies and is still going strong (see Box 1.5).

Box 1.5 ■ Supreme Court Continues Its Crime Control Rulings

Advocates of the crime control model should be pleased with recent appointments to the U.S. Supreme Court. President Reagan's appointments of Antonin Scalia in 1986 and Anthony M. Kennedy in 1988 and President Bush's appointments of David Souter in 1990 and Clarence Thomas in 1991 have strengthened the Court's conservative stance on constitutional matters. Here are some examples of recent rulings on criminal process:

U.S. v. *Leon* (1984): Established a "good faith" exemption to the exclusionary rule, establishing that illegally seized evidence may be used in court if the illegal police action is based on mistakes by judges or magistrates and not on an intent to violate a citizen's Fourth Amendment rights.

California v. *Greenwood* (1988): Police may search plastic garbage bags left at curbside for pick-up without first obtaining a search warrant.

U.S. v. *Robinson* (1988): Earlier statements by a witness who had subsequently lost his memory could be used in court in lieu of courtroom testimony without necessarily violating the defendant's right to confront his accuser.

Arizona v. *Fulminate* (1990): Unlawful use of coerced confessions as evidence against a defendant sometimes may be considered harmless error.

Florida v. *Bostick* (1990): Even without search warrants, police may board busses and ask passengers to consent to searches for drugs (but passengers can refuse).

California v. *Acevedo* (1991): Police may open luggage in a car without a search warrant if they have probable cause to believe there are drugs inside.

California v. *Hodari D.* (1991): Police may chase a person even without reasonable suspicion that the person committed a crime: A chase by police or an order to halt is not the same as a seizure, according to Judge Scalia, who wrote the majority opinion.

U.S. v. *Felix* (1992): Prosecutors may bring charges of criminal conspiracy even after they have tried the defendant on the crime around which the conspiracy was formed; double-jeopardy does not apply in such cases, Chief Justice Renquist wrote.

Three Principles of a Moral Criminal Process   Federal Judge David Bazelon (1981:1143–1170) has questioned whether it is necessary "to compromise the most basic values of our democratic society in our desperation to fight crime." He believes that a "truly moral criminal law" will be guided by three fundamental principles:

1. "The criminal process must always remain sensitive to the social realities that underlie crime." Bazelon calls this the *reality* principle, and he draws attention to the fact that the bulk of street crime, especially violent offenses, is committed by people whose lives have been shaped by the poverty and desperation of the underclass. Muggers, rapists, purse snatchers, and burglars "turn to crime for economic survival, a sense of

excitement and accomplishment, and an outlet for frustration, desperation, and rage." The fear of street crime must not lead society to lose sight
of the social inequities that help shape it.

2. The criminal process "must make meaningful the claim of 'equal justice
   under law'." This is the *equality* principle, and it challenges authorities
   to do something about the inequities in the criminal process, to practice
   what they preach. Those who accept these inequities, Bazelon writes, "are
   only donning moral blinders."

3. The criminal process "must, through a process of constant questioning,
   force the community to confront the painful realities and agonizing
   choices posed by social injustice." This Bazelon calls the *education*
   principle. He argues that the criminal justice system is in a position to
   encourage humane and intelligent responses to the crime problem by
   articulating and reaffirming fundamental moral values in its own actions
   with respect to the constitutional issues embedded in the Bill of Rights.

Bazelon's views are not shared by all, but they offer a challenge to those who
advocate more of the same as well as a strategy for balancing due process
interests with those of crime control.

Summary of Chapter 1

This chapter began with the observation that the media image of the crime
scene is highly distorted. The emphasis on crimes that are especially violent
or sensational helps fuel widespread fear of crime, which leads many people
to retreat behind locked doors, making the streets even more dangerous for
those who venture out.

Criminologists try to uncover the truth about crime, criminals, and the
criminal process. The chapter discussed various concepts, definitions, and
perspectives that criminologists have developed. The legalistic definition of
crime is behavior that violates the criminal law; criminals are people who
engage in that behavior. A more sociological definition is that crime and
criminal are labels attached to behavior, events, and individuals by people in
positions of authority or power.

Criminal law formally creates crime by defining it into existence. It is the
application of law, however, that criminalizes actual behavior, people, and
events. This process is influenced by interests, the things that people value.
When interests are in conflict, as they often are, law usually reflects the
interests of the more powerful groups in society. As later chapters will show,
even laws supported by broad public consensus—rape statutes, for example—
may acutally serve the interests of the more powerful (males) at the expense of
the less powerful (females).

Public policy on crime is shaped by historical forces as well as by the
attitudes and beliefs of people in power. The crime control model emphasizes
order with justice and pays most attention to the capacity of society to catch,

prosecute, and dispose of a high proportion of guilty defendants. The due process model emphasizes justice with order and sees the crime control function as secondary to the protection of individual liberties and the right to equal treatment under law.

American public policy on criminal matters is dominated by the crime control model. Government spending is used largely to improve apprehension and conviction of criminals rather than to prevent crime in the first place or to ensure that the rights of offenders and victims are protected. Privatization of policing and the correctional system and moonlighting by uniformed police are recent trends that blur the distinction between private and public responsibilities, widen the net of coercive control, and introduce the profit motive into crime policy.

Recommended Readings

William J. Chambliss (1973). "The Saints and the Roughnecks." *Society* 11:24–31.

Aaron V. Cicourel (1968). *The Social Organization of Juvenile Justice.* New York: J. Wiley.

Stanley Cohen (1985). *Visions of Social Control: Crime, Punishment and Classification.* New York: Polity Press.

Walter B. Miller (1973). "Ideology and criminal justice policy: Some current issues." *Journal of Criminal Law and Criminology* 64:141–162.

Herbert L. Packer (1968). *The Limits of the Criminal Sanction.* Stanford, Calif.: Stanford University Press.

Henry N. Pontell (1984). *A Capacity to Punish.* Bloomington, Ind.: Indiana University Press.

Wesley Skogan and Michael G. Maxfield (1981). *Coping With Crime: Individual and Neighborhood Reactions.* Beverly Hills, Calif.: Sage.

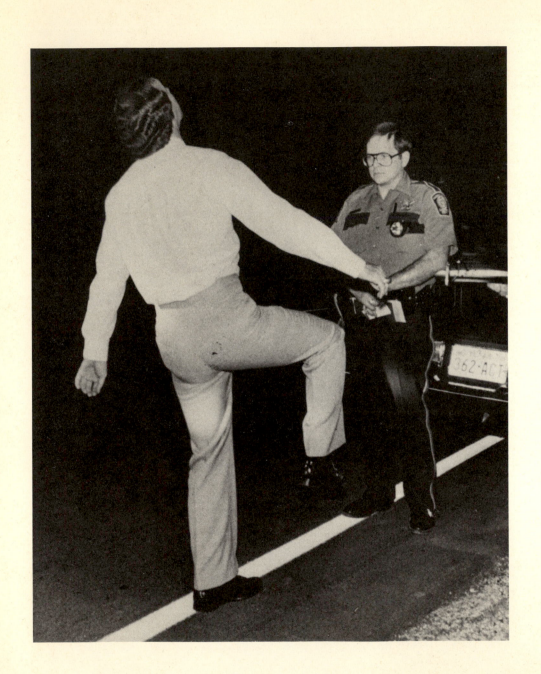

Chapter 2

Getting a Line on Crime: The Data and Methods of Criminology

Science involves the identification, collection, and analysis of data that are used to develop and test theories. In criminology this process is complicated by the nature of the subject. Criminology deals not only with human behavior, which is complex, difficult to observe systematically, and difficult to interpret, but also with behavior that is punishable, likely to be hidden, and often an embarrassment to offenders and victims. In fact, information on some crimes is so difficult to collect that even the most experienced researchers are intimidated by the task. Domestic violence, organized crime, and most work-related crimes are examples.

How Crime Data Are Produced

An individual who hears a burglar alarm sound is faced with a variety of options. One might think of various reasons for doing nothing at all. People rationalize that it's not their business; that someone else will notify the police; that the alarm may have tripped accidentally; that they are in a hurry; that they may get hurt; that they will be required to give a statement or testify; that police would not want to be bothered; that by the time police arrived it would be too late.

Most people probably have faced an opportunity to notify authorities of a possible crime but have not done so for similar reasons. More significant is the fact that many crime *victims* do nothing. The crimes officially ignored by victims are not, as one might think, minor ones. Many predatory crimes that result in substantial property loss or personal injury remain unreported.

Regardless of the reasons, when victims and witnesses fail to report possible crimes, the acts in question are "lost." They cannot become part of police records and cannot be studied as part of the official crime scene. Therefore it is important to note that the public has a major role in the production of crime data. Offenses that remain unreported are part of the so-called "dark figure of crime." This is the part that cannot be seen. Crime is like an iceberg—for most crimes the dark figure is much larger than the figure we can see.

The Production of Official Crime Data

For an act to become part of the data on crime someone must be told that it has occurred. To become part of the official picture, the act must be reported to agents of the government, which usually means the police.

Of course there are many crimes that police see themselves. Some of them would never become part of the official record if the police did not see them. So-called "victimless" crimes such as drug sales, prostitution, and many alcohol-related offenses are examples. Loitering and vagrancy also fall into this category. Another example is criminal conspiracy. Police use informants and undercover agents to discover many of these offenses. In other cases the crimes are discovered during routine police patrol. In both situations, however, the police observe only the tip of the iceberg.

In the case of predatory crimes involving property loss or injury, police rely heavily on the public's willingness to report that they have witnessed or have been victimized by a possible crime. It is estimated that only 3 percent of reported violent crimes and 2 percent of reported household crimes are actually discovered by the police themselves (Bureau of Justice Statistics, 1985a). If one had to rely on police observation of serious crime, one's information base would be small indeed. Yet national surveys indicate that little more than one-third of all serious crimes are reported to the police, and the situation is not much different in England (Hough and Mayhew, 1983). Clearly there is a vast amount of crime that the police do not know about even when someone else does. This observation applies equally today as it did 20 years ago (see Figure 2.1).

Reasons for Reporting/Nonreporting of Crime

Various reasons for deciding not to report hearing a burglar alarm have already been listed. But what if people were the victims of rape or robbery? Surely that would change their attitude.

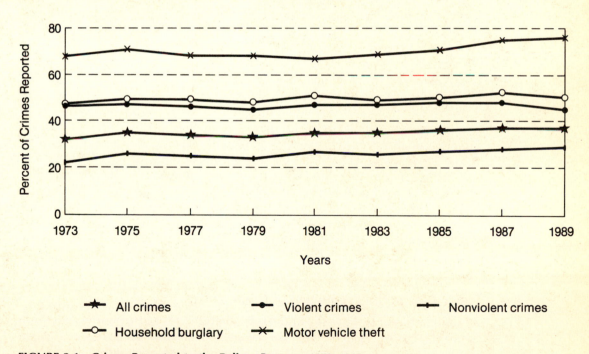

FIGURE 2.1 Crimes Reported to the Police. Percent, 1973–1989. *Source:* Compiled from Bureau of Justice Statistics (1990b). *Criminal Victimization, 1989.* Washington, D.C.: U.S. Department of Justice. Table 6.

Information collected by interviewing a sampling of Americans indicates that reporting behavior and the reasons for it vary from crime to crime, and it sometimes makes a difference if a person is a witness rather than a victim. As one might expect, crimes most likely to be reported are those involving the most serious losses (which are often insured) or injuries requiring medical treatment. Motor vehicle theft heads the list (73 percent in 1986), followed by aggravated assault (59 percent) and robbery (58 percent). Type of crime appears to have more impact on reporting behavior than either age, sex, or race of victims (Bureau of Justice Statistics, 1987:32). Violent crimes, however, are apparently more likely to be reported if they involve black or female victims (Bureau of Justice Statistics, 1985a) and if they involve the use of a weapon or result in injuries (Gottfredson and Gottfredson, 1988:26–29).

Another difference exists between "attempted" versus "completed" crimes: Completed crimes are much more likely to be reported than unsuccessful ones. On the other hand, it may come as a surprise that crimes committed by nonstrangers are more likely to be reported than those committed by strangers. The major exception to this is the crime of rape (Bureau of Justice Statistics, 1985b).

In general, the most frequently mentioned reasons for nonreporting are that the crime was unsuccessful, that it was not important enough, or that nothing could or would be done. In the case of violent crimes, composed mostly of assaults and robberies, the most frequent reason for nonreporting is that the matter was private or personal (Bureau of Justice Statistics, 1988a). Not surprisingly, this reason is much less likely to apply when people are attacked by strangers (Harlow, 1991a:3).

These reasons may hide a multitude of important distinctions in victims' minds, but one thing is clear: People shun interference from the "outside" even after they have been placed in danger. This decision may be based on an unpleasant past experience with police, embarrassment or fear, or a generalized belief that police are uncaring or incompetent. In the case of domestic violence, all three reasons may well be factors. Yet it now appears that calling the police helps prevent future victimization: National surveys from 1978 to 1982 show that wives who called the police after being assaulted by their husbands were three times less likely to be assaulted again than victims who did not call the police (Bureau of Justice Statistics, 1987:32). Many victims who report crimes apparently do so because they believe it will prevent a similar incident from happening again (Bureau of Justice Statistics, 1988a:86).

Police Role in the Production of Crime Data

Although the public have the initial responsibility for getting most crimes into the official record, the police have the last word. This is true of statistics on crimes as well as on criminals. Statistics on arrests, charges, adjudication, and sentencing are all affected by whether police officially recognize an event as a crime.

It cannot be assumed that a reported crime will be included in the official record. For one thing, police may decide that the reported incident was not a crime at all. The public cannot be expected to know all the technicalities of criminal law, a fact reflected in the vast number of emergency calls that turn out to be false alarms. The layperson is not always to blame, however. Sometimes callers describe events that police dispatchers list as murders, robberies, and aggravated assaults but which investigating officers cannot later verify as crimes. In one study, only 72.9 percent of the 23,136 classified violent crimes were subsequently confirmed or "founded" (Maxfield, Lewis, and Szoc, 1980:225). In an English study verification varied considerably by offense, from only 30 percent of reported bicycle thefts to 70 percent of reported burglaries (Bottomley and Coleman, 1981).

The police founding decision is a crucial one because only when an event has been officially recognized as a crime is it entered into the record, and only then will police consider recording information about a suspect. Unfortunately, the founding conclusion is not always accurate and at times may be intentionally falsified. An internal audit of the Chicago Police Department determined that many crimes had been incorrectly recorded as "unfounded." Of 377 rape cases, 18 percent were judged to have been incorrectly labeled as unfounded; of 649 robberies, 36.4 percent had been incorrectly labeled; and of 708 burglaries, nearly 50 percent should have been classified as founded but were not (*Chicago Sun Times*, April 1983). A study of Portland police estimated that 48 percent of serious personal and property crimes reported during the early 1970s had been incorrectly labeled as unfounded (Schneider, 1977).

The accusation of intentional falsification is difficult to document, but strong inferential evidence indicates that it happens routinely and not simply when police chiefs want to impress their superiors or the electorate (see Skolnick, 1966; Wolfgang, 1967). In one analysis of founding behavior by English police, the authors discovered several reasons why police would not record a reported crime as "found" though it was in fact an offense: (1) The police considered it too trivial; (2) they considered it unlikely that prosecution would be pursued by the victim; (3) the incident was determined not to be police business; (4) the crime was too difficult to investigate or prosecute; (5) the incident was not "real" crime (Kinsey, Lea, and Young, 1986).

The last reason deserves comment. Many people might believe that some crimes should not be considered as crimes: Marijuana use, prostitution, and gambling are examples. Crimes that involve violence or destruction of property, such as barroom brawls or the writing of wall graffiti are other examples. If people do not believe that an offense is "really" a crime, they are less likely to report it to the police.

When offenses *are* reported and police decide that they are not "real" crimes, then another problem arises. As private citizens the police are entitled to their beliefs, but their behavior as enforcers of the law cannot be dismissed lightly when it contradicts both the letter of the law and the wishes of the public.

The systematic underrecording of crime by police appears to be related to the type of crime involved and the people against whom it is directed. Kinsey, Lea, and Young (1986:60–61) observe that English police disparagingly refer to certain offenses as "rubbish" crimes, which are distinguished from true crimes in police perspective. Rubbish crimes typically involve lower-class, minority, or female victims who are assaulted in a domestic setting by a friend, lover, or relative or by an offender whom police regard as an amateur. A similar claim of police stereotyping has been made by Clifford Shearing (1979:6) in a study of a large Canadian police department. Shearing analyzed thousands of calls to police and communications among the police themselves. He found that police "made a fundamental distinction between 'the public' on the one hand, . . . and 'the dregs,' or more expressively, 'the scum,' on the other." By police account, the scum did not deserve to be served or protected.

Underrecording by police of crimes against minorities, women, and the lower classes has not been confined to petty offenses and minor acts of aggression (see also Elias, 1986:133–146). Largely because of the influence of civil rights activists and the women's movement, the police in many cities are more sensitive about minority victimization than they used to be and departments try to address racism and prejudice in their training programs. However, such positive steps must overcome two things. First, the police receive little reward for catering to victims, especially those without political clout (Elias, 1986:140–141). Second, stereotypes are remarkably enduring, and thus "rubbish" crimes can be expected to remain in the police lexicon despite official enlightenment.

For such reasons, crimes that victimize poor and minorities will remain underrecorded relative to crimes considered as "real." As Kinsey, Lea, and Young (1986) point out, the consequence is not merely a dark figure of crime, but the prospect that it will grow with time. That is because the lack of an official police response to citizen complaints feeds the belief that the police do not care or cannot be bothered with poor or minority victims. Thus the flow of crime information is reduced, further distorting the picture of crime that is drawn from official sources.

Police–Citizen Encounters   The police decision to record and investigate a complaint as an official offense may be influenced by the interaction between the responding officer and the complainant. Although police recording decisions are influenced primarily by the legal seriousness of a complaint, one must still account for the fact that many serious crimes are not recorded.

The first and most famous study of police recording behavior in the field was directed by Albert Reiss and his student, Donald Black. They discovered that police labeling of complaints as crimes was influenced by three factors besides legal seriousness: (1) the *demeanor* of the complainant—those people who demonstrated more deference to police were more successful in getting their complaints officially recorded; (2) the complainant's *preference for formal action*—those wanting official police action tended to get it; and (3) the

The official descriptions of crimes are constructed largely from police interviews with victims and witnesses. Police decisions about whether and who to interview, and about whether and what to report, clearly influence the picture of crime that is constructed, and therefore the official data that are available to criminologists.

relational distance between complainant and suspect—offenses committed by strangers were more likely to be officially recognized as crimes (Black, 1970).

The exercise of police discretion in reporting crimes is obviously substantial though it probably varies from jurisdiction to jurisdiction. At best, the number of so-called "crimes known to the police" is a poor approximation of the true amount of crime. In addition, police reporting reflects and perpetuates stereotypes of crime, victims, and offenders and may contribute to the disinclination of vulnerable people to call police after they have been victimized. From the perspective of victims, when the police do respond to calls for assistance they often do very little. A recent survey found that police asked few questions, even in cases of violent crimes, and in the case of burglary, they did not even "look around" in nearly half the incidents (Whitaker, 1989:6).

The Production of Official Data on Criminals All sorts of people commit crimes, and some do so many times. To become part of the official record, people must be identified and formally arrested by the police. Once a formal arrest has been made, a crime is considered "cleared" and the offender's name is entered into police record books.

The arrest data compiled by police is the only official count of criminals. Arrested individuals are the people officially doing official crime. This does not mean that they are actually guilty of the crime(s) for which they have been arrested, nor does it mean that they have committed only the offense(s) charged. Arrest data simply provide a count of the people who have been arrested as suspects in a crime. Arrest data chronicle police activity but tell us less about the nature of crime or criminals. Nor can these data provide information about criminals who are known to the police but not arrested. In addition, arrest data cannot describe the dark figure of crime nor the people who escape detection.

It may seem to contradict what was said earlier, but urban police tend to concentrate enforcement in poor and minority neighborhoods. These areas become "overpoliced" relative to other parts of the city (Hagan, Gillis, and Chan, 1978; Smith, 1986). To some extent this reflects the concentration in inner-city areas of violent crimes such as robbery, aggravated assault, and homicide. It also reflects and reinforces stereotypes of the origins, character-istics, and dangers associated with "real" crime and "real" criminals.

Because police concentrate enforcement in poor and inner-city neighbor-hoods, they discover not only more serious criminals there, but also more drunks, loiterers, vandals, and other petty offenders. The result is that arrest data in general are composed disproportionately of poor and minority indi-viduals. Even so, the probability of being arrested is uniformly low, regardless of race (Petersilia, 1985a).

Those most vulnerable to crime are also most vulnerable to arrest and prosecution. As an example, consider the situation facing black Americans in 1989. Although blacks constitute only 12 percent of the U.S. population, in that year they constituted 48 percent of the people arrested for serious violent crimes, 34 percent of those arrested for property crimes, almost 54 percent of those serving jail sentences, and 47 percent of those serving state prison terms (Maguire and Flanagan, 1991).

Police Clearance Rates   Recall that the neighborhoods in which significant underrecording of crime occurs are also the neighborhoods in which dispro-portionate numbers of arrests are made. This has a profound effect on what police call the *clearance rate*. The clearance rate is conventionally used as a measure of police productivity and is based on the number of recorded offenses that are cleared or "solved" by arrest. As noted previously, police consider a case solved for statistical purposes when *any* arrest has been made for that offense.

To compute the clearance rate for a crime category one divides the number of arrests per category by the number of recorded offenses in the same category. Usually the relevant arrests and offenses are for an entire year. To illustrate, suppose 1000 robberies were recorded in a certain city during 1988. Suppose also that during the same year the police made 200 arrests on

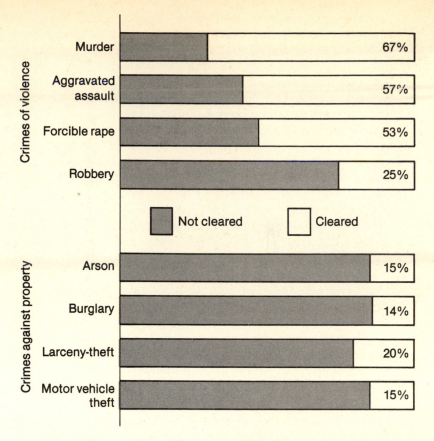

FIGURE 2.2   **Crimes Cleared by Arrest, 1990.** *Source:* Compiled from Federal Bureau of Investigation (1991). *Crime in the United States, 1990.* Washington, D.C.: U.S. Department of Justice.

robbery charges. The clearance rate for robbery would therefore be 200 divided by 1000, which is 0.20 or 20 percent. Figure 2.2 shows the clearance rates for various offenses as computed by the FBI for 1990. As one can see, the clearance rates for violent crimes are generally higher than those for crimes against property. Murder tops the list and not surprisingly—it is a heinous crime that people want to see solved, and the murderer is usually an acquaintance, friend, or relative of the victim and therefore not hard to find.

When the clearance rate is relatively high, the police look good. It should also be clear that the rate can be manipulated quite easily. If the number of arrests is inflated or the number of recorded offenses is decreased, the result is the same—the clearance rate goes up. Should the opposite be done, the rate goes down. Considering the close ties police officials have to government treasuries and to the fortunes of elected officials, it should come as no surprise that the clearance rate is sometimes the object of manipulation by high-level police administrators (Skolnick, 1966). If a department is requesting new resources, it might help to lower the clearance rate, thus showing that police are swamped by crime. On the other hand, to show that the department is successfully fighting crime, the clearance rate can be raised.

Police sometimes go to extraordinary lengths to "clear" crimes. A recent example illustrates the pressures they are under to inflate the clearance rate and the risks they encounter in doing so. Henry Lea Lucas was identified in 1983 as a serial killer who had confessed to nearly 100 murders around the country. By 1984 it was reported that he had confessed to 360 murders, and by 1985 the figure stood at an incredible 600 killings in nearly 30 different states (*TIme*, 1985). In that same year, however, the *New York Times* (April 18 and 24, 1985) reported that Lucas may actually have killed only one person, his mother! As the story unfolded, it became apparent that Lucas had been pressured by eager police into making confessions so that they could clear their books of unsolved murders. The truth will probably never be known, but most of the murders cleared by Lucas's arrest and "confessions" were not committed by him.

To return to the discussion of overpolicing and underrecording in certain neighborhoods, the resulting clearance rates present a distorted picture of experiences with crime. Underrecording downplays the suffering that occurs in inner-city areas and poor neighborhoods, while overpolicing subjects people living there to increased surveillance and risk of being arrested. The result is a sense of neglect on one hand and a sense of abuse by authorities on the other (for the American experience see Elias, 1986; for the English experience see Kinsey, Lea, and Young, 1986). The official clearance rate is inflated in the process and cannot be reliable for research purposes. What is known, however, is that the real clearance rate—the proportion of actual offenses actually cleared—is much lower than published statistics indicate (Kinsey, Lea, and Young, 1986).

Figure 2.3 illustrates the process by which official crime data are produced. As could be predicted by the preceding discussion, the numbers at the end of the process are considerably smaller than those at the beginning.

Kinds of Crime Data

There are three major sources of crime data: (1) information on crimes and the criminal justice system supplied by government agencies; (2) information on crime victimization gathered through interviews with citizens; and (3) information on crime and delinquency supplied through interviews with citizens who admit their own criminality.

The Uniform Crime Reports

The most widely used national data source on official crimes and criminals is the FBI's *Uniform Crime Reports (UCR)*. These reports were the brainchild of J. Edgar Hoover, late director of the Federal Bureau of Investigation. Over 50

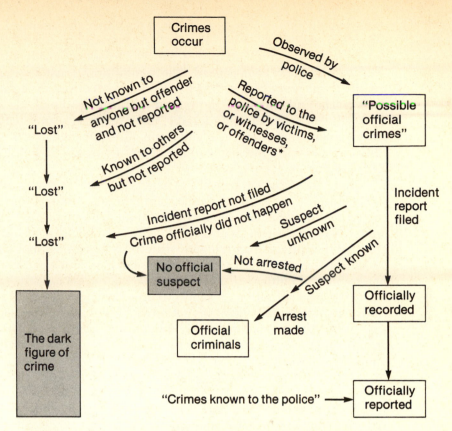

FIGURE 2.3 The Production of Official Data on Crimes and Criminals. *Some small but unknown proportion of offenders report their own crimes to the police, perhaps out of guilt or remorse or because of unintended consequences that the offender regrets.

years ago, Hoover recognized the need to compile nationwide data on crime as an aid to law enforcement and to basic research.

The UCR program was designed so that police departments from around the country would voluntarily compile and submit crime statistics according to a uniform system. The idea was to make the data comparable from jurisdiction to jurisdiction. At first, only the largest departments participated. Many smaller agencies found the process too costly or simply did not have the necessary personnel. Some police chiefs doubtless did not like the "Big Brother" implications. Nevertheless, the program gained acceptance as time passed, and with the development and growing use of computers it is now relatively easy for police to submit data to the FBI. Many send data first to a state or regional crime information clearing house, where they are relayed to the FBI for eventual publication in an annual report titled *Crime in the United States.*

Today the UCR contain information on crimes reported by police as well as on arrests and other topics ranging from the killing of police officers to crimes on university campuses. A major portion of the report deals with what are called "Part I" or "index offenses." Index offenses are serious crimes that are considered representative of the worst offenses and are therefore a "bellwether" of crime in general. The assumption is that if index offenses go up, the crime problem is getting worse; if they go down, the crime problem is easing. The index offenses now used are criminal homicide (murder and nonnegligent manslaughter), forcible rape, robbery, aggravated assault, burglary, larceny-theft, auto theft, and arson. (The appendix to this text gives the FBI's definitions of these and all the other offenses included in the Uniform Crime Reports.)

There are serious drawbacks to using the UCR. They are police data and thus subject to the criticisms and qualifications addressed in the preceding sections. Other problems should be mentioned, however. One issue concerns comparative research. Sooner or later most scientific research becomes comparative research as scholars search for generalizations, laws, predictions, and explanations. Comparative research on crime using official data is beset with difficulties.

First, legal definitions of some offenses vary from jurisdiction to jurisdiction. This is especially true internationally, but it is also true of states within the United States. To address the international problem. Archer and Gartner (1984) spent ten years developing the Comparative Crime Data File, which contains information on seven offense categories for 110 countries and 44 cities from 1900 to 1970. In general, the two major difficulties are these: (1) crime in one state may not be considered crime in another; (2) one jurisdiction may define a particular type of crime, such as burglary, differently from another, so what both report as burglary is not quite the same thing.

Second, comparisons across time are hazardous. The FBI's own offense classification system has changed through the years. In both 1958 and 1974, for example, the definitions of certain offenses were changed. Thus, statistics for offenses from prior years cannot be compared to post-change figures.

Another problem concerns the computation of the crime rate. Rates are used for comparative purposes because they reveal the amount of crime in proportion to a base, thus making comparisons more meaningful. Box 2.1 illustrates the computation and use of crime rates. Note that the traditional denominator is population. Accurate population figures, however, are notoriously difficult to calculate. Even census figures are estimates rather than exact figures.

For many years, official crime rates were computed by using population data from the most recently completed census. For example, crime rate figures for 1959 were based on population figures for 1950. If both population and crime had been rising during that decade but only changes in crime had been considered, the crime rates for 1959 would have been higher than if greater population figures had been used. Now the FBI uses yearly population estimates in the computation of rates.

Variations and periodic changes in data-recording technology, in police policy and practice, and in public reporting behavior also hamper the effort to do comparative research. One might ask, "why bother doing the research at all?" But comparative research is as important to criminology as it is to any other field. If ideas can be tested only in one place or with one group of people or for one period of time, then their applicability is diminished. Without comparative research the ideas themselves may not even surface. It is for these reasons that efforts to improve the comparability of data on crime and criminals continue.

It bears repeating that while official police statistics may be a poor indicator of criminal *behavior* they are, nevertheless, a perfectly good measure of organizational processes that shape the production of official criminality—they are "fully accurate indicators of police responses to crime and, by extension, rates . . . of criminalization" (Boritch and Hagan, 1990:571).

Finding Crime with Victimization Studies

The limitations of official data on crime and criminals have previously been documented. Fortunately, methods have been developed in an effort to fill in the gaps in the official picture and thereby uncover the dark figure of crime. In this section victimization studies will be discussed, and in the next self-report studies will be considered.

Victimization studies are designed to determine whether people have been crime victims. They are predicated on the assumption that an unrecorded crime can be uncovered by conducting direct interviews with the citizenry. In this way researchers try to develop an accurate picture of the extent and type of crime and of the circumstances surrounding it.

The National Crime Victimization Survey   Every year since 1973 the U.S. Department of Justice has sponsored a nationwide survey of 49,000 households to find out more about American crime. Called the National Crime Survey until October, 1991, and now called the National Crime Victimization Survey (NCVS), the program has become an international model.

The NCVS interview begins with a series of screening questions. These questions identify whether the respondent recalls being personally involved in a crime during the previous year. The questions help to jog the respondent's memory and also to identify the kinds of things that might be relevant.

The more detailed questioning that follows is designed to pinpoint specifics of incidents that respondents recall (see Box 2.2). Sometimes an incident is revealed not to be a crime; other times it may be determined to be a different crime than initially believed. For example, an apparent "breaking and entering" may have been vandalism. In addition, detailed questioning provides information about such things as the actions of offenders and victims, the extent of injury or loss, the type of weapon used, and whether the incident was reported to police.

Victimization surveys have their limitations, however. First, findings are based only on recall, and people's memories are often flawed. Second,

Box 2.1 ■ Numbers and Rates

Numbers indicate how many crimes have been recorded, but they fail to take into account the size of the population in which those crimes have occurred. Suppose two cities have officially recorded these numbers of crimes for 1989:

	City A	City B
Violent crimes	5,000	10,000
Property crimes	15,000	40,000
Other crimes	20,000	50,000
Total number	40,000	100,000

At first glance, City B has more crime than City A. If you wanted to move to one of these cities and decided to base your selection on the extent of crime, you might well choose City A over City B. But you might be making a big mistake.

Suppose you determine that the population of City A is 1 million and that of City B is 2.5 million. With this information you can compute a crime *rate* that takes into account the number of people in each city. If there are more people in one city than in another, you would expect more crime in the former.

With the population information in hand, crime rates for the two cities are computed by applying the conventional formula, which gives the number of crimes per 100,000 people:

$$\frac{\text{Number of crimes known to police} \times 100,000}{\text{Population}}$$

The crime rates, then, are as follows:

	Numbers of Crimes Per 100,000	
	City A	City B
Violent crime	500	400
Property crime	1500	1600
Other crimes	2000	2000
Total crime	4000	4000

It is now evident that the overall crime rates are the same, but the rate for violent crime is higher in City A than City B, while the rate for property crime is lower in City A than City B. If this were all the information available, your choice of city might well hinge on the type of crime you would rather avoid.

Other Types of Crime Rates. Though crime rates are often expressed in terms of total population, there are other useful ways of computing them. One way is to compute rates for specific categories of population—males, females; blacks, whites; young, old; and so on. Arrest data are commonly used, and the rates are computed as follows:

$$\text{Race-specific arrest rates (example)} = \frac{\text{Number of whites arrested} \times 100,000}{\text{Number of whites in population}}$$

$$\text{Age-specific arrest rates (example)} = \frac{\text{Number of 16–18-yr-olds arrested} \times 100,000}{\text{Number of 16–18-yr-olds in population}}$$

$$\text{Sex-specific arrest rates} = \frac{\text{Number of males (females) arrested} \times 100,000}{\text{Number of males (females) in population}}$$

Another useful way of computing crime rates is in terms of the risks of or opportunities for crime. Sarah Boggs (1964) was among the first to advocate this approach, arguing that it makes sense to express crime in terms of people or objects at risk. For example, two cities may have similar conventional rates of residential burglary but when one takes into account the number of residences rather than the number of people, the picture might look quite different. The following hypothetical data illustrate this:

	City A	City B
Number of residential burglaries	1,000	1,500
Population of city	100,000	200,000
Number of residences	30,000	40,000
Conventional crime rate for burglary	1,000	750
Opportunity-based crime rate for burglary	3,333.3	3,750.0

The two rates produce different results. The opportunity-based rate suggests that the risk of one's residence being burglarized is in fact higher in City B than City A, though the conventional rate might have led one to believe otherwise.

This rather superficial excursion into numbers and rates raises two questions about published crime statistics: (1) Are the crime data rates or absolute numbers? (2) If the crime data are rates, then are the rates expressed in terms of total population, specific population, persons or places at risk, or some other base?

Box 2.2 ■ The NCVS Questionnaire and the Reporting of Rape

As a household survey, the NCVS directs interviewers to ask each household member age 12 or older if he or she experienced a crime in the previous 6 months. If an individual says that he or she has been victimized by a crime, whether or not the incident was reported to the police, the interviewer collects information on the crime.

Each respondent is asked if he or she were attacked; and if so, how. If the respondent says that he or she was raped, the incident is classified as a completed rape. If the victim reports an offender's attacking and trying to rape her or him, the incident is classified as an attempted rape, even if the victim incurred injuries. If the offender threatened to rape the victim but did not attack, the incident is classified as an attempted rape. Rapes committed by nonstrangers, particularly those intimate with the victim, were less likely to be reported to the NCVS than rapes by strangers.

7b. Did the person(s) hit you, knock you down, or actually attack you in any way?

■ Yes
■ No

7c. Did the person(s) threaten you with harm in any way?

■ Yes
■ No

7d. How were you threatened? Any other way?

■ Verbal threat of rape
■ Verbal threat of attack other than rape
■ Weapon present or threatened with weapon
■ Attempted attack with weapon
■ Object thrown at person
■ Followed, surrounded
■ Other (specify) _____

7f. How did the person(s) attack you? Any other way?

■ Raped
■ Tried to rape
■ Shot
■ Knifed
■ Hit with object in hand
■ Hit by thrown object
■ Hit, slapped, knocked down
■ Grabbed, held, tripped, pushed, etc.
■ Other (specify) _____

Source: Caroline Wolf Harlow (1991a). *Female Victims of Violent Crime.* Washington, D.C.: U.S. Department of Justice, p. 10.

respondents may purposely deceive interviewers, though this is a risk that carefully constructed questionnaires and trained interviewers can reduce.

Deception may be increased for certain offenses or victims. For example, it is likely that the victimization of women and children is underreported by victimization surveys because of embarrassment or fear. "Indeed, their assailant may be in the same room at the time of the interview" (Hough and Mayhew, 1983:21). It has been found that the simple step of using female interviewers in a nonthreatening setting helps to uncover more domestic violence (Kinsey, Lea, and Young, 1986:63).

Comparison of UCR and NCVS   The UCR and NCVS data are not directly comparable. The two programs use different methods, measure different offenses, and provide different kinds of information. As a rule, far more crimes are discovered through the NCVS than are reported to police, but the differences are greater for some offenses than others.

For example, in 1986 the FBI recorded 91,460 forcible rapes, whereas NCVS data reported 129,940 rapes, over one-third more. (The definitions of rape were essentially the same, although the NCVS included homosexual rape and the UCR did not; however, less than 10 such cases were reported by those interviewed [Bureau of Justice Statistics, 1988a:16], so the difference is not due to that variation.) On the other hand, for the same year the UCR reported 834,320 aggravated assaults while the NCVS estimated that 1,542,870 such assaults occurred, nearly double. In the case of motor vehicle theft, the UCR reported 1,224,100 thefts and the NCVS 1,355,860, almost the same number.

If a research problem required the use of nationwide rape data, the investigator would probably look first to the NCVS rather than the UCR. On the other hand, a researcher searching for aggregate vehicle theft data could use either source without fear that missing data would bias the results. In the last analysis, the kind of data criminologists use is determined by the research problem they are addressing. As Lundman (1991:5) points out, one thing that UCR and NCVS show in common is that crime in America is predominantly crimes against property committed by young male offenders. In this respect they paint the same picture.

Because of the variety of questions that can be asked, victimization surveys provide information on a broad range of issues not available in the UCR. For example, one can learn about protective measures victims take when they are assaulted, robbed, or raped; about relationships between victims and offenders involved in robbery and rape; about family circumstances of crime victims; about spatial distribution of crimes; and about the risks of victimization and financial losses suffered by different segments of the population. New questions have recently been incorporated that investigate the nature and timeliness of the police response, and drug and alcohol use by offenders (Taylor, 1989; Whitaker, 1989).

Not surprisingly, the National Crime Victimization Survey provides virtually no information about crimes that victimize society rather than individuals—for example, drug offenses, prostitution, gambling, treason and espionage, and terrorism. It may be a surprise to learn that the NCVS contains no information about crimes committed in connection with one's work or social position: for example, embezzlement, fraud, pilfering, price-fixing, bribery and corruption, and so on.

Unfortunately, such information would severely complicate the design and use of victimization surveys and might prove impossible to document in some cases. In the first place, people are often unaware that they have been victimized by such crimes and if they do have suspicions, they are often unable to substantiate them or identify offenders. Although it may cost a victim much more, being the target of "bait and switch" at an appliance store is different than having one's pocket picked, purse snatched, or coming home to a ransacked house. Because victimization surveys deal mainly with crimes of assault and theft—and fail to detail equally important white-collar crimes—the public, the police, and some criminologists will continue to believe that these are the crimes that they should be most concerned about.

Self-Reported Criminality

In addition to victimization surveys, researchers explore the dark figure of crime by asking people to recount their involvement in criminal activities. The main purpose of these "self-report" studies is to assess the extent of criminality among different societal groups. Victimization studies are limited to a group of offenses that directly harm others. Self-report studies can provide estimates of those types of offenses and of the varieties that are essentially victimless or that harm only the perpetrators. They also provide estimates of offenses that are petty or are only crimes if committed by juveniles.

The usual self-report study employs a questionnaire listing a variety of deviant, delinquent, and illegal activities. Respondents are asked to indicate if they have engaged in those activities during a specified period of time, usually the previous year. Self-report studies have commonly focused on adolescents because much juvenile crime is hidden from official records and because schools provide easy access to representative samples.

The self-report technique also provides researchers with an opportunity to establish not only the prevalence of criminality, but also the *incidence* of crime. *Prevalence* is the proportion of a population that has committed any crime or a given offense during a period of time that might range from a year to a lifetime. If the prevalence of crime is greater among teenagers than among senior citizens, then proportionately more teenagers than senior citizens have committed at least one crime. *Incidence* is the number of times people have committed crime. If one says that the incidence of crime is greater among teenagers than among senior citizens, then one means that teenagers who commit crimes do so more often than senior citizens who commit crimes.

Interestingly, the crime rate for a population may be the same even though prevalence and incidence vary. Imagine that there are two societies, each with 100 people. Suppose that during the course of a year in society A each person commits 1 crime. Recalling Box 2.1, the crime rate is therefore 100 multiplied by 100,000 divided by 100, which equals 100,000. Suppose that in society B during the same year, 10 people each committed 10 crimes. Again, the crime rate is 100 multiplied by 100,000 and divided by 100, which is 100,000. Self-report studies are the only effective way to divide the population or group crime rate into its components of prevalence and incidence. Likewise, victimization surveys are the only effective way to divide a victimization rate into components of prevalence and incidence.

With adolescents as their target, self-report questionnaires usually include acts that would not be crimes if committed by adults. These "status" offenses represent an important component of juvenile delinquency. Yet many authors believe that their inclusion in self-report questionnaires has tended to trivialize juvenile crime and this explains why the prevalence of self-reported delinquency is similar across class, race, and sex lines (e.g., Hindelang et al., 1979).

More recent self-report studies of adolescent crime have sought to overcome the problem of trivialization. This is done by including a more extensive and varied list of predatory crimes along with the standard list of status offenses. The result can be seen in Box 2.3. The list of 47 items was developed by researchers at the Behavioral Research Institute of the University of Colorado for use in the National Youth Survey (NYS). This survey was conducted with a representative sample of American youth born from 1959 through 1965.

The National Youth Survey produced a wealth of information about delinquency, and criminologists are still learning new things from it. Because the study gathered information on both the prevalence and the incidence of delinquency throughout a number of years, it has been possible to identify the frequency of offending as well as its seriousness and duration (see Barlow and Ferdinand, 1992:45–49). The NYS has confirmed, for example, that while most delinquency is sporadic and minor in nature, a small group of "chronic" youth is responsible for a disproportionate amount of all types of self-reported delinquency (Dunford and Elliott, 1984). Although some authors have criticized general youth surveys because they underrepresent truly serious chronic offenders who are incarcerated (Cernkovich, Giordano, and Pugh, 1985), the NYS is generally recognized as one of the best.

During the past 30 years many small-scale self-report studies have been done, and despite deficiencies they have generally indicated the same thing: Crime and delinquency are not confined to any class, race, sex, or ethnic group. Until recently, however, they had not ventured into the executive suites of government and business. Price fixing, corporate fraud, tax avoidance, industrial pollution, monopolistic practices, violations of work safety laws, false advertising, computer fraud, and other white collar crimes were excluded.

Steven Box (1981:86) gives two reasons for ignoring white-collar crimes in self-report surveys: First, it is difficult to penetrate "the protective walls of secrecy behind which corporate executives conspire to commit crime"; second, it is "extremely unlikely that corporate executives would complete a self-report schedule, and certainly not for the inducement of £5 (less than $10.00) which often gets the hands of adolescents eagerly ticking away." As Box points out, a major irony is that the primary purpose of self-report studies is to improve on the deficiencies found in official statistics.

Two recent studies of corporate ethics and illegality have included interviews with executives (Clinard, 1983; Jackall, 1988). These studies are

20. Hit (or threatened to hit) a teacher or other adult at school.
21. Hit (or threatened to hit) one of your parents.
22. Hit (or threatened to hit) other students.
23. Been loud, rowdy, or unruly in a public place (disorderly conduct).
24. Sold hard drugs, such as heroin, cocaine, and LSD.
25. Taken a vehicle for a ride (drive) without the owner's permission.
26. Bought or provided liquor for a minor.
27. Had (or tried to have) sexual relations with persons against their will.
28. Used force (strong-arm methods) to get money or things from other students.
29. Used force (strong-arm methods) to get money or things from a teacher or other adult at school.
30. Used force (strong-arm methods) to get money or things from other people (not students or teachers).
31. Avoided paying for such things as movies, bus or subway rides, and food.
32. Been drunk in a public place.
33. Stolen (or tried to steal) things worth between $5 and $50.
34. Stolen (or tried to steal) something at school, such as someone's coat from a classroom, locker, or cafeteria, or a book from the library.
35. Broken into a building or vehicle (or tried to break in) to steal something or just to look around.
36. Begged for money or things from strangers.
37. Skipped classes without an excuse.
38. Failed to return extra change that a cashier gave you by mistake.
39. Been suspended from school.
40. Made obscene telephone calls, such as calling someone and saying dirty things.

How often in the last year have you used:

41. Alcoholic beverages (beer, wine, and hard liquor).
42. Marijuana—hashish ("grass," "pot," "hash").
43. Hallucinogens ("LSD," "Mescaline," "Peyote," "Acid").
44. Amphetamines ("Uppers," "Speed," "Whites").
45. Barbiturates ("Downers," "Reds").
46. Heroin ("Horse," "Smack").
47. Cocaine ("Coke").

Source: Delbert S. Elliott and Suzanne S. Ageton (1980). "Reconciling race and class differences in self-reported and official estimates of delinquency." *American Sociological Review* 45:108–109. Reprinted by permission.

discussed in Chapter 7; they are mentioned here because they demonstrate the feasibility of using interviews to uncover the attitudes and behavior of people who are traditionally secretive and self-protective about their work. As Clinard (1989) observed recently, elaborate steps had to be taken to ensure confidentiality. Jackall (1988:13–16) describes a variety of problems he encountered in gaining access to the corporate world and in finding people willing to divulge sensitive information about themselves and their colleagues.

The basis of both self-report and victimization studies is the one-on-one interview. The researcher usually sits face-to-face with the person being interviewed. Clearly, the situation is difficult for both parties, all the more so when questions are asked about incidents or activities that are embarrassing, humiliating, frightening, or strongly condemned by society. Yet it is only through such interviews that criminologists can examine the attitudes, experiences, and behaviors of those touched by crime. Two pioneers of American criminology, Edwin Sutherland (1937a) and Clifford Shaw (1930), were among the first to make use of extensive autobiographical interviews with offenders. Sutherland's interviews with a professional thief and Shaw's interviews with a "career" delinquent have become models for more recent research on diverse crimes, from fencing (Klockars, 1974; Steffensmeyer, 1986), to safecracking (King, 1972), to gang delinquency (Campbell, 1984), to drug addiction (Hills and Santiago, 1992).

Official Data on the Criminal Justice System

Suppose one wanted to know the number of Americans serving prison sentences, the reasons why they were in prison, and how long they had been in jail. Suppose one wanted to know about the physical, social, and health conditions in jails. Or suppose one was interested in comparing the social characteristics of prisoners with those of individuals in community-based correctional programs and those of people on parole and probation. Where would one find the information?

It was not until the late 1960s that authorities displayed much interest in the compilation of national data on the criminal justice system. The Omnibus Crime Control and Safe Streets Act of 1968 created the Law Enforcement Assistance Administration (LEAA), and over the next few years its budget grew to more than $1 billion. While the bulk of this money went to policing, millions of dollars poured into data collection and government support of crime research. Periodic fact-finding surveys of courts, jails, and prisons were conducted, and some of these eventually became annual reports.

Today, the Bureau of Justice Statistics (BJS) publishes bulletins and research monographs covering all aspects of the criminal justice process as well as the National Crime Victimization Survey. This text includes many references to BJS publications. Government sponsored data collection now covers all areas of crime and justice—victimization, parole, police practices, prisons, prosecution, all sorts of crime and delinquency, juvenile justice, prison alternatives, and (though much less extensively) crimes committed in the course of a person's work or occupation. People interested in tapping this information can call the Justice Department's National Criminal Justice Reference Service (NCJRS). Many publications are free.

Students wishing easy access to a broad range of data on crime and criminal justice issues, including public attitudes, juvenile delinquency, and drug abuse can consult the annual *Sourcebook of Criminal Justice Statistics* (e.g., Maguire and Flanagan, 1991). Compiled by the Hindelang Criminal Justice Research Center of Albany, New York, the *Sourcebook* was first published in 1973, and the authors take pains to make the data tables comparable over the years.

Recent developments in tracking criminal offenders have resulted in new data sources that can be tapped by criminal justice researchers. So-called "offender-based transaction statistics" (OBTS) are now available from 14 states. These data cover the processing and disposition of offenders from the point of arrest to their eventual release from the system. In addition, 45 states participate in the Criminal History Improvement (CHRI) program, which is designed to provide complete and timely records of offenders' criminal histories (see Bureau of Justice Statistics, 1992b). These data sources will be useful in basic research, but their real purpose is to help officials police and process offenders in line with prevailing justice policy.

Sometimes it is both necessary and desirable for researchers to collect their own data according to a specific research design (more on that in a moment). Scholars and practitioners recognize the need to keep abreast of developments in the field, and so they belong to professional associations such as the American Society of Criminology and the Academy of Criminal Justice Sciences. They also read journals relevant to their interests—a good many of these are available (see Box 2.4). In this way they keep aware of theoretical advances, new methodologies, and new evidence.

Though many important data sources are published by governmental agencies, it does not mean that private sources of data are unavailable or that important information about crime and criminality has not been collected by people working outside the government. But as is often the case, the government intrudes even here: Much of the research undertaken by private individuals and by universities or research institutions such as the Rand Corporation is approved and paid for by government agencies. The nature of the subject and the time and expense involved in doing original data collection virtually guarantee that government has a role in most criminological research.

In regard to the broad spectrum of criminological issues and problems, no one kind of data will serve the needs of criminologists. Criminology is a growing and changing field; new perspectives and new interests call for new methodologies, new data, new lines of inquiry. Throughout the remainder of this text the reader will see tradition and innovation side by side in the continuing quest for insights and explanations. If one recognizes the limitations of available (usually official) data on the crime scene, if one bears in mind that data provide limited information on some aspects of this subject, and if one knows when *not* to use them, then one will no doubt find an important place for them in the study of criminology. Certainly one should continue to strive for systematic, routine collection and dissemination of national, state, and local crime data.

Methods of Criminological Research

A variety of research methodologies is available to the criminologist. Some are used more commonly than others, often because of cost, time, and convenience rather than because of any inherent superiority. The choice of a particular research strategy is also influenced by the purpose of a study; by the availability of alternative strategies; by the nature and findings of prior research; and by the knowledge, skills, and training of the researcher. Much criminological research focuses on young people because teenagers and younger adults make up the bulk of common criminals and commit most of the crime that police and courts deal with. Taking this into account, and because it provides a common denominator for the discussion, the remaining sections focus on juvenile crime. They draw heavily from *Understanding Delinquency* by Barlow and Ferdinand (1992:23–38). (For a more comprehensive treatment of measurement issues in criminology, see Kempf [1990]).

Research with Human Subjects

Some research strategies involve direct contacts with the people who "do" crime or who do something about it. There are various difficulties in doing research with human subjects; three recurring problems involve ethics, reactivity, and attrition.

Ethics   Any research with human subjects involves ethical dilemmas. Since what is ethical is a matter of judgment and is relative, people do not always agree on what the dilemmas are, let alone on their resolution. The risks of being charged with unethical conduct are lessened, however, if criminologists follow these practices:

1. Avoid procedures that inflict physical or mental anguish or otherwise threaten the well-being of subjects.
2. Secure the voluntary, informed consent of participants, which means that they are told of possible dangers or risks associated with their participation and that they agree to participate without being pressured to do so.
3. Allow participants to withdraw from the research at any time.
4. Protect the anonymity of participants; this is especially important when the behavior in question is illegal and punishable.
5. Debrief participants after the research; this is especially important if the researcher has had to deceive participants as to the real purpose of the research. Deception may be the only way a researcher can protect results from being contaminated because subjects know what is going on.
6. Avoid practices that invite or encourage participants to break the law. Moral issues aside, when researchers participate in gang activities in order to study them, for example, their role as objective scientist may become confused with their role as participant.

Reactivity   People who are being studied may behave differently because of it. This is the problem of *reactivity*. Any researcher who intends to interview, experiment with, or observe other people must try to minimize reactivity. One way to do so is by deception; another is to conduct the research over a relatively long period of time in the hope that subjects have adjusted to, or forgotten, the fact that they are being studied; a third is for the researcher to be as unobtrusive as possible; a fourth—mainly appropriate in experimental research—is to use a "control" group (discussed later).

Attrition   The problem of attrition generally surfaces in projects that require subjects to participate over an extended period of time. Attrition occurs when people drop out of a research study, for whatever reason. Sometimes they move away; sometimes they decide not to participate after initially agreeing to do so; sometimes they cannot be found by researchers; and sometimes they simply forget. Attrition becomes a serious problem only if it distorts the representativeness of a sample or reduces its size significantly.

The remainder of the chapter discusses the main research strategies employed in the study of crime and delinquency. The survey method has already been touched on in the discussion of victimization and self-report studies, but we shall encounter further examples of its use in some of the research described below.

Cross-Sectional Studies

Much criminological research is *cross sectional*, meaning that data are collected at a single point in time or over a short period of time. For example, a researcher interested in the relationship between family life and self-reported delinquency might interview a sample of youths about conditions and relationships at home to see if they relate to differences in delinquency.

Two recent studies did just that. In one, Cernkovich and Giordano (1987) interviewed a sample of 824 male and female adolescents residing in private households in an urban area. The adolescents were asked about their family situations and their relationships with parents. They were also asked about

With her husband, Sheldon, Eleanor Glueck was one of the pioneers in criminological research, often combining a variety of different methods in a life-long search for the causes and correlates of juvenile crime and delinquency.

their involvement in delinquency and their relationships with friends. In another study (Johnson, 1986), over 700 male and female high school sophomores were interviewed about family conditions and delinquency. In addition, data were gathered on the youths' contacts with police, school officials, and other authorities.

The methods used in these two cross-sectional studies are conventional enough, but their findings challenged conventional wisdom as well as some earlier delinquency research. For example, both studies found that children from broken (i.e., single-parent) homes were not more prone to delinquency than others; nor were children with step-parents. The studies also found that girls and boys differ not only in the frequency and seriousness of their delinquency (boys are more delinquent in both ways), but also in the family factors that appear to influence their behavior. For example, Cernkovich and Giordano found that females were strongly influenced by belief that parents respected, supported, and accepted them and by parental disapproval of their friends; in contrast, boys were strongly influenced by parental control and supervision of their behavior and by the frequency with which they talked with their parents about their feelings, ideas, and future plans.

In the Johnson study, regardless of levels of self-reported delinquency, girls living in female-headed households had more official trouble than children living in intact, male-headed, or step-parent homes. This finding could not be accounted for by differences in race, class, quality of parent–child relations, or quality of school experiences. This suggests that "police and school and court officials . . . find it easier or more appropriate to officially respond to the behavior of daughters of single mothers . . ." (Johnson, 1986:73).

The fundamental limitation of cross-sectional research is the lack of a temporal dimension other than what can be created through questions about past events. Apart from the fact that people may not remember past events accurately—even if they want to—the behavioral links between past and present can only be inferred. If researchers wish to move beyond such inferences, or are interested in direct tests of causality, there are other strategies to consider. One is the experiment.

Experiments

When researchers wish to establish whether one variable causes another, they will think first of constructing an *experiment*. The experimental method is generally considered the ideal way to measure causation because the experimenter can control the research process. The "true" or "classic" experiment examines causation in the following way:

1. It establishes whether there is, in fact, a relationship or association between the key variables. The variable that is believed to cause the effect is usually called the *independent*, or *treatment*, variable and is conventionally denoted by the letter X. The variable that X affects or causes is

called the *dependent*, or *outcome*, variable and is designated Y. The first step in establishing causality is to show that a change in X is associated with a change in Y.

2. However, because two variables are associated does not necessarily mean that one causes the other. The design of a true experiment allows the researcher to establish that the change in X occurs *before* the change in Y. This is conventionally referred to as establishing the *temporal (or causal) order* of a relationship.

3. Showing that X and Y are related and that a change in Y followed rather than preceded a change in X still does not establish that X causes Y. This is because the change in Y might have been caused by something other than X. A true experiment allows the researcher to rule out "rival" causes. This is arguably the most difficult thing to do in social science research if for no other reason than that there are often many variables, some probably unknown, that could impact directly on Y or on the relationship between X and Y.

To satisfy the three criteria of causation—association, temporal order, and exclusion of rival causes—the true experiment is usually conducted in a controlled laboratory setting, with people ("subjects") randomly assigned to either *experimental* or *control* groups. Those subjects assigned to the experimental (or "treatment") group are exposed to manipulation of the independent variable, X, while those assigned to the control group are not. In both groups, the dependent variable, Y, is measured before and after the manipulation of X. If Y changes in the experimental group but not in the control group, or changes more in the former than the latter, the experimenter is reasonably confident that the change in Y is caused by the change in X. However, the experiment ought to be repeated with other subjects, just to make sure.

In the true experiment, then, the use of a control group helps ensure that any change in Y is due to the manipulation of X and not to something else. The before and after measurements establish the temporal order. The random assignment helps ensure that there are no preexisting differences between subjects in the two groups that might account for the experimental outcome. Even so, when only a few subjects are used in an experiment it is hard to ensure that the experimental and control groups are alike even with random assignment. In this event, the researcher tries to limit differences among subjects beforehand by using only people who are of the same sex, say, or the same race, or age, or economic or educational background.

This is just one way in which researchers performing experiments with human beings often have less than full control over possible rival causes. In many cases it is simply not plausible to bring representative samples of people into a laboratory for experimentation. In criminological research, the difficulties of carrying out true experiments are exacerbated by the very nature of the subject: Not only is it often not possible to isolate or manipulate important variables in a laboratory setting, but also there are many kinds of crime that one would certainly not wish to experiment with (even if one could).

Field Experiments   True experiments are rare in criminological research, as they are in the social sciences in general. Aside from the difficulties just mentioned, the more control researchers exercise over the experimental environment, the less that environment approximates the real world. Laboratory findings or experiments conducted in other controlled settings, such as prisons, halfway houses, and boarding schools, may have little validity outside those environments.

An alternative is to conduct experiments "in the field," where the environment more closely approximates the natural settings in which social behavior occurs. What they lack in researcher control, field experiments may gain in *generalizability*, that is, applicability beyond the experimental situation. And it should be pointed out that researchers usually try to construct field experiments so that they approximate as closely as possible the characteristics of true experiments.

The Provo Experiment   A classic experiment in delinquency research is the Provo (Utah) experiment designed to study the effectiveness of a community treatment program for youths who had committed serious offenses and/or were repeat offenders (Empey and Erickson, 1972; also see Lundman, 1984: 157–172). All 326 boys first went through an adjudicatory hearing where the judge assigned them to either probation or incarceration. At this point in a boy's hearing, the judge opened an envelope containing a randomly selected piece of paper marked either "experimental" or "control," and then announced the placement decision. In this manner each boy was randomly assigned to one of four groups: the probation experimental group, the probation control group, the incarceration experimental group, and the incarceration control group.

Those boys assigned to the experimental probation group were placed into a special community treatment program, while their control counterparts were placed on regular probation. Those boys assigned to experimental incarceration were also placed into the special community treatment program, while their control counterparts were placed in a state training school.

The experimental treatment program included daily guided group interaction in which the boys described and discussed their delinquent activities, debated their futures, and came to terms with their fears and emotions and considered how they might deal with them in nondelinquent ways. In addition, the boys in this group went home each evening and on the weekend. "On the street they had to choose between delinquent and conforming behavior. Moreover, they were making visible choices. Group members generally knew one another directly or by reputation, and were thus aware of what a member was doing apart from the group" (Lundman, 1984:166). Through the group sessions, some of the boys gradually learned that they could gain recognition and prestige by avoiding delinquent activities; they became informal leaders who looked after new arrivals and thus furthered their own involvement in and commitment to the process of treatment.

The results of the experiment for delinquency prevention were mixed. In terms of future trouble with the law, the boys "sentenced" to experimental probation could not be distinguished from the boys who had been placed on regular probation. On the other hand, those placed on probation had fewer future arrests than those sentenced to incarceration in the state training school. The boys initially sentenced to incarceration but then diverted into the community treatment program also had fewer future arrests than the boys actually incarcerated. Together, these findings suggested that community-based, group-centered treatment was more beneficial as an alternative to incarceration than as an alternative to regular supervised probation.

A variety of practical problems affected the performance of the Provo experiment and compromised its design as a result. The most important of these surfaced when the juvenile court judge proved reluctant to sentence youths to incarceration. It was soon apparent that there were too few boys to permit meaningful comparisons between the control and experimental groups among boys sentenced to incarceration. To solve the problem, Empey and Erickson sent all the locally incarcerated boys to the experimental treatment program and compared this group with boys sent to the state training school from other parts of Utah. This provided better numbers for purposes of comparison but violated the criterion of random assignment and therefore compromised the effort to rule out rival causes.

Practical problems reflect the operations of the real world, and most field experiments have to contend with them sooner or later. There is nevertheless a growing consensus in criminological circles that even with their problems, field experiments deserve more attention than they have received. Even scholars at odds on major methodological issues can be found in agreement on this point (see Gottfredson and Hirschi, 1987; Blumstein, Cohen, and Farrington, 1988a and b).

Longitudinal Research: Cohort Studies

Experimental research is sometimes longitudinal, and some longitudinal studies have included experiments along with other methodologies. A *longitudinal* study is conducted over time and is often designed to establish whether and when changes occur in the variables under investigation. Some researchers believe that longitudinal designs are a good way to address questions of causality, especially the temporal ordering of key variables. Others select longitudinal designs because they provide the only effective way of tracking developmental and historical changes.

A variety of longitudinal designs have been used in delinquency research. One of the most common is the panel study. A *panel study* involves gathering information about a group (panel) of people at two or more points in time. In order to avoid such problems as subject reactivity and attrition, some panel designs rotate people into and out of the sample as the study continues. The

National Crime Victimization Survey, discussed earlier, is an example of a panel study that uses this sort of rotation. However, most panel studies are done with much more limited samples and are designed to address specific research questions, for example, whether youths' perceptions of the risks of being punished for illegal behavior influence their subsequent conduct (see Bishop, 1983; Paternoster, 1987), or whether adolescent drinking influences delinquency involvement or vice versa (see Temple and Ladoucer, 1986).

One of the most interesting types of longitudinal research is the cohort study. A *cohort study* measures changes that occur over time among people who are in common circumstances or who share a similar characteristic. Because cohort studies are usually difficult, time-consuming, and expensive, they are relatively rare. This is especially true of *prospective* cohort studies, which are also long term. In this type of study, researchers measure changes in circumstances, experiences, and behavior as the people under study move through their lives. In some prospective cohort studies the measurements begin at birth; in others the cohort is composed of school-age children. Such studies may take 25 years or longer to complete.

The theoretical value of prospective cohort studies in criminological research lies in their ability to examine how and why some people become delinquent or criminal when others in similar circumstances do not. They are also valued for what they can tell us about the development of so-called *criminal careers.* For example, a rare consensus in criminological circles is that experienced adult criminals usually began their careers in crime as juveniles, and that the likelihood of such a career developing is greater the earlier the child gets in trouble with the law. On the other hand, many juveniles "mature" out of crime before they reach adulthood, and some youngsters dabble in delinquency without ever getting seriously involved. By repeatedly gathering information on an individual's family, school, health, economic circumstances, contacts with the criminal justice system, and other behavior patterns and comparing it with information on the rest of the group, cohort researchers hope to pinpoint the crucial factors that explain the emergence, character, and duration of delinquency involvement.

In the cohort research of interest here, the dependent variable is usually delinquent or criminal involvement, which can be measured in various ways, as we have seen. The independent measures vary from study to study, depending mostly on the specific research problem being addressed and on the training of the researchers. However, prospective cohort studies are generally broad in the range of variables they measure because the time, effort, and cost hardly justify anything less. Here are two excellent examples of prospective cohort studies.

The Cambridge Study in Delinquent Development   Begun in 1961, the Cambridge Study in Delinquent Development has become a classic. Led by Donald West, researchers in England contacted 411 boys aged 8 to 9 years, all of whom were attending one of six local primary schools in a working-class district of London (West, 1967). The sample was designed to be representative of the male population of the area. The boys were interviewed and given psychological tests at ages 8, 10, and 14, and were interviewed again at ages 16, 18, and 21. In addition, parents, teachers, and some of the boys' peers were interviewed periodically. Questions dealt with a range of issues, such as family circumstances; child-rearing practices; behavior and performance in school; truancy; and other boys' perceptions of their honesty, daring, and popularity. Delinquency involvement was measured by self-reports and also by official records of convictions.

Various reports have documented the emergence of delinquent careers in some of the boys, and further follow-ups (at age 24 and between 31 and 32) have examined the transition from juvenile to adult criminal involvement (see West and Farrington, 1977; West, 1982; Farrington, 1988). Barlow and Ferdinand (1992) cite many findings from this important study. One of the most significant is simply this: The minority of boys with self-reports of early delinquency involvement and early criminal convictions differed significantly from the rest on most measures used throughout the study and were significantly more likely to continue their criminal activity into adulthood and to be involved in life-styles considered deviant by conventional standards (Farrington, 1988:71–72).

The Kauai Longitudinal Study   The Kauai Longitudinal Study began even before its subjects were born and is remarkable because of the scope of its biological, cognitive, medical, behavioral, and social measures (see Werner et al., 1971; Werner and Smith, 1977). All pregnant women on the island of Kauai, Hawaii (population 32,000) were screened in 1954 on a variety of medical and psychological variables, and the 698 children subsequently born in 1955 were followed into their 25th year (Werner, 1987).

Half the children lived in chronic poverty, but even so, marked variations were found in the risks of delinquency even among the poorer children. Different combinations of factors were identified as delinquency predictors at different ages. For example, a child's health and temperament and its mother's health and age were found to be significant factors during infancy, but during adolescence the composition and coherence of the family and the presence of chronic family conflict were important predictors of a child's trouble with the law. Werner (1987:39–40) describes a major conclusion of the study as follows:

> Although most of the children who became delinquent were poor, it needs to be kept in mind that *poverty alone* was not a sufficient condition for the development of antisocial behavior. A low standard of living increased the likelihood of exposure of the child to *both* biological and psychological risk factors. But it was the joint impact of constitutional vulnerabilities and early family instability that led to serious and repeated delinquencies in *both* middle-class as well as lower-class children on Kauai. . . .
>
> Regardless of social class standing, children with "difficult temperaments" who interacted with distressed caretakers in disorganized, unstable families had a greater chance of developing delinquent behavior than children who

were perceived as rewarding by their caretakers and who grew up in supportive homes.

The two cohort studies we have reviewed meet four conditions that are considered desirable in longitudinal research (Farrington, Ohlin, and Wilson, 1986): (1) They are prospective, following the subjects as they grow up; (2) they involve collection of material from various sources, for example, self-reports, police and court data; and additional information from parents, teachers, and others; (3) the sample size is relatively large (over 100 subjects), thereby producing larger subcategories of subjects (e.g., chronic delinquents, sporadic delinquents, and nondelinquents) for analysis and enabling researchers to generalize the findings to similar groups in other places; and (4) they cover an extensive period of time, at least five years, in the lives of the subjects.

Despite all this, prospective cohort studies are not without their critics (see Esbensen and Menard, 1990), and not all researchers agree that these four conditions necessarily characterize good longitudinal research. For example, much can be learned from qualitative research in which single individuals or small groups of subjects describe and interpret their experiences and activities in their own words, as they live and recall them. Examples of this sort of research include Parker's (1974) study of The Roundhouse Boys in Liverpool, England, and the autobiographical account of Stanley, the "Jack-Roller," supervised by Clifford Shaw (1930) over sixty years ago.

Recently, two prominent criminologists have argued that longitudinal research may be overrated. Travis Hirschi and Michael Gottfredson (1983; also see Gottfredson and Hirschi, 1987 and 1990) direct their criticism primarily at longitudinal research on criminal careers, but in doing so they challenge various beliefs about the benefits of longitudinal research, including this one: that longitudinal research is superior to standard cross-sectional, one-point-in-time, designs as a means of establishing temporal or causal order among variables (see Gottfredson and Hirschi, 1987:586–606).

The heart of the Hirschi-Gottfredson critique is that longitudinal research has not in fact advanced our understanding of the causes of crime or delinquency beyond that already established through cross-sectional studies. Furthermore, they argue that the real reason some researchers (e.g., Farrington, Ohlin, and Wilson, 1986; Blumstein et al., 1986) advocate prospective longitudinal studies may be that the method fits their theories of crime causation, not because it contains inherent methodological virtues (Gottfredson and Hirschi, 1987:608). Thus the desirability of following individuals over time is grounded in the theory that crime results from changes in the characteristics, conditions, or experiences of individuals as they grow up. The upshot, according to Gottfredson and Hirschi (1987:610), is a blurring of the distinction between theory and method.

The debate sparked by Hirschi and Gottfredson (see also Blumstein, Cohen, and Farrington, 1988a and b; Gottfredson and Hirshi, 1988; Tittle, 1988; Hagan and Palloni, 1988) is unlikely to be resolved in the near future;

nor is it likely to dampen enthusiasm for longitudinal research. Indeed, Hirschi and Gottfredson appear to hold the minority position on this issue. As they themselves argue (1987:608), the use of any particular research design is guided by the theory being tested, and when the theory (whatever it is) purports to explain a crime in temporal terms, a longitudinal design is defensible when a cross-sectional design often is not. Blumstein, Cohen, and Farrington (1988a:72) undoubtedly spoke for many of their colleagues when they defended longitudinal surveys (such as the Cambridge Study in Delinquent Development) as "markedly superior to cross-sectional surveys in describing the natural history and course of development of a phenomenon, in studying developmental sequences, and in drawing causal inferences."

Observational Research

Some major advances in understanding delinquency and crime have been made by careful and systematic observation of that behavior *as it occurs*. Observational studies are especially useful if we don't know what to expect—usually because theory is weak or nonexistent—but they are also helpful in providing researchers with first-hand knowledge of behavior in the rich and often complex contexts in which it arises.

The use of observational research in the study of social deviance is controversial (and difficult) because people usually don't want to be watched by outsiders when they are doing something for which they could be punished. If people know they are being watched, they might try to fool the researcher by doing something quite different from what they would otherwise do. Observational research is controversial also because of abuses that have taken place. Although not everyone agrees on exactly what constitutes abuse, the famous study by Laud Humphreys (1970), cited in many sociology texts, comes to mind. Humphreys observed homosexual encounters as they occurred in public restrooms in a St. Louis park. In itself this might have raised eyebrows, but Humphreys also recorded the license plates of participants and had a contact in the police department provide names and addresses so that Humphreys could later interview the participants as part of the study. Clearly, this strategy entailed risks for the subjects and today would probably be illegal under federal privacy statutes.

Because much crime and delinquency occurs when there are no witnesses—at least no official ones—the usual observational strategy is for the researcher to become a *participant observer*. This does not mean that participant observers have to commit offenses but, rather, that they are present or nearby when they occur or that they participate in talk and other activities related to the routine behavior (including the crimes) of the people they are studying. A wide range of delinquent and criminal behaviors have been studied in this way, from organized crime (Ianni and Reuss-Ianni, 1973), to drug dealing (Adler, 1985), juvenile gangs (Spergel, 1964; Campbell, 1984), and less "formal" delinquent networks (Parker, 1974). Participant observation has also been used in the study of the interaction between police and suspects on the street (Piliavin and Briar, 1964; Reiss, 1971) and between defendants and others in the judicial process (Maynard, 1984; Daly, 1987a).

Participant observation puts the researcher close to the people and activities that are being studied, and as a result it provides insights that are often missed with other methods of research. A classic example of this is the work of William Foote Whyte (1943). Whyte spent over three years hanging around with a streetcorner group of ethnic Italian youths in Boston dubbed the "Corner Boys." Whyte noted that sociologists using conventional measurements of the neighborhood's social and economic character—including rates of crime and delinquency—would have written it off as a "disorganized slum." But through his participant observation, Whyte was able to show that the neighborhood was far from disorganized, although it was certainly poor. He discovered that the residents worked hard and took care of one another and that even among the boys there were clearly demarcated responsibilities, lines of authority, and mechanisms of social control to ensure conformity.

Whyte's study also showed some of the difficulties associated with participant observation. One important issue the researcher must decide is whether to reveal his or her identity. If people realize they are being studied they may behave differently (the question of reactivity); on the other hand, if they know they are being studied from the start, and are given time to adjust to the presence of an outsider and to establish trust, people may act "normally." To complicate matters further, ethical questions may be raised, for example, whether people have a right to know they are being studied. Whyte struggled with these issues, initially choosing not to reveal his true purpose, telling the boys he was writing a book about the history and customs of the neighborhood. Once his presence was accepted by most of the boys he became more open about his research.

Sometimes it is difficult to establish trust, especially when activities being observed are illegal and there is uncertainty about the researcher's true role. Irving Spergel (1964:190–198) documents this difficulty in his book about delinquent subcultures in three ethnic neighborhoods he dubbed "Racketville," "Slumtown," and "Haulberg." Spergel found that he had to define and redefine his role continuously, both to new people he met and to those he already knew who were still uncertain or uneasy. Some youths were openly suspicious, if not hostile:

> Little Augie raised a question about what I was doing in the neighborhood. He wondered whether I was a cop, a "stool pigeon," or a Youth Board worker. I tried to clarify my role as a researcher. Little Augie said that what I was saying to him wasn't clear and that he suspected my real motives. . . . He then said that he did not want to become a guinea pig for me. (Spergel, 1964:191–192)

On other occasions, Spergel found that the boys were testing him, which included "attempts to frighten me, 'baiting' or 'ranking' me, and . . . minor acts of physical violence." Spergel goes on to say:

> The testing behavior appeared to serve several functions: to demonstrate the group's uncertainty in the face of a new and strange relationship, to discover

whether or not I was a "right guy," and to determine my areas of personal weakness and of personal strength. (1964:193)

A researcher must show sensitivity, perseverance, and tolerance if uncertainties and fears are to be overcome. And the payoff can be substantial: The works of Whyte, Spergel, and the other participant observers mentioned above have provided knowledge about delinquency and crime that could not have been secured in any other way.

Biographical Research: Oral Histories

Participant observation is commonly referred to as a *qualitative* research strategy. Rather than measuring things that can be expressed as numbers—for example, how much Y changes when there is a change in X, or how many times people have been arrested, or the strength of association between delinquency rates and certain family or neighborhood characteristics—qualitative studies construct and interpret images of reality based on direct observation in the field and on the first-person accounts of participants. Because qualitative methods are more subjective and explorative than quantitative forms of measurement, some scholars believe they are of limited value in scientific research and are useful mainly in suggesting ideas that can be subsequently tested with "hard" (i.e., quantitative) data. In criminology and delinquency research, the debate has clearly been running in favor of quantitative techniques. One has only to consult methodology texts in the field to see that this is so (e.g., Hagan, 1982; Binder and Geis, 1983; Kempf, 1990).

This is in sharp contrast to the situation in the 1920s and 1930s, when *both* research strategies were widely used, often by the same investigators. A case in point is the work of Clifford Shaw. Shaw headed the Institute for Juvenile Research at the University of Chicago, and with his colleague Henry McKay embarked on an ecological study of delinquency in Chicago. Based on the geographic mapping of crime and delinquency, certain areas of the city were labeled "delinquency areas." These areas shared various features besides high crime rates: They were close to the central business district; they had high concentrations of minority and foreign-born residents; they were overcrowded and physically run-down; most of the residents were poor and unskilled; and there were few locally supported community organizations to which people belonged. Shaw and McKay believed that these conditions "combine to render difficult the development of a stable and efficient neighborhood for the education and control of the child and the suppression of lawlessness" (Shaw, 1931a:387). The term "social disorganization" was used to describe the inability of these neighborhoods to regulate themselves (Bursik, 1988:542).

Despite the voluminous quantitative data, Shaw and his colleagues could not tell what it all meant from the standpoint of individual youths growing up in delinquency areas. They believed, for example, that delinquency values were transmitted from one generation or group of residents to the next, but how was this accomplished? The answer could be gained, in their view, only by delving into the "life histories" of individual delinquents. So Shaw turned to qualitative research, eventually compiling over 200 life histories.

A life history (sometimes called an "own story") is a first-person account of behavior and experiences, usually given orally under the guidance of the researcher (for a comprehensive analysis of the use of life histories in delinquency research, see Bennett, 1981). Depending on the researcher's interest and the age of the subject, life histories can run to a few pages or to volumes. Many of Shaw's histories were short; however, three of the longer histories were turned into books: *The Jack-Roller: A Delinquent Boy's Own Story* (Shaw, 1930); *The Natural History of a Delinquent Career* (Shaw, 1931b); and *Brothers in Crime* (Shaw, McKay, and McDonald, 1938). Together, the life histories "enable a reader to *see* the process of transmission of delinquent practices from one person or group to another and the gradual evolution of those practices through further participation in delinquent groups" (Bennett, 1981:189).

Jack-Roller has become a classic in criminology and in sociological field research (Snodgrass, 1982:3). It is the story of "Stanley," who was 12 when he first met Shaw in 1921. Stanley had already run up an extensive arrest history and had spent almost half his life in institutions. By the time he was 17, Stanley had 38 arrests, most for petty offenses, but later ones for more serious crimes such as assaulting and robbing drunks or homosexuals—so-called *jack-rolling*. In Stanley's own words, "We sometimes stunned the drunks by 'giving them the club' in a dark place near a lonely alley. It was bloody work, but necessity demanded it—we had to live" (Shaw, 1930:85).

Through Stanley's story (and those of other delinquent youths) Shaw shows how delinquent attitudes and practices develop and are transmitted from boy to boy, and also how individual delinquent careers evolve. The acquisition of delinquent attitudes and practices is encouraged through friendships, by neighborhood traditions, and by the breakdown of parental controls, evidenced, for example, by Stanley's constant battles with his stepmother, who never displayed him any affection (see Snodgrass, 1982:79). In addition, Shaw used life histories to suggest appropriate treatment programs. In Stanley's case, this included finding a "sympathetic and informal" foster home; obtaining employment as a salesman (which did not last); helping him develop contacts with new, nondelinquent friends; and maintaining weekly contact with him. By Stanley's account of things as a 70-year-old (see Snodgrass, 1982), Shaw's efforts helped turn him away from crime, despite occasional relapses—one when he was 23 that resulted in yet another prison term. On a larger scale, Shaw's oral histories helped him construct the delinquency prevention program known as the Chicago Area Project, which focused on changing the delinquent child's social environment through neighborhood reconstruction organized via community self-help projects.

The Chicago work with life histories has not gone without criticism (see especially Bennett, 1981:179–210), much of which has focused on Shaw's failure to include oral histories of *non*delinquent youths living in high

Chicago in the late 1920s: The setting for biographical and ecological studies (see Chapter 14) that are now considered classics in criminology. An exemplary social research tradition at the University of Chicago has helped make the city a major site for comparative and historical research as well.

delinquency neighborhoods, the lack of comprehensive details about family and neighborhood characteristics, and the lack of information about the nondelinquent activities and associations of delinquents. Nevertheless, the life history research of Shaw and his colleagues at the Institute for Juvenile Research helped establish a form of qualitative research that has periodically produced very informative and influential studies of crime (e.g., Sutherland, 1937a; Chambliss, 1972; Klockars, 1974; Steffensmeier, 1986).

Life history research involves extensive interviews that tease out experiences and relationships in a subject's personal biography that are sometimes decades old. Needless to say, the focus on a single subject limits the generalizability of findings. Much useful information about the lived experience of crime can be uncovered through less extensive personal interviews with samples of criminal offenders who share common characteristics. A great deal of criminological research is based on some variant of the "open-ended" interview during which subjects are encouraged to give detailed answers and interviewers can pursue new (and sometimes unexpected) avenues.

Open-ended interviews with samples of offenders or criminal justice officials provide researchers with a rich body of data, but they are time-consuming and generally expensive to conduct. Even so, some notable studies have used this technique to great effect, providing new insights into the lived experience of crime and the criminal process. Good examples are Tunnell's (1992) and Shover's (1985; Shover and Honaker, 1991) interview-based research with persistent property offenders, and Johnson's (1990) study of the modern execution process. These studies are discussed in later chapters.

Comparative and Historical Research

Long ago, French sociologist Emile Durkheim ([1893] 1964b:65) observed that there is no known society without crime. "Its form changes," he went on, "but, everywhere and always, there have been men who have behaved in such a way as to draw upon themselves penal repression." In order to find out whether and how crime varies from place to place, or from time to time, criminologists use comparative or historical research. Ideally, *comparative research* compares different societies at the same point in time; *historical research* examines the same society at different periods in its history. The methodologies can be combined, though this strategy also combines their difficulties and limitations.

These difficulties and limitations include the costs and time involved (which are usually considerable), language barriers, political obstacles, lack or poor quality of available data, noncomparable definitions of crime and delinquency, and the ethnocentric tendency of researchers living in one society or time period to see their own as the "standard" against which to measure others. The last point is illustrated by the assumption, apparently held by some prominent criminologists, that American views of crime and delinquency can be applied everywhere. At the very least, researchers must be sensitive to the fact that in other societies and time periods, the actions and meanings associated with crime are likely to differ from their own (Beirne, 1983).

If these difficulties can be overcome, the benefits of comparative and historical research are considerable. Not only does this sort of research provide a way to measure the scope of theories—for example, does a theory developed to explain delinquency involvement in America also apply to, say, Germany, Israel, and India?—but it also places our own experiences with crime and delinquency in a larger perspective. Researchers today may learn from historical and comparative research about problems with crime and delinquency that have not yet surfaced, and perhaps how to avoid them. For example, the former communist block countries currently undergoing rapid social, economic, and political change may be able to learn important lessons

There is much less crime in Japan than in the United States. Comparative research helps us understand why and, in doing so helps us better understand crime in our own society.

in delinquency prevention from studying nineteenth-century Britain and America or contemporary Japan and Sweden (see Westermann and Burfeind, 1991; Barlow and Ferdinand, 1992).

Summary of Chapter 2

This review of data sources and research methods hardly does justice to a complicated topic. However, readers should now have a much better understanding of the strengths, weaknesses, and utility of the information about crime, delinquency, and justice presented in the chapters that follow. It is important to remember that no one research strategy or type of data stands above all the rest; each has its drawbacks and each has its benefits. In the last analysis, the appropriateness of a given methodology or body of data depends on the research question being addressed.

Recommended Readings

James Bennett (1981). *Oral History and Delinquency: The Rhetoric of Criminology*. Chicago: University of Chicago Press.

Anne Campbell (1984). *The Girls in the Gang*. Oxford: Basil Blackwell.

Kimberly L. Kempf (Ed.) (1990). *Measurement Issues in Criminology*. New York: Springer-Verlag.

Richard Kinsey, John Lea, and Jock Young (1986). *Losing the Fight Against Crime*. Oxford: Basil Blackwell.

Howard J. Parker (1974). *View From the Boys*. London: David and Charles.

Jon Snodgrass (1982). *The Jack-Roller at Seventy*. Lexington, Mass.: Lexington Books.

Kenneth D. Tunnell (1992). *Choosing Crime: The Criminal Calculus of Property Offenders*. Chicago: Nelson-Hall.

Donald J. West (1982). *Delinquency: Its Roots, Careers, and Prospects*. London: Heinemann.

Ted D. Westermann, and James W. Burfeind (1991). *Crime and Justice in Two Societies: Japan and the United States*. Pacific Grove, Calif.: Brooks/Cole.

Part II

Doing Crime

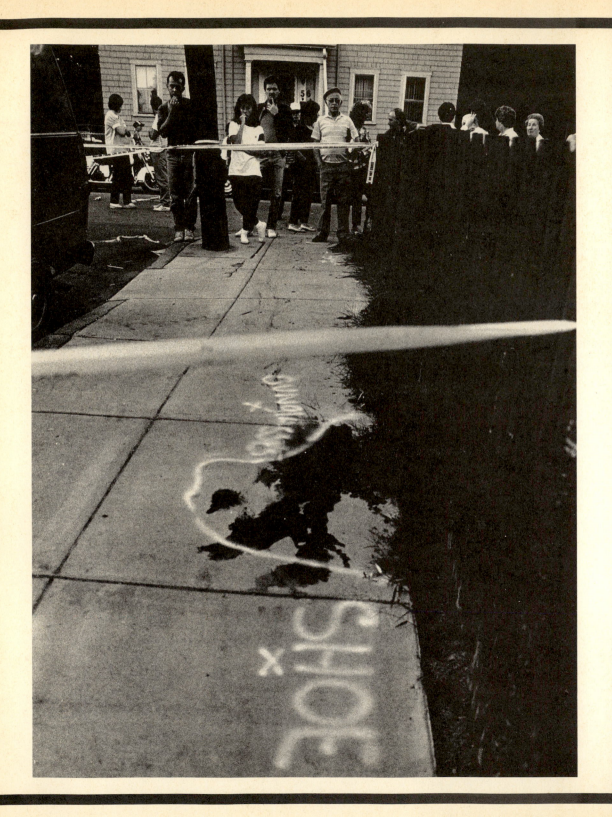

Chapter 3

Murder and Assault

This chapter is about everyday violence between people who get into arguments or disputes that end in injury or death. It is not about serial killers like Ted Bundy or Jeffrey Dahmer; nor is it about mass murderers like the man who killed 23 people at a McDonald's restaurant in California in 1987 or the man who drove his pickup into a restaurant in Killeen, Texas, in 1991 and opened fire with an automatic pistol. Serial killing has certainly become a hot topic in recent years, and there are claims that it is becoming more frequent (see Hickey, 1991; but see also, Jenkins, 1988). Good scholarship, however, has demonstrated no such increase, nor can it establish the extent and prevalence of serial murder (Egger, 1990:8–16).

Mass murders are more amenable to estimation because each event is bounded by time and space and attracts immediate publicity. It is argued that these, too, are on the increase (e.g., Levin and Fox, 1985), a fact that may largely reflect changes in opportunity and in the technology of destruction. An Uzi submachine gun or an AK47 assault rifle is capable of helping almost any motivated killer become a mass murderer. Whether anything else is responsible for the increase is a matter of speculation.

Interest in mass murder and serial killing is strong precisely because these events are aberrations. They are unexpected, sensational, often gruesome, and frightening. Many mass murders and all known serial killings involve strangers, another way in which they differ from the bulk of homicides. The killers themselves are presumed to be crazy: Who else would engage in sadistic, sexual, or cannibalistic practices or take the lives of complete strangers in a sudden fit of rage (Katz, 1988:275)? Whether juries agree, of course, is another matter and no more predictable than the phenomenon they are judging; expert witnesses make a very good living trying to convince them one way or the other.

The violence discussed in this chapter is mundane, and there is much, much more of it. The murderers involved rarely kill more than once (although they often have personal histories of violence), and they usually do not kill a stranger. (Box 3.1 shows definitions of criminal violence adopted by the American Law Institute's *Model Penal Code*. Although definitions of criminal offenses vary from state to state, the Model Penal Code is widely regarded as the standard, and will be cited throughout the text). The most common homicide around the world involves a male who kills another male with whom he is acquainted. In the United States, the killer is most often a young adult or older teenager.

Unlike Ted Bundy, the typical killer rarely shows ingenuity, and in many cases may not even intend to kill the victim. With the exception of participants' friends and relatives, perhaps, the ordinary murder is no one's big news. Daly and Wilson (1988b:124) observe:

On Sunday, September 7 [1980], the *Detroit News* reported that city's five Friday night homicides in a single brief story in Section B. Headlined was the stabbing death of a woman in her home. Four men who had been shot dead in four unrelated incidents around town got a few lines each.

Similar coverage can be found in any other big-city newspaper.

Box 3.1 ■ Definitions of Criminal Violence in the Model Penal Code

Criminal Homicide

(1) A person is guilty of criminal homicide if he purposely, knowingly, recklessly, or negligently causes the death of another human being.
(2) Criminal homicide is murder, manslaughter, or negligent homicide.

Murder: Criminal homicide constitutes murder when (a) it is committed purposely or knowingly; or (b) it is committed recklessly under circumstances manifesting extreme indifference to the value of human life. (Such recklessness and indifference is generally assumed when the defendant is committing a felony or attempting to flee from the scene of a felony.)

Manslaughter: Criminal homicide constitutes manslaughter when (a) it is committed recklessly, or (b) it is a homicide which otherwise would be murder except that it is committed under the influence of extreme mental or emotional disturbance for which there is reasonable explanation or excuse. The reasonableness of such explanation or excuse shall be determined from the viewpoint of a person in the actor's situation under the circumstances as he believes them to be.

Negligent Homicide: Criminal homicide constitutes negligent homicide when it is committed negligently.

Aggravated Assault

A person is guilty of aggravated assault if he:

(a) attempts to cause serious bodily injury to another, or causes such injury purposely, knowingly, or recklessly under circumstances manifesting extreme indifference to the value of human life; or
(b) attempts to cause or purposely or knowingly causes bodily injury to another with a deadly weapon.

Simple Assault

A person is guilty of assault if he:

(a) attempts to cause or purposely, knowingly, or recklessly causes bodily injury to another, or
(b) negligently causes bodily injury to another with a deadly weapon, or
(c) attempts by physical menace to put another in fear of imminent serious bodily injury.

Source: Excerpted from the Model Penal Code, copyright 1962 by The American Law Institute. Reprinted with the permission of The American Law Institute.

Violence in Historical Perspective

A better understanding of the present is accomplished through an awareness of the past. Obviously, violence is not unique to the twentieth century. History bears witness to its occurrence throughout the ages.

In primitive societies acts of physical aggression were typically handled privately by the injured parties or their kinfolk. Redress was sought through retaliation. If this retaliation was viewed by the original offender as an offense in itself, a bloody feud was likely to result. Feuds thus begun might last for a short time or they might last for generations. Feuds are not uncommon in some societies even today (Wolfgang and Ferracuti, 1967:280–282).

In ancient Rome, a civilized society by the standards of its day, violence was met with violence. The eye-for-an-eye concept of proper retaliation was invoked in the Twelve Tables. However, not all judicial violence was in retaliation for other violence: Anyone who stole by night was subject to death at the hands of the injured party. A. W. Lintott (1968:26, 29) says, "A general belief that private force was a proper instrument to execute private justice seems to have been in evidence at the time of the Twelve Tables." And "violence that was used to secure a man's natural or legal rights was recognized as a perfectly proper way of freeing him from undeserved restrictions." The Romans were accustomed to violence, and the upper classes in particular placed no great value on human life. Indeed, toward the end of the Republic, bands of strong-arm thugs roamed the streets acting on orders from their upper-class retainers.

In the Middle East, the Code of Hammurabi identified various acts of violence: kidnapping children, assaulting parents, and assaults resulting in miscarriage. The punishments for these offenses varied. If someone kidnapped another's son, he was executed; if a boy struck his father, his hand was cut off; if an assailant caused a miscarriage, he was punished according to the victim's status—the higher her status, the more severe the penalty. Generally, whenever an offense injured a person of higher status than the offender, the punishment was more severe. Women were regarded as socially inferior to men and laws reflected this. The Code of Hammurabi (Gordon, 1957:14) reads: "If a man's wife has caused the death of her husband because of another male, they shall impale that woman on a stake." No such law appears to have existed for cases of a man killing his wife for the sake of another woman—a mark of patriarchy, no doubt.

With the development of English criminal law, reactive violence slowly moved out of the hands of private individuals and into the hands of the state. Violence became legal and permissible in most situations only when perpetrated by state authorities. This was partly due to the political processes that accompanied the developing Norman grip on English society during the twelfth and thirteenth centuries. Since the Normans were in effect occupation forces, one of the first things on their agenda was to secure control over the routine use of force: "Private armies and bands of retainers were abolished;

manorial courts were squeezed out of existence; local bodies of law were absorbed or overriden" (Wolin, 1970:30).

All this did not signal a decline in violence. On the contrary, violence surfaced in disputes among political foes and in sports, from jousting matches to cock fighting, wrestling, and other pastimes, in the routine affairs of governments, in the judicial system, and in the efforts of peasants and outlaws to make a living. Notwithstanding its condemnation under law, violence was commonplace. One might think that the modern world is violent, but medieval England was certainly no paradise of tranquility. While it is virtually impossible to estimate the extent of violence in England during the centuries before industrialization, we do know that executions were commonplace—one indicator that the state sanctioned violence in the name of the people. And we now know that rates of homicide are affected by the level of officially sanctioned violence (see Williams and Flewelling, 1988).

Violence in American History

The Puritans came to America largely to escape forceful suppression of their exercise of religious preferences. Perhaps because of this, violence by New Englanders was generally a rare occurrence. Violence in the name of justice, however, was not. Consider what happened during the celebrated Salem witch hunts. In one year alone a score of deaths resulted from this repressive episode in judicial history—and more were to die before the witch scare died down (Erickson, 1966:149).

Some people believe that violence is never right, that it is immoral and without justification no matter what the circumstances. Others think violence can be justified, though only under exceptional circumstances, such as for self-defense. Others contend that violence can be justified by its accomplishments: a greater good or the prevention of a greater evil (Runkle, 1976). Much of the violence that has marked America's history has been justified on the grounds that it brought about important, constructive changes in American society. The Revolutionary War, the Civil War, the Indian wars, frontier vigilante justice, and labor violence have been called examples of "positive" violence (Brown, 1969). The fact that thousands of people were killed, maimed, orphaned, and left homeless has been played down. The end justified the means.

During the nineteenth century, riots plagued the major cities; feuds erupted in Kentucky, Virginia, West Virginia, and Texas; guerrilla bands roamed the Midwest in search of glory and fortune; outlaws plundered the frontier regions of the country, often chased by bloodthirsty posses; citizens formed groups of vigilantes; workers seeking the right to unionize took to the streets and were met by police and hired thugs; lynch mobs plagued the South and dealt their own brand of justice; and the mass destruction of Native Americans continued. Wherever it surfaced, conflict seemed destined to result in violence.

The use of violence for problem-solving continued into the twentieth century. The labor movement was marked by violence as it confronted stubborn bosses and politicians. Especially violent were the clashes in the country's mining areas. In one mining strike—against the Colorado Fuel and Iron Company, from 1913 to 1914—more than thirty men, women, and children lost their lives in fighting (Brown, 1969:55). The first half of the twentieth century also witnessed new forms of violence: During and after Prohibition, gangland killings became routine events in some cities, Chicago in particular; the Ku Klux Klan became a national organization and brought its hatred and prejudice to bear on blacks, Catholics, Jews, and "radical" whites in brutal beatings and killings.

The historical American experience involving individual rather than group acts of violence is more difficult to characterize because of the lack of national statistics on past levels and trends. In a report to the National Commission on the Causes and Prevention of Violence (hereafter called the National Commission), Mulvihill and Tumin argue that "there is no unequivocal evidence to suggest that recent levels and trends of violence per capita are significantly greater than in the more historical past" (Mulvihill, Tumin, and Curtis, 1969:49). Given the high level of group violence following the Revolutionary War, it is reasonable to think that individual acts of violence were at a high level and followed an upward trend during the nineteenth century. Mulvihill, Tumin, and Curtis (p. 52) conclude:

> If any general reported trend can be hypothesized, the available evidence suggests an initial high level of violence slowly rising in the late 19th century, perhaps leveling off for a period, rising to a new peak shortly after the turn of the 20th century, and then declining somewhat thereafter. The question of whether or not Americans have historically shown a propensity or impulse to acts of violence remains difficult to answer.

The Current Picture

Throughout the 1960s and 1970s overall levels of violent crime had been rising steeply in the United States. The National Commission found about a 47-percent increase in the official rates for murder and nonnegligent manslaughter between 1958 and 1968. Rates for aggravated assault showed even higher increases, around 100 percent. FBI data confirm that aggravated assault rates continued to rise during the 1970s, although more slowly. The most recent four-year period for which information is available shows that serious assaults and homicides are again on the rise after a leveling off period during the mid-1980s (Federal Bureau of Investigation, 1991:9, 24).

National crime survey figures for the 1980s suggest that the police picture overstates the increase in assault rates. In fact, fewer assaults have been reported in the most recent surveys than at any time since the NCVS program began in 1973 (Bureau of Justice Statistics, 1988b).

Official rates of murder and nonnegligent manslaughter vary around the country. New England states typically have the lowest rates, while Southern states lead the country. Rates also vary by size of city. The highest rates are found in cities with over 250,000 population, and the rates tend to decline along with city size. Homicide is primarily a large-city phenomenon. However, for many years, rural rates have been slightly higher than the rates for many small- and medium-sized cities. One reason may be that the distance from and quality of medical services in rural areas make assaults more likely to turn into homicides (see Doerner, 1983; Barlow, 1985a; Barlow and Schmidt Barlow, 1988).

More detailed information about official homicides is found in arrest data. Fortunately, official statistics on homicides are among the best available. Homicides rarely go unreported and suspects are usually apprehended and charged with the crime. Police departments generally take great pride in their ability to solve homicides, which is made possible by the existence of a corpse and the crime's typical circumstances. Although they have declined since 1970, probably due to increases in the proportion of stranger murders, clearance rates for homicide are markedly better than those for any other index crime (see p. 51).

More than half of the arrests for homicide occur in cities over 250,000; of all those arrested in 1990, 90 percent were males, 52 percent were under the age of 25, and 14 percent were under the age of 18. African-Americans are arrested around 55 percent of the time. According to FBI data, around 20 percent of those homicides on which information is available were committed in the course of other felony crimes, most often rape, robbery, or burglary. In most of these cases, the arrested suspect was white (Federal Bureau of Investigation, 1991:13).

The most common homicide situation starts when people get into an argument or altercation. Quarrels about money or over girl friends, disputes over "turf" or possessions, and fights erupting in bars are often the precipitating circumstances. The FBI estimates that nationally around 35 percent of all known homicides follow this pattern. An in-depth study of eight cities found that homicides were most likely to involve acquaintances, followed by family members, and finally, strangers (Riedel and Zahn, 1985).

The victims of homicides, national data show, are preponderantly male and usually between 20 and 30 years old. Most victims are of the same race and socioeconomic status as the offender, which often means poor and half the time means black. Most likely, the offender and victim are either relatives, friends, or acquaintances. FBI data show that a young black male living in one of the nation's larger cities has a better chance than anyone else of being arrested for homicide or of being the victim of one. Table 3.1 shows the lifetime probability of being murdered in the United States. Clearly, the risk is not shared equally.

Urban Studies   Although official statistics on homicide are valuable for assessing gross patterns and trends, those who wish a more complete picture will find a number of in-depth urban studies to which they can turn. The pioneering study of homicide was conducted by Marvin Wolfgang (1958) in

TABLE 3.1 Lifetime probability of being murdered

Lifetime Risk of Homicide	
1 out of:	179 white males
	30 black males
	495 white females
	132 black females

Source: Bureau of Justice Statistics (1988b). *Crime and Justice in America*, 2nd ed. Washington, D.C.: U.S. Department of Justice.

the mid-1950s. Wolfgang looked at homicides that had come to the attention of Philadelphia police from 1948 to 1952. He investigated a host of variables, including race, sex, age, temporal patterns, spatial patterns, motives, and offender–victim relationships.

Since the publication of Wolfgang's study, there have been quite a few other urban investigations of homicide. In America, the settings for these investigations have included Houston (Porkorny, 1965; Lundesgaarde, 1977), Dallas, Newark, N.J., and Memphis (Riedel and Zahn, 1985), Chicago (Voss and Hepburn, 1968; Block and Zimring, 1973; Block, 1976, 1987), Detroit (Fisher, 1976), Atlanta (Munford et al., 1976; Rose and McClain, 1981), greater Cleveland (Bensing and Schroeder, 1960), and Miami (Wilbanks, 1984). With few exceptions, these studies tend to confirm the following observations about homicide: (1) Young black adult males are most likely to be identified as offenders and victims. (2) Offenders and victims tend to be of low socioeconomic status and to reside in inner-city neighborhoods. (3) Homicides usually occur during the late evening and early morning hours of the weekend. (4) Around half of the known homicides occur in either the offender's or the victim's home. (5) Homicides do not follow consistent seasonal patterns— they do not, as prevalent myth has it, occur significantly more often during the hot months of the year (see also Cheatwood, 1988; Harries, 1989). (6) Offenders and victims are usually acquainted and often live in the same immediate neighborhood. (7) Strangers are killed most often during the commission of another felony, such as robbery or burglary.

With regard to homicide trends, three conclusions seem warranted on the basis of the evidence from available studies: (1) The homicide offender is getting younger—the proportion of offenses committed by persons under age 25 has been rising. (2) Interracial homicides seem to be on the increase, though the increases are small. (3) The proportion of homicides involving strangers has been increasing, though it still remains low relative to homicides involving people who know each other.

Homicide on the International Scene   The United States is certainly not alone in experiencing violence in interpersonal relations. True, violence among group members is rare or seemingly nonexistent in some societies—the

Arapesh of New Guinea, the Lepchas of Sikkim, the Eskimos, and the Zuni Indians are examples—but this is clearly the exception to the rule.

Nevertheless, the level of violence varies from society to society. Regardless of legal definitions, some societies do seem to be more violence-prone than others. The United States ranks first among Western and other industrialized nations and has done so for as long as data have been available. Recent U.S. homicide rates are five to six times greater than rates for England and Wales, Germany, Sweden, and New Zealand, and they are twice as high as rates for Northern Ireland, which has been experiencing a virtual civil war (Bureau of Justice Statistics, 1988e). A recent study of murders by Canadian youth found that although the characteristics of juvenile killings in Canada and the United States are similar in many respects (though not all), the *rate* of killings in the United States is 3 to 4 times higher, and in New York City it is *10* times higher than the rate in Canada (Meloff and Silverman, 1992). Whereas differences in classification and reporting practices may explain some of the variation, the more sizable differences are obviously a result of other factors.

Homicide is most often a crime of passion: It is rarely planned or committed in cold blood. In other countries, as in America, murders tend to occur during arguments. Homicides around the world share some other common features. First, offenders are almost always male, usually under 30, and poor. Second, they are likely to have known the victim, as a relative, friend, or acquaintance. Third, in countries with racial or ethnic heterogeneity, the offender and victim are usually of the same race or ethnic group. Fourth, many homicides appear to be victim precipitated, especially when the victim is male or the offender is female. The actions of the victim are instrumental in starting the physical fight or confrontation out of which homicide often erupts (Bohannan, 1960; Palmer, 1968). The most striking fact of all is that males kill males with more than ten times the frequency that women kill women. Daly and Wilson (1988b:146) observe, "There is no known society in which the level of violence among women even begins to approach that among men."

Disaggregating Homicide Even though most killings occur in the context of an argument or dispute of some sort, homicide is not a unitary phenomenon:

> Homicide is not one type of event, but many. Almost all acts of lethal violence begin as a confrontation—a spousal argument, a fight or brawl between acquaintances, a robbery, an act of sexual violence, a street gang confrontation—that escalates to death. While lethal violence is statistically rare, these nonfatal confrontations are not. Only some street fights end in murder; only some robberies end in murder. Homicides that begin as different types of confrontation have different characteristics, occur in different areas of the city, affect different segments of the population, and have different strategies for prevention. (Block and Block, 1991:6)

When homicide rates are compared across cities or countries or across time, the practice of disaggregating them uncovers important variations that would not otherwise be seen. *Disaggregating* simply means breaking down the total into different categories. Various criteria have been used to identify what those different categories might be, among them, the weapon used, the relationship between offender and victim, the time and place of occurrence, and the context or circumstances of the killing.

Studies by Block (1991) and Block and Block (1991) demonstrate the value of disaggregation in studying homicide trends. The Blocks broke down the aggregate Chicago homicide figures for the 25 years ending in 1989 into two underlying broad categories—"instrumental," where violence emerges out of a goal-oriented predatory attack (such as robbery) the purpose of which is not primarily to kill or injure, and "expressive," where violence erupts more or less spontaneously as part of a confrontation and as an end in itself.

These two categories are considered opposite ends of a continuum, and they "seldom occur in their pure form. Thus, the acquisition of money or property may occur as an afterthought in expressive violence, or it may be an additional way of hurting the victim" (Block and Block, 1991:7; see also Katz, 1988). They may also be further disaggregated into a variety of more narrowly defined categories, or "syndromes," as Carolyn Block calls them. She also discovered that the same homicide syndromes may be going down while others are going up, and vice versa. In similar vein, Block and Block (1991) found that areas of the city having high overall homicide rates have substantially different spatial distributions of individual homicide syndromes.

The Blocks' research in Chicago consists of disaggregating homicide rates within one city. Williams and Flewelling (1988) used a similar technique in a comparison of homicide rates across 168 cities. They divided homicide rates into offender–victim relationships and type of conflict and found that the social conditions influencing one type did not necessarily affect another the same way, or even at all. Other studies are confirming the importance of disaggregating the overall homicide rate. It now appears, for example, that different factors contribute to variations in homicide rates depending on whether women or men are involved, and that black female homicides differ significantly from those involving white females (e.g., Gartner, 1990). Much work still needs to be done, but all these studies warn against blanket generalizations about *the* homicide rate.

Aggravated Assault Aggravated assault is not as thoroughly researched as homicide. What is known about it, however, suggests a striking resemblance to homicide. Pittman and Handy (1964), the National Commission, and other sources agree that these two offense categories are alike in many important respects. This should not surprise anyone, because the essential difference between the two is the existence of a corpse.

Those arrested for aggravated assault are disproportionately young black males who come from low socioeconomic backgrounds and reside in large cities. The victims also fit this characterization. Wilbanks (1985), however, argues that black offenders are more likely than white offenders to commit assaults (and robberies and rapes) that are interracial. Most studies have focused on who is victimized by whom, and they show that whites and blacks are generally victimized by members of their own races. But Wilbanks turns the question around and asks, "Who do members of each race choose as victims?" His analysis of nationwide victimization data shows that whereas 81.9 percent of black victims were assaulted by black offenders (the usual way of looking at things), 55 percent of black offenders selected white victims. Whether this pattern holds for different regions and cities or for different time periods was not explored.

As with homicides, aggravated assaults often occur inside the home or around bars and street corners. Not surprisingly, knives are the weapons most often used (were guns more often used, assaults would more often be homicides). As with homicide, victim actions often contribute to the initiation of violence. Verbal confrontations between males, especially, are prone to result in physical attacks, not just in American cities but universally, it seems (e.g., Polk, 1991).

Family Violence

Many homicides and assaults occur in the home. If there are doubts that violence is widespread in the American family, consider the following facts: In Detroit, 50 percent of all homicides are domestic, and in Boston, police receive an average of 45 calls a day—that multiplies out to 16,425 a year—involving family disputes (U.S. Department of Justice, 1979). Nationally, an estimated 2.2 million children are physically abused by family members, and 2 million wives are beaten by their husbands. Indeed, "a person is more likely to be hit or killed in his or her own home by another family member than anywhere else or by anyone else" (Gelles and Straus, 1979:15).

Women are much more likely than men to become victims of domestic violence. The typical assailant is a husband, and the next most common is an ex-husband. Recent reports from the National Crime Victimization Survey indicate that once a woman has been exposed to violence from another family member, she has a 1 in 3 chance of being victimized again. Furthermore, when a woman is victimized, her injuries are usually just as serious as or more serious than those suffered in more than 90 percent of all rapes, robberies, and aggravated assaults (Bureau of Justice Statistics, 1988a:17).

Detecting family violence is not easy, partly because there is uncertainty and disagreement about what constitutes criminal violence in family settings. When does a spanking or other disciplinary action become abuse or crime? Consequently, even the most nonthreatening interviews often fail to uncover cases of family violence that respondents have not defined as such. This may explain why victimization surveys indicate that parental abuse of children is less often reported than spousal violence. In addition, many people believe that what happens within the family is a private matter. When people are asked why they did not call police after being attacked by another family member, this is the reason they most often give (Bureau of Justice Statistics, 1984b).

When young children are victims of family violence, the potential for serious injury is always present, even though fatality rates are relatively low. Typical child injuries from severe beatings include brain damage, skull and extremity fractures, internal bleeding, and other traumas. A nationwide survey of 2143 families found that during the year before the survey, over 20 percent had experienced parental assaults on children in which objects were thrown or in which children were kicked, bitten, or hit with clenched fists or with sundry other objects (Gelles, 1978). While this type of violence can be found in all social classes, evidence indicates that it is more commonly found in poor families. In this respect, family violence reproduces the uneven class representation found for homicide and aggravated assault in general.

Changes in Family Violence   In a national sample of 2143 American couples, Murray Straus and Richard Gelles, who pioneered survey research on domestic violence, found that at least one violent incident occurred in 16 percent of the families between 1975 and 1976, and in 28 percent of the families from the time of marriage. Most of the violence was minor—slapping or throwing objects, for example—but one-third of the cases involved kicking, biting, beating, stabbing, cutting, or shooting (Straus, Gelles, and Steinmetz, 1980).

In 1985 Straus and associates produced a second survey to determine whether rates of family violence had changed over the ten-year period. The use of half-hour telephone interviews rather than the hour-long face-to-face interviews of the first survey means that the two surveys are not directly comparable. Straus and Gelles (1986:472) argue, however, that the methodological differences do not seem to have biased the results. The principal findings indicate that both wife beating and physical child abuse *decreased* during the ten-year period, reported child abuse by 47 percent, and reported wife abuse by 27 percent.

Straus and Gelles (1986:473–475) believe the findings reflect *changing norms* (family violence is becoming less acceptable), *changes in family structure* (rising ages at which people get married and have children and a decline in the number of children per family), *changes in the economy* (lower rates of inflation and unemployment, hence lower levels of economic stress), and the *growth of support services*, for example, shelters and treatment programs for victims and offenders. In addition, it is possible that potential offenders perceive greater certainty and severity of punishment if they are reported to authorities. Many police departments have changed their methods of dealing with domestic violence from a more or less "do-nothing" approach to one in which domestic assaults are treated like any other assaults (see pp. 378–379).

Women Who Kill   Recent studies suggest that the reasons why women kill and the circumstances surrounding female violence are different from those attributed to males. For example, female homicides are often precipitated by the violence of the men they kill (Chimbos, 1978; Daniel and Harris, 1982; Wilbanks, 1983). Most spousal homicides follow this pattern, and the wives who eventually become murderers have often been physically abused by their husbands over a long period of time.

Angela Browne (1987) discovered that women resort to lethal counter-force because alternative solutions have failed and because they feel hopelessly trapped. Fifty-nine percent of her interview subjects also reported that they had been raped by their husbands (Browne, 1987:95). Compared to other battered wives, those who killed their spouses reported more severe sexual assaults. Often the women would wake up to find they were being beaten or raped. All the women believed they would be killed, and the fear grew as the husband's battering became more frequent and more severe. Ironically, the batterers were usually killed by their own weapons.

Unlike their male counterparts, women who kill rarely have extensive criminal histories, and they are rarely the first to use potentially lethal violence in an altercation. Also unlike males, women are most likely to kill their domestic partners. From 1980 to 1984 there were 76,048 homicides committed by men and 12,503 committed by women. Fifty-one percent of female homicides were directed against male partners, whereas only 14 percent of male homicides were directed against female partners (Browne and Williams, 1987:14; see also Silverman and Kennedy, 1988).

If women use violence largely in reaction to male aggression and do so only as a last resort, one would expect female rates of homicide to be higher in areas where rates of male violence are high and where there are fewer resources for abused women to find help. Browne and Williams (1987) found evidence to support this hypothesis for the period 1980–1984. The authors defined two indices of resources available to women at risk of domestic violence: One was based on whether a state maintained statutes providing civil and criminal remedies and financial support for victims of family violence. The other was composed of two variables—the number of shelters for battered women per 100,000 women in a state and the number of other services for battered women per 100,000 women.

The findings in both cases yielded interesting results: The higher the indices, the lower the rate of female homicide. From a practical standpoint, these findings suggest that rates of both female-perpetrated homicide and wife abuse will decline with improvements in the availability of legislative resources and support services to aid victims of domestic violence (see also Caringella-MacDonald, 1991).

Situational Elements in Violence

Before turning to explanations of violence that focus on etiology, it is important to recognize that whether or not people are predisposed to violence when they enter a situation, the likelihood of violence can be influenced by factors that are present in, or develop out of, the situation itself. Examples of situational elements that promote violent outcomes are guns, alcohol, victim precipitation, and the encouragement of witnesses.

Guns and Murder

Nationwide, about 60 percent of homicides are committed with a firearm, usually a handgun (see Figure 3.1). This picture has remained virtually unchanged since the late 1960s. When cities are compared, some exceptions to the general picture emerge: Riedel and Zahn (1985) found that in 1978, knives edged out handguns as the most common homicide weapon in Newark, N.J. (35.2 percent to 34.1), whereas in Memphis and Dallas over 60 percent of homicides involved handguns. Riedel and Zahn also discovered that handguns were most common in homicides involving strangers, perhaps because these homicides were more likely to occur in connection with some other offense, such as armed robbery. Around the nation, handguns are least likely to be used in family killings but are still the most commonly used weapon. As of 1990, only 14 states required handgun permits, though 21 required written applications and a waiting period before taking delivery, and 34 required a license to carry a concealed handgun (Maguire and Flanagan, 1991:133).

A study of 9054 handgun murder victims in 1986 found that half were blacks, a victimization rate nearly eight times that for whites (Rand, 1990). Blacks aged 20–34 were victimized at a rate nine times greater than the

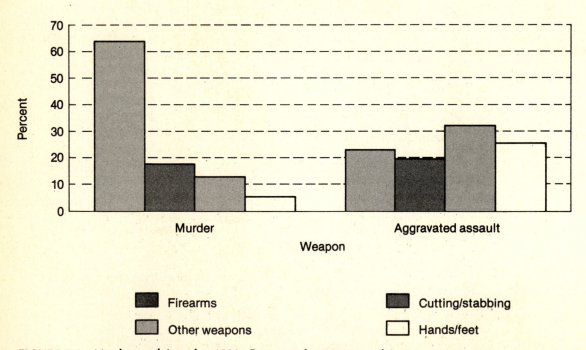

FIGURE 3.1 Murders and Assaults, 1990. By type of weapon used (percent). Compiled from Federal Bureau of Investigation (1991). *Crime in the United States, 1990.* Washington, D.C.: U.S. Department of Justice, pp. 12 and 24.

population as a whole, regardless of age. In contrast, white rates of victimization were only slightly higher than average. Male rates of handgun murder victimization were five times those for women. A majority of all victims were shot and killed during arguments, but nearly 30 percent were killed during a robbery or other crime.

Estimates of the number of firearms in private hands in America vary, and it is important to recognize their source. One should be wary of estimates made by people with financial or political interests in guns. Probably no one claims to know the exact number, and so any figure must be treated as a more or less educated guess. Having said this, academic estimates for the late 1970s place the figure at 120 million, plus or minus 20 million, with handguns making up about 30 percent of the total (Wright and Rossi, 1981). A more recent estimate of the number of handguns in private hands placed the figure at 65 million, roughly two for every household (*Newsweek*, October 14, 1985). National opinion surveys show that almost half of those interviewed report having at least one gun in their home (Maguire and Flanagan, 1991:202).

Wright and Rossi (1981) estimate that about 25 percent of private guns are kept for protection and self-defense. Clearly, many Americans are fearful for their lives or property. By comparison, relatively few people actually die from a firearm—around 30,000 annually. Still, an estimated 900,000 incidents occur annually in which guns are brandished or fired (Wright and Rossi, 1981). According to National Crime Victimization Surveys, an average of 837,000 crimes are committed with firearms each year. In roughly 70,000 of these (11 percent) the victim is shot at (Bureau of Justice Statistics, 1990c; also Robin, 1991:2).

One of the most troublesome issues regarding firearms in America is the growing interest in military assault guns capable of rapid fire. An estimated 620,000 such weapons are in private hands, including the Uzi, MAC-10, and AR-15 (*Newsweek*, October 14, 1985). The lethal capability of these weapons is awesome: A MAC-10 is large caliber (.45 or 9 mm) and can fire up to 1100 rounds per minute. It is very small, hence easily concealed, and costs less than $300. In semiautomatic form these guns may be legally owned in most states as of this writing.

Some claim that if Americans could not readily acquire guns, there would be less killing. Others argue that the availability of guns has no bearing on homicide rates—that people kill, not guns. The debate on the issue is fierce and seems unlikely to be resolved in the near future. Since guns are a fact of life in America and have been widely owned for at least two centuries, talk of civilian disarmament generally falls on deaf ears. Powerful interest groups such as the National Rifle Association (NRA) and the highly profitable gun industry, which earns over $2 billion a year, resist more stringent controls. In addition, opinion surveys consistently report that most Americans believe they have a right to own a firearm, though opinions are divided on whether *handguns* should be banned in the respondents' own community (Flanagan and Jamieson, 1988:173).

Guns are clearly a factor in American homicide (Klebba, 1975; Farley,

1980), but the causal significance of their availability is disputed (see Robin, 1991, for a review of the debate and evidence). Wright and Rossi (1981), for example, find no persuasive evidence that decreasing the availability of firearms would decrease homicide rates, and Wolfgang (1958:83) points out in his Philadelphia study that "few homicides due to shootings could be avoided merely if a firearm were not immediately present." But Fisher's (1976) study of homicide trends in Detroit shows a link between the increasing availability of firearms, especially handguns, and that city's rising homicide rate. Rose and McClain (1981:100) suggest that the relatively high proportion of handgun homicides among blacks in Atlanta, regardless of the circumstances of the incident, is due to the widespread availability of handguns in the black community.

George Newton and Franklin Zimring (1969:9–10) point out that known weapon ownership rates are highest in the South: Fifty-nine percent of all households owned weapons in 1968. On the other hand, only 33 percent of all households in the East owned firearms. In 1967, the official homicide rate for the South was almost ten per 100,000 people; for the East it was just over four per 100,000 people. A comparison of homicide and assault rates in Seattle and Vancouver confirms that the risk of being killed relates significantly to gun ownership, especially of handguns. People assaulted in Seattle were almost twice as likely to die as victims of assault in Vancouver. The risk of being murdered by a handgun in Seattle was nearly five times higher than in Vancouver (Sloan et al., 1988; but see Robin, 1991, for other studies on the link between gun availability and homicide).

The presence of a gun does not mean a murder will occur. Millions of Americans have access to guns, but relatively few kill or are killed by them. Yet the presence of a gun increases the probability that someone will die when violence erupts. The gun is a situational factor providing an easily accessible opportunity for murder.

The situational importance of guns to homicide is revealed in studies in Chicago (Zimring, 1972) and St. Louis (Barlow, 1983; and Barlow and Schmidt Barlow, 1988). Both studies found not only that guns were more lethal than knives but also that some guns were more lethal than others. In Chicago, .38 caliber handguns were twice as deadly as .22s; .32 caliber handguns were more lethal than .25s; and .25s were more lethal than .22s. The St. Louis study found that 47.7 percent of those victims shot by "large-caliber" weapons (i.e., .38, .357, .44, or .45) died, compared to 33.3 percent of those shot with .32 or smaller caliber handguns. In further contrast, only 18.5 percent of stabbing victims died.

It should be pointed out that the relative lethality of different firearms is affected by the location of the wound. In general, wounds to the head are more likely to be fatal than wounds to other parts of the body. However, Barlow's study also found that the difference in lethality between large-caliber and small-caliber handguns virtually disappeared in head-wound cases. Shoot someone in the head and it matters little whether the gun is a .357 magnum or a .25 caliber derringer (Barlow and Schmidt Barlow, 1988).

Alcohol

Just as guns turn up as the weapon used in most homicides, so alcohol emerges as a situational element in many homicides and assaults. Wolfgang found that alcohol was present in 63.6 percent of 588 homicide cases in Philadelphia. Other studies have found alcohol to be present in similar or greater proportions (Wolfgang, 1958:136). More often than not, both offender and victim had been drinking immediately before or during the fatal interaction.

Does this mean that alcohol in some way caused the killing? Most authors acknowledge the statistical association between alcohol and homicide but do not speak of the relationship in causal terms. True, alcohol is a psychoactive drug, meaning that it produces mental changes in people who consume it. The kind of changes and how extensive they are depend on numerous factors, including the quantity consumed, the consumer's physiological state, the consumer's tolerance for the drug, and whether or not he or she has just eaten.

In short, alcohol is best viewed as one likely precipitating factor in violence. To the extent that alcohol lowers social inhibitions and reduces anxiety and guilt, people who have been drinking may act more aggressively than otherwise would have been the case. The underlying dispute may have erupted anyway, and the individuals concerned may have been predisposed

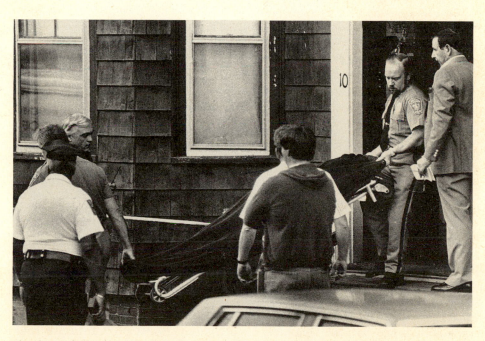

The facts about murder include these: almost all homicides involve suspects and victims who are male, under age 30, of the same race, and known to each other. In America, most homicides are also committed with the use of a firearm.

to seek a violent solution. With the situational influence of alcohol missing, however, fear, anxiety, guilt, and social inhibitions are there to serve as constraints. On the other hand, being drunk may be a factor in violence for an entirely different reason. People who anticipate getting into a dispute may prepare themselves by getting drunk. Being intoxicated may provide a convenient rationalization, besides the courage, for violence (Kantor and Straus, 1987).

Victim Precipitation

It is often argued that many homicide victims precipitate their own deaths. Many years ago Hans von Hentig (1948) said that killers are often driven to murder as much by their victims' actions as by their own inclinations. This is most likely to occur when those involved know each other well. Tensions and mutual aggravations reach the point where people see reconciliation only through violence. This can occur suddenly or develop over a long period of time. The violence is an outcome of *interaction* and not merely the result of a killer's actions.

A standard definition of victim precipitation is given by Wolfgang (1958:252):

> The term *victim-precipitated* is applied to those criminal homicides in which the victim is a direct, positive precipitator in the crime. The role of the victim is characterized by his having been the first in the homicide drama to use physical force directed against his subsequent slayer. The victim-precipitated cases are those in which the victim was the first to show and use a deadly weapon, to strike a blow in an altercation—in short, the first to commence the interplay of resort to physical violence.

Examples given by Wolfgang (1958:253), taken from Philadelphia police files, illustrate typical situations of victim-precipitated homicide:

- During a lover's quarrel, the male (victim) hit his mistress and threw a can of kerosene at her. She retaliated by throwing the liquid on him, and then tossed a lighted match in his direction. He died from the burns.
- A victim became incensed when his eventual slayer asked for money which the victim owed him. The victim grabbed a hatchet and started in the direction of his creditor, who pulled out a knife and stabbed him.

Identifying the number of victim-precipitated homicides is virtually impossible because doing so requires knowledge of the interaction between victim and offender. Because one party is dead, re-creation of the incident must rely on accounts by the killer or witnesses. Estimates have nevertheless been made, and these range from around 25 percent of homicides to upwards of 50 percent. The picture for nonlethal assaults is even more uncertain, especially since so many incidents are hidden. In all probability, a high proportion of assaults are precipitated by the victim's actions, but even pinpointing who the victim is may be moot since both parties may be injured and each is likely to blame the other for "starting it."

Violence as a Situated Transaction

All social situations possess unique characteristics, yet so many violent incidents look alike that the similarities lead one to ask whether there is some typical dynamic characterizing the events.

David Luckenbill (1977) looked at homicide incidents with just this question in mind. He found evidence of six stages in the "transaction" between actors in the typical homicide drama.

In the first stage, one person insults or offends another. To onlookers the action may not seem particularly offensive, but the person to whom it is directed is angered by it. In stage two, the offended individual sees that the insult is directed at him or her personally. Sometimes this clarification results from meanings assigned by onlookers or friends; sometimes it derives from the history of interactions between the parties involved, as when, for example, a husband has previously fought with his wife and now interprets the present situation as similar.

Stage three involves decisions about reactions to the insult or affront. The offended individual may excuse the other's behavior, rationalizing that the person is just drunk, joking, or acting "crazy." If such face-saving techniques do not work or are inappropriate, the individual must retaliate or back down. Retaliation is usually the route taken in homicide situations and those in which someone is severely injured.

In a search for the situational, proximate, or close-in causes of murder, Katz (1988:13) asks "What is the killer trying to do in a typical homicide?" He believes that many murders represent an impassioned attack, or "righteous slaughter," in which the killer makes a last-ditch effort to defend his basic worth. Insults about sexual prowess (for men) or continued sexual violation (of women) are felt to be deeply humiliating. When humiliation turns to rage, the would-be killer tries to settle things once and for all. In rage, the killer "confirms his humiliation through transcending it. In rage, he acknowledges that his subjectivity has been overcome by implicitly acknowledging that he could not take it anymore. But now the acknowledgment is triumphal because it comes just as rage promises to take him to dominance over the situation" (Katz, 1988:26).

Sometimes death or injury occurs in stage three. If not, a fourth stage may be entered, in which counterretaliation takes place. In stage four the original offender continues or escalates the insulting behavior, perhaps using violence. In this stage, onlookers may take sides in the dispute, escalating and even directing the conflict.

In stage five both parties are unable to back down without losing face, and weapons will be produced if they have not already appeared. In Luckenbill's study, many disputants already carried guns or knives with them. Others used bottles, pool cues, and other handy implements or temporarily left the situation to get a gun or knife. With weapons at hand, one party either kills the other quickly or a battle ensues.

Throughout these five stages, no one has given much thought to the police. In stage six the police enter the picture. Some killers flee, some are restrained by onlookers, some are aided by friends, and some call police themselves. The interactions themselves have thus created a new situation in which outsiders are involved and must be reckoned with.

This view of violent situations is not intended to describe all murderous encounters. However, as a depiction of the most "normal" homicide and serious assault it describes the dynamics well. Conflict, victim precipitation, face saving, retaliation and escalation, and the presence of weapons conspire to produce deadly violence. That many situations also involve alcohol, drugs, or partying makes defusing the process a difficult, if not impossible, task. One often hears about people who have tried to break up a fight only to be injured or killed themselves.

Explaining Violence

The explanation of violence has interested scholars and laypersons alike for centuries. Needless to say, many different theories have been advanced, and the search goes on. In this section some of the more prominent perspectives on violence will be reviewed.

Biosocial Views

Some biologists believe that people are instinctively aggressive, basing their claim on studies of animal behavior. According to Konrad Lorenz (1971), nature gave animals an instinct for aggression for three reasons: (1) to ensure that the strongest males succeed in mating with the most desirable females, thus ensuring a kind of genetic quality control; (2) to protect the physical space, or territory, necessary for raising the young, securing food, and the like; and (3) to maintain hierarchies of dominance and through them a stable, well-policed society.

Following Lorenz and Desmond Morris—the author of *The Naked Ape*—Pierre van den Berghe (1974:777) believes that human behavior is not "radically discontinuous from that of other species," and he advocates a biosocial approach to understanding human violence. Essentially, the argument is that humans, like animals, have predispositions to violence that are innate—that is, biologically grounded. Though conclusive proof of this is still unavailable, one promising indication is that aggression is a universal behavior pattern for a species: In humans, aggression has been observed everywhere, despite widely differing habitats, cultures, and technologies. The viewpoint receives additional support from the documented relationship between aggression and the male hormone testosterone and the discovery of "aggression centers" in the brain (van den Berghe, 1974; Bailey, 1976; Wilson and Herrnstein, 1985).

Robert L. Burgess (1979) has drawn on evolutionary theory to explain variations in child abuse and family violence. Burgess argues that mature humans have two related problems. The first is to pass on their genes through successive generations, and the second is to protect their offspring despite limited resources. The solution is for parents to invest most in those genetic offspring who show the best prospects for surviving and reproducing and least in nongenetic relatives and/or those genetic offspring who show the worst prospects of surviving and reproducing.

The problems and their solutions will produce greater risks of abuse and neglect in families with stepchildren, in poorer families, in those with less education, in families with many children, in single-parent families, and in families whose children have mental or physical impairments. Burgess cites studies both in the United States and abroad that confirm these predictions (see also Daly and Wilson, 1988b). However, it should be emphasized that child abuse is not inevitable in families with these characteristics and it is found in many families without them.

Daly and Wilson (1988a:520) make the following observation on step-relationships and violence:

> In view of the costs of prolonged "parental" investment in nonrelatives, it may seem remarkable that step-relationships are ever peaceful, let alone genuinely affectionate. However, violent hostility is rarer than friendly relations even among nonrelatives; people thrive by the maintenance of networks of social reciprocity that will make them attractive exchange partners. . . . The fact remains, however, that step-relationships lack the deep commonality of interest of the natural parent-offspring relationships, and feelings of affection and commitment are correspondingly shallower. Differential rates of violence are one result.

Personality and Aggressive Temperament

To say that people have an innate predisposition toward violence does not mean they will be violent, nor does it explain different levels and types of violence. The actual display of aggression is affected by *triggers* and *inhibitors*, controls that may be innate but also may be learned or situational.

Some psychiatrists believe that humans develop internal inhibitors during early childhood. According to Sigmund Freud, the individual psyche is composed of three parts: the ego, the id, and the superego. Behavior is motivated by those drives, Freud believed, that are innate: the sex drive, the aggression drive, and even the death drive. These make up the id. As one develops and interacts with others, the superego emerges. This part of the psyche consists of social ideals and rules that are internalized through socialization. Finally, the ego strikes a balance between the demands of the id and the constraints of the superego.

The aggressive drive is expressed as violence, Freudians believe, when disturbances occur within the psyche. Mulvihill and Tumin (1969:460–461) put it this way:

> The id may overflow with violent drives: the individual hates too much, enjoys pain too much, or wants to destroy himself. Sometimes the id is just too

much for the ego to control, and the individual breaks out into violent behavior. . . . Alternatively, the superego may be extremely overformed or underformed. If the superego tries to quash *all* expression of dislike or hatred, and to quell all fantasies about violence, the individual may build up a greater and greater reserve of unfulfilled desire, until he can no longer control himself. Then he becomes violent. If the superego is underdeveloped, the individual simply sees nothing wrong with violence; he will use it whenever the occasion seems to call for it. In the underdeveloped superego, we are not dealing with a "sick" man at variance with his environment; we are rather dealing with a sick environment which has encouraged violence as the "normal" mode of response.

Some psychiatrists locate the seeds of emotional disturbance in parent–child relationships. It is suggested, for example, that the "love bonds" between parent and child are important to regulating the aggressive drive and that destructive behavior is prevented by the formation of stable human relationships in early childhood (Chodorkoff and Baxter, 1969). By the same token, excessive physical disciplining undermines these bonds and, further, teaches youngsters that there is a place for violence in relationships with loved ones.

Although psychiatrists may have much to tell about aggression and violence among those who are "disturbed" or "sick," their work is not helpful in understanding types of violence for entire populations and societies. Indeed, some people question the applicability of the psychiatric approach to even extreme forms of aggression. They point out that violent offenders do not suffer from mental disorders as a rule. Summarizing the findings of investigations into mental disorders among murderers, psychiatrist Donald Lunde (1970:93) argues:

> I cannot emphasize too strongly the well-established fact that mental patients, in general, are no more murderous than the population at large. While it should not be surprising to find that psychotic killers have been previously hospitalized for treatment of psychosis, *the incidence of psychosis among murderers is no greater than the incidence of psychosis in the total population.* Furthermore, the percentage of murderers among former mental patients is actually slightly *lower* than that among persons who have never been in a mental hospital. Crimes committed by the mentally ill tend to receive disproportionate publicity, which reinforces a widespread myth about mental illness and violence.

Frustration-Aggression Theories

The frustration-aggression hypothesis was first advanced in the 1930s by psychologists at Yale University. Originally, the hypothesis asserted that "the occurrence of aggressive behavior always presupposes the existence of frustration, and . . . the existence of frustration always leads to some form of aggression" (Dollard et al., 1939:1). Frustration arises whenever something interferes with an individual's attempt to reach a valued goal.

It was soon recognized that this early statement of the frustration-aggression relationship required modification to accommodate the complexities of real life. Even though the impulse for aggression may be strong following some frustrating experience, the actual display of aggression may be inhibited by internal or external controls. Further, frustrations may be cumulative, one experience adding to another, and they may remain potent over a long period of time. It is now known that people evaluate frustrating experiences differently, according to whether they are arbitrary or unreasonable, for example. Finally, socialization teaches people how to respond to frustrations, and since the content of what is learned varies considerably from group to group and from society to society, the reactions to frustration can be expected to vary. In short, aggressive actions are not an automatic consequence of frustration, nor is the relationship between the two a simple one.

Violence and Economic Hardship

In recent years, a variant of frustration-aggression theory has been used to explain the relatively high rates of homicide and other violent crimes among blacks. In one account (Bowman, 1980), violence is an outgrowth of the frustrations stemming from the employment-related experiences of young black males. Taking a "dual" or "split" labor-market approach, Bowman argues that blacks are disproportionately employed in the secondary sector where pay is low, working conditions are inferior, and there is limited opportunity for advancement and little job security (see also Farley, 1988:225–226). According to Bowman, these stressful and frustrating conditions lead to high rates of drug and alcohol abuse and high rates of black-on-black violence.

Bowman does not adequately explain, however, whether the violence results directly from the frustrating job experiences or indirectly through the conditions and interactions associated with drug and alcohol abuse. Numerous studies of the relationship between homicide rates and economic hardship show conflicting results but, in any case, can only infer the psychological mechanisms that might be at work for an individual.

Scholars continue to explore the relationship between economic inequality and homicide rates, and confidence in the theory that violence stems from economic hardship remains strong (e.g, Blau and Blau, 1982; Williams, 1984; Sampson, 1987; Palley and Robinson, 1988; Messner, 1989; Kennedy, Silverman, and Forde, 1991). Blau and Blau (1982:126) assert that economic inequality "engenders alienation, despair, and pent-up aggression, which find expression in frequent conflicts, including a high incidence of criminal violence." Williams and Flewelling (1988) also favor this structural view of the causes of violence: The struggle for mere survival, they point out, leads to feelings of anger, anxiety, and alienation, which lead to increased use of physical aggression to resolve conflicts and to exercise control over one's destiny. Dealing specifically with violence among urban blacks, Sampson (1987:367) writes: "Variations in black crime are attributable to structural inequalities in income and jobs, which in turn lead to high and persistent rates of family disruption" (see also Wilson, 1987; Sampson and Wilson, 1991).

Still, why violence? And why is violence so often a *male* response, when women are subject to the same economic realities? Kenneth Polk (1991:13–14), who studies male-on-male confrontational violence among Australians, offers a partial explanation (he did not address female violence, or lack of it):

> For males at the bottom of the economic heap . . . the lack of access to economic resources has the consequence of rendering . . . their sense of masculinity as problematic. . . . [M]ales who are well-integrated into rules of economic success are able to ground their masculinity through methods other than physical confrontation.

Messerschmidt (1986:70) offers a similar view:

> Some marginalized males adapt to their economic and racial powerlessness by engaging in, and hoping to succeed at, competition for personal power with rivals of their own class, race, and gender. For these marginalized males, the personal power struggle with other marginalized males becomes a mechanism for exhibiting and confirming masculinity. . . . Members of the macho street culture have and maintain a strong sense of honor. As he must constantly prove his masculinity, an individual's reputation is always at stake.

Note, however, that Messerschmidt also brings in the idea of subcultural supports for violence with his reference to "macho street culture." This is an important argument that may help explain why most homicides involve young males, and also why most young men subject to economic hardship do not commit homicides or life-threatening assaults. Subcultural theory is addressed after we first consider the idea that violence is learned.

Learning to Be Violent

Many scholars believe that aggression is learned, just like any other behavior. One prominent theory is that people learn it by imitating or modeling the behavior of people they "look up to." Albert Bandura (1973) showed that the behavior of aggressive models is readily imitated by experimental subjects, whether observed in the flesh or via film. In one well-known experiment, Bandura played a film of a woman who beat, kicked, and hacked an inflatable doll. After witnessing the film, nursery school children, when placed in a room with a similar doll, duplicated the woman's behavior and also engaged in other aggressive acts.

Experiments such as these have established the existence of immediate imitation, but how enduring are the behaviors learned, and does each new situation have to be virtually identical with the one originally observed in order for similar behavior to occur? While the jury is still out on these questions, the evidence from work by Bandura and others (see Bailey, 1976) suggests that imitated behaviors do survive over time and that people will

Many children grow up learning that violence is rewarded. Of course,
most children who play with toy guns will not become murderers;
however, when coupled with other violent symbols and experiences in
a child's environment, these early games are among the building
blocks of violence.

generalize from the initial modeling situation to other, sometimes quite
dissimilar, situations.

Rewards for Violence   People tend to repeat activities for which they will be
rewarded and to avoid those for which they will be punished. They also tend
to copy others whom they see being rewarded. In this case the reward is
experienced vicariously. The sanctioning effect of rewards and punishments
may apply to any behavior. This "behaviorist" view of learning can be applied
to violence.

   Violent behavior has its rewards. Many people learn about them quite
early in life. They learn that conflicts can be won through violence, that
violence can be effective as a rule-enforcing technique, and that violence
helps people get their way in the face of resistance. They also discover that
respectable people often reward violence used in their interest, especially
against "outsiders" and people regarded as a threat. From history, they learn
that violence helped make America a better place to live. Closer to everyday
life, they see that successful use of violence often confers status, authority,
and even riches.

This brief list by no means exhausts the rewards associated with violence. As people grow up they have many opportunities to learn that violence is rewarded. But they also learn that it has its costs. William Goode (1973:162) looks at these from the standpoint of a growing boy: "A boy is punished more for using violence on a girl than on a boy, on a younger boy than on a boy his own age, on a teacher than on a stranger; more for imposing his will by violence than for defending his rights." Violence is costly, in other words, when used at the wrong time, in the wrong place, or against the wrong person. But since there are differences of opinion as to when the use of violence is wrong, the costs (and rewards) of violence in any given situation are perceived differently by members of different groups (Stanko, 1990). One cannot assume that because one person or group refrains from violence in a certain situation, others will too.

Subcultures of Violence

Lower-class, inner-city black males are found disproportionately in homicide statistics. It is also known that the typical homicide involves people who know each other, who are young rather than old, and who are of the same race. For many years, the homicide rate has been highest in the South, and it varies widely from country to country.

These patterns cannot be explained adequately by reference to the biological predispositions or psychic states of individuals. One also must consider the characteristics of populations and the relationships among individuals and groups.

An important theory advanced to account for variations in the prevalence and incidence of violence was developed by Marvin Wolfgang and Franco Ferracuti (1967) in their book *Subcultures of Violence*. In brief, their thesis is as follows: All heterogeneous societies have a dominant, or parent, culture accessible and attractive in varying degrees to its members. In America the dominant culture is commonly referred to as white, middle-class society. In addition to the dominant culture, societies often have various subcultures. These subcultures differ in degree, but never completely, from the dominant culture. Some are merely different—Amish settlements, for example—and others directly oppose the parent culture—the hippies of the 1960s or the Hell's Angels. The latter have been referred to as "contracultures" to emphasize the conflict between parent culture and subculture (see Vander Zanden, 1970:47–49).

Through socialization young people come to adopt the values and lifestyles of the subcultures to which they have been exposed. If the subculture is significantly different from the dominant culture, one's strong attachment to it may lead to complete dissociation from the values, attitudes, and lifestyles of the parent culture. Most people, however, are influenced by both the dominant culture and subcultures to which they have been exposed. For example, many communes in the 1960s failed because participants were unable or unwilling to break from conventional American culture.

People belong to a subculture of violence to the extent that aggression is expected and legitimated by the subculture in situations in which it is not supported by the dominant culture. Members of violent subcultures see violence as a significant element of their lives, an integral part of their lifestyles.

A subculture of violence is not something to which one can point, like a rock or tree. Rather, its presence is inferred by the existence of certain attitudes, behaviors, and conditions common to a group of people. In America a subculture of violence might be inferred to exist if one found the following:

- Relatively high rates of violence—homicide, assault, child and spouse abuse, sexual violence
- Common use or threats of violence in everyday disputes among friends and intimates
- Weapons carrying and other behaviors indicating anticipation of violence
- Relatively high rates of violence among the young, whose socialization exposes them to the subculture during their formative years
- Relatively high rates of victim precipitation—if violence is a dominant theme in life, people are likely to be "keyed up" for it and ready to provoke one another
- Criminal records and other personal histories indicating the repetition of violent crime
- The persistence of the above characteristics over time—subcultures do not develop nor do they disappear overnight.

The existence of a subculture of violence means that violence will have predictable features. Far from being senseless and random, aggression makes sense when viewed in light of the subcultural expectations governing its use. Actions that may appear trivial or senseless to outsiders are not so to group members. It is precisely because they are predictable that such actions endure over time.

Three real-life examples illustrate some of the features of violent subcultures listed above. The first case shows victim precipitation, weapons carrying, offender–victim acquaintance, violence in the family, and prior involvement in violence (Ward et al., 1969:881):

> The female victim was fatally stabbed to death by the defendant. . . . Both the defendant and the victim were in a bar when they exchanged some words, apparently about a mutual acquaintance. Defendant then left the bar and shortly thereafter re-entered, having changed her clothes. . . . As the defendant walked through the bar . . . the victim hit her on the head with a beer bottle . . . and after this attack, defendant removed a paring knife from her brassiere and struck the victim an unknown number of times.

> Defendant's arrest record shows four previous arrests for violent attacks. Two arrests involved fights with her husband. . . . The other arrests involved attacks on bar patrons; once she cut a man with a beer bottle and the second time she stabbed a man with a knife.

The second illustration comes from Wolfgang's (1958:188–189) study of Philadelphia homicides and shows the subcultural meanings, values, and expectations among different groups:

> [T]he significance of a jostle, a slightly derogatory remark, or the appearance of a weapon in the hands of an adversary are stimuli differentially perceived and interpreted by Negroes and whites, males and females. Social expectations of response in particular types of social interaction result in differential "definitions of the situation." A male is usually expected to defend the name and honor of his mother, the virtue of womanhood . . . and to accept no derogation about his race (even from a member of his own race), his age, or his masculinity. Quick resort to physical combat as a measure of daring, courage, or defense of status appears to be a cultural expectation, especially for lower socioeconomic class males of both races.

The juvenile gang provides the setting in which many young inner-city males explore violence. The ideals of masculinity, toughness, excitement, and reputation are stressed in gang activities (see Dawley, 1992). Members must show that they can take care of themselves when threatened or provoked, and much emphasis is placed on the conquest and dominance of women (an issue of great relevance to discussions of sexual violence).

The third illustration comes from a study of violent gang subcultures in Puerto Rico (Toro-Calder, 1950; see also Clinard and Abbott, 1973:59–60). Interviews with 98 males serving time for violent crimes uncovered the following features of gang life:

- Carrying weapons such as machetes, knives, or firearms, is common, accepted, and expected.
- Fighting and other aggressive behavior is common.
- Certain situations, especially related to gambling, reputation (personal and of family), and honor are defined as provoking violence.
- Individuals had witnessed fights in which weapons were used and had been involved in such fights, directly or indirectly.

A two-year study of urban youth gangs in Boston by Walter Miller (1966) shows further evidence of subcultural aspects of violent crime. Assaultive behavior occurred quite frequently, though it was less common than other activities, some of which were criminal, and it was often a matter of words rather than deeds. Gang members frequently expressed violent sentiments but rarely carried them out, indicating the existence of group norms governing the use of force.

Seven gangs were studied intensively, and Miller found that criminal violence was committed in groups rather than by individuals. Eighty-eight incidents were observed over the two-year period, and usually weapons were not used, adults were not assaulted, and targets were gang-affiliated. Contrary to the views of some other researchers (e.g., Yablonsky, 1966), gang violence was not erratic, unpredictable, or senseless. When approved by the group, violence was used as a means to achieve prestige, honor, and recognition— a difficult concept for most middle-class adults to grasp:

Gang members fight to secure and defend their honor as males; to secure and defend the reputation of their local area and the honor of their women; to show that an affront to their pride and dignity demands retaliation. Combat between males is a major means to achieve these ends. (Miller, 1966:112)

Viewed in this way, violence has positive consequences for male gang members. It deters rivals and improves a youth's competitive edge, while at the same time it enhances a member's reputation and social status (see also Horowitz, 1987; Daly and Wilson, 1988:129). Not only does violence help gang members gain a tough reputation for themselves and their gang, but it helps protect that reputation. Ruth Horowitz (1987:44) reports how members of a gang "gathered in an alley to discuss how they could regain the reputation they had lost when [two of their] members were beaten." All favored some sort of violent response.

The movies *Colors* and *Boyz 'N the Hood* brought gang violence to the attention of millions of Americans. These movies portray the world of rival gangs, focus on the violence that characterizes the rivalry, and underscore the almost hopeless task faced by police. Drugs and criminal enterprise are heavily emphasized, and gang members are depicted using semiautomatic weapons and sawed-off shotguns. Four hundred and fifty-two gang-related

Inner city youths suffering impoverishment, lacking conventional adult role models, and aware that their lives are unlikely to improve, find that aggressiveness bolsters feelings of self worth and helps them achieve status among similarly situated peers.

murders were reported in Los Angeles County in 1988, a record. A police official pointed to the growing use of high-powered weaponry: "Years ago you had five or six rounds [fired] in a drive-by shooting. Now you have 20, 40, 60 rounds. . . . When you have more shots fired, you have more people murdered" (*St. Louis Post-Dispatch*, January 20, 1989).

Two additional points about youth gangs need emphasis. First, drug trafficking and other criminal enterprises are commonplace activities of many big-city gangs (but see Klein, Maxson, and Cunningham, 1991). As a result, a certain amount of instrumental violence surfaces as gangs compete with rivals and try to protect themselves from police. Second, there is little evidence to suggest that youth gangs in general have adopted murder and mayhem as a way of life, or even that they are predisposed to violence. Youth gangs provide comradeship and a way to have a good time. While the adventures of adolescence often bring gang members into conflict with middle-class ideals and the law, most youths mature out of crime and go straight.

It is generally agreed that subcultural pressures leading to violence are often conditioned and reinforced by aspects of the dominant culture. Subcultures do not develop in a vacuum, and it would be a mistake to lay the blame for high rates of violence at their doorstep without considering the impact of the parent culture and of structural conditions that affect the quality of life (e.g., Sampson, 1985). In regard to the high rates of violence among inner-city blacks, Mulvihill and Tumin (1969:37) point out:

> . . . if the poor, young, black male is conditioned in the ways of violence by his immediate subculture, he is also under the influence of many forces in the general dominant culture. [Violence] is a pervasive theme in the mass media [that] tends to foster permissive attitudes toward violence. Much the same can be said about guns in American society. The highest gun-to-population ratio in the world, the glorification of guns in our culture, and the television and movies' display of guns by heroes surely contribute to the scope and extent of urban violence.

In addition, the experiences of black inner-city residents reflect conditions that have roots in American history and social structure (see Wilson, 1987). Lack of opportunities, overcrowding, physical deterioration, poverty and unemployment, transience, extensive police surveillance, and high rates of criminal victimization are typical ghetto conditions. These are problems that have a local impact but societal underpinnings. Given the combined cultural and structural pressures that eat away at a healthy self-concept and send young blacks into the streets in search of identity and worth, it is perhaps surprising that there are not more murders in America.

The high rates of violence in the South have been the focus of further applications of the subcultural view. Some believe that slavery, lynchings, post–Civil War adjustments, poverty, and long-standing traditions have spawned a cultural climate supportive of interpersonal aggression (Hackney, 1969; Gastil, 1971; Reed, 1971). John Shelton Reed (1977) has enumerated some of the features of "Southernness" that may help explain the difference in homicide rates between the South and elsewhere:

- The South maintains laws that permit an individual to assault another in certain situations.
- Certain forms of violence are regarded as natural in the South.
- Violence occurs more often than elsewhere in some situations, but less often than elsewhere in others: "The statistics show that the Southerner who can avoid both arguments and adultery is as safe as any other American, and probably safer" (Reed, 1977).
- Violence is found among well-socialized Southerners, the so-called upright citizens.
- Violence is more commonly found in Southern music, literature, and jokes than in the music, literature, and jokes of other American regions.

The Southernness explanation of North–South differences in homicide rates has been roundly criticized (e.g., Loftin and Hill, 1974; Lizotte and Bordua, 1980), but the many tests have failed to produce consistent results. Some of the inconsistency is due to methodological differences either in the nature of the data analyzed or in the methods used. Two recent studies comparing the homicide rates of Standard Metropolitan Statistical Areas (SMSAs) around the country show that regional effects persist even after taking poverty, percentage of blacks, and various other variables into account (Messner, 1983; K. Williams, 1984). Steven Messner (1983:1006) suggests that the controversy about the Southern subculture of violence will not be resolved until more sensitive measures of Southernness are used. He suggests measuring "subcultural orientations by means of the 'naturally' expressed preferences for art, literature, music, and leisure activities with predominantly violent themes." Another tack is to measure Southernness by the proportion of a population born in the South. This was recently done in a study of state homicide rates, and the findings indicate that Southernness helps account for variations in both white and black homicide rates (Huff-Corzine, Corzine, and Moore, 1986).

Societal Reactions to Violence

There is a clear duality in American values and attitudes regarding violence: It is supported, and yet it is also condemned. The popularity of contact sports and martial arts, of movies depicting slaughter and mayhem (*The Terminator* and *Rambo* films are recent examples), and the extensive ownership of firearms are cultural supports of violence. On the other hand, in law and in public opinion violent crimes are the most serious crimes that a person can commit, especially when someone is killed. Further mixed messages regarding violence have been conveyed by the criminal justice system. What happens when people kill others, for example, depends on who the offenders and victims are. Two early studies (Johnson, 1941; Garfinkel, 1949) showed that blacks who killed other blacks were likely to receive lighter sentences than were blacks who killed whites. In addition, whites who killed blacks were less likely to be indicted or given the death penalty than were blacks who killed whites. A study of Texas sentencing (Bullock, 1961) showed that although blacks generally received stiffer sentences than whites, in murder cases they received slightly shorter sentences. Bullock noted that most black murders involved black victims and suggested that local mores tolerated and perhaps even indulged black-on-black crime.

Research confirms that racial prejudice may be responsible for some of the variation in official responses to homicide. Almost half of the more than three thousand people executed for murder in the United States since 1930 were black, a proportion far exceeding their representation in the general population. When given the death penalty, whites are more likely than blacks to have their sentences commuted (Wolfgang and Cohen, 1970:85–86). In a study of homicide dispositions in Harris County, Texas, Louise San Marco (1979) found that although the offender's race did not seem to affect the outcome, the race of the victim did: Offenders who killed white victims, particularly females, received longer sentences.

Official reactions to violent crime are sometimes influenced by other nonlegal factors. A study of 125 "crime-specific" homicides (those occurring during the commission of another crime) found that young unemployed offenders who killed employed victims were more likely to be prosecuted than other offenders, a finding that remained true even after such legal variables as prior criminal record were taken into account (Boris, 1979). Studies of murder in Houston and in St. Louis (Lundsgaarde, 1977; Barlow, 1985b) show that prosecution, conviction, and sentencing are influenced by the degree of intimacy between offender and victim. In Houston, for example, 61 percent of murderous relatives escaped legal penalty. However, even in cases of domestic violence, dispositions varied considerably, prosecutors apparently considering the extent of prior family violence and evidence of victim precipitation.

As a general rule, prosecutors pursue the cases they are most likely to win, and the fact that someone has been injured or killed does not alter this strategy (Williams, 1978). The St. Louis study found that of 142 suspects arrested for murder or severe assault, 74 percent were not prosecuted or had their cases dismissed. Thirty-three offenders were eventually convicted, and the sentences they received were as follows: One received the death penalty, four got 15 to 24 years, eight got 5 to 14 years, eight received 4 years or less, and five received probation. It is noteworthy that all the cases involved either death or life-threatening injuries, and over 60 percent involved firearms (Barlow, 1985b).

In general, official reactions to domestic violence tend toward leniency, complementing the view that family affairs are private matters. Even when the victims are children, there is a considerable filtering effect, with most convicted offenders avoiding jail or prison. When imprisonment is imposed, the sentence is generally shorter than that received by other felony offenders (Bureau of Justice Statistics, 1984c). There are signs, however, that officials are slowly taking a more serious view of family violence. Today all but a few states have funds for sheltering victims, require more accurate police record keeping, or authorize the courts to issue protective orders. Iowa's statute regarding spouse abuse is characteristic of the more progressive legislation in this area:

> It allows the court . . . to order that the defendant grant exclusive possession of the residence to the plaintiff, that the defendant stay away from the plaintiff, and that the defendant pay a sum of money for the plaintiff's support. The statute also allows the court to issue an order determining temporary custody of minor children and establishing visitation rights. (Search Group, Inc., 1984a)

Homicide and serious assault are similar in many respects: Offenders and victims tend to be young, rates are highest in large cities and in Southern states, and both often involve cultural influence, victim precipitation, and the presence of alcohol. Yet in outcome they are different: Someone dies in a homicide.

In order to understand homicide, one must ask why some violent events result in death and others do not. Looking at violence as an event draws attention from etiological factors and toward the situational elements that are intrinsic to violent encounters—victim precipitation, weapon availability and selection, witness behavior, offender–victim interaction, number and location of wounds, action and reaction, and the impact of opportunity and ability. There is also the medical factor. When victims do not immediately die, there is a chance that emergency medical care can be delivered in timely fashion. In the last analysis this may make the difference between a homicide and a "merely" severe assault (see Barlow and Schmidt Barlow, 1988). Figure 3.2 illustrates how the intrinsic factors in violent events are linked with one another and also with extrinsic factors that are etiological (e.g., culture, social structure, experience, knowledge) and situational (e.g., victim assistance and the medical factor). One's understanding of homicidal violence may benefit from a perspective that emphasizes outcome as well as etiology.

There is still a long way to go before society understands violence and deals effectively with it. The material reviewed in this chapter shows that the problem has been a serious one in America and remains so. The mixed messages about violence may be the biggest obstacles to real progress. If this is true of murder and assault, it is certainly true of sexual aggression, the topic of Chapter 4.

Summary of Chapter 3

This chapter has explored the character and extent of interpersonal violence. The United States ranks first in homicide among industrialized countries and has for many years. Homicide offenders and victims are most likely to be young males of relatively low socioeconomic status who know each other. The same is true of nonlethal assaults, which are like homicides in most

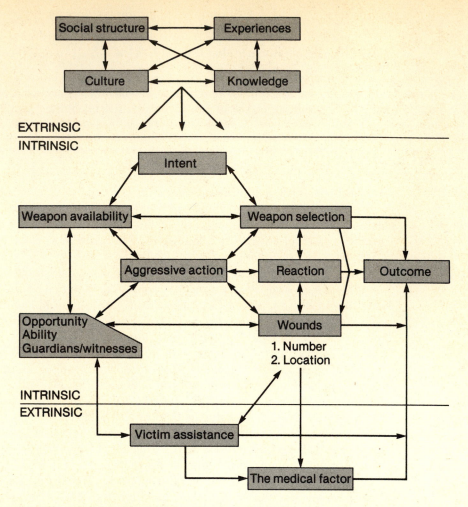

FIGURE 3.2   The Violent Event: Elements and Linkages

respects. The essential difference between a homicide and an assault is the existence of a corpse.

Certain situations are prone to turning violent: The presence of a weapon, the consumption of alcohol, and victim precipitation are examples of situational elements that contribute to violent outcomes. Many violent events follow similar stages in which someone is offended by an insult and the offended person retaliates in a face-saving ritual that in turn provokes a counterreaction.

Explanations of the etiology of murder and assault come from a wide range of sciences. Biologists believe that aggressive tendencies are innate and are triggered by events or circumstances that threaten an organism's survival or that of its genetic offspring. Psychiatrists have focused on the relationship between personality and aggressive temperament, although there is little evidence that violent offenders generally suffer from mental disorders or abnormalities. Some psychologists believe that violence results from frustration, while others believe that violence is learned through imitation or modeling, or because people have found that violence is rewarded.

Some sociologists have tried to explain why rates of murder and assault are disproportionately high among males who are young, poor, and black. One explanation is a variant of the frustration–aggression hypothesis, arguing that violence stems from the frustrations and strains generated by structural inequities; an alternative perspective emphasizes subcultural sources of violence, arguing that people who are exposed to lifestyles, norms, and values that support violence will tend to be violent themselves.

The chapter ended with the observation that there is a clear duality in American values and attitudes regarding violence: In some contexts violence is roundly condemned; yet in others it is supported. The resulting mixed messages do little to reduce levels of violence and probably contribute to the high rates of violence among youths, against women and children, and with firearms.

Recommended Readings

Dane Archer, and Rosemary Gartner (1984). *Violence and Crime in Cross-National Perspective.* New Haven, Conn.: Yale University Press.

Angela Browne (1987). *When Battered Women Kill.* New York: Macmillan.

Martin Daly, and Margo Wilson (1988). *Homicide.* New York: Aldine de Gruyter.

David Dawley (1992). *A Nation of Lords: The Autobiography of the Vice Lords,* 2nd Edition. Prospect Heights, Ill.: Waveland Press.

Jack Katz (1988). *Seductions of Crime: Moral and Sensual Attractions in Doing Evil.* New York: Basic Books.

Gerald D. Robin (1991). *Violent Crime and Gun Control.* Cincinnati: Anderson.

Murray A. Straus, Richard T. Gelles, and Suzanne K. Steinmetz (1980). *Behind Closed Doors: Violence in the American Family.* New York: Anchor Books.

Marvin E. Wolfgang, and Franco Ferracuti (1967). *The Subculture of Violence.* London: Tavistock.

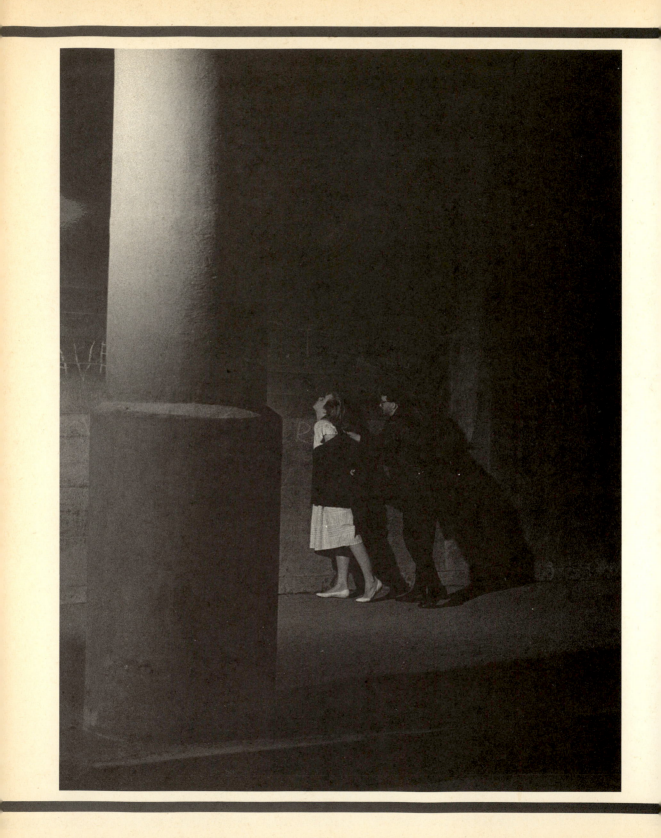

Chapter 4

Sexual Assault

Not long ago, rape and other sexual assaults were only mentioned in sensational news stories and discussed in secretive whispers. Even the scientific community kept the subject at arm's length. The sensitive nature of the subject may account for some of this, but the historical failure to address rape seriously may have a deeper meaning: It is women and not men who are the usual victims of sexual assault, and female problems are not viewed with urgency in male-dominated societies (e.g., Griffin, 1971; Brownmiller, 1975). In addition, it was long believed that sexual assault was a rare thing that cropped up from time to time, but not often enough to merit real concern, even among women.

In recent years sexual assault has become a major focus of writing and research. This development is largely due to the efforts of women who have sought to dispel the myths and mystique surrounding rape and the sexual abuse of children, and who have fought to help the victims. Elizabeth Stanko (1990:10) writes: "What feminist researchers have documented over the past 15 years is a continuous thread of violence and intimidation that runs through women's everyday experiences."

Rape: Violence with Sex

A major contention of some feminists is that a popular image of rape has been fostered by males and sustains certain myths about rape and the rapist. This popular image, portrayed in such films as *A Clockwork Orange* and Alfred Hitchcock's *Frenzy*, emphasizes the violence of male attackers who appear from nowhere to vent their repressed sexual desires by raping unsuspecting females who do everything possible to prevent the attackers from "taking" them. This image reflects and perpetuates cultural definitions emphasizing (1) male dominance and female vulnerability; (2) the idea that a woman's body, especially her vagina, is man's property, and, like any other property, can be stolen by those to whom it does not belong; (3) the view that "good" women must defend that property at almost any cost; and (4) the idea that normal males will not need to resort to force in order to acquire the sexual property represented by a woman—they learn to do it in other ways (Brownmiller, 1975; Russell, 1983).

The Legal Conception of Rape

Though laws dealing with the subject of rape have shown signs of change (see Box 4.1), the popular image of rape is mirrored in legal conceptions of it. Common law traditions have long emphasized lack of victim consent, physical resistance, the use of force, actual penetration of the vagina, and offender–victim sexual unfamiliarity. Force and victim resistance were fundamental. Physical injuries, torn clothing, and disarray at the scene of the alleged rape were just some of the things courts looked for in establishing that force occurred and was met by active resistance. Under common law, the victim

---

Box 4.1 ■ Changing Definitions of Rape

A small but growing number of states revised their rape statutes during the 1980s to accommodate some of the more recent theories about sexual assault. While the specific wording of statutes varies from jurisdiction to jurisdiction, as do the penalties, areas of change include:

- *Sex of offender and victim:* New laws are gender-neutral.
- *Penetration:* Many new laws include any intrusion, however slight and by any object at all, of genital or anal openings. Emission of semen is not required. Oral sex is included.
- *Force:* New laws focus on the behavior of the offender, including threats of violence and use of superior strength to restrain or confine a victim.
- *Resistance:* Victims no longer have to prove that they resisted. "Consent" means one thing only: agreement freely given. In some states a vestigial requirement of resistance remains in the notion of "reasonable" resistance, which is usually assessed in light of age, strength, and other factors.

---

was expected to resist vigorously and repeatedly. Modern courts, though recognizing that resistance is not a clear-cut issue, are inclined nevertheless to treat active physical resistance as an important factor in establishing that rape actually occurred. Prosecutors across the country tend to screen out cases in which evidence of force and resistance is considered weak (Law Enforcement Assistance Administration, 1977:30–31).

Offender–victim relationships are important also. Legal traditions are such that rape accusations are looked upon with some suspicion in cases in which there is anything more than passing acquaintance. In some states, a man who lives with a woman, even though they are not married, cannot be accused of raping her. Traditionally, a rape defendant who can show that he has had prior sexual intimacies with his accuser has a strong point in his favor if the case reaches court. However, with so-called *rape shield* laws, states are now allowed to bar evidence of previous consensual sex between victim and suspect. Writing for the majority in a 1991 case, U.S. Supreme Court Judge Sandra Day O'Connor said: "Rape victims deserve heightened protection against surprise, harassment and unnecessary invasions of privacy." This is a significant broadening of victim protection.

From the time of the earliest legal codes, the true rape victim has been pictured as a sexually naive woman, usually a virgin. Indeed, the Code of Hammurabi and the ancient Jewish laws specifically distinguished between virgins and nonvirgins in their treatment of rape. According to these early codes, a married woman could not be raped, but if she were sexually assaulted by someone other than her husband, both parties would be charged with adultery, a capital offense. Furthermore, ancient Jewish laws did not rely solely on the distinction between virgins and nonvirgins, for they ignored the virginity of those women raped within the city walls. In such cases, complicity was assumed, "for the elders reasoned that if the girl had screamed she would have been rescued" (Brownmiller, 1975:20).

The traditional view of rape has focused on penile-vaginal intercourse, but feminists have lately been successful in getting some states to change rape laws to include oral and anal sex and the use of any object to effect even the slightest degree of penetration. Russell (1983:43) comments on the traditional definition, saying,

> The focus on [penile] penetration of the vagina has often been seen as a vestige of an outdated patriarchal notion that female purity and virtue requires a vagina that has not been penetrated. According to this perspective, a female who has experienced all manner of "foreplay," including oral or anal sex, whether voluntary or involuntary, may still be regarded as a virgin.

The Official Record on Rape

According to official police records, 80 out of every 100,000 American women were victims of rape in 1990 (Federal Bureau of Investigation, 1991:16). Most experts agree, however, that the true rate of victimization is far greater. Estimates have placed the figure at from two to ten times higher than the official rate. This difference can be explained in large part by two things: victim reluctance to report offenses and police labeling practices.

Reporting and Nonreporting of Sexual Assault   Many victims of sexual assault fail to report to police what happened to them. Findings from the National Crime Victimization Survey show that during the period 1973 to 1987, almost half the 2,230,000 rapes cited by victims went unreported to police (Harlow, 1991a:13). The likelihood that a victim will not report the offense increases if she knows her attacker, if no weapon is used, and if she is not physically injured.

The most common reasons given for not reporting a sexual assault are (1) it was considered private or personal, or the victim would take care of it herself; (2) fear of reprisal; (3) police would be inefficient, ineffective, or insensitive; (4) lack of proof, no way to find attacker; and (5) the victim reported it to someone else. When victims did report the rape to police, the most common reasons were (1) to keep the incident from happening again; (2) to punish the offender; (3) to stop the incident from happening; (4) to fulfill a victim's duty; and (5) to get help.

Feminists are credited with bringing sexual assault into the open and with laying bare the myths and misogyny that have for centuries accompanied social and legal discourse on the subject. Their work has also encouraged women to come forward to report their victimization, and has resulted in changes in the way rape victims are handled by the criminal justice system.

The reasons for reporting or not reporting vary according to whether the victim was attacked by a stranger or an acquaintance. Victims of rapes by strangers are much less likely to consider the matter private or personal and are less likely to fear reprisal. Victims who did report rapes were more likely to cite punishing the offender or fulfilling one's duty when the rapist was a stranger (Harlow, 1991a:13). Other studies generally confirm these findings (e.g., McDermott, 1979).

Using victimization data, Lizotte (1985) concluded that factors likely to make the legal case strong—offender is a stranger, he did not belong where the rape occurred, and the victim sustained injury—weigh more heavily in the victim's reporting decision in rape incidents than in other assaultive crimes. However, Lizotte also found that white women raped by black men were less likely to report the assault to police. He speculates this may be due to humiliation and embarrassment, or to failure to appreciate that the chances of prosecution and conviction are increased in this situation.

Victimization surveys unlock the door to the dark figure of crime, but how wide the door is opened is a matter of debate, especially with regard to assaultive crimes such as rape and sexual molestation. Stanko (1990:11) found that much violence against women is hidden in that incidents are not easily called to mind even by victims who want to do so:

> One woman, a 63-year-old widow, assured me that she would not have very much to contribute to my study. When the interview was complete, she recalled being fondled by a shop owner when she was 8, feeling physically threatened by her brother as an adult, being attacked as a nurse while working at night in a hospital, and being hassled by men for sexual favors after the death of her husband.

As women began to talk more freely about rape, the manner in which rape complaints were received by police officials surfaced time and again as a factor in nonreporting. Rape victims are often subjected to intense and sometimes hostile questioning quite unlike that typically experienced by the victims of burglaries, robberies, and other crimes. One victim gave this account of her experience:

> They rushed me down to the housing cops who asked me questions like "Was he your boy-friend?" "Did you know him?" Here I am, hysterical, I'm 12 years old, and I don't know these things even happen to people. Anyway, they took me to the precinct after that, and there, about four detectives got me in the room and asked how long was his penis—like I was supposed to measure it. Actually, they said, "How long was the *instrument?*" I thought they were referring to the knife—how was I supposed to know? *That* I could have told them 'cause I was sure enough lookin' at the knife. (Brownmiller, 1975:365)

In court, rape victims are subject to the rigors of a cross-examination in which they are required to recall, in explicit detail, the humiliating and frightening encounter with the alleged rapist. Of course, rape is a serious offense in all jurisdictions, and defense attorneys quite naturally seek to discredit the testimony of victims and demonstrate that a real rape did not occur. But even so, from the standpoint of the victim who wonders whether to report her rape to the authorities the problem is a very real one and may only be resolved by a decision to keep silent. Here are the comments of two rape victims:

- I had heard other women say that the trial is the rape. It's no exaggeration. My trial was one of the dirtiest transcripts you could read. Even though I had been warned about the defense attorney you wouldn't believe the things he asked me to describe. It was very humiliating. (*Newsweek*, November 10, 1975)
- I don't understand it. It was like I was the defendant and *he* was the plaintiff. I wasn't on trial. I don't see where I did anything wrong. I screamed, I struggled. . . . (Brownmiller, 1975:373)

Important in the generation of police records on any crime is the decision to acknowledge formally that an offense has taken place. Where rape is concerned, police-reporting behavior has been congruent with the popular image of the offense. The police generally have been more likely to view rape allegations as "founded" when offender and victim are strangers, when there is physical injury, when the offense takes place in the open, when weapons have been used, when the rape did not occur on a date, when there was no prior sexual intimacy between the offender and victim, and when sexual acts other than intercourse were also inflicted on the victim (Law Enforcement Assistance Administration, 1977; see also Smith, 1989).

More compassionate treatment of victims may be encouraging more women to come forward, especially blacks and other minority women. In its victimization survey of 26 American cities, the Department of Justice found that 76 percent of minority victims reported to the police, compared with only 62 percent of white victims (McDermott, 1979:45). During the 1970s rape was the fastest rising crime of violence according to police statistics. Some of that increase may have been due to changes in victim reporting and police recording practices.

Data on forcible rape collected by the National Crime Victimization Survey show that rates of victimization have not changed significantly since 1973 for either households or individuals. The figure for completed or attempted rapes of females aged 12 and over has hovered near 140 per 100,000 females (Bureau of Justice Statistics, 1991b:1). Once again, the rise in police rates may be due to more complete reporting to or by the police.

Rape: People and Circumstances

During the 1960s and early 1970s, information collected independently in Philadelphia (Amir, 1971), Denver (MacDonald, 1971), and Memphis (Brown, 1974), and by the National Commission on the Causes and Prevention of Violence, suggested that the popular image of rape accurately depicts only a small portion of all rape incidents. The publication of more recent research has left some of the earlier findings in doubt. Since these later studies are primarily based on victims' reports, one is tempted to favor the newer evidence over that based on official police reports (so-called police-blotter rape). One should remember that rape characteristics may vary from area to area, however.

Before turning to the conflicting evidence, points of agreement should be reviewed. First, rape offenders and victims tend to be young, usually under 25. Second, offenders and victims tend to be of the same race and socioeconomic status. With some exceptions (e.g., MacDonald, 1971; Wilbanks, 1985), research shows that most rape, like most homicide, is intraracial. Linda Williams (1984) argues, however, that there may well be significant under-reporting of white rape of black females, something that has been largely ignored in the literature. Although the National Crime Victimization Survey data on 1,511,000 completed or attempted rapes from 1972 to 1983 cannot directly address Williams's point, they do show that: (1) Black women are as likely to report being sexually assaulted to the police as are white women; (2) when rape is interracial, it is more likely to involve white rather than black victims and to involve strangers (Bureau of Justice Statistics, 1985c; Harlow, 1991a).

In absolute terms, more white women are raped than black women, and more white men rape than black men. However, the probabilities of being a victim or an offender are significantly higher for blacks than for whites (Harlow, 1991a). The most likely victims and offenders in rape incidents, regardless of race, come from relatively low socioeconomic neighborhoods in the nation's larger cities, again mirroring other interpersonal violence (but see Harlow, 1991a:8).

As noted in the preceding chapter, Wilbanks' (1985) argument is that although blacks are victimized most often by other blacks, and whites by other whites, when one asks "Who do offenders choose to assault?" the answer is that black offenders select white victims as often as they select black victims. Figures 4.1 and 4.2 illustrate this situation with respect to rape. Harlow's (1991a) data on race victimization over a 15-year period are recomputed from (1) the victim's viewpoint (the usual way), and (2) the offender's viewpoint (Wilbanks' suggestion). Since the data are from the National Crime Victimization Survey, they pick up thousands of rapes that were not reported to the police. Note, however, that the offender's race is identified by the victim and not independently corroborated.

Figure 4.1 deals with single assailant rapes and Figure 4.2 with multiple assailant rapes. Read the figures this way: First, consider the victim's viewpoint, designated by the word "by." The first column of Figure 4.1 shows that 90 percent of black women were assaulted by black men; the third column shows that 10 percent of black women were assaulted by white men. The fifth and seventh columns show the figures for white victims: 22 percent of white women were raped by black men and 78 percent by white assailants. This is the classic intraracial pattern.

Now consider the offender's viewpoint, represented by the word "on." The second column shows that 51 percent of black assailants raped black

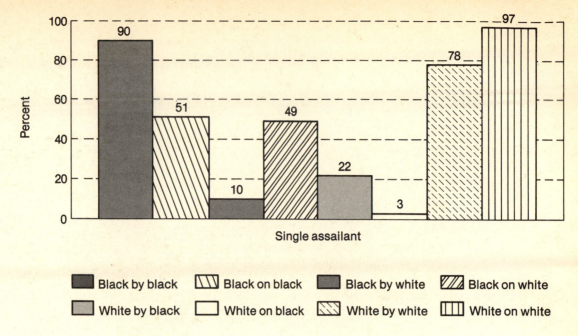

Single assailant

■ Black by black ◫ Black on black ■ Black by white ◩ Black on white

■ White by black □ White on black ◩ White by white ▥ White on white

FIGURE 4.1   Rape Victimization, 1973–1987. By race of victims and assailants. *Source:* Compiled from Caroline Wolf Harlow (1991a). *Female Victims
of Violent Crime.* Washington, D.C.: U.S. Department of Justice, p. 10.

women; the fourth column shows that 49 percent of black assailants raped
white women. The sixth column shows that 3 percent of white assailants
raped black women, and the eighth column shows that 97 percent of white
assailants raped white women. Read Figure 4.2 the same way.

Two things stand out: (1) Rape is predominantly an intraracial offense
when seen from the victim's viewpoint—black women are most often raped
by black men, and white women by white men. However, when viewed from
the offender's standpoint, around half the black assailants raped white
women and white assailants almost never raped black women. (2) The
percentage of rapes that are interracial—black on white or white on black—
increases considerably when there is more than one assailant (Figure 4.2).

The third point of agreement is that most rapes are likely to occur in
private or semiprivate locations such as homes, apartments, automobiles, or
parking garages. Although initial contact between the rapist and victim often
occurs outdoors or in public places such as bars and theaters, the single most
common location for the actual assault is inside a home, usually in the
victim's. Women living alone are most vulnerable to rape (Harlow, 1991a:8).
Fourth, rapists are most often unarmed. When they are armed, rapists tend to
carry knives. The presence of a weapon significantly increases the probability
that the rape attack will be completed. Finally, most rapes occur during the
evening hours of 6 P.M. to midnight (Bureau of Justice Statistics, 1988b:17).

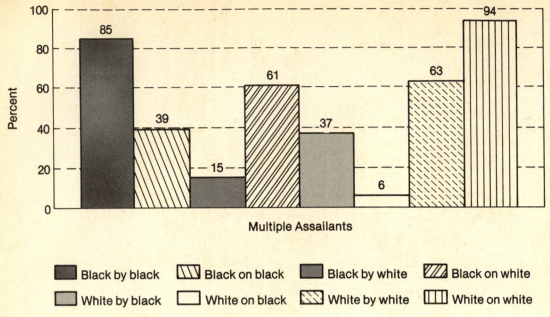

FIGURE 4.2 Rape Victimization, 1973–1987. By race of victims and assailants. *Source:* Compiled from Caroline Wolf Harlow (1991a). *Female Victims of Violent Crime.* Washington, D.C.: U.S. Department of Justice, p. 10.

Now for the points on which the evidence is conflicting or unclear. First, the earlier studies put the chances of being raped by someone known to the victim at around 50:50. However, more recent victimization surveys show a different pattern. McIntyre and Myint (1979) refer to three mid-1970 studies in which rape by a stranger was more prevalent than rape by an acquaintance. A national survey of victimization in 26 cities found that 82 percent of rapes and attempted rapes were committed by strangers (McDermott, 1979). The National Crime Victimization Survey mentioned above also found that stranger rapes were more common than nonstranger attacks (Harlow, 1991a). Thus there appears to be substantial support for the popular view that rape is committed by strangers (but see Smith, 1989). A word of caution is necessary, however. Many victims consider rape a private matter, and it could be that considerable numbers of nonstranger rapes are not reported to survey interviewers. In addition, the offender might be sitting in the same room as the victim being interviewed.

Second, there seems to be some question about the extent of injury associated with rape. There is no question that the psychological trauma associated with rape victimization is severe and potentially devastating, but what about physical injuries? Amir (1971) and MacDonald (1971) found that very few women suffer severe injury and that most injuries are a result of the rape act itself. A national victimization survey looked in detail at the injury question, and MacDermott (1979:36–38) concludes:

Briefly, most rape and most attempted rape victims who were attacked were injured. Injuries included rape and attempted rape injuries, as well as additional injuries. . . . [M]ost often the additional injury was in the form of bruises, cuts, scratches, and black eyes. These survey data on injury suggest that the element of violence in rape is the physical force used to attempt and/or achieve sexual intercourse with a woman against her will. Generally, it does not appear to be violence in the form of additional, capricious beatings, stabbings, and so forth.

This conclusion receives confirmation from other recent studies (e.g., Smith, 1989).

Both popular and legal images of rape place considerable emphasis on the violence of rape and the physical resistance of the victim. The impression gained from Amir's Philadelphia study is that rape victims put up token verbal resistance. The national victimization surveys, using a different categorization of resistance, established a rather different picture. Most victims took measures to protect themselves by screaming, by trying to use some form of physical force against the attacker, or by attempting to flee (Bureau of Justice Statistics, 1988c:64). A study of rapes in London also found that most victims took protective measures (Smith, 1989).

When potential victims resist a rape attack they increase the chances that the rape will not be completed, while at the same time they increase the chances that they will be seriously injured. This resistance–injury connection points to "an important danger in the popular notion (and some statutory requirements) that a victim of an attack should resist to her utmost" (Law Enforcement Assistance Administration, 1977:14–15).

Victims of rape by intimates fail to resist "forcefully" for three reasons, according to a study by Finkelhor and Yllo (1985): (1) Victims felt they could not prevent the attack no matter how hard they tried; (2) they feared being hurt even more; and (3) they felt some blame or responsibility for the attack and thus did not feel justified in resisting. A central goal of many of these victims was simply to keep the peace.

Third, speculation has generally held that rapes are usually not spontaneous. Some sort of planning is involved, and this seems most likely in situations involving multiple attackers. Amir (1971:143) found evidence of planning in 58 percent of single-offender rapes, in 83 percent of two-offender rapes, and in 90 percent of group rapes. On the other hand, a national survey of prosecutors found that only 25 percent of the cases presented to them by police showed any evidence of premeditation (Law Enforcement Assistance Administration, 1977:16).

This difference may be because few of the rapes in the latter study were committed by multiple offenders. The data here, and in the national victimization surveys, show that rapists generally act alone. Yet group rapes do account for a significant minority of reported rapes—around 16 percent according to Harlow (1991a)—a fact that should be kept in mind in assessing the view that rape is not so much sexual as it is an aggressive display of male power and domination over women.

Marital Rape Recent developments in some jurisdictions have led to a significant change in the scope of their rape laws: A husband may be held liable for rape if he forces sexual intercourse on his resisting wife. This possibility has existed for some years in Norway, Sweden, and Denmark and in many communist countries, but only recently has Anglo-Saxon jurisprudence seriously entertained the idea (Geis, 1978a). Two Australian states now prohibit marital rape—South Australia (in 1976) and New South Wales (in 1980)—and the Israeli Supreme Court in 1980 dismissed a husband's appeal of his conviction for marital rape, arguing that the Talmud prohibits forced sexual intercourse between a man and his wife (Russell, 1983:336).

In America today the possibility of rape in marriage is recognized in California, Connecticut, Delaware, Illinois, Iowa, Massachusetts, Minnesota, Nebraska, New Hampshire, New Jersey, Oregon, and Wisconsin, and the list grows every year. In 1985, the Georgia Supreme Court upheld the conviction of a man who raped and sodomized his wife, arguing that the marriage vow does not mean that a wife must always submit to a husband's sexual demands (Reid, 1989:152).

The issue bears comment for two reasons. First, it represents a significant departure from legal tradition going back hundreds of years. These traditions were born of patriarchy, with the wife always the loser. Matthew Hale, the seventeenth-century English jurist whose caution on rape (that it is easy to charge and difficult to defend) has guided judges and legislators, was unquestionably a misogynist, as Gilbert Geis (1978b) amply documents.

Second, the new changes reflect the influence of the feminist movement, showing yet again how important the pressure of organized interest groups is in the realm of law. The actual extent to which women's interests are met by the rape-in-marriage developments will depend on two factors: how widespread the change becomes and whether the courts support the change in their rulings on individual cases.

There have been few studies of rape in marriage, probably because of long-standing belief that there is no such thing. Recent studies by Diana Russell (1983) and by Finkelhor and Yllo (1985) are the best known, though Russell's is more extensive.

Russell conducted interviews with 930 women aged 18 and over living in San Francisco. Of these women, 644 were or had been married and were the major focus of her study. Russell defined rape as forced sexual activity that involves intercourse, oral sex, anal sex, or forced digital penetration. One in seven of these women had been the victims of at least one completed or attempted rape by a husband or ex-husband; 10 percent had been the victims of both rape and other forms of physical abuse; and 15 percent had been victims of either rape or other abuse, but not both.

The characteristics of Russell's rape incidents were as follows: 84 percent involved some physical force; 9 percent were threatened with physical harm; and 5 percent were unable to give consent, because they were asleep or drugged when the attack began. Weapons, usually guns, were used in 17 percent of the incidents. Force was generally minimal—that is, pinning or pushing; 16 percent involved hitting, kicking, or slapping; and 19 percent, beating or slugging. Most of the completed incidents involved penile penetration: 9 percent involved anal or oral sex. Thirty-one percent were isolated cases; but another 31 percent involved more than 20 different attacks, sometimes over a period of weeks or even over a period of more than five years. Alcohol was frequently present before or during the incidents, though Russell (1983:156–166) points out that no simple connection could be identified: Sometimes it appeared to be a factor and sometimes it did not.

The demographics of Russell's marital rape cases are particularly striking in light of other research on rape. White, not black, rapists were slightly overrepresented, and husbands were equally likely to hold lower-class, middle-class, or upper-middle-class jobs. Most of the husbands had at least some college education, and fewer than 20 percent were living at or below the poverty line at the time of the first incident. The majority of rapists were between the ages of 21 and 35. These findings depart from those commonly reported for rape in general. Russell warns against generalizations, however, as her study was plagued by refusals from many of the subjects initially contacted for interviews. On the other hand, it is probable that if cases such as those described by Russell were fully represented in victimization surveys, the demographics of sexual assault would look less young, black, and lower class.

Angela Browne's (1987) interviews with battered wives (see Chapter 3) disclosed that many had also been raped. But the interviews also disclosed that women who eventually killed their husbands were more likely to report they had been raped often and violently. Many of these women felt that the only way out of their fearful and humiliating marital life was by the death of their tormentor; yet most were also sorry that their husbands had died (Browne, 1987:140–141).

Finkelhor and Yllo (1985) conducted in-depth interviews with 50 women who had been sexually abused by their spouses. They constructed a typology of rapes based on their findings:

- *Battering rapes:* The sexual violence is part of a generally abusive relationship.
- *Nonbattering rapes:* The sexual violence grows out of other sexual conflicts, for example, a long-standing disagreement over the timing or setting of sex, or even the act itself.
- *Obsessive rapes:* These reflect bizarre sexual obsessions on the part of the male, perhaps related to pornography, sometimes a result of the need for force or ritual in order to get aroused.

Battering rapes were the most common, obsessive rapes the least.

Dating and Rape   A major way in which the American male is encouraged to adopt and act out the expectations associated with being a man is the institution of dating. Dating is an important social institution for both males and females. For the female it marks the conventional road to courtship and marriage and provides the opportunity to practice her "proper" role as the deferential, acquiescent, admiring, and passive partner. For the male, dating also provides the conventional road to marriage but in addition gives him the chance to demonstrate independence, masculinity, and action in this one-to-one relationship with a woman. As the expected initiator of sexual play, the male is encouraged to view his female companion as a sexual object to be won. His success is measured by how far he gets.

Of course the idea that the male will succeed in this particular demonstration of his manliness—"go all the way"—may not be shared by his female friend. When this happens, the interaction may become a physical confrontation. Influenced perhaps by the effects of a few drinks or by what he has wrongly interpreted as sexual acquiescence by his female companion, the rejected male refuses to back off once he has reached that point at which, in his own mind (and, he presumes, in the minds of other males), his masculinity is put to the test (see Weis and Borges, 1973).

Certainly, most dates do not end in physical confrontations and sexual assault. However, studies indicate that rape and attempted rape during a date are by no means rare, and their occurrences are not confined to dating situations involving lower-class males. Studies on college campuses have discovered that both male and female students—in some cases as many as 25 percent of those interviewed—could recall instances in which they had committed or been the victims of sexual assault during a date and as many as 60 percent recall unwanted petting, fondling, or kissing (Kirkpatrick and Kanin, 1957; Kanin, 1967; Christensen and Gregg, 1970; Murphy, 1984; Warshaw, 1989).

Elizabeth Stanko (1990:94) summarizes the dilemma for teenage girls this way:

> For many young women, negotiating adolescent heterosexuality is also negotiating sexual safety. How and when to say no or yes, without losing companionship, intimacy and the status involved in coupledom, is learnt from experience. Young women juggle sexuality and safety and, at the same time, keep their eye on their social responsibility.

Understanding Rape

Some dimensions of police-blotter rape bring to mind other forms of interpersonal violence, most notably homicide. For example, both rape and homicide are primarily intraracial acts of violence involving lower-class urban youths, many of whom are black, who assault victims from similar backgrounds. Noting this, some authors have followed Amir's lead in designating rape as yet another manifestation of a lower-class subculture of violence.

The idea is that lower-class urban youths learn to adopt violence as a legitimate means to settle disputes, acquire status and recognition, and bolster self-esteem. Further, they see the use of force as an acceptable alternative to which they can turn when their goals cannot be reached by other means. If it so happens that the goal they seek is identified as a challenge to their very identity as males, the pressure to overcome any obstacle will be considerable. Women are perceived as a challenge to manliness, not only because to "have" a woman is to be a real man, but also because it is expected that sexual advances will be met by at least some resistance, and this must be overcome. A man who cannot overcome that resistance is open to the derision of his peers, especially since prevailing definitions of womanhood include the idea that females are weak and vulnerable and should submit to men's demands. Then, too, "making it" is risky because the girl might get pregnant—another factor that raises the stakes and makes success all the more significant in confering status (Werthman, 1967).

Among lower-class males, some authors have argued, sex is treated combatively: Women are perceived as beings to be conquered and dominated, and sex is one of the prizes (Ferdinand, 1968). The important element in lower-class male–female relationships, however, is not so much the sexual aspect, but rather the demonstration that the male is indeed dominant and superior. A man gets what he wants from a woman precisely because he is a man. Thus, as W. H. Blanchard (1959) showed in a study of gang rape, the pressures to live up to lower-class conceptions of masculinity, superiority, and toughness may be resolved in the violent "taking" of a woman.

A Texas study of public opinions about rape found that black males differed sharply from whites and from black females. For example, blacks were more likely to believe that rape could be avoided if women did not provoke it, that women were curious and excited about rape, that a woman could not be raped by her husband, that most men were capable of raping, and that men were often falsely accused of committing rape (Williams and Holmes, 1981). These findings might indicate strong subcultural support for sexual violence among black males, but they remain to be confirmed in other studies.

The emphasis on rape as a behavioral manifestation of a lower-class subculture of violence has been criticized by some writers who say that rape statistics showing a preponderance of black lower-class offenders may not be an accurate reflection of the true rape picture. Furthermore, male aggressiveness toward females is by no means limited to one particular group of men. Thus, Charles McCaghy (1976:133) writes:

> [I]t is tempting simply to classify sexual assault as another instance of a subculture of interpersonal violence. But it is important to remember that the values supporting interpersonal violence have their roots in more general cultural values supporting violence as a means of solving problems. Despite the statistics, the case for assigning responsibility for sexual violence primarily to lower class, black males is not that convincing. Aggressiveness, if not open violence, by males toward females is pervasive in American society. Indeed, it may be argued that male sexual aggression in the United States has been the rule not the exception.

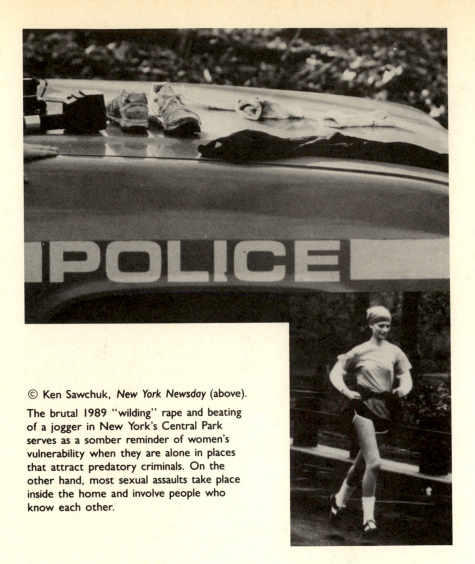

© Ken Sawchuk, *New York Newsday* (above).

The brutal 1989 "wilding" rape and beating of a jogger in New York's Central Park serves as a somber reminder of women's vulnerability when they are alone in places that attract predatory criminals. On the other hand, most sexual assaults take place inside the home and involve people who know each other.

The brutal 1989 "wilding" rape and beating of a jogger in New York's Central Park served as a somber reminder of the vulnerability of women when they are alone in places likely to attract predatory criminals. On the other hand, most sexual assaults take place in the home and many involve people who know each other.

Diana Russell (1983:108) makes a similar argument:

> The fact that Black men are greatly over-represented amongst those arrested for violent crimes is cited by some to justify their racism, by others to demonstrate the consequences of racism, either because they purportedly reveal discriminatory arrest practices, or because they show that racist oppression causes criminal behavior. What is invariably overlooked is that

the factor that is most highly correlated to violent crimes is not race, nor social class, but sex. Many theories that relate crime to lack of economic well-being, as well as other deprivations, overlook the fact that Black women should then be the most overrepresented group among criminals. But they are not. . . . The primary cause of violence in this country is related to notions that connect masculinity and violence, plus the power imbalance between the sexes that allows men to act out this dangerous connection.

In virtually all areas of American life—family, work, politics, sports, education, and so on—males have traditionally found themselves in positions of power, domination, independence, and self-determination. Women, on the other hand, are expected to take subordinate positions and to acquiesce to the decisions and demands made by men. The world of sexuality is no different. The prevailing cultural image of maleness supports the idea of men as being dominating, powerful, and active and as the instigators of sexual interaction; the female as weak, passive, and submissive. The so-called missionary position in sexual intercourse accentuates this asymmetrical relationship.

The adequacy of subcultural theories is challenged yet again in a study of self-reported sexual aggression by Christine Alder (1985). Using interview data from a cohort study begun in 1964, Alder found no relationship between social class and sexual aggression. However, she did find that having sexually aggressive friends increased the likelihood that a respondent reported being sexually aggressive at some time. This fits with associational theories of delinquency and crime, which stress the influence of an individual's circle of friends in the acquisition and performance of behavior (see Chapter 15; also Barlow and Ferdinand, 1992).

Myths and Misconceptions about Rape

Some males are quick to point out that rape can be justified. A number of myths and falsehoods mark the female as a legitimate target of male sexual aggression. Some women, it is said, need to be raped: They have stepped out of line; they are not passive or submissive and thus must be reminded of their place. Some women, it is said, deserve to be raped: They have been too submissive, and thus any man can have them, or they have (heaven forbid) rejected the male as a sex partner altogether. Then again, some men say, "When a woman says no, she really means yes" or "in their hearts all women want to be raped." A survey of Minnesota men provides evidence of the prevalence of such views. Seventy-one percent of the respondents believed that women have an unconscious desire to be raped, and 48 percent felt that going braless and wearing short skirts was an invitation to rape (Hotchkiss, 1978).

A survey of Los Angeles high school students found that 54 percent of boys and 42 percent of girls interviewed could think of situations in which "forced sex" was justifiable (*Los Angeles Times*, September 30, 1980; see also Smith, 1989:34). Among possible situations were:

1. The girl says "yes" and then changes her mind.

2. She has "led him on."
3. The girl gets the boy "sexually excited."
4. If they have had sex before.
5. If he is "turned on."
6. If she has slept with other boys.
7. If she agrees to go to a party where she knows drinking or drugs will be.

It is small wonder that women's groups are calling for urgent and continued efforts to educate people of all ages and backgrounds in the realities of sexual violence. This is one step toward removing the myths and confusion surrounding rape and other sexual abuse. William Sanders (1983:266) points out how absurd it would seem if the same list of "justifications" was applied to bank robbery. Among possible justifications would be:

1. The bank says "yes" to a loan and then changes its mind.
2. The bank has led the applicant to believe he/she will receive a loan.
3. Through advertisement, the bank has got the loan applicant "excited."
4. The bank has given the person a loan before.
5. The applicant "really needs" the money.
6. The bank has loaned other people money.
7. The loan officer goes to a party with the applicant where he knows drinking and drug use will be going on.

Even those who deal with rape professionally share many of the myths and help perpetuate them (Gager and Schurr, 1976). With culturally supported rationalizations to rely on, it is not surprising that convicted rapists rarely think of themselves as criminals and usually place the blame for their actions on their victims.

The conception of women as legitimate targets for rape fits nicely with prevailing views that the prevention of rape depends on women changing their behavior. "Don't hitchhike"; "Don't accept when a stranger or short-time acquaintance invites you to his apartment for drinks"; "Don't go out at night on your own"; "Don't wear sexy clothes"; "Don't initiate sexual play"; and, above all, "Don't promise what you won't deliver!" If you are a woman, be what you are supposed to be: vulnerable, demure, passive, dependent, and proper. So the wheel comes full circle. Men will be men, and women should be women.

Blaming the Victim These "appropriate" female responses to the risk of sexual assault and the myths that underlie them are manifestations of victim blaming. Victims are blamed for their suffering, and this practice diverts attention from the real causes of victimizing behavior (see LaFree, 1989).

Although victim blaming seems to be a generalized response to rape in our culture, it is most likely to surface when there has been a prior association between the assailant and victim, when the victim has behaved in a "bad" or nontraditional way, when the rape occurred close to the victim's home, when the community as a whole espouses patriarchal values and has rigid sex-role traditions, and when observers see themselves as vulnerable to rape but have followed "rules" to avoid it. An analysis of the infamous New Bedford, Massachusetts, "pool table" gang rape of a woman who stopped into a bar for a drink shows also that victim blaming can be linked to a community's efforts to defend itself in the glare of publicity (Chancer, 1987).

In the extreme, victim blaming becomes a denial that women are rapable. Consider this comment from a male juror as reported by LaFree (1989:225):

> I don't think a woman can be raped. . . . I ask why are they out at that time of the night? What did they do to provoke it? . . . A judge over in Ohio told me that a woman can run faster with her pants down than a man, and I believe that. . . . If you want to say rape, then she must be unconscious. She can scream and kick if she's awake and doesn't want it.

Pornography and Rape   According to many feminists, pornography is "an expression of a rape-prone culture where women are seen as objects available for use by men" (Scully and Marolla, 1985:253). Furthermore, rape is presented in pornography as a normal aspect of heterosexual relations in America, and despite the fear and horror associated with it, the victim is usually depicted as being aroused by the experience, if not actively enjoying it (Dworkin, 1981; Ashley and Ashley, 1984). Scully and Marolla (1985) interviewed 114 convicted rapists, and many justified their violent infliction of pain on the grounds that the victim had experienced an orgasm. "In fact, many argued they had been instrumental in making *her* fantasy come true" (Scully and Marolla, 1985:253).

If there is a causal relationship between pornography and sexual violence, it remains unclear despite (or perhaps because of) the 1986 report of the Commission on Pornography headed by former Attorney General Edwin Meese. This commission did no research of its own or even a comprehensive literature review, relying instead on testimony at six public hearings around the country. Much of the testimony was composed of horror stories (often accompanied by visual aids) from people claiming to have been victimized by pornography and from representatives of antipornography groups. Testimony from social scientists was inconsistent and often cautionary, but a majority of the commission's members chose to ignore this fact. Furthermore, as Nobile and Nadler (1986:310) have pointed out: "Social science research has not been designed to evaluate the relationship between exposure to pornography and the commission of sexual crimes; therefore, efforts to tease the current data into proof of a causal link between these acts simply cannot be accepted."

On the other hand, there seems to be growing consensus that the portrayal of women in pornography, especially pornography depicting force or violence, provides cultural approval of the sexual objectification of women and their subordination to the desires and commands of men. To that extent, pornography provides part of the culturally acquired vocabulary that can be used to justify and excuse male sexual violence directed against women. Scully and Marolla (1985:261, 262) discovered that many rapists saw women "as sexual commodities to be used or conquered rather than as human beings with rights and feelings." Rape, they conclude, "is not an idiosyncratic act committed by a few 'sick' men. Rather, rape can be viewed as the end point on a continuum of sexually aggressive behaviors that reward men and victimize women." They cite one man's comment as evidence of the contempt that lies at the extreme (confided to a female researcher, one might add):

> Rape is a man's right. If a woman doesn't want to give it the man should take it. Women have no right to say no. Women are made to have sex. It's all they are good for. Some women would rather take a beating, but they always give in; it's what they are for.

Rape and Culture The reasoning just presented argues that rape is best viewed not as a manifestation of lower-class values and expectations but, rather, as a behavioral consequence of general cultural values and images. According to these values and images, the male is dominating, sexually active, and independent. The female is dependent, passive, submissive, and a legitimate target of male sexual aggression. Further, institutionalized arrangements of our society (such as dating) give males the opportunity to act out their culturally supported prerogatives and hence are conducive to rape.

Building on this view, Chappell and his colleagues (1977) have argued that more sexually permissive societies may well find themselves experiencing higher rates of rape than less permissive societies. Their reasoning is simple. In a permissive society, in which casual sexual relations are more acceptable and presumed to be commonplace, the male will experience even greater threats to his image of self-worth and masculinity when his sexual advances are denied than he would in a less permissive society, in which that denial is expected and culturally valued.

Evidence in support of this view was obtained in a comparison of Boston (considered restrictive) and Los Angeles (considered permissive). In 1969, rape rates were 12.8 per 100,000 people in Boston and 25.4 per 100,000 people in Los Angeles. In a later paper, Gilbert Geis and Robley Geis (1979) present further evidence, this time from Stockholm, Sweden. The relatively high rates of rape in this city (18.9 in 1970; 22.9 in 1977) suggest support for the theory; however, the authors also found a different kind of support. In Stockholm many rapes occur after a pickup at some dance hall or bar and often involve a foreign man and a Swedish woman. After socializing the couple ends up at one or the other's residence, the man makes sexual advances, the woman declines, and a rape follows. The more sexually liberated Swedish woman exercises her prerogative of choice in sexual matters, and that decision is an affront to the foreigner who sees his masculinity severely challenged by the unexpected refusal. The authors conclude: "The irony is that the Swedish situation, which we think is a good thing, ends up looking bad in terms of rape rates" (Geis and Geis, 1979:320).

Psychological Profiles of the Rapist Most American males, presumably, do not commit sexual assaults, certainly not violent rapes. Hence the idea that those who do must be suffering from some sort of psychological pathology or disorder. This notion certainly fits well with the popular image of rape.

Research on the subject is inconclusive but generally does not support explanations of rape and sexual assault based on mental pathologies, brain damage, or personality disorder. Most studies show convicted rapists to be psychologically normal or, at most, suffering from some sort of neurosis (e.g., Ellis and Brancale, 1965; Gebhard et al., 1965). On the other hand, Nicholas Groth (1979:106–109) believes that 10 percent of his sample of incarcerated rapists were psychotic at the time of the assault and that 56 percent had various personality disorders. Generalizations are always questionable when based on groups of incarcerated offenders, as most of these studies were. More than likely, such studies overestimate the occurrence of mental pathologies and disorders among rapists in general, most of whom escape official attention.

Groth's study has been widely cited for his discussion of three major types of rape: (1) *power* rape, in which sexual aggression is an assertion of control and domination; (2) *anger* rape, in which coercive sex vents anger and frustration; and (3) *sadistic* rape, in which violent sex satisfies a pathological need to inflict suffering. In Groth's view, power rape is by far the most common type, and if anything, this would tend to support the view that most rapists are similar to, rather than different from, other males.

The other element that enters the picture in discussions of offender profiles is alcohol. Three theories are popular (Rada, 1975):

1. The man who drinks becomes disinhibited; he loses control and judgment and acts out normally unacceptable sexual fantasies and impulses.
2. Men drink to feel stronger rather than to reduce their sexual inhibitions; alcohol helps them exercise power and domination, to control the situation. The finding that many rapists rarely focus on the sexual aspects of the rape is considered support for item 2 rather than for item 1.
3. Alcohol "may have a direct effect on either the aggressive or sexual centers in the brain, since alcohol has been shown to increase the general level of activity in some animals" (p. 62).

Rada also suggests that a third, psychobiological, theory may have merit. It has been found that particularly violent rapists possess higher testosterone levels than other rapists, suggesting a connection between this male hormone and violence and sexuality (Rada, 1976). Research is continuing, however, and the fact that alcohol tends to *lower* testosterone levels makes further study important.

On balance, there is little impressive evidence that rapists are in general psychologically abnormal (Scully and Marolla, 1985:253). Some probably are—the particularly brutal, perhaps, or serial rapists who choose many different victims—but as a general explanation of sexual assault, psychic pathology or disorder theories are of limited use. The most promising approach is one that links structural and cultural factors with situational inducements, as was the case with explanations of violence in general (see Chapter 3).

If there is a common mental attitude among rapists, then Russell (1983:123) probably captures it best in her description of the "patriarch." When she speaks of husbands who rape, she makes it clear that the description would fit many American males:

> [Patriarchs] see themselves as superior to their wives because they are men; they believe their wives are their property and that it is the duty of their wives to accommodate them sexually whenever they want; they believe they should be the boss in the marriage, and that wives who behave in an insubordinate fashion deserve punishment . . . they subscribe to a sexual double standard in which it is acceptable for husbands to have other sexual attractions or affairs, but it is totally unacceptable for their wives to do the same.

Sexual Aggression and Evolutionary Theory   Notwithstanding the influence of culture and gender stratification, what of the argument that sexual aggression has biological roots? A theory advanced by Lee Ellis (in Ellis and Hoffman, 1990) explains male sexual aggression as an evolutionary trait spawned by the interplay of genetics and the environment. Briefly put, Ellis's theory is that males need expend little time and energy copulating, whereas women must invest more than nine months and considerable energy to produce offspring and keep them alive. Driven by the biological imperative to procreate, males emphasize quantity rather than quality and are pitted against each other as well as against the potentially resistant female. The appearance of sex-aggressive genes drives up the prevalence and frequency of rape, especially if female counterstrategies also evolve.

If procreation lies at the heart of sexual aggressiveness, which this theory argues, then rape should be ubiquitous among human and nonhuman animals. Ellis argues that it is. Furthermore, he contends that sex is the primary motivation in most rapes, despite what many authors and most, if not all, feminists claim (in Ellis and Hoffman, 1990:65). He supports this argument with the observation that the most likely victims of rape are women in their childbearing years.

Evolutionary theories of any behavior pattern should be treated seriously, especially so if the behavior is universal or cross-species. A basic conflict of interest exists between males and females that boils down to the ability to control their own bodies. Since men generally have greater physical strength than women and are the penetrators, they can force copulation on a woman; but since males are also in competition with each other over access to females, strategies evolve to moderate and control that competition without turning the tables in favor of the female, who might then be able to deny *any* male access to her body. From this perspective, rules about family relations, about incest and child sexual abuse, and about "appropriate" male and female behavior are social constructions with biological roots.

Sexual Abuse of Children

Although the most likely victims of rape are older teenagers and young adults, children, including the very young, are sometimes the victims of sexual assaults. Some authors claim that sexual abuse of children may even be more prevalent than nonsexual assaults such as child beating (DeFrancis, 1969). Such claims are difficult to assess, given the paucity of reliable information on either type of assault, but there is undoubtedly far more of both than is generally recognized. Estimates of the extent of child sexual abuse range from 1 in every 2 girls and 1 in every 5 to 6 boys, to 1 in every 6 to 8 girls and 1 in every 10 to 20 boys (Stanko, 1990:56).

As with the rapist, there is a popular image of the child molester. He is the stranger who lurks around playgrounds, parks, and other places where children wander and who lures or drags his victims into his car or home where he then sexually assaults them. This image is no more accurate than the one of rape and the rapist. For example, the child molester is not usually a stranger. In studies both here and abroad, researchers are finding that in most cases of child molestation the offender and victim are acquainted with each other (Stanko, 1990). In a New York investigation of Brooklyn and the Bronx, only 25 percent of the 250 sampled incidents involved strangers; in the remaining 75 percent of the cases, the offenders were either related to the child or were acquaintances such as neighbors, friends of the family, or baby-sitters (DeFrancis, 1969:66–68). Similarly, in a Wisconsin study of 181 convicted child molesters, 65 percent were at least casually acquainted with their victims (McCaghy, 1967:80).

Learning the details surrounding cases of child molestation is not easy, especially when very young children are victimized. Except when brutal physical abuses are involved (a small minority of known cases), even the nature of the sexual encounter itself may be difficult to determine. From the standpoint of criminal law, the nature and gravity of the offense hinge on the details of the encounter. Especially important when the victim is an older child, 14 or 15 years old, are the issues of resistance and consent. Did the child resist? Did the child consent to the sexual act or even encourage it? Was compliance secured by the use or threat of physical force? In dealing with those questions, investigators are often confronted with conflicting pictures of an incident. For one thing, the official account commonly departs from the account given by the suspect (Gebhard et al., 1965). Commenting on this discrepancy, Edward Sagarin (1974:147–148) notes:

> Both [accounts] are suspect. The child is old enough to understand that she will exonerate herself if she claims resistance or lack of encouragement in the courtroom; and since she is a prosecution witness, the prosecution encourages her in that direction in order to obtain a conviction. On the other hand, the defendant is anxious that the court, the researcher, and even himself believe that he was led on. Indeed, some defendants denied their guilt not only to the courts, but to the investigators as well.

Another problem with reconstructing sexual abuse incidents is that many children do not report the abuse until many years after it first occurred, and yet others may deny or retract statements made earlier to authorities.

A series of recent studies on the child testimony and related issues have been reviewed in a special issue of *Prosecutors' Perspective* (Vol. II, January 1988). The studies were performed by psychologists, social workers, lawyers, physicians, and sociologists and appeared in various scholarly journals. One of the major conclusions of these studies is that even young children remember details and testify more accurately than is generally believed. However, one potential problem for the prosecutor in sexual abuse cases is that child victims remember much more about the actions that took place than about where they took place or the identity of the offender.

A particularly alarming finding in one study (Jones and McGraw, 1987) is that many probably legitimate complaints of child sexual abuse are designated as "unfounded" by authorities. These authors looked at 576 reports of sexual abuse received by the Denver Department of Social Services and found that 47 percent had been designated unfounded. However, after review, the authors concluded that only 8 percent of these cases were probably fictitious reports. The remainder had been classified as unfounded primarily because of insufficient information or because appropriate suspicion could not be substantiated through investigation. If this sort of finding occurs in other cities, it suggests that vast numbers of child abuse reports are inappropriately closed.

Various strategies have been advanced to reveal the facts behind reports of child sexual abuse. These range from the use of anatomically correct dolls (see Freeman and Estrada-Mullaney, 1988) to videotaping testimony and the use of closed circuit television so that victims can testify in court from another room. These latter methods are controversial not only because they may not survive judicial review, but also because they may not be necessary in most cases of abuse. Yet prosecutors and courts feel pressured to use them routinely (see Whitcomb, 1985).

Many experts believe that molesters rarely resort to physical violence, and when a child does offer resistance it is most likely overcome by threats of deprivation (loss of love, affection, privileges) or by rewards (candy, money). Victim resistance and use of physical coercion by offenders most often occur in sexual incidents involving strangers, which is what one would expect. Victim compliance is problematic when love and affection or familial ties are absent.

Some important points of agreement among researchers are that child molesters come from all walks of life, are of varied ages, engage in different sorts of sexual acts, choose different types of child victims, and, as Donal MacNamara (1968:153) has noted, range "from senile old men, through drunken aggressors, to psychotic pedophiles, mental defectives, and adventitious offenders." About the only common characteristic is that they are most often males who choose young females (the most likely victim is 11 to 14 years old) as targets of their sexual demands (Vander-May and Neff, 1984). Relatively few known cases involve female offenders or male victims, although recent allegations of sexual abuse of children in day-care centers run by women suggest that there may be many more than suspected.

One attempt to identify types of molesters and to differentiate among them is by Charles McCaghy (1967). McCaghy's work uses information on the extent to which child molesters have interacted with children in the past and on the circumstances surrounding the offense situation. Four circumstances were considered important: (1) the amount of coercion used, (2) familiarity with the child victim, (3) form of sexual activity, and (4) the nature of the interaction between the offender and the child immediately before the offense. McCaghy identifies six types of molesters:

> 1. high interaction molester [described in the next paragraph]; 2. incestuous molester (whose victim is related and living in his residence); 3. asocial molester (whose molesting offense is but one segment of a lawbreaking career); 4. senile molester (whose older age and low educational level distinguish him from other molesters); 5. career molester (whose current offense does not represent his only arrest for molesting); 6. spontaneous-aggressive molester (whose offense characteristics are opposite those of the high interaction molester). (1967:87)

Though representing only 18 of the 181 subjects studied, the high interaction molester category is the one McCaghy feels best meets the typological criteria of internal homogeneity and isolation from other categories. As McCaghy (1967:79) describes them, molesters in this category have had life patterns involving "many contacts with children outside their own home and immediate neighborhood." They commit offenses against children with whom they are familiar; they do not use or threaten force; their interaction with the child begins on a nonsexual level; and the subsequent sexual activity is confined primarily to manual manipulation of their own or the child's genitals.

There is good reason to believe that the high interaction molester may be more prevalent than indicated by McCaghy's sample. First, offender–victim familiarity, coupled with the absence of physical coercion and the mildness of the sexual encounter itself, may render this offender less visible to authorities and to researchers and thus less easily discovered. In addition, evidence from other studies shows that parents of child victims are less likely to press charges when the offender is a family acquaintance or friend (DeFrancis, 1969:xi).

In cases in which family members or relatives of the molester are victimized, probably the most common situations of all, the offense is often not an isolated incident but has been committed over a period of weeks, months, or years. Given the ongoing nonsexual interaction between relatives and family members, this is not surprising. In addition, the sexual encounters themselves may have developed in an atmosphere of consensus and mutual affection. As one author has pointed out, incestuous desire on the part of both adult and child can be interpreted as a quite understandable consequence of close, personal, and satisfying relations between family members. What may begin as a loving nonsexual relationship between an adult and a child may, with the passage of time, expand to include repetitive sexual interactions (White, 1972:160–171).

Of course, most societies do not condone incest or noncoital sex acts between family members. By engaging in sex acts with any child, in fact, an adult departs from acceptable sexual roles. It is hard to imagine that molesters are, as a group, unaware that they have moved beyond acceptable boundaries of sexual conduct. A few may be mentally deficient or suffering from severe psychiatric disorders, but most are clearly aware of their transgressions, and like many other criminals they disavow their actions or try to justify them.

When asked to account for their actions, child molesters commonly explain away their conduct by either blaming it on a temporary loss of sense or rationality ("I was drunk"; "I didn't know what I was doing"; "everything went blank") or by blaming it on the behavior of the victim ("she wanted me to do it"; "he started it") or on conditions of family life or on other personal troubles. In his study, McCaghy found that the most common single response to the question "Why?" was to blame the offense on a temporary loss of rationality. The offenders most likely to deny their deviance in this way were those who had used force to obtain compliance and those who had molested female children.

Some molesters are quite candid about their conduct and do not attempt to deny their deviance or to justify it by appealing to external forces. Male offenders who molest boys and young men seem most likely to fall into this category. Explaining this, McCaghy (1967:82–83) argues:

> It appears that many homosexual molesters have previously accepted a homosexual role, which in itself represents a drastic departure from the sexual norms of conventional society. Being accused of molesting does not constitute a threat to their present self-concept as sexual deviants. Since deviant sexual conduct is already a way of life for them, they do not feel compelled to deny responsibility for their molesting offense. This interpretation was lent support during the author's interviews with these molesters. Many considered themselves to be first of all homosexuals. Their contact with a person under the age of fourteen was, to them, unfortunate and perhaps accidental, but only secondary to their basic sexual behavior patterns. Since they were already at odds with approved sexual norms, the molesting offense did not result in any need for serious self-examination.

Any complete and accurate picture of child molesting and the child molester is far away. Much research still is needed, and the greater willingness of people to talk about sensitive sexual issues will aid in that endeavor. Even so, most incidents of child molestation will remain hidden, particularly those offenses in which physical force and abuse are not employed and that involve offenders and victims who are familiar with each other and are associated in continuing relationships of a nonsexual kind.

Reactions to Rape and Child Molestation

Rape and sexual acts with minors have long been regarded as heinous crimes. Even when legal codes were in their formative stages, little sympathy was extended to rapists, child molesters, and those committing incest with children. The usual penalties were death, banishment, and, in recent years, long prison sentences. Notwithstanding this tradition, public and official reactions to offenders have not been clear-cut. Though generally punitive, reactions have depended on who the offender is, who the victim is, and what kind of interactions the two had.

Most state codes have at one time or another identified rape as a capital crime, and those offenders most likely to receive the death penalty have been blacks. Since 1930 there have been 455 executions for rape; of those executed, nearly 90 percent were blacks. To these legal executions one must add the hundreds of blacks who were lynched for alleged sexual offenses against white women (Valantine, 1956). The feeling among some whites, particularly in the South, seems to have been that only the most severe penalty matches the outrage committed when a black man violates the social taboos surrounding white–black relations and has sex with a white woman. Whether rape was actually committed—and in numerous cases this certainly was not established—seems to have been largely beside the point. A black simply did not

Thousands of blacks were lynched in the South during the late nineteenth and early twentieth centuries. Many were accused of raping a white female, and judicial proceedings, if any, were swift and always under the control of white males.

become "intimate" with a white, especially a white woman. The charge of rape justified the imposition of death, which matched the legal punishment for rape. Also important, it exonerated the white female, who, whites could argue, would never have consented to sexual intimacies with a black. The charge and the punishment thus reinforced racist practices.

The general sense of what "true" rape and molestation are affects trial and sentencing. Important to this image are the characteristics of the victim and how she behaved before and during the rape. If she is a virgin, a minor, or very old, and if there is circumstantial evidence that she put up resistance and was overcome by force, the offender is likely to be convicted and receive a severe sentence.

The moral categorization of women as "rapable/virtuous" and "non-rapable/unvirtuous" (MacKinnon, 1989:175) is a manifestation of patriarchy that is reproduced in courtroom behavior. In rape trials, patriarchy, law, and the dynamics of courtroom behavior blend together and reproduce the relations of domination that structure interaction between men and women in everyday life (Matoesian, 1993). Acquittals are often a matter of transforming a woman's rape into an act of consensual sex. Judges in a Philadelphia court, for example, admitted placing considerable weight on the victim and her behavior. They acquitted defendants when they perceived that the sex had been consensual (described by some judges as "friendly rape," "felonious gallantry," "assault with failure to please," and "breach of contract") or the result of "female vindictiveness" (Bohm, 1974).

But how did they arrive at this judgment? How do defense attorneys transform a woman's rape into a consensual act? In a new study, Greg Matoesian (1993) explores these very questions through an analysis of trial talk—the verbal exchanges between prosecution, defense attorney, defendant, victim, witnesses, and judge. Talk is "socially structured" in that "[w]ho gets to say what, when they get to say it, and how much they get to say is contingent upon the social organization of the courtroom system, the distribution of power among its participants, and the larger system of patriarchy within which these actions are embedded." Matoesian demonstrates that the moral categorization of the victim is not determined by virtue of her standards, but "according to male definitions through which rape is organized, interpreted, and legitimated." Through analyzing trial talk as it occurred, he shows how defense attorneys succeed and fail in convincing the court that the victim was no victim at all. The strategy is to impugn the victim's sexual/moral character, even though rape shield laws ostensibly forbid this. One illustration: In pretrial motions in one case, the judge ruled that the marital status of an unmarried pregnant victim could not be introduced; the defense attorney "consistently referred to her as 'Miss' during the trial."

Moral categorization of women from the vantage-point of male ideals is evident in this statement by a Wisconsin judge after he put a 15-year-old rapist on probation:

I'm trying to say to women, stop teasing. There should be a restoration of modesty in dress and elimination from the community of sexual gratification business. . . . Whether women like it or not they are sex objects. Are we supposed to take an impressionable person 15 or 16 years of age and punish that person severely because they react to it normally? (*Time*, September 12, 1977)

The judge was subsequently removed from office through a public referendum. Other judges with similar views are doubtless sitting in some of the nation's courts today. They are also sitting in courts in other countries: In England, for example, Judge Bernard Richards merely fined a rapist £2000 (about $3500) because he considered the victim guilty of "contributing negligence" (Box-Grainger, 1986:38).

Another illustration of the emphasis placed on the victim's own behavior is found in two cases reported by D. A. Thomas (1967) in a review of sentencing decisions in English rape trials and appeals. In one case, a girl of 16 had been forcibly carried into a van and subsequently raped by two men. In the other case, a girl of 20 accepted a ride from two men (both of whom had previous convictions for criminal offenses), whereupon she was driven to a secluded spot and raped three times, twice by one man and once by the other. The various defendants were found guilty, but those involved in the second incident received lighter sentences than did those in the first. According to Thomas (1967:515), "The difference in sentence between this case and the previous one can be explained by reference to the girl's acceptance of a lift, as opposed to being dragged forcibly into the car." On what grounds, one may ask, does agreement to ride with a man make his subsequent rape of the hitchhiker somehow less serious than if he had forced her into the car?

Post-trial interviews with jurors show similar versions of blame attributed to some victims of rape (LaFree, Reskin, and Visher, 1991). Defendants were more likely to be acquitted when there was evidence of the victim's drinking, drug use, or extramarital sex. However, these characterizations were cited most often in cases where the defense attorney had argued for consensuality or diminished responsibility. If the defense attorney does not impugn the victim's character as the story is reconstructed in court, it appears jurors accept the implication that she is rapable (see also Lafree, 1989:200–233).

Even when sentencing patterns suggest that judges do regard rape as a heinous crime—most offenders receive prison terms if convicted—the average length of the sentence is relatively short. In England it is less than 5 years (Box-Grainger, 1986) but may be getting longer (see Lloyd and Walmsley, 1989). In the United States, it is 15 years, but only 6 years will be served on the average (Bureau of Justice Statistics, 1990d:3).

Sexual assault of children commonly provokes severe reactions. The mere attempted sexual molestation of a minor was rated eighteenth in seriousness out of 204 offenses in the recent National Crime Survey of public attitudes (Wolfgang et al., 1985). Judicial attitudes toward sexual assault of young children are generally severe (see, e.g., Saunders, 1986). Even so, it is interesting to note that when children are the victims of sexual assault, an arrested offender is slightly *less* likely to be imprisoned for a year or more than if the victims are adults. In either case, the figure is less than 20 percent (Bureau of Justice Statistics, 1984h).

When pubescent children are involved, marked variations in official reactions have been observed. Again, much is made of the victims themselves and of their apparent role in triggering the offense. Two more examples from England illustrate. In one case, a young man had numerous episodes of sexual intercourse with a 14-year-old girl he had met at a dancing school. "It was accepted that the girl was a very willing participant." In another case, a married father of four children had repeated acts of sexual intercourse with his 15-year-old sister-in-law. Circumstantial evidence was entered to support the view that the girl "had been the real instigator." In both of these cases an appeals court reduced the sentences imposed by the trial judge on the major grounds of victim interest and participation (Thomas, 1967).

A retrospective study of 350 cases of child sexual abuse occurring in a Texas county from 1975 to 1987 found that prosecution and conviction was more likely when: (1) there was medical evidence to substantiate the charge; (2) the suspect made a statement of implication; (3) the time between the incident and the reporting of it was relatively short; and (4) the seriousness of the offense was greater (Bradshaw and Marks, 1990).

In general, the chances of obtaining convictions in cases of sexual assault, especially rape, are slim. When the victims are neither very old nor very young females, the chances are reduced yet further. The fact is that rape juries, as a rule, are dominated by males, not the usual situation in other criminal trials. According to a 1972 editorial in the *Yale Law Journal:* "The existing evidence indicates that juries view rape charges with extraordinary suspicion and rarely return convictions in the absence of aggravating circumstances, such as extrinsic violence" (Anon., 1972:1380). Indeed, most states require that witness testimony be corroborated by external evidence of sexual assault (torn clothing, physical injury, weapons, and so forth). The uncorroborated testimony of the victim, no matter how compelling, cannot be the sole basis for a conviction. Although these rules are being challenged in many states, and although there have been some reforms in recent years (New York State modified the corroboration rules in 1972), there remain doubts as to how successful these challenges will be (see also Caringella-MacDonald, 1991). At least two states (Georgia and Idaho) beefed up the corroboration rules, making prosecution and conviction in rape cases much more difficult.

There is no better way to sum up the tragedy of rape than from a woman's perspective. Elizabeth Stanko (1990:85–86) writes:

> Wherever women are, their peripheral vision monitors the landscape and those around them for potential danger. . . . For the most part, women find they must constantly negotiate their safety with men—those with whom they live, work and socialize, as well as those they have never met. Because women are likely to be physically smaller than men, as well as emotionally and economically dependent on them, they must bargain safety from a disadvantaged position. . . . The very people women turn to for protection are the ones who pose the greatest danger.

If the criminal justice "management" of sexual assault of women is to do more than merely mirror the sexism of a patriarchal society, argues Box-Grainger (1986:32), it must be recognized "that *all* women are entitled to be protected from rape and whatever a woman's behavior, *there is no justification for rape*."

Summary of Chapter 4

This chapter has discussed sexual violence directed against women and children. Both legal and scientific perspectives have been shaped by historical conflicts of interest between men and women, and by the societal dominance of males. In recent years feminists have led the way to more open and enlightened exploration of sexual assault. Research findings show that sexual assault is widespread, that it often involves people who know each other or are related, that victims are often humiliated and frustrated in their search for justice, and that reactions to rape are influenced by myths, stereotypes, and prejudices that generally serve the interests of men.

Current explanations of sexual assault focus on domination rather than on sex. The sex act itself is less important than what it represents—the humiliation of another person through intimate violation of that person's body and mind. Some people argue that high rates of sexual assault reflect the existence of subcultures of violence, while others suggest that aggressive male dominance of females is also valued in middle-class culture and encouraged through the institution of dating, through pornographic imagery, and by prevailing stereotypes of "proper" womanhood as weak, passive, and submissive to man.

Sexual assault of children is also widespread, and most of it remains hidden from authorities. Child molesters come from all walks of life, but the offenders are most often male, and the victims are more often girls than boys. When questioned by authorities or researchers, many heterosexual child molesters either disavow their actions or blame them on the victim or on forces beyond their control. Homosexual molesters, on the other hand, are more candid, perhaps because they have already accepted their deviant identity as homosexuals.

Recommended Readings

Susan Brownmiller (1975). *Against Our Will*. New York: Simon and Schuster.
Gary LaFree (1989). *Rape and Criminal Justice: The Social Construction of Sexual Assault*. Belmont, Calif.: Wadsworth.
Greg Matoesian (1993). *Reproducing Rape: Domination Through Talk in the Courtroom*. London: Polity Press.
Diana E. H. Russell (1984). *Rape and Marriage*. New York: Collier.
Elizabeth Stanko (1990). *Everyday Violence*. London: Pandora.

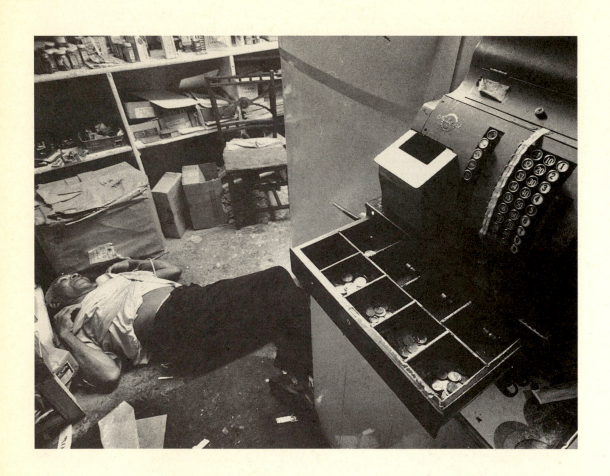

Chapter 5

Robbery: Theft by Violence

Crimes that involve physical force are called "heavy" crimes in street argot. Examples of such crimes are armed robbery, strong-arm robbery, hijacking, piracy, and extortion. The crime of robbery is defined in Box 5.1.

Robbery in Perspective

Anglo-Saxon and early Norman law maintained a distinction between robbery and theft. Theft was considered a dishonorable activity, because those who steal do so by guile, cunning, stealth, and deceitfulness. Those who rob, on the other hand, do so through direct confrontation with the victim, who is given an opportunity to fight in defense of his possessions. The robber runs the risk that his victim will resist and that he will be hurt or killed. This calls for "heart" and "guts."

While similar views are apparently held by some robbers today (see Katz, 1988), the prevailing view expressed by the public and in law is that robbery is one of the more heinous offenses. To explain why feudal England maintained a somewhat different view, one must look at the culture of the times. Physical confrontation permeated medieval England. It could be seen in the almost perpetual battles and wars being fought at home and abroad. It was encouraged as sport, and it had an integral role in the prevailing system of justice, whether in the form of self-help retaliation and feuding or trial by ordeal and the ubiquitous execution. If physical confrontation is an integral part of a society's way of life, the shape in which it is manifested and the kind of people who indulge in it may not matter much.

Heavy Crime in History and Law

Robbery is mentioned in Hammurabi's Code, in Roman law, and in the laws of various Anglo-Saxon kings. In Anglo-Saxon and early Norman law the

---

Box 5.1 ■ The Crime of Robbery as Defined in the Model Penal Code

A person is guilty of robbery if, in the course of committing a theft he:

 (a) inflicts serious bodily injury upon another; or
 (b) threatens another with or purposely puts him in fear of immediate serious bodily injury. . . .

 An act shall be deemed "in the course of committing a theft" if it occurs in an attempt to commit theft or in flight after the attempt or commission.

Source: Excerpted from the Model Penal Code, copyright 1962 by The American Law Institute. Reprinted with the permission of The American Law Institute.

---

physical confrontation in robbery distinguished it from mere theft. One of Henry III's judges, Henry de Bracton, felt it necessary to remind his colleagues that whatever else robbery may be, it is still a form of theft (in Pollock and Maitland, 1968:494). Bracton's influence was substantial, and after the middle of the thirteenth century, robbery was treated in common law as *aggravated theft.*

Bandits and Highwaymen Although medieval England may have shown grudging respect for the robber and his trade, lawmakers lost little time in designating robbery as one of the more serious felony crimes, punishable by death. As far as the evidence allows, there are two reasons for this turn of events: One concerns the frequency of offenses, the other the nature of the victims.

During the thirteenth and fourteenth centuries, banditry and plundering appear to have gained in popularity as a means of subsistence for oppressed serfs and peasants. These were hard times, made even harder by a pervasive inequality that kept the poor and lowly completely at the mercy of the rich and powerful. These were the times when tales about Robin Hood flourished, for the common people could find in his exploits solutions to their own miserable conditions. Robin Hood did all the things they wanted to do but could not. Most of all, these were times of resistance and innovation: Resistance found shape in the largely unsuccessful peasant revolts; innovation found shape in banditry. Robin Hood provided the *modus operandi*, and bands of marauding robbers plied their trade around the countryside. Joined by unemployed soldiers and men of fortune, the ranks of the robbers swelled as feudalism began to decay.

The victims were often the rich and the powerful. Though one has no way of knowing the actual distribution of robbery victims throughout the three great classes—nobility and landed gentry, churchmen, and peasantry—it is likely that most victims came from the first two classes. For one thing, these were the people most likely to travel from one part of the country to the next, making them easy prey for the robber whose territory was the field, the footpath, and the forest. Second, these were the people most likely to own valuable possessions or to have in their homes and churches possessions worth stealing. Third, these were the people at whose feet responsibility for the pervasive personal and collective troubles could be laid. What better victims could the robber find?

The growing incidence of heavy crime and the high status of its victims probably account for the severity with which robbers were handled under law. And severely handled they were: The scaffold continually felt the weight of the highwayman and bandit. By the sixteenth century, robbers were denied "benefit of clergy." Those who might previously have escaped the gallows because of birth or occupation now found it more difficult to do so. The removal of benefit of clergy may have been related to the appearance of a new category of highway robbers. During the highwayman's golden age, which stretched from the early sixteenth century to the early eighteenth century, many highwaymen were of noble birth or substantial means. Through highway robbery they were able to humiliate their peers and political adversaries and to make off with plunder in the process (Pringle, n.d.). It is not surprising that those in power should have made certain that the "gentlemen robbers," as they were popularly called, did not escape full punishment for their crimes.

Piracy   As the era of the highwayman declined, a new form of heavy crime made its appearance, this time on the high seas: piracy. Relatively unknown before the dawn of international sea trade and exploration, "piracy emerged in the Western Hemisphere in response to a unique interaction of many natural and social events" (Inciardi, 1975:87). The exploitation of the New World provided rich cargoes, the plunder of which was made viable by the existence of well-situated islands that provided cover for the pirates, and by the increasing mastery of the sea made possible by developments in maritime technology. As navies grew, more and more seamen possessed sufficient knowledge of the sea to make piracy an option.

Some of the same factors that helped piracy develop also ushered in its decline. Naval warfare, advances in technology, growth in national fleets, international maritime agreements, and the advance of civilization each placed obstacles before the buccaneer. His ships became outgunned, outmanned, and out of date; his escape routes and hiding places were controlled by treaties and regularly patrolling fleets; his seamen were press-ganged into legitimate service or volunteered for it; and the maritime frontiers closed. Piracy had largely disappeared by the nineteenth century.

Frontier Outlaws   In nineteenth-century America, meanwhile, heavy crime was flourishing in the form of cattle rustlers, bank and train robbers, marauding bands of outlaws, and lone bandits in search of quick money. For in America the frontier had been moving south and west, and with it went robbery, plunder, and violence. Just as robbery flourished in England during periods of social and political upheaval, so it did in America. The turbulent decades of the nineteenth century witnessed unprecedented lawlessness. First stagecoaches and then trains became the favorite targets of organized bands of outlaws and "road agents," as the highway robbers were called. For some, robbery was a form of moonlighting. Some road agents were small-town marshals and deputies who could use their police cover to advantage: "A man skilled with a gun might serve as outlaw, sheriff, and hero of his people at various stages of his usually short-lived career as a social bandit" (Lyman and Scott, 1975:139).

The sprouting mining camps on the edges of the western frontier were especially rough places, as people sought easy wealth by robbing company and individual alike of gold and silver. The nineteenth century was also the era of bank robberies. From Montana, the Dakotas, and Minnesota in the north, to New Mexico and Texas in the south, few banks were secure.

Earlier, when the Mississippi River was America's western frontier, robbery had flourished there too:

During frontier days, travelers faced daily threats to their lives and property from road agents who plied the stagecoach trails. Stagecoach companies and railroads hired armed guards to protect their passengers and goods.

Piracy and robbery increased with the spread of settlements. Both steamboats and river towns were looted not only by individuals but also by organized groups of desperadoes. The Chicester and Morrell gangs operated on the lower river, and the Timber Wolves and the Brown gang terrorized residents in Iowa, Illinois, and Missouri. Navou, the Mormon settlement, was felt by many to be the center of Middle Border crime. The steamer *Kentuckian* was robbed of $37,000 in September 1831, and a few months later a passenger on the *Peruvian* was robbed of a trunk containing $2,500. Such thefts could be multiplied many times over. St. Louis newspapers, as the decades advanced, regularly reported steamboat robberies. (Jordon, 1970:102–103)

Heavy crime reached its height following the conclusion of the Civil War. Thousands of discharged soldiers roamed the country, and many apparently found banditry a solution to their problems. Some Confederate soldiers organized into bands of plundering outlaws whose major victims were initially "Yankee enemies." As with the gentlemen robbers of seventeenth-century England, their crimes were shaped by a desire to get back at and to humiliate those they considered to be responsible for their woes.

Of the many factors that supported this era of heavy crime, probably the most important was the ready availability and common use of firearms. Even as late as 1890 few states considered the carrying or drawing of firearms a serious offense. Another influence was the natural environment itself—its geographic size and physical contours. Not only did the frontier have miles and miles of unsettled land in which outlaws could roam at will, but "the successful planning and execution of their crimes were made possible by the topography of confusing ranges of high mountains, segmented by wide deserts, and creviced with inaccessible canyons" (Inciardi, 1975:91). A final influence was the public sentiment of the period, one best summed up in the mystique surrounding the outlaws whose ties to the fallen Confederacy made them noble victims of tragic circumstance:

Characteristic of the mystique surrounding the noble robber is that he begins his career not as a criminal but as a victim of injustice, that he rights wrongs, that he robs the rich to feed the poor, that he never kills except in self-defense or just revenge, that he never deserts his people, that he is admired, aided, respected by his compatriots, that he dies because of betrayal, and, finally, that he is regarded as invulnerable. . . . No sooner is the bandit killed than popular legend restores him to life. (Lyman and Scott, 1975:139)

The Younger brothers, the Dalton boys, Frank and Jesse James, Henry Starr, and Sam Bass are but a few of the outlaws who became folk heroes. Even while the James brothers were carrying out their most ruthless robberies, observers laid the blame anywhere but at the outlaws' feet. This is certainly far from the popular sentiment regarding most robbers today.

With the dawn of the twentieth century, the era of the frontier outlaw was already on the wane. The frontier itself had disappeared as the railroads conquered the deserts and urbanization took hold of strategic points throughout the entire country. Disappearing, too, were some of the other conditions that had lent support to banditry. Large-scale unemployment vanished with World War I, law enforcement achieved unprecedented sophistication and professionalism, and the sociopolitical climate began to stabilize. While Prohibition and the depression years revived banditry for a time, John Dillinger, "Pretty Boy" Floyd, Bonnie and Clyde, and "Baby Face" Nelson were the last of a dying breed.

Robbery Today

In 1990, 639,271 robberies made up around 4 percent of the total index crimes reported by the FBI but accounted for 35 percent of those index offenses involving interpersonal force (Federal Bureau of Investigation, 1991:19). Although robbery rates increased steadily during the 1960s and 1970s, police-reported rates declined until the late 1980s, but now seem to be on the rise again. National Crime Victimization Survey data show similar trends in robbery rates, and so one can be confident that the changes háve been real (see Bureau of Justice Statistics, 1991b). The most likely explanation for the long decline during the 1980s is that there was a corresponding drop in the youthful population. Robbery is a crime of the young. An additional factor in the declining rates of victimization, however, is an apparent decline in robbery attempts that turn out to be unsuccessful (Bureau of Justice Statistics, 1987:1). This may mean that some opportunists are choosing to commit crimes other than robbery.

Data compiled by the FBI, as well as those produced by a number of in-depth studies of robbery (Conklin, 1972; Normandeau, 1968; Sagalyn, 1971; Bureau of Justice Statistics, 1987 and 1990a; Gabor et al., 1988) show the following picture of robbery in America:

1. *Robbery occurs most frequently in the more highly populated cites of the country.* Larger cities experience higher rates than smaller cities, and the lowest rates are found in rural areas.
2. *Robbery usually involves offenders and victims who are strangers.* Although the percentages vary from study to study, estimates of the proportion of incidents involving strangers reach as high as 90 percent.
3. *Robbery offenders tend to be young males.* Males between the ages of 15 and 25 predominate in arrest statistics for robbery. Black males are more likely than white males to be identified as the offenders in robbery incidents. Sixty-one percent of those arrested in 1990 were black and 38 percent were white, according to the FBI (1991:21).
4. *Robbery victims are usually white males over age 21.* Males are much more likely than females to be the victims of robbery. Whereas offenders are more likely to be black, the most likely victims are white males. However, the rate of robbery victimization of blacks is nearly three times higher than that of whites.
5. *Robbery tends to take place "on the street."* Although the percentages vary from city to city and from one part of a city to another, nationally, around 56 percent of recorded robbery incidents occur in the open—in alleys, outside bars, in streets, in parking lots, or in playgrounds.
6. *The robbery offender usually has a weapon.* The most typical robbery is an armed robbery with knives and handguns the preferred weapons. Black victims are more likely than white victims to face an armed robber, especially one armed with a gun. However, weapons are rarely used to inflict injury.
7. *The victim tends not to be injured or to be only slightly injured during the commission of a robbery.* Victimization data show that 7 out of 10 victims are not injured. One in 12 robbery victims, however, is seriously injured, from broken bones to rape or gunshot wounds. The most likely situation in which a robbery victim is physically attacked is when the incident involves two or more armed offenders who rob a female late at night. However, white robbery victims are more likely than black victims to be physically attacked. No matter who the victim is, resistance significantly increases the chance that the victim will be injured, but it also increases the likelihood that the robbery will be unsuccessful.

Violence in Robbery

The use or threat of physical force gives robbery its unique character and explains why it is viewed with fear and apprehension. Robbery comes to mind when people explain why they are afraid to go out alone at night, why they stay off the streets at night, and why they avoid talking to strangers. In his investigation of public views of crime, Albert Biderman (1967) found that most of those interviewed in Washington, D.C., thought of crime in terms of personal attacks, and similar findings have been uncovered in other studies. Beliefs about robbery appear to be little different today from these 1950 observations by journalist Howard Whitman.

> The hoodlum will bash in your head with a brick for a dollar and ninety-eight cents. The police records of our cities are spotted with cases of "murder for peanuts" in which the victims, both men and women, have been slugged, stabbed, hit with iron pipes, hammers or axes, and in a few cases kicked to death—the loot being no more than the carfare a woman carried in her purse or the small change in a man's pocket. (1951:5)

It is true that the kinds of assaults Whitman describes do occur in some robbery incidents. But how valid is this as a general description of robbery in America today? What role does violence play in robbery incidents? Why and when does the threat of violence become actual violence? Are robbers likely to injure or kill their victims as a general rule, or is physical assault a relatively rare occurrence in robbery?

As already seen, robbery incidents usually do not result in physical injury to the victims. When injury does occur, it is usually minor, requiring no hospitalization. In fact, from 1973 to 1979 only 2.6 percent of robbery victims required hospitalization, according to an analysis of National Crime Victimization Survey data by Philip Cook (1987). The degrees of violence that can occur in a robbery incident range from threat to fatal assault. This means that the designation of robbery as a "crime of violence" tends to ignore variations in the kind and degree of physical aggression actually found in particular robbery cases:

> There are many variations, ranging from an armed bank robbery in which several people are shot and injured to minor thefts such as purse snatching, where force or the threat of force is used. Dramatically profiling the lower end of the robbery spectrum was the report of an offense in which one of two 9-year-old boys twisted the arm of the other in the schoolyard in order to obtain 25 cents of the latter's lunch money. Because force was used, the police correctly recorded and counted the act as "highway robbery." . . . While these less serious events should be recorded, it does not seem reasonable to include them in the same category as the more serious offenses. (Mulvihill and Tumin, 1969:25)

The FBI distinguishes between armed and unarmed robbery. According to its reports, armed robberies outnumber unarmed robberies about three to two. This still reveals nothing about the actual use of violence, since the presence of a weapon does not mean that it will be used to inflict injury. Indeed, evidence from the National Commission and from Conklin's Boston study show that injury is more likely to occur in cases in which the offenders are unarmed than when they are armed. In the 18 cities covered by these studies, violence only infrequently involved shooting or stabbing. It was far more likely to involve kicking, shoving, beating, or knocking down. On the other hand, *fatal* injury is far more likely to occur in armed robbery than when robbers are unarmed (Cook, 1987:366).

The tendency for violence to erupt in unarmed robbery incidents is not hard to explain. First, the absence of a gun, knife, or club means that offenders have no obviously deadly weapon with which to intimidate the victim. To prove they mean business, unarmed robbers resort to displays of violence. With a gun or knife present, such a display may be unnecessary—the victim is sufficiently intimidated and offers no resistance.

Second, much unarmed robbery is of the sudden attack variety. A successful sudden attack robbery depends as much on the element of surprise and the speedy commission of the theft as it does on intimidation. The robber, bent on taking as much as possible as quickly as possible, uses violence in an instrumental way: It helps ensure that the victim is in no position to resist even if he or she wanted to do so, and it makes escape more likely. It may also lessen the chances that the victim will be clearheaded enough to identify the robber for the police.

Jack Katz (1988) argues that the violence in "doing stickup" is more than simply a means of securing compliance from the victim. "The more closely we examine violent interactions in robbery, the more we will appreciate that situational rationality will not do for the final analysis" (181). Katz believes that violence, especially killing, in robberies reflects "a commitment to be a hardman—a person whose will, once manifested, must prevail, regardless of practical calculations of physical self-interest" (187). The use of violence among "career" or "heavy" stickup men, Katz argues, is a way of demonstrating to victims and to themselves that they really mean it. However, "[t]he ultimate challenge for the would-be stickup man is to convince *himself* not to give up" (194).

The stickup man anticipates violence at any time, anywhere (see also Wright and Rossi, 1986). This is part of the "chaos" that career criminals live with, according to Katz. It is bound up with the constant threat posed by police, victims, other hardmen, and even the "action" lifestyle typical of hardmen: heavy drinking and partying, illicit sex, drugs, gambling, being "on the run," fast and heavy spending, and (consequently) persistent episodes of criminal activity week after week.

Katz constructs his picture of stickup men from the vantage-point of offenders themselves. What are they trying to do? His analysis is based on detailed police reports of Chicago robberies, ethnographies of street criminals, and autobiographical life stories such as that by John Allen (1977), whose criminal life began in his early teens and extended well into adulthood. The use of violence in these men's lives originates in the adolescent claims of the "badass" (see Katz, 1988: Chapter 3) and becomes increasingly a persistent aspect of an existence framed by chaos and the never-ending challenge of demonstrating control.

Viewed in this light, the apparently "senseless"—that is, unprovoked, unnecessary, irrational—violence described in accounts of some robberies takes on new meaning. In his Boston study, Conklin (1972) found that one in six robbers with guns and one in three with knives used force even though victims offered no resistance. A bank robber interviewed by Letkemann (1973:110) tells of seemingly gratuitous violence during a bank robbery:

> So they froze there—their reaction is one of extreme fear and they drop to the floor and sometimes we select the strongest person—the manager especially or another teller which is very big—a six-footer, or something like that, you know. And we won't say a word, we just walk up to him and smack him right across the face, you know, and we get him down.

Katz (1988:189) argues that for "both the offender and the victim, the perception of whether the victim is resisting or not, is not as clear-cut as researchers often assume. . . ." Katz illustrates with the following example:

> A 33-year-old male is sitting in his car when he is approached by a male of about 25, who opens the car door, displays a handgun, and demands money. The victim gives all his money. The offender then begins hitting the victim, requesting more money. The victim gives his wallet to the offender, who then runs off. (Katz, 1988:189).

Violence is a way to manage the uncertainties and suspense inherent in the robbery confrontation; however, the robber's understanding that he is able and willing to use violence (and that he is comfortable with it) transcends the specific event and is part of the "spiritual commitment" that transforms occasional and adolescent muggers into persistent offenders. The barrier to going on with robbery is the robber's inability to manage fear and uncertainty.

Management of a Mugging

Robert Lejeune (1977) has interviewed young New York City muggers, some with little experience and others claiming several hundred robberies during a six-year period. Lejeune calls mugging "a primitive form of crime . . . practiced by those too young, or otherwise too inept, to execute crimes requiring greater skill and knowledge." The mugger's success depends on skills and knowledge acquired on the street, where survival means being cool and tough and where interaction is often physical.

Lejeune describes how his subjects handled or "managed" their mugging activities. The *preconfrontation phase* consists of (1) managing their own fears and (2) selecting a victim. The very idea of confronting a stranger is fearful, especially to inexperienced muggers. With practice, however, young muggers learn to manage those fears by defining the activity as normal or routine. This process of "normalization" is facilitated by repeated successes, which help muggers lower their estimates of the risks and increase their estimates of the rewards, which for some muggers are intrinsic as well as extrinsic.

Muggers must contend with three threats to their safety: the police, the victim, and witnesses. Of these, victims are seen as the least predictable and controllable. Therefore, emphasis is placed on selection of the "right" victim. They generally look for those people who are least likely to offer resistance and most likely to be carrying cash. Lejeune found little consensus on just who fits the image of the right victim. Some muggers preferred women or old people, but others did not.

During the *confrontation phase* muggers must "denormalize" the situation for the victim and then maintain control. They accomplish the first task by inducing fear, shock, and disbelief through threats and sometimes by displays of force. A posture of toughness helps muggers maintain control, but in the event this control weakens, they may resort to "reactive" force, a display of violence designed to counteract what the muggers interpret (perhaps erroneously) as resistance. The following is how one of Lejeune's muggers justified his use of violence (1977:144):

> I went to take off his money. But I didn't go with the intention of hurting him—because I figured he was smart enough to give up the money. But what he did when I had him in the hallway: he screamed. And I got uptight, you know. And me being uptight, I used the knife. And other times people that I went to rob, they gave me a hard time. To get the money that I wanted to get I had to stab them.

Many of the same elements are present in the work of professional robbers, discussed in the following sections.

Robbery and Race

As noted earlier, robbery is predominantly an urban crime committed disproportionately by young black males. This observation applies not only in the United States, but in England as well. Why does this offense attract young blacks? Put another way, what do they get out of it?

Katz (1988) is one of the few scholars to address this question. However, before considering his analysis, some observations from England may provide insights. Jefferson and Clarke (1973) view robbery as both instrumental and expressive for young black males. They point out that young black males are much more likely than white youths to be unemployed or underemployed; they are also more likely to be undereducated and to live in substandard housing. These impersonal structural inequities are personalized for many young blacks through the racism they encounter in their everyday lives. In England, this ugly phenomenon has been directed primarily at people with Pakistani and West Indian origins. In America, the roots of racism go back to slavery, and remnants of that era are in evidence everywhere.

The future for most young blacks in England, Jefferson and Clarke argue, consists basically of three options: politics, crime, and drugs. Both politics and crime are self-assertive and confrontational; the former in its ideological commitment to raise black consciousness and pride and the latter in its violence and victimization.

Jefferson and Clarke argue that mugging is a desperate solution to a desperate situation. In the eyes of many young blacks it is the best available solution: It is a way to "make it," not simply in a monetary sense, but also as an expression of toughness and masculinity in a world where these are in doubt by all conventional standards. There is an added bonus: Robbery provides an opportunity to strike fear in whites, the dominant class. The imagery supported by popular reggae music, with its "Rudie" character, the supercool hooligan who always comes out on top, is undoubtedly a reinforcer of the defiant, aggressive behavior common among youth in the inner city.

Mugging is also relatively easy to commit, requires little special knowledge or skill, and can be staged on the spur of the moment. It offers the appeal of quick gains at minimal risk. Considering that they grow up in a milieu of chronic poverty and crime, are surrounded by signs of failure, and are confronted daily with the knowledge of a bleak future confounded by racism, it is small wonder more young inner city blacks do not take to the streets in search of victims to mug.

The racism aspect of this perspective on mugging may be the most vulnerable to attack. For example, it does not go far in explaining *intraracial* mugging, of which there is plenty. If the racial structure of victimization is important, it is more likely an artifact of the routine activities and better economic fortunes of whites than it is a result of muggers consciously bent on "getting even." Whites experience greater freedom of movement than blacks, and they are more likely to be carrying cash and credit cards worth stealing.

Katz (1988:249) makes two additional points. First, the use of violence to extort money is commonplace where illicit activity thrives, and since many victims—for example, prostitutes, "johns," drug dealers, and fences—are reluctant to notify the authorities, this sort of robbery is largely ignored in police and victimization data. Second, a significant but unknown amount of like-on-like robbery is missed either because the police themselves ignore it or because victims do not want it known that they have been "taken."

Katz characterizes the black stickup man as *parasitic* rather than racist. He is predatory within his milieu, and if whites happen to cross his path, or are owners of taverns and other small businesses in his neighborhood, they are "natural" targets. Straying from the home milieu is not characteristic of most young street criminals, black or white, but especially not blacks, who run the greater risk of standing out and being picked up by the police.

Katz suggests that what is special about black stickup is its relationship to the role of "bad nigger." The challenges faced by poor black males is to succeed in the struggle to transcend the devalued, denigrated status of "nigger." To be called a "bad nigger" by other blacks is to be recognized as having met that challenge. The "bad nigger" achieves a kind of moral superiority over other ghetto residents, and armed stickup both manifests and reinforces that achievement. But it is not the only way of "getting over":

> In the black ghetto street culture, being bad does not necessarily mean committing crimes. . . . Virtually any emphatically claimed moral competence can be bad. . . . A way of being becomes bad when it is understood to be daring and pretentious. . . .
>
> Being bad is, fundamentally, *not* acting criminally or immorally, or even acting with physical aggression, but something that is more precisely defined with a morally charged spatial metaphor: charting out a big space in public interactions and claiming to be able to fill it. . . .
>
> If being bad celebrates the maintenance of purpose in a morally challenging environment, we can understand how the project of committing stickups can be sustained even against the dictates of a rationally assessed material benefit. Doing stickup itself serves a larger, more widely embraced, fascination with the achievement of a morally competent existence. (Katz, 1988:271–272)

The Professional Robber

Conklin (1972) describes the professional robber as

> . . . the type of offender who reflects the image of the robber in the public's mind. He is portrayed in the media as the bandit who carefully plans his robbery, executes the crime with a group of accomplices, and steals large sums of money which are used to support a hedonistic life style. He exhibits a long-term deep-seated commitment to robbery as a means of getting money and carries out his holdups with skill and planning. . . .
>
> We will here define professionals as *those who manifest a long-term commitment to crime as a source of livelihood, who plan and organize their crimes prior to committing them, and who seek money to support a particular life style that may be called hedonistic.* (1972:63)

According to Conklin, two main types of professional criminals are involved in robbery: those who do it almost exclusively and those who have other "lines" (such as burglary) but may occasionally commit a robbery. The professional robber is one who engages in robbery almost exclusively and for whom it is the main source of income. Relatively few robbers are properly called professionals; nevertheless, they are responsible for a disproportionate number of armed robberies and for most of the big jobs.

It is conventional to distinguish between the professional criminal and one who commits crime habitually. Many robbers are habitual criminals in the sense that they engage in crime repetitively. They begin their careers in crime at an early age and remain largely unsophisticated in their choice of both the crime and the methods they use. As juveniles they quickly come to the attention of authorities, mostly for minor infractions of the law or because they are repetitively tagged as delinquent and incorrigible by parents, schools, and neighbors. Some may engage in robbery repetitively—evidence is considerable that a small core of repeaters is responsible for most robberies committed by juveniles. The robberies these repeaters commit are often of the street variety—mugging, "rolling" drunks, purse snatching—or they involve small stores and corner gas stations. The offenders are typically opportunists, and their commitment to robbery is transitory if it exists at all. If they carry their criminal careers into adulthood, some may emerge as professionals in the long run, but most do not. The majority probably spend their early adulthood in and out of jails and in and out of opportunist crime.

George Vold (1958:225) has described the distinction between the professional and the habitual criminal:

The professional criminal must be distinguished from the merely habitual one whose activity, while repetitive and habitual, has no other element of a profession. A lawyer "habitually" practices law; a doctor is in the habit of practicing medicine. We do not, however, speak of them as habitual lawyers or doctors, but as professional men of law or medicine. Similarly, the term "habitual criminal" is descriptive of a less specific and meaningful vocational identification with crime than is true of the professional. Such a person is often a repeater in crime, but essentially a failure in the practice of crime as a vocation and a way of life. He frequently gets caught, yet wants to work at crime and associate with other criminals, but often is not good enough to be trusted with any significant assignments. Consequently he sometimes has to work at legitimate employment between "jobs" and prison sentences. The merely habitual criminal, whose only accomplishment is that he has been caught several times, has no place and no status among truly professional criminals.

Although habitual offenders may skip from one type of activity to another, from legitimate enterprise to illegitimate enterprise, from burglary and shoplifting to mugging and assault, their involvement in criminal subcultures provides them with the slang and other trappings of the normative system, which help them feel at home among their fellows and offer group support for repetition in criminal activities. To be a *professional*, however, means to work at crime so that crime becomes work, a job, employment—a steady source of income.

Professionalism means more than quasi-membership in a criminal subculture. It means developing skills, talents, know-how, competence, viewpoints, a way of life, and assorted rationalizations and justifications. It means weighing risks, choosing among alternatives, planning, using caution, and subscribing to a code of conduct. Professionalism in robbery means that robbery is a part of one's way of life.

Werner Einstadter (1969) investigated the social organization of professional armed robbery. His informants were convicted robbers on parole in California. All of them had committed more than one armed robbery in the company of others; the robberies had been fully planned and calculated and were not incidental to some other form of crime; and all the subjects considered themselves robbers and had spent considerable time in that line of work.

Among the features of professionalization that Einstadter discovered were the following: Proceeds are shared equally, and anyone who participates receives a share. They usually have no financial backing but meet expenses themselves or by committing a series of smaller robberies. If arrested, team members are on their own—they are under no obligation to keep quiet, nor are their colleagues under any obligation to help them. If they do "rat," however, they will lose their share. The group has little cohesion. Members come in and leave the team as occasion necessitates, and leadership roles are filled more or less at will. Members of the team and other professional robbers are expected to deal honestly with one another, at least as it bears on the work itself. Members have a fatalistic attitude toward events that might transpire during a robbery. This is especially true of violence and of mistakes made by the inexperienced who have not yet learned the ropes:

> It's the "breaks" that count; you either have them or not. Fate is deemed to control the robber's destiny; when the cards are right, when the dice are right, when the *setup* is perfect, nothing can go wrong; but if luck is against you, "you haven't got a chance." It therefore becomes easy to excuse what would under normal circumstances be considered an unforgivable error. (Einstadter, 1969:69).

Other aspects of the professional robber's code and social organization concern cooperation, partnership consensus, planning the "hit," assigning roles (usually done on the basis of skill and knowledge), and decision making. (On pp. 206–212 it will be seen how professionalism in robbery departs in some ways from professionalism in nonviolent theft.)

The kinds of robberies that professionals usually commit are those likely to pay large dividends, though less lucrative jobs will be taken on if financial needs become pressing. The more lucrative jobs will be well-planned robberies, usually of commercial concerns, in which the partners work as a well-oiled team. This type of planned operation, as Einstadter calls it, works only when all contingencies are evaluated beforehand (fate rules anything else), when they have rehearsals or dry runs, when the target is fully studied, perhaps over a period of weeks, and when the partners know and trust one another well. The professional is interested in banks, loan companies, drugstores, large supermarkets, and liquor stores.

Although many professional robbers confine most of their work to the robbery of commercial establishments, some apparently specialize in the robbery of individuals. Professional purse snatchers, or "cutpurses," as they are called in the trade, are an example. Though looked down upon by many professional colleagues, some purse snatchers are quick to claim membership in the professional ranks, and, like other professionals, they distinguish themselves from opportunists, amateurs, and those who do not perform robbery for a living. One such professional cutpurse explains how the profession had been invaded by amateurs and other people:

> Like many a once-honored trade, the traditional art of the cutpurse has fallen on evil times. The profession is now overrun with amateurs, heavy-handed louts of small talent and even smaller character who would be better employed on a rock pile. Purse-snatching has become the catch-all of crime. It's a last resort for down-at-the-heel burglars, unemployed stick-up artists, and others who have lost the professional drive and are too lazy to go straight. It's a lark for high school kids, a source of party-money for juvenile delinquents, a spur-of-the-moment thing for drunks—and for many it's the outlet for something dark and vicious inside of them. (Dale, 1974:73–74)

Today many of the forms of robbery that in the past were the primary activity of professionals are now committed as often, if not more often, by amateurs—those who are unfamiliar with the skills, techniques, and other professional aspects of career robbery. Bank robbery is an example. Whereas bank robbery was once a favorite of the professional, today one sees growing indications that opportunists and other nonprofessionals are trying this extremely risky and difficult type of robbery. Much of the steady increase in bank robberies reported by the FBI for the period between 1977 and 1987 may be attributed to the nonprofessional. The amateur status of many contemporary bank robbers is confirmed by newspaper accounts of robbers who hold up tellers while cameras take clear pictures of their undisguised faces. Other accounts describe robbers who try to rob drive-up facilities in which tellers are protected by bullet-proof glass and are sufficiently hidden from view so that they can summon the police via silent alarm systems. According to one study of bank robbery today, most robbers do not use disguises; most do not inspect the bank before "hitting" it; and most make no long-range plans to avoid being caught (*Justice Assistance News*, November 1984:1).

Indications of amateurism in bank robbery are also found in estimates of the amounts of money lost in such robberies and in the arrest rates of the last few years. Not only are arrest rates higher now for bank robbery than for any other felony property crime, but the average amount lost has apparently decreased during the last few decades. In 1932, the average loss was $5583, compared with $3013 in 1987. Of course, some of the decline is due to changes in banking procedures in the handling of cash. A professional will know this, however, and will not waste time on petty "scores" unless hard pressed. Considering the impact of inflation, bank robbery is certainly less lucrative than it used to be.

Working at Robbery

One can learn more about the job of robbery by asking how professional, career robbers work. Although there are far fewer professional robbers than amateurs, they have been investigated more systematically. Hence, far more is

Bank robbery used to be the work of professional partnerships; now it is committed most often by lone robbers who are ill-prepared and who rarely get away with it. Large amounts of cash and no-resistance policies designed to protect employees and customers nevertheless increase the appeal of bank robbery notwithstanding the lengthy prison terms if caught.

known about their activities, work attitudes, and organization. In addition, the professional robber is important to study for he (rarely she) steals far more than the typical amateur and often has a lengthy career (despite concerted efforts to protect commercial establishments from him).

Since professionals make robbery their work, they cannot afford to fail or be caught. Therefore they emphasize careful planning, anticipation of difficulties that might arise, assessment of risks, and teamwork. To get some idea of how professional robbers pursue their work, one can look at four typical phases in the robbery attempt; going into partnership, setting up the robbery, the robbery itself, and the getaway.

Going into Partnership

First-time robbers, and even those who have robbed before, must often assemble a team before embarking on a robbery or series of robberies. What motivates first-time armed robbers (the usual kind of professional robbery) to get involved in this particular line? It might be at the invitation of an acquaintance who has some experience in armed robbery and needs a partner; it might arise during a conversation among experienced thieves who are looking for a new "line"; and it might come after a careful assessment of what best serves a person's needs:

> When my partner and I decided to go into crime, the first thing we had to decide next was just what branch of crime to go into. You've got car theft, burglary, stealing, stealing money or rolling drunks, armed robbery, other things. . . .
>
> . . . [I]n order to decide which branch we wanted to go into, since we were both inexperienced criminals at the time, we decided to do as much research as we could and find out which made the most money the fastest and that percentagewise was the safest. . . . We spent four days in the public library and we researched, and came up with armed robbery as the most likely for us. . . .
>
> We found . . . that armed robbery is by far the best as getting away with it is concerned because, unlike burglary or breaking and entering, you don't take anything that you have to convert into cash, thereby putting something in somebody else's hands, and you're not taking anything but *money*, which is spendable in any damned place. (Jackson, 1969b:20–21)

Einstadter found that partnerships might evolve as a result of casual interaction among strangers who find they have similar backgrounds and interests:

> You meet some guy and you say, I like him, and he likes you, and so you start horsing around, well you don't know each other, really, you don't know anything about each other, but eventually it comes out, you know. You let slip, you ask him about something—how do you like what you're doing—and he says—it's a whole lot better than doing time. Then I know, and I told him, yeah, and you're finally out on your backgrounds. So, we got to talking about an easier way to make money. . . . He says "I know a couple of guys, and we all got guns, and we can go out and hit a few places now and then. If we don't hit it heavy we won't get caught." So we started doing this stuff. (1969:68)

Groups of robbers with experience in this line of work also form partnerships before going into jobs. Sometimes the initial impetus to engage in a series of jobs will come from a transient robber who happens to be in town and makes contact with others. Here the choice of partners will probably be made on the basis of the kinds of skills needed for particular jobs.

Setting Up the Score

Once a partnership is established—and this may occur after a prospective heist has surfaced—planning consumes the partnership's time and resources. Many arrangements have to be made. Those who have been in the game for some time will make sure that they have personnel lined up for contingencies that might arise—doctors in case of injuries, lawyers in case of trouble with the police, and bondsmen to pay bail money.

The planning of the robbery may differ from one partnership to the next, but certain activities are typically involved. Among the things that must be set up are (1) the target—bank, supermarket, or liquor store; (2) role assignments for the job—someone to drive the getaway car, often called the "wheelman," someone to be the lookout, someone to be the "gunman," and someone to be his accomplice during the job; (3) stolen cars, false license plates, and routes to and from the robbery; (4) a place and time for splitting up the money; and (5) most important, "casing" the target and dry runs.

Casing the target may be done by the one who set up the robbery or by all members of the team. If done while driving around the area, attention will be paid to such factors as parking opportunities, entrances and exits, police patrols, and the movement of people into, out of, and around the target. Some groups even take special note of architectural arrangements:

> Bank robbers rely heavily on the architectural uniformity of banks. Banks are frequently located on street corners, and this is convenient for getaways. Glass doors permit the robber-doorman to see who is coming in, whereas, as a robber noted, the persons coming in have more difficulty seeing through the glass because of light reflection. The present trend toward low counters, possibly motivated by the bank officials' desire for a more personal and less prison-like atmosphere, is looked upon favorably by bank robbers. (Letkemann, 1973:94)

Quoting one of his interview subjects, Peter Letkemann continues:

> Well, sometimes you see, you might have to jump the counter. Well, if you get some of these real high counters, well, they're tough to get over. Well you lose a few seconds by getting over the counters, and some of these banks, like, they have these gates, like with—well you can't reach over and open them because the catch is too far down, so therefore you've got to jump over this counter, you see. (1973:94)

During casing, attention is paid to alarm systems, presence of guards, number of employees, and location of safes and cash registers. The timing of a robbery is also vital. If the job is in a small rural town, robbers are likely to have additional time to carry it out, whereas in an urban setting there is greater risk of police intervention, not to mention the coming and going of customers and employees. The extent to which some robbers go in planning their jobs is well illustrated in the memoirs of Blackie Audett (1945), who participated in nearly 30 bank robberies. He sometimes purchased special plans from a man who made his living supplying robbers with complete information on the target and on routes to and from it. The man also set up cars and other supplies for the job and for emergencies that might arise.

The Robbery

The actual procedures used during a robbery vary from one team to another and from one situation to another. If a job is in an urban area the robbers will typically do everything to avoid drawing attention to themselves, at least until the robbery is in progress. They may park their cars in legal places to avoid the risks of police interest, or they may wait until they are inside the target before donning masks or other disguises. If the target is in a small town or village, no such restraints may be necessary:

> . . . we don't care about parking, whether or not. We drive right in front of the bank where the door is closest to it, even if it's on the sidewalk, and there's a thing that goes on the sidewalk. And if there's one there we go right on the sidewalk. Period! Because we figure that as soon as we open the door of the car, we assume that the alarm is going off right there. (Letkemann, 1973:98)

In getting to the bank or other target a common ploy is to use stolen vehicles whose plates have been removed or changed. These cars will then be abandoned after the robbery. Often two such cars are used as security against breakdowns or other problems. A team driver will stay with the car and keep the engine running, while also being in a position to sound the horn in the event of trouble.

Once inside the target, team members assume the assigned roles to which they must adhere if things are to go smoothly. "The work positions are determined by the central concern of the operation, namely speed" (Letkemann, 1973:98). One person may be assigned to watch the door and to generally oversee the operation as it progresses, paying special attention to time. Another may have the sole job of keeping employees and customers out of the way, and hence out of trouble. In smaller teams this important task may be fulfilled by herding employees and customers into a room or vault that can be kept under surveillance but does not require the total attention of one person. In teams of four or more, two can usually be assigned to collect the cash.

Letkemann notes one important aspect that must be handled especially well if a robbery attempt is to succeed with maximum payoff and minimum trouble. He calls it *victim management*, and it has two dimensions: surprise and vulnerability, and establishing authority and managing tension.

The matter of surprise is crucial. When taken by surprise, employees and customers are more vulnerable than when they have been forewarned. Surprise, and the accompanying temporary paralysis of the victims, allows robbers to get matters under control and saves precious minutes. Some robbers, in fact, make a point of hitting banks and stores when employees are most likely to be sleepy and dull—early in the morning and preferably on Monday. As they see it, anything adding to surprise works in their favor.

Once things are underway the robbers must maintain control over the situation and manage the tensions that arise. The hysterical employee, the stubborn cashier, and the glory hunter each may react differently to the stress of robbery, and all must be controlled by the robber. How this is done differs from one situation to the next, but the tools used by the robber are generally limited to voice commands, appearance, and the use of force.

Robbers generally want to sound and look as if they are serious. As one robber put it: "They can tell by the sound of your voice, by what you say and how you go about things, whether or not you mean business. If you're shaky, they'll know" (Letkemann, 1973:111). Masks and hoods, besides concealing identity, also have a role in establishing authority and managing tension. To some robbers such elements are important because they help maintain the shock effect produced by the surprise entrance. To others they are useful because they conceal facial expressions and thus make it less likely that victims will detect a robber's anxiety.

The use of violence by the professional robber is apparently governed by two considerations. The first concerns completing the job as quickly and easily as possible. The second involves escape. Typical professionals seem to have no doubt that if necessary they will use force; if mere threat does not produce the desired results, the next step will be violence. But they will avoid using their guns if possible. Studies of violence among professional robbers support this contention. Apart from the fact that weapons usually make noise and thus attract attention, robbers have no particular desire to seriously injure or kill their victims—an attitude that may stem from the widely shared view that those from whom they actually take the money are not the real victims anyway. They have no animosity for the teller, the cashier, or the customer. As Einstadter puts it:

> The employee with whom the robbery encounter is made is considered to have nothing at stake since there is no personal loss for him; at most he is conceived of as an agent-victim. . . . [The robber] views the actual encounter as an impersonal matter for in doing so he is not robbing a person but some amorphous mass—a bank, a supermarket, a loan company. (1969:80)

It should be remembered that the robber is out for money, not blood. On those occasions when weapons are actually used—and these are rare—it is usually because the robber has been cornered or challenged by others with weapons, most notably the police. "Although the robber will hesitate to use his gun on a civilian, confrontation by the police is seen as resulting inevitably in a 'shoot-out' " (Letkemann, 1973:115).

The Getaway

The getaway is the most important phase of any robbery, for whether or not the attempt succeeds, the robbers must still escape. Those who have carefully planned their operations will have escape routes and contingency plans already mapped out.

As with the robbery itself, speed is paramount. The longer robbers remain at or near the scene, the greater the risks of apprehension. After abandoning their stolen getaway car at a prearranged point, they transfer to a vehicle owned by one of the team. If all goes well, the team may disperse for a time, move to a different town, or simply go underground until the "heat is off."

It is during the getaway that violence is most likely to erupt. The violence may include shooting, running roadblocks, or taking hostages. Robbers will make every effort to clear the scene and get as far away as necessary.

Understandably, the skills of the wheelman are especially important in this phase of the operation. Not only must the getaway vehicle be in top running condition, but it must be nearby with the engine running so that team members can hop in and clear the scene quickly. Once inside, the driver's skills and maintenance of a cool head may mean the overall success of the job (Conklin, 1972).

When robbery is studied as work, it does not look very different from many legitimate business pursuits. The popular myth depicting robbery as a senseless, violent act of plunder perpetrated by equally senseless and violent individuals can be upheld on some occasions. More accurately, though, robberies can be pictured as possessing characteristics that lie on a number of continua, of which three of the more important are *planning, organizing,* and *skill at victim management.* Those who make robbery a regular pursuit are likely to be found in robberies at the high end of these continua. Those who are opportunists, or who indulge in robbery in a repetitive but sporadic and unsystematic manner, will be involved in robberies at the low end. Thus robberies committed by professionals tend to exhibit high levels of planning, organization, and victim-management skills. Those committed by opportunists out for a fast buck tend to exhibit little in the way of planning and organization. It is in robberies committed by such individuals that confusion, fear, and disorder most often emerge.

Reactions to Robbery

Official reactions to robbery are usually severe, and they parallel public sentiments. Although police generally make arrests in only 25 percent of the incidents that come to their attention, the suspects who are arrested are almost always prosecuted. In the case of bank robbery, a federal offense, nearly 90 percent of those prosecuted are convicted (*Justice Assistance News,* November 1984). Nationwide data indicate that those arrested for any kind of robbery stand a one-in-four chance of being sent to prison (Maguire and Flanagan, 1991:519).

In many state prisons more people are serving time for robbery than for any other offense. In fact, a quarter of the nation's prisoners are convicted robbers. On the average, they are serving sentences in excess of nine years, though length of sentence differs widely around the country (Maguire and Flanagan, 1991:518). Of course, prisoners generally serve less than their maximum sentence. In the case of robbery, the average time served is three years (Bureau of Justice Statistics, 1988b:64), still longer than that of most prisoners. As already seen, robbery is an offense of the young, a fact that is illustrated by prison statistics. Half of all offenders confined in state prisons for robbery are under age 25, and nearly one-third are under age 18. Robbery is heavy crime indeed for those who are caught and convicted.

Official and public sentiments differ when one compares the robbery of commercial establishments, such as banks and loan companies, with the robbery of private individuals. Bank robberies are almost always detected, and almost always reported (Bureau of Justice Statistics, 1988a:18–19). It seems that those who rob institutions are more likely to be prosecuted and to receive long prison terms than are those who rob individuals (Williams, 1976). Yet the public seems less hostile toward the robbery of institutions than the robbery of individuals. Whereas Jesse James, the Dalton gang, and the "great train robbers" in England are accorded a sympathetic hearing, muggers are hated and feared. Robbery of institutions, like plunder in war, is more impersonal, its impact more diffuse. When the victim is also viewed in a somewhat negative light—as banks and loan companies seem to be these days—perhaps the public cares less that they are sometimes the victims of crime. Yet to authorities these establishments are the backbone of the economic system. To rob them is to threaten the very foundations of capitalism. Perhaps this explains the more punitive official reaction in the absence of corresponding public sentiment.

Summary of Chapter 5

This chapter has examined the crime of robbery. Robbery occurs most often in large cities and usually takes place on the street. The offenders are usually young males, and often are poor and black. Rarely do robbers venture far from their familiar milieu, and they often victimize people like themselves. The extent to which robbery is interracial is in dispute, but cross-race robbery—usually black on white—probably reflects the routine activity patterns and superior economic status of whites rather than racism or "getting even." Robbery by young black males may also provide a means for transcending devalued status.

Professional robbers regard robbery as work, and they demonstrate a long-term commitment to the crime, although they are likely to commit other crimes as well. They often work in teams and plan for all contingencies, including getting away and dividing up the spoils. Far more common are the opportunistic robbers, whose crimes are generally spur-of-the-moment and rarely very lucrative. Many hard drug users and alcoholics are occasional robbers, perhaps driven to it out of desperation or because a low-risk opportunity presents itself.

The threat of violence is always present in robbery, though injuries are relatively rare. When robbers are armed the weapon usually intimidates victims into submission: in strongarm robberies, however, a display of force is usual and injuries more likely. Victim resistance also increases the probability that violence will erupt. Katz (1988) believes that violence is not simply a matter of situational rationality, however. Shootings, stabbings, and other violent acts in the course of robbery are a stickup man's way of handling uncertainty and suspense and of establishing his willingness and ability to persist in an inherently chaotic and dangerous activity.

Recommended Readings

John E. Conklin (1972). *Robbery and the Criminal Justice System*. Philadelphia: Lippincott.

James A. Inciardi (1975). *Careers in Crime*. Chicago: Rand McNally.

Philip D. Jordon (1970). *Frontier Law and Order*. Lincoln, Neb.: University of Nebraska Press.

Jack Katz (1988). *Seductions of Crime: Moral and Sensual Attractions in Doing Evil*. New York: Basic Books.

Peter Letkemann (1973). *Crime as Work*. Englewood Cliffs, N.J.: Prentice-Hall.

James D. Wright, and Peter H. Rossi (1986). *Armed and Considered Dangerous: A Survey of Felons and Their Firearms*. New York: Aldine de Gruyter.

Chapter 6

Varieties of Nonviolent Theft

There are many different ways to steal. Only three conditions are necessary to make theft possible: goods or services capable of being stolen, someone from whom they can be stolen, and someone to do the stealing. Model Penal Code definitions of some of the offenses covered in this chapter are listed in Box 6.1.

Theft is the most common class of crime in most, if not all, societies. If people do not do it themselves, then they are its victims, or they hear about thefts involving someone else. Many people may be the victims of theft without even knowing it.

As one might expect, the legal notion of theft is not uniform across different societies. If property or material possessions do not exist, people are unlikely to have any notion of stealing. The types of possessions that can be stolen, the methods used, and the kinds of people who are victims all are influenced by culture, by the way people live, and by their attitudes and values.

In a society that places a premium on the acquisition of personal property, theft is likely to be a serious offense. However, those same values may also encourage the very behavior that is condemned. If possession of material wealth is highly valued, then people may stop at nothing to accumulate it. If people could acquire whatever they wanted through culturally acceptable channels, then theft might not exist. But when some people are systematically excluded from access to acceptable channels of acquisition or cannot acquire what they want even with such access, then stealing may be an alternative way to achieve material wealth. Though it is popular to think that thieves are primarily the poor and disadvantaged, people from all walks of life, even those with all kinds of advantages, steal from others. This will be the main topic of Chapter 7. This chapter concentrates primarily on forms of common theft committed outside the context of legitimate work.

Theft in History

Theft has a long and interesting history. In early legal codes theft was a rather vague term, though most known codes maintained laws identifying theft as punishable behavior. More interesting, perhaps, is that many of these early codes tried to distinguish among different methods of stealing and different classes of victims. For example, the Roman law of the Twelve Tables designated theft by night as a more serious offense than daylight theft. The Code of Hammurabi placed the interests of church and state above those of the citizenry as a whole: Those who stole from temples or royal palaces were punished by death, whereas those who stole from private citizens merely had to pay compensation.

It is mainly in English law that the roots of modern criminal law conceptions of theft are found. Even before the Norman conquest of 1066, theft was an offense. Many people are familiar with the adage "Possession is nine points of the law," but in early English law, possession was everything. It was in terms of possession that theft was identified and the thief so labeled. Ownership was a notion quite alien to early English society. One did not own something; it was in one's possession. To identify theft it was necessary to show, first, that the thief did not have lawful possession of the object in question and, second, that the person who claimed lawful possession could rightly do so. In practical terms this meant that to establish theft it was important to produce the thief, and the best way to do this was to catch the person red-handed.

Akin to the American "posse," the English chase was thus an integral part of the theft scene. If the suspect was caught while transporting stolen goods from the crime scene, then the theft was "manifest" and justice could be meted out swiftly and severely (and often was). If the chase was unsuccessful or the lawful possessor had failed to pursue the thief, then the theft was "secret" and justice was often slow and tortuous. All things considered, it was certainly in the interest of the victim to catch the thief in the act of fleeing with the loot.

Another important aspect of common law conceptions of theft was a civil law violation, *trespass*. The common legal term for theft was (and still is) *larceny*. Larceny was an extension of trespass. Under Roman law, larceny (*latrocinium*) was defined as almost any type of deceit and trickery, but this was not the case in England. Larceny meant laying hands on another's possessions without permission. "Simply to lay a hand on a man's thing without his permission would be trespass; therefore it was argued that there could be no larceny without trespass" (Turner, 1966:267). Larceny went beyond trespass in the notion of *animus furandi* (intent to steal); trespass turned into larceny when the trespasser intended to steal from the victim. The notion of trespass is still retained in many state laws dealing with theft.

Regarding what could be stolen, the idea of "movable" possessions remained central in emerging criminal law. The old charge that the thief "stole, took, and carried away" emphasizes this idea. In medieval times the most prized movables were agricultural chattels—farm animals such as oxen, cows, horses, and pigs, which often also served as money. Not surprisingly, these were the movable possessions to which early theft laws most often applied. But the creators of law have never been bound by tradition. One Anglo-Saxon king declared: "Men shall respect everything the king wishes to be respected, and refrain from theft on pain of death and loss of all they possess" (Attenborough, 1963:137). Though the king put the matter bluntly, the point is obvious: Those who shape legal conceptions of what can be stolen are in a position to impose their own ideas about what is valuable and to determine what will and will not be deemed stealable (Hall, 1952).

The actual value of goods has traditionally been irrelevant to the identification of theft. It matters little whether you steal a coat worth $5000 or one worth only five cents—a theft has still been committed. But value clearly does matter in what happens to the thief. From at least Anglo-Saxon times, distinctions in theft have been based on the value of the property taken. Just as today many states treat theft under $150 (or some other figure) as *petty theft* and anything more than that as *grand theft*, similar distinctions have been made throughout the history of theft laws. The penalties for grand theft, a felony, are more severe. If value is an indication of seriousness, which such

Box 6.1 ■ Varieties of Nonviolent Theft as Defined by the Model Penal Code

Theft by Unlawful Taking or Disposition

1. *Movable Property.* A person is guilty of theft if he unlawfully takes, or exercises control over, movable property of another with purpose to deprive him thereof.
2. *Immovable Property.* A person is guilty of theft if he unlawfully transfers immovable property of another or any interest therein with purpose to benefit himself or another not entitled thereto.

Theft by Deception

A person is guilty of theft if he purposely obtains property of another by deception. [Deception includes creating a false impression of value, law, or intent; prevention of another from acquiring information that would affect his or her judgment of a transaction; failure to disclose lien or other legal impediment to enjoyment of transferred property; failure to correct a false impression previously created or reinforced by the deceiver.]

Forgery

A person is guilty of forgery if, with purpose to defraud or injure anyone, or with knowledge that one is facilitating a fraud or injury to be perpetrated by anyone, the actor:

1. alters any writing of another without authority; or
2. makes . . . executes . . . or transfers any writing so that it purports to be the act of another who did not authorize that act, or to have been executed at a time or place or in a numbered sequence other than was in fact the case, or to be a copy of an original when no such copy originally existed; or
3. utters any writing which he knows to be forged in a manner specified in paragraphs (1) or (2).

Burglary

A person is guilty of burglary if he enters a building or occupied structure or separately secured or occupied portion thereof with purpose to commit a crime therein, unless the premises are at the time open to the public or the actor is licensed or privileged to enter.

---

rules imply, then such distinctions may be justified on the grounds that they provide a workable solution to the problem of "making the punishment fit the crime." Some authors have argued, however, that distinctions of value merely reflect the operation of class interests and ignore that what to one person may be a great loss to another may be trivial. More wealthy theft victims realize more in the way of "justice" than do poorer ones, whose losses may actually be more significant (Mannheim, 1946).

Receiving Stolen Property

A person is guilty of theft if he purposely receives, retains, or disposes of movable property of another knowing that it has been stolen, or believing that it has probably been stolen, unless the property is received, retained, or disposed with purpose to restore it to the owner. "Receiving" means acquiring possession, control, or title, or lending on the security of the property.

Bad Checks

A person who issues or passes a check or similar sight order for the payment of money, knowing that it will not be honored by the drawee, commits a misdemeanor. For the purposes of this section . . . an issuer is presumed to know that the check or order (other than a postdated check or order) would not be paid, if:

1. the issuer had no account with the drawee at the time the check or order was issued; or
2. payment was refused by the drawee for lack of funds, upon presentation within thirty days after issue, and the issuer failed to make good within ten days after receiving notice of that refusal.

Credit Cards

A person commits an offense if he uses a credit card for the purpose of obtaining property or services with knowledge that:

1. the card is stolen or forged; or
2. the card has been revoked or cancelled; or
3. for any other reason his use of the card is unauthorized.

Source: Excerpted from the Model Penal Code, copyright 1962 by The American Law Institute. Reprinted with the permission of The American Law Institute.

Interests and Theft Laws

Criminal law is constantly changing. For one thing, legal formulations prove inadequate when confronted by changing social conditions and interests. Theft laws have continually been revised and extended, and one result is that new forms of theft keep emerging. One particularly significant development in criminal theft occurred during the late 1400s, and it shows the impact on criminal law of emergent social conditions and interests (see Hall, 1952).

The "Carrier's Case" involved a man who was hired to carry some bales of merchandise to Southampton, an English port city. Instead of doing this he broke open the bales and took their contents. He was subsequently caught and charged with felony theft. As the larceny law then stood, however, his actions did not legally constitute theft: He had entered an agreement in good faith, and he thus had lawful possession of the bales. Under the possession rules he could not steal from himself or from the merchant who hired him. After much debate a majority of the judges in the case finally found him guilty of felony theft and in doing so extended the law of larceny to cover cases of "breaking bulk," as it was called.

Most people would probably argue that this verdict and the legal precedent it established are reasonable enough. After all, if you hire a truck driver to deliver goods, you would surely be angry if the driver stole them. But if no laws could be applied in your particular case, then what satisfaction could you hope to receive? To judge from the Carrier's Case, successful resolution of the problem would depend on how much pressure you could bring to bear on authorities to protect your interests. It so happens that at the time of the Carrier's Case, the judges were faced with a number of outside pressures:

> The most powerful forces at the time were interrelated very intimately and at many points: the New Monarchy and the *nouveau riche*—the mercantile class; the business interests of both and the consequent need for a secure carrying trade; the wool and textile industry, the most valuable by far in all the realm; wool and cloth, the most important exports; these exports and foreign trade; this trade and Southampton, chief trading city with the Latin countries for centuries; the numerous and very influential Italian merchants who brought English wool and cloth inland and shipped them from Southampton. The great forces of an emerging modern world, represented in the above phenomenon, necessitated the elimination of a formula which had outgrown its usefulness. A new set of major institutions required a new rule. (Hall, 1952:33)

So, as William Chambliss (1975:7) states: "The judges deciding the Carrier Case had, then, to choose between creating a new law to protect merchants who entrusted their goods to a carrier or permitting the lack of such legal protection to undermine trade and the merchant class economic interests. The court decided to act in the interests of the merchants despite the lack of a law."

The revision and expansion of theft laws continued to the present day. Many of the changes were designed to plug gaps and crevices in prevailing common law. Embezzlement, for example, emerged in its modern form in 1799 when Parliament passed a statute to cover cases of servants misappropriating goods placed in their possession in the course of employment. It was later extended to cover brokers, bankers, attorneys, and others in positions of trust as agents for third parties.

Embezzlement statutes covered only the illegal transfer of possession. For cases of ownership fraudulently acquired—as when one signs over property to another after being tricked into doing so—the law remained inadequate until a statutory decree in 1861 created the offense of obtaining goods by false pretenses. This new offense was basically an extension of the earlier common law crime "larceny by trick and device."

The Prevalence and Distribution of Reported Theft

Much theft remains beyond the reach of bureaucratic data collection. Accordingly, national data on theft are extremely difficult to assess and interpret. To obtain some idea of the problem, recall that estimates of the true rate of burglary alone begin at more than three times the rate reported by the FBI. When one also considers the fact that only a relatively minute number of thefts are ever solved, the difficulties become obvious.

Published national data provide an idea of the dimensions of the theft problem from the standpoint of the criminal justice system. In 1990, burglary, larceny-theft, and motor vehicle theft accounted for 12,655,486 of the index offenses reported by the FBI (1991). This represents 91 percent of all index offenses. Incidences of all three offenses steadily increased during the 1960s, with burglary and larceny continuing to climb, though more slowly, during the 1970s. During the 1980s all three offenses increased again, according to police figures. A closer look shows that while the bulk of offenses that make up the FBI's larceny category increased during the period (especially shoplifting, up 22 percent), some others actually decreased (for example, purse snatching, down 15 percent, and bicycle theft, down 16 percent). This warns against generalizations about trends in stealing, and we are reminded that larceny is a catch-all category (FBI, 1991:36).

The published national data indicate other characteristics of these three index offenses: Rural rates are substantially below those found in both cities and suburbs; suburban rates have been increasing faster than have large city rates; and, of those offenses reported, less than 20 percent are cleared by arrest.

National Crime Victimization Survey data show significant decreases in rates of burglary, larceny, and motor vehicle theft from 1975–1986, leveling off afterward (Bureau of Justice Statistics, 1991). Needless to say, this finding contradicts the police picture. The NCVS is picking up some of the dark figure of crime, which would lead one to consider its data a more reliable indicator of trends than that of the FBI. On the other hand, neither commercial larceny (mainly shoplifting) nor commercial burglary are included in the NCVS figures, and police report that both these crimes have been on the increase. A good deal of the downward trend in NCVS data would certainly be offset if these offenses were included, though how much is a matter of conjecture. In the next section different types of property crimes will be discussed and evaluated through the use of in-depth studies of each type.

Specialization and Varieties of Theft

Thieves rarely spend all or even most of their time in one particular line of theft (Bursik, 1980; Hartstone and Hansen, 1984). Explaining why most thieves diversify, one professional thief had this to say:

Stealing for a living isn't just being a burglar or stick-up man. You've got to be able to look around and recognize opportunities and be able to take advantage of them regardless of what the conditions are. A lot of people think once a stick-up man, always a stick-up man. Well, you can't run around stickin' up people every day of the week like a workin' man. Maybe something worthwhile sticking up only shows up every two or three months. In the meantime you're doing this and that, changing around, doing practically anything to make a dollar. (Martin, 1952:117)

Some thieves develop interests and talents so that they can concentrate on specific crimes. They "have a line." Some express interests in the theft of only certain types of merchandise—for example, credit cards, jewelry, or furs—and others see their talents put to the most productive (and secure) use in one line of work—picking pockets, sneak theft, forgery, or con games. On the whole, however, thieves are generalists rather than specialists. Some may even be adamantly opposed to specialization: It reduces the chances of remaining anonymous and increases the risks of being "fingered" for a caper known to be their style. Professionals give recognition to those who can say they "have a line," but this denotes their preference and skill rather than day-to-day activity. Letkemann (1973:33) suggests that concern for specialization is more likely to be found among aspiring young amateurs: "It may be that they carry over to the criminal world some of the square criteria for assigning status."

Varieties of theft involving high levels of skill, organization, and planning and those requiring substantial resources (some big cons) are usually outside the reach of the typical amateur. Many types of theft attract both professionals and amateurs, however. Within these types, some of the major characteristics distinguishing amateurs from professionals are arrest and conviction history, size of the heist, level of technical skill involved, and type of fencing arrangement employed. Amateurs tend to be arrested and convicted more often, to leave with smaller payoffs (or none), to employ little in the way of manipulative and technical skills, and to steal for themselves or for their friends. Both professionals and amateurs are involved in burglary, sneak theft, forgery, and auto theft. Amateurs rarely perform confidence swindling, counterfeiting, or extortion.

Shoplifting

When people steal from under the nose of their victims, it is commonly called *sneak theft*. Examples include shoplifting, pocket picking, and "till tapping" (stealing from cash registers).

Of the many varieties of sneak theft not committed by employees, shoplifting has no equal. The number of shoplifting incidents that occur throughout America during a given year is unknown and impossible to determine, but the estimates are staggering. Baumer and Rosenbaum (1984) estimated the figure at over 200 million in 1979, and there is no reason to believe that the number is any smaller today. In one English study, the authors estimated that the true number of shoplifting incidents that occurred in one store during one week was ten times higher than the number reported by the police for the *entire city and its surrounding communities* (Buckle and Farrington, 1984).

The cost of it all? The retail industry alone loses about $4 billion a year, $12 billion if thefts committed by retail employees are included (Baumer and Rosenbaum, 1984:16). The distinction is important if only because it demonstrates that those who are trusted are very often untrustworthy, a topic to which Chapter 7 is devoted. More important, it illustrates what is true generally of crimes committed on the job, that they exact a greater financial cost than do offenses committed outside employment or by the unemployed.

Historically, shoplifting is not new, nor have the methods changed much in a hundred years. To be sure, there have been changes in the architecture of stores and in the overall character of the shopping experience, but shoplifters still employ time-honored methods: concealing items under their clothes, hiding them in false-bottomed cases, "bad bagging" them (putting them in well-worn shopping bags), and using "booster boxes" (cartons and packages that appear sealed but in fact have an opening through which to put lifted items (see Edwards, 1958:4–15).

Shoplifting is dominated by amateurs and opportunists, and it cuts across age, sex, race, economic status, and educational distinctions. It used to be thought that females stole from stores more frequently than males did— reasonable, perhaps, in light of traditional sex roles. However, more recent evidence suggests that males steal just as often as females and tend to steal more items per visit (Buckle and Farrington, 1984).

Reactions to Shoplifting   Reactions to shoplifting and shoplifters reveal the most intriguing facets of this criminal activity. Time and again studies indicate that though most shoplifters are never apprehended, those that are caught often face little more than a scolding and are sent on their way after returning or paying for the merchandise. The shoplifter's chances of merely having a hand slapped depend on age, sex, ability to pay, attitude, apparent breeding, and whether or not he or she is a known or suspected professional.

Overall, it appears that the value of the stolen items is the best predictor of whether the shoplifter will get by with verbal scolding or whether police will be notified and prosecution pursued. Michael Hindelang's (1974) study of the referral behavior of a California private security agency shows that in both 1963 and 1968 those most likely to be referred to the police by victims had stolen items of relatively large value. But in this same study Hindelang discovered that when one controlled for the value of the item, the nature of the goods and how they were concealed were also important variables. The person who stole liquor, cigarettes, or fresh meat had a better chance of being referred to the police than one who did not. The person who used special methods of concealment also had a better chance of being referred to police.

Because detection and arrest of shoplifters are commonly the responsibility of store personnel, the decision on what people are arrested and what

Prominently displayed warnings, security personnel, and surveillance devices may deter rank amateurs and some children from shoplifting. However, ease and opportunity coupled with the rarity with which shoplifters are prosecuted and convicted help put shoplifting among the most commonly committed crimes.

happens to them is influenced in part by the policies and attitudes supported by store management. The typical store policy is usually one of caution and leniency. The primary objective is to deter shoplifting while avoiding anything that might hurt store business. Store management usually wants to avoid embarrassing situations on the shop floor that might adversely affect the attitudes and behavior of customers. Equally, it wants to minimize the time and expense involved in carrying through official prosecution of suspects. Finally, it wants to avoid unnecessary publicity that might mark the store as unfriendly, harsh, or as a place frequented by shoplifters (Waltz, 1953). If the store can recover the items or obtain payment through informal and discreet means, then its interests are partially met.

Other aspects of the informal approach should be kept in mind. Store management knows that most pilferers are amateurs and that when confronted with their attempted theft, most are shaken up so badly that they will do almost anything to avoid official attention. Further, they will probably refrain from stealing in that store, at least for a time. Studies have shown that typical pilferers are what the criminal subculture labels as "square johns," those who neither systematically involve themselves in criminal pursuits nor identify themselves as criminals. They are typically people who adhere to the dominant cultural values and spend most of their time in legitimate pursuits. When caught, amateurs (particularly adults) display their commitment to dominant values and strenuously deny that they have done anything wrong or that they are criminals. Cameron (1964:164) reports the following as a typical verbal response from the amateur on being apprehended:

> I didn't intend to take the dress. I just wanted to see it in the daylight. Oh! what will my husband do! I *did* intend to pay for it. It's all a mistake. Oh! my God! what will mother say! I'll be glad to pay for it. See, I've got the money with me. Oh! my children! They can't find out I've been arrested! I'd never be able to face them again.

Some pilferers dream up quite incredible accounts of their behavior: "The shop assistant took so long in coming"; "I thought my sister had paid for it"; "I only wanted to see whether things are properly supervised here" (Doleisch, 1960:4).

To arrest a misdemeanor suspect (the usual case in shoplifting incidents) is to do so at peril because lawsuits charging false imprisonment or false arrest may result (Waltz, 1953). Not surprisingly, retailers in recent years have pressured legislatures to amend regulations dealing with the apprehension of suspected shoplifters. Most states now permit store personnel to detain suspects under certain broad conditions and without fear of civil suits charging false arrest or imprisonment. This may mean an increase in police arrests (and thus, an increase in official rates of shoplifting), though the considerations reviewed in this section will continue to play an important part in management decisions.

Consequences of Informal Reactions   The informal handling of shoplifters may have important ramifications for the way shoplifting is viewed by those apprehended as well as by the general public. The fact that many shoplifters are generally law abiding suggests that in order to engage in shoplifting in the first place—which they recognize is wrong and illegal—they may have convinced themselves that in their case it is not really theft, certainly not crime. As already seen, many apprehended amateurs think of their actions this way. How do they arrive at this conception? How is it that what they do is not crime but what someone else does—for example, robbery and burglary—is crime?

What society views as crime is influenced partly by prevailing cultural conceptions of crime and partly by the consequences of criminal behavior. If people do things they expect will result in being labeled criminal, then to be so labeled comes as no surprise and reinforces the belief that the act is criminal. But if people are not sure that the actions are criminal or if they have adopted the view that they are not, there will be no reason to alter their view when reactions do not match what they think happens to "real" criminals committing "real" crimes. So, upright citizens who occasionally shoplift and who are treated informally and discreetly by store personnel will be under little pressure to alter their conception of themselves or their behavior: They believe that what they do is not criminal and the criminal is quite another sort of person.

Interestingly enough, American business practices may encourage amateur shoplifting in other ways. Businesses spend billions of dollars every year on campaigns designed to convince Americans that they need and want items offered for sale. Already attuned to the values of an acquisitive society, Americans are reminded constantly to spend as much money as they can. They are continually exhorted to buy now, buy more, buy better and pay later. During the Christmas shopping season, when shoplifting is at its yearly peak, the glitter and the temptation are at their height. Even if people cannot afford an item, they are discouraged from forgetting about it and instead are exhorted to find a way to buy it. When continually pushed to conceive of the meaning of life in material terms, people are measured by what they possess, what they can afford, and what they consume, rather than by who they are and what they are. Among the casualties of an acquisitive society are values of fairness, dignity, decency, concern for others, and feelings of contentment and well-being (Bredemeier and Toby, 1961).

Burglary

According to victimization surveys, burglary is the most common and, to many Americans, one of the most frightening among felony crimes. Victims often report that they felt as if their very person had been violated. People cherish the privacy and security of their homes and feel anger and resentment when these are breached. Women have a very special and justified fear: that an intruder will rape as well as steal. According to the Department of Justice, three-fifths of all rapes in the home are committed by burglars, and violence of some sort occurs in 30 percent of incidents in which someone is at home during the break-in (Bureau of Justice Statistics, 1988d:18).

The victims of burglary come from all walks of life, but the risks are not borne equally (see Table 6.1). National surveys performed from 1975 to 1987 show that blacks and Hispanics averaged higher victimization rates than whites, and the risks of being burglarized where much higher for families with incomes under $7500 living in rental property or residing in central city areas (Bureau of Justice Statistics, 1991b). Not surprisingly, the more valuable the stolen property is, the more likely burglary victims are to report the incident to police.

During the last few years the fears of middle-class homeowners have increased as suburban burglary rates have increased in relation to central city rates. Communities have organized "crime watch" groups to patrol their neighborhoods in an attempt to protect themselves from the burglar and other criminals.

TABLE 6.1 Burglary victimization rates in the United States, 1989

Household Characteristic	Rate[a]
Race/Ethnicity	
White	52.1
Black	88.4
Hispanic	85.2
Other	54.5
Household Income	
Less than $7,500	82.1
$7,500–$9,999	62.2
$10,000–$14,999	56.3
$15,000–$24,999	55.8
$25,000–$29,999	53.4
$30,000–$49,999	46.9
$50,000 or more	53.1
Residence	
Central city	77.1
Suburban	48.6
Nonmetropolitan area	44.2
Form of Tenure	
Home owned	45.2
Home rented	76.5

[a]Rate is number of victimizations per 1000 households.
Source: Excerpted from Table 8 in Bureau of Justice Statistics (1990b). *Bulletin: Criminal Victimization 1989.* Washington, D.C.: U.S. Department of Justice.

Whether committed in the suburbs, in rural areas, or in cities, most burglaries are the work of relatively unskilled individuals who commit occasional burglaries among a variety of other offenses, and who live in or near the places they burglarize (Shover, 1991). They look for cash and for items that can be readily disposed of via fences and pawnshops. Their methods are scorned by professionals. Professionals take pride in their ability to gain entrance without force and noise and to pull a job speedily and profitably. The unskilled, often youthful burglars are called "door shakers," "kick-it-in men," "loidmen," and "creepers," names that reflect their amateur techniques (Pileggi, 1968).

A number of research efforts during the past decade have aimed at identifying the major contours of burglary offenses and offenders. There is considerable agreement about the main characteristics. Losses are moderate,

Armed with a crowbar, almost any determined burglar can break into a home in a matter of seconds. Although it is usually a nonviolent crime, burglary leaves many victims feeling that their physical person has been violated. In fact, a woman at home alone runs a significant risk of being sexually assaulted by an intruder whose original purpose was "mere" burglary.

usually well under $500; most involve cash and cash-convertible items such as televisions, radios, and stereos; residential burglaries usually take place during the daytime, those of commercial establishments at night, often on weekends; and most involve forced entry. It is perhaps significant that the clearance rate (proportion of incidents resulting in arrest) tends to be higher for burglaries in which there is no loss at all or only a small one. Presumably these are uncompleted burglaries, whose numbers are higher than might be expected—up to 33 percent of all incidents in some studies (e.g., Conklin and Bittner, 1973). They are often the work of amateurs who cannot find what they want or who are discovered or frightened away before they have started work.

Those arrested for burglary are disproportionately young and black and almost always male. Shover (1991:87) points out that "[o]verwhelmingly, burglary is a male enterprise. . . ." Over 90 percent of arrested burglary suspects are male, a gender gap that is greater than for any index crime but rape. When women are involved, they are more likely than men to work in partnerships or in groups, although men also frequently work in teams. Most adult burglars have prior arrest records, often for burglary.

When professionals work, they choose targets that have been carefully cased; they work in well-oiled teams with each member assigned a specific role based on experience and expertise; and they work with quiet speed. In search of a lucrative target, the professional must deal effectively with security systems. The ability to disarm alarms separates the good burglar from both the amateur and the aspiring professional (Letkemann, 1973).

Once inside, there is the problem of finding the loot. If burglars are interested in cash, as many are, finding it is not always simple. Skilled burglars try to anticipate the behavior of their victims:

> In commercial establishments, [the burglar] may find it in the expected places, such as safes, cash registers, or in deliberately unexpected places, such as one shoe box among several hundred others. In residential dwellings, the burglar's task may be even more difficult, since the places where cash may be found are less predictable. A home does not have a cash register, nor, necessarily, a safe. Therefore, the burglar must make quick interpretations as to the most probable location of cash. The mental activity here is really a game of wits—or operating on the basis of reciprocal expectations. He proceeds on the assumptions he has regarding routine family behavior, and he anticipates uniformities in architecture as well as in styles of placing valuables. (Letkemann, 1973:55)

In professional burglary, safecrackers are at the top of the status hierarchy, and their work makes some of the greatest demands on a thief's skill. Safecracking has been explored in detail by Letkemann. Among the basic tools and equipment are "grease" (nitroglycerine), made from a combination of sulphuric acid, nitric acid, and glycerine; soap, which must be pliable and is used for funneling grease into the door; and "knockers and string" (detonators and fuses). The most common technique of safeblowing is the so-called jam shot, a procedure consisting of ten coordinated steps that, if done correctly, force the door of the safe to swing open on its hinges. When done incorrectly, the door is blown off the safe, or worse, the door and the safe buckle.

Professional safecrackers must remain knowledgeable about technological advances if they are to stay in business, and those who have been in the field long recognize the importance of information sharing. Safecrackers share information on jobs, on techniques, on new developments, and on any related aspects of their line. Letkemann suggests that the already fairly strong social bonds linking safecrackers have been strengthened as a result of greatly restricted access to dynamite (a ready source of grease), and the resulting need to make their own nitroglycerine: "It enabled leaders to screen new 'recruits' and necessitated the development of a stronger subculture based on mutual aid and group loyalty" (1973:88).

Sophisticated professional burglary has been swallowed up by the growing numbers of amateur burglaries committed by those in search of immediate economic rewards. It may be that increased activity secured and decreased use of cash as a medium of exchange will help drive all but the most organized and skilled burglars into other "professions." On the other hand, the low risks of arrest coupled with initial successes may encourage many inexperienced burglars to continue in this line. They build their skills, their pride, and their fencing contacts. As they develop friendships with other crooks and lose contact with "straight" friends, their commitment to burglary increases and they become new experts, replacing retiring or imprisoned professionals (Cornish and Clarke, 1986:13). This does not mean they drop other criminal activities; rather, they add burglary to a list of offenses they feel competent to commit successfully when the opportunity and incentive arise.

Forgery

It is estimated that in any given year, Americans lose from $500 million to more than $1 billion due to forgery (Foldessy, 1971). By far the most common form of forgery is "paper hanging." The term refers to the writing of bank checks when there are insufficient funds to cover them or when the signature has been forged. Since about 90 percent of all American money transactions are made with checks, there is a ready-made climate within which forgery can flourish. Actually, it is not just the abundant use of checks that provides a supportive environment for the check forger. Public attitudes toward checks and their use, the ease with which paper hanging can be accomplished, the unwillingness of banks and stores to prosecute, and the hazy line between criminal intent and mistake all make for a supportive atmosphere. In many respects, the factors that support shoplifting also encourage check forgery.

Naive Forgers Checks are commonly seen as "like" money but not as "real" money; hence their misuse may escape the public censure that the theft of cash receives. Two factors explain the seemingly pervasive public indifference to check forgery. First, it is not rare for a person inadvertently to cash or use a check without at that moment having sufficient funds to cover it. Second, check forgery does not have any of the earmarks of what one conventionally thinks of as a crime—it does not look like crime, so maybe it is not real crime (see Lemert, 1953). Most check forgers (*naive check forgers*, as Edwin Lemert calls them) do not think of themselves as criminals, cannot believe that anyone would have the audacity to call them that ("I would never hurt anyone!"), and come up with ready excuses or rationalizations for their behavior (from the more obvious "It was a mistake" to comments such as "No one is hurt by forgery because supermarkets make great profits and don't miss a little money lost through bad checks") (Gibbons, 1973:250).

Banks and stores, which provide checks and checking services, also help support forgery. Because they are in a business dependent on continued public good faith, they are unwilling to make too much of the typical case of check forgery. Rather than antagonize clients, banks and stores are more likely to treat most paper hanging as mistakes or oversights rather than what they legally are—felonies. More privately, they increase their efforts to ward off the forger. Commercial check cashers and issuers now find that insurance companies employ deductible clauses that can be invoked in cases of check forgery, another incentive for businesses to increase their vigilance (Foldessy, 1971).

Above all, check forgery is easy—access to a check is virtually all that is needed. It can be readily explained away as a mistake or oversight. Checks are currently the major means of dealing in money, and thus few people are surprised to see checks come into their lives or are suspicious of those who use them. Paper hanging has none of the earmarks of crime. Official reaction to it by banks, stores, and police is at best ambivalent. Arrests have hardly kept pace with population increases, let alone increases in the use of checks.

Although naive forgers are found in all socioeconomic classes and include both men and women, blacks and whites, and all ethnic groups, the people most often arrested as forgers are white males who hold white-collar jobs and have little identified criminality in their history. In addition, when compared with other known felons, the convicted forger appears to have higher-than-average intelligence and to have begun in crime at a much later age—late twenties and early thirties (Lemert, 1953).

Studies of naive check forgery suggest two factors that together may help explain why a particular individual is drawn into check forgery. One factor is the impact of situational conditions and the importance of forgery as a mechanism for coping with stress. Lemert discovered that the typical instance of naive check forgery occurs when the offender is under pressure to acquire money—he or she may be out drinking, be in a strange town and in need of cash, or be on a shopping spree. The pressures of the moment create stress that demands resolution, or "closure," as Lemert calls it. The forger achieves closure by passing a bad check, resolving the immediate problem, getting hold of cash or buying the desired item.

But why forgery? Why not enlist the help of friends or family? The answer is that naive forgers commonly have experienced considerable social isolation in their lives. Many forgers have experienced stressful and unproductive relationships that have progressively isolated them from conventional social bonds. They are often estranged from their families; many have experienced difficulties in marriage (Lemert found divorce in 40 percent of his sample). Some have encountered problems in employment and military service, and some have gambling losses. As these situational pressures build, victims find themselves unwilling or unable to break the chain of personal troubles by enlisting the support and confidence of others. Instead, they seek immediate closure. Remember, however, that society has provided an exchange climate in which forgery is easily and comfortably accomplished. Therefore, the choice of forgery as a closure device must be seen as a decision directed to some extent by this supportive exchange environment. The environment of support may be diminishing, however. The invention of "smart cards" for bill paying may greatly reduce the opportunities for forgery (Bennett, 1987:123). One wonders what bad check writers would do if check forgery were not available to them or if it carried the stigma of crime. Perhaps the naive forger would become a pilferer, if not one already.

Systematic Forgers Not all paper hangers belong to the category of naive check forger; some are professionals. Lemert (1958) prefers the term *systematic forgers*. For the systematic forger, forgery provides a steady source of income and is treated in a highly businesslike manner. Although forgery was once a well-established part of the repertoire of professional theft, today most systematic forgers are on the periphery of the world of professional theft. First, they most often work alone and therefore are not intimately involved in the organizational facets of professionalism—they do not need connections, accomplices, financial stakes, fences, or other aspects of group support. Further, theirs is not a criminal activity requiring special skills and tutelage, although this is not true of the skilled counterfeiter (Jackson, 1969a). Moreover, some professional forgers must guard themselves against association with the more common habitual amateurs—for example, petty thieves, alcoholics, and other drug users—who cannot be trusted when the chips are down and who are not welcomed by the professionals.

No accurate estimates have been made of the proportion of forgery efforts attributable to professionals. In all probability, they account for a small number of the total incidents of paper hanging. But systematic forgers stand out in the size of their rewards from forgery and in the persistence with which they pursue this line of work. Bloch and Geis (1970) tell of a female systematic forger who claims to work a 40-hour week in her line and who can expect to make about $100 a hour if things go well. One form of professional forgery requiring a little more planning and perseverance is "check kiting" described by James Inciardi (1975:27):

> *Check-kiting* is a swindle related to forgery that is directed against banks. This fraudulent operation involves the covering of bad checks with other bad checks. A professional bank swindler might open a series of checking accounts at scattered banks with deposits of $25. At *Bank Z* he cashes a $100 check drawn on *Bank X*, depositing $25 and pocketing $75. He then covers the *Bank X* check with a $250 check on *Bank Y*, depositing $125 and pocketing $125. This latter check on *Bank Y* is made good with a $500 check on *Bank Z*, with $300 deposited and $200 pocketed. Manipulations of this type have been executed by both individuals and organized groups of bank swindlers, with single operations accumulating thefts in excess of half a million dollars.

Confidence Games

Swindlers have been around for centuries. Swindlers and confidence artists rely on people wanting something-for-nothing, and they often say, "you can't cheat an honest man."

Variations on the con game are numerous: Lists of different swindles compiled through the years show as many as 250 variations (Inciardi, 1975). For at least 200 years, two of the most common con games have been "ring dropping" and "purse dropping." Both involve simple techniques of manipulation, and both rely on the victim's gullibility and greed. In ring dropping, a worthless piece of jewelry is dropped by one member of the con team (the "roper" or "steerer") near a stranger (the victim or "mark"). A second member of the team (the "insideman") rushes forward to pick up the jewelry and, after showing it to the mark, agrees to share the proceeds if the stranger will sell it. The mark is persuaded to leave something of value with the insideman as security—a token of good faith. The climax of the game is obvious—the insideman absconds with the security, leaving the mark to discover that the jewelry is worthless.

The game just described is one variety of swindles commonly referred to as "short cons." The aim in a short con is to fleece marks of whatever they have with them at the time or can obtain in a matter of minutes. In a short con, the amount of preparation needed and the size of the take are generally small. It can be put into motion at a moment's notice and the score is usually a matter of dollars and cents (Roebuck and Johnson, 1964). Another common version of the short con is the "pigeon drop," which operates along lines similar to ring dropping but requires more manipulative abilities by the confidence operator. In the typical pigeon drop, the victim is invited to share money that has supposedly been found by one member of the confidence partnership, but in order to qualify for a share the mark must first demonstrate good faith by putting up some of his or her own money.

The successful con artist must accomplish at least three things: (1) make the mark trust the con operator; (2) make the mark believe that his or her part in the enterprise will be rewarding; and, most important, (3) convince the mark to part ("temporarily," of course) with some of his or her own money. Clearly, a good deal of smooth talking and friendly persuasion is usually necessary. This is where good con artists excel (Roebuck and Johnson, 1964:236).

Those con artists who set their sights on lucrative swindles and are able and prepared to spend considerable time and energy in preparing and performing the swindle go after the big con. Big-con operators are at the top of the hierarchy of professional crime, and their line of work requires considerable skill and ingenuity. Big-con operators are shrewd entrepreneurs whose special talents lie in their acting ability and their knowledge of the limits to which people can be pushed in search of a fast buck. Big cons can reap large payoffs, as the experience of John Ernest Keely demonstrates:

> Keely, an ex-carnival pitchman, began a hoax in 1874 that reaped many fortunes and lasted for a quarter of a century. His nonexistent perpetual motion machine, "which would produce a force more powerful than steam and electricity," involved the financiers of many cities, the public of two continents, and the United States Secretary of War. Before his career ended, Keely had a 372-page volume written on his "discovery," over a million dollars in cash, a life of luxury for 25 years, and an international reputation. (Inciardi, 1975:24)

Most big-con operators adhere to a sequence of steps, each of which must be successfully accomplished if the con is to work. As each step is completed, it becomes more difficult for the con artists to abandon the enterprise and more likely that the swindle will succeed. Seven major steps in the sequence have been identified (Gasser, 1963:48–51):

Step 1: *Tying into the mark*—finding a victim, gaining his confidence, getting him ready for step two.

Step 2: *Telling the mark the tale*—showing the victim what is at stake for him, and how he can get hold of it.

Step 3: *Initial money gaff*—letting the mark make some money to show how easy it is.

Step 4: *Putting the mark on the send*—sending the victim for money.

Step 5: *Playing the mark against the store*—fleecing him of his money.

Step 6: *Cooling out the mark*—see explanation below.

Step 7: *Putting the mark in the door*—getting rid of the victim.

One of the most important steps in the sequence of events is "cooling out" the victim. Con artists recognize that victims will be angry when they discover they have been duped. Accordingly, they take a special step, the purpose of which is to reduce the chances that the mark will cause trouble. They hope the mark will be convinced to forget the whole incident.

Generally, con artists avoid using violence, even if it means losing the score (Roebuck and Johnson, 1964). How, then, do they cool out the mark? One method is to create a twist whereby victims become apparent accessories to a felony (sometimes murder) and hence think they have committed a crime. From being a victim, the mark is now a criminal, facing a prison sentence if caught. Of course, the whole situation is contrived; the con artists stage a fake murder. For example, the mark in the film *The Sting*, assuming himself to be an accessory to murder, was only too glad to forget the whole incident.

Erving Goffman (1952) has discussed a second method of cooling out the mark. This method relies on "the art of consolation." Instead of generating fear in victims, the con artists help them redefine the situation and themselves so that they feel more comfortable with the outcome. By emphasizing, for example, that it was extremely hard to con the mark or that the mark presented a real challenge, the con operators help the victim retain a positive conception of self. Although the stakes are higher, this method is rather like the situation in which a chess opponent who has just beaten you proceeds to commend you on your play and the challenge you offered. You have still lost the game, but you feel much better. Redefining the situation for the mark provides "a new set of apologies . . . [and] a new framework in which to see himself and judge himself" (Goffman, 1952:456).

Fencing Stolen Property

Along with the "fix" (see pp. 214–215), "fencing" overlaps the worlds of criminal enterpise and legitimate work. It binds theft to the larger social system. Without someone to dispose of stolen property, thieves would have to rely on their own connections, and the costs and risks of crime would increase substantially. For the rest of society, the fence provides an opportunity for people to buy something at less than market price.

The legal requirements for demonstrating that fencing has occurred are complex and help explain why police and prosecutors rely on highly specialized enforcement strategies in combating the crime. In America, as in England, there are four elements to the crime: (1) The property must have been stolen; (2) the property must have been received or concealed (though a fence may not have actually seen or touched it); (3) the receiver must have accepted it with the knowledge (in some states, merely the belief) that it was stolen; and (4) the property must have been received with criminal intent.

The "Sting"   Specialized enforcement has helped document just how widespread and lucrative fencing is. Much-publicized "sting" operations involve undercover officers acting as fences and thieves and using various electronic devices for monitoring transactions. "Customers" of the bogus fence run the gamut from amateur, opportunistic thieves to highly experienced professionals. Department of Justice figures show that when successful, these law enforcement efforts pay off in more than arrests: In the five years after stings were first used in the late 1970s, the police spent roughly $6 million but recovered more than $225 million in stolen property. Large-scale operations mounted by federal authorities are too expensive and too time-consuming for most police agencies, which concentrate their efforts in dealing with street crimes, traffic control, and requests for assistance. One must remember also that most fencing is carried on by "lay" or amateur fences, people who periodically deal in stolen property in networks involving family, friends, neighbors, and co-workers (see Hall, 1952; Klockars, 1974; Henry, 1978). Lay receivers may be essentially law-abiding ("square johns") or may dabble in other forms of crime (Shover, 1973). The thieves they connect with are often young, usually amateurs, and many will not know professional fences. They have no alternative but to unload their booty on friends and acquaintances.

Professional "businessman" fences and thieves are better organized and better connected than amateur thieves and lay fences. They buy from thieves with the intention of reselling, and they often keep a stock of goods on hand. The relationship between professional thieves and fences is one of mutual support. Though many professional fences remain on the periphery of professional theft, they are often a useful source of tips and information for thieves. By acting as a source of information, fences retain better control of their own business because they know what is "coming down," and which goods will be available. This works to the advantage of both fence and thief.

Networking   Connections are vital to the fence, whose business is essentially word-of-mouth. The importance of networking was first established by Marilyn Walsh (1977). She identified three types of networks: (1) kinship networks, dominated by family ties, often with young members stealing and

Pawn shops are an integral part of the "hidden economy" (see Chapter 7) in which goods and services are traded free from the rules and regulations of the legitimate marketplace. They are a favorite front for fences, but they are also a favorite target for opportunistic robbers looking for guns and cash.

older members selling; (2) work-a-day networks, often based on employer–employee relations, as when a fence with a legitimate business receives stolen merchandise from an employee; and (3) play networks, groups of "good" burglars and fences who meet socially and exchange information.

Walsh's work is limited, however, because she based her study on police reports and thus could give no first-hand details of the organizational and social-psychological aspects of fencing. Case studies by Carl Klockars (1974) and Darrell Steffensmeier (1986) do what Walsh could not. Klockars interviewed "Vincent Swaggi" (not his real name), a well-known fence in his city, while Steffensmeier interviewed "Sam Goodwin" (also an alias), a well-known fence in the fictitious "American City."

Steffensmeier shows that Sam's networking was extensive (see Figure 6.1). It was built on a foundation developed through word of mouth, referrals, and sponsorship by underworld figures. Sam played an active role in cultivating contacts with employee thieves and in developing long-term relationships with buyers. As a youth, Sam hustled and stole and was eventually arrested and imprisoned. He escaped from prison and settled in American City, where various jobs gave him the opportunity to continue hustling and making contacts throughout the underworld. His eventual opening of an antique and second-hand shop provided the needed front for systematic

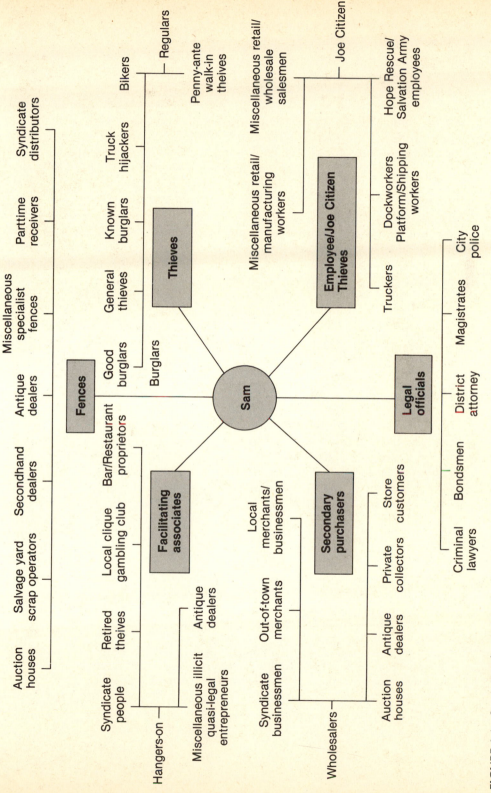

FIGURE 6.1 Sam's Fencing Network. *Source:* Darrell J. Steffensmeier (1986). *The Fence: In the Shadow of Two Worlds.* Totowa, N.J.: Rowman and Littlefield, p. 158. Reprinted by permission.

fencing. The shop was his bridge between legitimate and criminal society. His prison and burglary experience gained him acceptance by a local gang. Steffensmeier believes that the major factor facilitating Sam's networking was the existence of a fencing vacancy in the city. With his "larceny sense," street smarts, business skills, ingenuity, and charisma, Sam was able to capitalize on a need and turn it into a successful career.

As with professional thieves, the fraternity of business fences has gradations of status. At the top of the fencing ladder are "master fences." Their organization, facilities, and bankroll permit them to handle the biggest jobs. Master fences deal with all kinds of merchandise, and at a moment's notice they can arrange disposal of hauls too big or too general for the more common "specialty" fence. A good master fence can earn more than $250,000 a year.

Thieves who specialize in only one or two lines—for example, credit cards, clothes, or jewelry—prefer to deal with fences who specialize in the same goods. One professional fence estimated that in the city of New York there are 50 fences who specialize in jewelry (Pearl, 1974). At the bottom of the fence hierarchy are the neighborhood fences who are part of the vast network of fencing operations in any large city. What all these fences have in common is willingness and ability to run a rational, planned, business activity that plays off both the legal and illegal sides of the economy.

The Fence as Entrepreneur Walsh, Klockars, and Steffensmeier all describe fencing as an enterprise requiring resourcefulness, charisma, ingenuity, and a good grasp of market practices and the rules of economic competition. Pricing norms and prevailing market conditions are used to determine what is "fair," and a sense of justice is developed based on the risks borne by the thief. Yet neither Sam nor Vincent is above chicanery, and both take advantage of any opportunity to pad their profits. If the thief is desperate for cash or the goods are "hot," then the price the fence is willing to pay goes down. Klockars (1974:121–122) indicates that Vincent was proud of the tricks he sometimes played with quality, quantity, and price. In one transaction he duped a pair of small-time thieves who arrived with a Cadillac full of cigarette cartons into accepting $200 for goods worth at least $1800. Vincent worked his trick through a combination of fast talk and clever manipulation without divulging the true value of the merchandise:

> These two guys drive up to the store. They got a new Caddy, maybe a year old. Well, you wanna see it. Cartons everywhere . . . and the guy on the front seat's got one on his lap. He comes in an' asks if I'm interested, so I tell him to pull around the back an' let me see what he's got. They musta just run across an open truck, 'cause they had seven cartons, five big plus two little ones—all clothes. . . . All good stuff. So I put all the cartons in a line in my back room. Now here's somethin' to remember. You got this much stuff an' the guys bring it inside your store, they ain't gonna carry it all out. Just too much carryin'.

> Anyway, we start to go right down the line, just like an auction. First carton, shirts, Van Heusen. They're nice; in fact, I like 'em myself. "Whaddaya got? About three dozen? Thirty-five for this." Second carton, sweater sets . . .

retail approximately eighteen dollars. "Hmmm, sweaters. Three—no. I'll make it three-fifty. Let's see, that's about fifty, hell, make it sixty." Next carton, three-dozen boxes of men's socks. "Oh-oh, socks. Can't give you more than a quarter a pair. Let's see, a quarter a pair times three dozen," I ask the thief, "A quarter a pair times three dozen, how much does that come to?" He just looks at me. "Fifteen dollars, right?" He nods. "Wait a minute," I say, "not fifteen dollars, twelve. Twelve pair, twenty-five cents a pair, that's four a dozen times three is twelve dollars." By this time I got him so confused he don't remember there's nine dozen in the carton. Next carton, more socks. "Same deal on those, OK?" Then we come to two little cartons—men's gloves. "OK, ten apiece for these two little ones?" Then I stand up without sayin' nothin' about the next carton. I just opened the top an' sort'a hummed a little. "OK, what does all that come to? Thirty-five and a hundred for all the sweaters, that's a hundred thirty-five, plus ten apiece for the gloves, that's about a hundred fifty, plus fifteen each for the socks. Wait a minute, didn't I say twelve for the socks? Oh, make it twenty-five for both. Let's see, that's a hundred seventy-five." "Hey, wait a minute," they say, "you forgot the children's clothes here." "Oh yeh," I says, "see, I got grandchildren I was thinkin' of them for. How about you give me four for my personal use an' I'll give you two hundred for the lot. Take it or leave it." Then I start countin' out twenties. "OK now, here's a hundred for you an' another hundred for you." They took it. (Klockars, 1974:121–122)

The motivation for being fair with thieves is rarely altruism. It stems from the need to maintain a good reputation and good relations with valued customers. In this respect the fence is no different from anyone whose knowledge and power provide temptations to exploit others that must be overcome if the goal is long-term prosperity.

To leave the topic of fencing with the impression that it is primarily an entrepreneurial activity carried out by astute business people (like Sam and Vincent) who make a good living at it ignores the extensive hidden trading among "ordinary people." A word, then, about Stuart Henry's (1978) important work. Henry studied amateur fencing, or "on-the-side" trading, as he calls it. He used information provided by friends, fellow workers, neighbors, relatives, university colleagues, and even the local hairdresser.

Most of the amateur trading took place within loose networks of collusion, and a participant's job usually provided the opportunity and incentive to get involved. But Henry points out that the incentive was rarely need or greed. He believes that on-the-side trading is largely inconsequential, if not actually unprofitable, from a material standpoint: Things are sold for no more, and often less, than they cost. A beer or a promise of favors returned is often sufficient payment. As one participant put it: "No one really makes any money. Not real money. . . . The bloke who sells it is not actually making anything either" (Henry, 1978:89). The real profits are of a social nature—forging and maintaining good relations with acquaintances, neighbors, and workmates, and the fostering of "community spirit." To be sure, these social benefits may have a material side, but Henry's informants rarely mentioned it.

All this may help explain why amateur trading is so extensive and why participants do not think of themselves as criminals. They see themselves as ordinary people who are not doing anything really dishonest. Since they do not "need" to steal, the stereotype of the "real" criminal doesn't apply: "People in ordinary, honest jobs know that they do not have to fiddle, pilfer, or deal in order to earn a living" (Henry, 1978:76). Thievery is certainly more justifiable if its criminality can be defined away.

Professional Theft as a Way of Life

Professional theft has a history going back at least to Elizabethan times, when "conny-catching" (a type of swindling) was a full-time profession. Through the years other varieties of theft became the focus of professionalization, with shoplifting and pocket picking two of the more common ones. Much of what is known about professional theft and the professional thief has come from firsthand accounts by thieves (both practicing and reformed), many of which are of the "as told to" variety. Among the best known are *The Professional Thief*, edited by Edwin Sutherland; Ernest Booth's *Stealing Through Life*; and the more recent accounts, *My Life in Crime*, reported by John Bartlow Martin, and *Box Man: A Professional Thief's Journey*, as told to William Chambliss (1972). To those must be added an assortment of books and articles focusing on professionalism in specific types of theft—for example, confidence games, burglary, forgery, and pocket picking (e.g., Maurer, 1940).

By far the most influential work on professional theft has been Sutherland's *The Professional Thief* (1937b). Sutherland used the written accounts of one professional thief ("Chic Conwell") to illustrate the complex assortment of behavior characteristics, attitudes, organizational features, subcultural patterns, and views of the world that together make up a way of life shared by professional thieves.

In describing the world to which he belonged, Chic Conwell tells us that professional thieves (1) "make a regular business of stealing"; (2) acquire their skills and professional know-how through tutelage by and association with already established professionals; (3) develop highly skilled work techniques, the most important of which is the "ability to manipulate people"; (4) carefully plan everything they do in connection with their business; (5) look upon themselves as different from amateurs and superior to them, particularly those who indulge in sex crimes; (6) have a code of ethics that "is much more binding among thieves than that among legitimate commercial firms"; (7) are "sympathetic" and "congenial" with each other; (8) view successes and failures as "largely a matter of luck"; (9) have an established vocabulary of criminal slang, the main purpose of which is to enhance "we-feeling" and promote ease of intraprofession communication; (10) rarely engage in only one specialized form of theft (the notable exception being pickpockets, or "cannons"); and (11) usually operate in gangs, "mobs," or partnerships whose life span is generally short unless they are consistently successful (Sutherland, 1937b:2–42).

Summarizing Conwell's account of professional theft, Sutherland (1937b:ix–x) offers this conception of the profession:

> The profession of theft is more than isolated acts of theft frequently and skillfully performed. It is a group way of life and a social institution. It has techniques, codes, status, traditions, consensus, and organization. It has an existence as real as that of the English language. It can be studied with relatively little attention to any particular thief. The profession can be understood by a description of the functions and relationships involved in this way of life. In fact, an understanding of this culture is a prerequisite to the understanding of the behavior of a particular professional thief.

Becoming a Professional Thief

Sutherland's work describes the behavior system of professional theft as it appeared in the first quarter of the twentieth century, viewed through the eyes of one thief. A more up-to-date picture of professionalism in theft arises if one also looks at recent contributions to the literature.

Consider first how one becomes a professional thief. Put bluntly, "One gets into the profession by acceptance" (Sutherland and Cressey, 1974:285). Gaining acceptance represents the pinnacle of a maturation process for the emerging professional. During the process, newcomers learn to think, act, and be professional thieves. This means they must adopt these aspects of professionalism deemed important by those already in the fraternity, particularly those with whom they will spend much of their time.

One way aspiring professionals learn what is important is through others sharing the common store of knowledge. Although there is no formal or extensive recruiting of new members into the profession, the fraternity would die out if new members were not accepted on a fairly regular basis. It is by receiving shared information that many take their first steps toward membership. In earlier days "apprenticeship" sometimes took the form of systematic training and preparation, as when would-be pickpockets were formally schooled in the art, often at a young age and in groups. Today tutelage is a much more informal process, and though training in technical skills can still involve rather formal procedures, most of what is learned comes through continued association with professionals at work and play. Skills are picked up, experienced, and discussed but rarely taught. Simply by frequenting places where known professionals congregate, those interested will pick up details of the professional lifestyle, including many of the less tangible aspects. According to one thief: "I started hanging around with professionals and learned from them that you didn't steal from a home or small place of business; you stole only from a big place that could afford it" (King, 1972:12).

Needless to say, association with professional thieves is governed by the lifestyle of the professional fraternity itself. One very important facet of this lifestyle is the tendency of professionals to live, "hang out," and work in particular localities. This provides the profession with an ecological identity. Spending time in the same places provides an opportunity to form associations with professionals, even for "straights" and the police. Just as the nineteenth-century cities boasted favored places where the criminal underworld congregated, so do most urban centers today. New York's Tenderloin, Five Points, and Satan's Circus have given way to a 16-block area around Times Square; London's Hoxton has been replaced by Soho. According to James Inciardi (1975:51), the typical urban habitat of the professional is

> . . . composed of gambling and taxi dance halls, rooming houses and cheap hotels, houses of prostitution, third-rate bars, poolrooms, second-hand stores and pawn shops, or theatre, restaurant, and penny arcade complexes. Within these districts are the girls, the gaiety, and the excitement that attract victims of the pickpocket and confidence swindler. Every city has its *line*, its *tenderloin*, its *strip*. What is found in this area of the larger cities can also be found on a proportionate level in the smaller urban centers, the satellite cities, and the provincial county seats.

Professional crooks spend much of their time in these areas, and they reside in them unless they are on the move or unless they have reached the pinnacle of the profession and can afford a nice place in the suburbs. The specific hangout—bar, restaurant, poolroom, or barbershop—is partly a matter of custom, partly a matter of convenience, and sometimes a matter of security (Maurer, 1964).

Most information sharing occurs when the criminals themselves exercise control over the process. This is contrasted with the situation in prisons, where some learning of the professional way of life also takes place. In prisons, convicted offenders are thrown together and their interaction is geared to the constraints of formal prison arrangements, so what they do with whom is not entirely a matter of choice. In prison many amateurs, opportunists, or habitual thieves are exposed to aspects of professional crime.

The popular idea that more experienced inmates willingly and routinely teach others the skills and know-how of professional crime is far from the truth. It seems that learning comes primarily through friendship and acquaintance with imprisoned professionals, just as it does on the outside, and frequently those who share inside information with others do so with great caution and deliberation. Much consideration is given before other "cons" receive the information—whether they can be trusted, whether they will be useful contacts after release, and whether they show promise (Inciardi, 1975). Some prisons become known for the kinds of criminal skills and know-how that can be learned there (Letkemann, 1973).

Status and Prestige

A key feature of professionalism is the maintenance of a system that confers status and prestige. Status distinctions are based on a variety of things: type of theft engaged in, skill and technical competence, success, connections, and commitment. As in any other profession, participants confer prestige and recognition upon one another and distinguish the entire fraternity from outsiders, those who do not belong.

Within the ranks of professional thieves, certain specialties stand out. Confidence men and "box" men (safecrackers) have traditionally been considered at the top of the pecking order. Their work involves considerable skill and ability, and the payoffs can be substantial for those who succeed. Those who become known for their expertise in these areas are usually fully integrated into the professional subculture, for their work depends heavily on group effort, trust, connections, and esprit de corps. At the other end of the status hierarchy are those whose jobs usually have a small payoff, involve more modest levels of skill and risk, and whose victims are typically individuals or small businesses. Cannons (pickpockets), "boosters" (professional shoplifters), and small-time burglars are examples of low-status thieves. Here is how two thieves view shoplifting (King, 1972:81):

> A booster is just about the lowest thief there is. Nobody has much to do with them. I mean, I seen one yesterday as a matter of fact. I saw this one, then talked to this other guy who was a meter-robber; you know, a guy who robs parking meters. They make a lot of money. I was talking to this friend and he said he saw Charlie boosting the other day. I told him: "Gee, Charlie Jay? Man, I can remember when he was a real high-classed thief." "Oh," he said, "he's down at the bottom now." In our estimation he's down dragging bottom because he's boosting. And he used to be a real high-classed thief at one time.

Status distinctions are maintained even within theft specialties. Confidence men who operate the more sophisticated, complex games (the "big con") are considered superior to "short-con" operators who go in for quick swindles and usually small payoffs. Similarly, burglars distinguish among themselves, with high prestige going to the "good burglar," who (1) is superior in technical skills, (2) has a reputation for personal integrity, (3) tends to specialize in burglary, and (4) has been relatively successful in making money and staying out of prison (Shover, 1973).

When professionals refer to other crooks—the opportunists, habitual amateurs, sex offenders, and those who use spur-of-the-moment violence—they use a variety of names to designate their inferior status. These are the "bums," "young punks," "squares," "hustlers," "small-timers," "weirdos," and "amateurs." Unlike the professionals, their involvement in crime is unsystematic and sporadic; their skills are minimal; and "anything goes." Although some make it into the ranks of the professionals as they mature in crime, most do not. They remain bums in the eyes of professionals and, often, in the eyes of the public and the police as well.

It appears that "good" thieves also do not think much of women who venture into crime. In a rare investigation of the issue, Steffensmeier and Terry (1986) interviewed 49 male thieves, most of them experienced, some of them probably ranking as professionals. These thieves identified various traits that they felt were particularly important to their trade, but which women were perceived to lack (see Table 6.2). In their view, successful thieves are physically strong; they have "heart" ("guts" or courage); they are aggressive when they need to be; they have endurance; they can be trusted

TABLE 6.2 Likelihood of males or females having valued qualities helpful for being a successful thief/hustler/criminal

Attribute	Indicates Attribute Is Important %	n^a	Males Much More %	Males Somewhat More %	Males/ Females Equally %	Females Somewhat More %	n
Trustworthy	100	29	41	24	24	10	29
Physical strength	92	26	79	21	—	—	29
Calm and cool	89	27	46	46	7	—	28
Emotionally stable	84	25	39	43	10	7	28
Reliable	83	23	30	22	30	18	27
Endurance	80	20	43	25	5	14	28
Daring/guts	72	22	25	25	40	4	28
Aggressive	72	22	41	30	5	11	27
Leadership	70	24	44	33	18	4	27
Command respect	48	25	44	30	18	7	27
Intelligent	29	24	11	30	30	30	29

^{a}Totals do not always equal 29 because of failures to respond directly to the item.

Source: Darrell J. Steffensmeier and Robert M. Terry (1986). "Institutional sexism in the underworld: A view from the inside." Reprinted from *Sociological Inquiry*, vol. 56:3 (Summer), by permission of the University of Texas Press.

when the chips are down; they are emotionally stable; they stay calm and cool under pressure; and they command respect. Most thieves claimed to have committed crimes with women at one time or another, but in no cases were the women full partners in the crimes, being relegated instead to peripheral sex/service roles, for which they received a less-than-equal share of the "score." Even in crime, it seems, women are treated as second-class citizens.

Self-Images and World View

In distinguishing themselves from amateur thieves and other criminal offenders, professionals reinforce their feelings of importance and superiority and in this way bolster their self-esteem while erecting barriers against "outsiders." Yet, like other Americans, they brush their teeth, drive on the right side of the road, are consumers, lovers, and businesspeople, and are concerned about prices, politics, war, the state of their country, and their own successes and failures. Against this apparent conformity, they are committed to a life that continually brings them the threat of arrest, prosecution, and punishment by society. Though they are committed to crime as a profession, they have trouble accepting the idea that they are deviant, immoral, or unworthy of respect.

So, like others who have difficulty reconciling what they think of themselves with what others appear to think of them, professional thieves negotiate a path that emphasizes their adherence to the "American way" and devalues their critics and oppressors. The following comments by professional thieves illustrate how society is brought into focus along the path to self-respect and self-esteem:

> *A successful professional burglar:* You might laugh, but I'm for law and order. I don't hurt anyone, and anyway most of the people who lose stuff are insured, and I could tell you about the way they inflate their losses. But this mugging on the streets and rapes, and the way they have to coddle those creeps makes me sick. (Pileggi, 1968)

> *A "short-con" man:* You know how it goes in this dog-eat-dog world. You got to take the other guy before he takes you. You know, the real sharpie outwits the marks [victims]. Of course, it all depends on how you get ahead. My way was no different from, say, a lawyer or businessman. You know, a lawyer has a license to steal. The cops should lay off con men. We don't hurt nobody. You can't con an honest man. . . . The cops should do their job and clear the streets of the muggers, heist men, hopheads, and the rest. Why, it's dangerous for a decent man like me to walk down the street at night. (Roebuck and Johnson, 1964:242)

Consensus and Professional Ethics

The survival of any profession depends in part on the maintenance of a normative system to which its members adhere and in terms of which they interpret their behavior and that of their colleagues. Professional theft is no exception. Consensual understandings are expressed as expectations about and evaluations of the conduct of one's peers. Because they have their rules, maxims, and codes of ethics, as well as skills, high pay, and prestige, professional thieves have likened their careers to legitimate professions. Those who violate the rules and collective expectations are subject to the derision of their colleagues and, as in other professions, are punished in various ways and with varying degrees of severity.

Professional expectations and evaluations cover a wide range of topics, probably more extensive than that of many legitimate professions. The topics include work activities, treatment of professionals and nonprofessionals, relationships with the larger society, and relationships with family and lovers. Some of the more prominent expectations for conduct among thieves are that members will deal honestly with one another, stick to their assigned roles, give aid to others in time of crisis, and pay their debts. One of the long-standing principles of professionalism deals with informing or "snitching." A thief simply does not snitch on colleagues and expect to remain honored and respected, not to mention healthy (Inciardi, 1975). They also have the time-honored imperative, "Never grift [take] on the way out" (Sutherland, 1937b:13). This means that professional thieves will restrain their greed and take during a heist only what they have planned to take. Opportunistic plundering is the way of amateurs.

The "we-feeling" among career criminals provides a sense of solidarity and helps maintain group identity and security. Argot has a special place here. The slang used and shared by thieves is an expression of togetherness and facilitates communication among members of the criminal subculture. Many of the terms used have a long history, some going back to Elizabethan days. By adopting an artificial language, professionals are "able to determine in only a few minutes of conversation with a stranger whether he is acquainted with the underworld, what rackets he has experience with, and whom he knows" (Inciardi, 1975:56). This consensus in language is especially important when thieves are on the move and are setting up "connections." With few exceptions, professionals rely on an extensive network of contacts. Such connections are important not only as avenues of information sharing but also as a pool of potential partners—or, if they are lawyers and bondsmen, a pool of potential help when the law strikes. Recall the extensive network centered around Sam, the fence (Figure 6.1).

Although thieves clearly recognize the value of consensus, evidence indicates that much of the underworld code of honor among thieves may be crumbling. In his interviews with professional burglars, Shover (1973:512) found many spontaneous comments about the decline of "the Code." In part, this may be due to the fact that "the 'solid,' ethical career criminal seems to be giving way to the 'hustler,' an alert opportunist who is primarily concerned only with personal—as opposed to collective—security." But adherence to any code is severely tested when the chips are down, and thieves are certainly no different from the rest of society in this regard. It appears that pressures of the moment and practical considerations generally lie at the heart of any particular acceptance or rejection of professional codes or consensual understandings. Loyalty may have existed in the old days, but as one thief put it: "There is no loyalty among thieves today. There's no such thing at all. They have absolutely no loyalty. They'll beat one another to the money, you know, anything they can, they beat one another for their girls, or anything" (King, 1972:89).

When the rules are observed, when the code is followed, honor or loyalty may have little to do with it. As Inciardi (1975:70) stated,

> [H]onor among thieves? Well—yes and no. You do have some old pros who might talk about honor, but they're so well heeled and well connected they can afford to be honorable. But for most people, it's a question of "do unto others"—you play by the rules because you may need a favor someday, or because the guy you skip on, or the guy you rap to the cops about—you never know where he'll turn up. Maybe he's got something on you or maybe he ends up as your cellmate, or he says bad things about you—you can't tell how things could turn out.

Aging Property Offenders

There comes a time in most criminals' lives when they think seriously about "retiring" from crime. For some it comes relatively early, perhaps in their twenties or thirties; for others the decision may not come until they are in their fifties or sixties. Little is known about the later stages of criminal careers, a fact that Neal Shover (1983; 1985) has sought to rectify in a study of "ordinary property offenders." These are people who primarily commit nonviolent crimes of theft, though they sometimes venture into robbery or drug sales.

Shover interviewed 50 subjects, 36 of whom he classified as "unsuccessful" because their many crimes rarely paid off and they experienced multiple contacts with the criminal justice system. Shover classified 5 offenders as "successful"—they saw crime as a means of livelihood and were successful at it, though all had been incarcerated at least once. The remaining 7 were "uncommitted"; that is, they were infrequent offenders who rarely planned their crimes, rarely made much money from them, and did not think of crime as their occupation (Shover, 1985:24–26, 97). For uncommitted offenders, the experience of being arrested and jailed had a strong impact that usually jolted them into reaffirming their noncriminal identity.

Though based on a small sample, Shover's unsuccessful group probably mirrors the experience of many high-frequency offenders who begin their criminal careers at a relatively young age and persist well into adulthood when not confined in the penitentiary. In Shover's group, the youngest was 39 and the oldest 72. Four men were still involved in crime at the time of the interviews, though their current crimes paled in comparison to the burglaries and robberies of their youth.

Shover (1983) identified five experiential contingencies that influenced the criminal behavior of the "unsuccessful" property offenders as they aged:

1. *An identity shift*—Some subjects realized that crime was a dead end and they began to dissociate themselves from the "foolish," "dumb," even dangerous behavior of their youth.
2. *Incommodious time*—Many became aware that time was a diminishing resource and thus worried about how to make the best of their limited futures. Many feared dying in prison.
3. *Aspirations and goals*—Some developed new priorities and goals, such as family, "contentment," or a pension. One said:

   "I don't want to live that kind of life any more. I want peace. I want joy and harmony. I want to be with my children and my grandchildren. . . . I want to be with my mother. And when she passes on—I was in prison when my daddy died, I got to come home for five hours in handcuffs to see him—and when my mother passes on, I want to be there with her." (Shover, 1983:212)

4. *Tiredness*—Many grew tired of the problems and deprivations of crime and failure; they had simply had enough. If it was not age itself that weakened them, it was the criminal justice system that wore them down.
5. *Interpersonal contingency*—Ties to another person, such as the development of a satisfying relationship with a woman, and ties to a job, for

legitimate employment provides both immediate rewards and prospects of a secure future. Besides, the routine activities of work rarely leave time (or energy) for the criminal pursuits of the ordinary property offender.

Not all the men experienced all these contingencies, but for those who did, the change from a criminal lifestyle was likely to be abrupt and permanent. Even so, Shover (1983:216) concludes that "even offenders who committed serious crimes while young are capable of, and do, change as they get older." Shover believes that in essence the decision to refrain from crime is due to a perception of increasing costs and decreasing benefits (see also Cusson and Pinsonneault, 1986). As one subject put it: "I'd rather be a bum in the street, than a millionaire in the penitentiary" (Shover, 1985:124). The five experiential contingencies listed influence the decision-making calculus by making crime more of a risk.

The "Fix"

Most career criminals spend considerable time and energy negotiating their way around trouble with the law. For the professional, confrontations with the machinery of law are treated as normal, expected features of a thief's way of life. As a professional, however, the thief acts to minimize the risk of conviction and confinement. Whereas amateurs seem preoccupied with avoiding detection and arrest, professionals direct their energies to avoid conviction. Letkemann found that experienced criminals "didn't particularly mind if the police 'knew' they had pulled a particular caper. The important factor for the experienced criminal was that 'they have nothing on me.' That is, there must be no evidence that will 'stand up' in court" (1973:30).

The major method professionals employ to reduce the risks of conviction, and hence of confinement, is the "fix." The fix involves organization and resources, and it is the professional, as opposed to the amateur criminal, who is generally in a position to make it work. The fix works through manipulation of the judicial process. Efforts are made, therefore, to buy the help of those in a position to influence criminal proceedings. They include police, lawyers, bondsmen, politicians, court personnel, and even judges. An FBI undercover operation in Chicago code-named "Operation Graylord" exposed the largest judicial corruption scandal ever: By 1988, ten years after the investigation began, 90 judges, lawyers, and other court officials had been indicted and 70 convicted, including 14 judges (*St. Louis Post-Dispatch*, October 16, 1988).

In most large cities, professional fixers handle many of the legal problems faced by organized thieves. These persons generally hold respectable positions within the administration of justice and are often associated with the prosecution. As holders of occupational positions within the legitimate work structure of society, fixers represent one of the more important connections between the profession of theft and the larger society. It is through this connection that organized theft helps guarantee its own survival.

Without the fix, professional crime would lose one of its essential lines of defense against legal repression by the larger society. This is because as long as individuals with accepted membership in legitimate society also engage in illegitimate activities, the distinction between what is legitimate and illegitimate remains vague and contestable. It is therefore not surprising to find many thieves arguing persuasively that what they do is not that different from what respectable people do. Take away the fixer, and the thief's crimes stand out even more.

The perpetuation of thief–fixer relationships depends on a number of factors. Obviously, if each pays off as expected, both parties will meet the immediate demands of the relationship. From the fixer's standpoint this usually means money, but sometimes nonmonetary favors are involved. For the thief it means no conviction at all or the lightest possible sentence. But apart from these more obvious considerations are questions of personal security and mutual trust (which is not the same as respect!). The successful thieves and fixers are those who keep tight lips, who do not divulge confidences, and who can be relied on to fulfill their part of the bargain.

In making the most of fix possibilities, thieves display intimate knowledge of the ways of the world. They know, for example, that if it comes to a trial, court proceedings and sentence decisions may well be influenced by external factors, such as the way the media covers the proceedings. So, some knowledgeable thieves use the fix in dealings with newspaper reporters (Gasser, 1963). With some officials, indirect methods sometimes work more productively and safely than do blatant efforts to "put the fix in":

> If you were going to pay off a judge you wouldn't offer him any money, you do it indirectly. Say you had a big case coming up. If you're any kind of businessman at all, you don't put too much faith in your lawyer. Lawyers being what they are. So you go to your state committee man who don't hold any office at all, you go to your political boss and explain what your troubles are and you'd like to be pretty sure things were going to turn out all right and it would be worth so much if you could be sure things would turn out all right. He's the guy that put the judge's name on the ballot. So about ninety-nine times out of a hundred when you come back to his office the next day he tells you, "Don't worry about it, it'll cost five thousand, everything's gonna be taken care of." (Martin, 1952:171)

Although effective use of the fix may be less certain today than in the past, one study of professional criminals found that all had employed the fix quite frequently and generally with good results. The ratio of arrests to felony convictions was 100 to 5.8 and that of arrests to imprisonment for one year or more was 100 to 3.5 (Inciardi, 1975). The fix works for those who are in a position to use it and will remain available as long as people are willing and able to manipulate the judicial process for a price.

Summary of Chapter 6

This chapter has examined shoplifting, burglary, forgery, and confidence games, as well as fencing and the fix, which help support them. The social organization of professional theft was also examined.

Stealing has a long history and is found in some form in many societies. Without private property, however, the concept of theft is moot. Theft laws have been shaped by conflicting interests and by the power of property owners to protect that property. A society that values the acquisition of material wealth but also has gross inequalities in the distribution of material resources finds itself encouraging theft, as appears to have happened in the United States. Many thefts are not reported to the police, but even those that are usually remain unsolved. In this respect, most forms of theft are low-risk crimes, a fact that also contributes to high offense rates.

Most thieves are opportunists who sporadically shoplift, forge checks, or burglarize a business or residence with minimal planning or skill. Many do not think of themselves as criminals, either denying their crimes altogether or blaming their actions on situational pressures. Professional thieves, on the other hand, maintain a complicated system of roles and norms in terms of which participants gain status, prestige, and professional identity. In between the rank amateurs and the professionals are "ordinary property offenders," people who spend many years at crimes of all sorts, usually beginning at an early age, often spending considerable time in prison, and rarely making much money at crime. As they grow older they commit fewer crimes, and many eventually quit the largely unsuccessful criminal lifestyle to "go straight."

Fencing and the fix provide important links between legitimate society and the world of theft. Without them neither theft nor thieves would prosper, and with them it is possible for ostensibly "straight" society to cash in on the criminality of others. In both fencing and the fix, information networks are vital for the success of the enterprise, and this draws knowledgeable, connected individuals to the center of power relations in the underworld.

Recommended Readings

Abigail Buckle, and David P. Farrington (1984). "An Observational Study of Shoplifting." *British Journal of Criminology* 24:63–72.

Stuart Henry (1978). *The Hidden Economy*. Oxford: Martin Robinson.

Jack Katz (1988). *Seductions of Crime: Moral and Sensual Attractions in Doing Evil*. New York: Basic Books.

Carl B. Klockars (1974). *The Professional Fence*. New York: Free Press.

Peter Letkemann (1973). *Crime as Work*. Englewood Cliffs, N.J.: Prentice-Hall.

Neal Shover (1985). *Aging Criminals*. Beverly Hills, Calif.: Sage.

Darrell J. Steffensmeier (1986). *The Fence: In the Shadow of Two Worlds*. Totowa, N.J.: Rowman and Littlefield.

Kenneth D. Tunnell (1992). *Choosing Crime: The Criminal Calculus of Property Offenders*. Chicago: Nelson-Hall.

Chapter 7

Occupational Crime

This text's focus so far has been almost exclusively on what might be called "traditional" crime and criminality. Robbery, murder, assault, burglary, and other street property offenses are traditional crimes in a number of senses. First, they are among the activities that most readily come to mind when one thinks of crime. Second, they are the conventional targets of criminalization. Third, they have long been the prime focus of law-enforcement efforts. Finally, it is primarily around these kinds of crime that criminologists have framed their theories.

To say that robbery, burglary, and interpersonal violence are traditional crimes is not to say that they are the most common forms of crime nor that they have the greatest societal impact in terms of numbers of victims, economic costs, and damage to prevailing social institutions. The crimes discussed in this chapter arguably have far greater impact.

Occupational Crime in Perspective

As used here, the term *occupational crime* refers to illegal activities that occur in connection with a person's job. *Occupational crime* is preferable to the more conventional term *white-collar crime* because it makes no reference to the occupational status of the offender (for other views, see Braithwaite, 1985; Coleman, 1989; Wright and Friedrichs, 1991). When Edwin H. Sutherland (1949) coined the expression "white-collar crime," he had in mind crimes committed in the course of their occupations by persons of respectability and high social status. He observed that criminologists had virtually ignored the illegal activities of those in business, politics, and the professions, concentrating instead on the world of lower-class criminality emphasized in official statistics and in the normal routine of the administration of criminal justice. Lawbreaking, he argued, goes on in all social strata. Restraint of trade, misrepresentation in advertising, violations of labor laws, violations of copyright and patent laws, and financial manipulations were a part of what Sutherland called white-collar crime.

As some authors have noted, however, Sutherland's emphasis on high social status excludes other occupation-related crimes that are similar to his white-collar offenses in that (1) a person's legitimate occupation provides the context and sometimes the motivation for the offense and (2) the offense (and offender) largely escapes official processing at the hands of legal authorities (Newman, 1958). The broader notion of occupational crime thus includes criminal activities committed by anyone in connection with his or her job.

Many different examples of occupational crime readily come to mind. Apart from the illegal activities already mentioned (restraint of trade, unfair labor practices, and so on), there are embezzlement, a variety of consumer frauds, thefts by computer, music and record pirating, prescription law violations, employee pilfering, food and drug law violations, corporate tax violations, housing code violations, bribery and other forms of corruption by public officials, kickbacks, bid rigging, and real estate frauds—the list could go on.

Work and the Historical Development of Legal Controls

Gilbert Geis, one of America's foremost authorities on occupational crime, brings to his research an appreciation of sociology, law, and history. Guided by these perspectives, Geis discovered that the regulation of economic behavior was strenuous during the Middle Ages (and even before—see Box 7.1). Practical, moral, and historical forces promoted a collective appreciation of the dangers and injustices of unregulated marketplace behavior. It requires little imagination to see how important orderly and fair economic relations must have been during a time when most people lived in small villages and knew each other.

Box 7.1 ■ Early Economic Regulation

In early legal codes there is evidence of attempts to regulate occupations and market relations. The Code of Hammurabi, for example, lists a variety of work-related activities for which penalties and victim compensations were to be assessed. Here is a sampling:

- Laws 53–54 deal with the obligations of farmers. If a man has neglected to maintain the dike of his field, and has not kept his dike strong, so that a break has been found in the dike and he has let the water ravage the farmland, the man in whose dike the breach was opened shall make good the grain that he caused to be lost. If he cannot make good the grain, they shall sell him and his goods for silver, and the farmers whose grain the water carried off shall divide the proceeds.
- Law 90 deals with loans and interest rates and states that those lending grain or silver will forfeit the principal lent if they charge more than 20 percent interest.
- Laws 94–107 regulate commerce, the relations among business partners, and the activities of salesmen. Apart from setting penalties for shortchanging customers (Law 94), these laws establish what might be called the ethics of business.
- Laws 218–225 deal with physicians and veterinarians. For example, Law 218 specifies: If a physician has performed a major operation on a patrician with a bronze knife and has caused the patrician to die, or opened up the eye-socket of a patrician with a bronze knife and caused the destruction of the patrician's eye, they shall cut off his hand.
- Law 229 covers shoddy work in the building trade. If a builder has constructed a house for a man, but did not make his work strong, so that the house that he built collapsed and caused the death of the owner of the house, that builder shall be put to death. Law 230 states that if a son of the owner is so killed, the builder's son shall be put to death.
- Law 253 deals with the violation of trust and employee theft: If a man has hired someone to oversee his field, and entrusted him with feed-grain, and entrusted cattle to him, and has contracted with him to cultivate the field, if that person has stolen the seed or fodder and it has been found in his possession, they shall cut off his hand.

Source: Cyrus H. Gordon (1957). *The Code of Hammurabi: Quaint or Forward Looking?* New York: Holt, Rinehart, and Winston.

However, the Industrial Revolution pushed market exploitation "into the shadows, camouflaged by its remoteness, the diffuse nature of the harm it inflicted, and the obscurity of the source of the harm" (Geis, 1988:15). As a result, the public sense of injustice and indignation waned. As a fledgling capitalist society applied itself to the practical problems of making capitalism work, corporate power and wealth reached heights never before imagined. During the late nineteenth century there emerged a drive to check corporate power and the economic abuses spreading from it. First the railroads and later corporations in general became the target of regulatory reforms. However, rather than a systematic response to problems systematically understood, the regulatory movement was a response "to a series of disasters" (Geis, 1988:21), from coal mine explosions to deformed babies born to mothers who had taken thalidomide (see also Hills, 1971:151).

The Role of Interests The full flavor of laws relating to occupations is lost unless the role of special interests is considered. Besides the fact that many past laws were weighted in favor of higher-status individuals, so that the penalties for violation were less the higher one's social status, few laws formalized the obligations of masters and employers toward their servants, slaves, and employees. In addition, some laws were clearly designed to consolidate ruling-class control over economic and political activities and thus over the production and distribution of wealth and material advantages. Consider, for example, laws against criminal fraud.

Frauds When people induce someone to part with money or valuables through the use of deceit, lies, or misrepresentation, they commit *fraud*, or what was called a "cheat" in earlier times. Under English common law, criminal liability extended only to situations in which (1) some false token or tangible device of trickery was involved and (2) the activity was such that reasonable prudence could not guard against it and any member of the general public was a potential victim (Turner, 1966). Under common law, a personal fraud directed against a private individual was no crime, because it was customary to assume that individuals would exercise due caution in their financial dealings with others and because when an individual was deceived, civil remedies were available.

With the rise of capitalism, entrepreneurs throughout the business community urged Parliament to broaden the range of criminal liability associated with fraudulent practices. In 1757 a statute was passed establishing the crime of "obtaining property by false pretenses." Subsequently adopted in the American colonies, this law has remained one of the few specifically criminal statutes dealing with fraud.

In fact, fraud can be perpetrated in many ways; its mechanics are limited only by one's imagination and ability. The victim of fraud can be anyone, but the most commonly deceived persons are consumers acting on their own behalf as private individuals. This consumer fraud reaches all the way from small business to immense and wealthy insurance companies, retail chains, and manufacturers of consumer goods.

Despite the extensive victimization associated with consumer fraud, the courts until recently had operated on the principle of *caveat emptor*—buyer beware. The idea was simply that in making purchases, consumers have only themselves to blame if they are "taken." Reasonable as this may sound, it actually encourages victimization in the modern marketplace, where the complex nature of many products, services, and organizations are such that even knowledgeable purchasers find it almost impossible to protect themselves against fraud. For example, given modern supermarket packaging practices, shoppers can rarely inspect the products they want to buy in more than a superficial way.

The fight for protection against consumer fraud has been long and difficult. Consider the case of pure food and drug laws.

Pure Food and Drug Laws   The production, distribution, and sale of food and drug products are now regulated by a variety of laws aimed at the protection of public health and safety. Interest in the regulation of the food and drug businesses first gained prominence during the nineteenth century, as cities grew and consumers became increasingly removed from agricultural producers and the possibilities for adulteration, spoilage, exploitation, and fraud increased. Public awareness of the problem was stirred partly through the changing experience of buying itself, but mostly by newspaper editorials, and by articles and books that stressed the dangers of existing business practices, sometimes in lurid and frightening detail.

The first major federal legislation aimed at regulating the food and drug businesses was introduced in 1880 and soundly defeated, as were many subsequent bills. In his book *The Therapeutic Nightmare*, Morton Mintz (1970:78–79) observes: "It and other efforts like it were defeated by a durable alliance of quacks, ruthless crooks, pious frauds, scoundrels, high-priced lawyer-lobbyists, vested interests, liars, corrupt members of Congress, venal publishers, cowards in high office, the stupid, the apathetic, and the duped." When Congress finally passed the Federal Food and Drug Act of 1906, it was only the first step in what has turned out to be a long and hard battle between public interests and the food and drug industries.

The 1906 law declared it illegal to manufacture or introduce into an American state any adulterated or misbranded food or drug. Offenders could have their products seized, and those convicted of violating the law would be subject to criminal penalties. Thus a new area of occupational crime was born. But as Richard Quinney (1970:79) has observed:

> The need for revision of the act . . . became apparent shortly after its passage. The absence of adequate control over advertising provided an especially serious loophole for evasion of the spirit of the law, and labeling requirements of the law were such as to permit extravagant and unwarranted therapeutic claims for a product. Also, the 1906 act contained no provisions applying to cosmetics and failed to provide measures for safe and effective health devices.

Some of these inadequacies were corrected by the 1938 Food, Drug, and Cosmetic Act, passed by both houses of Congress despite heavy resistance from the industries involved. Still, by the 1960s, nearly a century after public interest was first mobilized, Americans could count on one hand the number of truly significant bills designed to regulate the powerful industries supplying their food, pharmaceutical products, and cosmetics.

If it were not for the efforts of Ralph Nader, the American public might still be buying meat products largely unregulated by legal controls. As long ago as 1906, Upton Sinclair described the disgusting conditions of meat slaughterhouses in his highly popular novel, *The Jungle*. Writing in 1967, Nader pointed out that "we're still in the Jungle." Following his own investigation of the meat industry, he concluded that Americans were still buying meat products that were adulterated with substances ranging from water and cereals to toxic chemicals and that were prepared under unsanitary conditions, contaminated with diseased and spoiled carcass pieces—even manure and pus—and often sold in a deceptive and fraudulent manner. In 1989, the State of Missouri charged a wholesale meat distributor with intentionally selling tainted meat to the state's various residential agencies (*St. Louis Post-Dispatch*, February 9, 1989).

The reason for appalling conditions in the meat industry, in Nader's view, is partly the inadequacy of existing federal and state laws and partly the pitiful efforts to enforce them. Both problems are blamed on the cozy relationship among the United States Department of Agriculture, state agriculture agencies, and the meat production and processing interests. When Congress passed the Wholesale Meat Act of 1968—bringing intrastate meat processing under federal jurisdiction and establishing stricter controls—another small victory for public welfare was achieved and the range of legal penalties extended. However, the Reagan administration systematically undermined the law by cutting back on expenditures for enforcement, and states have done no better.

The Costs of Occupational Crime

It is now appropriate to return to a matter raised in the opening paragraphs of this chapter: the costs of occupational crime to individuals and society. A brief look at some of these costs should support a more balanced view of the impact of crime in America and be a reminder that societal reactions to a particular form of crime are not necessarily an accurate reflection of its impact on people's lives, their communities, and their institutions. The same can be said of textbook coverage (see Wright and Friedrichs, 1991).

Financial Costs The financial costs of occupational crime far exceed those resulting from traditional crimes. This reflects the greater frequency with which occupational crimes are committed and also the fact that a single offense can result in losses running into millions of dollars (see Cullen, Maakestad, and Cavender, 1987:54–67). Recent estimates place losses resulting from traditional crimes such as burglary and robbery at $4 to $5 billion (Michalowski, 1985:363). By contrast, losses attributed to occupational crimes are estimated at over $100 billion per year, figures that do not include the costs of price fixing and other restraint-of-trade practices, industrial espionage, or violations of health and safety regulations. These offenses cost the public billions more. It is also extremely difficult to estimate the costs of employee crimes directed against employers. According to Michael Baker and Alan Westin (1987), even when employers are asked for figures, many reply that they do not even "cost out" the losses unless the problem is unusually serious. One executive hinted at the magnitude of costs when he observed: "We've got 24,000 employees; if half of them make $5 in forbidden personal calls a month, that's three-quarters of a million right there" (Baker and Westin, 1987:12). The overall costs of occupational crime may reach as high as $231 billion per year (Kramer, 1984:19).

Damage to Institutions and Moral Climate   Deception, fraud, price fixing and other monopoly practices, bribery, kickbacks, payoffs, and violations of trust not only undermine basic principles of honesty and fair play, they also foster a moral climate in which lawlessness provides little indignation—especially when its victims are vague entities such as "the public," "the consumer," "the corporation," and "the government"—and occurs largely free from any sense of guilt on the part of offenders. When those in positions of wealth, power, and prestige violate the law with relative impunity, their activities serve as a model for others and contribute to the "delegitimation" of prevailing institutions. Simply put, confidence in the integrity and strength of economic and political institutions is eroded. Looking out for number one, beating the system, getting something for nothing, or doing a favor for a price have become not disreputable approaches to life but, rather, the accepted and expected approaches for all social strata. When there is pervasive and unpunished thievery and corruption among leaders in business, the professions, and government, street criminals have easy rationalizations for their own illegal conduct. Their "betters" turn out to be surprisingly like themselves.

Personal Health and Safety   Finally, there are the costs to personal health and safety (for reviews of the literature, see Cullen, Maakestad and Cavender, 1987; Simon and Eitzen, 1990). Occupational crimes pose health and safety hazards in numerous ways. Landlords and builders who violate building code regulations expose their tenants to the threat of fire, building collapse, and disease; companies violating safety standards for their products (cars, tires, electrical appliances, toys, nightclothes, Christmas tree lights, or whatever) expose their customers to possible injury or death; physicians who do unnecessary surgery expose their patients to the risk of surgical complications; pharmaceutical companies conspiring to fix high prices threaten the well-being of those who need but cannot afford their products; mine and factory bosses who violate health and safety regulations expose their workers to injury, disease, and death; and companies manufacturing or selling contaminated food products or mislabeled drugs expose their customers to unnecessary health hazards. All these activities may result in severe psychological stresses for the victims.

There can be little doubt that when the health and safety of the population as a whole are considered, the threat posed by occupational crime far exceeds that posed by traditional crimes. This is not to minimize the physical dangers associated with violence, rape, robbery, and the like but, rather, to place the two broad categories of crime in perspective. It is easy to overlook the physical dangers posed by occupational crime because these are often less visible, less direct, and appear less concrete than those of street crimes. Yet they exist and are extensive. Take, for instance, the physical dangers associated with environmental pollution in the air, water, soil, workplace, and home. Millions of Americans are exposed every day to known carcinogens and other potentially lethal substances, often because corporations and businesses fail to meet environmental standards or find legal ways to circumvent them (see Green, 1990:135–136; Coleman, 1985:33–39).

In Missouri, the entire population of Times Beach was forced to evacuate because dioxin-tainted waste oil was sprayed on the roads to keep the dust down. Times Beach is now a modern ghost town, its people suffering the delayed effects of dioxin (called "Agent Orange" during the Vietnam War). Many thousands of industrial workers will become ill or die because they must work under conditions that needlessly expose them to the very real threat of cancer and severe respiratory ailments. Those in the rubber, steel, asbestos, coal, and chemical industries are especially vulnerable to such diseases. One of the most costly industrial disasters of all time has been tied to "unlawful, willful, malicious, and wanton" disregard for human safety—the December 1984 gas leak at the Union Carbide pesticide plant in Bhopal, India, which claimed 2000 lives and injured 150,000 to 200,000 more. In its recent judicial inquiry, the Indian government charged Union Carbide with moral responsibility and legal liability for the leak. For its part, the company has accepted moral responsibility but denies any criminal negligence (*St. Louis Post-Dispatch*, November 29 and December 1, 1985). It remains to be seen what the courts will decide.

As with most forms of crime, the risks and costs of being victimized by occupational crimes are not borne equally. The young, poor, and elderly are especially vulnerable to environmental crimes and to frauds of all sorts. As the population ages, we can expect to see more and more victimization of the elderly—not only by fast-talking salespeople, but also by corporate marketers who capitalize on their fear of change, their susceptibility to illness and need for health maintenance, their fear of having inadequate insurance, and their loneliness.

Recent congressional testimony has disclosed just how extensive is victimization of the elderly by the insurance industry (Associated Press, July 27, 1991). U.S. Representative Ron Wyden reported on a series of undercover investigations and random videotaping of sales presentations: "[N]ot a single one was truly straight with their elderly customers. Every single agent, selected at random, either misrepresented their policy, engaged in abusive sales practices or flat-out lied." The report indicts more than the individual salespeople, arguing that loopholes, fine print, marketing strategies, and rhetoric from the Health Insurance Association of America create an industry climate that fosters abuses. As for the business of insuring elderly people, the report noted that the profitability of long-term health insurance can be inferred from growth in the number of companies offering it: from 36 or so in 1980 to 143 or so in 1991.

Crimes for Personal Gain

This section explores occupational crimes that are primarily committed by individuals for their own gain, and in violation of loyalty to their employer or client. The crimes include embezzlement, many high-tech offenses, "fiddles," political corruption, and a host of small business crimes.

Embezzlement

As was observed in the preceding chapter, embezzlement first found its way into the statute books as a modification designed to plug gaps in the existing common law. Until 1529, criminal liability did not arise when servants kept valuable goods that were in their legal possession by virtue of their role as bailees for their masters. This meant that servants had committed no crime if they "stole" things from their masters that had come into their possession in their role as servants. Responding to the obvious risk posed for employers by this gap in the common law, Henry VIII made the "imbezilment" of such goods a felony.

Still, the new law did not cover cases in which a third party gave servants or employees cash or goods for delivery to their masters, only to have it pocketed by the servant. In these cases the only recourse for the employer was to institute civil proceedings against the "thief." The legal situation might well have remained this way had it not been for the expansion of commerce and trade and the subsequent rise of banking, accounting, and related businesses. The financial interests of the business community, coupled with its growing reliance on the role of the trusted employee/agent, moved members to look for additional protection under the criminal law. With interests at stake, the business community sought modifications in the existing laws. Thus in 1799 Parliament once again extended the embezzlement provisions and later added the crimes of "false accounting" and "fraudulent conversion" to cover other features of the business relationship between employers and those working for them in positions of financial trust.

As a percentage of all arrests, arrests for embezzlement are infrequent—only 0.1 percent in 1990 (Federal Bureau of Investigation, 1991:174). When arrests for embezzlement are made, the suspect is usually a white, middle-class, middle-aged male, quite unlike the prevailing stereotype of the criminal. However, this description of the typical official offender may not be an accurate portrayal of the bulk of people embezzling from their employers or clients (see Gottfredson and Hirschi, 1990).

When the embezzler is a woman, she is usually a lower-level employee rather than an executive (Daly, 1988). Indications are that male and female rates of embezzlement are converging (Hirschi and Gottfredson, 1987:961). It is not clear why this is so, but some believe it reflects increased employment of women in positions of financial trust, while others attribute it to the economic marginalization of many women, who find themselves in financial straits with families to support. It is probably a combination of both.

The embezzler has been called "the respectable criminal" (Cressey, 1965). Respectable or not, estimates of the frequency and costs of embezzlement are staggering. In 1967, the President's Commission on Law Enforcement and the Administration of Justice put the annual cost at more than $200 million; that figure is dwarfed by a 1974 estimate of $4 billion. Today's figure is certainly much higher.

The respectability of embezzlers mentioned by many authors acknowledges not only the relatively high occupational status of many offenders but also the fact that they rarely have a delinquent or criminal record prior to their embezzling activities and rarely think of themselves as real criminals. According to a study of 1001 embezzlers conducted some years ago, the typical male embezzler is the epitome of the moderately successful family man. He is ". . . thirty-five, married, has one or two children. He lives in a respectable neighborhood and is probably buying his own home. He drives a low or medium priced car and his yearly income is in the top forty percent of the nation's personal income distribution" (Jaspan and Black, 1960:24–25). The female embezzler also fits the picture of a respectable American, though her income was found to be in the bottom third of the nation's income distribution—a reflection of sex discrimination in jobs and salaries more than anything else.

In *Other People's Money*, Donald Cressey (1953) describes his interviews with 133 embezzlers in penitentiaries in Illinois, Indiana, and California. His findings regarding the "etiology" of embezzlement—the factors leading up to it—show that embezzlers typically committed offenses after (1) coming up against a "nonshareable" financial problem; (2) recognizing that they could secretly resolve the problem by taking advantage of their positions of financial trust; and (3) gathering an assortment of rationalizations and justifications, so that they could retain a self-conception in which they were still worthy of financial trust.

By a *nonshareable* problem Cressey means almost any kind of financial difficulty the individual feels cannot be resolved by enlisting the help of another. It could be some unusual family expense or gambling debts, once thought the major cause of embezzlement. It could even be linked to attempts to keep up a particular standard of living. Rationalization occurs before or during the act of embezzling. Many of Cressey's subjects, and especially those who had been independent businesspeople, reasoned that they would be merely "borrowing" the money or that it really belonged to them anyway. The embezzlers-to-be often argued that they were merely adhering to a standard business practice, borrowing against future earnings. Looked at sequentially, then, a nonshareable problem leads to the search for a personal and secret solution; a position of financial trust provides the means to solve the problem; and rationalization provides the excuse.

Cressey's explanation of embezzlement is not without its critics. One was put forward by Karl Schuessler (1954). Schuessler noted that Cressey's generalization, based as it is on an *ex post facto* (after the fact) inductive analysis using only actual offenders, sits upon a weak methodological foundation and cannot be verified:

> The finding that all cases in the sample had a single set of circumstances in common does not, unhappily, prove that all persons in such circumstances will embezzle. The empirical validation would require an unselected group of persons having in common the hypothesized circumstances who then should all subsequently display the expected behavior. Needless to say, Cressey's proposition is impossible to test. (p. 604)

A different criticism comes from Gwynn Nettler (1974), whose own study could not substantiate Cressey's emphasis on the nonshareable financial problem as an impetus to embezzlement. Nettler's embezzlers were apparently driven to their crimes by temptation and avarice, and their jobs provided the opportunity and the means. A study of female embezzlers also challenges Cressey's explanation. Dorothy Zeitz (1981) found that her subjects were more likely to justify their crimes in terms of family needs than in terms of a nonshareable problem.

Another point being made by some criminologists is that embezzlement is more likely to be trivial and persistent than a carefully thought-out, last-ditch solution to a pressing financial problem (Gottfredson and Hirschi, 1990; Croall, 1989). This view receives some support from private security experts, who recommend that the best way to find embezzlers is to give employees a vacation that requires someone else to take over their duties: Embezzlers will resist the offer for fear their schemes will be uncovered in their absence. A recent case came to light at my university precisely because the clerk involved had not taken a vacation for over a year and thus drew the suspicions of her supervisor. She had been taking relatively small amounts of money over the course of three or four years, though in the aggregate her embezzlement reached hundreds of thousands of dollars. In any event, it does not look as if the explanation of embezzlement is a matter of consensus yet.

"High-Tech" Crime: The Criminal and the Computer

Technological change advances criminal opportunities as well as noncriminal ones. Nowhere is this more in evidence than in the realm of electronics. In this era of high technology, electronic brains and silicon chips rule much of the behavior of people and machines. The more computers there are and the more things they can be used for, the more opportunities there are for computer crime. Estimates of the annual losses from computer-related crimes go as high as $5 billion, and in all likelihood the figure will go much higher (Kolata, 1982; Rockwell, 1990; McEwen, 1989).

The range of computer crimes is vast and growing. Examples of what criminally motivated people can do when they have access to computer technology are shown in Box 7.2. Embezzlement, industrial espionage, theft of computer services, invasion of privacy, copyright violations, destruction of information or programs, falsification of data, and a host of fraudulent transactions are just a few of the computer-related abuses that are possible.

The potential for computer crime is staggering, and that fact is now recognized in legislative and enforcement circles. Most of the preventive work so far initiated, though, is organized and paid for privately. Hundreds of companies have sprung up in recent years selling advice and technology to counteract the new breed of high-tech criminal. The 1980s have been a profitable decade for both computer criminals and those in the business of prevention.

As an instrument of crime the computer may be used to victimize individuals, one's own company, competitive companies, the government, the public at large, even other countries. Criminal use of computers may be incidental to the main purpose of a business; it may be the central activity of a business; or it may be an activity that violates loyalty and fidelity to an employer. Because of this variety it is more properly viewed as a means of crime rather than a type of crime. In addition, not all people with access to computer technology have the same opportunities to convert that access to criminal activity or the same ability to carry out the activity. It is likely that computer crime, like organized crime and some forms of professional theft, will be marked by conspiracy and organization, and as it becomes more difficult for individuals to counteract security measures, this characteristic should become even more marked.

Fiddling at Work: Part of the Hidden Economy

Operating within the legitimate world of work is a *hidden economy* in which goods and services are produced, stolen, or exchanged on the sly. There is no official record of this "fiddling," and the income obtained from it is rarely, if ever, taxed. Much of the activity is itself criminal, though rarely thought of as such by the participants or the general public. Stuart Henry (1978:4–5) illustrates the range of activities that make up the hidden economy:

> A number of specific fiddles make up hidden property crime. These include . . . taking company stock home to doing jobs "on the side." . . . Personal use of the firm's telephone, photocopying, or mailing service accounts for a certain amount of the kind of fiddling which may be claimed as perks, and overestimates of petrol [gasoline], food and travel allowances that appear as inflated expense accounts might also be seen in this light. In addition, there are a number of other . . . fiddles . . . such as short-changing, overloading, overestimating, under-the-counter selling, buying off-the-back-of-a-lorry [truck] goods, fiddling time, dodging fares, and smuggling duty-free goods. Nor should we neglect the numerous tax and social security fiddles involving undeclared income, falsely claimed allowances and misrepresented welfare

benefts and rebate claims; nor corporate fiddles, such as computer fraud and industrial bribery.

Collectively, these fiddles cost billions of dollars. In America, theft by retail employees alone costs close to $10 billion, and Gerald Mars (1983) cites estimates that 10 percent of the total U.S. gross national product is made up of unregistered production and service work, untaxed moonlighting, and other undeclared income. A recent survey of top management representing large and small firms across the United States found that no single generalization adequately describes the considerable differences in the nature and seriousness of employee crime across companies. However, executives were more likely to think that petty thefts, small frauds, and abuse of services are a more serious problem than large-scale thefts and frauds, violence, or sabotage (Baker and Westin, 1987).

This section focuses on pilferage on the job. There are many forms: Sometimes it is casual, sometimes systematic and repetitive; sometimes workers pilfer alone, at other times in more or less organized groups; and sometimes the pilferage victimizes the employer, sometimes the customer or client, and sometimes other workers. However, cash is rarely stolen directly, and the income obtained through fiddling at work is generally considered secondary to that obtained legitimately (Henry, 1978).

Mars (1983) argues that certain jobs are associated with certain kinds of pilfering and pilferers. He identifies four types of work situations depending on the extent to which jobs constrain and insulate workers or foster reciprocity and competition among them and the extent to which they give workers group support and control. Job pilferers can be categorized as hawks, donkeys, wolves, or vultures.

Hawks   Hawks are found in jobs that stress individuality, competition, autonomy, and creativity. The jobs also have weak group support because workers largely control their own activities. Independent salespersons, successful journalists, small-business people, academics, and other professionals are likely to be hawks, but so too are waiters, fairground buskers, and owner-operator cabdrivers. Hawk fiddles usually involve the manipulation of time and work performance, and the scale of the fiddle increases with the status of the fiddler. Mars shows how accountants, lawyers, physicians, management consultants, and even university lecturers are able to capitalize on their status and freedom from group control. Favorite fiddles of hawks are padding expense accounts and charging for work not actually performed. The risk that hawks face is generally not that their employers or colleagues will find out—they usually know about and accept fiddles as an integral part of the business—but, rather, that the public in general will find out and react with "envy, resentment, and occasional outrage" (Mars, 1983:49).

Donkeys   Donkeys are in jobs characterized by isolation and relatively rigid constraints. Assembly-line workers, supermarket cashiers, and retail sales-

Box 7.2 ■ Types of Computer Crimes

Given that computer crimes cover a variety of different illegal activities, it is beneficial . . .
to classify computer crimes into categories based on common characteristics. Five
categories are reflected [below]:

- Internal computer crimes
- Telecommunications and telephone crimes
- Computer manipulation crimes
- Computers in support of crimes
- Thefts of hardware and software

Categories of Computer Crimes

Internal Computer Crimes	**Support of Criminal Enterprises**
■ Trojan horses ■ Logic bombs ■ Trap doors ■ Viruses	■ Databases to support drug distributions ■ Databases to record client information

Telecommunications Crimes	**Hardware/Software Thefts**
■ Phreaking ■ Hacking ■ Illegal bulletin boards ■ Misuses of telephone systems	■ Software piracy ■ Thefts of computers ■ Thefts of microprocessor chips ■ Thefts of trade secrets

Computer Manipulation Crimes	
■ Embezzlements ■ Frauds	

Internal computer crimes are alterations to programs that result in the performance of
unauthorized functions within a computer system. These offenses, usually committed by
computer programmers, require an extensive amount of computer knowledge. A
programmer may, for example, change an existing program so that it appears to operate
normally but in fact performs unwanted functions whenever certain logical conditions
are satisfied. Under these conditions, the program may erase files, change data, or cause
the system to crash. Because these crimes have been around for years, they have been
given names, such as *Trojan horses, logic bombs,* and *trap doors,* to indicate different
programming techniques for performing the unauthorized functions.

    Viruses, the most recent type of internal computer crime, are sets of instructions that
not only perform unauthorized functions, but also secretly attach themselves to other
programs. With this self-propagating process, they spread through a system and to other
systems when the "infected" program is copied or transmitted. Viruses may be relatively
benign, such as a virus that merely displays an innocuous message on the computer
screen. . . . At the same time, the destructive instructions can be embedded in other
programs which may later be executed on other systems. . . .

    Telecommunications crimes involve the illegal access or use of computer systems
over telephone lines. A *hacking* program tries to find valid access codes for a computer

system by continually calling the system with randomly generated codes. With a valid code found in this manner, the system can be accessed and costs diverted to an innocent customer. Use of a hacking program constitutes unauthorized access to a system, and access codes generated by a hacking program are stolen property.

Misuses of telephone systems are another form of telecommunications crimes. *Phone phreaking* is telephone fraud carried out by electronic devices that emit tones signalling normal long-distance transactions to the telephone system. These illegal devices trick the telephone system into believing that long-distance charges are being legitimately processed. Another misuse of a telephone system is to take over a telephone line for one's own advantage. In [one] case . . . an individual found a way to avoid the internal accountability for long-distance calls and then sold time to friends for international calls. The increased sophistication in telephone systems has not served as a deterrent from trying to find new ways of avoiding long-distance charges.

Computer manipulation crimes involve the changing of data or creation of records in a system for the specific advancement of another crime. Virtually all embezzlements in financial institutions require the creation of false accounts or modifications of data in existing accounts in order to perform the embezzlements. The perpetrator need not know computer programming but must have a good sense of how to operate the system. The embezzlement offense will always be the main charge but computer crime charges (e.g., unauthorized access to a computer system) may also be made. . . .

Computer systems may also serve in *support of criminal enterprises*. In [one] case . . . a microcomputer system assisted the daily operations of a prostitution ring. . . . Data-bases developed by illegal drug operators for tracking distribution also fall into this category. . . .

Computer bulletin boards are another source of information to support illegal activities. Bulletin boards allow for the storing of information to be retrieved by someone dialing into the system. They are usually established for a specific audience, such as boards established by computer clubs to share information among members. There are probably over 10,000 bulletin boards now in exsistence across the country covering virtually every subject imaginable.

There are several examples of how bulletin boards have been used in support of criminal activities. In two . . . cases . . . bulletin boards were used to relay illegally obtained access codes into computer service companies. Pedophiles have been known to leave suggestive messages on bulletin boards, and other sexually oriented messages have been found on bulletin boards. Members of cults and sects have also communicated through bulletin boards. While the storing of information on bulletin boards may not by itself be illegal, the use of bulletin boards has certainly advanced many illegal activities.

Software and hardware thefts are the final category in this typology. A common offense is *software piracy*, defined as the unauthorized copying of a proprietary package. The most blatant form of piracy occurs when someone purchases a proprietary program, makes copies, and sells the copies for profit. Stealing *trade secrets* about products under development is another type of theft. . . . These offenses generally occur in parts of the country known for research and development of computer systems. Because these areas also manufacture computer products, *thefts of hardware*, from microcomputer chips to large mainframes, are not uncommon. While hardware and software thefts may be dismissed as merely thefts on a grander scale, they are computer crimes because the computers are the target of an illegal activity.

Source: J. Thomas McEwen (1989). *Dedicated Computer Crime Units.* Washington, D.C.: U.S. Department of Justice.

people are good examples. "The donkey type of fiddle is an appropriate response to this minimal autonomy. Since the job isolates the worker, the worker fiddles in isolation" (Mars, 1983:71). New workers may learn of fiddling among their fellows, but there is no group support for it, nor is it practiced as a group activity. Bar stewards who give short-measured drinks and pocket the difference between what each bottle would have brought in and actually does bring in, and cashiers who fiddle change or pocket money after ringing "no sale" on the till are examples of donkey fiddlers. Mars observes that donkey fiddles are often not motivated by material gain but, rather, by the worker's greater measure of personal control. In addition, the absence of group controls may give rise to excessive fiddling, as when a short-order waiter skimmed $150 a day for a year before being found out (Mars, 1983:87).

Wolves Wolf fiddlers operate in packs and are found in jobs in which the work is organized into crews: longshoremen, miners, prison guards, and garbage collectors are found in "wolfpack" jobs. The group comes to exercise a lot of control over the individual, and pilferage is organized and controlled by the group. Individualists are not welcome, and membership in the wolfpack is not automatic, but through acceptance by other members. Members are held together by mutual dependence and trust, with much testing of the latter.

Dock pilferage by longshoremen in Newfoundland is typical of the wolfpack. Longshore workgangs are close-knit, with controlled membership and a ranking system based on skill and trust that effectively controls any particular member's access to cargo by allocating work responsibilities. Only through access to cargo can a dockworker pilfer, and so jobs with such access are essential. On the other hand, the nature of dockwork makes it important for those with access also to have group support in order to pull off a fiddle. Since individual workers rarely have both access *and* support, dock pilferage remains group centered, and there is less room for the excesses sometimes found in the pilfering of donkeys and hawks.

Donald Horning's (1970) study of pilferage in a midwestern electronics assembly plant illustrates the power of the group in wolfpack jobs. Horning interviewed 88 operatives and found pilferage a common practice. However, group norms dictated what was pilferable and what was not. Three types of property were distinguished: (1) company property, consisting of buildings, fixtures, heavy machinery, power tools, and expensive electronic components; (2) personal property, consisting of anything known to belong to co-workers or marked with someone's name, such as wallets, lunch boxes, modified tools, and clothing; and (3) property of uncertain ownership, for example, unmarked clothing, nuts, bolts, scrap, waste, small tools, loose money, and so forth. Items of the third type, but not others, were considered fair game.

Widely shared definitions of the situation gave workers their rationalizations and justifications for their pilferage: "It's a corporation. . . . It's not like taking from one person"; or "The company doesn't mind, they've got plenty . . . they're not losing anything on what I take"; or "Everyone's doing it." Although it is not clear that these rationalizations are invoked before pilfering, as Cressey argued in the case of embezzlement, a number of factors point to this conclusion. First, group attitudes defining what is appropriate to steal prevail despite the arrival and departure of particular workers. Second, these attitudes are learned on the job, not brought to it, and they constitute the normative framework within which workers shape their own subsequent behavior. Third, the fact that pilferage of personal property is extremely rare, whereas that of property of uncertain ownership is pervasive, indicates that the appropriate distinctions were made before the thefts were committed. In other words, rather than rationalizations merely excusing behavior after it has occurred, the discrimination in choice of items suggests action guided by group definitions.

Vultures   Vultures hold jobs that offer autonomy and freedom but are subject to overarching bureaucratic control that encourages group influence. Vulture jobs are selling jobs, postal delivery, truck driving and other traveling jobs, taxi driving, and many service jobs. Fiddling tends to be exercised individually, but mutual self-interest keeps employees tied in a bond of sometimes uneasy cooperation. The relative instability of vulture occupations means that under the surface of cooperation there is competition, and when a particular fiddle threatens others' jobs, they close ranks against the offender.

I myself experienced a vulture fiddle. Many years ago I worked during a college vacation as a delivery driver for a well-known London department store. On the first day of work I learned from my co-driver that two breakfasts, a two-hour lunch period, and an hour-long afternoon tea break on top of seven hours of delivering always produced a healthy overtime check. I also learned that my co-driver expected me to conform to this schedule and that if I did not, it would not look good for the other drivers who were also doing the same thing. The company supposedly knew about the time fiddle, and so long as it did not become unreasonable, store management accepted it, I was told, in return for the drivers' staying nonunion.

Political Corruption

This chapter would certainly be incomplete if it ignored occupational crime in government and politics. Political corruption exists when office-holders in government and politics violate the laws regulating their official conduct so as to benefit themselves or their associates, or use the power and influence associated with their office to induce others to commit crimes (for a detailed discussion, see Coleman, 1989:102–112).

Forms of Political Corruption   Political corruption manifests itself in two different, though often related, forms: (1) activities designed to bring about economic gain and (2) activities designed to perpetuate or increase political power. Government officials who accept or demand monetary kickbacks in return for legislation favorable to some individual or special group are engaged in corrupt activities that promise economic gains. Politicians who arrange to have cronies stuff ballot boxes with the names of nonexistent voters are engaged in corrupt practices designed to keep them in office or to put them there. Needless to say, those who gain economically from corrupt activities may also gain political power, and those who gain political power may also gain financially. Thus it is sometimes difficult to separate the economic from the power dimension of political corruption.

It is pointless to speculate on the extent of political corruption. There is simply no way of knowing, and one is unlikely ever to find out with any certainty. In fact, it could be that the more corruption one knows about, the less there actually is, for corrupt practices thrive under a cloak of secrecy and indifference. What can be said with reasonable assurance is that the opportunities for corruption are probably greater today than they have ever been. As governments have come to dominate more and more areas of social life and have expanded their roles as employers, producers, consumers, taxers, and spenders, those in political jobs have found an expanding number of opportunities to reap illicit benefits from their position in the occupational structure.

Finding out about political corruption is not easy, and this is as true for the criminologist as it is for the general public. One reason is the insider-outsider barrier that politicians erect in their dealings with others who are not part of the political establishment. Another is the cronyism characterizing relations among politicians and their friends in business and government. This leads to a kind of "mutual aid society" and encourages a "politics is politics" attitude among insiders, who would rather look the other way than make public trouble for a colleague. During the entire history of the United States Congress, only 7 senators and 19 representatives have been censured by their colleagues, although others have resigned before they could be censured.

A third reason for the difficulty of learning about political corruption is that the agencies responsible for policing the politicians are themselves run by politicians. If an investigation of a particular official or agency is called for, it will usually be pursued without fanfare and rarely will result in the pressing of formal charges. Even when an investigation is reliably known to be underway, heads of the responsible agencies will often deny it. Fourth, there are no official statistics on the kinds of occupational crime committed by those in politics and government. One looks in vain for "official misconduct," "high crimes and misdemeanors," "bribery," "influence peddling," and so forth, in either the Part I or Part II offense lists published by the FBI in their annual *Uniform Crime Reports*. In fact, the only specifically occupational crime listed at all is embezzlement, which victimizes the establishment.

Political corruption is publicized primarily through the efforts of journalists and those who keep watch on government in the public interest, for example, Ralph Nader and Common Cause. Chicago has borne the brunt of media scrutiny for years, which has not blunted its reputation as the most politically corrupt city in America. From 1985 to 1988, federal grand juries indicted 265 public officials and government employees for corruption (*St. Louis Post-Dispatch*, October 16, 1988). Often, corruption comes to light because persons involved in it turn informer and approach the media or federal authorities. Someone who has been indicted may also "snitch" on others as part of a plea bargain.

Crimes for Money Political crimes that come to light are usually notable because they have been committed by high officials, have involved substantial losses to the taxpayer, or have represented a systematic and extensive violation of public trust or civil rights. During the last few years, political corruption at the national and international levels has so dominated the headlines that local scandals seem mild by comparison. Actually, the victimization brought about by local corruption may have a more far-reaching and harmful effect on the lives of Americans. When, as happened recently in a midsized Illinois city, school board officials misappropriate thousands of dollars in school funds, it may take years to overcome the damage to local education, not to mention public trust.

In the course of their political careers, government officials sometimes find their past catching up with them after they have moved to national prominence. Such was the case with former Vice-President Spiro Agnew, and former Labor Secretary Raymond Donovan. It was revealed in Agnew's case that while governor of Maryland, and earlier while a county official, he had received kickbacks from contractors doing business with the county and state governments. Upon these disclosures, Agnew resigned the vice-presidency and subsequently pleaded "no contest" to an income tax violation charge ("no contest" is not a plea of guilty but subjects the defendant to conviction). In Donovan's case, grand jury indictments charged him with fraud and grand larceny while he was in the construction business. Another case involved Judge Otto Kerner, formerly the governor of Illinois. Kerner was tied to an Illinois scandal involving offers of racetrack stock to politicians. Subsequently he was convicted of numerous criminal offenses, including perjury, and became the first federal judge ever to spend time in prison. These cases, in which bribery and kickbacks were prominent, clearly involve corruption for economic gain.

Political corruption for economic gain is encouraged by the tight links between politics and business. In addition to the fact that business provides financial support for political campaigns and governments disperse billions of dollars worth of contracts to industry, many government officials retain a financial interest in their business pursuits while in office. Members of Congress remain active in businesses ranging from real estate and insurance to construction, law, oil, and gas. Temptations to abuse their political connections abound, particularly when proposed laws or government contracts influence their personal finances and those of business colleagues.

The extensiveness of the connection between business and politics is illustrated by a 1976 international scandal involving payoffs to foreign government officials by multinational corporations based in the United States. Uncovered in the post-Watergate period of house cleaning, the scandal brought charges of payoffs to politicians and government officials around the world for their aid in granting lucrative government contracts to U.S. corporations. By early 1976, 40 corporations had been accused of such bribes and other questionable payoff practices, and some of the United States' largest corporations were admitting involvement. For example, Gulf Oil admitted paying $4 million to the South Korean ruling party and $460,000 to Bolivian officials; Burroughs Corporation admitted $1.5 million in improper payments to foreign officials. Aircraft companies such as Lockheed, Northrop, and McDonnell Douglas admitted by far the largest bribes, payoffs, and questionable commissions. As sellers of military and civilian aircraft, these companies stood to gain or lose billions of dollars in government contracts, and they aggressively pursued any avenue to acquisition of those contracts. Lockheed was charged with paying $202 million to foreign officials in Japan, the Netherlands, Turkey, Italy, and elsewhere. More recently McDonnell Douglas was indicted in federal court for paying $1 million in bribes to Pakistani International Airlines officials, and in 1985, General Dynamics and four other defense contractors admitted paying around $6.5 million to a South Korean general whose consulting firm helped the American corporations sell military equipment to South Korea (*St. Louis Post-Dispatch*, October 2, 1985).

Fraud and the Defense Industry   Companies like General Dynamics, Rockwell International, and McDonnell Douglas have prospered through government contracts. Indeed, it is from these contracts that many firms make most of their profits. For example, in 1984, Boeing made 93.7 percent of its profits from government contracts, McDonnell Douglas 97.8 percent, and General Dynamics 96.7 percent (*St. Louis Post-Dispatch*, December 15, 1985).

Because of the enormous sums of money involved—General Dynamics did $6 *billion* business with the Pentagon in 1984 alone—and the bureaucratic organization of government and large businesses, there are both the incentive and the opportunity for various types of fraud. The *St. Louis Post-Dispatch* (December 15–22, 1985) investigated the business of defense fraud and found many examples. In 1985, allegations of cost and/or labor mischarging were being investigated against McDonnell Douglas, Rockwell International, General Dynamics, Lockheed, Boeing, General Electric, United Technologies, Raytheon, Litton Industries, Grumman, Westinghouse, Ford, Northrop, Motorola, and others. In 1990, Northrop pled guilty to 34 charges of fraud, and was fined $17 million (*St. Louis Post Dispatch*, September 26, 5B).

When it seemed that the scandal had pretty well blown over, another flurry of subpoenas and warrants appeared, directed at many of the same companies. The newer charges have included claims that McDonnell Douglas received "inside" information from the Department of Defense to help the company in its efforts to sell over 170 F18 Hornet fighters in a fierce competition with General Dynamics (*St. Louis Post-Dispatch*, June 15, 1988).

Yet again, in November, 1991, more charges were filed against defense contractors (*St. Louis Post-Dispatch*, November 1, A1).

Another set of charges centered around Wedtech Corporation and its ties to U.S. Representative Mario Biaggi and former U.S. Attorney General Edwin Meese. Over a number of years, Wedtech received various defense contracts, some earmarked for minority-owned firms (which Wedtech was not), and some subcontracted from other firms. Investigation showed that Wedtech was primarily a racketeering venture in which millions of dollars changed hands in a series of bribes and extortion payments. Biaggi was subsequently sentenced to 146 years and fined $7,422,000. Edwin Meese has so far escaped indictment, though the conclusion of a special prosecutor was that his actions violated the spirit if not the letter of the law (*New York Times*, June 30, July 12, 16, 19, and August 5, 1988).

ABSCAM   The 1980s saw another major scandal involving crimes for money, this time by members of Congress. In the undercover FBI operation known as ABSCAM, one of its operatives posed as a wealthy Arab businessman seeking to obtain residency permits. Contacts were set up between the "Arab" and various congressmen to whom large sums of money were offered in exchange for help. The FBI videotaped the meetings, and when the prosecutions eventually took place, the public saw films of elected representatives glee-fully filling their pockets and briefcases with money.

Although all the offenders were initially convicted, some later filed successful appeals. These were heralded by many in Washington as the fitting end to an affair in which the FBI, not members of Congress, was the culprit. Accusations of entrapment and violation of privacy flowed from all sides, and if anyone emerged tarnished by the episode it was the FBI and the Department of Justice. Indignation like that directed at ABSCAM is noticeably lacking when similar police practices are directed at drug traffickers.

Crimes for Power   In regard to corruption for purposes of acquiring, retaining, or increasing one's political power, the Watergate scandal immediately comes to mind. Brought to light following the uncovering of a June 1972 burglary attempt at the Democratic National Committee headquarters in the Watergate hotel and apartment complex in Washington, D.C., the Watergate affair resulted in the first resignation of a U.S. president and touched people in all areas of national politics. Due in part to vigorous investigative journalism by *Washington Post* reporters Carl Bernstein and Bob Woodward, the American public was given a two-year, in-depth look at political corruption at its worst. Not only had the White House been deeply involved in the scandals, but also included were a former secretary of the treasury, the attorney general of the United States, officials of the FBI, CIA, and Internal Revenue Service, persons connected with organized crime, international terrorists, and even some street criminals.

The central theme around which the Watergate affair revolved was clearly one of political power. The involvement of the Committee to Re-Elect the

President, the activities of White House staffers, and the routine subversive manipulation of government agencies by Richard Nixon and his allies bear this out. Here was an incident, or rather a combination of incidents, in which maintaining and extending power stood as the central goal. The string of events began in early 1972, when the office of Daniel Ellsberg's psychiatrist was burglarized so that evidence from the files could be used to political advantage. During the presidential campaign of that year, Nixon's supporters and staffers committed various illegal actions: They used the U.S. Postal Service for fraudulent and libelous purposes, an aspect of the "dirty tricks" used to discredit Democratic opponents; the Watergate break-in itself was for the purpose of "bugging" the Democratic National Committee headquarters and scrutinizing its files; they pressured the IRS to harass political opponents and Nixon's alleged enemies; they encouraged the FBI and CIA to obstruct justice so that these and other criminal activities would not come to light and, if they were revealed, would not be linked with the White House; they paid "hush money" to the Watergate burglars; and they misused public funds and solicited campaign contributions in violation of federal laws. Eventually, White House staffers were fired and government officials forced to resign in a last-ditch effort to plug the ever-widening holes in the defenses around the Oval Office.

In the summer of 1974 the House of Representatives' Judiciary Committee voted to impeach President Nixon. He was charged with obstruction of justice and failure to carry out his constitutional oath and duty to uphold the laws of the United States. He resigned on August 9, 1974. Much still remains unknown about political corruption in Richard Nixon's administration. Nixon himself was pardoned by President Gerald Ford, making it unlikely that the true nature of his offenses will ever come to light. One is certainly left wondering whether anything would have come to light had it not been for the ill-fated break-in at the Watergate and the tenacity of two young reporters in search of news.

The Iran-Contra Affair Watergate centered on protection of the political fortunes of people in power. It was a domestic scandal, although had Nixon's cronies succeeded, the fall-out would have been international in scope. The Iran-Contra affair, arguably the worst scandal during the administration of Ronald Reagan, was an international conspiracy designed to secure the release of American hostages in Lebanon through illegal sale of arms to Iran, and to shore up the Contra rebels in Nicaragua through illegal diversion of the arms sales money to the rebels.

Investigations by congressional committees and by special prosecutors implicated members of the White House staff, the military, and the Central Intelligence Agency, and documented the involvement of businessmen and government officials from three continents. National Security Council aide Oliver North was at the center of the scandal, but other senior government officials were also implicated, though few have been charged and some convictions (including North's) were overturned on appeal.

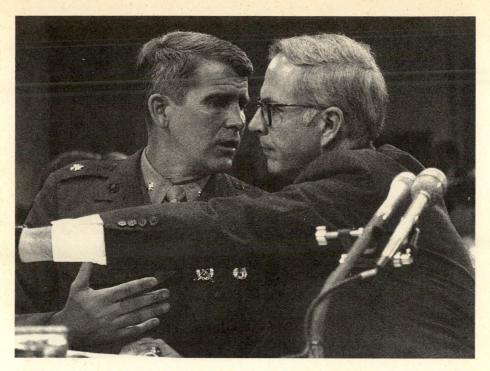

In hearings before Congress, Col. Oliver North and other witnesses involved in the Iran-Contra affair described an international conspiracy that is still under investigation by special prosecutors more than five years after it was first uncovered.

It is interesting that the defense most often presented in political corruption cases not involving personal gain is that "I did what I thought was in the best interests of the country." This appeal to national security diverts attention from the core issue (willful violation of the law by those entrusted to uphold it), protects the public image of the wrongdoers as people of honor who go out on a limb to protect the national interest, and conveys the idea that the accused have been wronged and are therefore the real victims. It also helps legitimize covert crimes by government officials and cloaks the secretive underside of national politics with an aura of decency and honor: The people are doing their best to protect "Good" against "Evil." Appeals to higher loyalty are not confined to political criminals, it turns out, but are also invoked by common-or-garden offenders and juvenile delinquents (see the discussion of "techniques of neutralization" in Chapter 15 for more on this).

Crimes Incidental to, and in Furtherance of, Business Operations

Some occupational crimes arise in connection with business pursuits but are not the central purpose of the business (Edelhertz, 1970:19–20). They are committed on behalf of business interests, sometimes by individuals, sometimes by groups; they surface among the self-employed and among executives of companies large and small. The discussion of such crimes here will concentrate on corporate activities that violate laws governing commerce and trade. Antitrust violations contribute to the persistence of a "closed enterprise system," the very antithesis of what American business is supposed to be (see Cullen, Maakestad, and Cavender, 1987:59).

Restraint of Trade

Among the occupational crimes committed by corporate decision makers on behalf of their organizations are those violating state and federal laws dealing with restraint of trade. The first relevant federal statute was the Sherman Antitrust Act of 1890. Designed to curb the threat to a competitive, free enterprise economy posed by the nineteenth-century spread of trusts and monopolies, this act made it a criminal misdemeanor for individuals or organizations to engage in restraint of trade by cominbing or forming monopolies to that end. In 1974, Congress made restraint of trade a felony, thus making it possible for convicted offenders to receive prison terms of a year or more.

There are three principal methods of restraint of trade: (1) consolidation so as to obtain a monopoly position, (2) price fixing to achieve price uniformity, and (3) price discrimination, in which higher prices are charged to some customers and lower ones to others (Sutherland, 1949). From the standpoint of those engaging in these practices, they make sense: The less the competition and the greater the control over prices, the larger the profits. But small and independent businesses will lose business, and the public at large will face higher prices and lose its discretionary buying power.

The most common violations of restraint-of-trade laws are price fixing and price discrimination. In Sutherland's investigation of 70 of the largest American corporations over a 50-year period, violations of this sort (including the illegal use of rebates) were the most prevalent restraint-of-trade activities. Interestingly, many of the suits charging restraint of trade through price fixing and discrimination were brought by private interests rather than by the Federal Trade Commission or the Department of Justice, the two agencies given primary responsibility for enforcing restraint-of-trade provisions. In this as well as in other areas of occupational crime in which corporate decision makers break the law on behalf of their organizations, officialdom has not been at its most aggressive in ferreting out violations and bringing charges. But this should hardly come as a surprise, given the close relationship between business and politics. Indeed, in Europe and the Far East, governments have historically encouraged cartels, whose price-fixing activities are legendary.

Price-Fixing Conspiracies In 1961, 21 corporations and 45 high-ranking executives in the heavy electrical equipment industry were successfully prosecuted for criminal violations of the Sherman Antitrust Act. They had been involved in a price-fixing and bid-rigging scheme that, over nearly a decade, had bilked local, state, and federal governments (and taxpayers) out of millions of dollars on purchases averaging nearly $2 billion a year.

In carrying out their scheme—called by the trial judge "the most serious violations of the antitrust laws since the time of their passage at the turn of the century"—executives of the conspiring companies would meet secretly under fictitious names in hotel rooms around the country. Referring to those in attendance as "the Christmas card list" and to the meetings as "choir practice," the conspirators arranged prices for equipment, allocated markets and territories, and agreed on which companies would supply the low bids on pending government contracts. The participants covered their tracks well and were discovered only because officials of the Tennessee Valley Authority had received identical sealed bids on highly technical equipment. The companies involved in the conspiracy ranged from such giants in the electrical equipment business as General Electric, Westinghouse, and Allis-Chalmers, to such smaller firms as the Carrier Corporation, the I.T.E. Circuit Breaker Company, and Federal Pacific (for more on this famous price-fixing conspiracy, see Ermann and Lundman, 1982:86–95).

This price-fixing conspiracy illustrates extensive collusion among corporations who have found a way to prosper without having to compete. Needless to say, cooperation is preferred when the benefits outweigh the risks of competition. Equally important, the cooperators usually gain over those who refuse to or simply cannot participate in the collusion. This advantage is precisely what restraint-of-trade laws are designed to curb, for its consequence is obvious: Fewer firms stay in business, and the prices of goods and services rise when the survivors exercise their monopoly power, keeping new competitors away and setting artificially high prices, in effect stealing from their customers. The cost of those higher prices can be staggering. In the heavy electrical equipment conspiracy, the cost approached $3 billion, "more money than was stolen in all the country's robberies, burglaries, and larcenies during the years in which the price fixing occurred" (Geis, 1978c:281). There are countless illustrations of price-fixing, although rarely will those accused of it admit the practice. Cullen, Maakestad, and Cavender (1987:60) argue that "conspiracy to set prices has become a way of life in some industries," and ample evidence indicates this is so (see also Coleman, 1989; Simon and Eitzen, 1990; Ermann and Lundman, 1982). Regrettably, such conspiracies usually victimize those least able to afford it: the poor, young, and elderly.

Another example of a price-fixing case is one involving pharmaceutical giants American Cyanamid, Charles Pfizer, and Bristol Myers. These companies were convicted of price-fixing and other monopolistic practices in the sale of antibiotics. For example, the conspiracy involving tetracycline resulted in a total markup of 3350 percent! One hundred 250-milligram capsules cost $1.52 to produce, $20.60 at wholesale, and $51.00 at retail. After the conspiracy ended in 1971, these same capsules sold for $5.00 at retail.

Corporate Fraud: The E. F. Hutton Scheme Many Americans periodically write checks on bank deposits that have not yet "cleared"—that is, during the time lag from when money is deposited in the bank to when it is credited to the individual's account. Technically, these new checks are worthless until the corresponding deposits have cleared. When a check occasionally bounces, at worst the individual may receive a note from the bank and perhaps a returned check with an overdraft charge. But what if someone knowingly and repeatedly wrote checks in this manner in order to obtain what in effect would be interest-free loans until the deposits cleared? Such a scheme would constitute fraud. A federal investigation determined that this is exactly what officials at E. F. Hutton had been doing at over 400 banks around the country from July 1980 through February 1982 (*Business Week*, May 20 and September 23, 1985). The scheme took advantage of normal delays in check clearing, and as a result the banks gave Hutton the use of billions of dollars in interest-free funds. Significantly, this was a period when interest rates were high, at 18 to 20 percent.

Prosecutors alleged that 20 to 25 people were involved. A plea bargain resulted in no individual prosecutions; however, the company was fined $2 million for 2000 counts of fraud and was assessed $750,000 for investigation costs. A subsequent internal investigation by former U.S. Attorney General Griffin Bell resulted in the suspension and fine of 14 mid-level executives. Of more significance for E. F. Hutton was the effect of the adverse publicity. For a while profits fell, and the company's stock tumbled. In seeking to regain public confidence, the company hired respected comedian Bill Cosby for its 1986 advertising campaign. It is likely that the adverse publicity eventually will be forgotten by the public, and those in the financial community will modify their rules of cash management and otherwise go about business as usual.

Insider Trading: The Ivan Boesky Affair Perhaps the worst scandal in the history of Wall Street was uncovered by the Securities and Exchange Commission (SEC) in 1986. Ivan Boesky, a 49-year-old stock market speculator, was at the center of the scandal. Boesky made arrangements with various Wall Street executives for inside information on merger negotiations and pending corporate takeovers (*Wall Street Journal*, November 17, 1986). Such information is not available to the general public and provides an advantage that allows speculators like Boesky to reap tremendous profits. In one of Boesky's arrangements he agreed to make cash payments to Martin Siegel, an investment broker, in return for inside information. In 1984 Siegel informed Boesky that the Carnation Corporation was very likely to be sold; Boesky made a $28.3-million profit from that information. Boesky also acquired information on merger negotiations between International Telephone and Telegraph and Sperry Corporation, Coastal Corporation's takeover of American Natural Resources, and McGraw Edison's buyout (*Wall Street Journal*, November 17, 1986).

Convicted in 1989 of insider trading and other federal offenses, investment broker Michael Milken and his employer, Drexel Burnham Lambert, were fined $650 million, the largest criminal fine ever imposed in a securities case. Even so, published estimates put Milken's earnings in a four-year period at over $1 billion. Everything is relative.

The media portrayed Boesky as a brilliant overachiever whose nickname was "Ivan the Terrible" due to his daring and usually successful speculations. He was regarded as a "workaholic," typically putting in 20-hour days. He married into a wealthy family, and friends speculated that he was determined to outdo his father-in-law, who reputedly considered him something of a bum. Others who knew him suggested he was insecure. One stated: "He wanted so much to be accepted and he thought money was the only way" (*Time*, December 1, 1986).

It is possible that Boesky was driven by an overwhelming desire to excell fueled by insecurity. A more likely explanation would also take into account the structure and culture of Wall Street itself. Networking his way through Wall Street's world of high finance and fierce competition, Boesky apparently had little difficulty obtaining inside information in exchange for money and favors. Since Boesky once claimed that "there are no easy ways to make money in the securities market ... there are no esoteric tricks that enable arbitragers to outwit the system" (*Time*, November 24, 1986), his own financial success naturally drew admirers and helped provide further access to corporate inner circles. People *expect* to make money on Wall Street, and their culture and organization reinforce and facilitate that expectation.

In 1986, Boesky's worth was conservatively estimated at $200 million. When convicted of insider trading in 1987, he was fined $100 million, the largest fine in SEC history at the time, and was sentenced to three years in prison. After a 16-month period in which to get rid of his holdings, he was also permanently barred from dealing with securities.

The Savings and Loan Failures   When savings and loan companies began to fail around the country in the late 1980s, alarm bells sounded in homes and businesses everywhere and in Washington, D.C. Long thought to be among America's most stable and trustworthy institutions, the local savings and loan suddenly looked weak and vulnerable. Since the government insures savings up to $100,000 in individual accounts, small investers were not hurt; however, the aggregate cost to taxpayers will be hundreds of billions of dollars when the dust finally settles, and many individuals and corporations holding stock in failed S&Ls have collectively lost millions.

Mismanagement and mistakes in operating a business are not necessarily an indication of criminal activity. Many observers believe that the S&L collapse was a product of systemic changes resulting from the deregulatory frenzy of the Reagan years and the rise of the junk bond market. According to this view, the opportunities and incentives for S&Ls to embark on risky ventures were simply too compelling given the freeing of controls and the prospects of huge short-run profits. Furthermore, changes in regulations meant the S&Ls could now give banks a run for their money, something they had lobbied hard for.

On the other hand, as details surrounding the collapse of Lincoln Savings and Loan—the largest thrift failure in U.S. history—emerged, it became clear that deceit, conspiracy, political corruption, and all manner of financial irregularities were involved. On December 4, 1991, a Los Angeles jury convicted owner Charles H. Keating, Jr., on 17 counts of securities fraud; on April 10, 1992, he was sentenced to 10 years in prison and fined $250,000. (*St. Louis Post-Dispatch*, April 11, 1992, A1). Keating still faces federal charges, and other states may prosecute him also. Keating may be the most infamous player in the S&L scandal, but no one argues that he is unique.

Consumer Fraud: Misrepresentation in Advertising and Sales Promotion

Consumers become the victims of fraud in many different ways, including misrepresentation in advertising and sales. Misrepresentation in advertising means that what prospective buyers are told about a product is untrue, deceptive, or misleading. Sometimes the misrepresentation is in regard to the quantity of a product or the actual contents of a package or container;

sometimes it concerns the effectiveness of a product; and sometimes it is a lack of information or insufficient information regarding a product or service such that buyers are misled. An illustrative case involved Chrysler Corporation. In 1987 the company admitted selling as "new" cars that had in fact been driven by executives. Another example is an ad campaign by Ralston Purina, the makers of Puppy Chow, in which the company seemed to be claiming that its product cured cancer (*St. Louis Post-Dispatch*, November 27, 1991:B1).

The fact that a fine line divides fraudulent from legitimate sales promotion becomes evident as one considers a problem faced by nearly all businesses: creating a need for their products and services. Many of the things considered necessities today—canned foods, refrigerators, automobiles, insurance policies—either did not exist a few decades ago or were thought of as luxuries, certainly not necessities. They have come to be thought of as necessities largely because the companies selling them have convinced the public to do so. When things are necessities, people "need" to purchase them.

In their efforts to convince people of a need for goods and services, businesses use a variety of different ploys. To use a fraudulent ploy is to make false claims as to the effectiveness of a product in doing what it is supposed to do. Those who believe the claims will see a need for the product. An example is the advertising plan followed some time ago by the makers of Listerine. In their campaign, the makers sought to create a need for Listerine as a mouthwash, a fairly new idea at the time; to establish that need, they presented fake claims as to the germ-killing powers of the mixture.

Less clearly fraudulent, though possibly more dangerous to health, were the sales promotions of vaginal deodorants, discussed here by Burton Leiser:

> The creation of a need is best exemplified by a new line of products that is just emerging. The advertisers have been going all out to convince women of the need for vaginal deodorants. Full-page advertisements have appeared in women's magazines recently, and on television as well, designed to convince women of the need for these deodorants and of the effectiveness of particular brands. (1973:39)

What makes these sprays potentially dangerous is that when used regularly they may mask vaginal odor, which can be a sign of infection or disease. Also, they can themselves contribute to skin irritations and other troublesome reactions. Leiser continues:

> We may suppose that nothing false has been stated in these advertisements. But lying behind each of them there is a suppressed premise—one that the reader is expected to supply for herself—namely, the assumption that women need vaginal deodorants. But this suppressed premise is false. To be sure, every woman can consult her physician to find out whether she really needs these products, but few will ever do so. Many, worried about their attractiveness, and insecure, perhaps, over a fear that they may have an unappealing odor that they themselves cannot perceive, will accept the suppressed premise uncritically and, in the process, make the marketers of Vespre and Easy Day and similar products rich. (1973:269–270)

Sales promotion strategies such as that just described may not be fraudulent. But it is only a short step from these strategies to those the common swindler uses. Consider the activities of the Holland Furnace Company. This company was in the business of selling home heating furnaces. With some 500 offices and a sales force in the thousands, the company put its resources to work on a fraudulent sales promotion involving misrepresentation, destruction of property, and, in some cases, what amounted to extortion.

> Salesmen, misrepresenting themselves as "furnace engineers" and "safety inspectors," gained entry into their victims' homes, dismantled their furnaces, and condemned them as hazardous. They then refused to reassemble them, on the ground that they did not want to be "accessories to murder." Using scare tactics, claiming that the furnaces they "inspected" were emitting carbon monoxide and other dangerous gases, they created, in the homeowners' minds, a need for a new furnace—and proceeded to sell their own product at a handsome profit. They were so ruthless that they sold one elderly woman nine new furnaces in six years for a total of $18,000. The FTC finally forced the company to close in 1965, but in the meantime, it had done some $30 million worth of busines per year for many years. (Leiser, 1973:270)

The activities of Holland Furnace Company salespeople differ, in Leiser's view, only marginally from those who sell mouthwash, vaginal deodorants, and a host of other "necessary" products.

> The difference between the cosmetic manufacturer who is trying to persuade women that they need vaginal deodorants and the exterminator who brings his own termites to display to customers whose homes he has inspected, claiming that he found them in the foundation of the home, is one of degree only. To be sure, the advertiser does not victimize any one person to the same degree. He gets rich by extracting a little money from multitudes of women, rather than by taking a lot from a very few gullible people. He has not pulled bricks from his victim's home or dismantled her furnace. But he has produced a pocketful of termites that weren't there when he arrived. (1973:271)

With more than $20 billion spent annually on advertising, businesses are making an enormous investment in the art of persuasion. Given such an investment it is not surprising that intense pressure exists to bend the rules. Misrepresentation, deception, and outright lies surface in all advertising media. It is not just the large corporations, with their immense advertising budgets, that find themselves charged with this kind of occupational crime. Small concerns advertising in local newspapers and on billboards are just as prone to the practice.

Fraud in the Maintenance and Repair Business

When it comes to the maintenance and repair of their property, consumers inevitably depend on the services of others. Those in the business of providing maintenance and repair services thrive on this consumer dependence, and some, if not many, are quick to take advantage of the many opportunities for fraud that that dependence generates.

Maintenance and repair attracts swindlers and opens up avenues for consumer fraud precisely because typical consumers do not usually have the time, resources, or know-how to repair things themselves. Even if consumers could fix or service their property, they are induced not to: Warranty specifications threaten lapse of the product guarantee if manufacturer-approved personnel or parts are not used; the manufacturer may withhold important information about the product and its repair, delay supply of replacement parts, or use special techniques and devices that are meant to guard against work by "amateurs."

The best opportunities for fraud arise in the maintenance and repair of expensive products and those so sophisticated or specialized as to be beyond the technical expertise of most consumers. Automobiles, electrical appliances of every sort, heating and air-conditioning systems, motorized garden equipment, and a multitude of home maintenance items can be included here. The area of home improvements bristles with opportunities for fraud: (1) because of its attractiveness to consumers—there is a ready-made, or easily encouraged, demand for improvement services; (2) because consumers expect that costs will be relatively high—meaning the swindler can pad the cost of the work or offer a deal that is hard to refuse because it costs far less than the victim had expected; and (3) because even costly home improvements are readily financed through second mortgages and are tax-deductible.

Fraudulent activities in the maintenance and repair business have been found not only among fly-by-night operators who descend on a town and swindle as many customers as they can before disappearing, but also among businesses with an established clientele, a permanent address, and even a respectable name in the repair field. The fly-by-nighters use a variety of techniques ranging from the offer of special discounts, prizes, and free services to tricky financial plans, the use of inferior products and parts, and promises of work that is never done. By the time the customer realizes that he or she has been duped, the swindlers have long since disappeared.

Such fraud is not new: In 1941, investigators working for *Reader's Digest* disconnected a coil wire in the engine compartment of an automobile and then took the car to a garage for repair. In all, 347 garages in 48 states were contacted; of these, 63 percent (218) either overcharged, did unnecessary work, charged for work not done or for unneeded parts, or perpetrated similar swindles. In a similar study, investigators took a radio in which a tube had been loosened to 304 repair shops. Once again, nearly two-thirds of the shops visited swindled the customer. In another study, a watch was taken to jewelry stores through the country. The investigators had simply loosened the small screw that holds the winding wheel to the internal spring of the watch. Nearly half of the repair shops visited deliberately cheated the investigators (Riis and Patric, 1942).

Though the *Reader's Digest* study was completed nearly fifty years ago, there is no good reason to believe that the situation has changed significantly since then. Though the extent of fraudulent activities among maintenance and repair businesses is unknown and unknowable—just as is the true rate of most other forms of crime—the meager data that do surface from time to time suggest that the problem is pervasive. One estimate places the costs of home improvement rackets alone at more than $1 billion a year (Rosefsky, 1973).

Although no one kind of repair business has a monopoly on fraud, the ease with which the typical motorist can be duped into paying for unnecessary repairs and services makes fraud an attractive option for auto dealers and service stations. As Leonard and Weber (1970) have shown, auto dealers are often financially dependent on the manufacturers, who control the purse strings and determine the framework within which dealers will operate. The dealer is expected to meet sales quotas, to push the sale of service parts, and to minimize expenses incurred by the manufacturer under new car warranties. The manipulative position of manufacturers is strengthened by the fact that most dealers are in debt to the manufacturer for the physical plant, equipment, and facilities of the dealership. Dealers are thus under considerable pressure to make profits any way they can. The situation is similar for service station owners who sell name-brand gasoline under lease arrangements with the major oil companies.

A person unfortunate enough to take a car to a disreputable dealer or service station could become the victim of tire "honking" (puncturing the tire in order to sell new ones), the "white smoke trick" (spraying chemicals into a hot engine to produce a cloud of smoke), "short sticking" (not putting the oil dip stick all the way down, so that it looks as if more oil is needed), and a host of other fraudulent practices. In 1992, disclosures from an undercover investigation in California showed that even reputable companies—in this case Sears—may be caught up in auto repair frauds. The investigation found that Sears auto repair shops did unnecessary repairs 90 percent of the time. Sears denied criminal wrongdoing, but agreed to a settlement that could reach $15 million nationwide (*St. Louis Post-Dispatch*, September 3, 1992:B1).

Crimes in the Health Fields

Physicians, lawyers, accountants, architects, dentists, pharmacists, and others in respected professions are not above illegal activities. Opportunities for fraud and other illegal activities are especially abundant in the various health fields. Because today's culture strongly emphasizes health and physical well-being and because most people learn to rely on experts when confronted with health problems, those in the business of health find a vast clientele for their services, and the unscrupulous among them have little difficulty taking advantage of this favorable position. Medical quackery thrives on customer fears, lack of medical knowledge, and promises of expert help. Medical fraud can be expected to increase as the proportion of the population that is elderly starts to rise sharply after 1995. Even now, health care fraud is estimated to cost 10 percent of all health care spending—or around $70 billion per year (*St. Louis Post-Dispatch*, May 8, 1992, B1).

A good example of quackery is Harry M. Hoxsey, a Midwesterner who claimed to have found a cure for cancer. Hoxsey, who was not a physician, listed himself with an Illinois chamber of commerce and set up "cancer clinics" around the Midwest to which the ill could come for miracle cures. Though more than once convicted for practicing medicine without a license, Hoxsey pursued his quackery for nearly forty years and in one year alone is estimated to have seen 8000 patients and grossed more than $1.5 million! Needless to say, his cure was no cure at all, but it was not until the 1960s that the Food and Drug Administration and the American Medical Association finally succeeded in putting him out of business (see Young, 1967).

Some unscrupulous practices take special advantage of the organization of legitimate medicine and the bureaucratic context within which most health care services are administered throughout the country. As C. Wright Mills observed some years ago:

> Medical technology has of necessity been centralized in hospital and clinic; the private practitioner must depend upon expensive equipment as well as upon specialists and technicians for diagnosis and treatment. He must also depend upon good relations with other doctors, variously located in the medical hierarchy, to get started in practice and to keep up his clientele. For as medicine has become technically specialized, some way of getting those who are ill in contact with those who can help them is needed. In the absence of a formal means of referral, informal cliques of doctors, in and out of hospitals, have come to perform this function. (1956:115–116)

The informal organization of medical referrals and the clique system provide a means by which less scrupulous physicians and dentists can take advantage of their patients. One well-known scheme is called "ghost surgery." A patient is led to believe that the surgeon will perform a needed operation. In fact, another surgeon (the ghost) performs the operation. The patient ends up paying an inflated price for the surgery because the original surgeon must pay the accomplice. Another practice made easier by the informal networks among physicians and dentists is fee splitting. Though illegal in most states, fee splitting is thought to be a fairly common practice. It involves kickbacks from specialists to the general practitioner who refers patients to them. Again, the patient is overcharged to accommodate the payoff.

With the extension of government involvement in medicine that came with the Medicare and Medicaid programs, many health services now operate in a complicated bureaucratic atmosphere that makes control of these services extremely difficult. Physicians, dentists, and those in such support services as lab testing and retail pharmacy sometimes take advantage of the unwieldy bureaucracy by claiming payment for services and products that were never provided, by issuing prescriptions in violation of federal regulations, and by performing unnecessary services, such as surgery, hospitalization, and lab tests. The annual cost of Medicare and Medicaid fraud is put at more than $1 billion (Coleman, 1989:116).

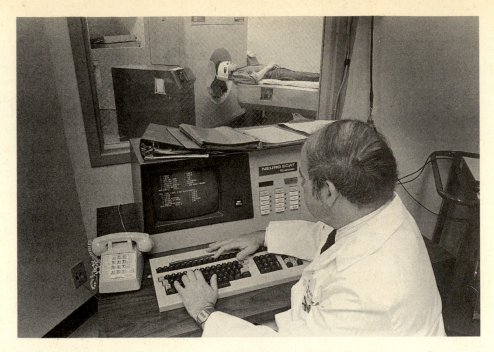

The use of expensive high-tech equipment in medical diagnosis and treatment creates opportunities and incentives for fraud. Patients are rarely knowledgeable or concerned enough to question procedures, and auditing by insurance companies and the federal government probably prevents only a small portion of medical fraud.

The special needs of the elderly create lucrative opportunities for Medicare fraud. For example, cataract surgery and pacemakers cost Medicare nearly $2 billion a year. Kickback schemes are commonplace between pacemaker salespeople and cardiologists, and between eye doctors and physicians who refer to them and the companies that manufacture and service products for the eye (Halamandaris, 1985). Because outpatient care does not have payment ceilings like those for care received in the hospital, cosmetic surgeons and ophthalmologists who own clinics can milk the insurance system almost at will.

One of the most alarming facets of medical fraud is the performance of unnecessary surgery. Although there is no accurate way of knowing how much surgery is unnecessary—even the most qualified physicians may not agree as to the need for a particular operation—evidence compiled over the past few years suggests that many physicians are quick with the knife and not always because the patient needs it. One study found that of 6248 hysterectomies performed in West Coast hospitals, 40 percent of the operations could be questioned for one reason or another, and 13 percent could not be supported by any available evidence (Doyle, 1953). Similar findings have been recorded for appendectomies, gall bladder operations, tonsillectomies, and other common surgical treatments. There is evidence that some hospitals are performing unnecessary cesarean sections and charging above average fees in the bargain (*Belleville News-Democrat*, June 21, 1991:3).

Unnecessary surgery is sometimes linked to declining occupancy levels in the hospitals and clinics to which the offending doctors are attached. When the occupancy level in a hospital declines, there is considerable pressure to reverse the situation; otherwise income declines while operating costs remain the same or increase. Economic decline is viewed with alarm not only because jobs are at stake but also because important support services may have to be curtailed or dropped, thus damaging health care delivery and public trust. From the standpoint of modern medical organization, anything threatening the hospital threatens the entire field of professional health care. For some doctors there is also the threat of personal financial troubles as their hospital investments turn sour.

Psychiatry is particularly prone to medical fraud, according to recent studies in California (Geis, Jesilow, and Pontell, 1982, 1985). Though psychiatrists constitute a small percentage of MDs, they have a disproportionately high rate of convictions for medical fraud. Their low case load leads them to inflate the amount of time they spend with patients. Many other frauds are documented through interviews with doctors and prosecutors in California and New York (Jesilow, Pontell, and Geis, 1993).

In his study of prescription violations by retail pharmacists, Richard Quinney (1963) showed how the existence of conflicting occupational roles can result in job-related crime. The organization of retail pharmacy is such that the pharmacist must fill two occupational roles: the business role and the professional role. The values and expectations embodied in the business role emphasize profit making; those in the professional role emphasize the correct procedures for such things as compounding and dispensing prescriptions and the proper relationship between pharmacist and doctor and pharmacist and customer. Quinney found that pharmacists tended to overcome the strains posed by these different roles by orienting themselves toward one role more than the other. Those who had adopted an "occupational role organization" stressing the business role were more likely to violate prescription laws than those with a professional role orientation.

It appears that occupational crime in the professions is inadequately accounted for by economic factors alone. Certainly, economic pressures can and do enter into the picture; yet economic pressures may just as well lead other professionals to pursue legitimate avenues of gain—working longer hours, improving one's skills, or writing books (Bloch and Geis, 1970). It seems that a more adequate explanation of occupational crimes among professionals is one that takes account of social structure; for example, the way occupations are organized, the interrelationships among them, and the normative contexts of work.

Crime as the Central Activity of a Business

The fly-by-night operators who defraud the American consumer by promising work they have no intention of doing, by charging exorbitant prices for shoddy and inferior services, by creating needs for a new furnace, a new roof, pest control, or aluminum siding where no need existed, or by selling products that do not exist are little different from the short-con operators discussed in Chapter 6. They commit fraud as their business. It is their work.

It is not only fly-by-nighters, however, who make fraud and deception their business. Over the years some businesses have made fraud their major purpose and yet they retain all the trappings of established respectability. They have permanent addresses, they are listed with chambers of commerce, they have boards of directors, they provide annual financial statements, and they may even issue stock for public purchase. The products and services these companies offer range from vacuum cleaners to swimming pools, from real estate to insurance. The Wedtech Corporation, discussed earlier, is a case in point.

The Equity Funding Corporation of America

One of America's most incredible corporate frauds was discovered in 1973. It involved the Equity Funding Corporation of America (EFCA) and centered on life insurance, the major business of the company and its subsidiaries (Dirks and Gross, 1974).

Established in the early 1960s, EFCA began as a new member of the legitimate life insurance business. For a while its business dealings were circumspect, though some of its operations would be illegal today. Yet by the mid-1960s, the company's top executives were not content to stay within the law. Instead they embarked on an ambitious program of fraudulent financial manipulations. On the surface EFCA remained, until its fall in 1973, a respectable company with growing assets and growing prestige in the world of high finance. In reality, however, the company's major business was fraud.

In November 1973, a federal grand jury in Los Angeles handed down criminal indictments charging 22 of the company's executives, including a number of its original founders, with 105 counts of criminal conspiracy for such illegal activities as securities fraud, mail fraud, bank fraud, interstate transportation of counterfeit securities and other securities obtained by fraud, electronic eavesdropping, and the filing of false documents with the Securities and Exchange Commission (Dirks and Gross, 1974:229).

At the heart of EFCA's fraudulent activities was a scheme involving the creation of fictitious insurance policies for the purpose of resale, in order to make the company seem worth far more than it actually was. Using the information contained in the files of their real policyholders, the company issued 64,000 phony policies, which were then sold to other insurance companies for cash. The companies that purchased the phony policies thought they were reinsuring bona fide policies with a total face value of $5 billion. In fact, they were buying nothing. In addition to this scheme, EFCA routinely faked its assets and earnings in its annual reports and in 1972 began printing counterfeit bonds with a face value of more than $100 million. The executives behind this last operation even established a "mail drop" in Chicago for their counterfeit bank bonds.

Transnational Crime: BCCI and Other Ventures

Occupational and business practices that are illegal at home may be legal in another country. This includes occupational health and safety, wage and employment practices, pollution control, banking and other financial activities, importing and exporting, construction and manufacturing, distribution and marketing. Other things being equal, the more restrictive (and enforced) the laws are at home, the more appealing the foreign country becomes as a place to do business. That appeal is heightened if the country also has a large population of poor but able-bodied workers or an abundance of natural resources.

Transnational corporations (TNCs) thrive on these conditions, but there is a downside: The costs to the host country may include hazardous working conditions, environmental pollution, worker exploitation, rampant bribery and corruption, and burgeoning rates of street crime and delinquency (Schwendinger and Schwendinger, 1985; Michalowski and Kramer, 1987). All is not necessarily rosy when an American corporation decides to build an auto or chemical or computer plant in a Third World country.

If legitimate businesses find opportunities abroad, so, of course, do shady businesses and enterprising criminals. For example, Block and Scarpitti (1986) describe the advantages to organized criminal groups found in the Caribbean, particularly the Bahamas:

- Secrecy in banking laws
- Low or nonexistent taxes
- Geographic proximity to the United States
- Involvement in large-scale criminal enterprises
- Secrecy in laws governing ownership, control, and operation of corporations
- Dependence on foreign investments and cooperation of public officials

Block and Scarpitti show that transnational criminal enterprises grow and prosper from collusion among politicians, business leaders, and criminal elements. Indeed, transnational crime is an activity that invariably draws legitimate businesses and organized crime into networks of collusion, and eventually blurs the boundaries between the two. Drug traffickers and other smugglers, casino operators looking to skim profits, terrorists, tax evaders, and corrupt politicians of every stripe do their business with bankers, industrialists, real estate developers, government officials, and all manner of entrepreneurs who may be breaking no laws in their own country but are fully aware of their complicity in ongoing criminal activities.

So it was with the Bank of Credit and Commerce International (BCCI). Established in 1972 by Pakistani financier Agha Hassan Abedi, BCCI became the first multinational bank originating out of the Third World. Headquartered until recently in London, regulated (in a very loose way) by Luxembourg, and backed by Middle East oil revenues, BCCI had by 1990 over $20 billion in assets in 75 countries with more than 400 branches and subsidiaries (*Newsweek*, July 22, 1991:37; *Time*, July 29, 1991:42). It gained a reputation for offering first-rate service to its large depositors, and for asking no questions. BCCI also knew exactly where to go in the political hierarchy of Western nations to get counsel and representation for its expansion—for example, to Clark Clifford, who "sat atop three branches of the capital's permanent government—law, money, and politics" (*Wall Street Journal*, June 14, 1991:4). Clifford, a man of formerly unquestioned respect and integrity, became chairman of First American Bankshares following its purchase by Saudi investors in 1981 with money loaned by BCCI. The investors eventually defaulted and BCCI (secretly, according to Clifford in Congressional testimony) became the owner of First American.

In 16 years of expansion, BCCI was not the legitimate banking operation it appeared to be. And there is evidence that officials in many countries, including the United States, England, Peru, and Argentina, knew it. They knew that BCCI was heavily involved in shady activities, and far from doing anything about it, found their own illegal uses for the bank.

Drug trafficking was arguably BCCI's downfall. Indicted by a federal grand jury in 1988 for laundering millions of dollars in drug money, BCCI eventually pleaded guilty and was fined $14 billion in 1990 (*Time*, July 22, 1991:46). Subsequent investigations produced an incredible array of charges: gunrunning, bribery and corruption, smuggling, terrorism, securities theft, property theft of all sorts, influence peddling, insurance fraud, covert operations for the CIA, bank fraud, espionage, extortion, kidnapping, and the violation of other domestic and international laws. The bank was closed down in July, 1991, its assets frozen. In January, 1992, BCCI pled guilty to racketeering; Clifford was indicted 7 months later, along with his law partner. and many more indictments and convictions will surely follow.

Reactions to Occupational Crime

One of Sutherland's (1949) major contentions regarding white-collar crime is that offenders generally escape the punitive action and criminal stigmatization evoked by other forms of crime. In the unlikely event that corporate crooks are brought before a judge, they rarely receive a prison term upon conviction. This situation has not changed much over the years. In fact, declines in the prosecution of white-collar crime have been observed over the past 50 years (Nader and Green, 1972; Stewart, 1987; but see Cullen, Maakestad, and Cavender, 1987). From 1940 to 1961 only 20 executives and businesspeople actually served jail sentences for antitrust violations (Dershowitz, 1961). More recently, the Joseph Schlitz Brewing Company was convicted of bribery amounting to more than $3 million; its criminal punishment was $11,000 following a reduction of charges to two misdemeanors (*Newsweek*, December 3, 1979). Marshall Clinard estimates that when convicted, the corporate criminal spends an average of 2.8 *days* in prison. In most cases, Clinard shows, offending corporations are merely issued warnings (Clinard et al., 1979).

Although occupational criminals tend to escape severe penalties, an offender's social status may bear on punishment. It is fashionable to refer to the pardon of ex-President Nixon and the prison terms given his aides following Watergate as an illustration of the link between status and punishment (see Table 7.1). It is also true that the 20 antitrust offenders mentioned earlier who received jail terms were not giants of the corporate world, but small timers and lower-level executives. In fact, of the 48 jail terms handed down in antitrust cases from 1890 to 1959, few involved higher-level executives of large corporations. Large defense contractors also manage to avoid strict enforcement and severe penalties, whereas smaller firms are fined and debarred into bankruptcy (*St. Louis Post-Dispatch*, December 18, 1985).

In a study of 1631 employee thieves, Gerald Robin (1967) found that although 99.5 percent were fired by their employers, only 17 percent were prosecuted. However, regardless of length of service and size of theft, a significantly larger proportion of lower-level employees than higher-level employees were prosecuted, and those prosecuted were almost all convicted. On the other hand, two more recent studies of the sanctioning of occupational crime show no association between socioeconomic status and sentencing (Benson and Walker, 1988), or that lower-level employees are more likely to be prosecuted and convicted than upper-level managers only when offenses are "most serious" (Shapiro, 1990). Similar contradictory findings are found in research on the sanctioning of traditional crime.

The relatively low probability of criminal sanctions being imposed, and the relatively high probability that they will be mild when they are imposed, is favorable not only to corporate offenders who violate regulatory laws, but also to those who steal from their employers, those who defraud the public, and those who violate public trust while holding political office. Compared with "traditional" criminals, occupational criminals generally face little organized enforcement. When exposed, they are ignored, handled informally and unofficially, ordered to "cease and desist," forced to pay a nominal fine, or placed on probation.

There are a number of reasons for the general absence of a rigorous and punitive reaction to occupational crimes and those who commit them. First, many of those who violate the law in connection with their work are simply not thought of as criminals. Not only are their crimes not the kinds of activities to which that label is culturally, or even legally, applied; they also do not often look like "real" criminals. They are not poor, transient, unemployed, black, inner-city, uneducated, lower-class people with a history of involvement in

TABLE 7.1 Watergate: Who got what

Richard M. Nixon	Unindicted co-conspirator	Pardoned	
Dwight L. Chapin	Convicted of lying to a grand jury	Sentenced to serve 10 to 30 months	Served 8 months
Charles W. Colson	Pleaded guilty to obstruction of justice	Sentenced to serve 1 to 3 years and fined $5000	Served 7 months
John W. Dean III	Pleaded guilty to conspiracy to obstruct justice	Sentenced to serve 1 to 4 years	Served 4 months
John D. Ehrlichman	Convicted of conspiracy to obstruct justice, conspiracy to violate civil rights and perjury	Sentenced to serve concurrent terms of 20 months to 8 years	Served 18 months
H. R. Haldeman	Convicted of conspiracy to obstruct justice and perjury	Sentenced to serve 2½ to 8 years	Served 18 months
E. Howard Hunt	Pleaded guilty to conspiracy, burglary and wiretapping	Sentenced to serve 30 months to 8 years and fined $10,000	Served 33 months
Herbert W. Kalmbach	Pleaded guilty to violation of the Federal Corrupt Practices Act and promising federal employment as a reward for political activity	Sentenced to serve 6 to 18 months and fined $10,000	Served 6 months
Richard G. Kleindienst	Pleaded guilty to refusal to answer pertinent questions before a Senate committee	Sentenced to 30 days and fined $100	Sentence suspended
Egil Krogh Jr.	Pleaded guilty to conspiracy to violate civil rights	Sentenced to serve 2 to 6 years (all but 6 months were suspended)	Served 4½ months
Frederick C. LaRue	Pleaded guilty to conspiracy to obstruct justice	Sentenced to serve 1 to 3 years (all but 6 months were suspended)	Served 5½ months
G. Gordon Liddy	Convicted of conspiracy, conspiracy to violate civil rights, burglary and wiretapping	Sentenced to serve 6 years and 8 months to 20 years and fined $40,000	Served 52 months
Jeb S. Magruder	Pleaded guilty to conspiracy to obstruct justice, wiretapping and fraud	Sentenced to serve 10 months to 4 years	Served 7 months
John N. Mitchell	Convicted of conspiracy to obstruct justice and perjury	Sentenced to serve 2½ to 8 years	Served 19 months
Donald H. Segretti	Pleaded guilty to campaign violations and conspiracy	Sentenced to serve 6 months	Served 4½ months
Maurice H. Stans	Pleaded guilty to five misdemeanor violations of the Federal Elections Campaign Act	Fined $5000	

TABLE 7.1 Watergate: Who got what (Continued)

James W. McCord Jr.	Convicted of conspiracy, burglary, wiretapping and unlawful possession of intercepting devices	Sentenced to serve 1 to 5 years	Served 4 months
Bernard L. Barker	Pleaded guilty to conspiracy, burglary, wiretapping and unlawful possession of intercepting devices	Sentenced to serve 18 months to 6 years	Served 12 months
Virgilio R. Gonzalez	Pleaded guilty to conspiracy, burglary, wiretapping and unlawful possession of intercepting devices	Sentenced to serve 1 to 4 years	Served 15 months
Eugenio R. Martinez	Pleaded guilty to conspiracy, burglary, wiretapping and unlawful possession of intercepting devices	Sentenced to serve 1 to 4 years	Served 15 months
Frank A. Sturgis	Pleaded guilty to conspiracy, burglary, wiretapping and unlawful possession of intercepting devices	Sentenced to serve 1 to 4 years	Served 13 months

Source: The Washington Post, June 17, 1982.

delinquency and street crimes. They are, instead, people with all the trappings of respectability, and some are wealthy and powerful.

Those occupational offenders with relatively high social status avoid criminal stigmatization, not only because they do not look like real criminals, but also because of their wealth, prestige, and power—and the interests they hold in common with those who create our laws and pass out sentences. Whenever new or more repressive legislation is under consideration in state or federal legislatures, it is remarkable how quickly it dies in committee, how easily it is held over to the next session, or how often it is amended into a completely different statute with plenty of loopholes.

When it is decided to prosecute upperworld crime, it is often the organization that is convicted rather than the executives who run it. John Braithwaite (1982) points out that when individuals are prosecuted, it is often those least deserving of punishment who take the rap. He claims to know of at least three transnational pharmaceutical companies with "vice-presidents responsible for going to jail" (p. 755). These people take a few risks in exchange for promotion to vice-president and, after a sufficient time in that position, are moved laterally to a safer vice-presidential position.

Another reason for the absence of a rigorous and punitive reaction to occupational crime in general is the "relatively unorganized resentment of the public toward" occupational crime (Sutherland, 1949:49). It is difficult to generate organized public indignation about occupational crime when the effects of much of this crime are diffused rather than simple and direct and when the acts themselves occur within a complex, often technically sophisticated economic or political context. As members of a Ralph Nader study group put it: "When one person is robbed face to face, the injustice and indignity are obvious. But when millions are deceived in a complex economic structure, when pinpointing the blame is difficult if not impossible, when crime grows so impersonal that it becomes 'technical'—then we lose our perception of the criminal act" (Green, Moore, and Wasserstein, 1976:554).

This does not mean that victims of occupational crime suffer no injustice or feel no anger. One study of the effects on victims of the savings and loan scandal found a range of responses, from feeling inconvenienced (the majority), to feeling "sobered," to being "devastated" (Shover, Littonfox, and Mills, 1991). The last group, although in the minority, were stunned, fearful, or severely depressed; they had difficulty sleeping, and many were extremely angry and resentful. These are common reactions of people who are mugged, raped, or burglarized—especially those victims whose history and lifestyle have not prepared them for it (see Elias, 1986:116–131).

Organized public resentment is also unlikely when cultural values support self-reliance, free enterprise, individual initiative, and the drive for profits and power. When the public learns that someone's financial achievements or political successes were based on shady practices, the inclination is to applaud the obvious commitment to American success values and to play down the dishonesty. John Hagan (1985:171–173) argues that this sort of rationalization helps foster a climate of moral neutrality. Upperworld indiscretions such as Watergate are thus regarded as worthwhile risks. An exploratory study conducted with 30 convicted white-collar offenders shows that normative pressures are easily neutralized if they do not actually condone illegality. Embezzlers and tax evaders denied that they had any criminal intent, while a common "claim" of antitrust violators was that their actions were "just normal business practice" and necessary given the realities of the economy (Benson, 1985; see also Jackall, 1988).

A climate of moral neutrality may not extend to all occupational crimes, however. Opinion studies reviewed by Braithwaite (1982) show that the public is often quite intolerant of corporate crimes that produce demonstrable harms such as pollution and government frauds. The National Survey of Crime Severity rating of offenses lists pollution resulting in multiple deaths as seventh in seriousness out of 204 crimes (Wolfgang et al., 1985). It should be emphasized again, however, that the existence of such feelings is one thing but organizing them into action against offenders is quite another.

When large, impersonal organizations are the victims of crime, public disapproval and indignation are minimal. Employee theft, embezzlement, tax evasion, and other activities victimizing corporations and government bureaucracies are more likely to be excused, if not condoned, because the victims are themselves unpopular and history has not provided strong ethical guidelines for relationships between large organizations and their employees and customers. Different individuals may have different reasons for disliking large organizations, but on the whole it seems that their unpopularity results from their impersonality, their power and influence, their wealth, and their emphasis on rule following as opposed to initiative and creativity. The unpopularity of organizations and lack of strong ethics governing the relationship between individuals and organizations not only dull public reactions to such crimes as employee theft, but they also serve as powerful justifications for potential offenders. When a sample of 212 adults in Indiana were asked what type of organization they would steal from if forced by necessity to do so, 155 respondents indicated they would prefer to steal from a large business (102) or government (53) than from a small business (Smigel, 1956). Large corporations are not in a totally pitiable situation, however: Hagan (1982b) found in Canada that when such corporations are victimized, they get more justice (if they want it) than individuals do, and they are more likely to be satisfied with the outcome.

Occupational crime is likely to flourish for a long time to come. Even if there were organized public resentment, major obstacles to preventing white-collar crime remain. One is the nature of work itself. Constant changes in the organization and technology of work provide new opportunities for crime. The inventive mind is able to take advantage of these opportunities and can often stay ahead of the law and its enforcement. This has happened with computer technology and now threatens to occur—with greater potential for injury—in the area of nuclear power (Bequai, 1978; Edelhertz and Walsh, 1978).

Prevention efforts are also frustrated by the close ties between business and politics mentioned earlier. The crimes likely to victimize most people, at greatest cost, are those dreamed up in corporate suites, in the offices of highly skilled professionals, and in back rooms where political deals are made. These high-status criminals are the people best able to capitalize on their occupational position. If they are caught they can hire the best lawyers, arrange the longest court delays, and manufacture the most compelling justifications for their actions. Usually it does not come to that; mutual protection serves mutual interests, and all parties benefit when matters are kept quiet and policing takes place from within. The Reagan administration will go down in history as a government that systematically eroded many of the protections against collusion, fraud, and occupational dangers of all sorts. Consider one outcome: There were more mergers and hostile takeovers during the Reagan years than ever before (*St. Louis Post-Dispatch*, November 16, 1988:B1).

There may be some public advantages to keeping corporations out of the criminal court and pursuing enforcement in nonlitigious or even extralegal ways. Braithwaite (1982:749–751) suggests that many unsafe practices are not covered under law, especially as rapid technological change far exceeds the ability of lawmakers to keep pace, and that even when laws exist, the enforcement apparatus often does not. If these practices are to be stopped, voluntary cooperation from the offending corporation may be the best avenue, and for this there needs to be a climate of goodwill. It is easy for corporations to exercise costly delays and to exploit the complexities of a situation so that prosecution costs become prohibitive. To avoid these problems it may be in the public advantage to use threats, revoke licenses, and give adverse publicity, rather than formal punishment, to secure compliance. Braithwaite further argues that those interested in preventing corporate crimes should explore how to harness the police power within corporate structures—help corporations regulate themselves internally, something many managers advocate as well (Fisse and Braithwaite, 1988; see also Baker and Westin, 1987).

The heart of Braithwaite's ideas on how to deal effectively with occupational criminals, especially those in upperworld jobs, is the process of shaming (see also Chapters 12 and 17). Shaming can take many forms, but the bottom line is that it provokes feelings of guilt, embarrassment, and humiliation. Punishment without shaming makes offenders feel mad but not bad (Braithwaite, 1991:27). And shaming can work in an organizational setting because the organization as a whole can be shamed—its reputation tarnished (see Simpson, 1990)—and "the shamed collectivity can not only pass on this shame by sanctioning guilty individuals after the event, it can also activate internal controls proactively to prevent future crimes before they occur" (Braithwaite, 1989a:127).

Summary of Chapter 7

This chapter has explored the many dimensions of occupational crime. Such crime occurs in connection with a person's job, with work providing the opportunity and sometimes the motivation for criminal activity. The financial, medical, and social costs of occupational crime far exceed those of such conventional street crimes as robbery, burglary, drug sales, murder, and assault.

Some occupational crimes are committed for personal gain. These include embezzlement, political corruption, and a host of other offenses ranging from simple fiddles to high-tech manipulations costing thousands of dollars. Other occupational crimes are committed on behalf of a person's employer. These are sometimes incidental to business operations, such as violations of antitrust laws and insider trading; at other times they may constitute the central activity of a business, as in the case of fly-by-night home repair operations and many real estate swindles.

No one theory adequately explains occupational crime, partly because the term covers diverse situations. It seems safe to argue, however, that many people who commit work-related crimes regard their behavior as normal rather than deviant. Situational incentives are reinforced by norms and values that define the behavior as appropriate, even expected. Under such circumstances it is the people who refrain from offenses who are regarded as deviant.

This sort of argument does not extend to all occupational crimes, especially those that make life difficult for fellow workers or which result in extraordinary losses or harm to the company. Even though many people doubtless have a grudging respect for Ivan Boesky and Michael Milken, Wall Street investors were quick to close ranks in condemnation of their activities. On the whole, however, official reactions to most occupational crimes are more lenient than reactions to most street crimes, and rarely will a convicted occupational criminal go to the penitentiary.

American culture strongly supports the drive for profits and power, and in doing so provides rationalizations for executives who bend the rules, for politicians who deal in favors, and for officials who look the other way. It should come as no surprise, therefore, that the factory worker, office clerk, and salesperson have little trouble justifying their relatively petty crimes. They are taking advantage of the opportunities before them in the same enterprising spirit. The irony is, however, that workers at all levels of responsibility and power actually have little choice in the matter: The structure and norms of work make occupational crime virtually inevitable.

Recommended Readings

Marshall B. Clinard, and Peter C. Yeager (1980). *Corporate Crime*. New York: Free Press.

James W. Coleman (1989). *The Criminal Elite*. 2nd Edition. New York: St. Martin's Press.

Francis Cullen, William J. Maakestad, and Gary Cavender (1987). *Corporate Crime Under Attack: The Ford Pinto Case*. Cincinnati: Anderson.

Gary S. Green (1990). *Occupational Crime*. Chicago: Nelson-Hall.

Robert Jackall (1988). *Moral Mazes: The World of Corporate Managers*. New York: Oxford University Press.

Paul Jesilow, Henry Pontell, and Gilbert Geis (1993). *Prescription for Profit*. Los Angeles: University of California Press.

Gerald Mars (1983). *Cheats at Work: An Anthology of Workplace Crime*. London: Unwin Paperbacks.

David R. Simon, and D. Stanley Eitzen (1990). *Elite Deviance*. 3rd Edition. Boston: Allyn and Bacon.

Chapter 8

Organized Crime

Most Americans are familiar with the term *organized crime*, yet it is unlikely that many of them know much about it. They probably have heard of Al Capone, Vito Genovese, Joe Bonnano, Joe Valachi, and Charlie "Lucky" Luciano. Most may also have heard of Eliot Ness, head of the "Untouchables," assigned to break up Capone's bootlegging operations during Prohibition. It is common knowledge that Chicago and the New York-New Jersey area are two major centers of organized crime activities. What most people have learned about organized crime, however, has come from the mass media. Apart from periodic news items, which are usually colorful and designed to demonstrate some special kind of inside knowledge, the entertainment industry has been a major window on organized crime. The success of *Goodfellas, The Godfather*, and "Miami Vice" is evidence of the strong appeal of organized crime as entertainment. At best, the information available to the public via the mass media is fragmentary, superficial, and misleading; at worst, it is patently false and purely titillating.

The Existence of Organized Crime

Over the years a belief has grown that there is in America a national alliance or cartel composed of organized groups of criminals, dominated by Sicilian- and Italian-Americans, and involved in an extensive range of illicit, often violent activities. As we shall see, this view is now strongly challenged. There is also controversy surrounding the definition of organized crime. Box 8.1 includes a definition adopted by the federal government in 1968. Note how vague the wording is. And many experts would quarrel with the term "highly organized," as we shall see.

The Case for a National Cartel of Corporate Crime Groups

In 1951 and then again in 1969, highly credible sources appeared to confirm that a national crime cartel does exist in America. First, the "Kefauver Committee" of the U.S. Senate reported that:

1. There is a nation-wide crime syndicate known as the Mafia, whose tentacles are found in many large cities. . . .
2. Its leaders are usually found in control of the most lucrative rackets in their cities.
3. There are indications of a centralized direction and control of these rackets, but leadership appears to be in a group rather than in a single individual.
4. The Mafia is the cement that helps bind the Costello-Adonis-Lansky syndicate of New York and the Accardo-Guzik-Fischetti syndicate of Chicago as well as smaller criminal gangs and individual criminals throughout the country. . . .
5. The domination of the Mafia is based fundamentally on "muscle" and "murder." The Mafia is a secret conspiracy against law and order which will ruthlessly eliminate anyone who stands in the way of its success in any

Box 8.1 ■ Organized Crime as Defined by the Omnibus Crime Control Act

In 1968 the Omnibus Crime Control Act added the following official definition of organized crime to the federal lawbooks:

> Organized crime means the unlawful activities of the members of a highly organized, disciplined association engaged in supplying illegal goods and services, including but not limited to gambling, prostitution, loan sharking, narcotics, labor racketeering, and other unlawful activities of members of such organizations.

Note that this official definition is uninformed by the wealth of scholarly work that has been undertaken in the past few decades and reflects the rather stereotypical views held in many academic and legal circles. Note also that the definition is vague and would be difficult to apply in practice. What, for example, do "highly organized" and "disciplined" mean? For further discussion of definitional problems see Howard Abadinsky, *Organized Crime*, 3rd edition: (Chicago: Nelson-Hall, 1990), Ch. 1.

Source: Section 601(b) of The Omnibus Crime Control and Safe Streets Act of 1968. United States Code, Section 3701.

criminal enterprise in which it is interested. It will destroy anyone who betrays its secrets. It will use any means available—political influence, bribery, intimidation, etc., to defeat any attempt on the part of law enforcement to touch its top figures or to interfere with its operations. (Tyler, 1962:343–144)

The findings of the Kefauver Committee were based on information supplied mainly by police officials and informants. Using basically the same kinds of information, Donald Cressey summarized his investigation on behalf of the President's Commission on Law Enforcement and the Administration of Justice as follows:

1. A nationwide alliance of at least twenty-four tightly knit "families" of criminals exists in the United States (because the "families" are fictive, in the sense that the members are not all relatives, it is necessary to refer to them in quotation marks).
2. The members of these "families" are all Italians and Sicilians, or of Italian or Sicilian descent, and those on the Eastern seaboard, especially, call the entire system "Cosa Nostra." Each member thinks of himself as a "member" of a specific "family" and of Cosa Nostra (or some equivalent term).
3. The names, criminal records, and principal criminal activities of about five thousand of the participants have been assembled.
4. The persons occupying key positions in the skeletal structure of each "family"—consisting of positions for boss, underboss, lieutenants (also called

"captains"), counselor, and for low-ranking members called "soldiers" or "button men"—are well known to law-enforcement officials having access to informants. Names of persons who permanently or temporarily occupy other positions, such as "buffer," "money mover," "enforcer," and "executioner," also are well known.

5. The "families" are linked to each other, and to non-Cosa Nostra syndicates, by understandings, agreements, and "treaties," and by mutual deference to a "Commission" made up of the leaders of the most powerful of the "families."

6. The boss of each "family" directs the activities, especially the illegal activities, of the members of his "family."

7. The members of this organization control all but a tiny part of the illegal gambling in the United States. They are the principal loan sharks. They are the principal importers and wholesalers of narcotics. They have infiltrated certain labor unions, where they extort money from employers and, at the same time, cheat the members of the union. The members have a virtual monopoly on some legitimate enterprises. . . . Until recently, they owned a large proportion of Las Vegas. They own several state legislators and federal congressmen and other officials in the legislative, executive, and judicial branches of government at the local, state, and federal levels. Some government officials (including judges) are considered, and consider themselves, members.

8. The information about the Commissions, the "families," and the activities of members has come from detailed reports made by a wide variety of police observers, informants, wire taps, and electronic bugs. (1969:x–xi)

In Cressey's view, these crime families are organized along the lines of what sociologists call *formal organization*. In this structure, the labor is divided so that tasks and responsibilities are assigned primarily on the basis of special skills and abilities; there is a strict hierarchy of authority; rules and regulations govern the activities of members and the relationships among them and with the outside world; and recruitment and entrance are carefully regulated. In short, the crime families are, like other formal organizations, rationally designed for the purposes of achieving specified objectives.

Former United States Attorney Rudolph Giuliani and many other law enforcement officials still favor this description of La Cosa Nostra (LCN). In testimony in federal court, Giuliani documented the existence of specific LCN families in New York, Philadelphia, Cleveland, Chicago, Milwaukee, Kansas City, and Los Angeles; and he described nationwide coordinated LCN control of the nation's largest union, the International Brotherhood of Teamsters (see Block, 1991: Chapter 10).

Much-publicized recent successes by federal law enforcement officials in prosecuting reputed LCN members, primarily through the extensive use of wiretaps, lend credence to claims of LCN's existence and of considerable interaction among Italian-American crime families. However, Alan Block (1991:13–14) believes they fall far short of proving the "big conspiracy," and he regards both the history of La Cosa Nostra and its sociology clouded in mystery.

An Alternative View

Not all authorities on organized crime agree entirely with Cressey's depiction of a national network of crime families. The alternative revisionist view, suggested by Daniel Bell (1965), John Conklin (1973), and Francis Ianni (1973), among others, emphasizes more or less organized local criminal gangs, some of whose activities inevitably bring them into working contact with groups operating elsewhere. These authors see no real evidence of any centralized direction or domination of these localized syndicates. In Block's view, "territory and organization are honored only in the breach" (p. 98). And there are, he says, "ceaseless disputes over rackets and territories" (Block, 1991:8).

Peter Reuter (1983) also rejects the notion of a formally organized, centrally directed, national alliance of Mafia families. He does not dispute the existence of Mafia families—most have continued in the same recognizable form for at least 50 years. Rather, Reuter believes that the relations among them are the result of occasional venture partnerships, occasional exchange of services, and attempts to reduce the uncertainty that arises when business takes a family into unfamiliar territory. Reuter (1983:158) also suggests that many of the connections among organized crime gangs resulted from Prohibition and from associations made while members served time in federal prisons.

Another point of contention concerns the degree and nature of organization. Some authors reject the idea that organized crime groups fit the formal organization model. In his in-depth study of one Italian-American crime family, Francis Ianni (1973:120–124) notes:

> Secret criminal organizations like the Italian-American or Sicilian *Mafia* families are not formal organizations like governments or business corporations. They are not rationally structured into statuses and functions in order to "maximize profits" and carry out tasks efficiently. Rather, they are traditional social systems, organized by action and by cultural values which have nothing to do with modern bureaucratic virtues. Like all social systems, they have no structure apart from their functioning; nor . . . do they have structure independent of their current "personnel." . . . Describing the various positions in Italian-American syndicates as "like" those in bureaucracies gives the impression that they are, in fact, formal organizations. But they are not.

A study of the South Philadelphia mob run by Angelo Bruno from 1959 until 1980, when he was assassinated, corroborates Ianni's finding rather than the picture drawn by Cressey. Haller (1991) analyzed all files of the Pennsylvania Crime Commission dealing with Bruno and his successor, Nicodemo Scarfo. He found that two organizational structures appeared to operate simultaneously: (1) a family structure comprising a network designed to help the individual enterprises of members and constituting a "shadow government" of rules and expectations that facilitate members' legal and illegal activities; and (2) an enterprise structure comprising the legal and illegal businesses run by individual members of the Bruno family. This enterprise structure involved cost, risk, and profit sharing (sometimes with non-family members), and most of the business was carried on informally, through "deals, negotiations, [and] whispered conversations," and through decentralized operations involving minimal oversight. According to Haller, this system not only fit the life-style of the men but also provided to each participant wide discretion in doing "business."

Although some crime families or syndicates exhibit some of the elements found in highly rationalized bureaucratic structures, as Cressey showed, most do not. This distinction is important when one considers the growing organized crime involvement of blacks and Hispanics, and of street gangs such as the Bloods and Crips of Los Angeles, whom law enforcement officials are now comparing to the mobsters of Prohibition days. Some of these groups display only rudimentary organization, mostly operating in loosely connected networks, but others are highly organized.

Illegal Enterprise

Reuter's (1983) study of loan sharking, gambling, and the numbers racket in New York City shows how illegality of products and services affects the organization of an economic market, keeping some enterprises localized and relatively small-scale. The illegal market differs from its legal counterpart in various ways: (1) Contracts cannot be enforced in a court of law; (2) assets associated with illegal operations may be seized at any time; and (3) participants risk arrest and imprisonment. These problems differ in significance from one illegal market to another, however; heroin trafficking carries more risk than operating a numbers game.

These problems call for control over the flow of information about the operation. Those who participate are at different risk and pose different levels of threat to others. The *entrepreneurs* who control operations are at greatest risk from their *agents* or *employees*, who know most about the business, but those risks are reduced by dividing up the tasks and responsibilities, by offering employees economic incentives, by ensuring that they are not employed elsewhere, by intimidating, and by recruiting based on family ties or the incorporation of employees into the family through rite or marriage. Risks to the employees come largely from other employees, thus encouraging entrepreneurs to keep operations small-scale and/or dispersed in time and space (Reuter, 1983).

Another problem faced by illegal enterprise is financing. Reuter (1983:120) found that credit works differently in illegal markets: (1) There are no accurately audited books; (2) the lender is unable to control any assets placed as collateral against a loan because the borrower is likely to demand secrecy, and, in any case, lacks court protection (as a financer of criminal activities); and (3) the loan is to the individual entrepreneur and not to the enterprise, which has no legal existence apart from its owner. Therefore, the lender would have difficulty collecting from any successor.

These problems also constrain the growth of illegal enterprises, especially those in loan sharking and gambling:

> Without smoothly working capital markets, the growth must be internally financed . . . out of profits. In the heroin importing business, where each successful transaction may double the capital of the enterprise, this may be a minor restriction. For the numbers bank, with a relatively modest cash flow and a need for maintenance of a substantial cash reserve, this may be a very important constraint. (Reuter 1983:121)

Mark Haller (1990), arguably America's foremost authority on the history of organized crime, reminds us that illegal enterprise existed long before La Cosa Nostra. Indeed, it shaped the underworld of American cities for over 100 years before the rise of Italian-American crime families. These enterprises included free-lance prostitution, street-corner drug dealing, and neighborhood bookmaking. Entrepreneurs sometimes got together in cooperative ventures giving rise to networks of collusion.

The cooperative ventures of illegal enterprise rested on three important factors, according to Haller: (1) police or politician oversight that involved regular payoffs (kickbacks), limited competition, and encouraged avoidance of scandals and participation in "honest" crime; (2) flexible partnership arrangements allowing several entrepreneurs to share risks, to pool resources, and to combine their capital, influence, and managerial skills; and (3) internal economics, that is, the need to develop cooperative relations between buyers and sellers in order to protect both from the vagaries of doing business in the illegal marketplace.

Distinguishing Characteristics of Organized Crime

It is unlikely that criminologists will soon reach a consensus on the issues under discussion here. Even if detailed and dependable information were forthcoming, how complete a picture could be drawn from it? When dealing with people who place a premium on secrecy and engage in criminal activities, one is rarely able to learn everything one needs to know. Even those in a position to know more than most—a participant who turns informant, such as Joe Valachi, whose testimony before the McClellan Committee was so influential (see Abadinsky, 1990:473–475)—may know the facts about only some aspects of their own organization and thus cannot be considered authoritative sources of information on other aspects or other organizations (see Maas, 1968). Even so, criminologists generally agree on some important features of organized crime that, when taken together, distinguish this type of criminal activity from others.

First, organized crime is *instrumental* crime, the purpose of which is to make money. To accomplish this, participants *organize* in more or less complex networks. Third, most organized crime activities offer *illegal goods and services*. This does not mean, however, that those in organized crime have nothing to do with "traditional" crimes such as burglary or robbery. As Stuart Hills (1971:138–139) points out:

> It is the syndicate that has mostly controlled the importation and wholesale distribution of narcotics that, together with prohibitionist laws and police activity, compel most addicts to engage in burglary, robbery, and larceny to pay the exorbitant black-market prices. And it is the "fences," aligned with organized criminal groups, who allow thieves to convert their booty into cash. Organized crime has also been known to promote bank robbery, cargo hijacking, arson, and burglaries, sometimes in cooperation with individual professional thieves.

This kind of crime has been called the "parasitic" activity of organized crime (see Abadinsky 1990:267–268).

A fourth important characteristic of organized crime is its connections with government and politics. *Organized crime makes political corruption an integral part of its business.* Indeed, political corruption is not merely a distinguishing feature of organized crime; it is critical to its survival.

The fifth feature of organized crime is its *generational persistence*. The syndicates or families involved in organized crime continue to operate despite the comings and goings of their members. Although the death or retirement of persons in leadership positions may result in significant changes, organized crime does not disappear, and individual organizations usually do not cease to exist. The persistence of organized crime can be explained in part by a sixth important feature: *sanctioned rules of conduct* (sometimes called "the code"). The survival of any group or organizatin is problematic if the behavior of members is neither predictable nor conforming to the evaluations of at least some other members of the group. Rules of conduct help establish conformity and predictability; sanctions for violations of the rules help ensure that conformity and predictability persist over time. Sanctions are related to a final characteristic: *ability and willingness to use force and violence* to accomplish the organization's goals. Reuter (1983) points out that reputation may be more important than actual behavior: A gang that has a reputation for violence can accomplish the same results with fewer bad consequences (see also Block, 1991:5).

When discussing what makes organized crime special, some authors emphasize its organizational features, while others note that organized criminals are able to commit a greater variety of crimes, on a larger scale, than are other offenders. Mark Moore (1986) believes that most recent research and policy has been guided by the first view rather than the second. For example, the Racketeer Influenced and Corrupt Organizations (RICO) Act of 1970 (see Box 8.2) focuses on the specific organization of criminal groups and their capacity to continue operations despite government opposition. "The Policy goal . . . is to weaken and frustrate the enterprise rather than control their criminal offending" (Moore, 1986:2). In addition, Moore argues, the organiza-

---

Box 8.2 ■ The RICO Statute

The provisions of the Racketeer Influenced and Corrupt Organizations Act (1970) include the following:

■ It shall be unlawful for any person through a pattern of racketeering activity or through collection of an unlawful debt to acquire or maintain, directly or indirectly, any interest in or control of any enterprise which is engaged in, or the activities of which affect, interstate or foreign commerce.

■ It shall be unlawful for any person employed by or associated with any enterprise engaged in, or the activities of which affect, interstate or foreign commerce, to conduct or participate, directly or indirectly, in the conduct of such enterprise's affairs through a pattern of racketeering activity or collection of unlawful debt.

■ It shall be unlawful for any person to conspire to violate any of [these] provisions.

[*Definitions:*] A "pattern of racketeering activity" means at least two acts of racketeering activity within ten years of each other (excluding any period of imprisonment).

"Racketeering activity" includes the following: (a) murder, kidnapping, gambling, arson, robbery, bribery, extortion, or dealing in narcotic or other dangerous drugs; . . . (b) any act indictable under provisions of Title 18, United States Code [i.e., the Organized Crime Control Act of 1970, of which RICO is a part], including those relating to bribery, embezzlement from pension and welfare funds, mail fraud, wire fraud, obstruction of justice, interference with commerce, robbery or extortion, racketeering, welfare fund payments; . . . (c) any act which is indictable under Title 29, United States Code, section 186 (dealing with restrictions on payments and loans to labor organizations) or section 501(c) (relating to embezzlement from union funds). . . .

---

tional focus draws attention to the parallels between organized crime and legitimate business enterprises. Interestingly, the Organized Crime Control Act of 1970 does not define "organized crime," nor does RICO define "racketeer" (Abadinsky, 1990:425).

The Code

There is no conclusive evidence that one particular code is shared by the various criminal organizations. Investigators have found numerous obstacles to a definitive statement of what the code (or codes) might be, the most important being the veil of secrecy that surrounds organized crime and the difficulty of gaining access to its participants.

Cressey (1969:175–178) combined snippets of information from informants with clues deduced from an analysis of the social structure of Cosa Nostra and suggested the following as the code of organized crime:

1. *Be loyal to members of the organization. Do not interfere with each other's interests. Do not be an informer.* This directive, with its correlated admoni-

John Gotti, head of the New York Gambino crime family was convicted in April, 1992, of racketeering and murder. In the sensational trial, a former associate and co-defendant, Salvatore "The Bull" Gravano, testified against Gotti. Gotti is now serving a life sentence without parole in the federal penitentiary at Marion, Illinois. His conviction is under appeal. Gravano, a self-confessed hit man responsible for 19 killings, received a 20 year sentence in exchange for his testimony.

tions, is basic to the internal operations of the Cosa Nostra confederation. It is a call for unity, for peace, for maintenance of the *status quo*. . . .

2. *Be rational. Be a member of the team. Don't engage in battle if you can't win.* What is demanded here is a corporate rationality necessary to conducting illicit businesses in a quiet, safe, profitable manner. . . .

3. *Be a man of honor. Always do right. Respect womanhood and your elders. Don't rock the boat.* This emphasis on "honor" and "respect" helps determine who obeys whom, who attends what funerals and weddings, who opens the door for whom, . . . and functions to enable despots to exploit their underlings. . . .

4. *Be a stand-up guy. Keep your eyes and ears open and your mouth shut. Don't sell out.* A "family" member, like a prisoner, must be able to withstand frustrating and threatening situations without complaining or resorting to subservience. The "stand-up guy" shows courage and "heart." . . .

5. *Have class. Be independent. Know your way around the world.* . . . A man who is committed to regular work and submission to duly constituted authority is a sucker. . . . Second, the world seen by organized criminals is a world of graft, fraud, and corruption, and they are concerned with their own honesty and manliness as compared with the hypocrisy of corrupt policemen and corrupt political figures.

In discussing the code, Cressey points out that it is similar to the codes adopted by professional thieves, prisoners, and other groups whose activities bring them into confrontation with official authority and generate the need for "private" government as a means of controlling the membership's conduct (see also Salerno and Tompkins, 1969:105–148).

Taking exception to Cressey's position, Ianni (1973:150–155) argues that the presumption of a shared code is based on the questionable belief that there is a single national organization, and that each individual organized crime group has achieved similar levels of organizational sophistication and has shared similar experiences. In Ianni's view, clues to organized crime codes are best discovered by the direct observation of members' behavior. His method "was to observe and record behavior and then seek regularities that had enough frequency to suggest that the behavior resulted from the pressures of the shared social system rather than from idiosyncratic behavior" (pp. 154–155). Family members were also asked why they and other participants behaved in certain ways.

From his two-year participant observation of one Italian-American crime family operating in New York (the "Lupollo" family) and his later research on black and Hispanic groups in organized crime, Ianni found evidence of different codes for different groups. In the case of the Lupollo family, there were three basic rules for behavior:

> . . . (1) primary loyalty is vested in "family" rather than in individual lineages or nuclear families, (2) each member of the family must "act like a man" and do nothing which brings disgrace on the family, and (3) family business is privileged matter and must not be reported or discussed outside the group. (Ianni and Reuss-Ianni, 1973:155)

Ianni found that black and Hispanic organized crime codes differed from the Lupollo rules, as well as from each other. For example, whereas the black and Hispanic groups emphasized loyalty and secrecy (as did the Lupollo family), some of these organized crime networks also stressed the rules "Don't be a coward" and "Don't be a creep" (in other words, "fit in" with the group). Some stressed the rule "Be smart" (know when to obey but also when to beat the system), and some stressed "Don't tell the police," "Don't cheat your partner or other people in the network," and "Don't be incompetent" (Ianni, 1975:301–305).

Which rules are stressed depends in large part on how the gangs came together in the first place. Gangs with shared family roots place a premium on rules supporting kinship ties. On the other hand, gangs with origins in youthful street associations and partnerships tend to stress rules underscoring personal qualities ("Don't be a coward"). Those originating in strictly business or entrepreneurial associations tend to stress rules emphasizing more impersonal, activity-oriented obligations ("Don't be incompetent"). The code adopted by a criminal organization reflects far more than the mere fact that it is a secret association engaged in regular criminal activities. How and why the participants came together in the first place, how long the organization has been operating, the cultural heritage of its major participants, and the nature and range of its activities all influence the code of a particular crime group.

The History of Organized Crime in America

One of the most important factors likely to influence the activities, structure, and code of an organized crime syndicate is the length of time it has been in the business of crime. The crime syndicates one reads about most often—those identified as Italian-American and operating primarily in the Midwest and East—have been around for three-quarters of a century; others are relative newcomers, and some are just emerging. Understanding organized crime today requires understanding how it was in the past.

The origins of organized crime can be traced to the gangs of thugs that roamed the streets of New York and other cities and followed the frontier west during the nineteenth century. In New York City the earliest gangs were made up of the sons of immigrant Irish families. These immigrants constituted the core of poor people and were also deprived of political power and were routinely discriminated against. In the eyes of many youths growing up during the period, survival and a path out of the ghetto lay in muscle and the willingness to use it. "The story of the early gangs—whether in New York, San Francisco, or the frontier—is told against a background of conflict; ethnic, economic, and political. It is the tale of men making their own law, legislating with their fists, striking out against real or imagined enemies" (Tyler, 1962:92).

From loafing and brawling the New York gangs moved into extortion. They soon discovered that money was easily made through the intimidation of brothel owners, gambling proprietors, and others in the business of providing illicit services. More money came, and with it power, when it was discovered that politicians and businessmen would pay for their muscle. Gangs were hired to break up picket lines, to intimidate voters, to stuff ballot boxes, and to protect establishments from harassment by other gangs, not to mention the authorities. By the 1850s the gangs were the muscle behind Tammany Hall, the Democratic headquarters and the political heart of the city. With this new power, the gangs were able to open doors that formerly had been closed to the Irish. The docks were under their control, which meant work for Irishmen; now city hall felt their power, which meant city jobs for their fathers, brothers, and cousins.

Rags to Riches and the Quest for Respectability

The history of organized crime in America is to some extent the history of people seeking riches and respectability, and of social, legal, and political conditions providing both the incentive and means to attain them. Whether one looks at the nineteenth-century Irish gang, the Italian-American crime family, or the emergent African-American, Puerto Rican, and Cuban crime networks, the picture is essentially the same. It is a picture of migration and the herding of newcomers into ghettos, with few legitimate avenues of escape; of poverty, discrimination, and degradation; of corruption in politics and government; of laws rendering criminal many goods and services in public demand; and of material things held up as legitimate symbols of success and respectability but denied to the newcomers. Identifying the ghetto as the social setting in which organized crime is spawned, Ianni (1975:89–90) writes:

> The social history of American urban ghettos documents how ghetto dwellers were forced to seek escape from underclass status into the dominant society through the interrelated and interdependent routes of crime and politics. The corrupt political structures of major American cities and organized crime have always enjoyed a symbiotic relationship in which success in one is dependent on the right connections in the other. In this relationship, the aspiring ethnic, blocked from legitimate access to wealth and power, is permitted to produce and provide those illicit goods and services that society publicly condemns but privately demands—gambling, stolen goods, illegal alcohol, sex and drugs—but not without paying tribute to the political establishment. The gangsters and racketeers paid heavily into the coffers of political machines and in return received immunity from prosecution. The ghetto became a safe haven in which crime syndicates could grow and prosper. Two factors—immigrant slum dwellers' alienation from the political process and society's characteristic attitude that so long as "they" do it to each other crime in the ghetto is not an American problem—kept the police indifferent and absent and added to that prosperity. The immigrant and his children found organized crime a quick means of escaping the poverty and powerlessness of the slums. The successful gangster like the successful politician was seen as a model who demonstrated to the masses of lower-class co-ethnics that anyone could achieve success and power in the greater society. And if they did this while defying the police and other oppressors, so much the better. Then, when political power came to the group, partly as a result of these same illegal activities, access to legitimate opportunities became enlarged and assimilation was facilitated. The tradition became one of up and out.

Italian-Americans in Organized Crime

Over the years virtually all ethnic groups have been involved in organized crime: the Irish, Eastern European Jews, Italian and Sicilian immigrants, Chinese and Cuban immigrants, Puerto Ricans, African-Americans, and WASPS, too, of course.

Of all these groups, the Italian-American immigrants made the most lasting impression on the organized crime scene and achieved, over the years, a dominating role in it. A study of the involvement of Italian-Americans in organized crime is thus particularly illuminating.

Immigration and Ghetto Residency   Between 1820 and 1930 an estimated 4.7 million Italians arrived in the United States. Many of the early immigrants traveled to the West and South and became farmers, fishermen, tradesmen, and craftsmen. Over 2 million Italians arrived between 1900 and 1910, 80 percent coming from southern Italy and Sicily. Poor, illiterate, and lacking occupational skills, many soon returned to Italy, but the majority remained in the East and congregated in "Little Italy" ghettos found in most urban centers, especially New York City. Like the Irish before them, they were desperate for a chance to improve their lot and achieve success and respectability in their new country. Also like the Irish, many found crime the easiest and quickest way up and out.

Unable to speak English, unfamiliar with American ways and big-city life, and dependent on one another for guidance and help, many Italian immigrants fell prey to exploitation. Apparently, crime among Little Italy residents was first of all crime against Italians: extortion, vendettas, and the kidnapping of brides. It was not, at first, organized crime, nor did Italian criminals often venture beyond the boundaries of the ghetto. As a member of the "Lupollo" family related to Ianni:

> Can you imagine my father going uptown to commit a robbery or mugging? He would have had to take an interpreter with him to read the street signs and say "stick 'em up" for him. The only time he ever commited a crime outside Mulberry Street was when he went over to the Irish section to steal some milk so that my mother could heat it up and put in my kid brother's ear to stop an earache. (Ianni and Reuss-Ianni, 1973:55)

Yet this intra-ghetto crime was the beginning of Italian involvement in organized crime. By using muscle and by cashing in on ghetto conditions and police indifference to what went on in Little Italy, some immigrants became rich and powerful. They began to extend their illicit activities and hired other men to help them.

One key to wealth and power was extortion. Sometimes alone, sometimes with others, the extortionist would select victims from among newly arrived neighbors. Some extortionists associated themselves with the infamous "Black Hand," a loosely connected band that terrorized vulnerable immigrants. A favorite tactic was to send a letter demanding money, the letter being signed with a drawing of a black hand. Other letters would follow, each successively more blatant in its threats of physical violence. The fearful victim would search for help, which often came in the form of a man who was himself associated with the Black Hand. Sometimes the victim was able to secure a loan from a local source, thus helping enrich not only the extortionist but also the creditor. In this way, "respectable" members of the community grew wealthy from the activities of criminals. In either case, the victim went into debt, becoming more dependent and more vulnerable.

The Mafia Connection   Sicilian-Italian immigrants brought their traditions with them. During the years of adjustment following their immigration, many naturally relied on their social and cultural heritage to help them, and the tendency to cling to old ways was heightened by the ethnic homogeneity of Little Italy. To understand Italian involvement in organized crime and the form it has taken, one must recognize the role played by the immigrant heritage itself.

Important to that heritage were the secret organizations that had flourished for years in southern Italy—among them the Mafia and the Camorra. The origins of the Mafia and the Camorra are generally traced to the early nineteenth century; the Camorra was centered in Naples, the Mafia in Sicily. Though their actual beginnings are unknown, they both flourished in large part because of the widespread political and social unrest characterizing the southern Italian and Sicilian societies during the nineteenth century (Block, 1974; Ianni and Reuss-Ianni, 1973:30–40).

The concept of *mafia* was also important to the heritage. It refers not to the organization but rather to "a state of mind, a sense of pride, a philosophy of life, and a style of behavior which Sicilians recognize immediately" (Ianni and Reuss-Ianni, 1973:26). To describe someone as a *mafioso* does not necessarily mean that he is a member of the Mafia; it may simply mean that he is a man who is respected and held in awe. He is a man who seeks protection not through the law but by his own devices; he is a man who commands fear; he is a man who has dignity and bearing; he is a man who gets things done; he is a man to whom people come when in need; he is man with "friends."

Though not all Italian immigrants were familiar with either the organization or the concept, those from southern Italy, especially western Sicily, undoubtedly were. Some of the immigrants themselves may have been mafiosi, in either meaning. In short, there is good reason to believe that Little Italy residents were familiar with Mafia ways and the spirit of mafia and that their behavior was affected by them. For example, Ianni noted that in the Italian ghettos, people went for protection or redress of grievances to informal "courts" held by mafiosi. In his testimony before the 1963 McClellan Committee of the Senate, Joe Valachi made much of the ties between the American Cosa Nostra and the secret organizations of southern Italy. One clear tie is the oath-taking ritual that changed little from that used in the early nineteenth century by both the Camorra and Mafia organizations:

> Flanked by the boss and his lieutenants, the initiate and his sponsor may stand in front of a table on which are placed a gun and, on occasion, a knife. The boss picks up the gun and intones in the Sicilian dialect: "Niatri representam La Cosa Nostra. Sta famigghia è La Cosa Nostra. (We represent La Cosa Nostra. This family is Our Thing.)" The sponsor then pricks his trigger finger and the trigger finger of the new member, holding both together to symbolize the mixing of blood. After swearing to hold the family above his religion, his country, and his wife and children, the inductee finished the ritual. A picture of a saint or a religious card is placed in his cupped hands and ignited. As the paper burns, the inductee, together with his sponsor, proclaims: "If I ever violate this oath, may I burn as this paper." (*Time*, August 22, 1969:19)

This is not to say that Italian immigrants imported wholesale the Mafia or the Camorra. Rather, they imported a knowledge of the ways of secret societies and the spirit of mafia. This spirit seems to have been particularly important during early ghetto life, for those who grew rich—whether through crime or by essentially legal means such as loaning money in exchange for a part interest in a business—were able to cash in on the mafia idea. These men became the mafiosi and, like those back home, were feared while at the same time respected and upheld as models for emulation by the young. Ianni suggests that it was in the role of mafioso that Giuseppe Lupollo, grandfather of the crime family he studied, gained much of his strength. Abadinsky (1990:32) describes the "boss" in a Mafia family as follows:

> The boss demands absolute respect and total obedience. His working day is spent in exchanges with numerous persons. With a word or two, a sentence, a shake of the head, a smile, or a gesture, he can set in motion a host of activities and operations involving dozens, if not hundreds, of persons. The boss is treated with a great deal of deference. People rise when he enters the room and never interrupt when he is speaking. If they are close to the boss, a kiss on the boss's cheek is considered an appropriate gesture of respect. If the boss rises and embraces an individual, this is considered a great honor, often reserved only for other bosses.

The Impact of Prohibition   Lupollo and other Little Italy residents grew rich and powerful through a combination of criminal and legal activities. Usually they worked alone or with other members of their families. No secret organization tied them together, and the immigrants did not form a new Mafia or Camorra on American soil. Ianni and Reuss-Ianni (1973:61) give three reasons why, until the 1920s at least, a Mafia-style organization did not emerge. First, they had not had enough time. The southern Italian immigrants were newcomers, and 20 years was hardly enough time to establish what had taken many decades at home. Second, the Italian immigrants had come mostly as individuals; hence they had to establish new patterns of organization and new sources of power and profit. Third, the traditional pattern of father-son respect and obedience was not reinforced in American schools and in church; especially in school, the lessons stressed individualism, not family loyalty.

The onset of Prohibition, however, added two of the missing ingredients. Prohibition provided the incentive and means to move outside the ghetto and offered substantial rewards to those who ventured into bootlegging and other liquor-related activities. The illegal market for alcohol provided the incentive for mafiosi to work together and establish contacts outside the ghetto. Prohibition also supplied new organizational models that replaced the traditional family model which older immigrants stressed but their American-born sons tended to reject. The organizational model was that of the American crime gang of Irish and Jewish thugs, which offered lower-echelon positions to Italian youths who had gained criminal experience in ghetto street gangs. A working relationship with non-Italians, frowned on by the older generation of immigrants—called "Old Moustaches" or "Moustache Petes" by the youngsters—became an important feature of the new Italian-American involvement in organized crime.

What emerged was an Italian-American participation in organized crime that combined aspects of the old Mafia and the mafia spirit with strictly American contributions. Unlike the Italian Mafia, the new crime syndicates operated beyond the boundaries of the local community and employed non-Italians. Yet strong ethnic bonds persisted and became especially important as Italians began to secure positions within legitimate government as councilmen, judges, and police officers. Slowly, the domination of the older mafiosi was weakened as ambitious second-generation Italian-Americans sought leadership roles and lucrative fields of operation (drugs, for example) over the objections of their elders.

Toward the end of Prohibition, internal dissension threatened the power and profits of the Italian-American crime syndicates, as the Old Moustaches fought for authority with their younger Americanized counterparts. The Castellammarese War of 1930–1931 marked the height of the conflict. Originating in New York between the older Salvatore Maranzano faction and second-generation gangs under Giuseppe Masseria, the feud spread to Chi-

Those in the higher echelons of organized crime are as likely to be removed by their own kind as by the authorities. With millions of dollars at stake, life becomes cheap.

cago and other cities. Although Maranzano was the victor, many of the Old Moustaches were killed, and it was Americanized gangsters such as Joe Adonis, Vito Genovese, Charlie Luciano, and Frank Costello who subsequently emerged as the powerful figures in the Italian-American syndicates.

After prohibition, Italian-American crime families continued to flourish and retain a dominant place in organized crime. This success was due to a number of events and conditions: the massive influx of Italian immigrants during the early decades of this century; the conditions of ghetto life to which they were subject; the indifference of authorities to what went on inside the ghettos; the immigrants' familiarity with, and fear of, the Mafia and mafiosi; the attempt by Mussolini to crush the Mafia and other secret societies, thus forcing mafiosi to seek shelter in America; the existence and successes of semiorganized American crime gangs; and widespread political corruption in urban areas. Most of all, it was due to Prohibition itself. Prohibition promised a quick and easy path to riches and provided the impetus for the mafiosi and other Italian-Americans to organize and venture outside the ghetto. Prohibition showed the criminal gangs in the ghetto how to increase their money and power. In short, Prohibition helped organized crime come of age.

The Money-Making Enterprises of Organized Crime

During Prohibition, crime syndicates made the manufacture, distribution, and sale of alcoholic beverages their major business. Although extortion, blackmail, robbery, prostitution, gambling, and the sale of protection had been lucrative enterprises, bootlegging outweighed them all. Suddenly the law had made illegal something much in demand by all segments of the population. Fortunes could be made by those who cared to break the law and could organize to do it.

When Prohibition came to an end in 1933 the black market quickly fell apart. This did not mean that no money was to be made by dealing in booze; only much less. Actually, organized crime continues to dabble in the liquor business. Some jurisdictions are still "dry," and others permit only beer or only certain labels to be sold. Even where liquor of any sort is legal, however, money can still be made. With the right connections, profitable liquor licenses can be bought on behalf of the syndicate; through control of bottling, warehousing, and distributing, syndicate liquor finds its way into legitimate outlets (Dorman, 1972:129).

Organized crime is not restricted to any one kind of activity, legal or otherwise, and, like any entrepreneur, must keep up with changing times or go out of business. To fill the void created by the repeal of Prohibition, organized crime turned its attention to new avenues of profit and has continued to branch out ever since.

Criminal Enterprises

The major enterprises providing illicit profits are gambling, usury (loan sharking), drug trafficking, theft, and racketeering. In all these areas the money to be made is enormous. Though one can only guess, it is generally held that profits from each one of these areas run into billions of dollars every year. Estimates of the annual gross from gambling enterprises go as high as $50 billion; drug trafficking is estimated to be a $75-billion business; and a conservative estimate of the gross from loan sharking is $10 billion. Even the sale of sex, not one of the big money-makers, is estimated to gross over $2 billion a year. Recalling that organized crime avoids most, if not all, of the overhead and taxes legitimate businesses have to absorb, these gross figures indicate tremendous incomes for organized crime—a conservative estimate of the net profits would be 30 percent of the gross.

Gambling   Though some speculate that the money-making possibilities of illegal gambling may be on the decline following the spread of state lotteries, gambling remains one of the principal sources of income for organized crime. Most of the money is made from the policy, or numbers, racket. Legend has it that the term *policy* originated from the nineteenth-century practice among the poor of gambling with money set aside for insurance policy premiums; Cressey, however, suggests that the term came from the Italian word for lottery ticket, *polizza*. Whatever the truth, one fact is clear: Policy, or numbers, betting is predominantly a feature of urban slum life. Nationally, the numbers racket is said to take in over $1 billion a year, with $200 million spent in New York alone (Reuter, 1983).

Numbers betting is a simple concept and easy to do. The gambler simply picks any three-digit number and bets that this number will correspond to the winning number, selected by some predetermined procedure. Over the years winning numbers have been computed from the number of shares traded on a stock exchange, the daily cash balance in the United States Treasury, and the payoffs at local pari-mutuel racetracks. At one time, the number was simply drawn from a revolving drum. The odds are 1000 to 1 against the bettor, whereas payoff never exceeds 600 to 1.

The numbers racket attracted organized crime not only because of the immense profits to be made from it but also because the game requires organization, money, and a good deal of corruption in the right places—things only organized crime had. Although small-scale games, involving small bets and a small betting clientele, have existed in the past, they were neither very profitable nor very secure for those who ran them. To work, the numbers racket needs organized crime. The boss of a New Jersey crime network explains why:

> Everybody needs the organization—the banker, the controllers, the runners, even the customers. Here's why. Only a big organization can pay up when the bank gets hit very hard. Suppose a lot of people play the same number one day. For example, when Willie Mays hit his 599th home run, a lot of black people played "600" the next day, figuring Willie was going to make it and so were they. If that number had come up, the banker would have been wiped out, and not only that, a lot of customers would have gone without their payoffs. The whole system would have collapsed. . . .

There was another reason why they needed the organization. Only the organization had the money and the muscle to keep the cops and politicians from breaking up the game and shaking down the players and operators. (Ianni, 1975:59–60)

Reuter (1983) found that New York City numbers games were not highly coordinated, though some apparently independent banks may have been branches of a single owner (see also Haller, 1991).

Though the specifics vary from place to place and from syndicate to syndicate, the numbers operation is organized along the following lines: The bets are picked up by "runners" from "numbers drops" in shops, factories, office buildings, and bars, or simply on the street. The runners pass the money and betting slips on to local "collectors," or "route men," in charge of their neighborhoods. The collectors pass the money and numbers tickets on to the "controller," who sends it on to the "district controller," who works for the "policy operator." The policy operator actually runs the enterprise and sometimes is known as the "'banker" or "owner." He or she is usually one of a number of operators, all of whom pay a commission to the crime syndicate under whose overall supervision and control and in whose territory the racket operates. These policy operators may or may not be actual members of the crime family. At payoff time, the money simply follows the reverse route, usually starting at the "branch" or "district bank" run by the policy operator.

Loan Sharking   Loan sharking thrives because some people who need loans are unable or unwilling to secure them through legitimate lending institutions. Loan sharks will lend them the money, for a price. To make loans one needs money; organized crime has it. To ensure that the money is repaid, with interest, one needs organization and the ability to make collections; organized crime has them. Because usury is illegal, a lender must be able to collect without resorting to legal channels and without the interference of the law; organized crime accomplishes this through muscle and corruption.

Borrowers who come to a loan shark usually want quick loans with no questions asked. They may be gamblers in need of money to pay off debts or finance further play; they may be businesspeople faced with bankruptcy or wanting to invest in risky, perhaps illegal, ventures; they may simply be poor people in need of small loans but lacking the credit or collateral required by licensed lending institutions. The interest they will pay depends on how much they borrow, the intended use of the loan, their repayment potential, and what they are worth to the mob if they cannot make their payments. Generally interest runs anywhere from 1 to 150 percent per week, with most smaller loans at 20 percent per week—the "six for five" loan, in which each five dollars borrowed requires six to be paid back at the end of a week. Usually a set time is established for payments, and if the required payment is not made on or before that exact time, the borrower will owe another week's interest, computed from the principal plus the interest already accrued.

Various members of the South Philadelphia Bruno family operated loansharking businesses, and Haller (1991) uses two of them to illustrate contrasting operations within one crime family. On the one hand, there was Harry Riccobene, whose loans were mostly small (less than $1,000) and made to local hustlers and merchants. "Within their culture, borrowing informally from a loan shark was a normal and accepted business practice" (Haller, 1991:10). When customers fell behind in their payments, as most did, Harry used a combination of gentle chastisement and renegotiated (lower) payment schedules. Some of his agents did not approve of Harry's leniency, but Harry's revolving credit system prospered.

Also prospering was the loan sharking operation of Frank Sindone, another Bruno family member. But Sindone's operation was different: He made much larger loans, up to $50,000 or higher, mostly to construction contractors and other legitimate businesses with credit and cash flow problems. He also took his operation further afield, to South Jersey and the Pennsylvania suburbs. His agents operated relatively independently, sharing in the profits, and together Sindone and his agents "had mastered the orchestrated use of vicious, vulgar, and convincing threats of violence to the borrower and the borrower's family" when dealing with delinquent loans (Haller, 1991:12).

It is unusual for a borrower to be killed, for death means the money is lost forever. Though a killing may be committed occasionally to make the victim an example to others, the loan shark wants the money first and foremost, and if this cannot be obtained with threats, the loan shark will look for other ways to get it. Indeed, loans are sometimes made—at very high interest rates—not in the expectation that they will be repaid but for other purposes. The mob may be looking to garner a controlling interest in a borrower's business, and when loan payments falter, this provides the leverage necessary to bring this goal about. The borrower simply turns over all or a part of the business in exchange for a temporary delay of the payments. The Bruno family's Sindone liked to operate this way (Haller, 1991:12). This is one of the ways that organized crime secures a footing in legitimate business enterprises, though Reuter (1983:101) thinks it is rare among the small-time loan sharks, most of whom would not know how to carry out profitable fraud schemes involving legitimate businesses.

Drug Trafficking   Organized crime is involved in drug trafficking at all levels, but especially in importation and wholesale distribution. The need for organization, contacts, and large sums of money puts the business outside the reach of most individuals and small criminal groups. This emphasis on importing and wholesaling does not mean, however, that organized crime is not interested in what goes on at the neighborhood and street levels of the drug scene. Since its own profits depend on a healthy drug traffic, it observes the street closely and helps keep open the channels through which the drugs flow. The syndicate also supplies loans to dealers—at least the bigger, more successful ones—and through loan sharking and fencing on the street endeavors to ensure that money circulates so that buys can be made. Today much of the local heroin trade is controlled by black and Hispanic criminal groups, and this has been one of the avenues giving these groups access to the world of organized crime. The world of illicit drugs is discussed in greater detail in Chapter 9.

In 1984 the so-called Pizza Connection was uncovered when Italian and American police arrested over 200 suspected Mafia members, including 28 in America, after a high-ranking mafioso named Tommaso Buscetta turned informant. Buscetta had extensive operations in Italy and Brazil, and he detailed the existence of a Sicilian-based organized crime network operating outside the established American Mafia families. This network is reputed to have imported over 1600 pounds of heroin since 1979, with a street value of $1.65 billion. Its American members were mostly pizza parlor operators—hence the name—located in rural parts of Wisconsin, Michigan, Oregon, and Illinois, and with connections in New York and Switzerland. In late 1988 another major drug ring was exposed, this one smuggling tons of marijuana into the United States from Colombia. Former race driver Randy Lanier and two associates were charged with engaging in a "continuing criminal enterprise," a federal charge carrying a mandatory life sentence. The three conspirators were said to have smuggled 646,000 pounds of marijuana over a seven-year period, and to have accumulated assets worth over $150 million (*St. Louis Post-Dispatch*, October 6, 1988).

Theft Organized crime has been interested in theft since its earliest days. Today most organized crime efforts are directed at the kinds of thievery that promise high returns while avoiding high risk, such as truck hijacking, car-theft rings, thefts from warehouses and docks, securities theft, and fencing. Once again the organization, money, muscle, and contacts of organized crime are major factors in explaining syndicate activity in these areas.

Much has been made of syndicate involvement in securities theft and manipulation. Millions of dollars in securities disappear every year from the vaults of major brokerage houses; most of the lost bonds are stolen. Testimony before the Senate Committee on Banking, Housing, and Urban Affairs indicated that securities theft is a major problem these days and that behind much of the thievery lie organized crime syndicates (see also Abadinsky, 1990: 291–294). While estimates of the actual amounts stolen are difficult to make, the yearly totals are generally thought to exceed $2 billion and may be much higher when thefts from the mails and manipulations during securities transfers are included (Conklin, 1973:121–127; Metz, 1971).

To accomplish the theft and manipulation of stocks and bonds, organized crime needs insiders, persons employed by brokerage firms who have access to vaults or who routinely handle securities. Sometimes these important contacts are indebted to loan sharks and steal securities in exchange for a respite from their payments; sometimes extortion and intimidation are used to frighten employees into working with the underworld; and sometimes the mob manages to place one of its own into a position of trust within a brokerage firm. Once in syndicate hands, the stocks and bonds are often converted into cash. This can be accomplished by using the stolen securities as collateral for loans, as part of a company's portfolio of assets, or merely by reselling them through brokers here or abroad.

Labor Racketeering

During the nineteenth century, organized criminal groups learned that money could be made in the fields of industrial organization and employee relations. Faced with the prospects of strikes and unionization, companies called on criminal gangs to help them combat these threats to their power and profits. The companies paid well for the gangs' muscle, and the gangs, in turn, were happy to oblige. Infiltration of the union movement by organized crime soon followed, and with it came money and power for leaders of the fledgling unions. First the building trades and then service industries fell under the influence and domination of corrupt officials backed by gangsters. Money was collected from both employers and employees, organized crime playing off each side against the other (Hutchinson, 1969).

Racketeering is explained not merely by the corruption of union and company officials nor by the fact that organized crime is in the buiness of making money any way it can. Rather, the spread of racketeering stems from a combination of conditions. Some are economic—for example, excessive entrepreneurial competition and an excess supply of labor. As Walter Lippmann (1931:61) observed many years ago:

> Given an oversupply of labor and an industry in which no considerable amount of capital or skill is required to enter it, the conditions exist under which racketeering can flourish. The effort to unionize in the face of a surplus of labor invites the use of violence and terror to maintain a monopoly of labor and thus to preserve the workers' standard of living. Labor unionism in such trades tends to fall into the control of dictators who are often corrupt and not often finical about enlisting gangsters to enforce the closed shop. The employers, on the other hand, faced with the constant threat of cutthroat competition, are subject to the easy temptation to pay gangsters for protection against competitors. The protection consists in driving the competition from the field.

Identifying additional conditions that support organized crime infiltration into unions, John Hutchinson (1969:143) includes (1) the traditions of frontier violence, (2) cultural values stressing individualism, (3) an entrenched philosophy of acquisition, (4) an admiration for sharp practices, (5) a tolerance of the fix, and (6) a legacy stressing politics as a source of personal profit. Companies and unions went along with the spread of racketeering because both saw benefits outweighing costs and because the conditions and temperament of the times presented no great obstacles. Actually, of course, both company officials and union leaders risk becoming pawns in the hands of organized crime syndicates. This is precisely what has happened over the years, with the costs borne not only by the union membership but also by members of the general public who hold company stock or who are simply consumers of the companies' goods and services.

Nobody knows for sure how much organized crime syndicates make from labor racketeering. In 1958, the Senate Select Committee on Improper Activities in the Labor or Management Field found that $10 million in Teamsters Union funds had been siphoned off into the pockets of union officials and their gangster friends (Salerno and Tompkins, 1969:295). The Teamsters Central States Pension Fund is widely acknowledged to have been under the control of syndicate figures. It is known that the mob helped pick Teamster presidents Jackie Presser and Roy Williams. Police informants have tied both men to organized crime groups in Chicago, New York, Kansas City, and Cleveland (*Los Angeles Times*, September 25, 1985). The pension fund is worth billions of dollars, and millions have apparently been spent without the knowledge of the rank-and-file membership, whose money it really is (see also Block, 1991; Abadinsky, 1990).

Pseudolegitimate Enterprises

Apart from their patently illegal enterprises, organized crime groups have infiltrated the world of legitimate business. Though any complete list of the different businesses in which organized crime is involved would be impossible to compile, the following have been specifically identified: banking, hotels and motels, real estate, garbage collection, vending machines, construction, delivery and long-distance hauling, garment manufacture, insurance, stocks and bonds, vacation resorts, funeral parlors, bakeries, sausage manufacture and processing of other meat products, paving, tobacco, dairy products, demolition, warehousing, auto sales and leasing, meat packing, janitorial services, beauty and health salons, lumber, horse breeding, nightclubs, bars, restaurants, linen supply, laundries, and dry cleaning. There may well be no type of legitimate business enterprise in which organized crime does not have a financial interest.

Organized crime has sought involvement in legitimate businesses for a number of reasons. First is the obvious economic incentive: Legitimate businesses are additional sources of income. Second, legitimate businesses can provide a front for illegal activities; owning a trucking firm, for example, gives a crime syndicate the means of transporting stolen property or a cover for bootlegging. Third, legitimate businesses can serve as an important outlet for monies earned through criminal activities. Profits from the latter invested in businesses under syndicate control appear to be "clean"; also, syndicate members can receive legitimate-looking salary payments from those companies with which they are associated. These salaries constitute the members' visible sources of income, and they declare this income on tax returns in a continuing effort to avoid federal prosecution. Needless to say, those receiving such salaries many contribute little or nothing to the actual day-to-day operations of the companies concerned.

A final reason that organized crime has sought holdings in legitimate enterprises is respectability. Crime is not respectable work, and the profits from it are dirty money. A long-standing goal among higher-echelon mobsters, especially Italian-Americans with their traditions of family honor, has been the acquisition of respectability for their children and grandchildren, if not for themselves. Legitimate businesses provide a route to social acceptance. Instead of following in the footsteps of their elders, the younger generation is able to acquire the trappings of respectability by working in enterprises with no apparent connection to crime.

Peter Lupsha (1981) suggests that the pull of respectability may have been overstated. He sees organized crime as rational behavior selected not so much as a last economic resort but because it fits "one perverse aspect of our values: namely, that only 'suckers' work, and that in our society, one is at liberty to take 'suckers' and seek easy money, just as one is at liberty to be one" (p. 22). Organized crime families are not leaving the business in droves, nor are the children of members all leading exemplary lives: "A sufficient number of family members and relatives do stay in the business so that family control is maintained" (p. 20). Penetration of legitimate businesses is guided more by economic motives than any interest in respectability, in Lupsha's view.

Certainly, the legitimate enterprises are rarely, if ever, completely divorced from a syndicate's illegal enterprises, and for this reason it seems more appropriate to call them "pseudolegitimate" enterprises. A certain real estate company may appear quite legal and aboveboard; if organized crime has anything to do with it, however, all is not what it appears to be.

Organized crime moves into its pseudolegitimate enterprises in various ways. Some use intimidation and force, and others use more normal avenues of business acquisition. When interested in a particular business, it is common for the syndicate to use the carrot-and-stick approach—in Don Corleone's words, "I'll make him an offer he can't refuse." Such a case was reported in the New York Court of Appeals in the late 1960s. An executive of several successful vending machine companies was simply told that he was to pass over to a certain family of interested persons a 25-percent share of his business interests. The request was backed up by assaults on his wife and various other forms of intimidation (Cressey, 1969:103). Another way to infiltrate businesses is to arrange, through extortion or bribes, to have syndicate associates placed in executive positions, so that eventually the company is controlled by the syndicate. Yet another way is to purchase large blocks of company stock through legitimate trading channels, though under the cover of fictitious names and companies. Finally, loan sharks may turn delinquent loans into a means of acquiring a controlling interest in a business.

The Survival of Organized Crime

Why does organized crime persist? The answer to this important question lies beyond the more obvious defenses that secret societies and groups erect against outsiders—secrecy, codes of conduct, mutual protection among members, and the like. Within the organization of crime syndicates are survival mechanisms that come into play whenever these more obvious defenses are inadequate. These include the roles played by public attitudes and behavior and the attitudes and behavior of those ostensibly responsible for combating organized crime. The nature of criminal law itself is a factor, especially as it focuses on moral choices and private behavior.

Role Imperatives

Two of the most important internal survival mechanisms appear to be the roles of "enforcer" and "buffer." These roles, assumed by select individuals in crime organizations, might well be called *role imperatives*, for without them (or something very similar) the survival of any crime organization would be threatened.

Donald Cressey (1969) goes so far as to argue that unless the division of labor provides for at least one enforcer, the organization in question is not a part of true organized crime. Ianni (1973), on the other hand, found only weak evidence of enforcer positions in the established division of labor and authority structure of the crime family he extensively studied. Methods of enforcement range all the way from verbal warnings to maiming or murder. A set of rules is not enough: From time to time threats must be enforced, and organized crime sees to it that they are. Organized crime has been likened to government in this sense: Not only do syndicates create their own rules; but, like states, they also have their own machinery for enforcing them and their own methods of doing it.

The "buffer" role identified by Cressey and others also enhances the organization's survival possibilities. The buffer is akin to the corporate "assistant to the president," whose tasks are primarily centered on internal communications and the flow of decisions in the hierarchy of authority. The buffer may also be likened to a spy, for he keeps tabs on what lower-level members do and say and reports back to his superiors. Without the buffer role, the smooth functioning of the organization would be impaired, and the decision-making process undermined. It is the buffer who keeps open lines of communication between leaders and followers, who passes down important messages from the top, who forewarns of internal dissensions and problems with operations at the street level, and who helps smooth out disagreements and conflicts.

Another role imperative is the "corrupter." Since organized crime syndicates are in the business of crime, their survival greatly depends on the fix. To put the fix in and maintain important connections with those in government and law, organized crime groups typically have one or more members assigned to corrupt officials in order to preserve good relations with them. Corrupters may be found anywhere in the organizational hierarchy, and their job is to bribe, buy, intimidate, negotiate, persuade, and sweet-talk themselves "into a relationship with police, public officials, and anyone else who might help 'family' members maintain immunity from arrest, prosecution, and punishment" (Cressey, 1969:251–252). Moore (1986) suggests that corrupter roles emerge in response to the organization of law enforcement itself. If there is one enforcement agency that has jurisdiction over a particular illegal activity, then a centralized corrupter role will tend to develop. If many agencies have jurisdiction, however, corruption will have to occur on more "local" levels to be effective.

Cressey (1969:248) calls the political objective of corruption the "nullification of government," and it is sought at two different levels:

> At the lower level are the agencies for law enforcement and the administration of justice. When a Cosa Nostra soldier bribes a policeman, a police chief, a prosecutor, a judge, or a license administrator, he does so in an attempt to nullify the law-enforcement process. At the upper level are legislative agencies, including federal and state legislatures as well as city councils and county boards of supervisors. When a "family" boss supports a candidate for political office, he does so in an attempt to deprive honest citizens of their democratic voice, thus nullifying the democratic process.

In his study of organized crime in Seattle during the 1960s, William Chambliss (1978) describes a crime network that extended from street hustlers, bookmakers, pimps, drug dealers, and gamblers to business-people, politicians, and law-enforcement officials. Hotel, restaurant, club, and bingo-parlor operators were fronts for gambling and vice; police officers and prosecutors took bribes and offered protection, falsified reports, and covered up investigations; and politicians took campaign contributions of "dirty money" and exercised their licensing and legislative powers in support of the rackets, "one of the largest industries in the state" (Chambliss, 1978:54). This crime network depended for its survival on corruption at all levels of government, and for many years the corruption was there.

For nullification of government to work there must be officials willing or able to be corrupted. Some persons obviously are willing to be corrupted, but even if there were no willing corruptees, organized crime's muscle and its willingness to use it would probably ensure viable corrupter–corruptee relationships. The truth is, however, that organized crime rarely has to use muscle to nullify government, no matter what level. The nature of politics and government is such that those acting in violation of the law and those ostensibly responsible for its creation and enforcement readily enter into mutually beneficial relationships. Just how successful and important these connections are is evidenced by the fact that since its very beginning, organized crime has made one of its first tasks the establishment of working relationships with those in politics, government, and law enforcement. Because it pays off in security, organized crime will continue to pursue the nullification of government.

Legislation of Morality

Organized crime will continue to flourish if lawmakers continue to enact legislation rendering illegal any activities, products, and services demanded by significant numbers of the population. Organized crime makes the bulk of its profits in supplying illegal commodities and services. Drugs, gambling, sex, and other so-called vices are profitable precisely because criminal laws have the effect of driving the activities underground and into the hands of those willing and able to carry out illicit business. In this way, criminal laws create the very conditions conducive to the emergence and spread of organized criminal activities.

The legislation of morality is, then, yet another factor in the survival of organized crime. But apart from encouraging the emergence of black marketeering, laws designed to repress what some people think of as vices also help give "a kind of franchise to those who are willing to break the law" (Schelling, 1967:117). This is what Herbert Packer (1964) called "the crime tariff"; it serves to protect those among us who will break the law by supplying drugs or gambling opportunities to those who are unwilling to do so but who will take advantage of their availability. Journalist and social commentator Walter Lippmann (1931:65ff) first drew attention to this unintended consequence of moral legislation when he noted more than 40 years ago that

> . . . we have a code of laws which prohibit all the weaknesses of the flesh. This code of laws is effective up to a point. That point is the unwillingness of respectable people to engage in the prohibited services as sellers of prohibited commodities. . . . The high level of lawlessness is maintained by the fact that Americans desire to do so many things which they also desire to prohibit. . . . [They] have made laws which act like a protective tariff—to encourage the business of the underworld. Their prohibitions have turned over to the underworld the services from which it profits. Their prejudice in favor of weak governments has deprived them of the power to cope with the vast lawbreaking industries which their laws have called into question.

Public Attitudes and Behavior

Organized crime depends for its profits and power on the widespread demand for its services. By demanding its products and services, the public helps organized crime survive and prosper.

In addition to public behavior, public attitudes and perceptions also help organized crime survive. How Americans view crime and criminals helps shape the crime scene itself. In the case of organized crime, public perceptions and attitudes are probably more fuzzy and mixed than anything else, but so far no evidence has been presented to indicate that the public perceives organized crime as a real problem deserving stringent control.

The lack of attitudinal opposition to organized crime reflects in part the fact that some of the public have used its services and that many others are not convinced of the harmfulness of the services it provides. Moreover, many people probably have only a vague idea of what organized crime really is, and popular films like The Godfather present a picture that hardly fits in with most day-to-day experiences or images of the world. Indeed, the mystery surrounding organized crime gives it a certain charm and appeal. Then again, even when people consume products and services supplied by organized crime, they rarely come in contact with persons who represent themselves as members of a crime family or syndicate, and those who are encountered have no distinguishing marks about them to suggest that they are part of organized crime. Stuart Hills (1971:130) points out: "Many of the customers who place a friendly bet with that nice old man in the corner bar do not perceive, in fact, that this criminal bookmaker is a businessman—not an unorganized individual gambler."

Perhaps the most important reason that public perceptions and attitudes are sketchy, stereotypical, and ambivalent is that those to whom society customarily looks for clues and guidance in thinking about crime have themselves presented a fragmented and warped picture. Government officials and law-enforcement agencies have tended to stress the individual character of crime and criminality and to downplay its organizational features. Beyond this, the stereotype of the dangerous criminal fostered by authorities fits the mugger, rapist, burglar, and dope pusher, not Vito Genovese, Carlo Gambino, or Sam Giancana. Whether government officials purposely play down orga-

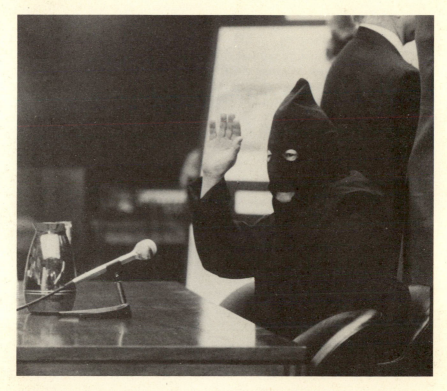

Information on organized crime activities is largely gathered through undercover work or through informants. To ensure their safety, the identity of witnesses is often concealed during testimony.

nized crime and systematically keep information about it from the public is hard to say. Salerno and Tompkins (1969:271) think that might be the case: "Too much effort spent exposing organized crime could be damaging in future elections." The healthy publicity given Rudolph Giuliani and other federal prosecutors may actually have diverted public attention from the mundane and parasitic activities of most organized criminals.

Future Trends

Organized crime is undoubtedly here to stay, at least for the foreseeable future. But changes are afoot, just as changes occurred in the past. Ethnic succession has brought Chicanos, Puerto Ricans, and Cuban-Americans into prominent positions in organized crime, especially in the highly populated Northeast and in Chicago and Miami. African-Americans have also claimed a more prominent place in organized crime, moving beyond their traditional urban numbers rackets into drug trafficking and prostitution. As yet they are neither as well organized nor as far-reaching in their activities as are Italian-American crime syndicates. But the die seems to be cast: Italian-American domination of vice should decline in urban centers where large populations of African-Americans and Hispanics are concentrated.

According to Ianni, the same ghetto conditions that spawned early organized crime helped produce the contemporary ethnic succession. In addition, the Italian-American crime syndicates themselves may have helped bring about change. Established organized crime groups inevitably came to employ ghetto residents as soldiers, lower-echelon pushers, and numbers runners in their own neighborhoods. Streetwise blacks, Chicanos, Puerto Ricans, and Cubans became vital links between the organization and street-level buyers of commodities and services. With involvement came knowledge, contacts, and, for some, wealth. With involvement also came efforts to control the business in one's territory. An added incentive for Cuban involvement was the establishment of a cocaine and heroin connection from South America through Cuba and Miami.

Although mainly restricted to their own ethnic neighborhoods, the crime networks of blacks and Hispanics are emerging as the new forces in the organized delivery of drugs and sex and are gaining more control over the numbers racket and loan sharking in the ghetto. In order to extend and expand, however, these newcomers will have to accomplish what the Italian-Americans did before them: "(1) greater control over sectors of organized crime outside as well as inside the ghetto; (2) some organizing principle which will serve as kinship did among the Italians to bring the disparate networks together into larger criminally monopolistic organizations; and (3) better access to political power and the ability to corrupt it" (Ianni, 1974:36). Although the first requirement may well be the easiest to meet because of their growing control over the drug traffic, much will depend on the willingness of established crime syndicates to allow a blossoming competition from these newcomers.

Peter Reuter (1983:136–137) believes that Mafia families are responding to the recent challenges to their power and profits with accommodation rather than conflict. He speculates this is because violence would bring even more police surveillance than is currently the case, dramatically pushing up the costs of doing business.

One can expect to continue hearing about organized crime. It should be apparent that organized crime is a consequence of numerous social, cultural, political, legal, and economic conditions, many of which seem destined to persist. Viewed from a rationality-opportunity perspective, organized crime will continue to flourish as long as illicit goods and services are demanded and capable people are willing to organize to supply them for a profit. As new opportunities for criminal enterprise appear, they will be grasped by criminally motivated individuals in a position to prosper from them.

Summary of Chapter 8

This chapter has explored the nature and role of organized crime in America. Criminals are considered part of organized crime if they combine into groups for the purpose of providing illegal goods and services or to engage routinely in illegal activities that profit the group. Political corruption is an integral part of organized crime as is the ability and willingness of participants to use force in pursuit of the organization's goals and to ensure that members abide by its rules. Although there is disagreement on the extent to which organized crime is *organized*, it is generally agreed that even rudimentary organization means that participants are able to commit a wider variety of crimes on a larger scale than are other criminals.

The history of organized crime in America is to some extent the history of people seeking riches and respectability, and of the social, legal, and political conditions that provide both the incentives and means to attain them. Over the years virtually all ethnic groups have been involved in organized crime, though Prohibition is probably the most significant event in its history. Prohibition helped organized crime come of age and lent it a distinctly American character while promoting the fortunes of ambitious Italian-American crime families. In recent years, trafficking in drugs from Mexico and South America has likewise promoted the fortunes of ambitious black, Hispanic, and Vietnamese crime groups.

Organized crime survives mainly because there is widespread demand for the illegal goods and services that it provides, because public officials are willing to be corrupted, and because moral entrepreneurs are successful in getting the authorities to criminalize activities that many people find pleasurable. In addition, however, the existence of marked ethnic and racial inequality in an acquisitive society helps explain both the appeal and suitability of black market enterprise for population groups isolated from the economic, social, and political mainstream.

Recommended Readings

Howard Abadinsky (1990). *Organized Crime*. 3rd Edition. Chicago: Nelson-Hall.

Patricia A. Adler (1985). *Wheeling and Dealing: An Ethnography of an Upper-Level Drug Dealing and Smuggling Community*. New York: Columbia University Press.

William J. Chambliss (1988). *On The Take: From Petty Crooks to Presidents*. 2nd Edition. Bloomington, IN.: Indiana University Press.

Mark H. Haller (1991). *Life Under Bruno: The Economics of an Organized Crime Family*. Philadelphia: Pennsylvania Crime Commission.

Francis A. J. Ianni, and Elizabeth Reuss-Ianni (1973). *A Family Business: Kinship and Control in Organized Crime*. New York: Russell Sage.

Peter Reuter (1983). *Disorganized Crime: Illegal Markets and the Mafia*. Cambridge, MA.: MIT Press.

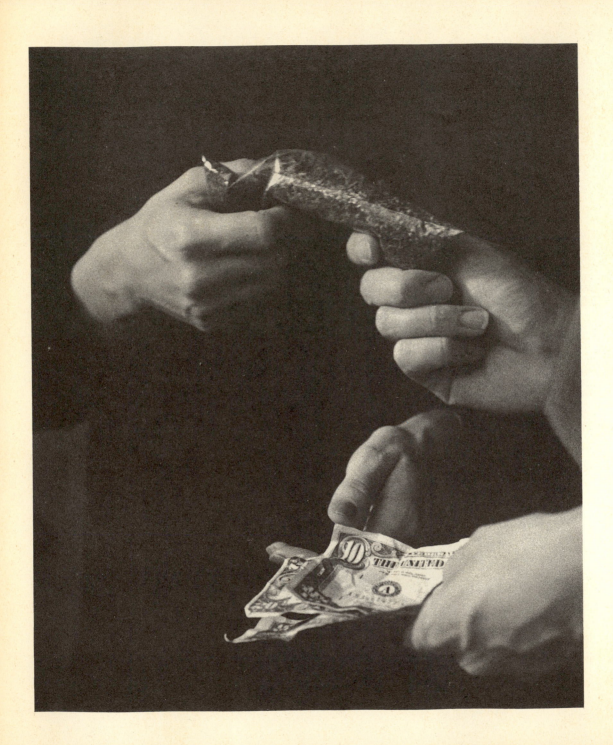

Chapter 9

Public Order Crime: Prostitution and Drugs

Nothing inherent in an act makes it a crime, though some crimes carry the stigma of "sin" as well as illegality. Over the centuries, societies have grappled with the problem of what to do about activities that many regard as sinful and yet many enjoy. As long as these behaviors are kept from public view, it is easy to deny that they really exist. Prostitution, pornography, drunkenness, and drug addiction are rarely hidden from the public eye, however, and for that reason are often considered threats to public morality and order and so are made illegal.

This chapter deals primarily with the public order crimes of drug use and prostitution. In their criminal aspects, drugs and sex have some marked similarities:

1. Participants in these crimes often do not view themselves as criminal, nor are they viewed as criminals by significant portions of the population.
2. The criminal sides of sex and drugs have legal counterparts that are sometimes difficult to distinguish from them except for their legality. For example, it is legal to buy and sell alcohol and caffeine but not heroin or marijuana. It is legal (in most places) to buy and sell *Hustler* and *Penthouse* magazines but not to dance nude in a bar.
3. Illegal sex and drugs are sources of pleasure and tremendous profits. The profits, more than the pleasures, are a direct consequence of criminalization. The black market drives up prices and profits, and entrepreneurs willing to take risks pay no taxes on their profits.
4. Illegal sex and drugs are prime targets of organized crime, with all three feeding off one another. For example, many prostitutes are drug addicts; most female drug addicts—at least poor ones—engage in prostitution; and organized crime controls large segments of drug trafficking and criminal sex, and through the profits it makes extends its control, protects itself from enforcement, and increases the market for its products and services.
5. The laws that apply to sex and drugs reflect both consensus and conflict, with special interests prominent in both their substance and enforcement.
6. Enforcement of laws dealing with drugs and sex requires a special type of policing: the use of informants and undercover police. It is also a major area of graft and corruption in the criminal justice system.
7. Much of the behavior that is criminalized in both areas is said to be "victimless," in that participants consider themselves willingly involved rather than being offended against.
8. Both areas of crime are prime targets of moral entrepreneurs, who see the behavior involved as evidence of declining morals and unreasonable permissiveness and who continually organize campaigns to broaden the laws and increase the penalties.

These, then, are some of the similarities. A more detailed, individual examination of these public order crimes follows.

Sex and the Criminal Law

Historically, criminal labels have been applied to sex on the basis of four considerations: (1) the nature of the act, (2) the nature of the sex object, (3) the social setting in which sex occurs, and (4) the existence of consent.

Some sexual behaviors are considered criminal regardless of the people and circumstances involved. In most states it is illegal to engage in anal intercourse or analingus (oral stimulation of the anus), and in many states oral sex of any sort is prohibited. However, the nature of the sex act itself is often coupled with other considerations in designating the behavior as criminal.

Most criminal codes limit legal sex to partners who are human, adults, and not members of the same family except as marital partners. Many states outlaw sex when the partners are not married (fornication) or are married but not to each other (adultery). Even when the act itself and the partners are legal, a crime may still be committed if the act is performed in public: sex in parks, restaurants, theaters, automobiles, trains, or anywhere else where it could reasonably be witnessed is usually an offense.

Last is the important question of consent. No matter what is done, with whom or where, a crime may be committed if a partner withholds consent or is legally considered incapable of giving it (he or she is mentally ill, for example, or drugged, or a child). However, as seen in Chapter 4, it is not a crime in many jurisdictions for a husband to force sex upon his wife.

The Shaping of Modern Sex Laws

In the earliest legal codes, relatively few sexual activities were illegal. Incest, adultery, fornication, and defilement of virgins were commonly prohibited.

With the spread of Christianity, an ever-increasing collection of sexual prohibitions emerged in law. As the church spread its gospel and increased its power in law and public policy, the foundations of modern sex laws were set in place. In England, for example, the church was quick to impose severe restrictions on sexual freedoms. At the heart of the church's stand was "a definite and detailed code of behavior regarded as obligatory [for] all Christian believers. At the center of the code was the fixed principle that pleasure in sex was evil and damnable. It was not the sex act itself which was condemned, but the pleasure which was connected with it" (Wright, 1968:20–21).

The church viewed sex in extremely narrow terms. Heterosexual copulation for the strict purposes of procreation was the rule, and then only within the framework of marriage. Any sexual activity or relationship not meeting these criteria was viewed as inherently wrong and evil. If the sex act was not "straight" intercourse, furthermore, it was considered "unnatural," "perverted" behavior.

These views and restrictions did not make the church successful in suppressing sexual expression. On the contrary, by all accounts it failed dismally. Even priests found it hard to abide by church rulings on sexual matters, and there are accounts of monks murdering their superiors when the latter sought to deprive them of heterosexual or homosexual outlets (Taylor, 1965). Even as late as the sixteenth century, the papal heads of the Roman Catholic church were notorious for their debauchery, incestuous conduct, and sexual adventures.

In England, developing common law left most sexual matters in the hands of the church. Despite certain exceptions—for example, rape, sexual assault on children, and sexual acts in public—sex was not a concern of criminal law. Morris Ploscowe (1951:138) describes the pre-sixteenth-century situation:

> The common law of crimes took a comparatively liberal attitude toward sex expression. A great deal of illicit sexual activity, both non-marital and extra-marital, was outside the domain of the common law and common-law courts. Fornication was no crime. Single men and women could copulate in secret without violating any penal provisions of the common law. Adultery was not a punishable offense. A man could two-time his wife or a wife cuckold her husband without having to fear the jailor or hangman. Men could masturbate each other in secret without running the risk of landing in jail.

Two things, however, seem to have provoked civil interest in sexual matters. First, the failure of the church and its ecclesiastical courts to control sexual expression left religious leaders searching for alternative ways to control sex. They turned to the state for help, reasoning, perhaps, that criminal law and its enforcement machinery would succeed where they had failed. Second, civil leaders grew less content to give the church sanctioning power over any area of human conduct, including sex. They saw punishment as the proper domain of the state, and besides, why allow the church to levy fines when these could be paid into the royal treasury?

Henry VIII was one of the first English kings to enact specific sexual legislation. His buggery statute of 1533 made it a felony for a male to have anal intercourse with another male or for a female to have intercourse with an animal. Urged on by Protestant and later by Puritan leaders—and quite in keeping with their statutory expansion of the criminal law—Henry's successors continued to enact sex laws. Thus by the eighteenth century almost every conceivable sexual activity and relationship could be made to fit common law or statutory provisions.

Vagueness in Sex Laws

Henry VIII's buggery statute was vague, leaving unclear whether anal intercourse with a female was included or whether male sex with an animal was a crime. Unfortunately, many of our sex laws today are unclear regarding what exactly constitutes a crime.

Part of the problem unquestionably derives from the reluctance of legal authorities to describe in plain language what have always been sensitive matters. Writing in the late sixteenth century, Sir Edward Coke found it hard to break with that tradition and may himself have contributed to its perpetuation. His attitude is summed up in his now famous reference to buggery as that "detestable and abominable sin, among Christians not to be named." In regard to a description of the penetration of the vagina during intercourse—an essential element in legal conceptions of carnal knowledge—he could only bring himself to say, in Latin, "the thing in the thing" (Gigeroff, 1968:11).

The U.S. Supreme Court has not improved matters much. Consider on the one hand its 1973 ruling in *Wainwright v. Stone*. In this case the Court supported the continued enforcement of a Florida statute outlawing sodomy, defined only as "an abominable and detestable crime against nature." On the other hand, there is the matter of obscenity. Here, in *Miller v. California* (1973), the Court appeared to have abandoned jurisdiction, leaving judgment largely up to "the average person," applying "contemporary community standards." From one perspective this might be hailed as progressive, since it allows for variations in community standards. From another it places considerable enforcement discretion in the hands of local authorities, does not reduce the likelihood of breaches of First Amendment freedoms, and encourages the activities of moral entrepreneurs, those who work for enactment and enforcement of moral prohibitions (see Becker, 1963).

Just what violates community standards depends, of course, on the standards themselves—which are essentially a matter of conjecture and disagreement. Certainly, one sees few attempts made to poll the moral views of the electorate, especially those pertaining to sex. In *Pope v. Illinois* (1987) the Supreme Court ruled that a work is obscene if a reasonable person applying objective social standards would find the work lacking in social value. Far from clarifying the question of standards, the case leaves undetermined what "reasonable" means, as well as "social value" and "objective." Justice Stevens, who dissented in this ruling, suggested that a work is protected if *anyone* finds merit in it.

Generally, all that is needed for a public morality law to appear on the books is pressure on legislators from those segments of the population that officialdom feels obliged to woo. Whether it is prostitution, homosexuality, massage parlors, or pornography matters little; the important point is that legal officials can generally accommodate moral entrepreneurs. The reason: Laws exist that are so worded (or interpreted) that almost anything can be brought under them. The best examples are vagrancy laws and those dealing with "disorderly conduct" and "public nuisances." Though often invoked in situations that have nothing remotely sexual about them, they are also used in cases in which the conduct is of a sexual nature. X-rated movies and movie theaters, strip joints, public nudity, homosexual encounters, and massage parlors all have been the object of criminalization under such laws. Today even zoning ordinances are used in some jurisdictions to suppress "undesirable" sexual activities. One example is Boston's "Combat Zone," where pornography, X-rated movies, massage parlors, and other sex-oriented commercial activities have been allowed to flourish in one small downtown area but are illegal elsewhere. More commonly, zoning laws are used to force all commercialized sex out of town.

Consensual Sex: Prostitution

Some sex offenses are victimless in the sense that they are between consenting adults who voluntarily engage in an activity that happens to be illegal. Homosexual encounters, adultery, fornication, the sale and purchase of pornographic literature, and prostitution are examples. This section focuses on prostitution.

One author estimated that as many as 600,000 full-time and 600,000 part-time male and female prostitutes are working at any given time in the United States (Esselzstyn, 1968). These figures may be high—other estimates

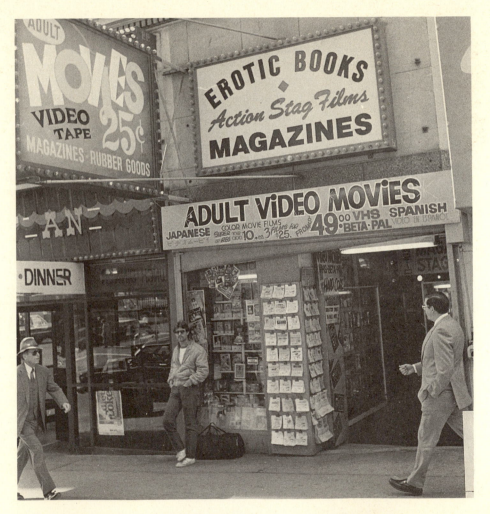

Catering to all tastes, the adult book and video market is booming despite creative efforts in many communities to outlaw sales. One strategy uses zoning ordinances to force retailers into designated areas or out of town altogether.

have placed the total number of prostitutes at around 250,000 (Sheehy, 1973). The United States undoubtedly has the largest prostitute population of any Western nation. Yet prostitution is in violation of criminal codes in all states except Nevada, in which county governments decide on legality.

Prostitution has not always been illegal in the United States (Daly, 1988:174), and in some Western societies it is tolerated today. In Germany, Holland, and Denmark, for instance, female prostitutes are pretty much left alone as long as they ply their trade in designated areas and fulfill other requirements such as licensing and payment of taxes. Describing the situation in Hamburg, Germany, Walter Reckless (1973:175) reports:

> On one enclosed small street (a block in length) of the Reeperbahn, the prostitutes are permitted to display themselves in the nude at every window of the houses on the narrow street. The entrance way at each end of the street has a sort of privacy screen which shields the prostitutes from view of pedestrians not entering the special section. The two privacy screens have posted notices indicating that only males over twenty-one years of age may enter the street. In addition, solicitation by prostitutes is permitted in certain cafes, especially around the central railroad station of Hamburg (the Haupt-bahnhof). On the side wall of each "booth" table is an "in-house" telephone. When male customers are seated in their booths, the phone rings and the woman at the other end asks for an invitation to join the party.

Some American laws may actually encourage prostitution, even though the prostitute herself breaks the law. In some states today, for example, the male client commits no offense when he agrees to buy sexual intimacies from the prostitute. Thus the risks of arrest are borne solely by the woman, and men in search of sexual fun can feel free to pursue their goal without fear of criminalization. Even in those states that have made it a crime to patronize a prostitute, the designated penalties are often greater for the prostitute than her client. In Victorian England, prostitution was encouraged because the existing laws left untouched the activities of those who stood to gain financially from prostitution and were in a position to recruit and protect the women. Although appearing on the surface to be a time of moral respectability, the period was one in which prostitution flourished and exploitation of women and girls prevailed (Wright, 1968:29).

Why is it that prostitution is outlawed while at the same time it is actually encouraged? The most obvious reason is that those responsible for creating laws are usually male and are potential clients. While paying lip service to precepts of moral decency, lawmakers remember that "men will be men," and that women are there to fulfill men's desires. In this sense, prostitution is, as feminists point out, yet another manifestation of male exploitation of females. It should come as no surprise that most inquiries into prostitution have focused not on the male client but on the prostitute herself. She, after all, is the deviant, the criminal.

Selling Sex: The Prostitute at Work   Prostitutes work in various ways (see Rolph, 1955; Winick and Kinsie, 1971; Sheehy, 1973). At one end of the spectrum are the *streetwalkers*, or *street hookers*. These women may be readily encountered on the street, particularly in those sections of cities where cheap hotels, bars, and mass transportation terminals are to be found. The streetwalker is at the bottom of the pecking order among prostitutes. She works where the risks are greatest, she has little or no control over what clients she takes, she must put up with all kinds of weather, she must generally give a good portion of her earnings away for "protection," and she must usually work long hours to make enough from her "tricks" (paying customers, sometimes called "johns") to meet her financial obligations. Even the classiest streetwalkers—those working office buildings or conventions—rarely gross more than $200 or $300 a day. The streetwalker does well to stay in business for more than a few years, and her earning capacity declines rapidly after she passes her twenty-second or twenty-third birthday. Bennett (1987:173) suggests that the prognosis for street prostitution is poor: AIDS, coupled with a more conservative ideology, may result in a decline in both demand for, and tolerance of, streetwalkers.

Next up the social ladder are prostitutes who work in *brothels* (also called *bordellos, cathouses,* or *whorehouses*). Until World War II, brothels were the major outlet for prostitution in the United States. In major cities, brothels numbered in the hundreds, and they were usually located close together in areas that came to be known as "red light districts." Run by *madams*, who themselves might have been working prostitutes at one time, these brothels sometimes had a "stable" of 20 or 30 women working in shifts. Since the 1940s, however, the number of brothels has declined, mostly as a result of cleanup operations by city councils pressured by local citizen groups. Brothels still operate as the major context of prostitution in Nevada (the state frowns upon the streetwalker), and most large cities in the United States have brothels that maintain themselves solely through a system of informal referrals. Gone are the days, though, when a visitor could simply appear on the doorstep of any of a string of houses and buy himself sexual pleasure. In fact, the closing of brothels made the business of prostitution more unpleasant and dangerous for both clients and prostitutes (Daly, 1988:199).

Toward the top of the prostitution pecking order are *call girls*. Though the operating methods differ, the established call girl usually secures her clients through individual referrals by customers or trusted friends (Bryan, 1965). She conducts the sexual transaction in her own apartment or in the office, home, or hotel room of her client. Many call girls work independently and exercise considerable discretion in their choice of clients. Most topflight call girls are in their early twenties; they are generally from middle-class backgrounds, and some have a college education. The successful call girl is physically attractive, well groomed, and articulate, and she makes a pleasant date for those men who can afford the $300 or $400 it takes to purchase her company for an evening.

Bars and Massage Parlors as Places of Prostitution   Public bars and nightclubs have long been frequented by prostitutes. Sometimes called *bar-girls* (or simply *b-girls*), these women often operate with the support of bar management. Not all b-girls are prostitutes—some are merely in the game of enticing customers to spend money in the hope of later sex (Cavan, 1966). Prostitutes do find bars good places for hustling, however. For one thing, they can work indoors; in addition, they have a constant flow of prospective clients, they can mingle with the crowd and thus not be too obvious, there are people around who can come to their rescue if trouble should arise, and they can choose their clients.

Massage parlors are a lucrative setting for prostitution. Though some establishments provide only therapeutic massages by trained personnel, many of the hundreds of parlors from coast to coast basically offer one service: sex. The range of sexual activities purchased extends from simple "hand-jobs"—which are permissible in some jurisdictions—to "blow-jobs," "straight" sexual intercourse, and anything else the customer may desire and the "masseuse" is willing to do (see Bryant and Palmer, 1975; Velarde and Warlick, 1973).

Massage parlors are good fronts for prostitution because they provide a legal setting for customer contacts. "Employees" need not solicit business; it comes to them. A typical customer is looking for more than a massage. Furthermore, the masseuses are not dependent on the customers' purchase of sex because they receive a commission (usually 30 to 35 percent) on any legal massage they give—and these can cost customers $100 an hour if they want frills such as nude masseuses, champagne, and special baths. Other advantages to prostitution in this setting include a comfortable work environment, a potentially speedy turnover in customers, and some protection against arrest and criminal conviction for prostitution. Massage parlor prostitutes are protected from arrest and conviction partly by the semiprivate character of the parlor and partly because by leaving it up to the customers to do the soliciting, they can minimize chances of a legal arrest. An undercover cop who first solicits sex and then arrests the masseuse may well be acting illegally under the rules of *entrapment*. These rules usually are interpreted as follows: Police may not entice a person into committing a crime and then use the offense and evidence of it to bring about a criminal conviction if the person would not normally have voluntarily committed the offense in question.

The Pimp A key position in the world of prostitution is held by the *pimp* (see Milner and Milner, 1972; Hill and Edelman, 1972). though there is no way of knowing exactly what proportion of prostitutes work under the control of pimps, it probably runs to over 70 percent. For a pimp, prostitution is the road to considerable financial success; he, not his "girls," reaps the real profits from the billion-dollar business. Despite the disproportionate monetary arrangements, many prostitutes would quickly fail in business without their pimp.

The pimp's importance comes partly from the nature of prostitution itself and partly from his own business acumen and ability to manipulate people. Because prostitution is illegal, those involved are constantly threatened by arrest. Pimps can help protect prostitutes from legal troubles as well as provide financial and other assistance such as posting bail. Pimps help defend their prostitutes against competition by establishing and maintaining control over a particular territory. Independent prostitutes do not have that kind of security. Pimps also offer protection against physical or financial threat posed by drunks, toughs, and customers who want something for nothing. Most prostitutes have little control over male access to them—indeed, they must make that access as free as possible—and when confronted by a troublemaker it is nice to have someone in the wings who can deal with the problem.

The dangers of prostitution open up a role for the pimp. Even so, his success also hinges on his adeptness in establishing and maintaining the prostitute's dependence on him and his control over her. Control and dependence are the central features of what is, at its heart, a relationship of exploitation. To establish that relationship the pimp demonstrates that the practicing or would-be prostitute needs him for both material and emotional reasons. He shows his importance in the material realm by taking care of room and board, clothing, medical and other expenses and by running the business profitably. On the emotional level, the pimp is at once father, brother, lover, and friend. He is there when the woman needs affection, advice, and love, but he also disciplines her when she falters. Once caught up in his grip, the prostitute quickly learns the extent of her dependence on him and the risks of attempting to leave the fold. If she does decide to leave she risks not only her financial security but also her physical safety. It is not uncommon for a pimp to maim or even kill a defecting or "retiring" prostitute (McCaghy, 1976:353–354).

Today pimps are predominantly African-American, at least at the street level. It is not clear just why blacks have come to dominate the pimping business, but the potential for financial success and status as well as a certain perspective on American society and women in particular suggest two explanations. In terms of money, a successful pimp can earn more than $500 a day. With that kind of money he is tempted to feel that he can do what he wants, when he wants, how he wants. He is successful by the standards that white society has set. In addition, the pimping role permits a black male the kind of domination normally reserved for those in the white-dominated world of legitimate business and professions. Instead of a subservient, dependent role, he assumes a role in which he pulls the strings. Furthermore, he can bolster his sense of manly pride by virtue of his relationship with his women and the fact that white men must pay him for their sexual pleasure. In the view of some black pimps, American society as a whole reeks of exploitation, in which one person pimps another. They are merely cashing in, in the tradition of free enterprise and individual initiative (Milner and Milner, 1972:242–244).

Entering the "Profession" Prostitutes risk not only police arrest and criminal punishment but also such work-related hazards as disease, injury, theft, and exploitation. Why, then, do some women become prostitutes? A conventional and long-standing explanation is that they are forced into prostitution by unsavory characters who use devices of compulsion ranging from kidnapping, blackmail, and forced heroin addiction, to the powers of love and dependency. One example of recruitment by force and deceit was reported in *Time* magazine some years ago and is summarized as follows:

> The report claimed that the ring of procurers had operated for ten years and that at least 35 murders of recruited girls had taken place. The girls were lured from poor families by the promise of domestic jobs with upper-class families. The girls were first raped and then sent to a training brothel. It was estimated that at least 2,000 girls had passed through the hands of the ring since 1954 (ten years before the report). The "sick" recruits were sent to [a "concentration" camp] at Leon [Mexico] to die, while the rebellious ones were also sent there for taming. (Reckless, 1973:169)

Doubtless some women are forcibly introduced to prostitution. But current thinking on the subject places less emphasis on the role of force and more on a voluntary, though often reluctant, decision to enter prostitution and the circumstances surrounding that decision. It seems likely that when considered as a whole, only a small minority of prostitutes are forced into the profession.

Prostition will continue to flourish as long as there are willing customers. Although it is a consensual crime and in this sense victimless, prostitution involves many elements of exploitation, most of which are suffered by the prostitute.

Nevertheless, a woman may feel that she has no real choice in the matter, and some look upon their entrance into prostitution as something forced upon them by circumstances beyond their control. One circumstance often mentioned is financial insecurity. Simply stated, some women enter prostitution because they need the money, as William Sanger observed in New York over a hundred years ago (see Daly, 1988:177). They may have a child to support; they may be out of work and unable to find a full-time job; or they may have pressing financial obligations, such as paying medical bills or financing a drug addiction, which they cannot hope to meet through conventional, legal kinds of work. Ronald Akers (1973:166) warns that one should not misinterpret the nature of the financial incentives in prostitution:

> This may sound trite or overly simplistic, but the nature of the monetary incentive in prostitution is often misunderstood. The woman need not be in dire or desperate economic straits; escape from poverty is only one way (and probably not the most frequent way) in which prostitution is economically inspired.

The choice, Akers argues, is not often between starving or becoming a prostitute but is more commonly between a low-paying, low-status, but respectable job and a relatively high-paying job that happens to be illegal and not respectable. The loss of respectability and the risks of arrest and criminal punishment are offset by the economic rewards believed to accrue from prostitution.

Most people to whom prostitution would offer financial attractions do not become prostitutes. For those few who do, it seems that additional considerations facilitate their entry into the prostitute role. Based on the evidence, one factor appears to be experience in sex at a relatively early age, and another is a set of verbalized opinions favorable to prostitution. Women who have had early sexual experiences have less difficulty accepting the idea of sex as normal, even among strangers. Opinions favorable to prostitution are bound to vary, but some notable ones are "prostitution is no worse than any other kind of job"; "people don't really look down on the prostitute"; "the prostitute is necessary, for without her marriages would fail, some men would have to commit rape to get laid"; and "the prostitute gives men what their wives and lovers won't" (Jackman et al., 1963; Bryan, 1966).

Becoming a successful prostitute is not easy. Not only must the novice learn how and where to find customers; she must also learn how to protect herself from disease, police, competition, and the customer and learn how to stay in business. In his study of call girls in the Los Angeles area, James Bryan (1965) found that most went through a kind of apprenticeship. Their initial entrance into prostitution was facilitated through personal contacts with an established call girl or a pimp, and from then on they were mentored by other call girls, some of whom ran "classes" in their apartments. Though there was apparently little training in sexual techniques as such, the new recruits were taught the "dos and don'ts" of the game and were helped in building an initial set of customer contacts. Among the rules learned were: Get the money first;

don't enjoy the trick or fall for the customer; don't be pleasant with the customer unless he has paid; don't engage in unnecessary interaction with him; get him "off" as soon as possible; and stay in good physical and mental health.

Reactions to Consensual Sex Offenses

Prostitutes are generally looked upon with mild intolerance by society and its legal officials. Unless community pressure to do something about prostitution builds up, police and courts rarely go out of their way to make life difficult for prostitutes. It seems that when police do take the trouble to arrest streetwalkers or to raid local brothels and illegal massage parlors, they do so more to harass them and get some "action" than to enforce the law. When prostitutes go before a judge, they typically pay a small fine and are back on the street within hours. FBI figures from 1990 show that 111,400 persons were arrested for "prostitution and commercialized vice." To put the figure in perspective, this represents less than 1 percent of all arrests, and just over 2 percent of the arrests for sex and alcohol/drug offenses combined (Federal Bureau of Investigation, 1991).

Reactions to Pornography   Pornography, like prostitution, arouses mild intolerance. The Supreme Court's 1973 ruling in *Miller v. California* left the problem of defining obscenity largely in the hands of juries applying "contemporary community standards," and there seems to be little agreement as to what those standards are. One Gallup poll found that a majority of 1020 Americans sampled favored being able to go to X-rated movies (60 percent), to buy magazines that show sexual relations (53 percent), and to buy or rent X-rated videotapes (68 percent). Yet a majority of those interviewed also believed that the depiction of sexual violence leads some people to commit sexual assault (76 percent) and that the law should prohibit pornographic violence (*Newsweek*, March 18, 1985).

The explosion in sales and rentals of pornographic videotapes and the success of sex-oriented cable and satellite channels indicate that many Americans want to view sexually explicit material, at least in the privacy of their homes. Middle-class people can now do in private what before necessitated a trip to the seamier parts of town. In this way they maintain a public front of decency while avoiding the dangers of predatory criminals in sleazy neighborhoods.

One major exception to this tolerance should be noted, and that is "kiddy porn," the depiction of children engaging in sexual activities with each other or with adults. Severe penalties have now been introduced by most states for offenses of this sort, and in *Ferber v. New York* (1982) the Supreme Court ruled in favor of state and local laws banning sexually explicit materials involving children.

The fight against pornography is continuing in some circles, and it has brought together strange bedfellows: On the one hand are such moral entrepreneurs as Citizens for Decency Through Law, who see pornography as a reflection of a larger moral decay (*National Decency Reporter*, October 22, 1985), and on the other are feminists who see pornography as a manifestation (and perpetuation) of sexual stereotyping, in which women are seen as "vile whores" who deserve, and probably want, to be sexually abused by men (Lederer, 1980; Dworkin, 1981). Both groups argue that at its best, contemporary pornography, with its "sexualization of violence" (Ashley and Ashley, 1984), trivializes male sexual aggression and at its worst actually encourages crimes of sexual assault.

It remains to be seen whether the war against pornography waged by these groups will succeed; the odds are long, however, because commercial sex is big business and growing bigger, and because America is a patriarchal society. Still, creative legislation keeps appearing: The Pornography Victim Compensation Act, introduced in Congress in 1991, would permit victims of sex crimes to sue people who produce, distribute, or sell obscene material, if the material is proven to be the "proximate" cause of the crime.

Reactions to Homosexuality   The public, police, and courts have traditionally displayed greater intolerance of and have made a more systematic effort to do something about homosexuality, than is the case with prostitution or pornography. With the exception of Illinois, Connecticut, and a few other states, homosexual acts, even in private and between consenting adults, violate state criminal codes and sometimes carry penalties equaling those for felonious assault, armed robbery, burglary, and even rape and murder. Compared with heterosexual offenses, the consequences of indulging in homosexual conduct are more demeaning, more punitive, and longer lasting. When there are victims, as in the case of a child molesting, the chances are that life will be made more miserable for a homosexual than a heterosexual offender. In one follow-up study of convicted child molesters, homosexual offenders served much longer prison sentences for essentially the same offense (Fitch, 1962).

Studies in Los Angeles, St. Louis, and elsewhere show that police often routinely harass suspected gays and lesbians on the street and in bars, nightclubs, and dance halls catering to the gay community. Public restrooms in parks, railroad stations, and bus terminals have been the setting for more perverse police practices. These have included the use of male decoys whose job is to lure other males into making sexual advances (sometimes accomplished by the decoy making a show of fondling his own penis), and use of peepholes drilled in walls and ceilings, and the use of still and movie cameras hidden behind two-way mirrors or ventilation screens (see Gallo, 1966; Humphreys, 1970). A police operation at a highway rest area in Michigan resulted in the arrest of 42 men whose sexual activities had been secretly videotaped during a ten-day surveillance period (UPI, March 20, 1986).

In their study of male homosexuality in the United States, Denmark, and the Netherlands, Martin Weinberg and Colin Williams (1975) point out that despite the availability of felony statutes (the so-called sodomy laws) providing for severe penalties, the common practice in the United States is to charge homosexual offenders with misdemeanors. At first glance one might think that this practice reflects an attitude of leniency and tolerance. On the contrary, these authors argue, the use of misdemeanor charges is preferred because these laws are easier to apply and give a greater likelihood of conviction.

Many of those arrested for homosexual acts are first offenders, in the legal sense, and hence have little experience of the judicial process. This inexperience, coupled with fears about publicity, makes them easy prey for disreputable or greedy officials. Sometimes they are blackmailed by corrupt police; sometimes they become patsies in a scheme of kickbacks involving police, bonding services, and corrupt attorneys. More often they find themselves in the hands of lawyers who make their living off the fearful and inexperienced who daily get in trouble with the law. Such lawyers, often called "courthouse regulars," get business by referrals from bondsmen, police, or court officials or by hanging around police stations and misdemeanor courts and routinely charge $500 or more just to plead their client guilty. Under a hard sell and promises of no publicity, no conviction, and the like (falsehoods, or in any case not under the lawyer's control), a suspect finds it hard to refuse the "help" offered by a seemingly sympathetic, knowledgeable, and experienced attorney.

There is evidence that public and official attitudes toward homosexuality have moved in a more tolerant and permissive direction (see McCaghy, 1976:366). The National Survey of Crime Severity ranks consensual homosexual conduct fourteenth from the bottom out of 204 crimes. Opinions, however, may be changing again, and new laws have already been passed restricting homosexual conduct. The reason is AIDS: acquired immunological deficiency syndrome.

By the end of 1991, AIDS had been clinically diagnosed in over 110,000 Americans and in many more worldwide. The *Morbidity and Mortality Weekly Report* published by the Centers for Disease Control in Atlanta keeps tabs on AIDS cases, and by the time this text is published, the figure for the United States will be well over 120,000. In addition, there are an estimated two million Americans who have been exposed to the virus but who have not developed clinical symptoms. All will eventually develop AIDS unless effective treatment is discovered. World-wide, the situation is even more grim: 2.6 million already have AIDS and 13 million are HIV positive; by the year 2000, 38 million to 110 million adults, and more than 10 million children will be infected with the HIV virus (*Associated Press*, June 4, 1992).

Among diagnosed AIDS patients, homosexual males are the largest group, consistently around 73 percent of the total. This fact, together with the deaths of Liberace and actor Rock Hudson, has brought considerable attention to homosexual lifestyles. Studies in New York and San Francisco, where around half of all American AIDS cases are located, show that homosexuals with highest risk of being infected are those who engage in anonymous sex with many different partners and those whose sexual activities include anal-receptive intercourse without a condom and the ingestion of semen (Darrow, Jaffee, and Curran, 1983; Jaffee et al., 1985).

Many of these high-risk activities take place in gay baths and clubs, leading authorities in New York to empower city health officials to investigate and close them down if sexual activities are observed. In Texas, the state health commissioner asked for the power to quarantine AIDS patients who refuse to discontinue their high-risk sexual activities (Associated Press, December 16, 1985). In October 1985, the U.S. Defense department established mandatory screening of all recruits and active duty members of the armed forces, and prison officials around the country are initiating similar programs for inmates (United Press International, October 29, 1985).

Most authorities agree that the transmission of AIDS will continue unless there are drastic changes in sexual lifestyles, especially among homosexual men. The evidence collected so far indicates that there have been changes but also that these have been selective and nonuniform. A follow-up study of 301 gay males found that the proportion reporting unsafe sexual practices had decreased; nevertheless, 36 percent said they had had more than one sexual partner during the past 30 days, and 7 percent had exchanged semen (Centers for Disease Control, 1985). A survey of 655 gay males in San Francisco found that men who considered themselves monogamous were unlikely to change their high-risk sexual activities and that other men showed more significant reductions in oral-genital contact than in unprotected anal intercourse (McKusick, Horstman, and Coates, 1985). The conclusion reached in this study was that knowledge of the risks was not sufficient to produce significant changes in the sexual behavior of subjects. Even with the considerable publicity about AIDS in recent years, many well-educated people resist change in their sexual behavior. Surveys at the University of Texas, Austin, and at Oregon State University found that a majority of sexually active students did not use condoms, and in Austin, 94 percent of those interviewed did not consider themselves at high risk of getting AIDS (*Chronicle of Higher Education*, September 28, 1988).

Without evidence of voluntary changes in sexual lifestyles, authorities are likely to rely more and more on law as a weapon in the fight against AIDS. Public health and criminal justice officials will no longer treat anonymous homosexual encounters as victimless offenses because it is now clear that the risk of being infected with the AIDS virus is a real danger to the participants and that each new case of infection increases the risks for the heterosexual population. It is also likely that drug addicts and prostitutes will be subject to more rigorous surveillance and prosecution, because they, too, are in high-risk groups.

There is increasing alarm about the spread of AIDS among African-Americans and among heterosexual young people. Blacks are at higher risk because rates of intravenous drug use and prostitution are high in inner-city communities where disproportionate numbers of blacks live. AIDS is now the second leading cause of death (after murder) among black males aged 16 to 34. The Centers for Disease Control (CDC) reports that while the disproportionately high rate of HIV positives among black (and Hispanic) groups is related to the prevalence of IV drug use, it is high even allowing for drug abuse. The speculation is that these populations, especially in the inner city, are less resistant to HIV infection because of factors related to inner-city life itself: "poor diet, unsanitary living conditions, crowding, . . . , lack of adequate medical care typical among the poor, and the promiscuity associated with impoverished life styles" (Kelly, 1991:51).

Among the young heterosexual population generally, the fear is that AIDS will spread at an ever-increasing rate as a function of unprotected sexual experimentation involving growing numbers of youths who are HIV positive but unaware of it. The publicity surrounding basketball star "Magic" Johnson's revelation that he is HIV positive has helped turn the spotlight on heterosexual behavior. Some communities are taking aggressive steps to educate youngsters about the risks of contracting AIDS, and some school districts and many colleges now provide easy access to condoms. Even so, strongly held religious beliefs and the persistence of myths and fears about the causes, transmission, and treatment of AIDS make the challenge of prevention a formidable one.

Unfortunately, some lawmakers have taken a repressive approach to sexuality, rather than one of sensitivity and enlightenment: In a controversial 1986 ruling, the U.S. Supreme Court upheld a Georgia law that prohibits consenting adults from engaging in oral or anal sex and makes the offense punishable by 20 years in prison. The case in question involved two men arrested by a policeman who entered their bedroom with a warrant on an unrelated matter and saw them engaged in oral sex. The consitutional issue concerned the right to privacy, and by its 5-to-4 decision the high court ruled in effect that no such right extends to homosexual acts. Many gays interpret the decision as clear support for renewed repression of homosexuals.

Others fear that the reasoning of the court in the Georgia case could be extended to the private sexual practices of consenting heterosexuals. As of a 1986 review, 24 states and the District of Columbia have laws regulating consensual sex between adults, with penalties ranging from 30 days in jail to 20 years in prison (*Newsweek*, July 14, 1986). The Supreme Court decision may encourage some states to join the list, and others to increase their penalities.

The weight of historical evidence leaves little room for doubt that legal repression of human sexuality is doomed to failure. Hard as it is to curb male sexual aggression toward females, it is even harder to control consensual sex. Even so, there seems to be no end to legislative and enforcement efforts to criminalize those who seek sexual pleasures in ways that are publicly denounced. In 1976, Harry Reems was prosecuted and convicted under federal obscenity statutes for his part in the widely seen X-rated movie *Deep Throat*. Though the conviction was subsequently reversed, the affair extended the scope of legal repression of essentially personal matters of moral choice. If pursued, this attack will produce more criminals, but is unlikely to reduce the incidence of the behavior in question. The same has been said about societal reaction to drug abuse.

Drugs and Crime

This chapter began with the assertion that nothing inherent in any activity makes it a crime. Rather, activities and those who engage in them become criminal when they are so labeled by persons with the authority to do so. Sometimes acts similar in substance are labeled differently—some are called crimes; others are not. This is especially true of drug-related acts. Most Americans are consumers of drugs, but some do nothing illegal, whereas others do. The world of drugs, then, has two sides, the legal and criminal. Although this is a criminology text and as a such focuses on crime, one cannot hope to grasp the realities of the criminal side of drugs and their use without at the same time considering the legal side. Indeed, understanding the legal use of legal drugs gives insights into the illegal use of drugs and drug-related crime.

Here the word *drug* will refer to any psychoactive substance. A *psychoactive substance* is one having the capacity to alter mental states, and hence influence behavior. Identifying an "altered mental state" requires a subjective assessment by the drug user, which sometimes complicates the identification of a substance as a drug. However, there is widespread agreement on the following examples of currently abused drugs: alcohol, nicotine, caffeine, opiates, hallucinogens (LSD, DMT), cocaine, barbiturates ("downers"), amphetamines ("speed"), marijuana, tranquilizers, and analgesics (pain killers).

Drug Use and the Law

Psychoactive substances have been a part of American life since the founding of the country, but only in this century have drugs become a significant aspect of the crime scene. An understanding of today's picture requires some knowledge of the recent past.

The history of drug use in America is a history of politics, big business, prejudice, and hedonism. Consider the narcotics: opium, heroin, and morphine. Opium use steadily increased from colonial days to the late 1800s, by which time morphine had been extracted, and both were readily used for a variety of medicinal purposes. Morphine addiction came to be known as the "soldier's disease" as a result of its use with the Civil War wounded, and opium-based medicines were widely available both by prescription and over the counter. Nineteenth-century America was, in the words of Edwin Brecher (1972), a "dope-fiend's paradise." The sale of opiates was big business.

Whether or not the general public realized it, opiates were everywhere, and many thousands became addicted. By the last quarter of the nineteenth century, as many as 1.25 million Americans were regularly using opiates in one form or another (Terry and Pellens, 1970). Although it is not known how many were addicts, there would have to be as many as 8 million opiate users today for an equivalent usage rate. This is more than eight times most current estimates.

Sanctions against opiate users first appeared in local ordinances forbidding the smoking of opium in so-called opium dens. San Francisco adopted a prohibition in 1875, and other cities soon followed suit. But opium smoking was outlawed not so much for the drug itself as for the circumstances surrounding its use. In San Francisco, for example, opium smoking was primarily a pastime of Chinese railroad workers. Being immigrants and non-English speaking, the Chinese were treated differently almost as a matter of course. When they settled in San Francisco, their visibility increased, and their "strange" lifestyle and willingness to work for a pittance soon drew hostility from many townsfolk. When white Americans, especially women and persons of "respectable" background, began visiting Chinese opium dens, officials of the city succumbed to the cries of outrage and outlawed the dens.

By the first decade of the twentieth century, the legal importation of opium had grown to more than 14,000 pounds per year, and countless more was smuggled in (Brecher, 1972). The various prohibitions seemed to have little effect. At the same time, there was considerable pressure on Congress to join other nations in an effort to curtail the opium trade, although this pressure seems to have had more to do with international politics than with morality or fears about the drug itself. The Hague Convention of 1912 culminated a series of international conferences regarding trade and political cooperation among states, and American participation had been strongly advocated by opponents of isolationism (Lindesmith, 1967). In Congress, the Harrison Narcotics Act of 1914 was heralded as a way to implement the Hague Convention while also demonstrating America's willingness to fulfill its international obligations.

Alcohol Prohibition   Five years after the Harrison Act, Congress ratified the Volstead Act, and National Prohibition, the "great experiment," had begun. Unlike narcotics prohibition, the new federal laws restricting alcohol were the culmination of over a hundred years of crusading by temperance groups with roots in Methodist and Quaker teachings. By 1869 the Prohibition party had become a powerful force in American politics (Sinclair, 1964).

Pragmatic as well as moral concerns impelled the Prohibition movement. Excessive drinking had a demonstrably negative impact on family life, on work, and on the quality of interpersonal relations generally. Besides, scientific research showed damage to nerve cells, impairment of mental functions, weakening of blood vessels, lowered resistance to illness and disease, adverse effects on digestion, and impaired judgment and reaction time. More recent research catalogues an even longer list of medical dangers (Brodie, 1973). The medical and social ills associated with alcohol became potent weapons in the hands of the Prohibition party and helped bring about the 1919 Prohibition victory.

Effects of Early Drug Legislation   The immediate consequence of the Harrison and Volstead acts was to create a new set of crimes, and although neither law specifically criminalized the act of consumption itself, the end result was to turn users into criminals because obtaining the drugs meant breaking the law. The use of the drugs apparently fell off for a while, partly because the customary sources of supply dried up, partly because the risks of being labeled criminal were simply too great for some people to accept, and partly because some people believed in obeying the law. More striking than the effects on consumption rates, however, were the effects of the laws on the social context of drug use, on the population of users, on public attitudes, and on economic interests. In the case of alcohol, these effects culminated in the repeal of Prohibition in 1933; in the case of narcotics, they produced new ills and an expanding repression.

The repeal of Prohibition provides a good illustration of the role of special interests in the decriminalization of behavior. There was considerable public demand for alcohol, and many people continued to drink and and were willing to pay inflated prices for their pleasure. This demand was incentive enough for the black marketers, and, as seen in the preceding chapter, Prohibition was a major factor in the development of organized crime. The black market in turn fostered corruption and gang warfare, hardly anticipated by the temperance lobby.

These repercussions played into the hands of the liquor interests, who before Prohibition legally produced and sold billions of gallons annually (Benson, 1927). For them, even a month of Prohibition was too much. Armed with evidence of the evils of Prohibition, supported by politicans clamoring for states' rights and by a growing public opinion that the experiment had failed and probably would never work, the liquor interests got their way.

Narcotics, on the other hand, remained outlawed, and the laws were even tightened during this period. The pharmaceutical industry was able to produce and market alternative drugs, which physicians were happy to dispense in light of increasing risks of arrest they faced in supplying patients, particularly addicts, with opiates. Erich Goode (1972) estimates that between 1914 and 1938 as many as 25,000 physicians were charged with violations of drug laws.

Many previous opiate users now became heavy users of, if not addicted to, barbiturates. Because opiates were widely dispensed for so-called female problems, middle-class, middle-aged white women had been the largest group of opiate users before the Harrison act. After the act, they became the largest group of sedative users, and they remain so today (Goode, 1972:193). In the meantime a new class of opiate addicts began to emerge: inner-city blacks and Hispanics. A relatively small black-market demand grew along with inner-city decay and the emergence of a subculture of intravenous heroin use. The tightening laws and subsequent refusal of physicians to dispense opiates to addicts pushed narcotic distribution into the ghetto, where an anonymous and concentrated population, ravaged by the Depression, became a new, profitable market for the unscrupulous. The illicit use of "hard drugs" was seen as a growing problem by the same people who had urged the repeal of Prohibition.

Marijuana and the Drugging of America

There are two trends in America that together explain much of the current drug problem, in particular its criminological aspects. First is a growing recreational use of drugs, especially among the young; second is a marked growth in the production and marketing of *legal* drugs. In the opinion of many experts, the first has been helped along by the second.

In Search of Self: Marijuana   The preeminent illegal youth drug is marijuana. According to national surveys of use among high school students, 14 percent of high school seniors in 1990 claimed to have used the drug during the 30

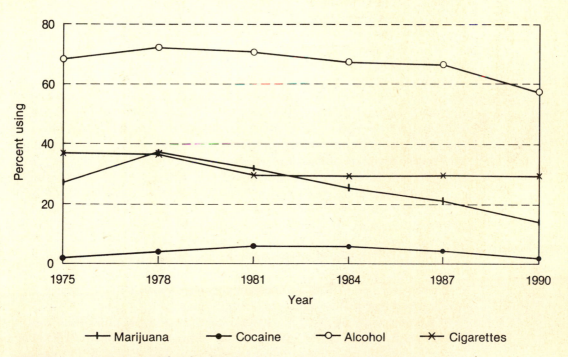

FIGURE 9.1   Drug Use: High School Seniors. Percent using during last 30 days. *Source:* Compiled from Kathleen Maguire and Timothy Flanagan (1991). *Sourcebook of Criminal Justice Statistics.* Washington, D.C., U.S. Department of Justice, p. 329.

days before being interviewed (see Figure 9.1). Around 5 percent of the seniors were classified as daily users. After 1969, marijuana use grew steadily among all segments of the U.S. population, reaching a peak in 1978 of over 22 million people who considered themselves current users. Figures 9.1 and 9.2 show a decline in use among youth over the past decade, and the most likely reasons are an American "health craze" and a decline in peer support for any kind of smoking. Nonetheless, marijuana is readily available: Around 85 percent of high school seniors surveyed think it would be easy to buy marijuana where they live (Maguire and Flanagan, 1991:220).

Marijuana comes from the Indian hemp plant (*Cannabis sativa*) and has been used for centuries. The resin, called *charas* by Hindus and known as *hashish* today, was used for spiritual purposes by Native Americans and as a medicine by the ancient Chinese. When the top leaves of the hemp plant are cut and dried, they can be eaten or smoked. The mixture is less potent than hashish, and the Indians called it *bhang*; it is now called marijuana, grass, or pot, among other terms. Over half of the marijuana supply in the United States comes from Colombia (National Narcotics Intelligence Consumers Committee, 1985). Much of the remainder is locally grown.

Hemp was used by American pioneers in the manufacture of rope, and a number of authors have suggested that it was grown for the psychoactive resin as well (see Andrews, 1967). By the mid-nineteenth century, marijuana was used freely as a medicinal preparation, and many home medicine chests contained some. Around the same time, marijuana and hashish became a popular recreational drug, and "hashish houses" sprang up in many larger cities.

Prohibition gave marijuana a boost as a substitute for alcohol. By the late 1930s New York City claimed 500 known marijuana peddlers, and in Harlem alone there were an estimated 500 "tea-pads" where people gathered to smoke pot (Mayor of New York's Committee, 1944). Many accounts of marijuana use linked the drug to those whose lifestyles were already considered deviant by mainstream America: musicians, sailors, artists, prostitutes, delinquents, criminals, and minority groups. The evils of marijuana use were widely reported in the press, and a "new menace" was born (Walton, 1938).

State and local governments began passing legislation outlawing the drug, and their efforts were spurred on by officials of the newly established Federal Bureau of Narcotics, under the directorship of Harry J. Anslinger. In 1937 Congress passed the Marijuana Tax Act, modeled after the Harrison Act, and by the 1950s, all states had adopted severe penalties for the cultivation, purchase, sale, or possession of marijuana. People spoke widely of marijuana addiction and marijuana-induced sex and violence.

How, then, did marijuana emerge as America's most popular illicit drug? The answer lies partly with the growth of countercultures during the late 1950s and subsequent confrontations with "the Establishment" on college campuses during the 1960s. The "beat" generation that emerged in New York and San Francisco in the 1950s emphasized an alternative lifestyle of autonomy, drugs (especially pot), music, free sexual expression, aversion to

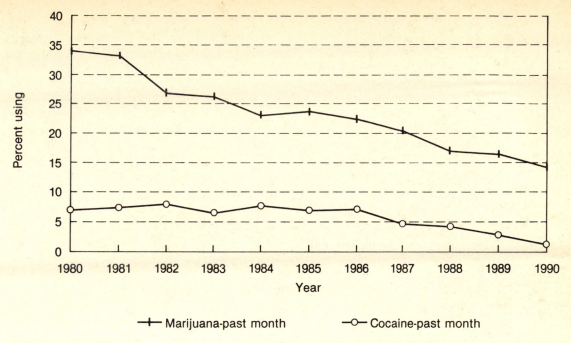

FIGURE 9.2 **Self-Reported College Drug Use.** Marijuana and cocaine, 1980–1990. *Source:* Compiled from Kathleen Maguire and Timothy Flanagan (1991). *Sourcebook of Criminal Justice Statistics*. Washington, D.C.: U.S. Department of Justice, pp. 330–331.

routine employment and politics, and disregard for the law (Polsky, 1967). Hippies succeeded the beats and made famous the Haight-Ashbury district of San Francisco. They claimed a similar lifestyle, though jazz was replaced with acid- or folk-rock, and marijuana was joined by LSD. Hippies also enjoyed "putting on straights" and "blowing their minds" by rejecting all that was valued by the dominant, middle-class culture. By the end of the 1960s the hippie culture, if not its ideology, had spread to all parts of the country, and rock music was one of its major vehicles.

Another factor in marijuana's increasing popularity was the growing disenchantment among young people, especially college students, with the policies and practice of American government. Use of illegal drugs became a way of underscoring their opposition to the Establishment. In addition, marijuana and psychedelics were touted as a way to "expand the mind," to "trip," to "get your head right." They were perfect for the "now" generation, those who searched for meaning and heightened self-awareness (Carey, 1968).

Drugs as a Way of Life   A second trend that encouraged illicit drug use was the growth of drug use in general. In America, drugs have become a way of life for the healthy as well as for the sick. Beer, wine, liquor, tea, nicotine, coffee, and myriad pills and potions are daily fare for many respectable Americans. Even children are targets: Aspirins are named after saints, vitamins are made to look like cartoon characters, and beer that is not really beer is marketed as if it were beer.

With the exception of caffeine, and perhaps aspirin, alcohol and tobacco are the drugs used most often. Caffeine is a stimulant found in coffee, tea, hot chocolate, cola beverages, and in over-the-counter pills for dieting and preventing sleep. The per-capita consumption of coffee is around 10 pounds per year, of tea just under 1 pound, and of soft drinks (most of which contain some caffeine) nearly 40 gallons. Americans drink an average of between three and four cups of coffee a day (U.S. Department of Agriculture, 1983).

Even though most other legal drugs are intended for medicinal uses, stimulants, sedatives, and tranquilizers are widely used for nonmedicinal purposes. The National Commission on Marijuana and Drug Abuse (1973:57) concluded that "the preponderant use of sedatives is for experimentation and enjoyment," whereas tranquilizers are used as "coping" mechanisms, and stimulants often to stay awake or "just to see how they work." A study of New York state households found that more than 70 percent of those using such drugs obtained them by prescription. The typical user was a white, middle-class female between 25 and 45, precisely the same class of people who regularly used opiates before 1914 (Chambers, 1971).

Drugs are big business. Twenty years ago, Richard Blum and Associates (1972) estimated that $25 billion a year was spent on over-the-counter drugs, including aspirin, tobacco, and alcohol. Today the figure is certainly higher. In addition to this, America spent $34 billion on medicines in 1987, a figure that does not include government and hospital purchases. In 1987, the pharmaceutical industry employed 123,400 people with an annual payroll of $4 billion (U.S. Bureau of the Census, 1990:737). Another measure of the economics of drugs in America is the expenditure on advertising. In 1988 the following amounts were spent by the various media (U.S. Bureau of the Census, 1990, Tables 899, 935, 936):

Magazine advertising:	$213,000,000 on beer, wine, and liquor
	145,000,000 on drugs and remedies
	352,000,000 on tobacco products
Television ads:	$480,000,000 on beer and wine
	794,000,000 on proprietary medicines
	1,000,000 on tobacco products

The message conveyed by advertisers is that drugs are normal, natural, and good for you. Often, they are shown making problems and difficulties go away. Drugs bring "the good things in life" and even confer respectability, the ads proclaim, subtly or otherwise. People will feel better and look younger and fit in with others if they use drugs, though the word *drug* is rarely used, of course.

With so many drugs around, with so many respectable people selling and using them, it is small wonder that America has a drug problem. People grow up anticipating a place for drugs in their lives. That first cigarette, puffed courageously in some secluded spot, that first can of beer, downed with much bravado in a friend's car, are milestones along the road to adulthood. Most youthful experimenters know they are breaking the law, but that merely adds to the adventure. What is "cool" about doing something that children are supposed to do? Anyway, there must be something to smoking, drinking, popping pills, for why else would parents and other adults spend so much time and money doing it, and why would all those advertisements encourage it? According to Erich Goode (1972:126–128), "The legitimate drug industry is, both directly and indirectly, responsible for much of the illegal drug use taking place today. The 'pusher' should be sought not only on the street but in the physician's office, the pharmacy, the tavern—and the home."

Those likely to use illegal drugs are precisely those who have grown up in a social environment in which legal drugs are commonly used. No matter whether it is cocaine, heroin, marijuana, or the psychedelics, studies consistently show generational continuity in drug use and in the progression from legal to illegal drugs (see Goode, 1972:34–35; also Brecher, 1972). Of course, thousands of those who use legal drugs do not "progress" to illegal ones, and many who do usually discontinue their use after one or two episodes (they do tend to remain consumers of legal drugs such as alcohol). The important lesson is that illegal drug use is most likely to be found in a climate favorable to drug use in general. In fact, the most significant correlate of illegal drug use is the consumption of legal drugs.

Cocaine

Cocaine is America's new drug problem (see Figure 9.3). Cocaine is not a new drug, however. It is extracted from the leaves of the plant *Erythroxylon coca*, which is found in South America. Coca leaves have been chewed for at least 3,000 years by South American Indians. Cocaine use in America is not well documented but does not seem to have been particularly extensive until recently. It was first used medicinally as an anesthetic in eye surgery in the early 1900s. It is now said to be a popular "yuppie" drug, and its street use is growing (Grabowski, 1984).

The major site of coca cultivation continues to be Peru, but trafficking is dominated by Colombia, where the raw paste or cocaine base is converted into cocaine hydrochloride (HCl) for distribution to the United States. Generally, cocaine HCl is 90 percent pure when imported. Between 55 and 76 metric tons of cocaine were consumed in the United States during 1984, up from an estimated 33 to 60 tons in 1981 (National Narcotics Intelligence Consumers Committee, 1985:26–27).

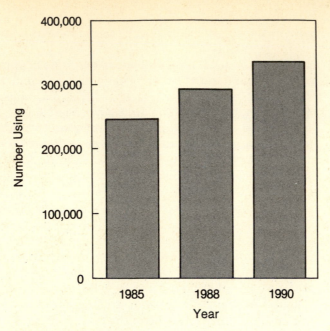

FIGURE 9.3 Estimated number of cocaine users in the United States. *Source:* National Institute on Drug Abuse. Reprinted in *The Compiler.* Summer 1991, page 16.

Cocaine confiscations by the Drug Enforcement Administration (DEA) have increased every year, from 399 pounds in 1977 to 82,042 pounds in 1987. U.S. Customs seizures of cocaine have also increased, from 952 pounds in 1977 to 52,000 pounds in 1986 (Flanagan and Jamieson, 1988:402–403). As it becomes more abundant, cocaine is getting cheaper and purer. The estimated cost of 1 gram of cocaine on the street is now $100; in 1982 it was $600. In 1983, street cocaine was 35 percent pure; now it is 70 percent pure (Flanagan and Jamieson, 1988:289). The same is also true in Great Britain (Wagstaff and Maynard, 1988).

Cocaine use has been controlled since the Harrison Narcotics Act of 1914 restricted its manufacture, distribution, and sale. It is illegal in all states. Cocaine is not, in fact, a narcotic; it is a stimulant that acts directly on the "pleasure" or "reward" centers of the brain. It is so powerful that it undermines the brain's ability to regulate such functional necessities as sleeping, eating, and handling stress. Users describe the "high" as elation, warmth, vigor, friendliness, and arousal (Grabowski, 1984). Because the subjective effects are so pleasant, cocaine is considered a prime target for abuse, though it is not physiologically addictive.

If anything accounts for the explosive growth in cocaine use in America it is crack—a cheap, smokable form of cocaine. Crack, like other forms of cocaine, is getting cheaper: In New York City in 1985, a vial of crack cost $40;

it now costs only $15 (*Newsweek*, November 28, 1988). Crack is easy to make, relatively cheap, and extremely fast acting. It is produced by processing street cocaine with ammonia or baking soda to remove hydrochlorides. The resulting crystalline mixture gets its name from the crackling sound that the residues of baking soda make when the mixture is smoked (Inciardi, 1987).

Crack was initially confined to major East and West Coast cities, but it now appears to have spread across America. Federal authorities report that it is now the number-one street drug sold in Denver, where there are reputed to be fifty "crack houses," many serviced by Jamaican dealers who supply high-yield cocaine hydrochloride. Denver police also believe that dealers associated with Los Angeles street gangs are moving in, and both the supply and the competition in the crack market are likely to increase. Similar concerns have been expressed by Kansas City police (*NCTAP NEWS*, April, 1988) and by authorities in St. Louis (*St. Louis Post-Dispatch*, February 12, 1989). In 1988 St. Louis police labs processed 15 times the number of cocaine specimens that were processed in 1984. In suburban Montgomery County,

Crack cocaine is simple and cheap to make, hence the flourishing "crack houses" in many American cities. Frustrated and fearful, residents in some neighborhoods have taken action against local crack dealers with proactive armed patrols, and in some cases have burned crack houses to the ground.

Maryland, crack cocaine is now the second most popular drug after alcohol. Whereas Denver and Kansas City users are primarily inner-city youths, most of the Montgomery users who have been identified are middle-class adults between the ages of 20 and 40 (*NCTAP NEWS*, October, 1988).

Although self-reported cocaine use has been declining among young people in the last few years (Figures 9.1 and 9.2), this optimistic account is surely an artifact of who is being asked. Surveys of high school seniors and college youth will not tap drop-outs and the millions of poor Americans who never get to college. An inference about the extent of crack use among young adults in the inner city can be drawn from the results of random drug testing of arrested individuals. For example, results from the first three months of 1991 show a majority of male and female arrestees testing positive for cocaine in Manhattan, Chicago, Atlanta, Houston, Philadelphia, and Washington, D.C. (National Institute of Justice, 1991:2–3).

Furthermore, the opportunities and incentives for crack cocaine use have not decreased; if anything they have increased. A quarter gram of rock cocaine now costs between $10 and $25 on the streets of Los Angeles. "This lower price, the flood on the market, the ease of rock manufacture, transportation, carrying, hiding, and the rapidity and intensity of the high all conspire to make the rock form of cocaine preferable to the produced form" (Klein, Maxson and Cunningham, 1991:625). And most high school seniors report that it is easy to get cocaine in one form or another (Bureau of Justice Statistics, 1991c:19).

Drug dealing structures are not well studied, but some similarities appear to exist across drug types and may help explain the rapid spread of crack:

> First, the structure of distribution is better characterized as groups of dealers and individual entrepreneurs throughout, rather than as a single, highly organized and centralized criminal operation; and second, entrance and acceptance into dealing groups are based on familiarity, friendship ties, situational factors ("the right place at the right time"), and available capital. (Hunt, 1990:181)

Crack can be manufactured in anyone's kitchen, and the "step from crack manufacturer to crack user is a short one" (Hunt, 1990:179). Thus the entire crack business can be a local, neighborhood affair.

The presence of neighborhood gangs and cliques facilitates the production and distribution of illegal drugs. True, illicit drugs have been a feature of street-corner society for decades (see Merry, 1981; Schwendinger and Schwendinger, 1985), but the intensity of trafficking activities seems to have escalated since crack appeared on the scene. Traditions of street drug use, black market enterprise networks, protection of "turf," anonimity, and high rates of truancy and unemployment combine with ease of manufacture to promote gang-related trafficking in crack (compare with Klein, Maxson and Cunningham, 1991).

Designer Drugs

During the 1980s a new breed of drugs appeared on the streets of some cities—the "designer drugs." Underground chemists, who seem to work mainly in California, manufacture "analogs" of compounds available in existing pharmaceutical products.

> For instance, the compound fentanyl is a powerful narcotic manufactured under the tradename Sublimaze by Janssen Pharmaceutica of Belgium. Fentanyl is about 100 times as potent as morphine. It is very short-acting [and is used] as an anesthetic in, by one estimate, up to 70 percent of all surgical procedures in the United States. Fentanyl is also jsut as addictive as heroin or morphine, and the "high" associated with it, though shortlived, appears to be very similar to that associated with heroin. (Baum, 1985:7–8)

The underground chemist tinkers with the molecular structure of fentanyl and produces a chemical that may be just as powerful in its effects but is technically legal since no laws apply specifically to it. The motivation is not new discoveries for medicinal science, but profit: By one account, an investment of $2000 in glassware and chemicals will produce about one kilogram of heroin worth $1 million in the street; similar investment can be turned into a kilogram of 3-methyl fentanyl worth about $1 *billion* on the street (Baum, 1985:8). A limitation is the fact that the manufacture of fentanyl analogs is a dangerous process apparently requiring a highly sophisticated chemist.

The pharmacology professor who invented the term "designer drugs" believes that a single "world-class medicinal chemist" was responsible for the fentanyl analogs that have appeared on California streets (Baum, 1985:10). Congress passed the "Designer Drug" Enforcement Act in 1986, but it remains to be seen whether the problem escalates or disappears. One clue may be that formulas and instructions for their use have been found in raids on clandestine laboratories, suggesting an information chain that threatens to spread designer drugs around the country.

Heroin: "Tragic Magic"

The millions of Americans who routinely consume psychoactive substances with little thought that they are addicts, or even drug users, stand in stark contrast with the estimated 500,000 heroin addicts, who spend an estimated $5 billion annually on their habit (Kaplan, 1983). Heroin bears the brunt of public and legal intolerance, and the world of most heroin addicts is quite different from that of other, "respectable" drug users. It is a world in which getting the "shit" (or "horse," "smack," "Hi," "junk," "tragic magic") and staying alive and out of jail consume much of every waking day (see Box 9.1).

The heroin that an addict craves has often traveled thousands of miles and passed across numerous links in a complex underground chain of importation and distribution. Over the past decades, the primary foreign sources of heroin

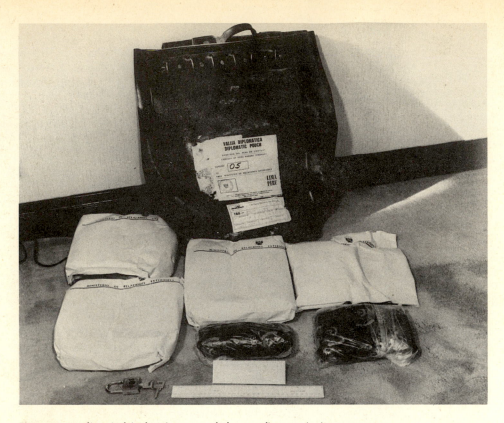

Drug smuggling is big business and the profit margin is enormous. Small wonder that people from all walks of life are involved, from Presidents (General Noriega of Panama) to lowly peasants who bring drugs across the U.S./Mexico border by mule, auto, or even inside their own stomachs. The diplomatic pouch is surely safer, but apparently not foolproof.

have been the Middle East, Afghanistan, Pakistan, India, the Far East, and Mexico. During the 1970s, Mexico emerged as the major foreign source, with an estimated 80 percent (10 tons) of the 1975 domestic supply originating there. Today, Pakistan and Afghanistan compete with Mexico and the "Golden Triangle" (Burma, Laos, and Thailand) as the major U.S. sources (Pace and Styles, 1983). In 1984, an estimated 6 metric tons of heroin were consumed in the United States, about the same as in the preceding two years together (National Narcotics Intelligence Consumers Committee, 1985:45).

The mechanics of importation vary according to the location and availability of raw opium—Mexico became an important source only after America withdrew from Vietnam and the Turkish government cracked down on opium production. Local dealers and vendors always remain the important final links in the chain and effectively control dealing at the street level. It is the pusher, the small-time vendor, who provides the addict and user with heroin.

Box 9.1 ■ A Day in the Life of an Inner City Heroin Addict

The scene is the "marketplace" where heroin deals are struck: a dilapidated inner-city black neighborhood with a few shops and perhaps a take-out restaurant or two run by immigrants from the Far East or Latin America. People come there to buy marijuana, cocain, Dilaudid, Quaaludes, amphetamines, barbiturates, Valium, and heroin (or "tragic magic," as some call it). The trafficking itself takes place at the curbside "copping corner," and some users then go to "shooting galleries"—nearby houses or abandoned stores where they shoot up with others, sharing needles and the other "works."

Early morning. For users careful to save some heroin from the day before there is first the wake-up fix, "just to get straight." for most, however the day begins with reefer. Those with jobs follow the routines of conventional society; those without head for the marketplace, many to team up with other addicts, find out what has been going on (i.e., who got busted, who is dealing, who has the best drugs), and plan the day's hustles.

Midmorning. After teaming up with other junkies, addicts look for ways to earn enough money to buy a day's supply later in the afternoon. They will try begging, borrowing, conning, and stealing; they are flexible. Many have legitimate jobs for at least a few hours a day, running errands, fetching and carrying, washing dishes, and the like.

Noon. The marketplace becomes a bustling street as workers come to make purchases during their lunch hours. Many whites come into the area to buy, feeling it safe to do so. A hierarchy of marketplace participants is evident: "Vultures" or dope fiends are at the bottom—dirty, unkempt, strung out and sick, mostly relying on handouts. Hustling users take care to look more casual and presentable, mainly because they do not want to draw attention to themselves. Those in the dealing hierarchy are stylishly dressed, with designer jeans and lots and lots of fine jewelry.

Midafternoon. By early afternoon most addicts have acquired enough money for their day's purchase and are trying to connect quickly with a dealer they know personally. As soon as possible after they have scored, they will shoot up. Most will avoid shooting galleries as too risky and noisy; they want to relax, enjoy the effects of heroin, and perhaps listen to music. They will head for a friendly bar or go home or to a friend's pad.

Evening. The evening hours are spent back on the street. Straights come home from work, change, and are on the street to join the action. Hookers appear, "johns" start driving through, and the police come out, too. The heroin trade continues, with clusters of people conversing, dealing, negotiating, and sometimes arguing, but always alert to the police. James Walters (1985:47) describes the closing of the day:

> As the evening nears midnight, most [of the addicts interviewed] . . . look back on a full, even rewarding day. Once again they have met the challenges of poverty and addiction. They have parlayed their wake-up dollars into enough money to satisfy their "jones" (habit) one more day. For one more day they have avoided being burned, busted, or spasmed by withdrawal. And along the way they have had adventures, high times and maybe even some loving.

Source: Compiled from George M. Beschner and William Brower, "The Scene"; and from James M. Walters, " 'Taking Care of Business' Updated," in Bill Hanson et al., eds. (1985). *Life with Heroin.* Lexington, Mass.: Lexington Books.

Pushers are usually addicts themselves; they finance their own drug purchases through sales to others (Preble and Casey, 1969).

How Addicts Finance Their Addiction

Heroin can cost an addict as much as $100 a day, though most probably spend around $25 a day on their habit (Walters, 1985). This amounts to nearly $10,000 a year and does not include food, rent, clothing, utilities, and other essential living expenses. Where do addicts get their money?

Most addicts finance their addiction through a combination of legitimate work and various sorts of hustle: begging, borrowing, stealing, drug pushing, and prostitution. In a Florida study, selling drugs ranked first, followed by (for men) burglary, shoplifting, and robbery and (for women) prostitution, shoplifting, and prostitute theft from johns (Inciardi, 1979). It was estimated that in one year alone, the sample of 356 Florida addicts committed a total of 118,134 offenses.

A study of the lifestyles of 124 black, male, inner-city heroin addicts in Chicago, New York, Washington, D.C., and Philadelphia (see Box 9.1) presents an up-to-date picture of the economics of heroin addiction, at least for blacks (Hanson et al., 1985; for another view, see Faupel, 1991). Most of the addicts interviewed were unskilled opportunists who rarely began the day with any money. Their "overwhelming preference" was to get money in the quickest, least violent, and least risky way (Beschner and Brower, 1985:36). As with the Florida addicts, legitimate work was an important, but usually insufficient, source of income. To supplement it, most addicts engaged in a variety of hustles, some legal, some not. For half the addicts the main hustle consisted of thefts, robberies, or con games; most would also try to borrow money from family and friends.

The Hanson study (1985) distinguished four types of addict hustlers:

1. *Opportunistic hustlers* will take any opportunity, legal or not, that comes along. They start early in the morning so as not to miss any opportunity, but beyond that they do little planning. Versatility is their hallmark, and the target is open.
2. *Legitimate hustlers* seldom engage in crimes, raising money by offering goods and services in the neighborhood to people they know. No job is rejected, no matter how menial, and their day is dictated by the routine activities of the neighborhood. They are also versatile and prepared to take drugs in exchange for services. They do not generally deal with strangers.
3. *Skilled hustlers* engage in crimes and hustles that require more skill and risk but are also more lucrative: picking pockets, specialized shoplifting, burglary. Targets are selected for vulnerability, the addicts usually work with a partner, and hustles are planned.
4. *Dope hustlers* raise money through drug trafficking. They are usually lower-echelon participants, getting drugs on consignment and selling

them to fellow addicts in their own neighborhood. They may also offer services to others in exchange for dope.

A Fields and Walters interviewee (1985:64) explicates the services a dope hustler might offer:

> Like sometimes there are people that don't know where to cop. We get their money and cop for them and get a taste. My biggest advantage is that I know, uh, I am real tight with most of the people that get in big quantity. I always know when the [good] stuff is comin' through. I always have people who want me to get it for 'em. I'm like the middleman, I got a credit line with most guys.

Besides "copping," dope hustlers may also "steer" customers to sources or "route" them to a particular dealer in exchange for drugs or cash (Johnson et al., 1985).

Addiction as a Career

Many drug users appear to have a career of use during which they are initiated into a drug's use, become regular users, and then "mature" out of using it. Trevor Bennett (1985) analyzed heroin addiction according to these career stages and the decisions that users and addicts make. His approach is predicated on the assumption that people are self-determining, deliberate, and responsible and that their behavior is goal-directed, episodic, self-limiting, and mundane.

1. *Initiation.* Bennett discusses three popular theories in conjunction with the initiation stage of career addiction. (1) Hard drug use is preceded by and may be the result of using other drugs—the escalation or stepping-stone view. Research does not support this view, Bennett claims, and though it is true that many heroin users also use marijuana or other drugs, few users of other drugs go on to use heroin. (2) Heroin users are initiated through pressures brought by pushers. This view also finds little support in the literature. (3) Initial use occurs among friends and under the influence of a normative structure providing justification and support for its use. This theory is the preferred view, and Bennett correctly points out that some of the normative supports may exist before the drug is ever taken. Bennett's own study of six groups of addicts from 1982 to 1984 found that 90 percent were introduced to the drug by friends or acquaintances, and many had made a conscious decision to try heroin some time before they actually did so.

2. *Continuation.* Heroin users generally progress slowly toward addiction, some taking many months to reach that point. The majority of Bennett's subjects took over a year from first use to the point where they were using heroin daily, and many reported long gaps without use in between. "One addict reported that he usually gave up opioids during the summer months so that he could pursue his favourite sports. During the winter months he injected heroin on a daily basis" (1985:25). Bennett also found

considerable variation in the amount consumed from day to day, suggesting purposive decision making.

3. *Cessation.* Other studies (e.g., Winick, 1962) have shown that addicts can mature out of addiction, quitting heroin for a variety of reasons: because of a new job, family responsibilities, or an effort to change lifestyles. In Bennett's Cambridge study, all the subjects were current users, and half said they had no interest in quitting permanently. The others were confident they would quit within ten years, but only if certain other things occurred, for example, if they moved away from their associates and contacts or if their lives changed dramatically in some other way.

Bennett's study indicates that the behavior of heroin users can be self-regulated and manageable. Furthermore, they are not slaves to their addiction in the sense of having lost all self-determination. A similar position was taken by Fields and Walters (1985:71–72) in a study of black heroin addicts in America. Other, more rewarding, things may temporarily supplant an addict's use of drugs, may lead to reduced levels of use, or may lead the addict to quit altogether (see also Shaffer and Jones, 1989). Unfortunately, studies of ghetto use indicate that many of the conditions most likely to result in cessation—a good job, a stable family life, involvement in "straight" society—are out of reach of many inner-city addicts (Hanson et al., 1985). The problem is exacerbated by, and is partly the result of, the criminal involvements of many ghetto addicts. Submerged in crime, an addict's horizons rarely extend beyond the neighborhood and a small group of drug-using friends.

These observations are in line with a study of 32 hard-core heroin addicts (including 14 women and 23 blacks) by Faupel and Klockars (1987; see also, Faupel, 1991). Copping, dealing, and shooting heroin take place at the intersection of conventional and criminal roles and are structured by the availability of the drug. Faupel and Klockars describe a pattern in which "stabilized junkies" (addicts whose routine activities have incorporated regular and controlled heroin use and who have relatively easy and predictable access to the drug) may become destabilized—often after a binge of "free-wheeling" heroin use—and find themselves caught up in a ceaseless round of hustles, opportunistic crimes, and (consequently) arrests, and able to score only "street dope," heroin that is diluted ("stepped on") many times. This is the archetypical street junkie, whose life is "a continuous but typically unsuccessful effort to stabilize life structure and increase heroin availability" (Faupel and Klockars, 1987:64). For the inner-city street junkie, respite from this struggle often comes only with jail (temporary) or death.

Criminal Drug Use and Police

The existence of drug laws calls for an enforcement response to people who violate them. A number of factors, however, work to make enforcement of drug laws extremely difficult. For one thing, the possession, sale, and use of illegal drugs are in essence *victimless crimes*; that is, they usually involve willing participants. Police do not usually have an aggrieved person who will complain that he or she has been the victim of a crime. They must typically discover drug law violations on their own. To make enforcement more difficult, an individual can violate a drug law without being detected. Who is to know that a person carries two or three joints, some illegal pills, or a day's supply of heroin?

The "Narc" and the Informant

Because illicit drug offenses are mostly consensual crimes and because they are not readily observed, police enforcement strategies place a premium on infiltration and the cultivation of police informants. Through infiltration into the ranks of users, undercover drug agents are able to develop trusting relationships with users, addicts, and pushers and thus keep tabs on the people, events, and places having to do with illegal drugs. To maintain a cover, the "narc" must learn and adopt street ways—the rules, language, and nuances of the criminal drug scene. Narcs must virtually live among those they are charged with catching. Following his investigation of the junkie's world in New York, Houston, Austin, and Los Angeles, Bruce Jackson (1969b) concluded that narcs found it hard to separate themselves from that world, even though they may despise it and their purpose is to destroy it.

Helping police are the informants. Usually active participants in criminal drug activities, informants are cultivated by police, who rely heavily on the information they pass and on the contribution they can make to "good busts"—arrests that hold up in court. Informants' own crimes are often used as a means to induce them to work for the police. Under threat of arrest and a jail sentence, prospective informants find their options limited and unattractive. Besides, the police can always threaten to let the word get around that they are informants (whether true or not). If the threat of jail is not enough, this will be added inducement to turn informant.

A common feature of drug enforcement strategy is for undercover agents to spend months developing information on drug use and traffick so that when they are ready, police can pounce on many suspects at the same time. These dragnet raids usually take place in the early morning hours and not uncommonly produce scores of arrests. Often out of uniform, police from federal, state, and local agencies form together for the raid and systematically root out those on a list of suspects. Apart from producing relatively large numbers of simultaneous arrests, there is no real evidence that raids of this kind greatly reduce the availability, sale, and use of illegal drugs. They do, however, result in much local publicity, and the public is reassured that the police are working hard in their fight against the drug criminal.

Police have met with little success in their efforts to reduce the availability of drugs such as heroin, marijuana, and cocaine. The drug pipeline is not easily breached, not only because major importers, wholesalers, and distributors are well organized and equipped, but also because the profitability of small quantities of these drugs make large shipments unnecessary. It is like looking for the proverbial needle in the haystack. The diversity of drugs is also a factor. As Kleiman and Smith (1990:73) observe:

> This last point ought to be enough to keep a responsible official awake at nights. Crack, powder cocaine, heroin, PCP, "pills"—each drug type has a different volume, different user demographics, a different relationship to dealer and user crime. . . . [Yet] the distinctions among drugs occupy little of police managers' thoughts. They want "good," that is, valid and prosecutable felony arrests. . . .

One line of attack against the illicit drug scene is to crack down on "head shops," places where drug paraphernalia are sold. the drug paraphernalia industry is big business, estimated at several hundred million dollars annually (*Newsweek*, November 26, 1979). This law-enforcement effort may help reduce the chances of any respectability rubbing off on illicit drug use, but it is doubtful it will greatly curb it. In fact, it will probably add to the social problem of drug use, for business will once again move underground, bolstering the black market as well as profits in organized crime.

Many states have recently passed forfeiture laws that enable officials to confiscate various types of property if these have been used in drug trafficking or manufacture or are the fruits of such activities. In some states (e.g., Alabama, Arkansas, Kansas, Nevada, New York, Oregon, and 14 others), confiscated property may be kept for law-endorcement use. When this is not done, the property is sold, with the proceeds usually going to local or state governments (Stellwagen, 1985). It remains to be seen whether forfeiture laws will have any material effect on illegal drug trafficking. In all probability, the risk of forfeiture will merely become another of the costs of doing business, unfortunate but accommodated.

Asset seizures are growing in frequency according to the United States Drug Enforcement Agency (DEA), and it is clearly big business. For 1990, nondrug seizures were reported as follows (Bureau of Justice Statistics, 1991:1):

	Number of Seizures	Value
Currency	7622	$363,717,740
Vehicles	5674	605,790,075
Property	1599	345,617,695
Vessels	187	16,522,303
Airplanes	51	25,586,000
Other	2716	206,376,219

The popularity of asset forfeiture among law enforcement officials is understandable: There is a material reward for their drug enforcement efforts.

JUST SAY 'NO'
TO THE
BILL OF RIGHTS
1791-1991
(R.I.P.)

IMPOUNDED

ANTI-DRUG COPS

FIFTH AMENDMENT
...No person shall be deprived of... property without due process of law

ENGELHARDT
©1991 St. Louis Post-Dispatch

'We May Not Get Many Drugs, But We Sure Do Get A Lot Of Other Valuable Stuff'

However, an investigation by the *St. Louis Post-Dispatch* (April 29–31, 1991) found an array of questionable practices by Missouri police departments. For example, although the law requires the return of assets seized if a suspect is not convicted, some St. Louis area police departments were returning property only after the owners paid various kinds of "charges," sometimes in the thousands of dollars. In addition, suspects were sometimes told that the charges would be dropped if they signed over the seized property to the police. The title of the series, "Hooked on the Drug War," seems apt.

The major obstacle to effective control of drug trafficking at home and abroad is the simplest to identify and the hardest to overcome: Illicit drugs are in high demand, and people are willing to pay the price. The lure of high profits means there will always be plenty of people willing to pit themselves against authorities. Even as the authorities become more organized and sophisticated in their enforcement efforts, so do the traffickers. Drug interdiction efforts have generally been unsuccessful in curbing international trafficking. The General Accounting Office reports that the $100 million spent on antidrug efforts in Bolivia and Colombia has been "almost entirely useless" (*NCTAP NEWS*, January, 1989:4). (For more on drug interdiction efforts, see Moore, 1990).

Drug Arrests

Notwithstanding the overall failure of drug enforcement efforts, police do make many drug arrests (see Figure 9.4). In fact, if all such arrests are combined in any given year more arrests are made for drug-related offenses than for any other broad type of criminal offense, major or minor. In 1979, 34 percent of all criminal arrests were drug related. In 1990, the percentage was virtually the same, amounting to 4.5 million out of a total 14 million arrests. (Federal Bureau of Investigation, 1991:174)

These figures include arrests on charges relating to alcohol, which far outnumber other drug arrests. Over 80 percent of all drug arrests can be linked to alcohol, whether the offense involves public drunkenness, the violation of liquor laws governing sale and consumption, or driving while intoxicated

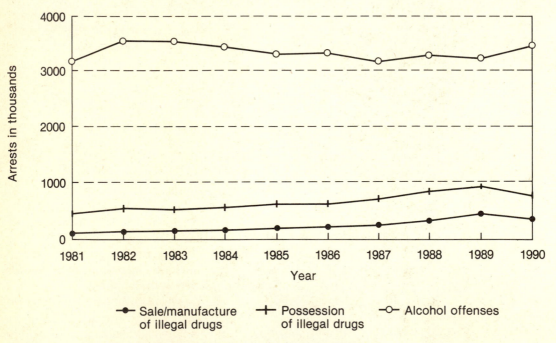

FIGURE 9.4   Drug and Alcohol Arrests. Yearly totals, 1981–1990. *Compiled from:* Bureau of Justice Statistics (1991), *Fact Sheet: Drug Data Summary.* Washington, D.C.: U.S. Department of Justice; and Federal Bureau of Investigation (1982–1991). *Crime in the United States.* Washington, D.C.: U.S. Department of Justice.

(now the number-one alcohol offense). In terms of police arrests, alcohol-related offenses are America's number-one crime problem.

Most drug-related arrests occur among larger urban populations. Easy accessibility to drugs, concentrated user populations, and more extensive and sophisticated police surveillance all contribute to the higher arrest rates found in larger cities and their suburbs. In the case of alcohol-related arrests, especially those for drunkenness, the typical arrestee is an adult over 30 years of age. In regard to heroin, marijuana, and other illegal drugs, the typical arrestee is under age 30. In fact, the age at which drug arrests peak (20 to 24) is identical to that for street crimes in general (Bureau of Justice Statistics, 1991d:8).

The Link Between Drugs and Crime

Where there is illicit drug use, there is often other crime, some of it to finance the drug use (see Blumstein et al., 1986; Inciardi, 1986). This *instrumental* crime is most likely to be found among people who are poor, unemployed, or unemployable and among those who are heavy users. Many inner-city heroin addicts belong to both groups (Hunt, 1990).

Recent studies in Baltimore and Harlem confirm that heroin addicts who are frequent users commit crimes at a much greater rate than lower-level users. In Harlem, addicts participated heavily in drug distribution, with daily users averaging 316 drug sales per year plus 564 episodes of copping, steering, or routing. In all, daily users generated an average of $11,000 *in cash* per year from crimes of all sorts (Johnson et al., 1985). In Baltimore, a sample of 354 known users drawn from 7510 users arrested or identified by police between 1952 and 1976 committed four to six times the amount of crime when frequently using than when not using or using occasionally (Ball, Shaffer, and Nurco, 1983). The Baltimore addicts admitted to nearly 750,000 offenses, mostly thefts, drug sales, and various cons, over the course of nine and a half years.

The relationship between level of drug involvement and crime is confirmed in a study by Anglin and Speckart (1988). These authors found not only that as the level of use increased, so did the amount of criminal activity, but also that a shift seemed to occur in the criminal activities of high-level users to more profitable types of crime. Daily use of a narcotic drug was the best predictor of stepped-up criminal involvement among the 671 male addicts studied. However, even after addiction was terminated, a "subsistence" level of crime continued (see also Nurco et al., 1988).

There is little argument that drug use and crime are related. What is a matter of dispute is the direction of that relationship. In fact, drug use and crime may be connected in various ways: (1) Drug use may give rise to crime; (2) crime may give rise to drug use; or (3) drug use and crime may be reciprocal—each giving rise to the other. All three views find support in criminological research, as does another: (4) commitment to a life of "action" produces *both* drug use and crime.

Most studies of chronic criminal offenders find heavy drug use and drug sales in their backgrounds, often beginning in their early teens (Peterson, Braiker, and Polich, 1980; Dunford and Elliott, 1984). What is not clear is how much of that crime is explained by their drug use. The financial pinch that forces many drug users—especially the young and poor—into instrumental crime is clearly a factor; but it is difficult nevertheless to disentangle the offenses that are driven by drug abuse from those that are not and would have occurred anyway. As far as violence is concerned, it appears that drug (and alcohol) users who commit violent acts were likely to have been aggressive *before* they started using drugs (Fagan, 1990). So, too, one should recognize that there is a kind of systematic violence associated with the world of illicit drug use—violence that derives from the milieu rather than the drug-using behavior of individuals within it. Territorial fights, robberies of dealers and subsequent retaliation, the elimination of informers and punishment for selling adulterated (or fake) drugs, are examples (Hunt, 1990).

Crime may lead to drug use. This makes intuitive sense:

> (1) people who "earn" money like to spend some of it on pleasurable things; (2) a risky but successful venture should be celebrated; (3) a risky venture may need some special courage or other mental preparation; (4) the peer networks that facilitate delinquency and crime also facilitate drug use; and (5) drugs may substitute for cash or other profits. (Barlow and Ferdinand, 1992:109).

Studies have shown that serious drug use is more likely to be an aspect of the lifestyles of chronic delinquents and criminals than chronic criminality is of the lifestyles of serious drug users. In part, this reflects the better economic backgrounds of chronic drug users compared to those of chronic delinquents. On the other hand, as illegal income increases, so does discretionary buying power, which means more money is available for drugs (Collins, Hubbard, and Rachel, 1985; also see Faupel, 1991).

For various reasons people cling to the idea of a casual connection between drugs and antisocial behavior. The idea helps one account for criminal behavior without imputing criminal intent. If a person were not "under the influence," a crime would not have happened. The drug becomes an excuse, a rationalization and justification. Another reason pertains to enforcement: It is because people believe that (mostly) illegal drugs cause terrible crimes that they accept and support severe penalties and secretive police tactics used against drug offenders. Ordinarily, people abhor "snitches" and distrust those who go about in disguise pretending to be what they are not.

Public Opinion and the Punitive Reaction to Illegal Drug Use

When a substance is alleged to be linked with crime, condemnation of it is encouraged. However, if that substance happens to be widely used and is considered legal and socially acceptable, fears and condemnation will be appropriately toned down. Thus although alcohol shows the strongest links with crime, people remain less concerned about its availability and use than they are about illegal and socially unacceptable drugs such as heroin and LSD. They do not want to believe that alcohol is as bad as these drugs, no matter what the evidence.

Drunk driving stands as a constant reminder of the dangers of complacency toward alcohol. The majority of all auto fatalities and accidents are attributed to drinking before or while driving. The carnage on roads has stirred some citizens to outrage, especially when courts hand down lenient sentences to those convicted of vehicular manslaughter. Recent years have seen a nationwide mobilization of public and private resources to combat drunk driving. Private efforts such as MADD (Mothers Against Drunk Drivers) and SADD (Students Against Driving Drunk); and government-sponsored campaigns such as RID (Remove Intoxicated Drivers) have combined to pressure lawmakers into revising drunk-driving laws. All states have passed new laws or toughened existing statutes (Lundman, 1991). As with all legislative efforts, success will depend on the reactions of both the public and those who enforce the laws on streets and in courtrooms. Judging from experience in other countries, the deterrent effect of such laws is likely to be temporary, if there is any at all (Ross, 1982). Nevertheless, the risks of being arrested while driving intoxicated are less than 1 percent. And then even when people are stopped by the police, the effect is opposite that predicted by the deterrence doctrine (Lanza-Kaduce, 1988; see also Linsky et al., 1986).

The recent declines in drug and alcohol use among young people (see Figure 9.1) make good press for groups such as Mothers Against Drunk Driving. Richard Lundman (1991) has looked more closely at the relationship between MADD and drunk driving and tells a different story. He agrees that city police in the early 1970s were not much interested in drunk driving and made "driving under the influence" (DUI) arrests infrequently. With the founding of MADD in 1980, DUI arrests initially grew, but then declined from 1984 through 1989. Lundman argues that the long-term increase in DUI arrests from 1960 to 1989 resulted not from MADD but from two factors: (1) There were more police; and (2) there were more people at the crime-prone ages of 18 to 39. .

National surveys show Americans to be most concerned about illegal drugs and much less concerned about alcohol. Not surprisingly, the public supports punishing sellers and users of illicit drugs. In one Gallup poll, 80 percent of those interviewed thought that heroin vendors should receive prison terms, and nearly 70 percent felt the same way about users. A 1987 survey found that 90 percent of respondents felt that a jail or prison term of at least one year was appropriate for cocaine sales, and 60 percent would give jail time for mere use. In a *New York Times* poll, 43 percent felt that jail time of a year or more was right for a first offense of selling crack (Bureau of Justice Statistics, 1988b:28).

Given this climate of opinion, a continuation of repressive drug enforcement and severe penalties for illegal drug sale and use is likely (see Box 9.2). In federal prisons, violators of laws dealing with narcotics, primarily heroin

Box 9.2 ■ Stricter Drug Laws: The Illinois Case

In a series of measures over recent years, the Illinois State Legislature has created new drug offenses and extended the penalties for drug-related crimes. Some examples follow.

- Sale or delivery of any item of drug paraphernalia has been upgraded from a misdemeanor to a Class 4 felony carrying up to three years in prison and minimum fine of $1000 for each item.
- The Secretary of State is required by law to cancel the driver's license of anyone under 18 who is convicted of a drug offense while driving an automobile.
- Use of a cellular phone to traffic in controlled substances is a Class 2 felony with a maximum fine of $100,000.
- Assets, including cash and conveyances, are subject to forfeiture if used in violation of state controlled substance laws and for violations of the Cannabis Control Act.
- Parents may lose custody of a child born with evidence of controlled substances in blood or urine.
- Prison terms are subject to being doubled if person 18 or older uses or employs a person under 18 in trafficking drugs.
- Penalties for delivering illicit drugs within 1000 feet of a school may be a Class X felony, carrying a mandatory ten-year sentence and maximum $500,000 fine.
- State agencies will not contract with any employing individual or organization that does not provide a drug-free workplace.
- Licenses of physicians or pharmacists who violate the Illinois Controlled Substances Act will be revoked.
- Any amount of drug or drug by-products in a driver's blood or urine is evidence of driving under the influence and subjects the offender to mandatory revocation of his or her driver's license.
- Criminal conviction records, including drug convictions, are now available to potential employers, landlords, and other members of the public previously excluded from such records.

and cocaine, serve more time than most other offenders. In some states the penalties for possession and sale of illegal drugs, including marijuana, are equaled or surpassed only by those for murder, rape, and kidnapping. In Georgia, Indiana, and New Jersey, extended prison terms are now provided for certain drug offenses (Bradley, 1984). In 1990, Congress passed the Omnibus Drug Initiative Act, which emphasizes drug education, denies loans to students with drug convictions, and requires capital punishment for certain drug-related murders.

As long as authorities condemn the use of heroin, psychedelics, marijuana, cocaine, and other such drugs reactions will continue to be punitive, as they are with street crime generally. Those features of drug use linked with criminalization will therefore persist. Users will be labeled and treated as criminals; black-market supplies and high prices will flourish; fear, illness, suspicion, and instrumental crime will fill users' lives; and users will be outcasts in a society of drug users. Alternative strategies, such as the Dutch policy of fostering a controlled, decriminalized drug climate with restrained enforcement (see Gottman, 1989), are frowned upon here, despite their positive results.

Summary of Chapter 9

This chapter has examined prostitution and offenses involving drugs and alcohol. To some extent, these activities are prohibited as violations of prevailing moral standards and because they threaten to interfere with the orderly functioning of society. The discussion in this chapter has shown, however, that special interests also play a major role in the creation and enforcement of these so-called public order crimes.

There are many similarities in the criminological aspects of drugs and sex, including the fact that participants usually do not think of themselves as either criminals or victims. Prostitution thrives because there is widespread male demand for sexual encounters and a more or less organized network of suppliers prepared to meet that demand for a price. If there is a victim in prostitution it is the prostitute herself. Among the various participants— prostitute, customer, pimp or procurer—it is the prostitute who runs the greatest risk of arrest, jail time, assault, robbery, disease, and dependency.

Many authors believe that prostitution results from, and contributes to, a system of gender stratification in which women are subordinate to, and serve the interests of, men. Even though few women are forced into prostitution, the economic options open to many poorer women, especially single mothers, are such that prostitution is a rational choice from among a restricted number of unpromising alternatives.

Reactions to prostitution are generally lenient, as one might expect in a society where laws are created and enforced primarily by men. The same is largely true of reactions to other consensual sex crimes, although enforcement of laws prohibiting prostitution and homosexual activity may well become more systematic and repressive as the AIDS epidemic grows.

Offenses involving alcohol generally enjoy lenient reactions on the part of both the public and legal officials. This is hardly surprising given widespread social drinking, the failure of Prohibition, and the fact that powerful liquor interests spend millions of dollars advertising the pleasures of drinking and lobbying state and federal officials on their behalf.

In contrast, offenses involving heroin, cocaine, hallucinogens, and to a lesser extent marijuana, are the focus of extensive enforcement efforts and can result in penalties that are more severe than those given to burglars, robbers, and rapists. Influenced by fears of a crumbling morality among youth and by the view that drug use causes other crime, the current furor over illicit drug use largely obscures the fact that much of the current drug problem in America is explained by three related historical processes: growth in recreational use of drugs; growth in the production and marketing of legal drugs; and the selective creation and enforcement of prohibitions dealing with essentially similar behaviors. This observation does not deny that the growing use of crack is a serious problem that needs to be solved, but it serves as a reminder that crime is invariably shaped by social, political, and economic history rather than by the criminal motives of evil, or merely weak, individuals.

Recommended Readings

Kathleen Daly (1988). "The Social Control of Sexuality: A Case Study of the Criminalization of Prostitution in the Progressive Era." *Research in Law, Deviance and Social Control* 9:171–206.

Charles E. Faupel (1991). *Shooting Dope: Careers and Patterns of Hard-Core Heroin Users*. Gainesville: University of Florida Press.

Bill Hanson, George Beschner, James M. Walters, and Elliott Bovelle, eds. (1985). *Life With Heroin*. Lexington, Mass.: Lexington Books.

James A. Inciardi (1986). *The War on Drugs*. Palo Alto, Calif.: Mayfield.

Laura Lederer, ed. (1980). *Take Back the Night*. New York: Bantam Books.

Michael Tonry, and James Q. Wilson, eds. (1990). *Drugs and Crime*. Vol. 13 of *Crime and Justice: A Review of Research*. Chicago: University of Chicago Press.

Part III

Reacting to Crime

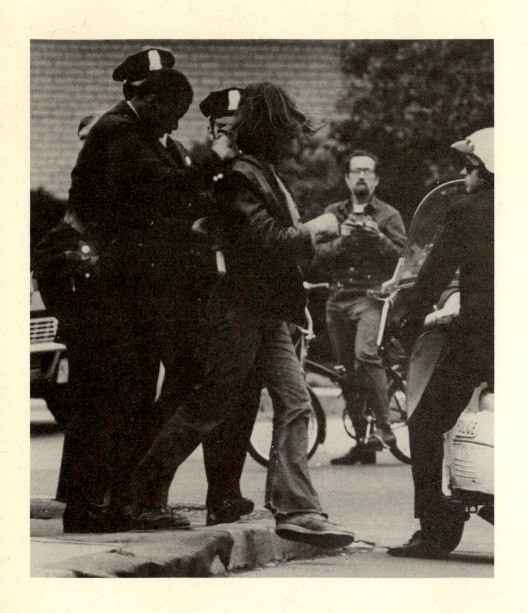

Chapter 10

Policing Society

The job of uncovering law violations, apprehending violators, and seeing to it that order is maintained rests with the police. As a practical matter, police must assume the burden of routinely translating law on the books into law in action.

To civilians the police officer is the law. Not only are police officers expected to interpret, investigate, and take action in matters of law and order, but they are also the typical citizen's most common and direct contact with the social control aspect of government. Once officers are present, a situation takes on new meaning—the "long arm of the law" has entered. Police officers carry symbols of the law and confirm in no uncertain terms what it represents. Their uniforms and badges symbolize their authority to take action in the name of the state; their weapons symbolize the availability of coercive force to back up their commands; their handcuffs symbolize the state's power of detention.

What the police do and do not do carries more weight in the legal process than the actions of any other single agency of criminal law—perhaps more than all others put together. It is *whether* and *how* laws are enforced that most directly and completely shape the working character of the legal process. The police are clearly at the heart of the criminal process.

The police, in their capacity as "first-line enforcers," make the important decision whether or not to take official action when confronted by people and events the law defines as criminal (Turk, 1971:67). If they choose not to identify an act as a crime, if they choose not to label a person as a suspect, or if they choose not to take official action, then for all practical purposes the act or person is not criminal. By decisions not to invoke the legal process, police effectively determine the outer boundaries of law in action (Goldstein, 1960:543). As a rule, the police are the first to apply the official labels *crime* and *criminal*. Whatever might happen at subsequent stages in the legal process can happen only after that crucial action has been taken.

Police not only merit serious attention in criminology as part of the official machinery of law, but they also shape the crime scene itself. In their roles as crime detectors, crime investigators, and crime preventers, police make crime a part of their work, just as does the professional thief. This is not to say that the police commit crimes (although such acts do occur from time to time) but, rather, to draw attention to their work in dealing with criminal matters, complainants, witnesses, suspects, and victims and the impact this work has on the character of crime within their jurisdictions. The unique contribution police make to the overall shape of crime is found in how they perceive and do their jobs. Aspects of police work such as patrolling practices and techniques, discretion, use of force, training, departmental norms and policies, and the operation of specialty details (vice, traffic, or intelligence) help create the social reality of crime.

The History of Policing

The police force as known today is of relatively recent origin. Most students of the police trace its modern origins to the rapid industrial expansion and population growth in the late eighteenth and early nineteenth centuries in western Europe, particularly England.

Origins and Growth of Modern Police

For centuries, England relied for law enforcement on the services of volunteers and patronage appointees. Together with the military, these early constables and sheriffs saw to it that the interests of landowners, nobility, and monarchy were protected. Considerable time and energy were spent collecting taxes and making sure that villagers and townspeople ran their personal and community affairs on behalf of the wealthy and powerful. Since the tradition of self-help justice was slow to die away, the essential responsibility for doing something about crime was placed on the shoulders of the citizenry. Individual towns and villages were held accountable for the enforcement of laws and prohibitions, and enforcement, such as it was, was largely a collective affair. As towns grew, able-bodied men (especially property owners) were expected to volunteer for nighttime duty as watchmen. These unpaid citizens were expected to look out for disruptions of public order or threats to property and were to guard the moral standards of the day. The constables worked at upholding law and order during the day; the watchmen took their turns at night.

Though constables and watchmen were accorded the powers of arrest and in some towns were armed, little public protection and crime control was apparently expected of them, and little was delivered. As time passed many property owners who had participated as watchmen found ways to escape what was seen as an onerous responsibility; those who stayed on the job made the most of it through a variety of corrupt and unlawful practices. Over the centuries, public and corporate faith in the reliability of the constable and watchman system steadily declined.

The rise of capitalism changed economic and social conditions dramatically and painfully. The migration of countless thousands of hopeful workers into already crowded towns and cities added new tensions to the hardships suffered by the masses. Brutal living conditions, small wages and long hours for those lucky enough to have jobs, growing poverty in the midst of growing affluence, and the ideology of laissez-faire contributed to social disorder. Add to this periodic crime waves, vagrants and beggars by the thousands, and an extremely punitive system of laws, and the scene was set for a breakdown in the existing police system.

Matters came to a head with a series of militant demonstrations and riots in which the disadvantaged and disaffected citizenry sought to improve their lot. The property owners and emerging middle class saw growing opposition and resistance, and felt that the very foundations of the new industrial era were under attack. It became popular to refer to the poorer classes—the unemployed, the disadvantaged, the menial factory workers—as social scum or the dross of society, and these unfortunates were lumped together with petty criminals under the title "dangerous classes." It was to contain and suppress these dangerous classes that many advocated police reforms and innovations (Critchley, 1972:34–42; Silver, 1967).

The English were reluctant to accept the notion of an organized, professional, paramilitary police force, feeling it would seriously threaten traditionally prized liberties (Banton, 1973:18). Despite this reluctance, the reform proposals of men such as Patrick Colquhoun eventually gained widespread support. Colquhoun (1806) proposed that a well-regulated, full-time, centrally administered police organization be set up to prevent crime by patrolling the streets of London. Its officers would be salaried men under the direction of commissioners accountable directly to the government. In 1829, Parliament, under the leadership of Home Secretary Robert Peel, enacted the Metropolitan Police Act. This act followed the model for police organization and strategy long advocated by Colquhoun. The forerunner of the modern police force had been born.

Policing in America

In America, meanwhile, the larger cities were facing some of the same problems that so alarmed the English propertied class. Though industrialization and modern capitalism were slower to appear on the American scene, by the early 1800s many American cities were experiencing rising rates of poverty, unemployment, migration, and crime and were feeling signs of growing unrest. Riots and demonstrations erupted in Boston, New York, and elsewhere, and the police came under attack for ineffectiveness in controlling the dangerous classes (Bacon, 1935; Lane, 1967).

During the early colonial period, American towns and cities had relied on constables and watchmen. The protection of life, property, and public order was considered a civic responsibility, as it had been in England. Able-bodied property owners were expected to assume constable and watchman duties on a rotating basis. These policing methods soon acquired a dubious reputation; as towns grew and abuses of duty became commonplace, city officials sought to improve crime control efforts. In 1772, Williamsburg, Virginia, instituted one of the first municipal night patrols, composed of four "sober and discreet people" who were its permanent, paid members. Their job was "to patrol the streets of this city from ten o'clock every night until daylight the next morning, to cry the hours, and use their best endeavors to preserve peace and good order, by apprehending and bringing to justice all disorderly people" (Weston and Wells, 1972:6). Boston and New York soon followed suit, and the new patrols were given authority to enforce all laws and to stop and question anyone suspected of criminal designs (see Bacon, 1935).

These moderate reforms failed to satisfy the demand for order and crime control voiced in many quarters. American authorities looked to England for help, The London "New Police," as they were called, seemed to be doing a good job, so why not try the same system in America? In New York, an 1845 ordinance established a police force with around-the-clock patrol and law-enforcement duties. The force was administered by a board of police commissioners (composed of the mayor, the recorder, and a city judge), a model adopted by New Orleans in 1853, Cincinnati and San Francisco in 1859, Detroit, St. Louis, and Kansas City in 1861, and Buffalo and Cleveland in 1866.

It became patently clear, however, that police commissions were little more than political tools in the hands of the parties in power. Further, they proved ineffective in managing the administrative affairs of their departments, with the result that they quickly fell into disfavor. By the early 1900s many cities had abandoned commissions in favor of a single public official acting as police executive.

One marked difference between the organization of English and American police has been the "home rule" jurisdictional structure in America. Although local and regional hierarchies administer the day-to-day operations of English police forces, the police nevertheless retain a national character, in that Parliament and the Home Office oversee operations and local police have jurisdiction in what here would be called federal matters. In America, the Constitution reserves the bulk of criminal law matters for state control and makes a clear distinction between federal and state laws and their enforcement. Law enforcement operates under a complicated system of jurisdictional controls, with local, county, state, and federal political units exercising varying degrees of authority and retaining varying amounts of autonomy in police affairs.

One consequence of this division of authority is the *politicization* of law enforcement. Police operations are not divorced from politics in England; in America, however, they are firmly entrenched in politics, and day-to-day political interference at all levels is a risk, if not an inevitability. The association between machine politics and police work has been well documented in the case of Chicago (see, e.g., Haller, 1976). At the turn of the century, when Chicago was experiencing unprecedented growth and industrial development, the law-enforcement apparatus was an indispensable part of machine politics. Police promotions as well as judgeships were dependent on the demonstration of party loyalty. All police employees paid a portion of their salaries into the party treasury and were required to do its bidding, even if this meant occasionally breaking the law. Today the connection between politics and police may no longer be so blatant, but it is there nonetheless.

Over the past few decades, American crime control agencies have mushroomed in number, personnel, and budgets. Today more than 40,000 federal, state, and local police agencies employ over 500,000 officers and operate with a combined budget in excess of $28 billion. These figures do not include the more than one million people working in private police agencies (such as Pinkerton's) and in the various inspection services employed by public authorities (such as game wardens or bank examiners).

One of the most noteworthy aspects of the growth of American police services has been the expansion of federal involvement in crime control. Although the Constitution reserves the bulk of general criminal law matters for the states, congressional action over the past 75 years or so has made extensive federal participation in law enforcement inevitable. Today, around 90,000 criminal suspects are handled by the federal system each year (MaGuire and Flanagan, 1991:475).

The Police at Work

Policing in America is different from that found in many other countries. Therefore, what is described here may not necessarily apply elsewhere (see Archambeault and Fenwick, 1983). In addition, police organizations and police work itself differ from agency to agency and around the country. These caveats aside, a general picture of recruitment and training practices, the exercise of police authority, and styles of policing in America can be drawn.

Recruitment and Training

Much police work is "dirty work" (Hughes, 1964:23–36), something that respectable or good people shun, prefer not to have to think about, and leave for others to perform. It is work that is both demanded and rejected; it is work that is both disgusting and indispensable; it is work that protects the in-group from the out-group, but those who consider themselves "in" hire outsiders to perform it; it is work society regards as essential, yet fails to reward adequately.

The dirty aspects of police work—handling drunks, dead bodies, accident victims; dealing with child abusers, muggers, and other "deviants"; and sometimes using violence in the process—merely reinforce the view that such work is not for respectable citizens (Harris, 1973:5–6). To most citizens it is precisely this facet of police work that identifies the real job of the police. How often do police officers hear: "Instead of bothering me, why don't you go and arrest real criminals like we're paying you to?" or "Why don't you clean up the streets so that respectable people can walk safely at night?"

In view of all this it is reasonable to wonder whether there is anything particularly striking about those who enter the occupation. Is there a pool or supply of individuals who are ready candidates for police work? Do they share social and personality characteristics that make them somehow different from other citizens? Are only certain types of people actively recruited by police agencies?

There are few indications that police recruits are particularly different from those who enter other occupations. It is true that they show a fair degree of homogeneity in their educational, occupational, and family backgrounds. The recruit typically comes from a lower-middle- or working-class background, has no more than a high school education, and has previously worked in clerical, sales, or manual jobs (McNamara, 1967). For many, police work represents a step up the occupational status ladder. These traits, though, are shared by millions of other American workers.

The evidence on personality traits again offers no sound basis for distinguishing recruits from their nonpolice peers. Some have argued that the police recruit exhibits traits associated with the "authoritarian personality." Among these traits are conventionalism (rigid adherence to middle-class values), cynicism (a view that "things are going to pot"), aggression, and stereotypical thinking. Administering the F-scale (designed to measure authoritarianism) to 116 New York City police recruits, Arthur Niederhoffer and John H. McNamara found a relatively high mean score of 4.15 (the highest possible score is 7.0). This score was almost identical, however, with previous scores for general working-class samples, indicating nothing exceptional about the recruits, considering their predominantly working-class backgrounds. Niederhoffer concluded that although police officers may well develop strong authoritarian personalities, once they have been exposed to training and the demands of the job, nothing suggests "self-selection among authoritarian personalities prior to appointment" (Niederhoffer, 1967:159). This conclusion still stands today.

Why, then, do individuals enter police work? Niederhoffer suggests they do so for reasons such as security, decent working conditions, adventure, and relatively good pay, which make the job attractive to those with little formal education, few marketable skills, and lower-class backgrounds. David Bayley and Harold Mendelsohn (1968:32–33), investigating Denver police entrants, echo this interpretation:

> One does not need a special theory to explain why men go into police work. . . . One explains recruitment to the police force as one explains recruitment to any occupation, namely, in terms of its status, rewards, minimal educational requirements, and conditions of service. . . . Recruits bring to police work the same kinds of evaluations of the police made by people generally. They are neither more starry-eyed nor more cynical. They choose to be policemen because it fits their potentialities and promises the kinds of rewards considered by them commensurate with their background and training. By and large, it represents an advance over what their parents obtained. One understands police recruitment, then, in terms of a practical upward step in social mobility as well as an improvement in life prospects.

When questioned about their reasons for joining the force, officers voice many of the same reasons that move people to seek nonpolice jobs. Among the most often cited reasons are security and retirement benefits. Few officers speak of excitement, action, or dirty work as reasons for joining, and few recruits are drawn to police work for idealistic reasons, such as helping rid society of criminals or contributing to law and order. These findings reinforce the view that those who enter police work are in no way a special category of people and are not different from others with similar backgrounds.

Most police agencies exercise considerable control over who is accepted for police work. The days when departments were willing to take just about anyone are long over. The typical police agency now requires applicants to pass a standard civil service exam, undergo a battery of other tests and examinations (sometimes including lie-detector tests), and pass checks on health, background, and character. Many agencies place considerable weight on these last checks, and a good portion of recruits never make it past one or another of these hurdles (Harris, 1973:16–17).

None of these procedures is without controversy, and this is especially true of psychological testing. Such tests have been criticized on methodological grounds—what do they really tell us?—and also because they are thought to infringe on the rights (including privacy) of applicants. However, court challenges to the use of psychological tests have generally failed (Inwald and Kenney, 1989:39).

Interviews are especially important as a means of weeding out "undesirables." The interview is usually conducted by senior officers, and it permits recruiters to reject applicants who might otherwise be acceptable (Bent, 1974:16). In this way, recruits who display undesirable values or whose political attitudes and ethnic backgrounds conflict with those dominant in the force can also be weeded out. This tends to perpetuate the class, ethnic, and value characteristics of those already employed. Such homogeneity in personnel makes it easier for departments to retain already fashioned policies and practices, to reduce potential internal disruptions, and to maintain more complete control over their policing operations. From the standpoint of the officers themselves, it cements distinctions between the in-group and out-group and aids in the development of predictability, solidarity, and secrecy. These three important dimensions of organization and work are further emphasized as a recruit becomes a full-fledged police officer.

Recruitment of Women and Minorities

In 1910 the first woman was sworn in as a police officer in the United States (Milton, 1972). Even so, it took over 60 years before women had an equal legal right to a law-enforcement career, and many court battles have been fought in a continuing effort to halt discriminatory employment practices.

Susan Martin (1989) has reviewed the recent history and current status of women in policing. She observes that there seem to be two opinions about how far women have come since the 1972 Amendments to the Civil Rights Act of 1964. On one hand it is argued that female entry into criminal justice professions has not kept pace with changes in other occupations traditionally dominated by males (such as law); on the other hand there are those who believe that dramatic changes in the sexual integration of policing have already occurred (see, for example, Fyfe, 1987).

There has certainly been growth in the number of female police officers in the 1980s. That growth looks more impressive in absolute than in relative terms, however, and some communities have fared much better than others. Although the number of female city police officers grew from 7383 in 1980 to 28,335 in 1990, they still constituted only 8.3 percent of all city officers (Federal Bureau of Investigation, 1991:242). Notably, the percentage increases for smaller cities and suburban counties have been smaller than those for large cities. Gender discrimination goes hand in hand with traditionalism, which is inversely related to urbanization.

Another aspect that has not changed much is sex differences in rank. Over 20 years ago, Milton (1972) observed that few women were to be found in higher ranks or administrative positions. Today's situation is only a little better. Female officers are still predominantly found in police jobs that fit stereotypical images of the female role—dealing with juveniles, for example, or helping rape and sexual abuse victims, or being on mediation teams called out to deal with family violence. These jobs are apparently not the best track to promotion. Judging from experiences in other occupations, even those women who do well by institutionalized standards may find that they are less likely to be promoted than their male counterparts (see Martin, 1989:324– 326). Evidence suggests that the deck is stacked against women in the design of performance evaluation itself (Morash and Greene, 1986). For example, evaluation of patrol performance is geared toward traits that males tend to value such as physical prowess, initiative, and aggressiveness (see Bloch and Anderson, 1974). Women do tend to make fewer arrests than men, but even this finding is open to various interpretations (Martin, 1989:317):

> For example, the women's lower arrest rates may mean that women are not taking enough initiative. Alternatively, it might indicate that women handled the situations better than male officers, if the latter caused incidents to escalate into confrontations which resulted in unnecessary arrests. A third explanation is that when a more experienced male patrolled with a female rookie, he tended to take charge of the situation and take credit for arrests more frequently than with male rookies. Thus, it is necessary to look beyond the numbers to an interpretation of their meaning.

Despite mounting evidence that female officers perform their police duties as well as and sometimes better than their male counterparts, they must still face blatant sexism (Morash, 1986). While most of the opposition to women is expressed in terms of physical inadequacies ("they are not strong enough to deal with mostly male suspects"), Martin (1989:319) suggests that "women also pose a threat to work group solidarity by penetrating the emotional masks men wear and inhibiting their use of 'raunchy' language." Until sexism and the male fears behind it are overcome, women will continue to experience an uphill battle in their efforts to achieve equality and equity in policing.

The situation is somewhat different for African-Americans, though their battle has also been an uphill one. Around the turn of the century few black police officers were to be found, especially in small cities and rural areas. Sullivan (1989) observes that little progress was made until blacks mobilized politically and organizationally and could thus bring pressure to bear on police and municipal administrators (see also Kuykendall and Burns, 1980). Even so, most blacks were hired to police black areas, and their arrest powers were often restricted.

The race riots of the 1960s and growing numbers of lawsuits put police officials on notice that their hiring practices had to change. Coupled with the emergence of black police associations formed to represent minority interests, these events had a profound impact. Table 10.1 shows that from 1970 to 1985 black (and also Hispanic) representation among the nation's sworn police officers grew to full proportionality. What the table does not show, however, is that the majority of black officers are hired by large city departments.

Minority officers, like their female colleagues, find it hard to get favorable duty assignments and promotions. "Too often," writes Peggy Sullivan

Recruitment (and promotion) of women and minorities still lags far behind their proportions in the population as a whole, though the situation has vastly improved over the past decade, especially in big city departments and in state and federal police agencies.

(1989:341), "the prejudice that would have kept minorities from being hired in the first place now functions to keep them from getting good assignments, performance ratings, and promotions."

It is almost impossible to obtain good information on assignment and promotion practices. Certainly, there are no national data, and individual departments have not been diligent in making information available, even if they have kept proper records. The consensus is that minority members are severely underrepresented in higher ranks, and a variety of court cases confirm the picture. The outcome of these cases has generally been favorable for blacks, though reverse discrimination suits and other challenges have increased in recent years. In some communities black officers who qualify for promotion are allowed to jump to the next higher rank; others have a policy that every time a white officer is promoted a black will be too. Needless to say,

TABLE 10.1 Percentage of blacks and Hispanics in population and among all police and detectives in the U.S.

	Blacks		Hispanics	
	% in Population	% of Police	% in Population	% of Police
1970	11.1	3.9	4.5	2.7
1980	11.8	8.4	6.4	4.0
1984	12.0	13.1	6.4	4.0
1985	12.1	13.5	6.4	6.1

Source: Statistical Abstracts of the United States, 1987, 1985, 1981, and 1971. Reported in: Peggy S. Sullivan (1989), "Minority Officers: Current Issues." In Roger G. Dunham and Geoffrey P. Alpert (eds.), *Critical Issues in Policing* (Prospect Heights, Ill.: Waveland Press), p. 335.

such practices are disquieting to many white officers, and therefore they carry the risk of increasing hostility and ill-feelings among police officers.

One of the most difficult issues to resolve concerns written tests used in hiring and promotions. It has long been recognized that blacks do not compete well with whites in these tests, and so some departments have changed the requirements. This brings the charge that standards have been lowered at the risk of jeopardizing performance. On the other hand, poor scores on written tests may hide a person's potential for leadership.

Society is a long way from resolving the difficulties surrounding these issues. The battle against racism (and sexism) is still to be won. If the statistical picture continues to improve, the fact that females and minorities make just as good police officers as males and whites will be more widely recognized and will help dismantle prejudicial practices that discriminate against them. However, the growing number of "reverse discrimination" suits and a conservative Supreme Court are not encouraging.

Training and the Acquisition of Police Perspectives

Most police officers assert that the only way to learn about police work is by doing it; experience counts for all. Although this view is by no means unique to police officers, many features of police work not found in most other occupations underscore the importance of experience. Police carry guns and other weapons that can be used with deadly results. They are subject to other people's aggressions and hostilities just because they are police officers. They are given authority to act in situations in which other citizens must stand back. In many jurisdictions, they are expected to be police officers 24 hours a day. If they make mistakes, they may be subject to criminal and civil suits.

Because most recruits are ill prepared for the demands of police work and also because there are insistent pleas for professionalization of the police, many police agencies offer extensive training courses for their new recruits. If they have no police academy, they send them to universities and colleges with special law-enforcement curricula. These training programs introduce the newcomer to the legal, ethical, organizational, and operational facets of police work. It is while enrolled in the programs that a recruit gets a first taste of what it means to be a police officer. An intensive socialization process begins and the "cord binding the rookie to the civilian world is cut" (Niederhoffer, 1967:43).

In training by police instructors, rookies see for the first time something of the ambiguities and conflicts inherent in police work. They learn that they are expected to enforce all criminal laws but that in practice they must be selective. They learn that the public is like an enemy—they are told to be suspicious, always on the lookout for a setup, and never to rely on any help from citizens—but that they must serve and protect its members. They learn that although the authorities demand that they combat crime and arrest criminals, those powers also insist that police officers follow procedures, even if that sometimes means the escape of a criminal, the commission of a crime, or perhaps injury and death. They learn that police work is also public relations work and that valued attributes such as zeal and honesty may get them into trouble with their superiors. Most important of all, perhaps, they learn that what they are told in class often differs markedly from what they know from experience as private citizens. Whatever idealism they brought with them is soon forgotten—often permanently.

Defensiveness, Professionalism, Depersonalization One of the primary goals of formal police training is the development of uniform behavior among officers so that there is less room for personal judgment and individualized behavior (Harris, 1973). Recruits must be stripped of their identity and taught to assume a police identity—to think and act as a police officer. Richard Harris suggests that three themes emerge during training to help generate in recruits a proper police perspective. The first, perhaps most important, is *defensiveness*—to be alert to the many dangers of police work and to build defenses against them. These dangers are not merely physical. They include the dangers of procedural violations that can lead to criminal charges, civil suits, reprimands, lost cases, and dismissal. They include the dangers of corruption, inefficiency, and emotional involvement in police–citizen encounters as well as the danger of provoking hostile and punitive reactions by members of the public who are in a position to make trouble for the department.

In a major study of the police at work in three Southern California counties, Michael Brown (1988) documents the "schizophrenic existence" that embroils patrol officers and stimulates this defensiveness. The police, he finds "must cope not only with the terror of an often hostile and unpredictable citizenry, but also with a hostile—even tyrannical—and unpredictable bureaucracy" (p. 9). He overheard one exasperated officer complain to his sergeant: "I'm getting jabbed in the ass by the public and jabbed in the ass by the department" (p. 81).

The second theme is *professionalization*—the development of a professional image, techniques, esprit de corps, service ideals, and a sense of "us" as opposed to "them." The third theme is *depersonalization*, which has two sides. On one side, recruits learn that the public and their own supervisors often treat them as faceless, lacking an individual identity; they are less persons than objects. They also learn that some occupational demands necessitate the denial of personal qualities—police officers dare not personalize their official relationships with the public and must beware of those who try to personalize that relationship. The other side of depersonalization involves the officer's own adoption of stereotypes, black-and-white distinctions, and intolerance of out-groups, whose members, in turn, become faceless.

In Harris's view, one important product of defensiveness, professionalization, and depersonalization is the cultivation of solidarity among recruits: "a subjective feeling of belongingness and implication in each other's lives" (Harris, 1973:163). This solidarity, the we-feeling that comes with group identity and belonging, firms up and helps preserve the police identity fostered during training (see also Alpert and Dunham, 1988:Chapter 5).

Danger, Authority, Efficiency In a study of city police at work, Jerome Skolnick argued that police officers typically develop a distinctive "working personality" (1975:42–70). A unique combination of work elements foster in police a particular way of looking at the world and responding to it. The key elements identified by Skolnick are *danger, authority,* and *efficiency*. Together they encourage the development of suspicion, social isolation, and solidarity—central characteristics of the police officers' relations with the world in which they work. They become suspicious of the events, persons, and things they learn to associate with danger, and the defensive posture caused by this suspicion moves them to erect barriers between themselves and the world. Even if they might not wish to erect barriers—as in their relations with neighbors, family acquaintances, civilian friends, and members of the opposite sex—they find that barriers may be erected for them, because their work makes them less desirable as a friend.

It has been suggested that there are two paradoxes inherent in the police role in relation to danger (Cullen et al., 1983). First, many officers view their role as both safe and unsafe—safe because in reality relatively few officers are killed or seriously injured, unsafe because the job always carries the potential for harm or death. Second, there are two apparently contradictory consequences of danger—one is that the police officer must be constantly alert; the other is that this alertness contributes to stress and sometimes produces psychological disturbance.

One should also remember that perceptions of danger differ among the general population, from which all police recruits are drawn. Middle-class people see their environment differently than inner-city residents who learn constantly to assess their surroundings for tell-tale signs of danger (Stanko, 1990:15). Thus many police recruits must be taught *how* to see the signs of danger. Unfortunately, once they have learned to do it, their quality of life, like that of inner-city residents, is reduced.

The social isolation of police is enhanced by their role as enforcer of public order and public morality: "Typically, the policeman is required to enforce laws representing puritanical morality, such as those prohibiting drunkenness, and also laws regulating the flow of public activity, such as traffic laws. In these situations, the policeman directs the citizenry, whose typical response denies recognition of his authority and stresses his obligation to respond to danger" (Skolnick, 1975:44). Expected to enforce laws that they may not agree with or that are resented by large segments of the population, police officers' official authority once again encourages erection of barriers and contributes to social isolation.

Added to the effects of authority and danger is a persistent pressure to be efficient—to produce, to demonstrate that they are living up to the expectations of their superiors. Sometimes required to fill quotas for such things as traffic tickets (Skolnick reports that motorcycle patrol officers were required to write two tickets an hour) and vice arrests (a "rigidly enforced" expectation in some cities), police officers find themselves further alienating the public as they seek to meet demands for efficiency.

With barriers between themselves and the general public, police seek support and reciprocity among their colleagues. To counteract the threat of danger and the effects of public hostility and to fulfill the persistent demands that they produce, officers are drawn together in relationships of mutual dependence and self-help (see Manning, 1977). The solidarity thus encouraged becomes a central facet of police working relationships, and officers draw on their we-feeling as they act out their roles. Sensing that they can rely on neither the public nor their higher-echelon superiors, they turn to one another, further separating themselves from the world around them. Loyalty becomes a core value of police culture. In return, the patrol officers receive protection and honor (Brown, 1988:83).

Stereotyping and the Exercise of Police Authority

The police deal in stereotypes and this means that police authority is sometimes exercised in situations that would not warrant it if all the facts were known. Police feel that the undesirable consequences of this are outweighed by the benefits. From the first day of training through the rest of their careers, police find little reason to discover all the facts before acting, nor can they afford to. If anything, they learn that facts are less important than initial appearances and that the best way to approach appearances is to have ready a set of categories for them.

As noted already, suspicion is central to police officers' approach to their work. It is toward people, objects, places, and events labeled suspicious that the police direct much of their attention. Perceptual categorization and simplification are important devices in defining what is suspicious—police cannot suspect everything and everyone. Werthman and Piliavin (1967:68–

By its nature, police work sometimes puts officers in situations of imminent danger to life and limb. Thankfully, surprisingly few officers are killed while on duty; nationwide, the annual risk is approximately .0002, although the actual risks vary by place, time, and situation, and by characteristics and work patterns of the police themselves.

69) suggest that police arrive at their categorization of persons and things as suspicious through *pragmatic induction*:

> Past experience leads them to conclude that more crimes are committed in the poorer sections of town than in the wealthier areas, that Negroes are more likely to cause public disturbances than whites, and that adolescents are a greater source of trouble than other categories of the citizenry. On the basis of these conclusions, the police divide the population and physical territory under surveillance into a variety of categories, make some initial assumptions about the moral character of the people and places in these categories, and then focus attention on those categories of persons and places felt to have the shadiest moral characteristics.

In this way police create a self-fulfilling prophecy: The official criminals come from precisely those areas and groups that fit the stereotype. On the other hand, those areas and groups that do not fit the stereotype retain their "clean" look and continue to receive modest police scrutiny.

English sociologist Dennis Chapman (1968:56) tells of a case in which for six months residents of an upper-middle-class neighborhood removed building materials from a construction site: "Each evening and every weekend, after the workmen had departed, the site was visited by between 5 and 15 men with motor-cars or wheelbarrows. They removed bricks, tiles, paving slabs, timber, mortar, and other building materials systematically, and often in large quantities." When asked by an observer why he did not intervene, a police officer who happened to witness one evening's thievery replied that he assumed they all had permission! Neither the thieves nor the circumstances fit police stereotypes of suspicious persons and activities.

Contrast this case with an incident Alan Bent (1974) observed during his investigation of the Memphis police at work. Some police officers were under pressure to produce following an uneventful evening. Officers in four cars descended on an area adjoining a converted warehouse in which a dance was being held. The officers made numerous attempts to uncover evidence of illegal activity by teenagers moving around the area or parked in their cars. Eventually four adolescents were discovered with a couple of joints, and a bust was made. The stereotype linking young people, play, and crime (in this case illegal drugs) had worked and was thereby reinforced.

The fact that considerable energy and resources are spent dealing with members of selected segments of the population—usually the poor, the inner-city residents, the young, and the black—should not be taken to mean that police-enforcement practices reflect only *police* prejudice, stereotypes, and decisions. On the contrary, police are conforming to culturally supported stereotypes, prejudices, and policies rather than deviating from them. One must look beyond the police for an explanation of their behavior. American police operate in a culture that generally rewards those who conform to middle-class values. Middle-class America looks not to itself for the criminal but, rather, to the underclass and especially to minorities.

Some evidence of police conformity with prevailing middle-class standards comes from Bent's study in Memphis. Bent found much agreement in self-appraisals and attitudes toward the others between the police and white middle-class samples, despite the disparate background of the two groups. Though police views of some subjects differed from those of the white middle-class sample, their views differed most consistently from those held by blacks and students. Both the police and the typical white middle-class respondents held to an "order-stability" value structure, stressing crime control, improved police efficiency and production, and enforcement patterns aimed at preserving order and stability. This value system is contrasted with the "democratic-active," which emphasizes service responsibilities, social needs, due process, justice, human dignity, and respect for human differences. The order-stability group—represented by the white, middle-aged person with at least a high school education who earns over $15,000 (1972 dollars) a year—held "warm feelings" toward the military, conservatives, Republicans, police, whites, and the National Guard. So did the police sample. The group held "cold feelings" toward liberals, blacks, feminists, and other persons and groups most closely associated with social innovation. So did the police. Since white, middle-class individuals typically are in the best position to influence the activities of governments and their agencies, it should come as no surprise that police share a similar set of values and engage in behavior in support of them.

It is interesting to note that programs of higher education have been advocated as a means of broadening police attitudes, of reducing prejudice, authoritarianism, stereotyping, and hostility toward those with whom they come into contact as enforcers. In 1966, 184 colleges and universities offered degree programs in criminal justice; in 1978, there were 816 such programs (Kobetz, 1978:1). Yet it appears far from conclusive that higher education for police greatly changes their attitudes and behavior. Indeed, "there is strong evidence that the value of police education may be nullified by the realities of the police role as it is now constituted" (Weiner, 1974:323; for other views see Eskridge, 1989). The nature of police work, especially the need to be suspicious and to pattern enforcement in terms of arrest-productive stereotypes, coupled with pressure from middle-class law-and-order interests, seems to be blocking any real liberalization of police attitudes and behavior.

The Los Angeles Police Department (LAPD), long regarded as one of the most professional and well-educated departments in the country (see Brown, 1988:60–64), illustrates this point. The 1991 Rodney King beating, videotaped by an onlooker and shown numerous times on national television, involved members of this department. The Christopher Commission that investigated the incident remarked on "the frequency and bravado with which far too many LAPD officers used the in-car Mobile Digital Terminal system to communicate their scurrilous racial, ethnic, and sexual sentiments. . . . These were conscious statements . . . typed on a keypad with little, if any, concern for the possibility that they would ever be disclosed or judged" (*Los Angeles Times*, September 14, 1991, M1). Fairly clearly, this statement implies that police higher-ups condoned, or simply did nothing about, rampant and prejudicial stereotyping among LAPD patrol officers. Some of the responsibility for the subsequent "not guilty" verdict and the rioting that followed must surely be borne by those higher-echelon officers within the LAPD whose professional conduct reinforced prevailing prejudices and contributed to feelings of resentment and fear among African-Americans and among members of the community at large.

Styles of Policing

In his influential book *Varieties of Police Behavior*, James Q. Wilson (1968) describes three styles of policing: (1) watchman, (2) legalistic, and (3) service. By his own account, Wilson (1988) entered criminology "through the back door," in response to invitations to study the police in Chicago, and later in Boston and in Oakland, California. Through these inquiries he discovered that the social and political characteristics of a community determine in large part how its police define and carry out their duties.

Police departments that can be characterized as *watch* departments harken back to the days when police acted as reluctant maintainers of order. They tend to be found in older cities with large populations of poor and minorities. Patrolling officers avoid rather than seek out law violations (Lundman, 1980:43). They would rather ignore traffic violators (unless there is something in it for them), juvenile delinquents, and crimes that occur among the poor and minorities. Vice is tolerated, if not encouraged. When faced with serious crime they can be tough; on other occasions their enforcement is informal and variable. Corruption is a frequent problem in watch departments, primarily because of the tolerance of vice and the dominance of machine politics, but also because patrolling officers are largely unsupervised. Chicago under Mayor Richard Daley and Philadelphia under Mayor Frank Rizzo had watch-style departments.

The *legalistic* style of policing may also be found in some older cities with large concentrations of poor and minorities, usually because reform-minded administrators have replaced the old machine, as happened, for example, in Los Angeles. However, the legalistic style is most often found in newer and more affluent communities—for example, Oakland, California and Highland Park, Illinois (Lundman, 1980:46). Such communities want unobtrusive yet professional policing; they want laws enforced and public disorder controlled. Police in legalistic departments are careful about their appearance and image, and they emphasize arrest and ticketing of violators without regard to race, affluence, or age. Organized corruption is rare, mainly because vice laws are routinely enforced.

Service departments are found primarily in white, middle- and upperclass suburbs. Lundman (1980:47) identifies Lakewood, Colorado and Burnsville, Minnesota as service departments; Wilson (1968:200) singled out Nassau County, New York. In these departments police are proactive (see below) in generating contacts with citizens and suspects, but they also emphasize their duty to respond to all calls for assistance. Their response to less serious offenses is likely to be noncustodial: Warnings, counseling, mediation, and referrals to nonpolice agencies are typical. Service departments emphasize good community relations, and each officer is expected to work toward that end.

Lundman (1980:47–49) illustrates the three styles of policing in relation to domestic disputes and traffic violations. The distinctions he makes are summarized in Table 10.2. However, it is important to remember that the three styles are "ideal types," which means they may not exist in the real world exactly as depicted, and some departments may have elements of more than one style. The distinctions Wilson has drawn are nevertheless important for an understanding of variability in police practice and its relationship to community organization, political structures, and police-citizen relations.

Brown's Typology of Operational Styles   Moving beyond Wilson's analysis to a consideration of how patrolling police respond to the pressures and demands of a professional police force, Brown (1988) used interviews, field observa-

TABLE 10.2 Typical police responses by type of department and problem

Type of Department	Problem and Typical Police Responses	
	Domestic	Traffic
Watch	Ignore/minimize/separate and warn not to call again	Ignore/honk horn and yell out window/opportunity for money
Legalistic	Potentially productive of serious criminality/law enforcement problem/arrest possible	Traffic citation
Service	Opportunity to counsel and refer citizen/"crisis intervention"	Counsel and advise

Source: Richard J. Lundman (1980). *Police and Policing: An Introduction* (New York: Holt, Rinehart and Winston).

tions, and official police statistics in developing a typology of operational styles. "An operational style," Brown (1988:244–245) asserts,

> represents a patrolman's initial response to the uncertainties of attempting to control crime and the demands of police administrators. . . . An operational style structures action, it leads a patrolman toward some alternatives and away from others, and it is frequently the decisive factor in determining his choices.

Brown identified four operational styles, constructed from the combination of two characteristics: "*aggressiveness* in pursuit of the goal of crime control, and *selectiveness* in the enforcement of the law" (p. 223).

Old style crime fighters are high on aggressiveness and selective in their enforcement of laws. They regard felonies as the only crimes "worth" pursuing since they involve "real" police work involving technical skills and "street sense." They are ruthless and aggressive in their street behavior: "Most of their free time is spent prowling down darkened streets, often with their car lights out, and stopping any vehicle or individual that looks even remotely suspicious" (Brown, 1988:226). However, if they do stop someone for a minor violation, they rarely write a citation or made an arrest. They devise schemes to avoid such order-maintenance activities as breaking up fights and removing drunks, and they are unwilling to do service calls. The old style crime fighter prospers in a large department such as LAPD, which permits independent action and honors officers who demonstrate skill and ability to do the job. "In a way, the old style crime fighters earn the right to flout the rules to which other policemen are subject," but the price is that they are "brutal and often given to the worst abuses of police power" (p. 229).

Clean beat crime fighters are high on aggressiveness and dislike order-maintenance and service calls. While they also agree with the old style crime fighter that crime prevention and control is the primary function of patrolling, they look "for all kinds of violations . . . , from jaywalking to homicide, and make as many stops as [they] can." They believe in "the rigid and unrelenting enforcement of the law" (p. 229). The clean beat crime fighter possesses none of the skill and finesse of the old style crime fighter but "is something of a rogue elephant . . . , the kind of officer who will make a lot of felony arrests but will be consistently in trouble" (p. 230). He is always trying to "dig something up," always on the move, always stopping cars and people. Brown offers an example:

> [T]wo clean beat patrolmen in the course of an evening cited one jaywalker; made three traffic stops, two of which resulted in citations; arrested six drunks, although two were the result of backing up a vice unit in a bar; stopped and interrogated one suspected heroin addict; and made two other investigative stops in "suspicious" circumstances. This was in addition to handling a moderate number of calls for service. (p. 231)

Subject to departmental constraints and a hostile public, the zealous clean beat patrol officer is often frustrated and resentful.

Professional style patrol officers are also broad in their enforcement of the law, but they are low on aggressiveness. "These patrolmen are legalistic without being rigid" (p. 233). They presume neither guilt nor innocence, but regard their role as serving a public that has a right to courtesy, impartiality, and compassion. Field interrogations are the exception rather than the rule, and all calls for service are treated with thoroughness, even trivial ones. Police professionalism is emphasized, but unlike the clean beat officer, the professional style patrolman follows departmental rules and policies and believes "that a policeman can enforce the law and cope with crime while maintaining rapport with the people in the community" (p.235).

Finally, the *service style* patrol officer comes in two forms, both low in aggressiveness and selective in enforcement of the law. In one form, officers take the line of least resistance and do the minimum work necessary to please their supervisors. "Their code was to take problems as they occur and above all stay out of trouble" (p. 236). In its other form, service style officers do not think that crime control is the primary goal of policing and emphasize, instead, helping people solve their problems within the framework of the law: They "combine the best of the beat cop and the professional policeman" (p. 236). Vice laws are downplayed, but violence is a fundamental concern. Because service style officers are skeptical of "present approaches to police work," they are not afraid to criticize fellow officers.

There is not space to present adequately Brown's intriguing work; suffice it to say that his typology needs further examination in the context of diverse police environments and will probably undergo refinement as a result. Because it is based on field observations and interviews, it adds an important experiential dimension to the analysis of styles of policing that was missing up to now.

Proactive Policing

The traditional police response to crime is largely reactive. Crimes occur and the police respond. However, reactive policing is inappropriate for many types of crime:

> It cannot . . . deal with consensual crimes such as drug dealing behind closed doors. Nor can it deal with crimes such as extortion and loan sharking where the victims are too afraid to report crimes. A reactive strategy cannot deal with sophisticated white collar crimes or political corruption where the losses associated with the crimes are so widely distributed that people do not notice that they have been victimized. Finally, a reactive strategy cannot deal even with traditional street crimes in those parts of cities where confidence in the police has eroded to such a degree that the citizens no longer call when they are victimized. (Moore, Trojanowicz, and Kelling, 1988:6)

To fight these crimes, police adopt a proactive strategy. The police find out about crime by uncovering it themselves. Various methods have been employed:

- *Decoys:* Sometimes police pretend to be participants in crime, thereby inviting the real offenders to commit crimes in their presence. This strategy has been used for consensual crimes involving homosexual acts as well as in sting operations used against money-laundering activities of drug traffickers and the transactions of fences and thieves. In some situations the police act as inviting victims, hoping to lure potential rapists and muggers into committing a crime.
- *Directed patrols:* A long-standing strategy employed when certain crimes have reached epidemic proportions, or when citizen complaints have become politically embarrassing, the directed patrol involves a concentration of patrol officers in particular locations or in surveillance of particular individuals or groups.
- *Special units:* Police response to some crimes must be especially sensitive, while the response to others is very complicated or dangerous. The police have developed special units to deal with such situations. For example, sex-crime and domestic-assault units are now common-place in larger cities, and "SWAT," organized crime, white-collar crime, and repeat offender (ROP) teams have sprung up around the country. Since these special units often employ undercover methods and recruit informants, they may not be widely known in the community; naturally, they have little deterrent function. However, as they generate intelligence about crime, they provide direction for proactive police enforcement.

Deterrence Aggressive policing such as that advocated in some proactive strategies is believed to contribute to crime reduction through its deterrent effect. Simply put, the argument is that the risks of arrest are increased: "By stopping, questioning, and otherwise closely observing citizens, especially suspicious ones, the police are more likely to find fugitives, detect contraband (such as stolen property or concealed weapons), and apprehend persons fleeing from the scene of a crime" (Wilson and Boland, 1978:373).

Wilson and Boland also believe that aggressive policing can lower crime rates by influencing the perceptions people hold of the likelihood of being arrested. As Sampson and Cohen (1988:165) put it:

> The general public has only a vague notion about the actual probabilities of arrest, and in fact arrests for serious index crimes (e.g., robbery) are relatively rare. Consequently most potential offenders rarely witness an index crime arrest. In contrast, the vigorous intervention by police on driving violations, drunkenness, and public disorder is a very visible indicator of police activity in an area. Aggressiveness in police patrol practices thus in all likelihood sends a signal to potential offenders that one's chances of getting caught are higher than they actually are.

Thus proactive policing may have a direct effect on crime by causing potential criminals to reconsider.

Sampson and Cohen (1988) tested the Wilson and Boland thesis by relating police arrest rates for public disorder crimes (disorderly conduct and DUI) to the robbery rates for 171 American cities. They found that aggressive policing had a direct negative effect on robbery rates in general, and especially for robberies committed by adults and by blacks. The authors argue that proactive policing may be more visible to blacks than to whites because they see it not only in their own neighborhoods but also in downtown and commercial areas where most whites are arrested. This may explain the observation that proactive policing of whites influenced black robbery rates more than did proactive policing of blacks themselves. Sampson and Cohen (1988:182) conclude that "police aggressiveness in controlling disorder by both whites and blacks has a pervasive crime reduction effect in adult robbery."

Other Considerations   Proactive policing has its drawbacks (Moore, Trojanowicz, and Kelling, 1988:7–8). First, some critics believe that it is too obtrusive, especially in its more aggressive forms. Second, some contend that surveillance and other offender-oriented practices raise serious constitutional questions regarding individual freedoms. The decoy technique raises the issue of entrapment: Are the police encouraging people to commit crimes who would not normally do so? Third, since the proactive role is one of seeking out crime, there are worries that police might actually manufacture evidence for it. Finally, some scholars argue that aggressive policing helps create a self-fulfilling prophecy since individuals who have repeated police contacts are at greater risk of continued offending (e.g., Shannon, 1991).

In addition to these problems, Moore, Trojanowicz, and Kelling (1988) cite three others: (1) Police are reluctant systematically to build explanations of crime into enforcement strategies—awareness of precipitating causes of criminality and criminal events has tended to remain anecdotal and the domain of intellectuals rather than practitioners; (2) police are reluctant to encourage neighborhoods and communities to develop their own self-defense capability—block watch programs and property marking campaigns were token efforts, but police strongly resisted inroads from private security forces and from volunteer groups such as the Guardian Angels; (3) police often fail to realize that community support is vital to the success of police anti-crime efforts. In Chapter 2 it was shown that police rely heavily on the public for information about crime. If the information loop from community to police is shut down, all aspects of the police function deteriorate, from protection to service. Intelligence gathering is at the heart of much proactive policing, and this rests upon solid community support of the police. Support in turn rests upon how the police behave in their everyday encounters with the public (Kinsey, Lea, and Young, 1986).

New Initiatives   Moore, Trojanowicz, and Kelling (1988:8–10) discuss some initiatives in proactive policing that are designed to meet the criticisms outlined above. These initiatives are sometimes referred to as neighborhood or community policing. Among the new techniques are *enhanced police presence,* including the use of conspicuous foot patrols and routine contacts between police and all (not just suspect) citizens; *close surveillance and monitoring* of dangerous offenders—suspects in current crimes and even parolees are placed under continuous surveillance, and the public is canvassed by local police for information about them (which in itself may deter potential offenders who learn from others that the police are keeping tabs on them); and *shoring up community institutions,* where the local police participate in efforts to strengthen schools, churches, neighborhood and community organizations, local businesses, and family relations. An example:

> A local school is plagued by dropouts who continually hang around the school intimidating both students and teachers. Crime has increased in and around the school. The principal decides to crack down on the problem. The neighborhood police officer becomes involved in the efforts. He teaches a course in youth and the law, increases his surveillance of the grounds, consults with teachers about handling problems, and invokes other agencies to become involved with youths who have dropped out of school. (Moore, Trojanowicz, and Kelling, 1988:10)

It remains to be seen how well these innovations will work in reducing crime (for a review of research see Greene, 1989). In many ways they represent a return to the neighborhood-centered social control of the nineteenth century, except that modern technology and a more impersonal society complicate the picture. In large measure they rest on the initiative and willingness of patrol officers, and the willingness of department chiefs to decentralize authority and decision-making structures despite some loss of control and undermining of the long-valued reactive mode of policing. The new initiatives also depend on the public's willingness to be partners in the effort.

The bulk of available evidence indicates that the public feel safer when they know that officers are patrolling their neighborhoods on foot (Moore and

Trojanowicz, 1988:4–5). City and police officials in Flint, Michigan, however, are sufficiently skeptical about the benefits of foot patrols that they have pushed to abandon their community policing program despite the fact that citizens have twice funded police foot patrols through the ballot box. Apparently those officials prefer the "old order" of centralized systems of control, standardization of procedures, and fast patrol car response times (Kelling, 1988).

On the other hand, Peter Manning (1989) warns that all sorts of pragmatic and ideological considerations underlie the police initiatives loosely referred to as community policing (see also Williams and Murphy, 1990). Many of these have not been, and some cannot be, evaluated empirically. Manning suggests, further, that there are managerial, moral, and legal questions that any fundamental change from today's "bureaucratic" policing to community policing would inevitably raise. For example, Manning (1989:403) writes:

> Community policing urges egalitarian, intimate and nonauthoritarian communal relations. The further one pushes horizontal democratic relations, the more community policing appeals. Community policing would require a change in the uses of law; in the standards used to apply the law and order enforcement; in the overall contracts governing police and the public and the degree of centralization, structure, hierarchy and formalization of such matters as recruitment, evaluation, promotion and rewards in police departments.

Nevertheless, neither Manning nor other critics (for example, Walker, 1989) are prepared to rule community policing dead. Rather, they see a long, tortuous road ahead.

Police Exercise of Discretion

In their daily work, police are faced with two related decisions whenever they enter a situation. The first is whether to take any action at all, and the second concerns the kind of action to take. It is in making these decisions that police invoke their awesome discretionary powers. The exercise of discretion lies at the heart of real police work, and its ramifications touch the entire legal process, not to mention the people immediately involved.

Discretion is, of course, exercised at all levels of the legal process:

> Police officers decide what "suspicious" persons to "stop and frisk," to round up in a "dragnet raid," to warn, or to arrest. Judges pass on the guilt of suspected offenders, make decisions on whom to release and whom to hold for further hearings (in jail or on bail), and determine the kind and length of sentence. Prosecuting attorneys exercise considerable latitude in what cases to prosecute and when to negotiate with the defense attorney over pleas, charges, and dispositions. A sifting and sorting operation occurs in which certain persons are processed through the legal machinery, with a steadily

increasing attrition as suspected offenders move through the various procedural stages of the criminal justice system. At each of these stages, decisions
made by certain legal officials will limit the alternatives for those operating in
subsequent stages. (Hills, 1971:22)

In routine law enforcement the police are typically the first officials to
exercise discretion. Their decisions shape law in action and the official
character of the crime scene. Furthermore, "through the exercise of discretion
patrolmen define and redefine the meaning of justice" (Brown, 1988:7).

Constraints on the Exercise of Discretion

Discretionary decisions are possible in all police operations. Some scholars
have argued that the most important discretionary decisions are the negative
ones, such as not to arrest, not to investigate, or not to bargain. When police do
take action, their decisions are often subject to review and examination, but
this is seldom the case for decisions not to invoke the legal process, for these
decisions are usually of low visibility (Gottfredson and Gottfredson, 1988:50).
Negative decisions, then, can remain largely free from scrutiny by interested
people and by other police officers, particularly superiors. This covertness
promotes secrecy in police operations while lessening both internal and
external control.

Given the low visibility of police decisions not to invoke the criminal
process, information about such discretionary actions is hard to find. However, work by Brown (1988) and others provides some clues to why and when
nonenforcement decisions are made. It is useful to frame discussion around
seven observations made by Mortimer Kadish and Sanford Kadish (1973:
74–75).

First, police may believe that the legislative purpose behind a particular
law "would not be served by arresting all persons who engage in the
prohibited conduct" (Kadish and Kadish, 1973:74). Examples are gambling
laws, various sexual prohibitions (especially those concerning consenting
adults), and laws considered obsolete. Second, some enforcement selectivity
is inevitable given the limitations of police resources. These resource limitations involve more than police time, money, personnel, or equipment: If there
is not enough jail space, police arrests and bookings may decline. In her study
of skid-row alcoholics, Wiseman (1970:71) found a negative relationship
between the number of people that the police arrest and the jail's level of
occupancy.

Third, police may be aware that some laws prohibit behavior that is
acceptable and expected in some subcultures of society and thus treat
violators selectively on that basis. Fourth, in some situations, victims are
more interested in restitution than criminal sanctions (recall the discussion of
shoplifting in Chapter 6), and the police accede to victim interests. Fifth,
police shape their enforcement patterns to some extent on the basis of
community preferences. An excellent illustration of this by Ernest Alix

(1969:332–339) describes police enforcement practices in a run-down river town. Rather than bust taverns and other commercial violators of liquor and vice laws on each violation, the police responded to community pressures by rotating their raids, thus keeping offending businesses open and revenue flowing into the town's meager bank account.

Sixth, the police routinely make use of informants, and many of these informants are known offenders whom the police decide not to arrest or charge in view of their potential usefulness:

> [The police officer's] steadiest source of information is what he collects as rent for allowing people to operate without arresting them. "Prostitutes and faggots are good. If you treat 'em right, they will give you what you want. They don't want to get locked up, and you can trade that off for information. If you rap 'em around," a very skilled patrolman said, "the way some guys used to, or lock 'em up, you don't get nothing." At a lunch counter another officer said, looking at the waitress who was getting his order, "She thinks I don't know she's hustling the truck drivers. She'll find out tomorrow. I don't care if she makes a few bucks on her back, but she is gonna tell me what I want to know." (Rubinstein, 1973:207)

Finally, there are some occasions when officers do not invoke the criminal process because "the personal harm the offender would suffer on being arrested outweighs the law enforcement gains . . . achieved by arresting." Such decisions usually have to do with the status of the offender (age, occupation, and community standing) and are most likely to be invoked for nonstreet crimes such as shoplifting. They are unlikely, therefore, to be invoked in dealings with those segments of society stereotypically linked with serious crime—namely, the poor and relatively powerless.

To these seven clues concerning discretionary nonenforcement practices one should add the impact of relationships between the police and other criminal justice personnel. Police work cannot be divorced from what goes on among prosecutors, judges, and other legal reactors. If the choice is whether or not to arrest a suspect, a negative decision may well be influenced by police expectations regarding how the case will be handled at subsequent stages in the criminal process: "Whatever their own views of the importance of particular crimes might be, if it is common knowledge that local magistrates take a very different view which is reflected in their sentencing decisions, the police will often not wish to 'waste' time on arresting individuals who may subsequently be given a merely nominal sentence by the court" (Bottomley, 1973a:41).

Steven Box (1981:162–163) argues that police discretion is further constrained by interpretational issues, by ideological and theoretical considerations, and by occupational and career worries. Worries about personal safety may lead an officer to withdraw from a situation, but a more general influence, Box suggests is the *symbolic* threat posed by certain citizens. These are the ones who police believe will go over their heads and appeal to higher-ups if street decisions are not to their liking. Denver police interviewed by Bayley and Mendelsohn (1968:102) held a clear image of who those citizens are: the wealthy, the connected, and those in professional jobs.

Police Use of Deadly Force

Police exercise of discretion is inevitable and desirable. It also carries with it enormous responsibility. Exercised humanely, cautiously, and in the service of all the people, discretion makes for law enforcement that is just and responsive to social needs. Exercised inhumanely, incautiously, or in the service of prejudice or special interest, discretion becomes intolerable and must be curbed.

Nowhere is the problem of discretion more acute than in the decision to use deadly force. Police in America and in many other (but not all) countries are armed with guns and are prepared to use them. The law in most states now requires that one of the following conditions be met for police legitimately to use deadly force: (1) A suspect is engaged in a forcible felony; (2) a suspect is fleeing the scene of a forcible felony; or (3) a suspect is resisting arrest and has placed the officer or a civilian in mortal danger.

Shootings by police officers require justification before the public and sometimes the courts. However, the use of deadly force must also be justified before one's fellow officers. Here there is a difference: Whereas the public and the courts expect the justification to be couched in terms of legal rules or formal procedures, the police themselves hold to a perspective that allows for negotiating the meanings of rules and procedures so that an officer is protected from censure and allowed flexibility in applying the rules to any given situation (Waegel, 1984; Hunt, 1991).

Research on police use of deadly force generally support's three conclusions. First, rates of police shootings vary considerably from one jurisdiction to the next. In one comparison of nine American cities, a 1500-percent variation was found even after taking account of the level of community violence and the number of arrest incidents involving violent felonies and, therefore, some risk to arresting officers. Another study found police shootings to be twice as high per 1000 police officers in Memphis as in New York (Fyfe, 1982:707–722; see also Knoohuizen, Fahey, and Palmer, 1972).

Second, the percentage of shooting incidents involving black suspects is disproportionately high. In the case of fatal shootings, blacks are anywhere from 5 to 13 times more likely than are whites to be killed by police action. When one looks at the young (10 to 14 years) and the elderly (65 and over), the disproportionate representation of blacks is even more stark: Paul Takagi (1979:34) found that "black youngsters and old men have been killed by the police at a rate 15 to 30 times greater than that of whites at the same age."

A third finding describes the most likely shooting situation among urban police forces:

> The most common shooting of a civilian by a police officer in urban America is one in which an on-duty, uniformed, white officer shoots an armed black

male between the ages of 17 and 30 at night in a public location, in connection with an armed robbery. Typically, the shooting is subsequently deemed justifiable by the police department following an internal investigation. Even if the officer is criminally prosecuted, a jury is unlikely to convict. (Geller and Karales, 1981:1818)

Two caveats must be held in mind when considering these findings. First, they are based on data and methodologies that in most cases cannot be compared. To mention one important variation, there are different ways to compute rates of police shootings: (1) in terms of population, such as the number of shootings per 100,000 residents; (2) in terms of police personnel, such as the number of shootings per 1000 police officers; or (3) in terms of police–citizen encounters involving risk, such as the number of shootings per 1000 violent felony arrests. Studies using different measures of shooting rates should not be lumped together. Another important difference among studies is the source of information on police shootings. Some studies rely only on official police accounts, whereas others have sought to include recollections of witnesses and survivors.

Second, many studies have not really tapped the situational component in police shootings. It is probably safe to say that no two shooting situations are ever the same, and decisions are often made on split-second judgment with all sorts of influences crowding in on the officer's thoughts, affecting the officer's actions, and pushing the event in perhaps unpredictable directions. The same can be said of other participants in the encounter, and since it is an *interaction*, what one person does materially affects what others will do.

Jurisdictional variations and racial issues in police shootings cannot properly be evaluated in the absence of detailed incident-by-incident information, both on situations in which officers fire and on those in which they do not fire their weapons. In fact, different police departments may experience similar rates of shootings but vary considerably in terms of the situations in which those shootings occurred.

James Fyfe suggests that an important distinction can be made between police–citizen encounters in which use of deadly force is *elective* and those in which it is *nonelective*. Elective shootings are "those in which the officer involved may elect to shoot or not to shoot at little or no risk to himself or others." Nonelective shootings are "those in which the officer has little real choice but to shoot or to risk death or serious injury to himself or others." Fyfe calls elective shootings "real exercises in discretion" (1982:710).

Any shooting situation falls somewhere along a continuum from nonelective to elective. By hindsight an officer may put an encounter closer to the elective end than he or she actually did when in the situation; similarly, observers may later define a situation differently from how they did at the time; finally, persons who later hear the "facts" may interpret a situation differently from either the officer involved or any witnesses. This shows how difficult it is to construct a picture of an encounter that does justice to both the subjective interpretations of participants and the objective characteristics of the event. Nowhere is this dichotomy more germane than when an officer shoots a suspect who is actually unarmed and could not in fact have placed either the officer or any other party in personal jeopardy. Second-guessing is a luxury that only those not involved in an encounter can afford.

With these interpretive difficulties in mind, Fyfe believes that incidents falling close to the elective end of the continuum are more likely to be influenced by such things as departmental rules and policies, the attitudes and prejudices of officers, and their level of training in firearms, methods of nonlethal control of suspects, and human relations. These factors are internal to police organization and work. On the other hand, incidents falling close to the nonelective end are more likely to be influenced by factors *external* to police work and organization, such as the amount and type of crime in a jurisdiction and the participation rates of different population groups in activities likely to precipitate shootings.

In comparing New York and Memphis shootings, Fyfe found that the elective-nonelective distinction was very useful in contrasting the two cities. In New York, over 60 percent of the shootings that occurred between 1971 and 1975 were interpreted by officers to have been in "defend life" (nonelective) situations; in contrast, over 50 percent of the incidents in Memphis from 1969 to 1974 occurred in situations in which officers were seeking to apprehend suspects in property crimes, not violent crimes (which in Memphis were classified as "defend life" situations). The data showed that police in Memphis were 14 times more likely to shoot at property crime suspects than officers in New York. That difference was explained mainly by the much more liberal shooting rules in effect at the time in the Memphis police department.

Further analysis of the Memphis situation showed that 85.7 percent of those shot at were black and 14.3 percent white. Rates of shooting per 1000 officers showed that blacks were 6 times more likely than whites to have been shot at and missed, 13 times more likely to have been shot at and wounded, and over 3 times more likely to have been shot at and killed. Rate differences by race remained when calculated in terms of population and by felony arrests. Notably, the disproportionate representation of black victims in police shootings in Memphis was greatest in the case of elective shootings. In addition, between 1969 and 1976, 50 percent of those killed who were black were killed in nonassaultive situations, versus only 12.5 percent in the case of whites (Fyfe, 1982:712–721).

The Memphis findings leave little room for doubt that internal influences—in that city's case department policies and racial attitudes among police—are a major factor accounting for the frequency and character of police shootings. However, this is only one city in one state, and until further comparable data are secured, Memphis should certainly not be used as a basis for generalizing about police attitudes and conduct.

A very detailed study of Chicago police shootings (Geller and Karales, 1981; 1982) tells interesting things about that city's experience and warns once again about judging events on the basis of gross impressions. The Chicago study is especially significant because it represents the first time a major American city opened up its shooting investigation files to public scrutiny.

Some of the major findings from that study are as follows: (1) The most common shooting situation was one in which a suspect used or threatened to use a gun (51 percent), followed by flight without other resistance (17 percent), and use or threat of force other than with a gun (14 percent). Notably, 10 percent of the incidents (52 cases) involved accidents, and 3 percent involved stray bullets. (2) When calculated in terms of population figures, blacks were from 3.8 to 6.6 times more likely to be shot than whites, but when calculated in terms of forcible felony arrests, blacks were only slightly more likely to be shot. (3) Blacks were more likely than whites to be involved in gun use and threat situations, and almost 3 times *less* likely to have been shot accidentally. (4) Although 70 percent of all shootings involved white officers, the rate per 1,000 officers was higher for blacks, and blacks were much more likely to shoot black suspects than were white officers. (5) Black officers were more likely than white officers to shoot while off duty and 29 times more likely to shoot civilians in high-crime areas than off-duty white officers.

These findings point to two conclusions. First, most of the shootings in Chicago appear to be nonelective, at least according to police accounts. Second, the disproportionate involvement of black victims and off-duty black police officers suggests that many Chicago police shootings may be patterned according to the residency of black officers in areas where opportunities for and risks of violent crime are highest. In short, the authors show no evidence of a significant racist factor in police shootings in Chicago.

It is possible that many police shootings involve the clash of two violent subcultures. On the one hand there is the subculture of police violence—a legitimized subculture associated with rule enforcement—and on the other, an inner-city subculture of the ghetto—an outlawed subculture at odds with the Establishment and deemed a threat to it. Many inner-city black youths expect violence in their daily lives and come prepared for it. Police who live in or enter these same areas also expect and come prepared for violence. There are compelling reasons to believe that violence reinforces violence. Surveys have shown that respondents who would accept relatively high levels of police violence are themselves likely to have been involved in violence and accept it in a variety of interpersonal situations (Blumenthal et al., 1972).

Public support for police use of violence in dealing with the "criminal element" is bound up with the catch-the-criminal-at-all-costs theme. Emphasized by television and movie portrayals of cops and robbers, the theme has a cherished image: the police hero firing a .45-caliber revolver at a fast-disappearing crook, felling the crook with one shot. The fact that most police do not carry forty-fives is only one of the distortions of the image. What may be especially dangerous about it is its impact on impressionable youths, especially those who have come to see themselves as having trouble with the law. "Be prepared for violence," television tells them, "because the police are!" In sum, "catch the criminal at all costs" is not a sound doctrine for either the police or the public to support. One consequence is police fatalities and injury, the subject of the next section.

Shootings of Police

Relatively few police officers are killed while doing police work—around 0.01 percent annually (Federal Bureau of Investigation, 1991). From 1976 to 1983, just over half the 903 police officers killed on duty were shot (Schmidt, 1985:6). The shooting *of* police officers is the other side of the police violence coin, and from the police standpoint it is the most important side. Police may be prepared for violence—they may even expect it—but when it happens to one of their own, they all share in the hurt and resentment. The threat of danger to oneself or one's colleagues is at the heart of the police personality.

One of the few good studies of police shootings by civilians is by Geller and Karales (1982), the authors who investigated shootings by police in Chicago. In the city they found that nearly half of all police shot between 1974 and 1978 (187) were off duty; 27 percent shot themselves, mostly by accident, but 11 were suicides, a rate higher than that for the general population. Twenty officers (11 percent) were shot by fellow officers, mostly accidentally. More than half of the off-duty officers shot were black (compared with 17.5 percent representation on the Chicago Police Department as whole); 91 percent of the black off-duty officers shot were shot in medium- and high-crime districts where they lived. Black officers off duty were 13 times more likely to be shot in high crime areas than off-duty white officers; by contrast, off-duty black officers were only twice as likely to be shot in low-crime areas as white officers. These findings reflect the residency patterns and routine activities of black and white officers.

In Chicago, black officers who were shot were ten times more likely to survive than be killed; among white officers the difference was half as much. On the whole, officers shot by civilians stand a better chance of surviving than civilians shot by police (an 86-percent survival rate versus a 74-percent rate for civilians). This is probably due to factors such as caliber of weapon, marksmanship, number of shots fired (more by police), and the type of ammunition used (police in Chicago used hollow-point bullets, a very lethal form of ammunition).

Shootings of police in the Chicago study were primarily intraracial: Black civilians shot black police officers, white civilians shot white officers. Interestingly, during the period of the study no Hispanic or black officer was shot by a white civilian. Yearly variations in shootings show that what happens one year is not a good predictor of the next year, for both shootings of and by police. These variations demonstrate the importance of situational factors in violence, a matter discussed in Chapters 3 and 16. In an unusual variation, in 1976 Chicago police "actually were placed in greater jeopardy by themselves and their colleagues than by armed criminal suspects" (Geller and Karales, 1982:353).

Geller and Karales were particularly concerned with off-duty shootings, both of and by police. They concluded their long and detailed investigation of both types of violence with the following recommendations (1982:373–374):

1. Off-duty officers should generally be prohibited from carrying guns when they anticipate consuming alcohol beverages.

2. Greater restrictions should be imposed on the types of weapons that may be carried by officers, and consideration should be given to tightening the minimum standards of proficiency required of officers with these weapons.
3. Police officers may need additional guidance in the kinds of incidents to which they should respond when off duty and special reminders about the dangers of resolving their own disputes by taking police action. The unavailability to off-duty officers of police radios with which they could instantly summon assistance and check information . . . may make it inadvisable for off-duty police to intervene in situations which do not obviously require immediate police attention.

Geller and Karales were perhaps too cautious in their recommendations (they made others as well). The goal in police shooting situations, for both police and suspects, is *outcome*. If society clings to the goal of catching the criminal at all costs, then that outcome is almost inevitably going to include injuries and deaths. Unless someone is directly and immediately put in mortal danger by the actions of a suspect, "it would seem more prudent to allow them to escape [temporarily at least], as many criminals do anyway" (Rubin, 1965:528).

Crime Victims and Police Discretion

The relationship between citizens' calls to police and police discretionary practices has only recently come under scrutiny. It appears that police decisions are often influenced by a variety of factors that have little or nothing to do with legal issues; for example, the complainant's demeanor, preference, and relational ties with the suspect (see pp. 48–49). Another important set of factors concerns victim decisions to appear as prosecution witnesses and to sign formal complaints when these are needed. The police may refuse to pursue a complaint from those they know or believe will back away from these responsibilities.

When citizen complaints come in on police switchboards, the responsibility for directing the police reaction rests on police dispatchers. They are in a position of considerable power and responsibility. Their decisions determine whether or not official action will be taken, the initial nature of that action, and the time lag between call and response. Their discretion has a profound effect on enforcement efforts. Because police departments typically take steps to monitor incoming and outgoing communications, dispatchers have less discretionary leeway than their colleagues working the streets. In one U.S. city studied, the operatives are like assembly-line workers:

> They are timed to the second on every break by the computers; they are supplied work by an automatic computer that shifts calls their way as soon as they are 'free'; the order of their work is technologically determined and demand driven. . . . [T]hey work for the machines that lurk behind them, glow in front of them, click and buzz in their ears, and fill the air with dull electronic sounds (Manning, 1988, cited in Erikson, 1990:78).

The modern police communications center is filled with sophisticated computers and radio equipment. How different things were in the early days of electronics! What has not changed nearly as much is the substantial discretionary power and responsibility that rests with the police dispatcher.

But even while technology is "ominous," according to Peter Manning (1988), the occupational culture of policing is even more important in the construction of meaning in communication among citizens, dispatchers, and patrol officers. When messages move among citizens, police operators, police dispatchers, and patrolling officers they are transformed as the different participants seek to create order and meaning out of chaos. The essential problem for citizens and police operatives alike is how to create a "visualization" of events and situations so that meaningful information is conveyed.

Police culture constitutes a resource of unwritten symbols used to organize and to justify police activity. Together with the interpretive acts of individual officers, police culture provides definitions and meanings that curb the impact of technology (or take advantage of it as we saw on p. 361) and subvert or modify departmental rules and official police codes. Despite sophisticated technology, and regardless of the availability of resources, citizen calls for assistance may end up unanswered, responses may be delayed, or complainants may simply be "put off."

Needless to say, sending a patrol to every call for assistance—even those coming in on emergency numbers—would result in absolute chaos. There are simply too many calls, and many of these turn out not to be emergencies.

Police are asked to deal with barking dogs, lost cats, personal problems of a noncriminal nature, and a host of other things (Cumming, Cumming, and Edell, 1965). These are support services that police often consider to be a drain on resources and a hindrance to their crime-fighting mission. "Most patrolmen define their task largely as the responsibility for controlling crime, and include almost nothing else" (Brown, 1988:135).

Another view held by many police officers is that certain groups do not deserve their service (Grossman, 1974). Clifford Shearing (1979) has reported on a six-month study of the communications center of a large Canadian police department. After observing and recording thousands of communications between citizens and the police and among police officers themselves, Shearing found that police officers "made a fundamental distinction between 'the public' on the one hand, and 'third- and fourth-class citizens,' 'the dregs,' or more expressively, 'the scum,' on the other. . . . The public were people the police felt duty-bound to serve and protect" (p. 6). The scum, on the other hand, were troublemakers; they needed police control and hence were viewed as an enemy of the police. Armed with this view, police are unlikely to respond energetically to calls for assistance by persons identified as scum or those who, because of their "stupidity" or "ignorance" about what the police should really be doing, are only marginally part of the "public."

The Minneapolis Experiment: Domestic Violence

Police must walk an awkward line in dealing with domestic violence. Most people consider what happens inside the home to be a private matter; even many victims feel this way (Bureau of Justice Statistics, 1988b; 1988c). For this reason, police may be viewed as intruders even though they are at a home in response to a call for help. In addition, many police believe that handling domestic disturbances is particularly dangerous to them. While some recent FBI data suggest that the danger may have been overstated (Garner and Clemmer, 1986), officers may fear personal injury or death if they confront the parties or try to make an arrest.

Lawrence Sherman and Richard Berk (1984) conducted an experiment with Minneapolis police to see whether police actions affected the likelihood of future domestic assaults. Officers were randomly assigned to three experimental conditions: In one they used mediation, in another they ordered the assailant out of the house, and in the third they arrested the assailant, who spent a night in jail. The police officers were given no special training, being instructed to apply their existing knowledge and experience. After a domestic call was completed, Sherman and his colleagues tried to contact each victim every two weeks for the following six months. Any evidence of new incidents of violence was noted. They also checked the records of assailants and victims for any official evidence of repeat violence.

In the end, the experiment found that those assailants who were arrested were less likely to commit repeat violence over the six-month period. While the authors make no claim that their experiment justifies a change in police policy, some major cities have adopted the position that officers should always make an arrest when a victim alleges that an assault has occurred, even if there are no obvious injuries and the victim does not want to press charges. St. Louis takes this approach. Atlanta, on the other hand, allows the use of discretion in making arrests, and emphasizes mediation in dealing with most simple assaults.

Atlanta's approach may actually turn out to be the better one. Replications of the Minneapolis experiment in six other jurisdictions (Dade County, Florida; Atlanta; Charlotte, North Carolina; Milwaukee; Colorado Springs; and Omaha, Nebraska) have not uniformly confirmed the earlier findings. In the Omaha study, for example, random assignment of domestic assaults to mediation, separation, or arrest produced no differences in the prevalence or frequency of domestic assault six months after intervention (Dunford, Huizinga, and Elliott, 1990).

Another study by Sherman and colleagues (1991) found that a policy of arresting domestic assault offenders may backfire in the long run despite short-run benefits. Varying the length of time offenders were held in custody from an average of 2.8 hours to an average of 11.1 hours, these authors discovered a long-term crimogenic effect for short-duration arrests and no long-term effect (good or bad) for arrests of longer duration. Clearly, the troublesome issue of how best to deal with domestic violence is far from being resolved.

Corruption and Abuses of Police Authority

The sensitive and controversial issue of police corruption has followed the police from their earliest origins. An 1816 report to England's House of Commons described corruption among constables and sheriffs' deputies:

> [The] deputies in many instances are characters of the worst and lowest descriptions; the fine they receive from the person who appoints them varies from ten shillings to five pounds; having some expense and no salary they live by extortion, by countenancing all species of vice, by an understanding with the keepers of brothels and disorderly ale-houses, by attending courts of justice, and giving there false evidence to ensure conviction when their expenses are paid, and by all the various means by which artful and designing men can entrap the weak and prey upon the unwary. (Pike, 1968:464)

The practices referred to in this report—extortion, perjury, protection, and more—are merely a few of the activities included under the rubric of police corruption. To these have been added brutality, neglect of duty, nepotism, racism, and bribery.

Depending on whose opinion is accepted, almost any police activity can find its way onto the list of things identified as corrupt police practices. Historically, much of the concern about corruption has focused on blatant abuses of police authority such as the misuse of force, extortion, the taking of bribes, and perjury, but some authors now include many common police practices. Examples are "police perks" such as free meals and discounts at certain stores, the use of abusive or profane language, stopping and questioning citizens, and intraorganizational practices such as payoffs for favors granted by police colleagues. In 1972, the Knapp Commission report to the mayor of New York added another dimension of corruption in arguing that "even those who themselves engage in no corrupt activities are involved in corruption in the sense that they take no steps to prevent what they know or suspect is going on about them" (p. 3).

One of the most useful typologies of police corruption is that by Roebuck and Barker (1974:118–127). These authors distinguish types of police corruption on the basis of: (1) the kinds of norms violated, (2) the amount of peer group support, (3) the extent of organization needed to put the practices into effect, (4) who is involved in the corruption apart from the police, and (5) departmental reaction. Eight types of police corruption were identified (see also Lundman, 1980:143–157):

1. *Corruption of authority* means receiving unauthorized, unearned material gains by virtue of police officer status. This includes free liquor, meals, discounts, and payments by merchants for more police protection. The corrupters are respectable citizens, there is considerable peer group support, there is little adverse departmental reaction, little organization is required, and the violation involved is primarily that of departmental regulations.

2. *Kickbacks* involve receipt of goods and services in return for referring business to a variety of patrons (doctors, lawyers, bondsmen, garages, taxicab companies, service stations, and so on). Corrupters are usually respectable persons who stand to gain from the scheme. Departments tend to ignore it, or actually condone it, depending on the respectability of the corrupter, though the practice is usually in violation of formal departmental rules. Peer group support is often substantial, though its degree may depend on the reputation and trustworthiness of the patron. The organization involved is relatively simple and "inheres in the collusion between businessmen and policemen."

3. *Opportunist theft* is the illegal taking of goods from arrestees, victims, crime scenes, or unprotected property. It involves no corrupter and is clearly in violation of criminal laws as well as departmental rules. Reaction from departments is usually negative but may depend on value of goods or cash taken, public knowledge, and willingness of the victim to prosecute. Peer group support depends on informal norms governing distinctions between "clean" and "dirty" money. Little organization is involved; the activities result from situational decisions.

4. *Shakedowns* are opportunistic behaviors that occur when the police know about a crime but accept money or services from suspects in exchange for doing nothing. The corrupter may be respectable or known to be habitually involved in criminal activities. Shakedowns violate legal

and departmental norms, and though peer group support is necessary for the routinization of shakedown operations, that support is often contingent on what the suspect is known to be engaged in—bribes from narcotics pushers and robbers are apparently frowned upon. Secrecy in peer group relations is a prime element of shakedowns.

5. *Protection of illegal activities* refers to corrupters who seek to continue their illegal operations free from police harassment. The corrupters can be respectable or nonrespectable; in either case they are doing something illegal, which makes protection important. Protection violates criminal and departmental rules and involves considerable collusion, peer group support, and organization (for instance, officers have to know which businesses are protected). Though departmental reaction is often severe (suspension, dismissal, or criminal charges), the severity and consistency of negative reactions may depend on the degree of community support of the illegal activities being protected.

6. *The fix* refers to either quashing legal proceedings or "taking up" traffic tickets. Corrupters are arrestees attempting to avoid police action that would probably embarrass them in one way or another. The fixer is often not a patrol officer but someone with access to the investigative aspects of police work. The fix, of course, violates legal and departmental rules, and reaction is usually severe when cases are brought to light. The authors suggest that in departments where the fix occurs frequently and with considerable regularity it is a highly organized activity.

7. *Direct criminal activities* involve no corrupter, as the police alone are parties to the corruption. Direct criminal activities include crimes by police officers against suspects, victims, pedestrians, or whomever, and against property. Lack of peer group support and severe departmental reactions generally underscore the blatant criminal character of these practices. For these activities to continue, some organization is necessary, and therefore they are unlikely to persist as opportunist efforts by individuals or teams. Drug enforcement provides a major incentive for police crime. Pocketing drugs seized from suspects on the street or from smugglers is reputedly a routine occurrence (see Abadinsky, 1990:401–402), and everyone has heard of the theft of 57 pounds of heroin from the property office of the New York City police department. The stolen heroin was among that confiscated during the famous "French Connection" case.

8. *Internal payoffs* involve bribes within the police department for such things as assignments, hours, promotions, control of evidence, arrests, and so forth. Some officers are in a particularly advantageous position to take payoffs, as Jonathan Rubinstein's (1973:85) comment on the police dispatcher shows:

He has numerous little favors he can grant a man that will ease the burdens of the tour. For instance, the patrolman can go to "lunch" (policemen [in Philadelphia, at least] refer to all their meal breaks as lunch, regardless of the hour) only with the dispatcher's permission. If the dispatcher wants a man to remain in service, he simply tells him that he cannot go. The men are not supposed to eat together and the dispatcher is responsible for seeing that they do not gather. A sympathetic dispatcher will allow several men to share their lunchtime by permitting one man to give a location where the dispatcher knows the police do not eat.

The internal payoff system is usually highly organized, particularly in departments under pressure to produce and in those in which lucrative and corrupt practices such as shakedowns and protection are regular aspects of police work. Peer group support is usually considerable. Departmental reaction is tolerant if it means a more satisfied work force, and if officers involved in the payoff system are not in violation of high-priority regulations or the criminal law.

The value of Roebuck's and Barker's typology lies in its applicability across departments, jurisdictions, and cultures, and in its attempts to specify some of the dimensions in terms of which corruptions can be analyzed. This brief review of one typology shows that police corruption is hardly to be understood only by reference to what the police do. The roots of and supports for corruption lie not in the police per se, but in the larger social, cultural, economic, and political climates in which they operate (Chambliss, 1971).

Brutality and Misuse of Force

One aspect of police operations continually appears in discussions of corruption and abuse of police authority—the use of coercive force. Police are charged from time to time with brutality and abuses of their authority to employ coercive force. The beating of Rodney King by members of the Los Angeles Police Department certainly comes to mind here, but other examples could be cited and many will remain hidden.

What is meant by brutality and misuse of force? As one might guess, there is hardly consensus on their meaning. Albert Reiss (1970) suggests that almost any routine police action will be interpreted by someone as an instance of police brutality. He argues, further, that if brutality is the actual use of force, the police themselves have no clear-cut guidelines. Police training films, such as Motorola's *Shoot, Don't Shoot,* endeavor to instruct the police in the matter of using deadly force, but most officers are rarely faced with situations in which such force is either authorized or used. At lesser levels of violence, police rely on the notion of *reasonable force,* but what constitutes reasonable force? A rule of thumb adopted by most police agencies, and supported by the courts, is that reasonable force means that force necessary to secure a legal goal without endangering innocent citizens. Any unnecessary force is therefore unreasonable and may be illegal. But these are difficult distinctions to apply in practice, particularly under pressure.

Some people apply the term brutality only to those situations involving force, but others include situations of "psychic violence," resulting in loss of self-respect and other emotional hurt. Although "third degree" techniques are no longer condoned, the questioning of suspects may seem unnecessarily brutal (see Box 10.1). Some people abhor the use of trickery, deceit, and other psychological devices designed to give police the upper hand—procedures quite acceptable to police officers, and taught at the academy.

The line between brutality and misuse of force is hazy. Though all brutality may well be a misuse of authorized force, not all misuse of force is brutality. An officer who fires at a fleeing felon (a legal action in many jurisdictions) and hits instead an innocent bystander would probably be considered to have used deadly force inappropriately, but is this police brutality? *Brutality* may perhaps best be used in reference to situations in which police knowingly and intentionally use force in order to satisfy personal or group whims, prejudices, and interests. *Misuse of force*, then, can be applied to situations in which police use force in a manner that goes beyond that required by law or department policy, though the intent is to satisfy those obligations and not personal whims and prejudices.

One is more likely to be dealing with brutality, then, if the police assault citizens who offer no resistance or are in no position to offer any resistance (they are handcuffed), or if a number of officers join in the assault of a lone citizen who clearly can be subdued with less forceful means (Reiss, 1970). The Rodney King incident is an example. Another example of brutality is the following account of an incident in Philadelphia. A man suspected of sexually molesting a child was treated to the following at the hands of his police captors:

> Any squad member who wished was allowed to beat the suspect from the ankles to the armpits with his stick. Men came in off the street to participate in the beating and then returned to patrol. Before he was taken downtown, the suspect had been severely battered, although he had no broken bones. At no time did he utter a complaint, ask for mercy, or curse the police. Without a murmur he absorbed a brutal beating, which caused him to foul himself and drew the admiring comments of several men who admitted he could "really take it." (Rubinstein, 1973:183)

A less shocking situation, but nevertheless in line with the definition of brutality, is the following, again reported by Rubinstein. Suspects who are arrested are often transported in wagons. They are handcuffed and sit on benches with no handrails or other devices on which to rely for support during the ride. The driver of the wagon can give prisoners a very uncomfortable ride merely by swerving hard and braking without warning. "Rarely is a prisoner injured by any of these methods, but anyone who runs when he is told to halt, swears or spits at a policeman, or threatens him in any way may find himself chastened by these methods" (Rubinstein, 1973:329).

Police misuse of force is likely to surface if police are under relatively extreme pressure, if they are acting overzealously, or if they have misinterpreted actions they have witnessed. In addition, poorly trained and inexperienced police officers are probably more apt to use excessive force than the more experienced. Firing warning shots in the air or shooting at fleeing suspects, practices not officially condoned by most police agencies, may be triggered by one of these factors.

Box 10.1 ■ Sticks and Stones . . .

If you dislike foul language, then you won't appreciate what follows. But if you dislike police abuse even more, then read on.

Below are segments of the transcript of a tape made by [two] police officer[s] as they questioned a young black man about the murder of a police officer. Another man was later convicted, perhaps wrongly, of the crime. [The police] asked that the name of the suspect, who has become an informant, not be disclosed. The suspect played no role in [the officer's] murder.

Detective: OK. Do you know why you are here?

Suspect: They said robbery.

Detective: Robbery first degree, assault first degree. Now, I'm going to tell you a little secret, right here and right the fuck now. I don't like you. I think you're fucking puke. Do you understand me?

Suspect: (inaudible)

Detective: And I'm going to tell you something else that somebody's told me. Do you know what that is?

Suspect: (inaudible)

Detective: You know what that is? Don't fuck around with me, puke breath! You were there the night my sergeant got killed. Don't, don't fuckin' play.

Suspect: I ain't playing.

Detective: Hey, listen to me, shithead! You're probably wondering what took them so long to get your fucking black ass up—

Suspect: I ain't, I wasn't—

Detective: No, you lying piece of self-shit, motherfucking cocksucker, whore dog! Turn around here. Let me see your ear. Did you ever wear an earring?

Suspect: No. Never.

Detective: Never, huh? What happened to your fucking schnoz?

Suspect: I did this when I was—

Detective: How come you stink so bad? Don't you take a fucking shower?

Detective: OK. I'm going to tell you a little fucking secret. You know and I know you were there that night.

Suspect: You're fucking lying.

Detective: Listen to me. I'm talking, bitch. You were there that night. Gerald's down in the fucking prison. He's running his fucking mouth. We had three or four, we had Gerald. Gerald said, "Fucking (suspect's name) was the trigger man."

Suspect: No.

Detective: Hah, I'll be honest with you—we ain't got nothing fucking to put you up on charges like that. Not us. We're going to put the fucking charge on you.

Suspect: I wasn't there.

Detective: Shut up! We ain't got nothing to put that charge on you. Right now. But I'm going to tell you something. What we've heard Gerald has said in the prison. . . . You know Gerald. Gerald's a friend of yours. Isn't he?

Suspect: I know.

Detective: You know he's a friend of yours, motherfucker. You run right over there at Evans and Vandeventer.

Suspect: No. I don't run over there.

Detective: What that guy tell us? Evans and—what did the guy tell us? He said Evans and Vandeventer, didn't he?

Suspect: I live at (gives address).

Detective: No. I didn't say, "Where do you fucking live?"

Suspect: I don't lie to you. You know you want to sit up there and order me to turn—

Detective: No, I don't want to order, I want you to shut the fuck up and listen to me, OK?

Suspect: No.

Detective: And you're a fucking killer.

Suspect: No.

Detective: Yes, you are. There's a killing.

Suspect: I don't know.

Detective: You were there.

Suspect: I wasn't there. I ain't, don't know nothing about it.

Detective: You want to try and get my gun?

Suspect: No.

Detective: I'm a little bit bigger than sergeant was, ain't I?

Suspect: I don't even know him.

Detective: Oh, fuck you, punk. Stand the fuck up.

Suspect: You think I'm lying, huh?

Detective: Get over here! Turn the fuck around. Don't look back here. Don't look fucking back here! Man.

Suspect: I ain't did nothing. I ain't did nothing. You want to beat—

Detective: I ain't going to beat you up.

Suspect: I didn't did nothing, sir.

Detective: I'm talking about murder! You getting mad at me, boy? You want to fucking hit me?

Suspect: No.

Detective: You want to fucking hit me?

Suspect: No.

Detective: Because you ain't fucking man enough to come at me straight on, head on, are you, boy?

Suspect: I don't—

Detective: You fuckers coming up from behind and shoot like this! Fuck you, lying bastard!

Suspect: I ain't lying. You know I ain't lying.

Suspect: Now, I don't give you any problems. Now don't give me no case.

Detective: Shut the fuck up. I don't give nobody no case. I'm a nice man. If everybody was like me in this fucking world, it would be a lot better. Wouldn't be no scumbags like you out there. Rob . . . hey, you robbed somebody, bitch!

Suspect: That was six years ago.

Detective: That makes him a good man now. That makes him a good man now.

Suspect: Oh, you ain't never, you ain't never made a mistake in your life. Just say that.

Detective: Nah, I've made one fucking mistake all right. Taking this fucking job and having to deal with—

Suspect: I'm talking other than your job.

Detective: I've made a mistake before, but I've never put a gun in somebody's face and robbed them.

Suspect: Man, that was six years ago.

Detective: No, let me tell you something. You fuck up once, you fuck up the rest of your life. You're a scumbag and you're going to be a scum for the rest of your fucking life. You were there when my sergeant, you were there when my sergeant got killed.

Suspect: No, I wasn't. . . . Man, I don't know. I haven't did anything. I don't know anything about it. You know, cause, you know. All I know is what the paper said, what you all had in the paper they did. The police murder and that was it. I didn't get into the details. I don't know anything. I was too far at the time of getting my life together.

Second Detective: Why don't somebody else come down to this station and tell me? You did it.

Suspect: People say shit, you know, every day. I can't help that.

Second Detective: Why would they say you?

Suspect: Man, I ain't got the slightest idea. . . . I don't know. I ain't never judged people. You think I'm crazy or something. I've been gone six years and you think I'm going to walk out of here and do something crazy? Man, I've been through so many—

Detective: Oh, yeah, that's right, you went to prison, you went to prison, now you're reformed. Right.

Suspect: Not exactly.

Detective: You're reformed, right. You went to prison. Everybody that goes to prison, everybody that goes to prison never does another crime.

Suspect: Not everybody.

Detective: Let me ask you this, though. Detective will give you a polygraph. Are you going to take a polygraph? Do you think you can pass a polygraph?

Suspect: What do you mean, pass? I ain't getting nothing. As long as I got a lawyer here, you know.

Detective: You can't have a lawyer there. It would just be in your own free will. Otherwise we keep investigating.

Suspect: No, I would like to have a lawyer then. Cause, you know, I don't understand about the polygraph.

Detective: You're going to need a lawyer if you killed the policeman.

Suspect: I didn't kill the policeman.

Detective: Then what do you need a lawyer for?

Source: The Riverfront Times, October 2–8, 1991, pp. 12–13. Reprinted with permission of Hartmann Publishing Co.

Misuse of force and, on occasion, police brutality can be linked to a police officer's need to gain control in encounters. Police efforts to gain the upper hand in dealings with suspects, witnesses, and victims are given high priority in police operations (Bottomley, 1973a:51). In the effort to gain control, police may sometimes misuse or abuse their authority to employ coercive force. Also, if police control is threatened, it is likely to be perceived by officers as a challenge to their authority, an issue to which police are particularly sensitive. It is not too surprising, then, that excessive use of force tends to surface if police perceive that their control of a situation is threatened.

The "Stop"

Police authority to use coercive force is most often invoked when an arrest is taking place. In addition to actual arrests, police also exercise this authority whenever they make a routine "stop"—that is, stop a citizen for questioning. Subjects may not know that failure to heed an officer's command to stop makes them liable for arrest on charges of refusing to obey a lawful command by a police officer. Behind the officer's authority to make the stop lies the authority to use force if needed.

Because of boredom, an intrinsic part of police work, stop situations often are contrived events (Brown, 1988:143). Bent (1974:17–18) observed this in Memphis:

> Occupants of a police car actively looked for "deviants" on their beat to break the monotony of a quiet evening. To these officers, deviants included anyone whose clothes, hair length, mannerisms, or race did not conform with an officer's standards of acceptability. Thus, youths with long hair or garish dress—"hippies," as defined by the policemen—transvestites, and blacks were stopped and questioned at the pleasure of the patrolmen:

> A typical scenario in a two-man squad car during periods of prolonged inactivity went something like this: Patrolmen Harry and Jack have had an uneventful evening when a car driven by some teenagers goes by. One of the youths stares (or smiles, or grimaces, or sneers, etc.) at the police car. Patrolman Jack turns to his partner and says, "Harry, let's pull that car over. Those kids are guilty of 'contempt of cop'!" Or one of the officers spots a pedestrian who appears likely to provide some "activity" and turns to his partner saying, "Jack, let's stop the fag (or hippie, or whore, or nigger, etc.) and ask him a few questions. That ought to liven things up."

Lying scarcely beneath the surface of police abuses involving force are stereotypes of "bad guys," and beneath the stereotypes lie racism and ethnic prejudices. Although no good statistics exist, qualitative studies lead to the conclusion that members of minority groups, drug users, and homosexuals bear the brunt of police excesses. It was the conclusion of the Christopher Commission in Los Angeles that racism was rampant and that a confrontational street posture and excessive use of force received implicit support from the police hierarchy, notably Chief Daryl Gates himself (*Los Angeles Times*,

July 10 1991:1). Not far away, in Inglewood, California, Brown (1988) discovered that many officers made no bones about characterizing blacks as not only inferior but prone to crime.

A confrontational street posture and images of bad guys are fostered not simply from within police culture but by the larger society as well—in films, by the news media, and especially by people who make a living from violence. The makers of "Second Chance" bullet proof vests advertised their product with comic strips depicting a smiling cop dreaming about two hoodlums who are stabbing a judge who just gave them probation for shooting a cop ("Second Chance," 1973). Calibre Press, producers of police training videos, recently sent a flyer around (one came to me) advertising "action-filled" self-defense videos for use at home. The flyer speaks authoritatively of "knife culture" offenders and identifies members as "new immigrants from Latin and Asian countries," and "crazies on the streets." The knife culture "has you [people in law enforcement] as its target," the flyer asserts, and in a highlighted box adds:

> For any gift-giving occasion or just to say "I Care," Surviving Edged Weapons makes an ideal present. ORDER TODAY.

Extent of Police Corruption and Abuse of Force

The extent of police corruption and abuse of force is unknown and unknowable. To remove the cloak of secrecy surrounding police operations, particularly the unlawful ones, requires powers beyond the control of even congressional committees and those who head police agencies. Serious investigations into these matters are also hampered because the time and money required for in-depth research are beyond the grasp of most criminologists, assuming they could raise the veil of secrecy. Even police officers themselves find it difficult, if not dangerous, to bring corrupt practices to light. The movie *Serpico*, which dealt with corruption in New York and was based in part on the Knapp Commission investigations, brought some of these difficulties and dangers to wide public attention. Some evidence shows that those who try to remain aloof from corruption are placed under considerable pressure to conform with the practices of their colleagues (Stoddard, 1968).

The meager evidence that exists suggests two things. First, as the Knapp Commission concluded, corruption is widespread and is likely to remain so given prevailing stereotypes of the criminal, long-standing traditions in police work, and demands that police enforce laws over which there is considerable disagreement and resentment. Second, excessive use of force by police seems to be less prevalent than many appear to think. Albert Reiss (1970:142) found that out of 5012 police–citizen encounters, around 10 percent involved what was considered police misconduct, and in most of these cases abusive language and ridicule constituted the misconduct. He did discover one very alarming fact, however. Around 33 percent of the incidents in which excessive force was used occurred while the suspect was in police custody, under physical control. Just how much violence occurs behind closed doors is impossible to ascertain.

Summary of Chapter 10

This chapter has examined the nature of policing. Even though strongly influenced by the English experience, the social, political, and technical dimensions of modern American policing give it a unique character. In America the Constitution reserves the bulk of criminal matters for state control, and yet within states policing also falls under the jurisdiction of city and county governments. At the federal level, policing has grown considerably over the years, as the passage of more and more federal laws has increased the enforcement obligations of federal agencies.

The bulk of this chapter examined police recruitment, training, and practice in urban settings. Police work is dominated by white males, and even though efforts are underway to increase the representation of women and minorities, most agencies still have a long way to go, and it is unlikely that proportionate representation will be achieved any time soon, if ever. Police are, after all, the enforcement arm of government, and so long as the exercise of political power is dominated by white males, police work will be too. Even when women and minorities are hired, stereotypes and institutionalized discrimination make it difficult for them to achieve positions of leadership.

Much of the day-to-day work of policing involves making discretionary judgments, and the decision not to enforce the law is as important as the decision to investigate a crime or to make an arrest. Discretion is exercised in an environment of suspicion and danger, where events and people are placed into categories calling for different kinds of action. Stereotypes and other cultural forces come into play here, too, for like other citizens the police are influenced by the norms and values of the people with whom they associate and of the larger society. They are also required to protect the organization they represent as well as the people whose interests crime threatens.

Despite these universals in police work, styles of policing differ according to the social and political character of the community. Watchman, legalistic, and service styles result in different kinds of enforcement practice, which determine in turn how victims, suspects, and citizens in general experience police work. Contemporary innovations in policing include the development of proactive strategies which authorities hope will bring citizens and police together in a sort of crime prevention alliance which will help in both the solution and deterrence of crime. Whether such strategies improve the quality of life for all citizens is an open question, but if they result in greater public oversight of policing the benefits may range from fewer shootings of and by police to greater sensitivity to the special needs and problems of minorities and the underclass.

Recommended Readings

Michael Brown (1988). *Working the Streets: Police Discretion and Dilemmas of Reform*. New York: Russell Sage.

Roger G. Dunham, and Geoffrey P. Alpert eds. (1989) *Critical Issues in Policing*. Prospect Heights, Ill.: Waveland Press.

Richard N. Harris (1973). *The Police Academy: An Inside View*. New York: Wiley.

Richard Kinsey, John Lea, and Jock Young eds. (1986). *Losing the Fight Against Crime*. Oxford: Basil Blackwell.

Peter K. Manning (1988). *Symbolic Communications: Signifying Calls and the Police Response*. Cambridge, Mass.: MIT Press.

Jonathan Rubinstein (1973). *City Police*. New York: Farrar, Straus, and Giroux.

Chapter 11

The Judicial Process

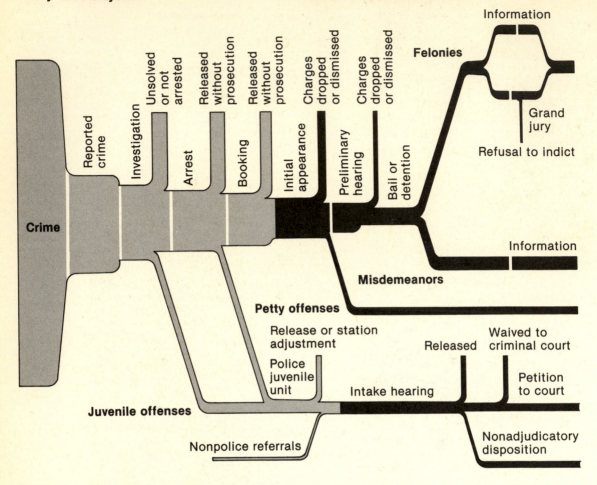

Entry into the system

Prosecution and pretrial services

Crime

Reported crime

Investigation

Unsolved or not arrested

Released without prosecution

Released without prosecution

Arrest

Booking

Charges dropped or dismissed

Charges dropped or dismissed

Initial appearance

Preliminary hearing

Bail or detention

Felonies

Information

Grand jury

Refusal to indict

Information

Misdemeanors

Petty offenses

Release or station adjustment

Police juvenile unit

Intake hearing

Released

Waived to criminal court

Petition to court

Juvenile offenses

Nonpolice referrals

Nonadjudicatory disposition

FIGURE 11.1   A General View of the Criminal Justice System.   *Note:* This chart gives a simplified view of caseflow through the criminal justice system. Procedures vary among jurisdictions. The weights of the lines are not intended to show the actual size of caseloads. *Source:* Adapted from President's Commission on Law Enforcement and the Administration of Justice (1967). *The Challenge of Crime in a Free Society.* Washington, D.C.: U.S. Government Printing Office, pp. 8–9.

Once arrested by police, a criminal suspect is eligible for further processing by the state. This change in status is symbolized not only by physical detention but also by the warning that "anything you say can and will be used against you in a court of law."

The judicial process can be thought of as a series of decision stages through which suspects pass. Figure 11.1 shows the various stages in detail. Notice that there is considerable attrition as defendants pass from arrest to

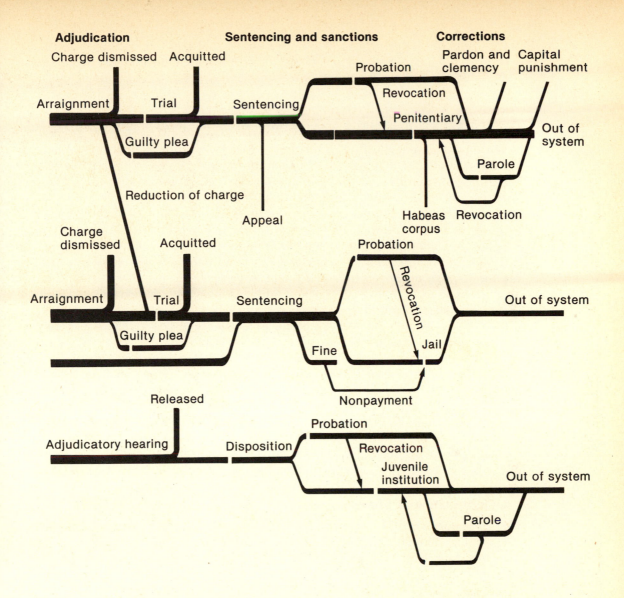

Adjudication

Charge dismissed   Acquitted

Arraignment   Trial   Sentencing

Guilty plea

Reduction of charge

Appeal

Sentencing and sanctions

Probation

Revocation

Penitentiary

Corrections

Pardon and   Capital
clemency   punishment

Out of
system

Parole

Habeas   Revocation
corpus

Charge
dismissed   Acquitted

Arraignment   Trial   Sentencing

Guilty plea

Probation

Revocation

Fine   Jail

Nonpayment

Out of system

Released

Adjudicatory hearing   Disposition

Probation

Revocation

Juvenile
institution

Out of system

Parole

sentencing to punishment. Of course, jurisdictions differ in their rates of attrition, but even in felony cases it is not unusual to find dropout rates after arrest of 40 or 50 percent, and even higher.

Overview of the Judicial Process

Different jurisdictions may use various procedures and terminologies in the handling of criminal suspects, but a general sense of the major decision stages in the American judicial process can be obtained from the following overview. It mainly applies to adult felony offenders, but significant differences in the judicial handling of people suspected of misdemeanors and petty crimes are noted.

Initial Appearance Before a Magistrate

Within a "reasonable time" after they are arrested and charged by police, suspects must be brought before a magistrate or judge for consideration of bail. In *Riverside County* v. *McLaughlin* (1991), the U.S. Supreme Court ruled that police can detain suspects for up to 48 hours without a hearing.

The initial appearance also provides indigent defendants with the opportunity to secure counsel. The court will assign a public defender or court-appointed attorney if the defendant claims indigency. However, taking indigency on faith can prove a mistake: An Idaho man who claimed he was too poor to hire a laywer to defend him was seen driving away from the courthouse in a Corvette. A check of motor vehicle records revealed that he also owned a Triumph sports car, a Ford, a boat, a motorcycle, and two trailers. Under oath, he had valued his assets at $600. The judge gave him a three-year prison sentence for perjury (Associated Press, May 23, 1991).

In minor cases such as drunkenness, disorderly conduct, vagrancy, traffic offenses, and violations of local ordinances, the initial appearance may also be the occasion defendants plead guilty to the charges brought against them; if they do so, a summary disposition is entered by the court. For those arrested on more serious charges, no plea is involved at this stage, although the court may review the circumstances of the alleged offense and hear testimony relating to the sufficiency of the evidence ("probable cause").

Determination of Charges

Following the initial appearance, the prosecution must decide what charges to pursue. Initial determination of charges is made by studying police reports regarding circumstances of the case. If the decision is made to prosecute, formal charges must be lodged against the suspect. Sometimes this is done through *grand jury* proceedings, in which the prosecution (only) presents evidence in support of the case to a jury of 12 to 23 citizens. If the grand jury agrees with the prosecution, it will hand down an *indictment* specifying the charges, or it may reduce or alter the charges or grant no formal indictment. However, a grand jury rarely disagrees with the recommendations of the prosecution.

In states without a grand jury system, and in offenses not requiring grand jury proceedings, the prosecution formally presents charges before a magistrate or judge in a *preliminary hearing*, sometimes called an *information* proceeding. Unlike the grand jury situation, the defendant may challenge the evidence presented in support of the charges and, in some jurisdictions, may elect to waive the hearings altogether.

Arraignment and Plea

Upon indictment, or when the defendant is bound over for trial on an information, a time is usually set for formal plea making. A judge asks the defendant for a plea, and if the judge accepts it, a trial or sentencing date will be set. A judge is not bound to accept a plea of guilty or *nolo contendere* (no contest); however, a judge *must* accept a plea of not guilty.

Trial

For those who have formally entered not-guilty pleas, guilt or innocence is usually decided in a court trial. All defendants are entitled to a jury trial, though this right may be waived for most offenses in most states. Trial procedures, however, are basically the same, regardless of whether or not a jury is sitting.

The trial is an *adversary* proceeding during which the prosecution and defense seek to convince the judge and jury that their presentation of the facts surrounding the case best accords with the truth. The onus of proof lies with the prosecutor, who must demonstrate that the evidence implicates the

Attorneys argue points of law out of earshot of defendant and jury.

defendant *beyond a reasonable doubt*. Although trial proceedings are acted out within a fairly rigid set of rules, the presiding judge may rule on matters of procedure, evidence, testimony, and trial conduct. The judge cannot, however, overrule a jury's finding of not guilty.

Normally, felony defendants wait weeks or even months before they come to trial. In federal cases the delay currently averages around three months (Garner, 1987:239). Unfortunately, there are no comparable data for state courts.

Appeals

Upon conviction, the defendant has the right to appeal the case to a higher court. If an appeals court refuses to consider the case or makes a negative ruling, the defendant may appeal to even higher courts. The end of the appeals road is the U.S. Supreme Court. The basis for an appeal may be procedural or evidentiary or may involve basic questions of substantive law, such as the constitutionality of a particular criminal statute. In most jurisdictions, defendants also have the right to appeal their sentences.

In its disposition of a case, an appellate court may (1) uphold ("affirm") the lower court's ruling; (2) change ("modify") part of the ruling; (3) set aside ("reverse") the lower court's ruling, without requiring any further action; (4) overturn the lower court's ruling and require further action from the lower court ("reverse and remand"); or (5) send it back ("remand") to the lower court without overturning it but requiring proceedings such as a new trial. The activity of state appellate courts grew an average of 107 percent from 1973 to 1983, with more than 400 percent growth in Alaska, Connecticut, Hawaii, and Louisiana (Bureau of Justice Statistics, 1985e).

Sentencing

After conviction, the defendant faces sentencing. In some states, and for some offenses, a jury may set the sentence, while in other circumstances sentencing may be decided by a panel of judges. Usually, however, the trial judge decides the offender's fate. In most felony cases a time interval between conviction and sentencing is provided so that the defendant's background, present circumstances, and criminal record can be investigated. These investigations are intended to aid the judge in deliberating sentencing alternatives, if they are available.

These, then, are the major decision stages in the American judicial process. The decisions made at any one stage determine whether criminal suspects will move to the next one. Most suspects do not go through all the stages that are available to them. How and why the decisions are made become central issues in determining what actually happens to those who enter the judicial process.

Becoming a Legal Criminal

With a reasonable time after arrest, suspects must be given the opportunity to gain release from custody, pending future proceedings against them. In Anglo-American law, the traditional route to freedom is posting a money bond. Those "bailed out" in this manner forfeit bail if they fail to appear at a specified later date. However, many states and countries permit the use of releases based merely on the promise to reappear, called *release on recognizance*. This is usually reserved for suspects charged with less serious offenses.

Bail and Pretrial Detention

To give someone the opportunity to post bail does not guarantee release. First, the suspect must raise money. The actual amount of bail, whether $500 or $50,000, is beyond the reach of many arrested suspects. Those who cannot raise bail themselves can turn to bondsmen and bonding agencies. For a cash fee, usually 10 to 20 percent of the bail, these bonding services guarantee the full amount of bail. The fee is nonreturnable, which means that suspects are out of pocket whether or not they appear in court as scheduled. Not all states permit bondsmen to operate, and in those that do not, the defendant is usually required to put up only 5 to 10 percent of bail and in some cases may put up assets rather than cash.

Many criminal suspects cannot raise the bonding fee. A 1988 study of the 75 largest American counties found that eight of every nine suspects detained before trial had failed to make bail (Bureau of Justice Statistics, 1991d). Caleb Foote's (1958:633) pioneering study of bail practices in New York showed that 25 percent of all defendants failed to make bail at $500, 45 percent failed at $1500, and 63 percent failed at $2500. The 1988 survey shows the impact of inflation: 22 percent failed to make bail set under $2500, 45 percent failed at $5000–$9999, and 68 percent failed at $20,000 or above.

Those who cannot afford bail are punished for their lack of financial resources in a variety of ways. First, they are deprived of freedom. Second, they are often placed in overcrowded and understaffed jail facilities, which provide few comforts, and which are dangerous places, especially for young inmates. Third, they are deprived of significant personal and social relationships on which they rely for support and emotional sustenance. Fourth, they lose some of the advantages that freedom brings when they seek legal services and prepare for the judicial proceedings ahead. Fifth, they are often forced to spend hours, days, and even months in the company of people they might normally have nothing to do with. Sixth, they are subject to a regimented daily routine that strips them of ordinary decision-making opportunities and undermines their identities. Seventh, they are deprived of privacy in dealing with personal affairs and suffer forced exposure to the personal activities of others. In sum, jailed suspects suffer innumerable deprivations, even though they have not yet been legally declared criminal.

Bail Decision Making   Although some jurisdictions have predetermined limits governing the setting of bail, bail proceedings are generally characterized by on-the-spot decisions involving considerable discretion. Police, prosecutors, and magistrates all influence bail decisions, and the amount of bail in any given case depends heavily on the factors influencing these legal authorities. A study of bail decisions in federal courts found that three major factors influenced the amount of bail, in this order: (1) seriousness of the offense, (2) the district in which bail is imposed, and (3) the suspect's criminal record (Bureau of Justice Statistics, 1985f).

The fundamental consideration in setting bail is the question of non-appearance: Will the defendant abscond once freed? But a judicial tradition has emerged over the years emphasizing other issues as well. For example, weight is given to the nature of the charges and the suspect's criminal record. Further, bail decisions are often influenced by extralegal considerations that have no foundation in law, such as whether or not the suspect's freedom will impede further police inquiries and whether or not the prosecution feels that the accused is obviously guilty. In only 33 percent of the bail deliberations observed by one author did the prosecution mention the question of non-appearance (Bottomley, 1970:59–73).

The recommendations of the prosecutor are not to be ignored, for when they go against the defendant, the judge usually agrees. By agreeing with prosecution recommendations, the judge may hope to defuse potential criticism and can argue that others must share in the responsibility for the decision. Of course, if the matter of bail is to be decided strictly on the basis of nonappearance, then the task is no simple one, and one should recognize the difficulties that magistrates face. Martin Friedland (1965:176) argues, "A system which requires security in advance produces an insoluble dilemma. In most cases it is impossible to pick a figure which is high enough to ensure the accused's appearance in court and yet low enough for him to raise; the two seldom, if ever, overlap." On the other hand, few suspects flee or "willfully" fail to appear in court. Neither the likelihood of a severe punishment nor a high bond appears to have much effect on court appearances (Goldcamp, 1979).

Preventive Detention and the Dangerous Offender   Over the years, considerable attention has been paid to the widespread European practice of refusing bail on the grounds that suspects pose a threat to the community if released. In American federal courts, preventive detention has generally been authorized when the accused is charged with a capital crime, is insane, or is an alien awaiting deportation proceedings (Altman and Cunningham, 1967:178). In addition, federal judicial approval has been extended to bail denial in cases in which there is a threat to witnesses or some other obstruction of justice. State courts, however, have generally assumed greater leeway in the denial of bail; judicial opinion has consistently held that defendants in state courts have no automatic right to bail. In 1987 the U.S. Supreme Court appeared to move in a similar direction. In a 6-to-2 ruling, preventive detention was upheld in a case involving a robbery suspect who turned out to be innocent, but was held in jail for 71 days (*Newsweek*, June 8, 1987).

Whatever the legal and constitutional dilemmas posed by the bail issue, and there are many, judges who see fit to keep suspects in custody may do so indirectly by setting extremely high bail. In this way, the accused is typically prevented from securing release because he or she is unable to raise bail. A 1988 study found that defendants charged with violent crimes were three times more likely than other defendants to have bail set at $20,000 or more (Bureau of Justice Statistics, 1991d). This practice is inherently discriminatory: "If the dangerous defendant can raise the bail sum, he goes free. By its nature, therefore, the system succeeds in retaining only the 'dangerous poor.' The 'dangerous rich' post bond and are released" (Altman and Cunningham, 1967:179).

Advocates of preventive detention are concerned that dangerous offenders will jeopardize the lives and property of community members. Certainly, some suspects will commit crimes they could not have committed in jail. Some may commit crimes during the period between arrest and trial to pay off bonding fees they have incurred in obtaining pretrial release. There is also evidence that the probability of crime increases with the length of time that suspects remain on bail, with the extensiveness of their criminal records, and with their involvement with drugs (Bureau of Justice Statistics, 1985f).

Predicting dangerousness is no easy matter, and conventional wisdom is little help. A recent study illustrates. Chaiken and Chaiken (1991) distinguished "high-rate dangerous" offending from mere habitual offending and from periodic crimes of violence (see Figure 11.2) and looked for characteristics of criminals that would predict it. The authors gave the following example of high-rate dangerous offending: "A person who has committed three assaults, two robberies, and a burglary in the past month" (Chaiken and Chaiken, 1991:2). Using self-report and official data on 452 male defendants, they found that displaying or using a gun to threaten a victim, alcoholism, prior arrests for drug distribution or possession, previous imprisonment, previous parole or probation revocation, and previous adult convictions were *not* associated with high-rate dangerous offending. Nor were age at first arrest, race, or employment status, though these factors did predict habitual offending.

The authors found some factors that predicted high-rate dangerous offending: The victim in the present offense was female; a knife was used or brandished; the defendant was wanted for failure to complete a previous sentence; the instant offense was committed in a public place; the defendant had one or more juvenile convictions for robbery. It is not immediately obvious why this group of factors, and not the first, should predict high-rate dangerous offenders. The authors regard their findings as a step toward constructing preventive detention policies, but they stop short of proposing solutions to this controversial problem.

Some might argue that if pretrial detention can prevent even one predatory or violent act, preventive detention will have served a useful purpose.

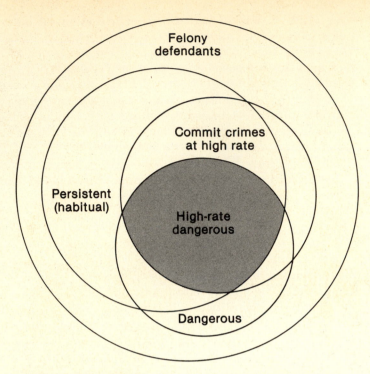

FIGURE 11.2 Candidates for Career Criminal Prosecution.
Source: Marcia R. Chaiken and Jan M. Chaiken (1991). "Priority prosecution of high-rate dangerous offenders," *NIJ Research in Action* March:
1–8.

Against this view, however, is the specter of a judicial process operating on
the basis of fear, speculation, and stereotypes. This problem arises because
criminal justice authorities have so far been unable to predict accurately
which suspects will in fact commit crimes upon release (Angel, 1971;
Monahan, 1981). Failing this ability, suspects are released if they "look right"
and detained if they do not. In fact, bail has been made more difficult in most
states over the past few years (Bradley, 1984).

Prosecution

Legal confirmation of a suspect's criminality comes with conviction in court.
Upon conviction, defendants officially lose their status as law-abiding citizens and are subject to punishment at the hands of the state. A conviction
justifies the efforts of police and prosecution: "The policeman's triumph
comes when the court vindicates his judgment by a conviction. . . . At any
rate, a conviction reassures him of his own competence and at the same time
of the worth of his job. . . . It provides for him a reassurance as to the
correctness of his judgments" (Westley, 1970:81). (Or so it has long been

Sensational crimes get a lot more attention than run-of-the-mill offenses, and attorneys on both sides find that the publicity can do wonders for a career. Here a packed court listens to testimony in the trial of serial killer Jeffrey Dahmer.

argued. One of the few studies to address the issue found that detectives and police supervisors show little interest in the proportion of their cases that are accepted or rejected by prosecutors. "In many instances, the detectives did not know whether suspects they had arrested were convicted or acquitted" [Petersilia, Abrahamse, and Wilson, 1990:33]. What follows after the arrest is someone else's responsibility.)

In America, all criminal defendants have the right to plead not guilty and to ask for trial by a jury of their peers. The trial provides the setting for the adversary proceedings that, in theory, are the heart of the Anglo-American judicial process. The trial is also the setting for review of previous actions against criminal suspects. It is the place where justice supposedly reigns; where fairness, impartiality, and due process guide the judgments of others. Fans of *Perry Mason* and *L.A. Law* may be surprised to learn that most criminal defendants never go to trial. Instead, they plead guilty, virtually ensuring their own conviction. In fact, around 90 percent of all convictions are the result of guilty pleas, though the actual percentage varies from place to place (Bureau of Justice Statistics, 1988b:41). This means that only about 10 percent of criminal convictions occur in the adversary setting of a public trial. To understand how criminal convictions usually come about and to understand how one becomes a legal criminal, one must focus on those pretrial phases of judicial decision making in which charges and pleas are considered.

The decision to prosecute, or more correctly, *not* to prosecute, is perhaps the most crucial in the entire criminal process. For defendants, an unfavorable decision often guarantees conviction; the only remaining question is whether something can be done to reduce the negative consequences likely to follow. For police, the decision to prosecute vindicates their judgment and efforts, though it may put their methods on the line. If there is no prosecution, there can be no adjudication of guilt or innocence, and certainly no official criminal punishment. It is no exaggeration to say that the prosecutor has become *the* criminal justice official (McDonald, 1985:9).

The Decision Not to Prosecute   Many criminal cases that come before prosecutors are screened out at an early stage or end up being dismissed (Table 11.1). The decision not to prosecute is often made at an initial prosecution screening. Two reasons for rejection appear most often: problems with the evidence and problems with the witnesses. Evidence problems are most likely to be either insufficient testimonial corroboration—willing witnesses could not substantiate the charges—or lack of physical evidence, such as stolen property or weapons. Apparently, relatively few cases are dropped because of due-process "technicalities," such as suspected violations of the rules governing police searches and seizures (Brosi, 1979:18–19). When due process is an issue, it is most likely to surface in drug offense situations. The violation of due process here may be a consequence of negative attitudes toward drug offenders generally, coupled with the pressing need to secure physical evidence of possession or delivery.

Criminal charges may be dropped after cases have passed initial screening and after official charges have been filed. When this happens the major reasons are again either evidence or witness related. In many cities the failure of witnesses to appear in court or to make themselves available to the prosecution accounts for most of the dismissals as well as the refusals (Brosi,

TABLE 11.1   Typical outcome of 100 felony arrests brought by police for prosecution in 37 jurisdictions, 1982

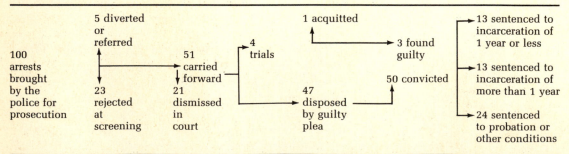

Source: Bureau of Justice Statistics (1988b). *BJS Data Report, 1987.* Washington, D.C.: U.S. Department of Justice, p. 42.

1979). However, the impact of witness and evidence problems seems to vary by offense and from jurisdiction to jurisdiction. For example, in murder cases, witnesses were more of a problem in St. Louis than in Los Angeles or in New Orleans. In drug cases, witness problems were cited as the reason for 80 percent of dismissals in Washington, D.C., but for less than 10 percent in most other jurisdictions (Bureau of Justice Statistics, 1983c).

Regarding witness cooperation it should be noted that designation of witnesses as "uncooperative" may be a result of prevailing offense stereotypes. That is, it may be that prosecutors associate certain offense situations with uncooperative witnesses and decide not to prosecute a certain individual because the case fits the stereotype. An example is assault. Here victims often consider the problem a personal matter, especially if it involves relatives or friends. Many victims are unlikely to follow through with official complaints or to appear as witnesses for that reason. Both police and prosecutors know this, and it colors their handling of assault cases. It is easy for them to ignore or drop cases, citing lack of witness cooperation even when no attempt actually had been made to establish that prospective witnesses would in fact be uncooperative if given the chance to testify.

Is there evidence of such a gap between prosecutor perceptions and witness intentions? Frank Cannavale (1976:50) sought to find out in a study of witness cooperation in Washington, D.C. His conclusion was that "prosecutors were apparently unable to cut through to the true intentions of 23 percent or more of those they regarded as uncooperative and, therefore, recorded the existence of witness problems when these were premature judgments at best and incorrect decisions at worst."

The decision to prosecute is sometimes influenced by private individuals and groups who are able to put pressure on the district attorney's office. In his study of prosecutors in King County, Washington, George Cole (1970) found that staff members routinely took steps to protect the district attorney from public criticism. These steps included manipulations of the bail system as well as the vigorous prosecution of certain forms of crime—for example, child molestation. Prosecutors' charging practices can be expected to reflect community influences in those areas of enforcement where they are in substantial agreement with public opinion.

Bargain Justice

Many guilty pleas, perhaps most, are entered as a result of an agreement between the prosecutor and defense counsel. The agreement means that both sides see themselves as better off with the plea than they would have been without it.

A number of different "bargains" are possible: A guilty plea may be exchanged for (1) a reduction in the charge(s); (2) a promise of leniency in sentencing; (3) for concurrent consideration of multiple charges—the defendant serves one sentence for a number of different crimes; or (4) for dropped charges—the defendant pleads guilty to (usually) the major charge, and other lesser charges are dismissed. William McDonald (1985) has shown that different jurisdictions emphasize different types of concessions (see Figure 11.3).

In addition to these bargains, the defendant might exchange a guilty plea for release on bail or in order to avoid a future problem. For example, a prosecutor in one jurisdiction will sometimes offer a deal to a defendant who is also wanted in another jurisdiction, using the threat of returning the defendant to that jurisdiction to induce a guilty plea (Newman, 1966:85). Finally, there is what Arnold Enker (1967) call's the "tacit bargain." Though no explicit negotiation is involved, defendants may plead guilty because they believe the court will show greater leniency if they do. A guilty plea saves the state time and money and indicates that the defendant is prepared to pay for

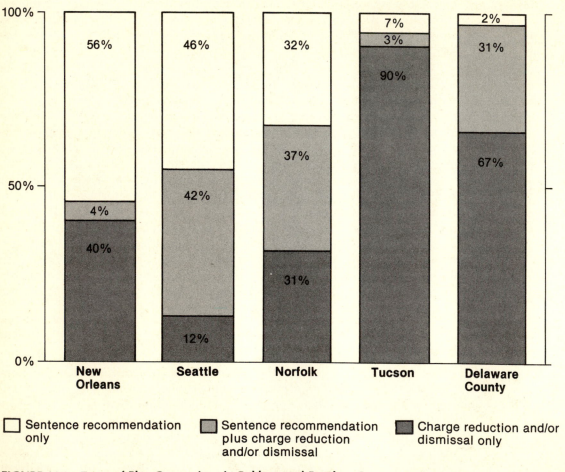

FIGURE 11.3   **Types of Plea Concessions in Robbery and Burglary Cases by Jurisdiction.**   *Source:* William F. McDonald (1985). *Plea Bargaining: Critical Issues and Common Practices.* Washington, D.C.: U.S. Department of Justice, p. 27.

the crime. There is evidence that prosecutors and judges agree that guilty pleas should be rewarded (Mendelsohn, 1956; Vetri, 1964; Bottomley, 1970:120–122; Rosett and Cressey, 1976).

Defendants may feel pressure to "deal" for other reasons: (1) They want to avoid the publicity of a trial—a likely concern for offenders who are employed or have families—(2) they want to avoid the unknowns of adversarial proceedings; the outcome of a trial is influenced by many factors beyond the defendant's control, and so why take the risk of things going wrong? And (3) a guilty plea usually gets things over with more quickly than a trial does, and some defendants may feel this is important.

McCarthy and Lindquist's (1988) study of 619 defendants indicted for murder, rape, aggravated assault, and robbery in Alabama suggests that proneness to plead guilty reflects the need to reduce uncertainty about outcome and/or to get the best result possible, and that type of offense may play a significant role in determining the benefits of a guilty plea. For example, rapists and murderers received the greatest gains by pleading guilty while only slight gains were made by assault offenders.

The Prosecution and Guilty Pleas The advantages and pressures considered by defendants are well known to prosecutors who often use them as carrots in negotiations. One particularly effective method used to encourage guilty pleas is to bring up the defendant on as many charges as possible. These "multiple-count" indictments include the major offense(s) and all the so-called lesser-included offenses. For example, an armed robbery indictment might include various assault, larceny, and weapons charges as well as the major offense. An offer to drop the lesser charges could save the defendant many years in prison, a deal hard to refuse.

If a guilty plea favors the defendant, why would the prosecutor be interested, as is usually the case? One obvious explanation is that with current budgets and personnel, it would be virtually impossible to prosecute and try every case police brought in. Most of the time court calendars are full, with cases set months in advance. Under such conditions prosecutors have little choice but to divert cases from the courtroom (McIntyre and Lippman, 1970).

The judicial enterprise itself brings pressures to deal. Organizational demands go beyond time and money, and they include *productivity* and *reciprocity*. Convictions are a measure of how productive one is as a prosecutor, and a good track record is important. Henry Pontell (1984:35) writes:

> Because prosecutors are elected to their positions, their "track" records (convicted defendants), which reflect how well they are protecting the public, strongly influence their future careers. They must produce conviction statistics that place their activities in the best possible light. This is likely to take precedence over other concerns of due process, social justice, and deterrence. Prosecutors strive for high rates of conviction, and correspondingly low rates of acquittal and dismissal, once cases are accepted. This is, in part, accomplished through the semi-official practice of plea bargaining.

Reciprocity is important in any group or organization, for it helps bind members and ensure that goals are met. The organization of criminal justice consists of interdependent roles connected by obligations and expectations. Reciprocity is high when these obligations and expectations are met. When the police produce arrests that hold up in court—and many do not (Bureau of Justice Statistics, 1983c:11)—the prosecutor's job is made easier. When the prosecutor speeds cases through the system so that police are not tied up in court, police work is made easier.

The Defense Attorney and Guilty Pleas Defense attorneys are often the first to suggest that their clients plead guilty and in many cases convince defendants to change initial not-guilty pleas to guilty (Casper, 1972). Though this means a client's conviction, the defense counsel recognizes a professional obligation to do what is best for the defendant. If this can be accomplished by copping a plea, then the defense attorney will recommend it. The plea bargain is attractive, if not obligatory, when the client is guilty and the case is strong enough to produce a conviction. If a lighter sentence can be achieved through a deal, then this is the route any responsible defense attorney will take.

Yet this is not the whole picture. Defense attorneys are subject to some of the same organizational demands as prosecutors. Whether a public defender or a private attorney, the defense counsel's career is dependent on good relations with other actors in the system. The result is that defendants are often manipulated to serve the professional interests of those within the organization. Defense attorneys must cooperate or risk losing insider status and the rewards that meeting reciprocal obligations brings. If they persist in bucking the system, sanctions will be applied. Attorneys may be excluded from information sharing and from conferences. Chambliss and Siedman (1971:402) recount an occasion in which a young public defender was "read the riot act" by the chief justice of his state because he refused to plead an unusually large proportion of his cases. He was warned of the necessity of cooperating with the prosecution and the bench.

There are also economic advantages to pleading a client guilty. George Cole (1970:340) argues that the criminal attorney's salable product is influence rather than technical proficiency in the law: "[King County, Wash., attorneys] hold the belief that clients are attracted partially on the basis of the attorney's reputation as a fixer, or as a shrewd bargainer." In addition, private criminal attorneys usually make money in their offices, on the phone, or in the prosecutor's office, but rarely in the courtroom. Time is money, and the time spent in court is the least profitable. The more clients one can handle in a given day, the more money one can make and the wider one's contacts will become.

Criminal law is generally not a profitable business for private attorneys, nor are most lawyers well trained in it (Downie, 1972). There is also evidence that criminal law attracts less competent and less ethical lawyers (Carlin, 1968), many of whom become so-called lawyer regulars. Blumberg (1967:18) describes them as:

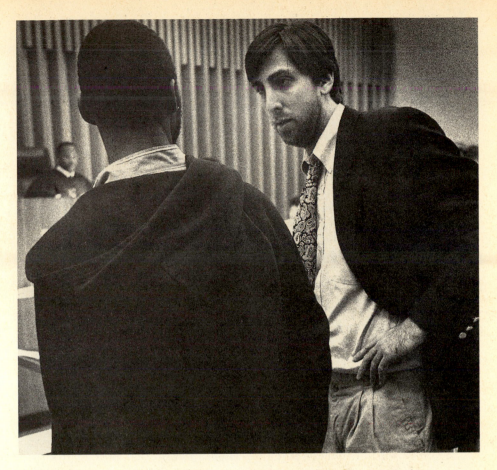

A public defender consults with his client during arraignment proceedings. Many criminal defendants never see their attorney outside the courtroom or courthouse hallway.

. . . highly visible in the major urban centers of the nation; their offices—at times shared with bondsmen—line the backstreets near courthouses. They are also visible politically, with clubhouse ties reaching into judicial chambers and the prosecutor's office. The regulars make no effort to conceal their dependence upon police, bondsmen, jail personnel, as well as bailiffs, stenographers, prosecutors, and judges.

In the hands of these attorneys, the interests of the client may be subordinated to self-interest, and the bargain actually struck may be no bargain at all.

Backroom deals and negotiations hurriedly carried on in courthouse corridors paint a picture of *sub rosa* decision making in the judicial process which may no longer be as accurate as it once was. The U.S. Supreme Court stands behind plea bargaining (see Box 11.1), and the whole process is much more open than it used to be. Furthermore, while commonsense reasoning and some factual sleight of hand may lead negotiators beyond the formal rationality of procedural law (Maynard, 1982), it seems that prosecutors and defense counsels nevertheless place greatest weight on strictly legal issues: the seriousness of the crime, the criminal past of the defendant, and the strength of the evidentiary case (see McDonald, 1985). The increasing role played by judges may have a lot to do with bringing plea bargaining out of the closet. Based on a study of 711 plea negotiations and on interviews with over 200 judges, prosecutors, and defense attorneys, McDonald (1985) believes that having judges involved has resulted in more careful and deliberate negotiations and that defendants are more likely to be advised of their rights in the process.

Judges and Bargained Justice   Nowadays, judges quite often take an active part in bargaining. In some states a judge's participation is mandated by statute. It should come as no surprise that judges are routinely involved in bargained justice. After all, they are actors in the same play, as it were, and they are more likely to be impartial than anyone else. In addition, judges are subject to direct pressures from outside the immediate court organization. Their continued appointment or reelection depends on how well the court's business flows. When things get bogged down, pressure from the media, their political bosses, and the higher judiciary weighs heavily on their shoulders. Like the roles of prosecutor and defense attorney, the judge's role in the judicial process often leads to an administration of the law best characterized as a cooperative endeavor aimed at the speedy, predictable confirmation of a suspect's guilt.

The Future of Bargained Justice   In recent years there has been more and more criticism of plea bargaining, both inside and outside legal circles. In one criminal justice text (Robin, 1987:259) 16 criticisms are listed, and one could probably find more. The author concluded:

> There is something deeply disturbing about a criminal justice system in which lawyers avoid the due process model like the plague, in which the outcome of cases depends on the personal interests and administrative convenience of the practitioners, and in which sentences are unrelated to the crimes committed or to the defendant's genuine correctional needs.

On the heels of increasing criticism of the system, some jurisdictions moved to abolish plea bargaining. Alaska was one of the first, with a complete ban in 1975. Other jurisdictions adopted partial restrictions, for example, banning its use in cases involving career criminals, repeaters, and serious violaters, or in cases involving specific heinous crimes such as rape or the killing of law enforcement personnel.

It appears that the effects of reduced bargaining were not exactly as expected, at least in Alaska (Rubinstein, Clarke, and White, 1980). After the prohibition went into effect the number of court trials remained small, the court docket did not bog down (actually, cases were processed faster than before), and the proportion of defendants pleading guilty remained pretty much the same as before the ban. The overwhelming modes of disposition continued to be dismissal and guilty plea. "In the final analysis, most guilty pleas and dismissals were entered because the parties simply did not perceive any better alternative" (p. 223).

If these findings were unexpected, so were the ones dealing with the severity of sentences. True, sentences for some classes of offenders did increase drastically—237 percent for drug offenses; 117 percent for fraud. But in the case of burglary, larceny, and receiving stolen property, sentences actually declined for experienced, older offenders charged with more serious offenses and increased for young first offenders whose charges were the least serious in this group. Furthermore, the sentences given to violent offenders remained basically unchanged.

These findings suggest caution in anticipating the consequences of reduced plea bargaining. Certainly, it appears from the Alaska experience that the response of the judicial system cannot be taken for granted. Even so, doubts and cautions should not prevent the contemplation and testing of alternatives to the present system, however far-fetched they might seem. John Griffiths (1970:397) has demanded: "What is so inconceivable about a process which includes a trial (perhaps a shorter and neater trial) for *every* defendant?" Perhaps the judicial process would seem less like a game to many participants, as Casper (1972:18) discovered:

> The system as it operates in practice is seen by defendants in this study as an example of their life on the street. Outcomes do not seem to be determined by

principles or careful consideration of persons, but by hustling, conning, manipulation, luck, fortitude, waiting them out, and the like. . . .

How well you do in this world depends upon what you've got and how well you use it. The criminal justice system, like the streets, is a game of resource exploitation. The defendant typically has little in the way of resources and doesn't win. He can, though, with luck and skill, lose less than he might. In this way . . . the system has no real moral component in the eyes of the defendant. It is an extension of life on the street and the other participants— the police, defense attorney, the prosecutor, the judge—are themselves playing a game that is perceived as existing on the same moral level as that of the defendant.

Sentencing

All offenders who are convicted of a crime face sentencing. In this section the behavior of judges and the constraints within which they operate will be discussed. But a word of caution is necessary. Although officially, it is the magistrate or judge who decides the sentence a convicted criminal must serve, in reality it is often the prosecutor who largely determines the sentence. This is so because the prosecutor is in control of the charges. A suspect who is arrested for armed robbery may be formally charged with some other, lesser, offense. In this way the prosecutor has reduced the possible sentence.

Sentencing Disparities

Sentencing decisions in felony cases must address three questions: (1) Should the defendant be incarcerated? If yes, then (2) in a local jail or in a prison? and (3) for how long? There is little consistency from jurisdiction to jurisdiction and from judge to judge in the answers to these questions, even when the offense is essentially the same. There is, in short, considerable sentencing disparity in America.

The extent of the problem is only now being fully documented, though it has been recognized for years. One study of judges in New York, Connecticut, and Vermont (the U.S. Court of Appeals for the Second Circuit) used actual presentence reports by probation officers and asked each judge to assign a sentence in 20 different cases. The range of sentences among the 50 judges interviewed was considerable, and the sentences for identical cases could not be predicted (see Robin, 1987:309). In a similar study, 47 Virginia judges were given identical descriptions of five criminal cases (Austin and Williams, 1977). They were asked to determine a verdict and assign a sentence as if the situation were real. There were high rates of agreement on the verdicts but wide variation in the sentences. Using different methods, other studies have produced similar results.

A comparison of average prison terms in four jurisdictions with similar sentencing structures, that is, with similar rules governing judicial discretion,

Trials are adversarial proceedings in which advocates for the defendant and for the state each try to convince a judge or jury to accept their version of the criminal event and the defendant's role in it. Most cases never come to trial, however, and most guilty verdicts result from plea bargains.

found wide variation for the same offense categories (see Table 11.2). Furthermore, the likelihood of being sent to prison in the first place shows considerable variation around the country for similar offenses. In robbery cases, for example, 100 percent of those convicted were sent to prison in Iowa, versus only 57.7 percent in Wyoming—and both states are predominantly rural.

The Presentence Investigation

In both Europe and America, presentence investigations are often used as an aid to sentencing. Though rarely used in dealing with misdemeanants, presentence reports are intended to help the judge choose a sentence more appropriate to the particular case. In some states, a presentence investigation is mandatory; in others it is available at the request of the judge.

A presentence report contains information about the convicted offender considered relevant to guiding the judge toward an appropriate sentence within the jurisdiction's statutory framework. The information is usually collected by probation officers or other trained social workers employed by the state. What is contained in the report depends in part on the jurisdiction,

TABLE 11.2 Average minimum and maximum sentence lengths (in months), circa 1980

	Illinois		New York		Pennsylvania		Wyoming	
	Min.	Max.	Min.	Max.	Min.	Max.	Min.	Max.
Homicide	346	743	130	156	42	112	146	195
Rape	125	154	67	156	53	136	70	127
Robbery	55	108	38	91	24	68	56	99
Burglary	21	60	25	61	19	52	28	58
Larceny	16	40	18	42	7	25	21	47

Source: Bureau of Justice Statistics (1984). *Special Report: Sentencing Practices in 13 States.* Washington, D.C.: U.S. Department of Justice.

in part on administrative policies, and in part on the experience, talents, hard work, competence, and perspectives of the investigators. "In theory [the report] is a neutral document, its purpose being neither adverse nor favorable to the sentencing fate of the defendant" (Remington et al., 1969:696). It is intended to provide accurate and relevant information on aspects of an offender's personal and family history—police record, prior convictions, employment history, and family situation—that are thought to make a difference in choosing from among sentencing alternatives.

In practice, presentence reports may be neither neutral and accurate nor filled with only relevant information. According to one study, reports often contain misinformation, prejudicial statements, and "facts" based on hearsay and rumor. Here are some illustrations, taken from presentence reports:

1. "While [the defendant] apparently never engaged in any serious criminal conduct before, and while he has never shown any tendency to use violence, it is rumored in the factory, and evidently widely believed, that about two years ago he murdered his boss's wife."
2. "His wife reports that he is given to murderous rages."
3. "In my opinion [as an experienced, graduate-trained probation and parole agent], he is the type of person who, if not checked soon, will kill somebody someday."
4. "There is a broad, deep base of sexual psychopathy in this boy. His offense may technically be burglary but he is basically a sex deviate."
5. "He is a loser, plain and simple. He is sexually inadequate, vocationally inadequate, and mentally inadequate. He has failed in everything— school, jobs, military service, with his family, and with his wife. He has even failed as a crook. There is absolutely no reason to think he can make it on probation and probably prison won't help him much. The only thing I can recommend is incarceration for as long as possible and then hope for the best." (Remington et al., 1969:697–98)

There is no reason to believe that all investigators take such liberties. However, many probably do, for three reasons. First, many jurisdictions and administrative policies require or encourage investigators to recount feelings and attitudes, and to present opinions and recommendations. Second, those who write the reports sooner or later see themselves as experts, professionals whose opinions should be taken seriously. Third, investigators are subject to organizational pressures and they try to avoid rocking the boat. If police are particularly anxious for a certain disposition, for example, investigators may feel obliged to tilt their reports accordingly. Remember, participants in the judicial process work together.

Ralph Blankenship (1974) shows how special meanings are attached to language used in the case records that accompany individuals throughout their official careers as deviants. Presentence reports, probation records, prison records, and mental hospital records are put together by professionals who share language "registers," words and phrases having special meaning for them. When compiling case records, they present an image of the subject that fits *their* perception of the criminal, psychotic, or delinquent reality: "[T]he professional does not use his register to describe, but as a means of constructing his social reality" (1974:255). Blankenship points out how direct quotations from labeled deviants give the appearance of letting the deviant tell the story, but to those in the know they serve to discredit the story at the same time.

Impact of Reports on Sentencing All this matters little if presentence reports have no impact on the actual sentences handed down. The question is, then, are judges influenced by presentence reports and, if so, to what extent?

Data on the impact of presentence reports provide few conclusive answers. Some studies show that presentence reports are influential in the sentencing process. Thus Carter and Wilkins (1967) found in California that judges and probation officials were in broad agreement about major sentencing criteria and that judges accepted 86 percent of investigators' recommendations. Other studies have found similar evidence of strong correlations between sentencing recommendations and actual sentences (e.g., Frazier and Bock, 1982).

On the other hand, Hogarth (1971) reports that Canadian magistrates were likely to use reports and other sources of information in a selective manner, when it was consistent with their own philosophy, attitudes, and preconceptions regarding the case. However, presentence reports tended to be requested when judges already considered a case difficult, when they saw themselves likely to give sentences out of keeping with their normal practice. Hogarth speculates that the presentence report gives judges the opportunity to justify a decision *they have already made.*

Hogarth observed an important difference in the use and impact of presentence reports. He found that urban magistrates tended to react negatively to probation officers' recommendations, whereas rural judges appeared more likely to accept them. He explains the difference by referring to the rural judge's easier work load, greater self-esteem and community status, greater informality, less punitive orientation, and the closer ties between court and probation services in rural areas. In summing up the value of presentence reports, Hogarth (1971:262) concludes:

> . . . if the presentence report is to have the impact on sentencing that was originally intended, and indeed often assumed, certain favourable conditions for its proper use must exist. Magistrates must have the time to read reports carefully. They must also have the opportunity, when the need arises, to discuss their contents informally with probation officers. Most important, they must have a set of attitudes and beliefs which are consistent with the rationale underlying the use of the presentence report, namely, the individualization of justice.

Extralegal Factors in Sentencing

The existence of sentencing disparities would probably not be of so much concern were it not for the fact that much of the variation is thought to be the result of bias rather than objective features of the offense and offender as recognized in law. The widely divergent sentences imposed for essentially the same crime cannot be adequately explained by differences in the law, in the circumstances of the offense, or in the criminality of the offender. What, then, are some of the extralegal factors thought to influence the sentencing decisions of judges?

Gender, Race, and Class Scholars have documented sentencing disparities by race (e.g., Sellin, 1935; Wolfgang and Cohen, 1970; Thornberry, 1973) and class (e.g., Hood, 1972; Thornberry, 1973), and of late the question of gender bias has received increasing attention (e.g., Datesman and Scarpitti, 1980; Morris, 1987). This section reviews some of the evidence on these extralegal factors in sentencing.

Race and social class are intertwined in American society, as are gender and class. African-Americans and women tend on the whole to have lower socioeconomic status and power than whites and males, respectively. This makes distinguishing their individual relationship to sentencing more difficult. A further complication is the age factor; many studies have focused on juvenile offenders, making generalizations problematic. Of course, given that people under age 21 constitute the single largest group of people arrested for crime—30 percent of all arrests in 1990 (Federal Bureau of Investigation, 1991:190)—we are certainly interested in whether race, class, or gender influences what happens to them if they are convicted.

With regard to gender, a recent review of available research on juvenile court dispositions concludes that girls receive harsher treatment than boys for lesser crimes but not for more serious offenses (Barlow and Ferdinand, 1992:130–134). To some extent this reflects the impact of gender on referrals to juvenile court. In an extensive national study of juvenile court data, Snyder and Finnegan (1987) found that girls were three times as likely as boys to be referred to juvenile court for status offenses (acts that would not be crimes if committed by adults). Once there, however, girls were also more likely to be incarcerated than boys charged with status offenses. Meda Chesney-Lind (1987a; 1987b; 1988) has shown that this difference is historical.

A new study (Johnson and Scheuble, 1991) looked at gender bias in 36,680 juvenile court dispositions in Nebraska over a nine-year period. Hypotheses were derived from two competing theoretical perspectives: *sex role traditionalism* and *chivalry (paternalism)*. Sex role traditionalism predicts harsher punishment for females based on the argument that girls and women who commit crimes have violated traditional definitions of the female role as gentle, complaint, and dependent. The chivalry (paternalism) model predicts an opposite gender bias: more lenient sentences for females because males (who also dominate the criminal justice system) try to protect the "fairer sex."

The findings of this study support both models of gender bias. Overall, girls received more lenient dispositions than boys, suggesting a chivalry effect. On the other hand, harsher penalties for girls were found in the case of repeat offenders who committed more serious offenses, suggesting a sex role effect. Over the nine years, however, the trend was toward greater leniency— "higher odds for girls being dismissed and higher odds for probation and lock-up for boys" (Johnson and Scheuble, 1991:695).

One of the few studies to analyze at sentencing practices as they take place in the courtroom is by Kathleen Daly (1989). She found that courts in New York City and Seattle placed considerable weight on the *family ties* of defendants. Black women with family ties benefitted most from sentencing leniency, and single and married men with family ties also did better than other men. Thus, the greater leniency shown certain defendants may have more to do with judges' beliefs about the importance of family than about gender or race (see also Bickle and Peterson, 1991).

If the findings on gender bias are complex, those on race and class are equally so. The impact of race and class has also been found in the sentences given to juvenile offenders. In one study, the records of 9601 juvenile court dispositions in Philadelphia were analyzed. It was discovered that even when legal variables such as severity of offense and prior record were taken into account, blacks were more likely than whites to be prosecuted and institutionalized, and offenders of low socioeconomic status were more severely penalized than others (Thornberry, 1973).

In a study of early releases from prison under a "shock probation" program* in Ohio, Peterson and Friday (1975) found race to be the most important factor in determining releases in certain situations. For example, when the probation department had recommended against early release, whites were twice as likely as blacks to be released, even after controlling for a variety of legal variables.

---

*Shock probation allows an incarcerated offender to appeal to the court of conviction for early release from prison as a form of probation. The offender must appeal within sixty days of the original sentencing date.

Much of the research on judicial disposition of cases seems to support the view that race and class are often taken into account in sentencing. Even so, in a review of recent studies, Steven Box (1981) found 10 showing no association between class and disposition and 17 studies showing no association between race and disposition.

Many of the studies dealing with judicial disposition of criminal cases employed different methods. Caution must therefore be exercised in any attempt to arrive at general conclusions regarding the impact of social status on sentencing. When the data in some earlier studies have been reanalyzed and controls for such "legal" variables as prior record introduced, different conclusions have been reached. After his reanalysis of 20 studies purporting to show race and class effects, John Hagan (1974:379) concluded that "while there may be evidence of differential sentencing, knowledge of extralegal offender characteristics contributes relatively little to our ability to predict judicial dispositions."

Gary Kleck (1981) also reevaluated published research on criminal sentencing. He focused on racial bias in both capital and noncapital cases and reviewed more than 55 studies, mostly from the 1960s and 1970s. He concluded that there was little evidence of any general, overt racial discrimination in noncapital cases, but strong evidence of discrimination in capital cases in the South when the offense was rape. However, Kleck also observed that black defendants sometimes are treated more *leniently* than whites, and especially so when their victims are also black. Kleck offers various explanations of this: (1) that blacks are devalued crime victims, hence offenses against them are deemed less serious; (2) that there exists a sort of white paternalism; and (3) that some judges may feel guilty about past discrimination or may be compensating for institutionalized racism or for any prejudice they might have. These hypotheses remain to be tested, however.

Some support for the hypothesis that blacks are devalued victims comes from Paternoster's (1983) study of decisions to seek the death penalty in South Carolina. Although Paternoster looked at prosecutorial decisions, and not at the sentencing decisions of judges, the findings illustrate the posture of court officials. Table 11.3 compares death penalty requests for various racial combinations of offenders and victims. It clearly shows that when blacks killed blacks their offenses were least likely to be classified as capital murders, and if they were, the prosecutor was least likely to request the death penalty.

A number of authors have pointed out that prior criminal record is itself a product of previous discretionary judgments, which may themselves have been influenced by social considerations. Furthermore, when introduced as a factor in court deliberations, a prior record influences outcome indirectly by affecting a defendant's ability to secure bail and competent private counsel and to negotiate a reduced charge. In sum, the finding that legal variables account for most of the variation may actually reflect the accumulated disadvantages of being black and lower class (Box, 1971:194; Kleck, 1981:799).

TABLE 11.3 Death penalty requests by prosecutors, South Carolina, 1977–1981

All Homicide Cases

Offender/Victim Combination	Number of Homicide Acts	Number of Death Requests	Probability of Death Request	% That Are Capital Murders[a]
Black kills White	148	54	0.365	75.0%
White kills White	580	46	0.079	19.5%
Black kills Black	894	8	0.009	8.5%
White kills Black	54	7	0.130	29.6%

Capital Murder Cases

Offender/Victim Combination	Number of Capital Murders	Number of Death Requests	Probability of Death Request
Black kills White	111	54	0.486
White kills White	113	44[b]	0.389
Black kills Black	76	8	0.105
White kills Black	16	7	0.438

[a]Capital murder cases are the only homicide cases for which the death penalty may be sought. They involve the commission of a willful homicide in conjunction with at least one other aggravating circumstance as defined by South Carolina's death penalty statute.

[b]Two cases are missing here because neither the SHR nor police incident report could verify the existence of a statutory aggravating circumstance. In both cases guilty pleas were accepted in exchange for a life sentence and the death penalty request could have been a ploy in plea bargaining negotiations.

Source: Raymond Paternoster (1983), "The decision to seek the death penalty in South Carolina," *Journal of Criminal Law and Criminology* 74:754–787.

The evidence on status discrimination in sentencing permits no firm conclusions. Yet even if there were incontestable evidence against the conventional wisdom that there is discrimination, the fact is that the penalties assigned by law to predominantly lower-class crimes (robbery, burglary, assault, heroin pushing) are, in general, higher than those for predominantly upper-class crime (corporate fraud, misrepresentation in advertising, restraint of trade, environmental crimes). This indicates built-in bias against lower-class offenders and raises the likelihood that lower-class offenders will receive harsher penalties than higher-class criminals, even if the crimes are similar in consequence or, worse, even if occupational crimes have more serious consequences.

In similar vein, Petersilia (1985a:22) points out that even if no discrimination was to be found in sentencing, "corrections is a closed world in which discrimination could flourish." She discovered that in Texas black inmates consistently ended up serving more time than whites, and they received less educational treatment than whites despite their demonstrably greater need for education.

Community Characteristics   A person's attitudes and beliefs are shaped by a variety of influences. Some of the more important ones derive from the immediate social environment in which the person lives and works (Meyers, 1988). Studies of judicial sentencing behavior bear this out. Almost all such studies show that it makes a great deal of difference where a judge lives and works. Hood (1962) found that judges in rural or small-town communities were more inclined to sentence offenders to prison, this policy fitting in well with community sentiments and the "peaceful" lifestyle of rural communities. Emile Durkheim ([1893]) 1964a:102–108) argued long ago that deviance stands out like a sore thumb in village communities, and the collective sentiments that it threatens require immediate and forceful reaffirmation:

> We have only to note what happens, particularly in a small town, when some moral scandal has just been committed. They stop each other on the street, they visit each other, they seek to come together to talk of the event and wax indignant in common. . . .

> It is necessary that [solidarity] be affirmed at the very moment that it is contradicted, and the only means of affirming it is to express the unanimous aversion which crime continues to inspire, by an authentic act which can consist only in suffering inflicted upon the agent.

The relationship between community characteristics and sentencing may be more complex than Hood and Durkheim believed. Indeed, Hogarth (1971) found that sentencing in rural areas was less, not more, severe than in urban areas. But Nagel (1967) found that sentences in rural areas were not less punitive for all offenses—rural courts were less punitive in assault cases but more so than urban and northern courts in cases involving larceny.

Hogarth (1971) believes that sentencing behavior largely boils down to how judges define their role, what they see as the purpose of punishment, how they perceive the various social and legal constraints to which they are subjected, and how they view the relative merits of different sentencing options. If wide judicial discretion is allowed, one can expect to find more room for the impact of attitude and philosophy. Within the boundaries of legal constraint, judges will attempt to organize their sentencing behavior in congruence with their perceptions of legal, situational, and social realities (Hogarth, 1971:209–210).

Curbing Judicial Discretion

No one argues that sentencing is easy or expects judges to behave like robots. Judges are human, and there is nothing that adequately prepares them for the awesome responsibility of deciding the fate of other human beings. Whereas most experts acknowledge the need for some judicial discretion, they nevertheless support efforts to curtail it in the hope of reducing sentencing disparities and excesses.

Directed mostly toward the sentencing of felony offenders whose crimes carry statutory prison terms of more than a year, these efforts have resulted in a variety of sentencing reforms. In some states juries are empowered to decide sentences. In others a panel of judges (often called a "sentencing council") is formed to consider penalties. In yet others a sentencing board, composed of lawyers, social workers, psychiatrists, and others with professional interest in the legal process, meets to decide sentences. The value of the last two methods lies mainly in the opportunities they provide for sharing views, philosophies, and knowledge regarding sentencing, thereby promoting greater uniformity than is found when judges act individually.

Sentencing Guidelines One promising reform is to give judges guidelines based on a jurisdiction's actual sentencing practices to give structure to the exercise of discretion. Leslie Wilkins and colleagues (1978) devised reference tables that can be used to determine the average or model sentence given by judges in cases of similar offense and offender circumstances (see Table 11.4). Similar tables are now in use around the country, and in January, 1989, the U.S. Supreme Court ruled them constitutional for use in federal courts.

Using information about the seriousness of the offense and the prior record and "social stability" of the offender, judges can determine scores for offense and offender according to a prearranged formula. To find the model sentence for any particular combination of offense/offender scores, the judge simply finds the cell that lines up with the two scores in the table. Suppose an offender in Colorado has committed a Class 4 felony (for example, a robbery) and is given an offense score of 6 and an offender score of 10. What would be the model sentence?

Wilkins considers the plan to be a middle course between the current lack of consistent policy and the much more restrictive system of mandatory flat sentencing described below. The model or guideline sentence is to be considered advisory, but judges are required to give written reasons if they decide to go outside the guidelines in a particular case. Wilkins and his co-authors see the plan "as a means to guide and structure—not eliminate— judicial discretion, so as to aid judges in reaching a fair and equitable sentencing decision" (Wilkins et al., 1978:vii).

The federal sentencing guidelines adopted in 1987 have resulted in a changed profile of offenders sentenced to prison. In particular, the proportion receiving longer prison terms has gone down, as has the proportion of inmates convicted of violent crimes (which probably goes a long way to explaining the declining prison terms). On the other hand, the proportion of inmates with drug offense convictions has gone up, and now constitutes 68.8 percent of the federal prison population (Federal Bureau of Prisons, 1991). The sentences for some specific crimes have gone up; for example, the typical term for robbery (the second most common inmate offense) is now 78 months, up from 48.8 months prior to 1987.

There is some suggestion that African-Americans are not receiving equi- table treatment under guideline procedures. For example, a study by Kramer and Lubitz (1985) in Pennsylvania found that nonwhites generally had slightly higher incarceration rates and longer average minimum sentences

TABLE 11.4 Sentencing guidelines, Felony 4, Denver

Offense Score	Offender Score				
	−1 −7	0 2	3 8	9 12	13+
10–12	Indeterminate minimum 4–5 year maximum	Indeterminate minimum 8–10 year maximum	Indeterminate minimum 8–10 year maximum	Indeterminate minimum 8–10 year maximum	Indeterminate minimum 8–10 year maximum
8–9	Out	3–5 month work project	Indeterminate minimum 3–4 year maximum	Indeterminate minimum 8–10 year maximum	Indeterminate minimum 8–10 year maximum
6–7	Out	Out	Indeterminate minimum 3–4 year maximum	Indeterminate minimum 6–8 year maximum	Indeterminate minimum 8–10 year maximum
3–5	Out	Out	Out	Indeterminate minimum 4–5 year maximum	Indeterminate minimum 4–5 year maximum
1–2	Out	Out	Out	Out	Indeterminate minimum 3–4 year maximum

Note: Colorado uses a penal code that contains five levels of felonies (with Felony 1 being the most serious and Felony 5 the least serious) and three levels of misdemeanors. Typical crimes that fall within the Felony 4 category are manslaughter, robbery, and second degree burglary. The statutory designated maximum incarcerative sentence for a Felony 4 offense is 10 years. No minimum period of confinement is to be set by the court. The term "out" refers to a nonincarcerative type of sentence such as probation, deferred judgment, or deferred prosecution.

Source: Leslie T. Wilkins, Jack M. Kress, Don M. Gottfredson, Joseph C. Calpin, and Arthur M. Gelman (1978). *Sentencing Guidelines: Structuring Judicial Discretion.* Washington, D.C.: U.S. Government Printing Office, p. xv.

than whites. Petersilia and Turner (1986) point out that sentencing guidelines are supposed to reduce discrimination, but not the disparities due to differential rates of offending. Blacks, they argue, have disproportionate rates of serious crime, and because of this the guidelines will generate higher sentences. In any case, the procedures have not been around long enough to form conclusions about the race (or class) aspects of sentencing guidelines.

Determinate Sentencing Statutory changes in favor of determinate sentencing (sometimes called "flat" or "fixed-term" sentencing) have been one of the more notable products of concern about sentencing practices. The first state to enact fixed-term sentencing was Maine, in 1975. California, Illinois, Indiana, New Mexico, and Washington (in its 1977 juvenile code) soon followed suit.

Determinate sentencing is advocated in many quarters as a solution to unfair (that is, excessively lenient or harsh) and disparate sentencing. It is supposed to eliminate judicial discretion but in some cases does so only after the judge has decided on a particular type of penalty (usually imprisonment). In other words, a judge is free to decide whether or not an offender should receive probation or some other penalty, but once the judge decides on prison, the law sets the term of imprisonment. The defendant serves a specified term with time off for good behavior; however, parole is abolished. In the federal system today, there is no parole.

Slightly different is the *mandatory* sentencing system. Here a minimum sentence is required for certain offenses, usually those involving armed, violent, repeat, or drug offenders. "In 25 states imprisonment is mandatory for certain repeat felony offenders. In 30 states imprisonment is mandatory if a firearm was involved in the commission of a crime. In 45 states conviction for certain offenses or classes of offenses leads to mandatory imprisonment; most such offenses are serious, violent crimes and drug trafficking is included in 18 of the states. Many states have recently made drunk driving an offense for

New York State appellate judges confer on cases before them. Most criminal cases do not result in appeals, although the number of criminal appeals has been growing steadily over the past two decades. Most appeals have to do with procedure and successful appeal of sentences is rare.

which incarceration is mandated (usually for relatively short periods in a local jail rather than a state prison)" (Bureau of Justice Statistics, 1988a:91). Maine and Illinois have combined mandatory and fixed-term sentencing. Other states have retained combinations of mandatory and indeterminate sentencing or have made sentences fixed-term but not mandatory (Bureau of Justice Statistics, 1983d:3).

As with any reform, this approach to sentencing has its critics. Some claim that discretion is not really curbed but is simply shifted from judge to prosecutor. Indeed, the California determinate-sentencing laws have been called a plea-bargainer's paradise, for they give prosecutors all kinds of leverage in securing guilty pleas (Alschuler, 1978:73). Rather than receiving sentences intended by reformers, offenders escape them through the bargaining process. In addition, some critics argue that the mandatory sentences are uniformly too high and, despite rhetoric to the contrary, will be avoided by prosecutors and judges because correctional resources are inadequate to handle the influx of new prisoners (Foote, 1978:133–141).

A study of the Indiana experience with determinate sentencing is instructive. The 1977 penal code provides for certain specific terms of imprisonment for seven classes of offense, with enhancement for aggravation (such as use of a weapon or brutality) and reduction for mitigation (such as victim precipitation). Under the code, for example, the maximum possible sentence for a Class A felony such as armed robbery or forcible rape would be 30 years *plus* 20 years' enhancement for aggravation; the minimum would be 30 years *minus* 10 years' mitigation. Once in prison, the offender would be able to build credit toward future release in the form of "good time," thus reducing the actual time served (Clear et al., 1978).

The authors of the study point out that the code increases sentencing discretion in two ways. First, enhancement and mitigation rules greatly extend the bargaining flexibility of prosecutors who can play the carrot-and-stick game while pressuring for a plea. Under this system a lesser charge or fewer elements of aggravation add up to years off the sentence. Second, the use of credit time as the only way a sentence can be reduced once it is being served gives sentencing discretion to prison authorities. "Thus, a great deal of effective control over the inmate's sentence has been placed directly in the hands of the correctional officer who watches over him" (Clear, Hewitt, and Regoli, 1978:440).

"In fact," the authors continue, "that control has been formalized by the new law, and, even assuming the best intentions on the part of all concerned, the result may be a more repressive atomsphere for inmates" (p. 440). Not only that, the authors show what could happen to first offenders under the new code as compared with the old. Even assuming the offenders had earned all the available credit time, they would still end up serving an estimated 47.4 percent *more* prison time if sentenced under the new penal code. In the case of some offenses the percentage difference is more, in others less. In two cases—negligent homicide and check forgery—offenders would serve less time under the new system.

The authors' own conclusion best summarizes this study:

The new Indiana Penal Code provides such wide discretion, coupled with untenably heavy penalties, that a most likely result will be the creation and solidification of a formal system of decisions and rules that barely conceals a low-visibility, busy, and pragmatic system of informal decisions regulating the actual sentence, largely in the control of prosecutors, judges, and correctional officials. The new sentencing scheme may come to bear a strange resemblance to what reformers hoped to eliminate. (Clear, Hewitt, and Regoli, 1978:443)

Selective Incapacitation

The decision to send a felon to prison may be taken out of a judge's hands by statute, as may the length of sentence. However, whether by statute or by judicial discretion, many experts believe that these decisions should be guided by a formal policy. One policy that has attracted considerable attention has been recommended by Peter Greenwood and Allan Abrahamse (1982). It is called *selective incapacitation*.

As shall be seen in the next chapter, one of the ways in which punishment may prevent crime is to incapacitate the offenders, that is, to take them out of circulation. Imprisonment does this. Greenwood believes sentencing policies can be constructed to maximize this function of imprisonment for whom it is most needed: offenders who are most likely to commit crimes if released. Incapacitation would therefore be selective: "some offenders would be imprisoned for a longer period than others convicted of the same offense, because of predictions about their *future* criminality" (J. Cohen, 1983:3).

Greenwood (1984; Greenwood and Abrahamse, 1982) studied robbery and burglary inmates in California on behalf of the Rand Corporation. He found that robbers who had *four or more* of the following characteristics committed an average of 31 robberies per year on the street, compared with an average of 2 robberies per year for inmates with only one of these characteristics:

1. Prior convictions for robbery or burglary.
2. Being incarcerated for more than half of the preceding 2 years.
3. Juvenile conviction prior to age 16.
4. Commitment to a State or Federal juvenile facility.
5. Current heroin or barbiturate use.
6. Heroin or barbiturate use as juvenile.
7. Employed less than half of the preceding 2 years, excluding jail time. (1984:6)

Selective incapacitation policy would use this seven-item "scale" as the basis for setting prison terms at sentencing.

Advocates of selective incapacitation believe one of its major advantages is that judges would be able to base sentencing decisions on information most relevant to the crime proneness of convicted offenders rather than on a hodge-podge of information and opinion, much of it irrelevant to gauging the risk of sending them to prison for short terms, or not at all. By incarcerating the "right" offenders, the community would be spared the large number of crimes that otherwise would have been committed. At the same time, those offenders identified as low risk would benefit by avoiding long-term imprisonment.

Opponents of selective incapacitation have both pragmatic and moral objections (J. Cohen, 1983; von Hirsch, 1984). A common ethical objection is that two persons convicted of the same offense deserve a similar punishment. Another opponent questions whether it is fair to send a person to prison for crimes not yet committed. On the practical side, there are serious doubts whether accurate predictions of future criminality can be made. Indeed, the errors that have appeared in past efforts suggest that around half the offenders evaluated as high risk in fact are not. A methodological objection to the Greenwood approach helps explain why many experts lack confidence in it: He studied only incarcerated offenders and based his predictions largely on self-reported information. It has not been established whether the same results would hold with offenders at large, and as Jacqueline Cohen (1984) points out: "At sentencing, one could not confidently rely on information provided by the offender."

Samuel Walker (1985:62–63) makes a rather different criticism of selective incapacitation. He observes that according to the proposed seven-point scale, unemployment carries the same weight as prior conviction offense and all the other items. It is therefore possible for a person's unemployment to make the difference between jail or prison. He goes on:

> It is outrageous that anyone could seriously recommend imposing criminal penalties for unemployment. But that is precisely what the Rand formula does. The policy would take us back 300 years to the days of imprisonment for debt. . . . The Rand data are undoubtedly correct: unemployment does correlate with criminal activity. The way to deal with that problem—the rational, effective, and humane way—is to provide employment.

The controversy about selective incapacitation rages on, all the more so because it has received considerable publicity. As with all efforts to curb judicial discretion, there will be some judges who welcome the assistance in a most difficult task and others who reject it as unwarranted infringement on their role. In the last analysis, the daily sentencing decision may be more influenced by the system's capacity to handle criminals than by any formal policy (Pontell, 1984).

Intermediate Sentences

In recent years more and more alternative criminal sanctions have been explored. These alternative "intermediate" sentencing options are often advocated as a means to reduce the high cost of imprisonment, but they may also have rehabilitative possibilities. First-offenders and those convicted of property crimes are considered good prospects for these programs because they are bad risks for probation, but not so dangerous that they require imprisonment. Critics of current penal practice (e.g., Morris, 1991) believe that too many offenders are sent to prison who would be better handled in the community and that, conversely, too many offenders are given probation who should be placed in a more controlled environment. Intermediate punishments are advocated as a solution to these problems.

The public is often skeptical of such programs. Some people believe that anything less than imprisonment is too lenient. Nonetheless, the programs are generally designed to be safe, punitive, and inexpensive. Some even allow for restitution to victims and for community service (Petersilia, 1987).

Three examples of alternative sanctions reviewed by Petersilia (1987) involve a "shock" program, restitution, and electronic surveillance. The Oklahoma Regimental Inmate Discipline (RID) Program was developed at Lexington Correctional Center in Oklahoma. This "shock" treatment centers around a "boot-camp" for young first offenders. Offenders undergo rough physical conditioning, stringent dress codes, minimal idle time, and vocational testing which can build self-esteem and a sense of responsibility. Authorities hope offenders will be impressed by the seriousness of their crimes and "shocked" or deterred from future crimes.

The Texas Residential Restitution Program is for felony offenders who are employable. Offenders acquire employment and pay victim restitution from earnings along with a room and board fee. During off-work hours they perform community service. They are evaluated by the court every three months for a period of six months or more. The offender is released to intensive probation if successful in this program.

The San Diego Electronic Surveillance Program allows low-risk offenders to go to work and to perform necessary business such as going to court, but confines them to their homes during the rest of the time. An electronic transmitter strapped to the ankle or wrist emits signals to a dialer/receiver within a 150-foot range. Computers monitor the signals and will indicate if the offender has left that range.

The sanctioning process itself will be discussed in detail in the next chapter. If they become widespread, the new sentencing initiatives may change the punishment picture for years to come. At present, however, they remain under evaluation and are unlikely to displace the conventional penalties of probation, fines, and imprisonment for most felony offenders.

Summary of Chapter 11

This chapter has explored the judicial process through which criminal defendants pass after they have been arrested by the police on felony charges. The major decisions concern bail and pretrial detention, the nature of charges, whether or not to prosecute, the plea and plea negotiations, trial and jury selection, sentencing, and appeal. Defendants sometimes play a major role in decisions concerning pleas, trial, and appeal but have little, if any, role in bail determination, prosecution, and sentencing. The major actors in the judicial drama are, of course, attorneys, and it is only through jury duty that most citizens can expect to have much impact on the outcome of a particular case.

This does not mean that the judicial process is unaffected by public sentiments or by the lobbying efforts of private citizens. A prosecutor or judge who violates powerful special interests or widely cherished values is liable to feel the impact of the mistake, and since in America these judicial positions are tied to the electoral process, decisions are not easily divorced from political and economic influence.

Aside from external influences, the judicial process is subject to internal influences, some of which stem from its bureaucratic context. The reciprocal obligations of police and prosecutors, and of prosecutors, defense attorneys, and judges, create an environment in which actors must play by the rules if they are to survive and prosper. Among other things, the rules help to ensure that the judicial system accomplishes its formal objective—punishing guilty defendants—with minimal strain and resistance. Bargain justice thrives in part because it helps in the accomplishment of this objective, but also because all parties (even some crime victims) see that the copping of pleas can be made to serve their interests: The prosecution secures a conviction, judicial resources are freed up, police suspicions are confirmed, and defendants are punished less than they would otherwise have been, a deal that happens to save defense attorneys considerable time and effort, which the typical defendant could not pay for anyway.

The judicial process is not a game, but it surely has winners and losers. At sentencing the most likely losers are minority members with lengthy criminal records; the winners are white collar offenders without criminal records but whose crimes are often far more costly to society. It is certainly a matter of debate whether justice is served in either case. Efforts to reduce judicial discretion in turn may create new opportunities and incentives for injustice. Many people advocate bringing victims back into the judicial process (see Chapter 1), but even this strategy can do little to address inequities in the system that are rooted in larger socioeconomic conditions, or in the nature of bureaucratic organization itself.

Recommended Readings

Jonathan D. Casper (1972). *American Criminal Justice: The Defendant's Perspective.* Englewood Cliffs, N.J.: Prentice-Hall.

William F. McDonald (1985). *Plea Bargaining: Critical Issues and Common Practices.* Washington, D.C.: U.S. Department of Justice.

Douglas W. Maynard (1982). *Inside Plea Bargaining: The Language of Negotiation.* New York: Plenum.

Allison Morris (1987). *Women, Crime, and Criminal Justice.* Oxford: Basil Blackwell.

Joan Petersilia (1987). *Expanding Options for Criminal Sentencing.* Santa Monica, Calif.: Rand.

Henry N. Pontell (1984). *A Capacity to Punish.* Bloomington, Ind.: Indiana University Press.

Chapter 12

Punishing the Criminal Offender

The two preceding chapters discussed how the police and courts process criminal suspects. This chapter investigates what happens to those who are found guilty of crimes. At the outset it should be noted that most criminals are never caught, and many of those who are apprehended end up being filtered out of the system before penalties can be applied. For most crimes, punishment is actually the exception rather than the rule.

The Definition of Punishment

Punishment can be defined as any action designed to deprive a person or persons of things of value because of something that person is thought to have done. Examples include "liberty, civil rights, skills, opportunities, material objects, less tangible forms of wealth, health, identity, life, and—perhaps most crucial—significant personal relationships" (Turk, 1969:19).

Criminal Punishment

There are three major categories of criminal punishment. The first, *official criminal penalties*, consists of punishments provided for by law and imposed by lawful representatives of a state, community, or group according to the directives of law. Examples of official criminal penalties are fines, prison terms, probation, and the death penalty.

The second category can be designated as *extralegal penalties*. These punishments, though not illegal, are not provided for by law nor designated as punishments to be applied by officials of the state. Extralegal criminal penalties are diverse. Examples are refusal to marry someone because of his or her criminality and harassment of a prisoner by a guard.

The third category consists of *illegal penalties*. These are punishments that are themselves illegal (such as torture) or that are applied illegally (such as the lynching of a convicted murderer).

The Relativity of Punishment

Punishment is relative, first, in the sense that what is a deprivation for one person or group may not be for another. For example, although most people would probably consider a stay in jail as a significant deprivation, this view may not be held by everyone or by members of other societies. Second, it is relative in the sense that different people may have different views on which deprivations are more severe than others. Although most people would probably consider a jail sentence a more severe penalty than a fine, this view is apparently not shared by everyone. It is not uncommon for skid-row drunks to see fines as far more punitive than workhouse or jail terms (Lovald and Stub, 1968:525–530). For one thing, they see a jail sentence as an opportunity to recuperate from the ravages of their lives; a fine, on the other hand, means giving up drinking money.

Punishment is also relative in terms of its imposition and the sorts of deprivations involved. There are variations in the degree to which certain punishments are used. Some are used more frequently than others, and there are variations in the amount of deprivation depending on time, place, and situation. Like crime, punishment is affected by law, politics, culture, social structure, and situation.

Legal Punishment: Justification and Aims

When convicted criminals are punished today, they are punished by the state in the name of its people. Crimes are conceived of as public wrongs, and in criminal law the state is the victim. The real injury to the real victim of a crime is formally ignored. The state prosecutes, the state adjudicates, and the state determines the possible penalties. The result, Bittner and Platt (1966:81) suggest, is that punishment has become "an abstract measure of justice," in that the penalty for a crime is not assessed in terms of the real harm experienced by its immediate victims. This situation raises the need for a moral justification of punishment that goes beyond victim compensation. Over the years, two major arguments have been offered in support of legal punishment. The first stresses the ideas of moral responsibility and just deserts; the second justifies punishment in terms of its capacity to deter or to reform. Both perspectives seek to justify legal punishment in general and in its particular application.

Retribution: The Justice Model of Punishment   It is a mistake to believe that retribution is synonymous with revenge. According to its advocates, retribution emphasizes justice and due process, not the subjective passions of punishers seeking vengeance. Punishment is deserved when responsible people are guilty of willfully violating the moral order of the society in which they claim membership. For its part, society has the moral right, and the duty, to punish the guilty. It has the right to punish because the integrity of its moral order has been violated; it has the duty to punish because not to do so negates the very idea of crime and renders moral responsibility meaningless. None of this means that penalties will necessarily be severe. A distinguished panel of educators and lawyers concluded that the only just system of punishment is one based on retribution and proposed a maximum penalty for all crimes of five years imprisonment except for murder (von Hirsch, 1976:136).

Retributivists see only one possible basis for justifying particular penalties for particular crimes. A particular penalty is justified when the guilty person has received a punishment matching the gravity of the offense. The two issues of guilt and making the punishment fit the crime provide the grounds for arguing that any particular legal punishment is a "just desert."

But how does society make the punishment fit the crime? Various possibilities have been offered: (1) Make the punishment mirror the crime itself (*lex talionis*, an eye for an eye); (2) adjust the severity of penalties according to the social harm resulting from different offenses; and (3) link the penalties to the moral outrage or indignation felt by a majority of citizens.

From a practical standpoint, none of these proposals would be easy to follow. What kinds of penalties would accurately mirror robbing a bank of $20,000 or possessing 2 grams of heroin? On what basis are things considered socially harmful, and who makes the relevant judgments? Moral outrage may offer more hope, in that public sentiments can be tapped. In one attempt, wide agreement was found in rating the seriousness of 141 offenses (see p. 12). Even so, a practical problem arises: Two identical acts might generate different degrees of outrage, depending on their circumstances. Should society expect judicial authorities to poll the public every time a criminal conviction is handed down? Surely this would be the only just way to deal with the problem of moral indignation.

The Utilitarian Doctrine: Deterrence and Prevention   Today few people in the public eye speak of retribution when addressing the problem of punishment. This is certainly due in part to the popular misconception that retribution stands for revenge. The emphasis today is almost always on punishment as a means of preventing or reducing crime.

One of the first to outline this view was the Italian philosopher Cesare Beccaria (1963) writing in the second half of the eighteenth century. Although ambiguous on many points (see Newman and Marongiu, 1990), Beccaria was extremely concerned about the rampant injustices in eighteenth-century penal practice. Yet he saw, too, that crime was apparently escalating and that something had to be done. Punishment, applied rigorously but fairly, he thought, had to be the answer.

A just punishment, in Beccaria's view, is one that is proportionate to the offense *and* sufficient to outweigh the pleasure derived from it. The second part is important, for it lies at the heart of the *utilitarian* doctrine, which Beccaria espoused, and helps explain how punishment is thought to prevent crime.

Simply put, the utilitarians argued in favor of a guiding principle: the greatest happiness of the greatest number. Any action can produce pleasure or happiness for someone, just as it can also produce pain. Whereas crime produces pleasure for its perpetrator, it produces pain for others—considered a bad or evil thing by utilitarians. Punishment also brings pain, and so it, too, is a bad thing. Yet if punishing the criminal prevents crime, the group as a whole is given more pleasure at the expense of those whose behavior is bad in the first place. One can justify the use of punishment along utilitarian lines, then, if the group as a whole is better off.

This brings us to the ways in which punishment is conventionally thought to prevent crime. First, punishment is a way to *reform* criminals so that they will not commit crimes in the future. The original penitentiary was an early application of the idea that punishment reforms. Second, punishment is a way to prevent crime by *incapacitating* offenders so that they are in no position to engage in criminal activity. Death, banishment, and other penalties that remove an individual from access to opportunities to commit crimes are incapacitating penalties.

Third, there is the question of *deterrence*. The early utilitarians, especially Beccaria and Jeremy Bentham (1948), believed that punishment could be made to deter individuals from committing crime. Like Beccaria, Bentham believed that punishment was justifiable if it prevented crime. The important remaining question is: How? The answer, they believed, was obvious: Since people seek pleasure and avoid pain, they will tend to avoid those things that bring pain, especially if pain outweighs pleasure. Accordingly, punishment can prevent crime by threat of pain. Simply put, people are scared away from crime by fear of the consequences.

Official Criminal Penalties

The range of legal punishments throughout history has been vast. Not so long ago the list included all sorts of things: torture, branding and other public humiliations, maiming, deportation, banishment, loss of property, corporal punishment, forced labor, coerced penitence, self-denial, and, of course, death.

In this section, three major types of legal punishment's will be reviewed: (1) removal from the group, (2) shaming, and (3) fines. *Intermediate* punishments were discussed in Chapter 11.

Removal from the Group: Death

Death, banishment, transportation, and imprisonment are examples of removal penalties; they remove individuals from their familiar social worlds, if not from life itself.

In early criminal codes, death was the penalty for a wide range of offenses. Both the ancient Mosaic code and that of Hammurabi prescribed death for witchcraft, incest, kidnapping, certain forms of theft, and negligence. In Greece, Rome, and among the Germanic tribes governed by the laws of Tacitus, death was also a common penalty, and Durkheim (1900:65–93) noted its extensive use by the ancient Egyptians, Assyrians, and Hindus. Death was usually inflicted by stoning the condemned. In his fascinating book, *Death Work: A Study of the Modern Execution Process*, Robert Johnson (1990:6) writes:

> The impression to be gained from the Bible, which includes accounts of a number of stonings, a few of them impromptu, is that those executed in this manner somehow came to terms with their terrifying punishment, bearing their fate with some resemblance of dignity. And terrifying those executions must have been. Following the lead of witnesses, the citizens would arm themselves with stones and surround the offender, perhaps also taunting and ridiculing him before launching their onslaught of bruising rocks; they would only stop when the offender's bloody and lifeless form lay buried under the

stones. In this manner, the community would act as one, cleansing itself of the guilt of the criminal and putting things right with God.

It has been said that during the reign of Henry VIII, 72,000 people were executed, many of them for trivial offenses (Calvert, 1971:4). The popularity of this penalty seems to have reached a peak during the sixteenth century, when it dropped off only to rise again by the end of the eighteenth century. At that time, England had more than 200 capital offenses. The list of capital crimes included arson, rape, sodomy, murder, forgery, highway robbery, pocket picking, shoplifting, burglary at night, stealing horses, cattle, and sheep, setting fire to coal mines, cutting down trees in a public avenue, destroying silk or velvet in the loom, sacrilege, mutiny, desertion, concealing the death of a bastard child, sending threatening letters, and returning from exile (Blackstone, 1962). Until well into the nineteenth century, it was not uncommon for children to be hanged. By the 1840s, however, things took a turn away from death as the principal penalty. "Only" 20 offenses were designated as capital crimes, and the execution of children was abolished.

In America, capital punishment has traditionally been reserved for a mere handful of crimes in comparison with England. Even so, the death penalty was not limited to violent and heinous offenses, for one of its earliest uses was as a punishment for sacrilege and witchcraft.

Until recent times executions were generally carried out in public. As if it were not enough to die, often miserably, the condemned were made a public spectacle, which often had all the trappings of a family picnic, a fair, and even a wedding (see Hay et al., 1975:114). Yet the often cruel and public aspects of capital punishment were conditioned by history and culture and based on what authorities felt were both reasonable and practical considerations. A particularly heinous crime would bring its perpetrator a crueler death than would, for example, a simple case of robbery.

Why execute in public? Here again there was reason behind the procedure. The issue was framed in terms of *deterrence* and *moral education*. The idea was that witnessing executions would deter observers from committing capital crimes by exploiting their fear of death. It also would reinforce the belief that their crimes were indeed wrong, sinful, and damnable.

John Lofland (1977) suggests that the contemporary Western way of executing personifies the art of concealment, thereby losing any deterrent effect it might otherwise have, besides depriving the condemned the opportunity to publicly display courage and dignity at the time of death. In America, the condemned are permitted few visitors; the time of execution is inconspicuous (for example, five o'clock in the morning); the place of execution is secluded; few witnesses are allowed; the technique is reliable, fast, and relatively quiet; the executioner is anonymous and impersonal; the announcement is terse; and the body is removed quickly.

By past practices, the modern execution process probably appears humane. However, some critics believe this is nothing more than an illusion— the dispassionate, ritualistic, impersonal, assembly-line procedures "actually make modern executions distinctively brutal and dehumanizing" (Johnson, 1990:25). Robert Johnson (1990) has written a vivid and eloquent account of modern executions, an excerpt from which is reproduced in Box 12.1.

Executions in America   Many countries have abolished the death penalty altogether. In 1972, it looked as if the United States might never execute again. The last execution had been in 1967, and then in 1972 the Supreme Court ruled in *Furman* v. *Georgia* that the death penalty violated the Eighth Amendment's prohibition of "cruel and unusual punishment." However, a majority of judges did not object to the death penalty per se but to the arbitrary and often discriminatory way that it was applied. This left the door open for legislatures to enact new statutes to meet the Court's objections. In January 1977, Gary Gilmore was killed by firing squad in a shed outside the Utah State Prison, the first execution in ten years. By January 1991, 143 executions had taken place (most in the South), and nearly 2500 inmates are currently on death row (see Figure 12.1). Among the 35 states that now allow capital punishment, most laws prescribe it for murder during a sex offense (all 35 states); murder for gain (all); murder of a police officer (all but one); and murder during a kidnapping (all but one). Twenty states authorize the death penalty for persons who have a previous murder conviction. In the federal system, a new crime bill passed by Congress in July 1991 extended the death penalty to over 20 new offenses, including drug-related killings, and also contained provisions for banning nine types of semiautomatic assault weapons.

Of the 4002 executions between 1930 and 1991, just under 90 percent were for murder, with rape accounting for most of the remainder. Nearly 2300 executions occurred in the South, as did all but 12 of the 455 executions for rape. Overall, more blacks than whites have been executed, and nearly 90 percent of those who died for rape were blacks. Since 1976, not one white person has been executed for killing an African-American. Of the 16,000 documented executions in U.S. history, only 30 involved a white sentenced to death for killing a black (*Time*, April 4, 1991:68).

These data clearly raise questions of racial discrimination. The charge of racial discrimination has been the main issue in the National Association for the Advancement of Colored People's (NAACP) long fight to have the death penalty abolished. Evidence accumulated from 1930 to 1960 seemed to support its contention (see Wolfgang and Riedel, 1973:119–133). Following careful analysis of data going back as far as 1890, William Bowers (1974:102) believes that the findings point "unmistakably to a pattern of racial discrimination in the administration of capital punishment in America." That discrimination has been concentrated in the South, he argues, where blacks have been executed for less serious crimes, as well as for crimes less often punished by death (such as rape) when committed by whites. Further, the blacks who have been executed were generally younger than their white counterparts and were more often executed without appeals.

Box 12.1 ■ The Execution

At 10:58, Jones entered the death chamber. He walked quickly and silently toward the chair, his escort of officers in tow. Three officers maintained contact with Jones at all times, offering him physical support. Two were stationed at his elbows; a third brought up the rear, holding Jones's back pockets. The officers waiting at the chair described the approaching Jones as "staring off in a trance, with no meaning in his stares. It was like he didn't want to think about it." His eyes were cast downward. His expression was glazed, but worry and apprehension were apparent in the tightly creased lines that ran across his forehead. He did not shake with nerves, nor did he crack under pressure. One could say, as did a fellow witness, "Anybody who writes anything will have to say he took it like a man." But a scared and defeated man, surely. His shaven head and haggard face added to the impression of vulnerability, even frailty.

Like some before him, Jones had threatened to stage a last stand. But that was lifetimes ago, on death row, with his fellow condemned to lean on. In the death house, alone, Jones joined the humble bunch and kept to the executioner's schedule. At the end, resistance of any kind seemed unthinkable. Like so many of those before him, Jones appeared to have given up on life before he died in the chair. His execution, like those of the men who preceded him, was largely a matter of procedure.

That procedure, set up to take life, had a life of its own. En route to the chair Jones stumbled slightly, as if the momentum of the event had overtaken him, causing him to lose control. Were he not held secure by the three officers, he might have fallen. Were the routine to be broken in this or, indeed, any other way, the officers believe, the prisoner might faint or panic or become violent, and have to be forcibly restrained. Perhaps as a precaution, when Jones reached the chair, he did not turn on his own but rather was turned, firmly but without malice, by the officers in his escort. Once Jones was seated, again with help, the officers strapped him in.

The execution team worked with machine precision. Like a disciplined swarm, they enveloped Jones, strapping and then buckling down his forearms, elbows, ankles, waist, and chest in a matter of seconds. Once his body was secured, with the electrode connected to Jones's exposed right leg, the two officers stationed behind the chair went to work. One of them attached the cap to the man's head, then connected the cap to an electrode located above the chair. The other secured the face mask. This was buckled behind the chair, so that Jones's head, like the rest of his body, was rendered immobile.

Only one officer on the team made eye contact with Jones (as he was affixing the face mask), and he came to regret it. The others attended to their tasks with a most narrow focus. Before the mask was secured, Jones asked if the electrocution would hurt. Several of the officers mumbled "no" or simply shook their heads, neither pausing nor looking up. Each officer left the death chamber after he finished his task. One officer, by assignment, stayed behind for a moment to check the straps. He mopped Jones's brow, then touched his hand in a gesture of farewell. This personal touch in the midst of an impersonal procedure was, in the warden's opinion, an attempt to help the officer himself live with the death penalty. The warden noted that it also by implication helped the team of which he was a part. "It's out of our hands," the gesture seemed to imply. "We're only doing our job."

During the brief procession to the electric chair, Jones was attended by a chaplain from a local church, not the prison. The chaplain, upset, leaned over Jones as he was being strapped in the chair. As the execution team worked feverishly to secure Jones's body, the chaplain put his forehead against Jones's, whispering urgently. The priest might have been praying, but I had the impression he was consoling Jones, perhaps assuring him that a forgiving God awaited him in the next life. If Jones heard the chaplain, I doubt that he comprehended his message. At least, he didn't seem comforted. Rather, he looked stricken and appeared to be in shock. Perhaps the priest's urgent ministrations betrayed his doubts that Jones could hold himself together. The chaplain then withdrew at the warden's request, allowing the officers to affix the mask.

The strapped and masked figure sat before us, utterly alone, waiting to be killed. The cap and mask dominated his face. The cap was nothing more than sponge encased in a leather shell, topped with a metal receptacle for an electrode. Fashioned in 1979 in replica of a cap dating back to the turn of the century, it appeared decrepit, presumably from sitting in brine for a number of years. It resembled a cheap, ill-fitting toupee. "It don't fit like a normal hat," said the officer responsible for securing this piece of hardware to the prisoner, in a matter-of-fact tone, "it's for a person with no hair." The mask, also created in 1979 and modeled on a turn-of-the-century original, was made entirely of leather. Somehow it, too, looked well-worn, perhaps because it was burned in places—from saliva that had spilled from the mouths of some of the executed prisoners, then been brought to a boil by the heat of the electricity coursing through the chair and its appurtenances. The mask had two parts. The bottom part covered the chin and mouth; the top, the eyes and lower forehead. Only the nose was exposed. The effect of the rigidly restrained body, together with the bizarre cap and the protruding nose, was nothing short of grotesque.

A faceless man breathed before us in a tragicomic trance, waiting for a blast of electricity that would extinguish his life. The internal dynamics of an electrocution are quite profound. As the electrician affiliated with the team made clear to anyone who would listen, in one swift and violent instant twenty-five hundred volts of electricity, at five to seven amps, shoot through the body, starting at the head, passing through the brain, then on to the heart and other internal organs, some of which explode, before the current comes to ground through the ankle. Jones presumably did not know the details, but the general picture is vividly impressed in the minds of all condemned prisoners facing death by electrocution.

Endless, agonizing seconds passed. Jones's last act was to swallow, nervously, pathetically, his Adam's apple bobbing. I was struck by that simple movement then and can't forget it even now. It told me, as nothing else did, that in Jones's restrained body, behind that mask, lurked a fellow human being who, at some level, however primitive, knew or sensed himself to be moments from death.

Jones sat perfectly still for what seemed an eternity but was in fact no more than thirty seconds. Finally, the electricity hit him. His body stiffened spasmodically, though only briefly. A thin swirl of smoke trailed away from his head, then dissipated quickly. (People outside the witness room could hear crackling and burning; a faint smell of burned flesh lingered in the air, mildly nauseating some people.) The body remained taut, with the right foot raised slightly at the heel, seemingly frozen there. A brief pause, then another minute of shock. When it was over, the body was inert.

Three minutes passed while the officials let the body cool. (Immediately after the execution, I'm told, the body would be too hot to touch and would blister anyone who did.) All eyes were riveted to the chair; I felt trapped in my witness seat, at once transfixed and yet eager for release. I can't recall any clear thoughts from this time. One of the officers later volunteered that he shared this experience of staring blankly at the execution scene. Laughing nervously, he said,

It's a long three minutes. It hits him and then you wait. The [current] goes on a couple of times. And you wait three minutes after the machine goes off; the doctor comes in and checks him. You just, you just, you just watch the whole thing. There's nothing really (pause) going through your mind.

Had Jones's mind been mercifully blank at the end? I hoped so.

Source: Robert Johnson (1990). *Death Work: A Study of the Modern Execution Process*. Pacific Grove, Calif.: Brooks/Cole, pp. 109–111. Reprinted by permission.

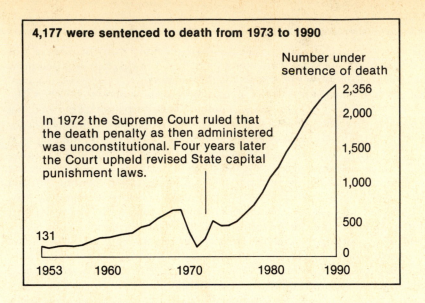

4,177 were sentenced to death from 1973 to 1990

Number under
sentence of death

2,356

2,000

In 1972 the Supreme Court ruled that
the death penalty as then administered
was unconstitutional. Four years later
the Court upheld revised State capital
punishment laws.

1,500

1,000

500

131

0

1953   1960   1970   1980   1990

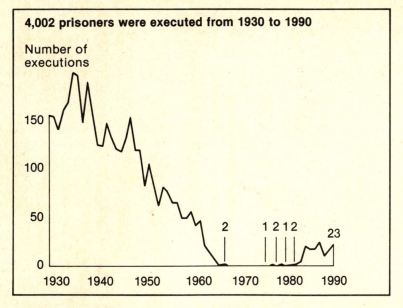

4,002 prisoners were executed from 1930 to 1990

Number of
executions

150

100

50

2   1 2 1 2   23

0

1930   1940   1950   1960   1970   1980   1990

FIGURE 12.1   The Death Penalty in America: Recent History.   *Source:*
Bureau of Justice Statistics (1991d). *National Update.* Washington, D.C.: U.S.
Department of Justice, p. 4.

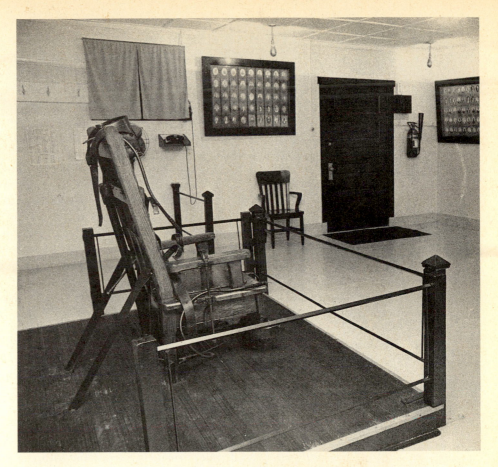

The Ohio electric chair photographed in 1973. Note the framed pictures of condemned prisoners executed in Ohio. Fifteen American states and many foreign countries have abolished the death penalty altogether.

A finding of racial discrimination at the aggregate level does not inevitably mean that the practices of individual courts are discriminatory. The U.S. Supreme Court ruled in *McCleskey* v. *Georgia* (1987) that while the link between the victim's race and the death penalty was established at the system level, this did not mean that in an individual case the death sentence was given only because the victim was white. Although this is true, civil rights advocates are concerned that the preponderance of white prosecutors and white judges and the relative rarity of black-on-white homicide raise the risks of discrimination. In Columbus, Georgia, for example, prosecutorial discretion to seek the death penalty is held in the hands of four white men, who have exercised it most often (78 percent of the time) when victims were white, despite the fact that in Columbus, blacks are victims 65 percent of the time (*Time*, April 4, 1991:69).

The picture from the northern and western regions of America shows considerably less evidence of racial discrimination, but those who are executed are characteristically of low social status. Robert M. Carter (1965) has drawn a composite sketch of the men executed in California over the years, and it shows a person who from early childhood has had little going for him. Thirty-four years old when executed, the death penalty victim comes from a rural background of poverty and alcoholism. He will have been tagged delinquent at an early age, will drop out of school by age 14, and leave a broken home by age 17. With few occupational skills he will drift from job to job and will soon be arrested for some unsophisticated, unplanned property crime. When he is convicted, his young marriage will break up and he will again be in and out of jobs and jail. Back to crime, this time with a partner, he will be arrested again, this time getting five years in prison. Out in two years and on parole with no marketable skills, he will work intermittently, drink more, and begin to think of himself as worthless, a no-good bum. The culmination of a life devoid of love and security comes quickly, as the frustrated criminal is found pulling a robbery for fast money, killing the gas station operator in the process. Caught 3 days later, he is sentenced to death and executed two years, eight months, and 28 days after his arrest.

Public Opinion and the Death Penalty   Public opinion surveys show that a majority of Americans favor the death penalty for some crimes. During the 1970's support of capital punishment grew steadily. Polls by the Gallup organization show that in 1970, 60 percent of respondents favored the death penalty for people convicted of murder. By 1982, the figure was 74 percent, and it has remained stable since then (Maguire and Flanagan, 1991:200–201). Joseph Rankin (1979) believes the high level of support reflects the emergence of a "law-and-order syndrome," resulting from heightened concern about violent crime. There was much publicity during the 1970s about rising rates of violent crime, and periodic reports of mass murderers hardly eased a worried public's fears.

Some people favor mandatory death sentences for certain offenses, for example, the killing of police officers. Among other things they believe that such an approach would prevent discrimination in the administration of the death penalty. On the other hand, both the spirit and the intent of mandatory death sentences can be circumvented through the discretionary charging that rests in the hands of prosecutors. The question is moot, in any case, for the U.S. Supreme Court ruled in *Woodson* v. *North Carolina* (1976) and again in *Roberts* v. *Louisiana* (1979) that mandatory death sentences violate the Eighth Amendment.

In 1986, the U.S. Supreme Court furthered the cause of death penalty advocates by ruling that "death qualified" juries are not unconstitutional; that is, opponents of the death penalty may be excluded from juries hearing capital cases. Since juries composed of people who support the death penalty are considered more prone to convict, this step is seen as increasing the likelihood that more convicted criminals will find themselves on death row.

TABLE 12.1 Types of felony sentences imposed by state courts, 1988

Most Serious Conviction Offense	Percent of Felons Sentenced To:						
		Incarceration			Nonincarceration		
	Total	Total	Prison	Jail	Total	Probation	Other
All	100%	69%	44%	25%	31%	30%	1%
Murder[a]	100	95	91	4	5	5	—
Rape	100	87	69	18	13	13	—
Robbery	100	89	75	14	11	11	—
Aggravated assault	100	72	45	27	28	27	1
Burglary	100	75	54	21	25	25	—
Larceny[b]	100	65	39	26	35	34	1
Drug trafficking	100	71	41	30	29	28	1
Other felonies	100	62	35	27	38	37	1

[a] Includes nonnegligent manslaughter.

[b] Includes motor vehicle theft.

Note: For persons receiving a combination of sentences, the sentence designation came from the most serious penalty imposed—prison being the most serious, followed by jail, then probation. "Prison" includes sentences to death. Sentence designation "other" includes unknown sentences (0.7% of cases). Less than 0.5%.

Source: Bureau of Justice Statistics (1990). *Bulletin: Felony Sentences in State Courts, 1988.* Washington, D.C.: U.S. Department of Justice, p. 2.

Removal from the Group: Imprisonment

Today, some form of imprisonment is imposed on the vast majority of convicted felons (see Table 12.1). However, ancient societies rarely used physical detention, and when they did it was not as a punishment in itself but, rather, (1) as a means of pretrial detention and surveillance, (2) because offenders had not paid their fines, or (3) because secure physical confinement was necessary if certain kinds of penalties (torture, execution, banishment) were to be imposed.

Today the essential accomplishment and raison d'être of prisons is simply to deprive offenders of their freedom. This modern conception of imprisonment gained ground during the eighteenth century, as penal reforms took shape both here and abroad.

Development of Prisons in America   The Walnut Street Jail in Philadelphia is usually identified as America's first state prison and its first penitentiary. Opened in 1773, the jail received its first state prisoner in 1790. This historic occasion rewarded the hard work and dedication of a group of Pennsylvania citizens, many of them Quakers. These citizens abhorred the cruelty and degradation of existing punishments and felt that an alternative could be devised that was both humane and reformative. The group embraced the

Quaker view that criminals should be made to contemplate the evil of their ways in unrelieved solitude. Under conditions of solitary confinement day and night, inmates would immerse themselves in self-reflection and penitence—or so they asserted. Work, necessary for regeneration of the spirit, would be performed alone in one's cell.

Built inside the existing jail structure, the new penitentiary was an awesome place. Crude efforts were made to segregate women, capital offenders, and debtors, vagrants, and other petty criminals. The inmates were housed individually in tiny whitewashed cells measuring 6 feet wide, 8 feet long, and 9 feet high. A small grated window could be seen high up on the outside wall, and the toilet amenities consisted of a lead pipe in the corner of each cell. The convicts were preached to on a regular basis but were denied any form of recreation. For their part, the guards were forbidden to use chains, irons, weapons, or canes.

Ten other states soon constructed prisons along the lines of Philadelphia's Walnut Street Jail. Although particular procedures varied somewhat from state to state (in Massachusetts, for example, the guards were issued guns, bayonets, and cutlasses), the basic architectural design was the same, as was the emphasis on enforced solitude. Eventually, overcrowding in most of these early prisons forced administrators to give up the idea of solitary confinement for all. Instead, it was used more and more for those who had violated prison rules.

Support for a penitentiary system embodying solitary confinement was reaffirmed in the 1820s when the Pennsylvania legislature authorized two new prisons—Western Penitentiary in Pittsburgh and Eastern Penitentiary in Philadelphia. The structures were monolithic, the cells small and ranged along the outside walls, and the solitude, for all intents and purposes, was total. Charles Dickens, on visiting Eastern Penitentiary, wrote of the inmate: "He sees the prison officer, but with that exception he never looks upon a human countenance or hears a human voice. He is a man buried alive; to be dug out in the slow round of years; and in the meantime dead to everything but torturing anxieties and horrible despair" (cited in Goldfarb and Singer, 1973:26).

The "Pennsylvania System" was tried and soon abandoned in New Jersey and Rhode Island. These states turned instead to what is known as the "Auburn System," after Auburn Prison in New York. In that prison, opened in 1817 but enlarged and modified by 1823, inmates were locked in separate cells at night but worked together in small groups during the day. Complete silence was maintained both day and night, however, and regimentation was complete. The prison contained tiered blocks of tiny cells with narrow galleries encircling them. All was surrounded by an outside wall of stone over 2½ feet thick. Almost all early American prisons were fashioned after Auburn. In contrast, most European and Southern American countries adopted the Pennsylvania system.

Another example of early prison design, this time from England, was the Panopticon Plan created by Jeremy Bentham. Called a "dinosaur of the penal world" by Goldfarb and Singer (1973:32), there are nevertheless some living examples, one at Joliet, Illinois. Basically, the panopticon consists of tiers of cells arranged along the outside of a larger circular structure. Besides the innovative architecture, Bentham had plans for heating, care of prisoners, health and educational services, and food and clothing as well. As it turned out, however, Bentham found few takers.

The Reformatory Movement   From around 1870 to the early twentieth century, the so-called reformatory movement held sway in American corrections. The movement's principles were outlined at the first meeting of the American Prison Congress in 1870, and included the idea that *reformation rather than suffering* should be the cornerstone of penal practice and that *indeterminate sentences* should be adopted to enable authorities to release early, or keep longer, those inmates who had succeeded, or failed, in demonstrating rehabilitation. Inmates were to be put into three classes, depending on their achievements and conduct: (1) First Grade, meaning that they had earned sufficient "marks" to make them eligible for parole; (2) Second Grade, mostly for new entrants who had not yet shown their true colors; and (3) Third Grade, for those whose disobedience and lack of improvement suggested the need for sterner measures.

The first prison organized to apply these principles was the Elmira Reformatory in New York, opened in 1876. Elmira was primarily designed for young first offenders, 16 to 30 years old. Its superintendent was Zebulon Brockway, a confident and determined administrator who left no stone unturned in his efforts to prove the success of this new penology (Brockway, [1912] 1969). Encouraged by early results and the prospect of succeeding in the battle against crime, other states soon followed suit, and by 1913 some 18 state reformatories had been organized around the country.

Yet the old style of harsh prison discipline, hard labor, and strict regimentation continued to dominate prison life. At least 16 major state prisons of the Auburn variety—including Menard in Illinois, Folsom in California, Walla Walla in Washington state, and Brushy Mountain in Tennessee, all in operation today—were opened between 1870 and 1900. By the 1900s the reformatory movement was on the decline. It failed for a number of reasons: (1) lack of high quality leadership and staff, especially in the key area of education; (2) continued acceptance, despite the rhetoric, of the idea that the prison experience should be punishing; (3) lack of recognition that reformation and architecture might somehow be related—the reformatories were by and large monolithic stone fortresses; (4) overcrowding, which led to a breakdown in already clumsy efforts at classification, grading, and behavior modification; (5) overemphasis on the custodial functions of prison by administrators; and perhaps most important, (6) lack of official commitment to the movement in the form of supporting policy and resources.

Prisons Today   In America today one sees an agglomeration of prison philosophies, goals, and architectures. There has, in fact, been little consequential innovation over the last 50 years. With the exception of so-called community corrections, discussed in a later section, the form and character of incarceration are pretty much what they were decades ago.

There are some 250 prisons housing adult offenders and administered by either state governments or the Federal Bureau of Prisons. In 1969 an attempt at classification was made. At that time, about 708 percent of the 214,000 inmates were housed in "work-oriented" prisons, about 23 percent in "rehabilitation-oriented" institutions, and about 7 percent in "special-function" institutions such as prison hospitals. Thirty-one of the rehabilitation prisons housed women, 58 housed men. Of the 77 maximum security prisons in 1969, 12 were built before 1850, 33 between 1850 and 1899, and 32 since 1900 (Goldfarb and Singer, 1973:49). In 1976, some 50,000 adult felons were serving time in maximum security prisons built before 1900. That figure represents almost one-fifth of all adult inmates in state and federal prisons on any day that year (Hawkins, 1976:42).

At year's end in 1990 there were 771,243 state and federal prisoners (Bureau of Justice Statistics, 1991j). This represents an overall growth rate of 133.8 percent since 1980. (see Figure 12.2). The South shows the highest rates

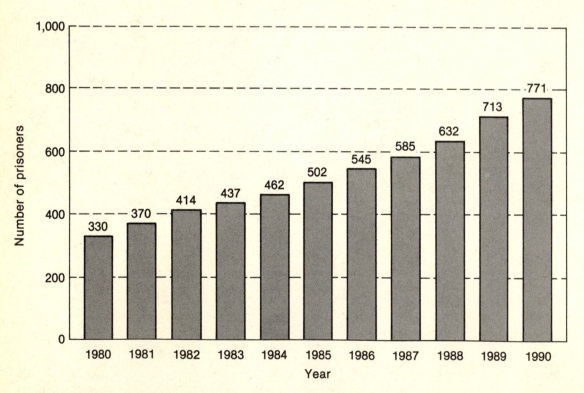

FIGURE 12.2 American Prison Population. On December 31 each year (1000s). *Source:* Bureau of Justice Statistics (1991j). *Prisoners in 1990.* Washington, D.C.: U.S. Department of Justice.

TABLE 12.2   Lifetime probabilities of being imprisoned

		Estimated Chance		
Males	from	1 in 40	to	1 in 25
Females		1 in 588		1 in 370
White males		1 in 67		1 in 42
White females		1 in 556		1 in 409
Black males		1 in 10		1 in 6
Black females		1 in 167		1 in 100

Source: Bureau of Justice Statistics (1985j). *Special Report: The Prevalence of Imprisonment.* Washington, D.C.: U.S. Department of Justice.

of imprisonment, with 315 inmates per 100,000 population, compared with 232 in the Northeast. There is also considerable variation from state to state. The rates for North Dakota and Minnesota were 67 percent and 72 percent, respectively. At the other extreme were South Carolina (451), Maryland (347), Louisiana (427), Nevada (444), and Washington, D.C. (1,125).

It has been estimated that the lifetime probability of any particular American between the ages of 13 and 84 serving time in a state prison is from 1 chance in 77 to 1 chance in 48. However, the risks are not borne equally, as Table 12.2 shows. The highest probabilities are for black males, the lowest for white females. Joan Petersilia (1985a) found in California that a strong predictor for receiving a prison term is the number of prior adult crime convictions. Offenders with *three or more* of the following characteristics had an 80-percent chance of going to prison:

- Current conviction on two or more counts
- Two or more prior adult convictions
- Being on parole or probation when arrested
- Being a drug addict
- Being armed in the current case
- Using a weapon in the current case
- Seriously injuring the victim

Around the nation, males account for roughly 93 percent of prison inmates. Most are under age 30, and a majority have not graduated from high school. Although a majority of inmates were employed during the month before arrest, their jobs were nearly always manual or lower-skill service work, with wages rarely above minimum. Nearly half America's prison inmates have never been married. This profile has not changed materially since the first comprehensive survey in 1974. What *has* changed over the years is the proportion of prison inmates who are African-American. As Figure 12.3 shows, white and black prison admissions have been converging for most of the Twentieth century. Black rates of imprisonment have become increasingly disproportionate, due, one suspects, to their greater rates of

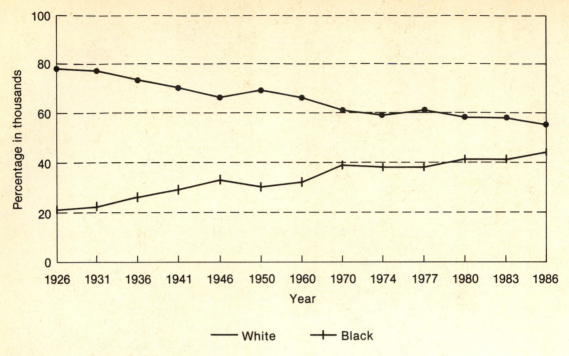

FIGURE 12.3 Prison Admissions, 1926–1986. State and federal, by race. *Source:* Graph compiled from data in Patrick A. Langan (1991). *Race of Prisoners Admitted to State and Federal Institutions, 1926–1986.* Washington, D.C.: U.S. Government Printing Office, p. 5.

violent crime and, recently, to the government crackdown on street drug trafficking, which largely affects the inner cities.

Most inmates in state prisons are serving time for robbery, burglary, or homicide. In the federal system drug offenses and bank robbery account for 75 percent of the prison population. The difference reflects the fact that most street crimes are handled in state courts, whereas bank robbery is a federal crime, and intense federal law-enforcement effort is currently directed at drug trafficking.

Prison terms handed down in court are quite misleading as a measure of the punitiveness of American penal practice. First, the experience in prison varies considerably from prison to prison and in any case cannot be predicted merely by knowing the sentence. Second, the actual time served by most offenders is much shorter than the length of their sentence. Where sentences to state prisons are concerned, the average time served for a felony conviction is two years. By contrast, the average prison sentence is nearly seven years (Bureau of Justice Statistics, 1990d:3).

One penologist, John Conrad (1975), sees the rise in inmate populations as stemming from a new "hard line" in the administration of justice. He believes that the hard line reflects various things; first, an escalation in public anger at the criminal; second, an increase in public disenchantment with social meliorism, represented in part by widespread use of probation and parole and in the recent advocacy of community corrections; and, third, rising crime rates in urban areas have helped exacerbate already high levels of social conflict in the cities. Once again the law-and-order syndrome noted earlier with respect in the death penalty is manifesting itself.

Women in Prison Although the proportion of total prison inmates who are female has not changed dramatically since the early 1970s (from 4 to 5.7 percent), the female inmate population grew faster than the male population during the 1980s (Bureau of Justice Statistics, 1991i:7).

Men and women prison inmates are similar in most respects, although women are more likely to have been married and less likely to have been employed prior to incarceration. The racial breakdown is virtually identical: 57 percent are African-American. However, female violent offenders are much less likely than their male counterparts to have had prior correctional sentences or prior convictions as either juveniles or adults. Women are also more likely than men to have been incarcerated for property and drug offenses (Bureau of Justice Statistics, 1991i).

This may reflect sex-role bias in sentencing (see pp. 416–417) in that the instant offense seems to be a more important determinant of imprisonment for women than it is for men. Another way in which women and girls suffer unfairly in the correctional process is in the facilities and programs available to them. Gordon (1991:3) argues that the adult female inmate "has been ignored in terms of facilities, programs, and security," a charge that has also been levied at juvenile detention (e.g., Chesney-Lind, 1988).

Jail as Punishment Jail time is generally used as punishment only for those convicted of misdemeanors and petty offenses. Sometimes a judge will allow time spent in jail while awaiting trial and sentencing to be counted toward the eventual sentence. If less than a year is left for a felony offender, that time will usually be served in a county jail.

The 1987 Annual Survey of Jails (Bureau of Justice Statistics, 1988f) discovered that 295,873 people were being held in the nation's 3493 jails. Of these, 52 percent had not been convicted of a crime. These inmates were awaiting formal adjudication proceedings; most had simply been unable to make bail. The remaining 48 percent were serving sentences, awaiting transfer to prison or other correctional facility, or involved in postconviction proceedings. The majority of jail inmates are young men in their early twenties. Most have not completed high school. Slightly less than half are black, and only 8 percent are women.

Urban jails in general are overcrowded places lacking even modest amenities. Critics contend that jail time is generally more punitive, dangerous, and degrading than time in a maximum security prison. There is, in addition, the mixing of technically innocent people with convicted offenders,

In the United States, local jails house over 300,000 inmates on any given day. Less than half of those detained in jails are actually serving a sentence. Many urban jails are overcrowded and dangerous, and inmates are often mixed together indiscriminately.

not to mention petty offenders with hardened criminals. Experienced convicts say they would rather do time in prison than in jail.

Shaming

Arrest, prosecution, trial, conviction, and the levying of penalties are all punitive responses to transgressions of the criminal law, even though only the last is specifically designed to punish. The entire criminal process is punitive because it stigmatizes and degrades defendants in the eyes of others, for example, parents, friends, neighbors, school officials, fellow workers, and employers. In so far as an experience lowers a person's esteem or reputation in the eyes of others, *shaming* has taken place. John Braithwaite (1989a:57–58) describes shaming as follows:

> It can be subtle: a frown, a tut-tut, a single comment, a turning of the head, a laugh; it can be a direct verbal confrontation in which the offender is admonished about how guilty she should feel or how shocked her relatives and friends are over her conduct; it can be indirect confrontation by gossip which gets back to the offender; it can be broadcast via the mass media or by

a private medium (as when the feminist paints a slogan on the front fence of a rapist); it can be officially pronounced by a judge from the bench or by a government which names a wrongdoer in an official report or in the chamber of the legislature; it can be popularized in mass culture by a film which moralizes about a certain act of wrongdoing.

Historically, shaming and criminal punishment have been explicitly coupled. For example, branding and mutilation flourished during the medieval period, and they were used in colonial America for a variety of offenses: burglary, robbery, religious crimes, and hog stealing (Earle, 1969). Until the nineteenth century, the stocks and pillory were used extensively in England and America for such minor crimes as drunkenness, disorderly conduct, prostitution, blasphemy, lying, swearing, and threatening. In Sweden, miscreants were sometimes tied on a wooden horse and left to be ridiculed by their neighbors (James, 1817:236–239).

Although Western society no longer brands, maims, or pillories its criminals, many nations still incorporate shaming as part of legal punishment. For example, certain offenses carry automatic penalties that deprive offenders of civil rights or common privileges: citizenship, employment, inheritance, and even marriage (Damaska, 1968).

Shaming is a key element in probation and parole, although most people probably do not think of these penalties as particularly punishing. The degradation may be less public, but probationers and parolees experience it nonetheless. Although conditions vary depending on jurisdiction, probationers and parolees have been told they cannot marry without permission; they must attend church; they cannot spend their earnings on certain things; they must not drive a car; they must dress a certain way; they must not smoke or drink; they must not travel certain distances or to certain places (Imlay and Glasheen, 1971; Czajkoski, 1973). In short, they are required to lead an exemplary life, much more so than ordinary citizens. But even while they are exhorted to get control of their lives, they are denied effective control over their daily affairs. In effect, the conditions of probation and parole may undermine an already fragile sense of worth and lower the individual's esteem in the eyes of others. The risk is that rather than fostering independence and self-control, parole and probation lock the individual into a condition of dependency (see Erickson et al., 1973).

Braithwaite (1989a:59–60) contends that Western societies have systematically uncoupled punishment and shaming by removing most of the public aspects from the penal process. To be sure, this was partly done because of the cruelty of onlookers during whippings, executions, and other public punishments (Babbington, 1968:13), but it has removed opportunities for the criminal to receive his deserts with courage and dignity witnessed by the community, and for the community to participate in the process of reconciliation. As we shall see in a later section of this chapter, Braithwaite believes that shaming should be brought back into the penal process in a special way.

Medieval punishments included the pillory. Used primarily for petty offenses, this uncomfortable and humiliating punishment exposed offenders to public ridicule—and sometimes rocks, bottles, and vegetables hurled at them by onlookers.

Financial Penalties

Today fines are the most commonly imposed criminal penalties. Although no accurate national data exist, estimates usually place fines at about 75 percent of all criminal convictions. In other countries, too, the fine is the most widely used criminal penalty (Davidson, 1965; Gillespie, 1980).

The fine has existed in penal law for centuries. Under early law monetary payments in the form of damages or compensation were made to the victims of wrongs. Monetary compensation eventually replaced the long-standing tradition of self-help justice that allowed victims to retaliate directly against those who wronged them, often with disruptive and bloody consequences. By the thirteenth century, the king received the payments in criminal cases, and victims of wrongs could receive compensation only through civil courts. The growing popularity of the fine is partly explained by the fact that financial penalties were an important source of revenue for the royal treasury.

Today, fines are regarded with favor because they are inexpensive to impose, can be paid back if wrongly imposed, can be readily adjusted according to the gravity of the offense and the financial capacity of the offenders, and can be substituted for more stigmatizing and incapacitating punishments such as imprisonment.

Interest in the fine as a penalty for more serious crimes has gained strength in recent years as a result of prison overcrowding and heavy probation caseloads (Hillsman et al., 1987). A survey of 126 judges around the country found that most imposed fines routinely, often in combination with other penalties. First offenders with ability to pay were the most likely people to be fined. The offenses ranged from sale of an ounce of cocaine to auto theft, embezzlement, and passing bad checks (Hillsman et al., 1987:2).

In justifying why he rarely imposed fines, one judge said, "After paying $56 in court costs, $10 fee to the Crime Victim Compensation Fund, $200 public defender fee, and $100 to $500 in probation supervision fee, the defendant will be sufficiently punished" (Hillsman et al., 1987:3). When asked what sentence they would likely impose on a 24-year-old, single, male janitor with three previous larceny convictions who pleads guilty to shoplifting a $40 pair of slacks, very few judges picked a fine only, while most opted either for jail or prison time alone, or for incarceration *plus* a fine.

Much of the current criticism focuses on the use of jail and prison terms as penalties imposed for nonpayment of fines and on the built-in inequities that characterize monetary punishments. Studies show, for example, that around 50 percent of those fined end up in jail or prison for nonpayment. These are usually the poor. In effect, the imposition of fines discriminates against those with low incomes and insecure financial status. Further, nonpayment often entails additional suffering avoided by those who can pay their fines. A jail term may mean loss of job and loss of housing, not to mention the multitude of other deprivations incurred through incarceration. By contrast, fines are a relative boon to those who can afford them and thus avoid alternative punishments. Fines are imposed extensively in cases involving consumer fraud, antitrust violations, and a host of other occupational crimes. For the middle-class offender or the corporation, a fine is often akin to a slap on the wrist and, in light of prevailing criminal stereotypes, merely reinforces the view that it is the "dross of society," the "dangerous classes," who belong in jail.

Fines are often given together with other penalties: Sometimes they are levied with jail time, and sometimes offenders placed on probation are also fined. Although they are the most common penalty, however, little systematic research exists on the use and effects of fines. A recent effort by Gordon and Glaser (1991) looked at fining in municipal courts of an urban California county. The authors compared three situations: fines levied alone, fines given with jail time, and probation given alone. Not surprisingly, money penalties without jail were most likely to be given to low-risk offenders. The single most important determinant of type of sentence and the amount of any fine was the seriousness of the offense. However, a second consideration influencing the amount of any financial penalty was the offender's employment status: Those who could afford to pay were fined more than those who could not.

The authors took these various findings as evidence that municipal judges in this county, at least, were acting rationally. Furthermore, they argue that the "light touch of the law" represented by most fines is more worthwhile than jail time since the odds of an offender being subsequently arrested and jailed for a new offense are lower for those fined than for those given jail time. This may largely reflect the fact that jail time almost certainly results in loss of employment.

How Punishment Can Prevent Crime

Jack Gibbs (1975:57–93) identifies ten different ways that punishment can prevent crimes. First, certain forms of punishment *incapacitate* potential offenders by removing or diminishing their opportunities to commit crimes. Incapacitation is absolute when an offender is executed but is relative for other forms of punishment. Consider imprisonment: Although putting someone behind bars reduces the opportunity to commit crimes, it does not rule out all manner of offenses and may actually encourage some, for example, homosexual rape.

Second, some punishments can prevent crimes because they place offenders under *surveillance*. The conditions of probation and parole often have this effect. Surveillance can prevent crimes simply because it increases the visibility of an offender's behavior. Gibbs acknowledges, however, that surveillance of probationers and parolees probably does not prevent a substantial amount of crime. However, recent experimentation with electronic monitoring of probationers and parolees is heralded by some as a breakthrough in preventive surveillance (see Lilly, Ball, and Wright, 1987). Transmitters strapped to offenders' ankles emit signals that warn officials that the wearer has moved outside permissible territory or has removed the device (see Ford and Schmidt, 1985).

Enculturation is the third preventive mechanism associated with punishment. The idea is that people acquire knowledge that a certain behavior is illegal by experiencing, witnessing, reading about, or being told of the punishment for doing it, and this knowledge furthers their respect for the law. Simply put, people refrain from committing a criminal act because they have learned that it is wrong or bad through the punitive response to it.

The fourth crime-preventive mechanism of punishment is *reformation*, the idea that the experience of punishment alters an offender's behavior: He or she "no longer contemplates criminal acts." Essentially, the argument is that punishment conveys a sense of shame and remorse to some offenders, and this promotes subsequent conformity. Even an arrest, Gibbs notes, may produce a "moral jolt," as seen in the case of amateur shoplifters.

In his discussion of reformation, Gibbs (1975:72) notes that the terms reformation and rehabilitation have usually been considered interchangeable. He argues that "the meanings of the terms should be distinguished. Criminal *rehabilitation* is the alteration of an offender's behavior by nonpunitive means, so that he or she no longer violates laws. Criminal reformation is the alteration of an offender's behavior through punishment, so that he or she no longer violates laws" (p. 72). As discussed in the preceding chapter, early American prison systems clearly emphasized reformation of offenders. Modern correctional practice tends to favor the rehabilitation of offenders, at least in principle. Work release programs and halfway houses are examples.

The fifth way in which punishment can prevent crime is through *normative validation*. This notion echoes an argument advanced many years ago by Emile Durkheim (1964a, 1964b). He saw punishment as the opportunity to reaffirm, and possibly intensify, condemnation of an act. Indeed, this is a "function" of punishment, according to Durkheim. When society punishes, people are reminded that the rule of law is valid, that the violation of it continues to be condemned.

The sixth alternative is *retribution*. This may come as a surprise, especially since the previous discussion specifically distinguished between punishment as retribution and punishment as crime prevention. Gibbs asserts that when there exists a demand that the guilty be punished, not to do so would encourage private vengeance, the extreme form of which is armed vigilantism. The "subway vigilante," Bernard Goetz, exemplifies what Gibbs has in mind.

Stigmatization is Gibbs's seventh crime-preventive mechanism in punishment. Because it identifies a perpetrator as "criminal"—often publicly and dramatically—punishment "thereby becomes a *criterion* for subsequent social condemnation" (1975:84). An individual may refrain from crime not because of the punishment itself but, rather, because of the anticipated stigmatization. Presumably, the stigmatizing impact of public punishment is greater than that of private or secretive punishment. Another important issue is that stigmatizing effects may be linked to class or ethnic status: Blacks, Hispanics, and low-income people "are less prone to view punishment as a stigma than are upper-class Anglos," Gibbs (1975:85) suggests.

The eighth preventive mechanism is *normative insulation*. Consider Edwin Sutherland's theory of differential association: that people may learn attitudes and values favorable to law violation in their intimate associations with others (see pp. 522–526). The more one associates intimately with persons who are not law-abiding, the more one is likely to adopt their normative orientation. If one could somehow escape their influence, perhaps one's own normative orientations would be more law-abiding. In Gibbs's view, at least three punishments have the effect of insulating society from the normative influence of offenders: execution, imprisonment, and banishment.

Habituation, the ninth way in which punishment is thought to prevent crime, has been discussed by Zimring and Hawkins (1973:85), among others. These authors argue that people develop the habit of conforming to law.

Punishment comes in because it contributes to both the development and maintenance of habits. Efforts to reduce the speed at which Americans drive on the nation's highways illustrate the effects of habituation. By all accounts, many drivers are not abiding by the speed limit, but driving *is* slower than it was before national speed limits were lowered in 1973, especially in states with systematic enforcement. Though it is difficult to separate habituation from deterrence, habituation is implied when drivers tend to follow speed limits in the absence of patroling police or after enforcement has abruptly ended for some reason.

Deterrence is the tenth way in which punishment can prevent crime. Before discussing this preventive mechanism, it is appropriate to ask whether any of the preceding nine mechanisms have been shown to work effectively. Gibbs's presentation is rather discouraging here, for it is clear that there has been little research on any of them. Gibbs also makes it clear that research to establish if and how they work is obstructed by conceptual and methodological problems, especially when efforts are made to identify the effects, if any, of deterrence.

Obviously, if one thinks only of individual offenders who are caught and convicted, then incapacitation through execution would be a sure way to prevent *their* further criminality. It is preposterous to suggest this remedy for all types of offenses, and it would certainly be rejected by some even for premeditated murder. For any other type of punishment, incapacitation is a matter of degree. Among other conventional penalties imposed in the Western world, only imprisonment can be considered incapacitating, and then only temporarily in most cases. Indeed, it is possible that in some instances a prison sentence provides opportunities to acquire additional skills and abilities that may be put to criminal use upon release. It is doubtful that this is a major consequence of imprisonment, but the idea is part of conventional wisdom.

One of the ways teachers, judges, and other authorities attempt to explain their choice of punishment is by saying: "I'm going to make an example out of you!" This remark may be thought of as an attempt to raise fear in others who are potential offenders; in this case one would correctly think of deterrence. There is more to the remark, however, for the speaker is alerting others to the fact that punishments such as this *will be* applied to wrongdoing. The intended audience—a class of schoolchildren, workers in a factory, people in general—are reminded how they ought to behave and what the appropriate reaction will be if they do not. This is normative validation.

In the minds of many, normative validation is the hidden agenda in punishment. If society can reinforce and perhaps intensify conformity to the law, then there will be less violation of it. Gibbs (1975:82) argues, however, that:

> [i]f punishments validate laws and thereby reduce the crime rate, they do so only to the extent that they are publicized. But in the United States and many other countries, actual punishments are not publicized systematically, and the citizenry is informed only at the whim of the news media. The situation is

all the more remarkable because publicizing punishments might further both normative validation and deterrence.

One might well ask, Has normative validation been given a chance? The answer is probably no.

A Closer Look at Deterrence

In the preceding section, deterrence, the tenth way in which punishment can prevent crime, was discussed in general terms. A more detailed discussion is in order for two reasons: (1) There appears to be widespread belief that it works, a view held by many experts as well as by members of the public; and (2) deterrence has become a major research focus in criminology, giving it not only scientific standing as a cause célèbre, but also a tremendous amount of empirical scrutiny, which is not the case with the other nine preventive mechanisms.

It has become conventional to distinguish between *specific* (or *individual*, or *special*) deterrence and *general* deterrence (Andenaes, 1974). The distinction recognizes two classes of potential offenders who may refrain from crime because they fear punitive sanctions: (1) those who have directly experienced punishment for a crime or crimes they committed in the past— specific deterrence; and (2) those who have not experienced punishment but are deterred from crime by the threat of punishment—general deterrence.

The distinction is important because the deterrent effect of experienced punishments may be quite different from that of threatened punishments. Even so, not all authors agree with this conventional distinction between specific and general deterrence, and it in no way exhausts the typological possibilities. For example, Gibbs (1975) distinguishes between *absolute* and *restrictive* deterrence. Some people refrain from a particular criminal activity throughout their lives because they fear punishment (absolute deterrence), whereas others may modify or curtail their criminal activities for a period of time because they see a growing risk of punishment if they persist (restrictive deterrence).

Properties of Punishment: Severity, Certainty, Celerity

In their early work, Beccaria (1963) and Bentham (1948) made a significant contribution to the development of ideas about deterrence when they focused on three properties of punishment. They recognized that criminal penalties can be more or less *certain*, more or less *severe*, and more or less *swift* in their imposition. They believed that the deterrent impact of punishment will be greater the more certain, severe, and swift the penalties. Of the three properties, severity of punishment was considered less important than the others, and this idea fit the growing view in the late eighteenth century that penalties were too harsh, while suggesting an alternative policy focus on certainty and swiftness.

Does Punishment Deter?

Deterrence is probably the most widely researched of any single issue relating to penal practice. Yet experts would probably agree that we are still a long way from establishing an answer to the question: Does punishment deter? The inability of the scientific community to substantiate or reject the conventional wisdom that punishment deters—especially if it is swift, certain, and severe—must be difficult for many people to understand. Most of us can think of anecdotal illustrations of deterrence, but serious researchers have found the going very rough indeed. Indeed, scholars are still hotly debating basic methodological questions (for example, see Gibbs and Firebaugh, 1990).

It seems that the more scientists delve into the problem the more complex it becomes. For many years, researchers focused only on the "objective" side of the issue. For example, do rates of particular crimes correlate inversely with variations in the properties of penalties actually imposed on offenders? If robbery rates are higher in communities where penalties imposed are less certain or severe, and lower in communities where penalties are more certain or severe, this was regarded as evidence in support of the deterrence argument. The most that can be said of this research is that few studies demonstrated support for deterrence, and when they did, it was a moderate to weak association between crime rates and the objective certainty of punishment. It will certainly interest some readers to learn that more than 50 years of research has yet to uncover a deterrent effect for capital punishment (see Beyleveld, 1980; Archer and Gartner, 1984; Peterson and Bailey, 1991).

There are many different ways of researching the relationship between objective properties of punishment and crime rates, and probably all of them have been tried at least once (for good summaries, see Gibbs, 1975; Blumstein, Cohen, and Nagin, 1978; Beyleveld, 1980). Because of the many variations in data and methods, however, the findings are rarely directly comparable. Furthermore, it is now recognized that deterrence is really a social psychological theory, properly tested only with evidence on perceptions—a subjective, cognitive phenomenon (Erickson, Gibbs, and Jensen, 1977:305). The essential mechanism presumed to restrain a potential offender is fear of the threat of punishment. This fear is grounded in people's knowledge or beliefs about what happens to those who commit crimes.

Over the past 20 years much research has attempted to probe the perceptual side of the deterrence model. Here, again, the issue has proven to be more complex and intractable as more is learned. It has become apparent, for example, that the threat of formal sanctions (such as imprisonment) is less salient a concern than the threat of *informal* sanctions imposed by relatives, friends, co-workers, or other close acquaintances (see Tittle, 1980; Braithwaite, 1989a; but see Minor, 1978). Shlomo Shoham (1970:9) was one of the first scholars to argue this point:

> The fear of stigma is probably much stronger than the fear of punishment for the average law-abiding citizen. He is afraid of losing his job, of being ostracized by his business associates and friends, of the possible alienation of members of his family, of having to leave his neighborhood or even his town.

To demonstrate that deterrence works on the perceptual level it is necessary to show that individuals who have not committed a crime did not do it out of fear of punishment. This is a tall order for various reasons, one of which is simply this: "deterrence is inherently unobservable. . . . We do not observe others refraining from a criminal act because of fear of punishment" (Gibbs, 1975:13–15). At best, evidence of a deterrent effect can only be inferential. Furthermore, if we ask people who recall having contemplated committing a crime why they did not follow through (surely every adult?), a recollection referring to possible penalties does not rule out other compelling reasons (for example, recognition that the act was illegal, or too difficult, or "not worth doing," or simply "not right"). Indeed, research on the decision-making of criminals (see pp. 541–552) finds that all sorts of situational factors structure decisions and that worries about punishment are apparently not high on the list.

The claim that fear of punishment deters must also address the problem of causality. Although some researchers have tried to place the relevant variables in the right causal order—fear of punishment precedes the decision not to commit a crime—this is generally done by asking people to reconstruct past events or to predict future behavior. Since perceptions apparently do not remain stable over time (Minor, 1978), there are serious questions as to the validity of findings based on this kind of research.

While criminologists struggle with these various problems, the research on perceptual (and objective) deterrence continues. Once again, the overall picture is not promising for the deterrence doctrine—especially as it relates to formal punishments imposed by the criminal justice system. Concluding their review of recent "panel" (longitudinal) research, Nagin and Paternoster (1991:561) find generally "no evidence of a deterrent effect of either perceived certainty or severity of punishment."

Reintegrative Shaming   Before leaving the topic of deterrence it is worthwhile considering one more issue—shaming. As already noted, the stigmatization that accompanies arrest, conviction, and legal punishment may be more compelling as a deterrent than fear of the formal sanctions themselves.

Braithwaite (1989a) has capitalized on this idea and proposes that the process of shaming (see p. 450 for examples) be recoupled with punishment not simply as a potent deterrent to crime, but also as a mechanism of normative validation and conscience formation: "Shaming is a social process which leads to the cognition that a particular type of crime is unthinkable" (p. 81).

However, shaming by itself does not promise that an offender will develop a conscience, let alone commitment to the law. One-sided moralizing, as Braithwaite (1989a:81) puts it, does not encourage potential offenders to embrace the rules; more likely they feel estranged, cut off, or rejected from the group. Accordingly, Braithwaite advocates reintegrative shaming: The act of shaming is bound up with ceremonies of forgiveness and repentence in which offenders and the community participate and that strengthen the bonds that bind them. The "blame" is not suffered only by the offender but is borne also by the collectivity. The context for shaming is positive, supportive, even loving, rather than punitive, negative, and destructive. This, after all, is how children are effectively socialized within a family setting, and some societies—Japan, for example (see also Barlow and Ferdinand, 1992)—stress reintegrative shaming at all levels of society. Contrasting the American and Japanese responses to crime, Braithwaite (1989a:63) writes:

> The fact that convicted American offenders are more than twenty times as likely to be incarcerated as convicted Japanese offenders says something about the respective commitments of these societies to outcasting versus reintegration.

Braithwaite is careful to point out that some offenders may be beyond the influence of community shaming—some belong to subcultures of offending in which there are strong social supports for crime. Public chastisement produces no loss of esteem, and one's prestige may even grow as a result of criticism by authority figures. On the other hand, in communities where such subcultures do not exist or are emergent, a policy of shaming without reintegration may actually encourage the rise of criminal subcultures, because devalued individuals find solace with those who will accept them. And so Braithwaite advocates a penal policy of reintegrative shaming for all manner of miscreants; and if society must imprison, "maximum effort to integrate the prison with the community—work release, study release, easy access for family visits—is recommended" (Braithwaite, 1989a:180). We shall return to Braithwaite's important work in Chapter 17.

Reformation and Rehabilitation: Do They Work?

It has become conventional to speak of "corrections" when referring to incarceration or some form of direct supervision. Hence the American Correctional Association is primarily composed of professionals in prison, parole, probation, or community treatment jobs. The word *corrections* means just what one would expect: to put right someone who has gone wrong.

Needless to say, if one is trying to change someone it helps to have a firm idea of what "right" behavior looks like. In primitive societies, or in those headed by totalitarian regimes, it is relatively easy to assert what is right and wrong. Attitudes and behaviors tend to be cast in the same mold and are confined within narrow limits. In modern complex democracies, definitions of right and wrong, of what is and is not desirable, are harder to pin down and consensus is less likely. When there is no strongly entrenched sense of what right is, the goal of corrections is largely what those in charge say it is.

Despite these difficulties, it is conventional to use recidivism as a way of evaluating correctional outcomes. The word *recidivism* means "relapse into crime"; hence recidivists are those who once again commit crime. The *rate of recidivism* is the proportion of offenders in a population who relapse into crime after having experienced correction. Recidivism rates are used to measure the success of correctional programs.

Before examining recidivism, it should be pointed out that no one has yet isolated the effects of correctional efforts from other forces that affect the behavior of criminal offenders. Apart from the other possible consequences of punishment (incapacitation, deterrence, stigmatization, and the like), many things are likely to influence a person's behavior after release from a correctional institution. These are often beyond the control of correctional authorities: There is nothing they can do about an offender's past record of crimes, age at first offense, race or sex, job history, marital status, or any precorrectional experience. It is extremely difficult, therefore, to demonstrate any direct causal link between experiences with reformation or rehabilitation and subsequent recidivism.

Recidivism Recidivism is a relative matter, but this fact is hardly ever recognized. Offenders may relapse into more or less serious crimes than they committed before imprisonment; they may relapse into more or less frequent criminal activity; they may relapse almost immediately after they are released or only after a considerable time has elapsed. Visualizing recidivism in this way, as a matter of kind and degree, may help in the construction of specific rehabilitation and reform programs. Although the total eradication of recidivism is an impossibility, more reasonable designs might stress reduction in only certain forms of criminality (for example, violence) or in the probability that offenders will "graduate" to more serious crimes than those for which they have been punished.

Most studies of recidivism look at the proportion of offenders released from prison who are subsequently rearrested and/or returned to prison. Needless to say, this approach uncovers only those offenders who have been unfortunate enough to get caught. Two problems should also be mentioned. First, reimprisonment does not necessarily indicate that a person has committed a new crime. From a national sample of male parolees, David Greenberg (1975:551) found that "many of the returnees were sent back to prison for behavior that is not forbidden to the general public, for suspicion of an offense where guilt was not proved in court, and at least sometimes when the parolee had already been tried and acquitted." Only 25 percent of those returned to prison during their first year of release were reimprisoned for new felony offenses.

Second, low recidivism rates do not mean that inmates are "corrected." Even if problems of discovery are excluded—that is, of establishing whether or not they have committed new crimes—one cannot be sure that ex-inmates would have committed new crimes had they not been subjected to correction. Remember, correction is not the same as incapacitation, though it is usually attempted while offenders are incapacitated. The belief that much crime is prevented through incapacitation is strengthened by recent studies showing that nearly half of those reentering prison for new offenses would still have been in prison had they fully served their last sentence and therefore been unable to commit the new crime (Bureau of Justice Statistics, 1985c). But again, this is the incapacitative effect of imprisonment, not the corrective effect.

The figures on recidivism are not encouraging. An Illinois study of 1983 prison releases found that 48 percent were rearrested within 18 to 20 months after release, and 37 percent of those people were rearrested more than once. New property crimes accounted for 34 percent of the arrests, and violent crimes for 21 percent. Offenders with the longest criminal histories were those most likely to be rearrested (Illinois Criminal Justice Information Authority, 1985). A national survey of prison readmissions estimated that 29 to 38 percent of prisoners released for the first time would return to serve another term. Second-time prisoners had a 40 to 46 percent chance of returning, and third-time prisoners a 42 to 53 percent chance (Bureau of Justice Statistics, 1985c).

Prisons and Rehabilitation   There are several schools of thought concerning the connection between correctional efforts and recidivism. There are those who argue that reform and rehabilitation simply will not work in a prison setting. Part of the problem relates to prison organization and management: "Wardens are paid for running quiet prisons, not for reforming inmates. Any attempt to establish rehabilitation programs in prison are opposed by both staff and inmates because it makes life more difficult for all concerned" (Jeffery, 1977:88). Gordon Hawkins (1976:48) points out that "the actual experience of imprisonment for most persons imprisoned in this country in this century has been simply punitive." Furthermore, prisons isolate inmates from the communities into which they will later return, often by hundreds of miles. A 1971 survey by William Nagel (1973) found even the newest correctional facilities for men located in sparsely populated areas, far from the largest cities in their states. Prison construction is largely a matter of politics—it means money and jobs for some, danger and deviance to others—and almost never a matter of what is best for correctional efforts.

In the early 1970s, Badillo and Haynes (1972:178–179) observed that New York State could boast the highest concentration of psychologists and psychiatrists in the world. Yet the state's penal system had none on its regular staff, and there were only 60 for the entire American prison system. Further, of the nation's correctional budget, only five cents of every dollar was actually spent on "correcting" inmates. Badillo and Haynes concluded: "We do not have in America, and never have had, any rehabilitation program on a significant scale for a significant length of time." This is the "we haven't done enough" argument, and it has many adherents. The solution, they suggest, "is simply a more full-hearted commitment to the strategy of treatment" (Martinson, 1974:49).

From another side comes the view that physical confinement breeds its own version of tyranny, expressed in the relationship between guards and prisoners and among the prisoners themselves. Philip Zimbardo's well-known experiment in the basement of a Stanford University building has helped document what he calls the *pathology of imprisonment*. In this experiment, 24 "mature, emotionally stable, normal, intelligent college students from middle-class homes" (Zimbardo, 1972:4) were arbitrarily assigned

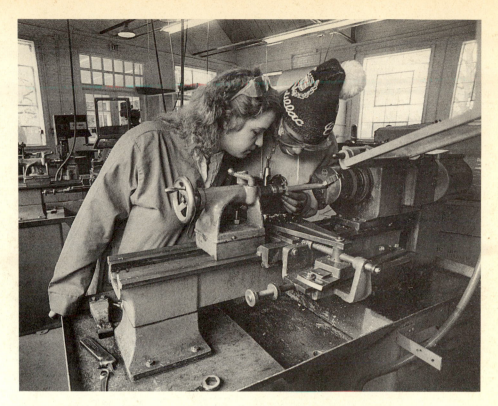

By and large, prison educational and training programs are poorly
funded and serve only a small proportion of inmates. Even so, most
experts agree that prisoners who participate have a better chance of
making it on the outside than those who do not.

as prisoners or guards. The guards were instructed to prepare rules for
maintaining law and order, and were allowed to improvise new ones as they
saw fit throughout the course of the experiment. Without warning, the
prisoners were picked up by real policemen at their homes, taken to the Palo
Alto police station, stripped, searched, handcuffed, fingerprinted, and then
blindfolded for the trip to the "jail."

The experiment was called off at the end of six days because "it was no
longer apparent to most of the subjects (or to us) where reality ended and their
roles began" (Zimbardo, 1972:5). The guards (students) and prisoners (students) adopted their respective roles in "every aspect of their behavior."
Initial solidarity among the prisoners eventually gave way to each man for
himself; some guards became tyrannical, while "good" guards stood by and
did nothing. Zimbardo (1972:7) observes:

> In a sense, the good guards perpetuated the prison more than the other guards
> because their own needs to be liked prevented them from disobeying or violating
> the implicit guards' code. At the same time, the act of befriending the prisoners
> created a social reality which made the prisoners less likely to rebel.

One manifestation of the tyranny of imprisonment has been the use of prisoners in research involving drugs, shock therapy, and even psychosurgery. In "Clockwork Orange in a California Prison," R. T. Trotter (1972) describes three brain operations performed in 1968 on inmates of Vacaville State Penitentiary. Richard Speiglman (1976) has documented the use in the California prison system of powerful depressants such as Thorazine, Prolixin, and Acetine. Whether in this form or in day-to-day prison life, the tyranny of confinement is viewed by many as antithetical to reform and rehabilitation. No amount of behavior modification, drug therapy, group counseling, or correctional techniques can overcome the pathology of imprisonment. "*Prisoners adjust to the environment of the prison, not to the environment of free men,*" C. Ray Jeffery (1977:86) claims; like many others he advocates the community, not the prison, as the key to rehabilitation.

Halfway Houses   One outgrowth of interest in community-based alternatives to prison has been the *halfway house* movement. Although it began over a hundred years ago with the purpose of providing temporary shelter, food, clothing, and counsel to ex-offenders, the movement really got going in the 1950s and early 1960s. Today no single description adequately conveys the myriad forms the nation's halfway houses have taken. Sometimes called community treatment centers, the facilities provide housing for psychiatric patients, delinquent children, alcoholics and other problem drug users, neglected children, homeless adults, and the mentally retarded, as well as criminal offenders.

Early halfway houses were not really part of the correctional system, but today there are close ties between the two, for these reasons: (1) recognition among those involved in community corrections that their very survival and success depend in large part on a close association with mainstream corrections and (2) increasing state and federal involvement in community corrections (McCartt and Mangogna, 1976b:554–555). The correctional bureaucracy is vast and now encompasses the community as well as the more traditional institutions.

Where community correction clearly has the edge over imprisonment is in the opportunity it provides for an offender's continuation of many of the social relationships that free people take for granted. Another particularly damaging aspect of imprisonment is that the removal of individuals from society interrupts their normal or expected progress through the cycles of life, especially those pertaining to work. Most inmates are young and would normally be embarking on a series of important economic and social "moves" in life to ensure their "making it." It is not the prison regimen or efforts at rehabilitation that really affect recidivism rates but, rather, the degree to which those important moves are interrupted. It is easy to fall behind in a highly technological age.

A measure of this nation's failure to take seriously the challenge of rehabilitation is the vast number of criminal offenders with whom virtually nothing constructive is done. Each year millions of offenders are placed on probation, and although this may be suitable and sensible in many cases, especially for minor miscreants, there is growing sentiment, and some evidence, that the widespread use of felony probation poses serious threats to public safety. Joan Petersilia's (1985b) study of California felony probationers shows that during a 40-month period after sentencing, 65 percent were rearrested and 53 percent were formally charged with new crimes. Those most likely to recidivate were property offenders, suggesting that correctional specialists would do well to take criminal histories into account when developing crime-prevention strategies.

In the face of steeply rising crime rates during the 1960s and early 1970s, it was easy to agree with Martinson (1974) that "nothing works." Support for a get-tough-while-being-fair "justice model" emphasizing deterrence and just deserts began to replace the treatment model as the cornerstone of penal policy. Some scholars now claim that Martinson's analysis was flawed (Mair, 1991), and debate over his famous conclusion is vigorous (see, e.g., Whitehead and Lab, 1989; D.A. Andrews et al., 1990; Lab and Whitehead, 1990). It remains to be seen whether real efforts will be made to resurrect rehabilitation, but the ambitious prison construction program now underway, the growth in prison and jail populations, and the toughening of criminal codes makes that resurrection unlikely for the foreseeable future. Prison is central to American crime control policy, not a last resort.

The Effects of Imprisonment: A Closer Look

There are those who charge that far from "correcting" criminals and preventing crime, prisons may actually be contributing to the rate of crime through their effects on inmates. In an age in which rationality is thought to rule, it would certainly be ironic if one of the major forms of punishment produced precisely what it was penalizing. The problem directs attention to what really goes on in prison.

The "Pains of Imprisonment"

In a study of life in a maximum security prison, Gresham Sykes (1958) wrote about the "pains of imprisonment." He observed, as others had before him, that prison means much more than mere deprivation of freedom. First, there is a deep sense of rejection by the free community. Every day the inmate remains cut off from society, he or she is reminded of this rejection and the psychological toll is heavy. Second, prisons are not hotels, as some seem to think. They are places of involuntary confinement that lack most of the amenities that free people take for granted. The prisoner lives under extreme material deprivation. In the larger society the possession and use of myriad goods and services is taken as a sign of one's status; not to have them, or not to be able to control their use, marks the individual as incompetent, a loser.

Deprivation of heterosexual relationships is a third pain of imprisonment. The inmate is "figuratively castrated by involuntary celibacy" (Sykes, 1978:523). Apart from physical pleasures there is the psychic pleasure that sex with a loved one involves; both are denied the inmates of most prisons.

Fourth, there is the deprivation of autonomy, the lack of independence that is typical of "total institutions" such as prisons, mental hospitals, and military installations. There are rules and regulations to cover virtually everything. Seemingly, the inmate's most trivial actions are brought under the control of someone else.

The fifth pain of imprisonment is forced association with other criminals, often for long periods of time and always under conditions of deprivation. This involuntary association has many aspects, but those likely to be most threatening are those that undermine an inmate's sense of physical security. In an analysis of prison violence, Hans Toch (1977:53) draws a stark picture of this facet of prison life:

> Jails and prisons . . . have a climate of violence which has no free-world counterpart. Inmates are terrorized by other inmates, and spend years in fear of harm. Some inmates request segregation, others lock themselves in, and some are hermits by choice. Many inmates injure themselves.

> The "testing out" of new arrivals by their peers leaves many a first offender feeling vulnerable. Rumors of danger are rife. In jails, inmates who have already spent time in the "pen," or who claim to know what happens there, spread horrifying tales about brutality. Recipients of such accounts arrive in prison expecting to struggle for their survival. Such fears cause problems beyond the immediately obvious ones. In prison, fear is a stigma of weakness, and it marks men as fair game for exploitation . . . Inmate norms contain implicit threats of violence. Unpaid debts call for violence; group loyalties prescribe retaliation for slights to group members. There is also the norm of "fight or flight": Beleaguered inmates are told (by both fellow inmates and staff) to do battle unless they wish to seek refuge in segregation.

Toch warns of the probability that prison violence will increase as a result of recent trends in criminal justice. Overcrowding means that only the more hardened and violent offenders get prison terms. Hence prisons are being filled with inmates who are aggressive, tough, or bitter. In addition, determinate sentences and tougher parole policies have reduced the stakes that inmates have in remaining nonviolent. Being passive, quiet, obedient, and nonaggressive is no longer good for an early release.

Toch may have overstated the impact of overcrowding, and he certainly did not anticipate the huge increase in prison terms for drug offenses. One prison expert (Gaes, 1991) believes that prison overcrowding is rarely the sole cause of serious inmate problems. Reviewing available research, Gaes concludes that there is no convincing evidence that overcrowding per se leads to a decrease in the quality of inmate life. He found no major effect on inmate health, violence or recidivism. While this controversial finding may fuel claims that the overcrowding "problem" has been promoted by special interest groups—prison administrators, guards and their unions, prisoner rights activists, reformers, and inmates themselves (see Bleich, 1989)—this is an area crying for competent research.

Victimization of Prisoners

Sociologist Lee Bowker (1978:1–2) has depicted the inmate experience as one of *victimization*, "a continuous process extending through all hours of the day and the night." Any transaction is seen as victimizing when "a relatively more powerful individual receives more goods, services, or other advantages from a relatively less powerful individual through the coercive exercise of superior strength, skill, or other power resources." Victimization of prisoners involves four systems, according to Bowker: the biological, the psychological, the economic, and the social.

Biological Victimization Included in biological victimization are acts of murder, rape, and assault. These are more likely to characterize relationships between inmates than guard–inmate relationships. However, recent discussions of prison life have spoken of a "trench warfare climate" and have taken special note of the physical intimidation of guards by inmates. Inmates are often prepared for violence, as evidenced by the routine carrying of assaultive devices such as knives and iron bars, called "headknockers" (Guenther, 1975).

Homosexual rape and other sexual assaults have long been associated with prison life, and the reasons are not hard to find. The problem may be even worse in jails. In one study of sexual assaults in the sheriff's vans and jails of Philadelphia, Alan Davis (1968) estimated that 2000 rapes had occurred in a 26-month period in the late 1960s. The exchange of sex for protection has been widely documented both here and abroad. In a twist to this common theme, Davis discovered that many of the aggressors he interviewed felt they had to continue participating in gang rapes to avoid becoming victims themselves.

Bowker suggests that there may be even more violence in juvenile institutions than in adult ones. If true, one explanation could be that youths are still in that period of life of proving themselves, especially their masculinity. Life in the detention home and reformatory is an extension of life on the street, but a more intense one. The opportunities for asserting one's manliness are probably more frequent, and the constant surveillance by adult keepers merely increases the likelihood that demonstrations of "coolness," "toughness," and independence will be highly valued in interpersonal relationships. John Allen's (1977) account of his experiences at Junior Village, an institution for juveniles, illustrates all these points. "The institution simply exposed Allen to more concentrated doses of the same sort of things he was experiencing on the street" (Barlow and Ferdinand, 1992:72).

Psychological Victimization Combined with other forms of victimization, psychological victimization primarily consists of manipulation and intimidation for the purposes of achieving status, prestige, authority, and power. The new prisoner (often called a "fish") is likely to be scared, confused, and vulnerable to demands made by more experienced cons. Among the types of psychological victimization described in one study of a juvenile institution are "threat-gestures," "ranking," and "scapegoating" (Polsky, 1962). Bowker (1978:7) describes them in this way:

> In threat-gestures, threatening verbal commands and denigrating gestures are used to keep lower status boys in a constant state of psychological turmoil. Ranking is the use of verbal insults to remind weak boys of their social inferiority. Scapegoating combines threat-gestures, ranking, and physical aggression toward certain individuals who have come to permanently occupy positions at the bottom of the social hierarchy. Once a boy has been manipulated into the scapegoat role, it is very unlikely that he will be able to reestablish himself as a viable member of the community of prisoners.

There are various ways in which guards and other staff members victimize prisoners through manipulation and intimidation. It is the guards who control the flow of information and materials inside the prison. They are in an excellent position to intimidate and disrupt the psychic equilibrium of prisoners. Refusing to allow inmates to shower, make telephone calls, receive mail, and eat certain foods are deprivations that take on added significance in a prison setting. Similarly, purposely deceiving and exploiting inmates by breaking promises and using information against them intensify the pains of imprisonment.

Economic Victimization   Material deprivation leads to the development of a "hidden economy." Economic transactions between inmates and between inmates and guards involve all sorts of goods and services, from sex to drugs to books to wages. Earlier, the use of inmates for drug research as an aspect of the tyranny of imprisonment was mentioned. Bowker sees it as an example of economic victimization.

In addition, there is constant thievery of personal possessions whenever inmates' backs are turned, and simply getting commissary purchases back to one's cell may entail running a gauntlet of would-be robbers. Those inmates who give up any attempt to protect their economic rights become fair game for exploitation and harassment.

Social Victimization   By social victimization Bowker (1978:14) means the victimization of prisoner groups rather than specific individuals. He identifies three bases for the victimization: race and ethnicity, religion and ideology, and nature of offense.

In Bowker's view, racial and ethnic group victimization is the most significant and widespread. It used to be that the minority black inmates were the object of victimization, but now it appears that in many prisons it is the whites, especially the middle-class whites, who are victimized by black inmates. Leo Carroll's (1974) research at a New England state prison confirms the direction of interracial aggression, as does a study of Stateville, the Illinois penitentiary at Joliet. In Stateville, James Jacobs (1977) found four highly cohesive gangs whose reputations and power dominated interracial contacts and radiated throughout the prison. The Black P. Stone Nation, the Devil's Disciples, and the Vicelords are black gangs; the Latin Kings is made up of Hispanic inmates. Their exploitation of other prisoners is extensive.

Certain offenders are singled out for special victimization by other inmates. In particular, child molesters, child rapists, and homosexuals are at the bottom of the pecking order and consequently receive the most systematic victimization by other inmates as well as by guards. In contrast, violent offenders who commit murder, adult rape, and robbery stand at the top of the hierarchy; unless they subsequently demonstrate otherwise, their reputations for being tough and cool are valuable in this world dominated by streetwise felons.

Power and the Prison Guard

Prison guards have been called "forgotten men" (Hawkins, 1976), and little is known about how they perceive prison life. With few exceptions (one is Jacobs and Retsky, 1975), prison research has tended to focus on the inmates or on organizational structure rather than on the values and attitudes of the guards.

This oversight is now being rectified, and one recent paper examines the important question of power. John Hepburn (1985) distinguishes five types of power, each with a different basis of obedience. *Legitimate* power is obeyed because the guards' position in the authority structure gives them the right to expect obedience. *Coercive* power is obeyed because prisoners perceive that guards have the ability to punish disobedience. *Reward* power is obeyed because prisoners recognize that guards are in a position to reward them, sometimes formally, as in committee or program assignments, and sometimes informally, with friendship or by overlooking petty violations of the rules.

Expert power is obeyed because guards are recognized as having special skills, knowledge, or expertise and can make professional judgments of prisoners' needs. Finally, *referent* power is obeyed because prisoners respect or admire guards' performance of duties.

In order to assess which sort of power guards perceived themselves as exercising, Hepburn asked 360 guards at five male prisons to fill out self-administered questionnaires. He found that the guards were most likely to mention legitimate and expert power as the reason that prisoners obeyed them and that they were least likely to mention reward or coercive power: "Prison guards believe their control over prisoners to be based largely on their position as guards and on their reputation for competence and good judgment" (Hepburn, 1985:154). This appeared true for all five prisons. However, those guards more likely to see their jobs as custody oriented were also more likely to emphasize coercive power. Research like this helps provide a more complete picture of the dynamics of prison life and may lead to the creation of more stable, productive, and humane conditions in our prisons.

Prison Tomorrow

By all accounts the correctional future looks bleak. There may be more prison disorder and rioting such as that which occurred in New Mexico in 1980 and in Oklahoma in 1985. According to Irwin (1980), two factors helped promote the prison unrest that culminated in earlier revolts at the Missouri State Penitentiary and at Attica, New York, and that set the stage for the turmoil of the 1970s. First, prisons began housing more and more blacks, who by the 1960s were becoming more assertive, and finally militant. This fueled white fears and prejudices, stirring up more tension between races. Second, many inmates grew disenchanted with rehabilitation and its promise: "After years of embracing rehabilitation's basic tenets, submitting themselves to treatment strategies, and then leaving prison with new hope for a better future, they discovered and reported back that their outside lives had not changed" (Irwin, 1980:63). Prisoners, educated by the very programs they came to despise, spread their indictment of rehabilitation and taught themselves to "see through things" and to fight "the system."

Today, Irwin (1980:195) believes, a new prison hero has emerged: the "convict."

> The convict or hog stands ready to kill to protect himself, maintains strong loyalties to some small groups of other convicts (invariably of his own race), and will rob and attack or at least tolerate his friends' robbing and attacking other weak independents or their foes. He openly and stubbornly opposes the administration, even if this results in harsh punishment. Finally, he is extremely assertive of his masculine sexuality, even though he may occasionally make use of the prison homosexuals or, less often, enter into more permanent sexual alliance with a kid. . . . To circulate in this world, the convict world, one must act like a convict and, with few exceptions, have some type of affiliation with a powerful racial clique or gang.

Prisons today are full of hate, with "dope fiends, pimps, bikers, [and] street gang members" competing for power and respect. It is hard to imagine that anyone can emerge from prison and "go straight."

Summary of Chapter 12

This chapter has examined the nature, types, and consequences of criminal punishment. Advocates of the justice model of punishment argue that people who willfully commit crimes deserve to be punished commensurate with the gravity of their offense. Supporters of the utilitarian doctrine, on the other hand, believe that punishment is justified if it prevents or reduces crime, and therefore the consequences of punishment should be considered in the designation of penalties.

The official criminal penalties currently used in most industrialized nations today consist of fines, imprisonment, probation, and in rare cases, the death penalty. Death and imprisonment remove offenders from society, and are reserved for criminals who commit the most serious crimes or who are repeat offenders. Fines and probation are by far the most commonly used penalties, and fines are often used in addition to jail or prison time.

The United States is one of the few industrialized nations that uses the death penalty, although not all individual states do so. Debate rages over whether the death penalty has been used fairly, an issue sparked by the fact that more blacks than whites have been executed and that almost all executions for rape have been of black defendants. A law-and-order syndrome has been sweeping America in recent years, and growing numbers of executions are likely through the foreseeable future.

The new hard line in attitudes toward crime and punishment seems to have touched rates of imprisonment, which have been increasing steadily, as well as sentence lengths, which also have been increasing. On the other hand, prison overcrowding has resulted in the early release of many inmates, and the probation population continues to grow around the country. This apparent contradiction in penal practice reflects an overburdened judicial system, and there is little doubt that the new prisons now being constructed in many states will be filled as soon as their doors open.

Discussions of the consequences of punishment generally focus on its deterrent or rehabilitative effects and on its human impact. Deterrence is a problem that seems to defy generalizations, and this mainly reflects the complexity of the subject. Rehabilitation is no easier nut to crack, and studies of recidivism are hardly encouraging fare for its advocates. Research on the human impact of imprisonment reveals a victimizing experience that deprives inmates of much more than their physical freedom. As prisons are increasingly filled with violent and repeat offenders, many with gang histories, the human toll can be expected to grow, with no hard evidence of any gains in terms of crime reduction or prevention.

Recommended Readings

Lee H. Bowker (1977). *Prisoner Subcultures*. Lexington, Mass.: D.C. Heath.

John Braithwaite (1989). *Crime, Shame and Reintegration*. Cambridge, England: Cambridge University Press.

Jack P. Gibbs (1975). *Crime, Punishment and Deterrence*. New York: Elsevier.

John Irwin (1980). *Prisons in Turmoil*. Boston: Little, Brown.

James B. Jacobs (1977). *Stateville: The Penitentiary in Mass Society*. Chicago: University of Chicago Press.

Robert Johnson (1990). *Death Work: A Study of the Modern Execution Process*. Pacific Grove, Calif.: Brooks/Cole.

Graeme Newman (1978). *The Punishment Response*. Philadelphia: Lippincott.

Part IV

Explaining Crime

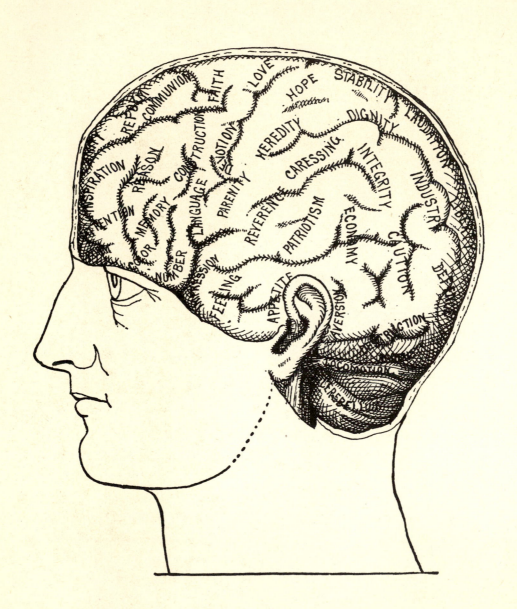

Chapter 13

The Foundations of Criminological Theory

Criminology dates back little more than a hundred years. The pioneers in the field were trained in a variety of disciplines. Cesare Lombroso (1835–1909) was a physician and surgeon; Raffaele Garofalo (1852–1934) was a professor of law and a magistrate; Enrico Ferri (1856–1929) was a criminal lawyer and member of the Italian Parliament; Gustav Aschaffenburg (1866–1944) and William Healy (1869–1965) were psychiatrists. Although people from many disciplines continued to make important contributions to the field over the years, criminology found its primary academic home in departments of sociology, where it remains today.

Criminological Theory

The orientation of this text is sociological, which means that crime and criminality are discussed in terms of social structures and social processes. Individuals are part of the analysis, but only to the extent that they are connected with other individuals in social relationships.

For example, a sociologist might study the amount and kinds of crime committed by a class of people, or the relationship between the criminal behavior of people and the sorts of friends they have. Alternatively, a sociologist might ask how the characteristics of situations affect people's chances of being victimized by crime, or why the rate of a certain crime varies in space and time or from one group or class of people to another. A sociologist might also study the social origins of criminal definitions, as well as how their enforcement affects group life, including crime itself. Some sociologists are interested in why certain events and people are labeled criminal and others not; other sociologists look into the *process* of constructing criminal definitions itself—among scientists, perhaps, or on the street or in the courtroom.

Some account of nonsociological perspectives in criminology is necessary to cover adequately the field's history and the diversity of current theories of crime. As we have already seen, psychology, geography, biology, economics, philosophy, and history have added a wealth of knowledge to the field, but their contributions are secondary to the sociological thrust guiding this text.

Ideology and Criminology

The way criminologists visualize their field and its subject matter reflects their particular set of beliefs and values. These beliefs and values—called *ideology*—affect decisions about what to investigate, what questions to ask, and what to do with the knowledge gained. The intrusion of ideology is a normal aspect of scientific enterprise, and the study of crime is no exception. Three competing ideological perspectives are generally acknowledged in criminology: conservative, liberal, and radical (or critical) (Gibbons and Garabedian, 1974; Jefferson and Clark, 1975).

Conservative Criminology Conservative criminology is identified with the view that criminal law is a codification of moral precepts and that people who break the law are morally defective. Crimes are seen as threats to law-abiding members of society and to the social order on which their safety and security depend. The "right" questions to ask about crime include: How are morally defective persons produced? and How can society protect itself against them? The causes of crime are located in the characteristics of individuals. The solution to the crime problem is couched in terms of a return to basic values wherein good wins over evil. Until well into the twentieth century, most criminological thinking was conservative.

Liberal Criminology Liberal ideology began to emerge as a force in criminology during the late 1930s and early 1940s, and it has remained dominant ever since. The most influential versions of liberal criminology explain criminal behavior either in terms of the way society is organized (social structure), or in terms of the way people acquire social attributes (social process). Social structure is discussed in detail in Chapter 14 and social process is covered in Chapter 15. Here, a brief introduction to major theories within the liberal perspective will suffice.

Social structure theories include strain theory, cultural transmission theory, and conflict theory. Strain theory argues that when people find they cannot achieve valued goals through socially approved means, they experience stress and frustration, which in turn may lead to crime. Cultural transmission theory draws attention to the impact on individuals of the values, norms, and lifestyles to which they are exposed day to day. Delinquency and crime are learned through exposure to a criminogenic culture, a culture that encourages crime. According to conflict theory, society is characterized by conflict, and criminality is a product of differences in power exercised when people compete for scarce resources or clash over conflicting interests.

Social process theories include associational theory, control theory, and labeling theory. Associational theories assert that people become criminal through close association with others (family members, friends, co-workers) who are criminal. Control theory asserts that crime and delinquency result "when an individual's bond to society is weak or broken" (Hirschi, 1971:16). More room is allowed for individual deviance when social controls are weak. Labeling theory suggests that some people become criminals because they are influenced by the way other people react to them. People who are repeatedly punished for "bad" behavior may eventually accept the idea that they are bad, and their subsequent behavior is consistent with that identity.

Radical Criminology Liberal criminologists locate criminogenic forces in the organization and routine social processes of society, yet they do not call for any change in its basic economic structure. Radicals do. Radical criminologists reject the liberal doctrine, which they believe has "served to strengthen the power of the State over the poor, Third World communities, and youth"

(Platt, 1974:3). To radicals, crime and criminality are manifestations of the exploitative character of monopoly capitalism, and current efforts to control crime are poorly disguised attempts to reduce freedoms and to divert attention from the real culprits—those who control capital.

All three ideological positions are represented in the theories reviewed in this and the next three chapters. Sociological criminology has been dominated by liberal perspectives, but the field has also benefited from important insights from the conservative and radical camps.

Types of Theory

Before reviewing particular theories of crime and criminality, it is helpful to consider other general ways in which sociological theories differ (for discussions, see Farley, 1992; Williams and McShane, 1988). Theories can differ in level of analysis and in applicability.

Macrotheories and Microtheories   Some theories deal mainly with large-scale social patterns such as social change or the social, economic, and political organization of society. Crime is viewed as a property of whole groups of people rather than as a property of individuals. Because they focus on how societies are organized, these theories usually relate crime to social structure. They are called *macrosociological* theories, but this does not mean they lack relevance for the everyday lives of individuals. Rather, such theories attempt to make sense of the everyday behavior of people in relation to conditions and trends that transcend the individual, and even the individual's neighborhood and community.

Some other theories focus on the ways individuals interact with others and with the groups to which they belong. These are called *microsociological* theories, and most share an interest in the way social interaction creates and transmits meanings. They emphasize the social processes by which people and events become criminal. For example, as people move from situation to situation, they are confronted with all sorts of messages, rules, and expectations, some of which are not obvious. Through a process of sending, receiving, and interpreting messages, individuals help construct the social reality of which they are a part. An interesting application of this perspective is Luckenbill's (1977) analysis of homicide, which was discussed in Chapter 3. Other prominent examples of microsociological theory in criminology are Hirschi's control theory and Sutherland's differential association, both discussed in Chapter 15.

Some theories seem to bridge the two levels. An example is the subcultural theory of violence (Wolfgang and Ferracuti, 1967), discussed in Chapter 3. Recall that this theory relates broader cultural patterns to the interactions of people in their immediate social environments. Another bridging theory is proposed by Laub and Sampson (1988). In their theory, Laub and Sampson predict that structural factors such as household crowding, economic dependence, residential mobility, and parental crime influence the delinquent behavior of children through their effects on the way parents relate to their children day by day.

General and Restricted Theories   A second important way in which theories differ is in the range of phenomena they purport to explain. *General* theories are meant to explain a broad range of facts. They are also not restricted to any one place or time. A general theory of crime, for example, is one that explains many (if not all) types of crime and can be applied to a variety of social and historical settings. Examples are Cohen and Machalek (1988), Braithwaite (1989), and Gottfredson and Hirschi (1990). These theories will be discussed in Chapter 17.

A general theory subsumes more *restricted* theories; that is, theories designed to apply to a narrower range of facts. A restricted theory of crime might apply to one type of crime, or to various types under a limited set of circumstances. Most modern theories in criminology are regarded as restricted, but the development of general theory remains an important goal, and recent efforts are promising (see Chapter 17).

Scientific Foundations of Criminology

The birth of criminology as science is usually traced to nineteenth-century Europe. By the latter half of that century the scientific revolution was well under way. Armchair philosophizing was grudgingly giving way to the logic and methodology of science. Observation, measurement, and experimentation were the basic tools of the scientific method, and their use in the study of human behavior heralded the development of disciplines now taken for granted—biology, anthropology, psychology, sociology, political science, and statistics. Thus was born the Age of Positivism, and crime was placed under the microscope of science. Theories now had to be spelled out, quantified, and falsifiable.

Positivism and Early Criminology

The notion that crime could be studied through the methods of science was established early in the nineteenth century by two authors whose work earned them an honored place in the annals of criminology. Working independently, Adolphe Quetelet (1796–1874) and André Michel Guerry (1802–1866) compiled the first criminal statistics and used them to make predictions and comparisons about crime. Others soon followed suit, and these early ventures into social statistics became a model for the later work of Emile Durkheim. "For the first time in history," Leon Radzinowicz (1966:35) has observed, "crime became thought of as a social fact moulded by the very environment of which it was an integral part." This was an important break with the classical theorists, who viewed criminal behavior as stemming from the exercise of free will in the pursuit of pleasure (see Chapter 16).

Cesare Lombroso (left) helped establish criminology as a field of scientific study. Strongly influenced by Charles Darwin's (right) theory of evolution, Lombroso spent decades searching for the criminal type.

A major impetus to the rise of positivism was Charles Darwin's work on animal evolution. Darwin's followers argued that human behavior is largely determined by *Homo sapiens'* position on the evolutionary scale and by the ongoing battle for survival. However, the specific impact of these forces on an individual was considered a matter for empirical investigation.

Today positivism has become "little more than a derogatory label" in some quarters (Gibbs, 1987:4). The objections to positivism are varied, but primarily they consist of the argument that the so-called "objective" depiction of "concrete facts" in the world obscures a reality that is socially constructed by the participants in it. The facts are "constructed meanings produced within specific cultural, political, and economic contexts" (Michalowski, 1988:18). Even the nature of crime itself cannot be taken for granted.

The debate about positivism versus social constructionism is unlikely to be resolved in the near future (see also Gibbs, 1988; Nettler, 1988), and it is certainly possible for both to live side by side, and for criminology to profit from their contributions to our knowledge and thinking about crime. Gibbs (1988:4) makes an important point, however: How else are scientific theories about crime to be assessed, if not by testing their predictions against a body of empirical data? This was the great insight of the early positivists.

The Search for the Criminal Type

Influenced by positivism, early criminologists were convinced that they could uncover the causes of criminal behavior if they could apply the methods of science to the study of human beings. Devlance, they believed, was caused rather than chosen (Pfohl, 1985). The major figure was Italian physician Cesare Lombroso (1911). Like many of his contemporaries, Lombroso believed that criminals must be different from law-abiding people in some important way. The problem was to find out *how* they differed, and the search for the criminal type consumed much of his career.

As a physician attached to the army and later to prisons and asylums, Lombroso examined thousands of individuals. Profoundly influenced by the evolutionary doctrine, he searched for physiological evidence of the link between deviant behavior and biological forces. In 1870 he claimed a triumphant discovery: In his view, many of the criminals he had studied were *atavistic*—biological throwbacks to a more primitive evolutionary state. Such "born criminals" could be identified by five or more physical stigmata, or anomalies: an asymmetrical cranium, a receding chin, a low forehead, large ears, too many fingers, a sparse beard, protruding lips, low sensitivity to pain, and deformities of the eye.

But the born criminal was not the only type Lombroso identified, nor did he argue that criminal behavior was solely the result of biological forces. He distinguished other categories of criminals, including *insane criminals* (idiots, imbeciles, alcoholics, degenerates), *criminaloids* (those with less-pronounced physical stigmata and degeneracy, but pulled into crime by situation or environment), and *criminals by passion* (those who were neither atavistic nor degenerate, but drawn into crime by love, politics, offended honor, or other intense emotions).

Though the core of his theory was biological, Lombroso recognized the importance of precipitating situational and environmental factors. He mentioned poverty, emigration, high food prices, police corruption, and changes in the law as nonbiological determinants of criminal behavior (Wolfgang, 1961:207). However, it remained for one of his followers, Enrico Ferri, to undertake serious investigation of the impact of environmental factors (see Sellin, 1937).

Lombroso and his followers had a tremendous impact on the emerging field of criminology. Especially important was the impetus their work gave to research on the individual criminal offender. For more than 50 years, scholars concentrated their efforts on describing and classifying criminals and on distinguishing them from noncriminals.

Many felt that such research would identify traits and characteristics peculiar to criminals. One monumental study was done by anthropologist Earnest A. Hooton (1939). He studied 13,873 male criminals from ten different states, as well as 3023 individuals regarded as noncriminals. His study claimed to show that criminals are organically inferior to noncriminals, though Hooton did admit that environmental factors could be precipitating influences. Most controversial was Hooton's claim that certain types of crimes are committed by certain physical types of individuals: Tall, thin men tend to commit murder and robbery; short, heavy men are prone to commit assaultive and sexual crimes; and men of small frame commit theft and burglary. It all sounds fanciful now, especially as one recognizes that the main difference between most assaults and most murders is the presence of a corpse, and a major difference between one type of stealing and another is the presence of an appropriate opportunity. But there are still serious scholars who argue that biological characteristics such as body type predispose individuals to commit crimes (for reviews of this work, see Wilson and Herrnstein, 1985).

The search for biological correlates of criminal behavior was largely discontinued in America during the 1950s and 1960s, partly because studies of human behavior in general came more and more under the influence of the social and behavioral sciences, but also because the necessary research became too costly. There were also many people who believed its pathological focus was simply inaccurate (Pfohl, 1985:118). Although Scandinavians have maintained a continued interest in this area (see Christiansen, 1977a, 1977b; Mednick, Garbrielli, and Huthings, 1984), American criminologists basically lost interest in it until the 1980s.

The biological perspective in criminology is by no means a unified approach (Ellis and Hoffman, 1990; Fishbein, 1990). Its advocates draw on research from a variety of behavioral sciences, including behavioral genetics, physiological psychology, psychopharmacology, and endocrinology. Among the theoretical perspectives found within the biological camp are (1) evolutionary theories—for example, antisocial behavior is an adaptation to abnormal environmental conditions; (2) genetic theories—for example, antisocial behavior is the result of inherited defects; and (3) biochemical theories—for example, antisocial behavior is the result of hormonal imbalance.

Fishbein (1990:55–56) concludes a critical review of theory and research from the biological perspective with both caution and optimism.

> Caution against the premature application of biological findings is clearly called for. The weakness in design, sampling techniques, and statistical procedures . . . preclude drawing definitive conclusions, and results are frequently contested and unreliable. . . .

> Overall, evidence to suggest that biological conditions have a profound impact on the adaptive, cognitive, and emotional abilities of the individual is compelling. . . . The capability to identify and predict the factors responsible for maladaptivity may eventually enable society to employ innovative methods of early detection, prevention, remediation, and evaluation.

The Biosocial View

Advocates of the biological perspective in criminology have been swimming against the tide for the past 40 years. However, a recent book by James Q. Wilson and Richard Herrnstein (1985) helped spark renewed interest in the

	Endomorphic	Mesomorphic	Ectomorphic
Body Type	Soft & round	Muscular & strong	Thin & fragile
Temperament	Relaxed, sociable & fond of eating	Energetic, courageous & assertive	Brainy, artistic & introverted

The search for personality types led William Sheldon to propose a theory based on body build (somatotype). Sheldon applied this theory to criminal types and believed that mesomorphs were most likely to become criminals. Subsequent research has not validated his theory, although there are still authors who believe that a person's physical attributes, together with personality characteristics, may influence behavior.

relationship between biology and criminal behavior. The tide hasn't turned, by any means, but a healthy research interest in biological correlates of crime has emerged (Fishbein's review cited over 200 studies, most published since 1980).

Studies of chronic delinquents (see Barlow and Ferdinand, 1992:18–41) have found that when compared with less delinquent youths, the chronic offenders are more likely to suffer from minor birth defects, to have abnormal electrical activity in the brain, or to suffer various other neurological deficits (see Buikhuisen, 1988; Burchard and Burchard, 1987). These correlates of chronic delinquency are believed to influence behavior through their impact on the socialization process. They impede a child's ability to learn and to develop attitudes and behaviors consistent with self-control, deferred gratification, and restraint. The interaction between biology and social environment lies at the heart of *biosocial* perspectives.

Biology and Environment   Wilson and Herrnstein take a biosocial approach. They argue that certain constitutional factors, some of which are genetic, predispose people to commit crimes, but also that these predispositions are influenced by social forces as well as by the individual's own personality. In their view, neither biology nor environment alone is sufficient to explain why some people commit crimes and others do not, or why some people commit more crime than others. There is certainly no "crime gene," which means there is no "born criminal" (1985:69). However, Wilson and Herrnstein emphasize that biological factors cannot be overlooked:

> The existence of biological predispositions means that circumstances that activate criminal behavior in one person will not do so in another, that social forces cannot deter criminal behavior in 100 percent of the population, and that the distribution of crime within and across societies may, to some extent, reflect underlying distributions of constitutional factors. . . . [C]rime cannot be understood without taking into account individual predispositions and their biological roots. (1985:103)

Wilson and Herrnstein infer the existence of biological influences from two observations: First, there is the widespread finding that street crimes such as murder, robbery, and burglary are mostly committed by young males who are disproportionately black and of lower intelligence. The most striking differences are observed for sex: Males are up to 50 times more likely to commit crimes than are females (1985:460). Second, there is a large body of research suggesting something biologically distinctive about "the average offender." The typical male offender is more muscular than other people and is likely to have biological parents who are themselves criminals.

Wilson and Herrnstein review a vast amount of research to substantiate their claims, but how exactly are biological forces thought to influence criminal behavior? The authors are cautious on this point, as well they might be, since many of the findings they review can be explained by other theories. However, their answer seems to be in the impact biological factors have on (1) the things people consider rewarding; (2) the ability (or desire) of people to think about rewards and punishments that might come in the future; and (3) the ability of people to develop internal, moral constraints—the "bite of conscience." Aggressive drives and needs are dominant in males; younger and less intelligent people are more inclined to be impulsive, to want rewards now rather than later; and the cognitive skills involved in the development of conscience grow with age and are positively related to intelligence. People who are aggressive, impulsive, opportunistic, and less constrained by conscience are at greatest risk of committing crimes.

Wilson and Herrnstein's theory of criminal behavior is mentioned here both because it is a theory of individual differences and because it uses biological factors in the explanation of criminal behavior. Although Wilson and Herrnstein are not emphatic on the point, the two biologically based factors that most strongly predispose people to commit crimes appear to be aggressive temperament and level of intelligence. Aggression was discussed in Chapter 3. Here we concentrate on the connection between intelligence and crime.

Intelligence and Crime One of the most enduring arguments found in scientific and popular literature is that antisocial behavior is more likely among people with low intelligence. There is little disagreement that intellectual defects (and abilities) are heritable (Fishbein, 1990:44), and much of the research on intelligence and crime has concluded that boys with lower aptitude are more likely to become involved in delinquency and crime (see Hirschi and Hindelang, 1977).

When a certain group of people is found to have disproportionate involvement in crime, the natural inclination is to look for things the people have in common and then attribute the criminal behavior to these things. This is the sort of reasoning that has linked intelligence to the disproportionately high rates of serious (especially violent) crime among blacks compared with whites (see Hindelang, 1978; Hindelang, Hirschi, and Weiss, 1979). Blacks consistently score lower on intelligence tests than whites, and it is a short—but incorrect—step to concluding that blacks are less intelligent because they are black (Jensen, 1969). The higher rates of serious crime among blacks are then explained as a result of biological differences in intelligence or aptitude.

Wilson and Herrnstein (1985:470–472) correctly point out that intelligence varies among blacks (and whites) much more than it does between the two races. Furthermore, environmental differences such as neighborhood, upbringing, economic conditions, schools, and nutrition could well account for most of the difference in measured intelligence between blacks and whites.

One recent study that attempted to ferret out the impact of IQ in the race-IQ-delinquency puzzle concluded that IQ was "the potent variable" in explaining black–white differences (Gordon, 1987). However, the author's measure of delinquency was based on court referrals and commitments—hardly good measures of the behavior of offenders.

The unresolved issue for the biosocial perspective is, of course, to establish how constitutional and environmental factors come together to influence criminal behavior. Certainly, the intelligence-criminality puzzle remains to be solved. Some authors do not hold much hope that low intelligence will explain crime in general: "It does not account for fluctuations in crime rates in the population at large or within a specific group, and it fails to take into account white-collar crime, organized crime (particularly its leadership), and political crime—all of which require considerable intellectual ability" (Bernard in Vold, 1979:97).

Is There a Criminal Personality?

Intelligence is linked with personality, and personality is directly related to behavior. Not surprisingly, psychologists and psychiatrists have had much to say about criminal behavior. It is assumed that criminal behavior is tied to mental process that reflects a bundling together of emotions, thoughts, drives, desires, and inhibitions. Because criminal behavior is considered harmful to its victims and reflects a violation of rules to which severe punishments may be attached, theories of the link between personality and crime have often emphasized the "bad side": mental disease, mental disorder, emotional instability, sociopathy, psychopathy, and all sorts of other mental defects (for reviews, see Vold and Bernard, 1986). Against this view, recent epidemiological research suggests that neither the amount of mental disorder among criminal offenders nor the amount of criminal offending among the mentally disordered is larger than for the general population (Monahan and Steadman, 1983).

The search for a criminal personality continues, nevertheless. It is not hard to see why: Most people are reluctant to believe that rapists, serial murderers, child molesters, and those who commit hundreds of crimes during adolescence and early adulthood have "normal" personalities.

When Samuel Yochelson and Stanton Samenow (1976, 1977) published the results of their decade-long research at St. Elizabeth's Hospital in Washington, D.C., the two-volume work was received with much fanfare. Here, at last, seemed to be confirmation that a criminal personality did indeed exist. The goal of their work was to devise a strategy for changing the behavior of 240 hard-core adult offenders confined to the psychiatric hospital. Apart from the authors' conclusions, the work is interesting because it represented a break with more traditional psychiatry (for example, there were no lengthy "couch sessions" in which the doctors attempted to draw out the emotional burdens of childhood) and because it rejects environmental influences on behavior in favor of free will. Yochelson and Samenow write:

> It is not the environment that turns a man into a criminal. Rather, it is a series of choices that he makes starting at a very early age. . . . There is a continuity in his thinking and action regardless of setting. . . . Crime does not come to him; he goes to it. . . . He seeks out other delinquents. . . . By the time he is apprehended, he has more than likely committed hundreds, if not thousands, of offenses. . . . The excitement that is involved [in crime] is what is important. (1976:247)

Throughout their account, Yochelson and Samenow stress the calculating, hedonistic personality of their subjects. Consistent with this, they firmly believe that crime can be deterred. However, while conventional views of deterrence stress the use of external threats and sanctions, Yochelson and Samenow favor the development of internal deterrents: Deter the person from thinking in criminal ways, and you will reduce the likelihood of that person acting in criminal ways.

The theory seems credible, but there are major problems with Yochelson and Samenow's account. Bernard (in Vold, 1979:155) criticizes their methodology:

> The assertion is made that criminals think in a certain way, and this statement is supported with several examples to illustrate it. That format has no scientific validity, since literally any statement can be made in a similar way. One can say: "All criminals come from bad home environments—for example, Joe's father beat him, and his mother drank" and so on. No terms are operationally defined, no indication is given as to how it was ascertained that all these thinking patterns were present in all the 240 subjects involved in the experiment, or why it is thought that these traits, which are found in a highly selected population, would be found in the general population of criminals.

Equally questionable is the authors' failure to show how criminal thinking arises in the first place. Since environmental influences are apparently ruled out, is one to believe that the source is something in the criminal's biological makeup? Unfortunately, the authors do not address this important point.

Taking the position that a scientific criminology demands empirical evaluation of its theories by independent researchers, George Vold (1958:125) has criticized the entire field of psychiatry in its applications to crime: "A methodology under which only the patient knows the 'facts' of the case, and only the analyst understands the meaning of those 'facts' as revealed to him by the patient, does not lend itself to external, third-party, impersonal verification or to generalizations beyond the limits of any particular case."

The foregoing should not be taken as a general indictment of psychogenic approaches to the study of crime, nor does it mean that personality has no relevance in the explanation of criminal behavior. But it is precisely when the social dimensions of life are ignored that explanations of human behavior become suspect. What, after all, is personality if it is not partly a product of the experiences and interactions a person has in his or her social environment?

The importance of looking for sociological elements in explanations of behavior is nicely illustrated in recent studies by behavioral geneticist David Rowe (Rowe and Osgood, 1984; Rowe, 1986; Rowe and Rodgers, 1988; Rowe, Osgood, and Nicewander, 1990). It is now recognized that a lot of crime happens within families; that is, family members are either victims of other family members or they commit crimes together as "partners" (see Lincoln and Straus, 1985). However, Rowe has been interested in uncovering the hereditary (biological) dispositions underlying criminal behavior. What he found in his study of siblings living in Ohio was that the mutual interaction that occurs among siblings (twin, non-twin, same or different sexes) tends to modify the influence of genetic factors in behavior. Thus, any hereditary predispositions to crime may be enhanced or weakened by the activities that siblings engage in together (Rowe and Rodgers, 1988).

Another recent study serves as a final illustration of the value of keeping sociological variables in mind when investigating biological or developmental (personality) factors in criminal behavior. Deborah Denno (1985) examined a sample of 800 black children who were at high risk for developing learning and behavioral disorders. After controlling for various biological and psychological factors, Denno found that delinquent behavior was most strongly related to problems experienced by the children in school. Various factors appeared to give rise to school problems, but low intelligence was not one of them. The most important was "lack of behavioral control," a factor that could be aggravated by minimal brain dysfunction and hyperactivity, two common afflictions in the sample. On the other hand, definitions of and rewards for appropriate behavior in school are in the hands of teachers and other students with whom the child interacts. Denno concludes that social dimensions of a child's life must be included in any comprehensive explanation of behavior (see also Denno, 1990).

The major stumbling block to any definitive biosocial theory is the difficulty of disentangling biological and environmental influences. Studies of the childhood experiences of chronic delinquents and career criminals illustrate the difficulty. Poor parental supervision and inconsistent discipline; lack of love and emotional support; parental perception that a child is incorrigible, neurotic, or simply refuses to learn; and differential distribution of family resources may all hinder effective socialization in the absence of any underlying biological impediment. The same can be said of negative labeling by teachers and peers. All these conditions show correlations with chronic delinquency (Buikhuisen, 1988; Werner, 1987; Loeber and Dishion, 1983).

The same is true of family characteristics such as large size and low income, and these may even help *produce* some of the biological impediments we have been discussing. Low income and large family size may result in malnutrition, poor prenatal and postnatal care, and inadequate parental monitoring of a child's behavior and welfare. Poverty exacerbates the developmental impact of biological impairments and negative family or school experiences because it makes the search for socially acceptable solutions more difficult. Options available to middle- and upper-class families are often not open to lower-class families, if they are even thought of at all.

Multifactor Approaches

An immediate and long-standing criticism of the early biological and psychogenic approaches to crime was that much of the work centered on the search for a single factor that could account for all criminal behavior. At one time or another, scientists held up biological degeneracy, or feeblemindedness, or psychopathy, or body type as *the* cause of crime. Critics argued that if one of these is the cause of crime, the others could not also be a cause.

From this reasoning grew the *multifactor* approach. The underlying assumption was that criminal behavior is a product of many factors—biological, psychological, and social—and that different combinations of factors are likely to have correspondingly different effects on behavior. Hence

By the early twentieth century, criminological theory and research centered increasingly on environmental factors in crime. Whereas early criminologists were often trained in medicine and the natural sciences, today the field is dominated by behavioral and social scientists.

the "proper" approach in criminology is an eclectic one, emphasizing the identification and analysis of multiple factors.

One of the best-known multifactor studies was undertaken by Sheldon Glueck and Eleanor Glueck (1950). In *Unraveling Juvenile Delinquency*, the Gluecks published the results of a study that matched 500 "delinquents" with 500 "nondelinquents" on a number of dimensions, including residence, age, and general intelligence. They then looked for delinquency factors in an extensive analysis of social background, home life, body type, intellectual ability, psychiatric states, emotions, and temperament. Their conclusion: Although many factors showed a statistical association with delinquency, the major causes of delinquency were problems in the home. These problems included parental separation or prolonged absence, parental drunkenness and other mental or physical ailments, poor home management, poor supervision of children, and little parental display of affection toward their child or children. Family problems are still regarded, over 40 years later, as important causes of delinquency and crime.

This discussion of multifactor theories should not be abandoned without acknowledging their critics. The most frequent criticisms have been cataloged by Albert Cohen (1951). First, advocates of the approach have failed to seek integrated theories; yet they have criticized as too narrow the explanations offered by others. Cohen believes multifactor theorists have confused explanation by means of a single theory with explanation by a single factor. A list of factors does not explain crime, but neither does a single theory necessarily explain crime in terms of a single factor. Theories are concerned with *variables*, characteristics that vary in quantity or quality, and a single theory usually incorporates a number of different variables. Theories are needed to explain crime, and when formally stated these consist of logically related statements asserting particular, testable relationships among different variables.

A second objection is that factors found to be statistically associated with crime may not be a *cause* of crime. The Gluecks recognized this, but many multifactor studies have not. Causal power cannot be assumed merely because a certain factor, or combination of factors, is statistically related to crime. A conclusion that variables A and B (say, parental drunkenness and poor school grades) cause variable C (criminal behavior) requires that a change in A and B occur before a change in C, and that the change in C is not caused by some other, perhaps unknown, variable. Needless to say, cause is extremely difficult to establish. The best hope is to use an experimental approach, in which variables are manipulated under controlled circumstances; even here there may be unknown factors influencing outcomes.

Finally, Cohen observes that many multifactor studies seem to be mired in the "evil causes evil" fallacy. The fallacy is that evil consequences must have evil causes. In other words, crime (an evil thing) must be caused by sordid living conditions, biological anomalies, low IQ, pathological mental states, or other equally "evil" conditions. The tendency to think this way has dogged criminology from its beginnings: Lombroso did not expect to find crime among people of sound biological or mental states.

Summary of Chapter 13

This chapter began with a discussion of the nature and types of criminological theory. Theories reflect the values, beliefs, and academic disciplines of those who propose them. Conservative criminological theories explain crime in terms of the moral defectiveness of individuals. Liberal theories explain crime in terms of normal social conditions and processes that characterize group life. Radical theories explain crime in terms of the exploitative character of capitalist society.

Theories differ in other ways. Macrotheories deal with large-scale social patterns; microtheories focus on the interaction of individuals and on the manner in which meanings are created and transmitted in social situations. General theories explain a broad range of facts; restricted theories apply to a narrower range of facts. A general theory thus subsumes more restricted theories. However, the development of general theory is extremely difficult, and most modern theories in criminology are regarded as restricted.

The scientific foundations of criminology are traced to nineteenth-century Europe and the rise of positivism. The development of new techniques of data collection and analysis and Charles Darwin's work on evolution spurred the application of science to problems of human behavior.

A brief review of biological, psychological, biosocial, and multifactor perspectives on crime raised a number of points. First, there is little evidence to support the notion of a criminal who is either biologically or psychologically distinctive. Second, explanations of criminal behavior that do not incorporate sociological variables must deal with the fact that human behavior rarely, if ever, occurs in a social vacuum. The organization of group life and the processes by which individuals interact and become social beings leave a profound imprint on behavior and are themselves affected by it. Third, a major weakness of some multifactor studies and of personality theories such as that of Yochelson and Samenow is the imputation of cause and effect when there is neither theory nor methodology to warrant it.

Recommended Readings

John D. Burchard, and Sara N. Burchard, eds. (1987). *Prevention of Delinquent Behavior*. Beverly Hills: Sage.

Deborah W. Denno (1990). *Biology and Violence from Birth to Adulthood*. Cambridge: Cambridge University Press.

Lee Ellis, and Harry Hoffman, eds. (1990). *Crime: Biological, Social, and Moral Contexts*. New York: Praeger.

Stephen J. Pfohl (1985). *Images of Deviance and Social Control*. New York: McGraw Hill.

George B. Vold, and Thomas J. Bernard (1986). *Theoretical Criminology*. New York: Oxford University Press.

James Q. Wilson, and Richard J. Herrnstein (1985). *Crime and Human Nature*. New York: Simon and Schuster.

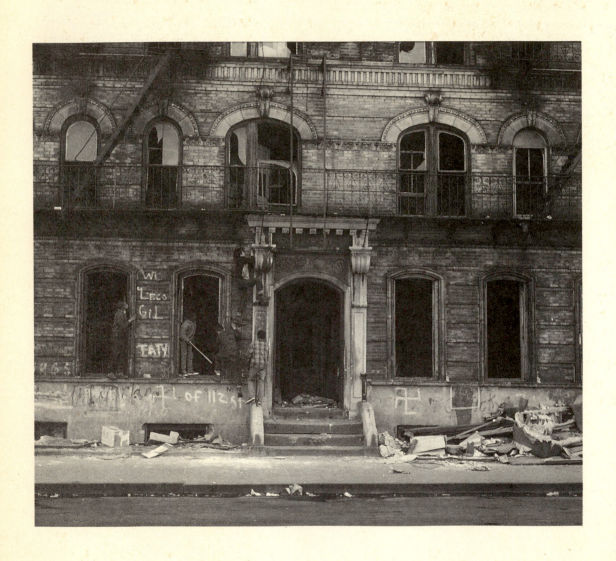

Chapter 14

Crime and Social Structure

This chapter and the next examine sociological theories of crime and criminality. As noted earlier, sociological theories emphasize the social aspects of human behavior, including the organization and culture of group life as well as the interactions that occur among individuals and groups. Theories of crime that focus on social structure are generally macrosociological. They emphasize social conditions and patterns that transcend the immediate social situation. Theories of crime that focus on social interaction explain crime in terms of social process and are generally microsociological. They emphasize how the immediate social situation shapes the behavior of participants, and is in turn shaped by it. This chapter focuses on social structure, the next on social process.

There are two strains of liberal thinking. The earliest, and most influential, emphasizes the behavior of criminal offenders, and explains that behavior in terms of social structure, or in terms of social process.

The second strain of liberal thinking deals more with the causes and consequences of the application of criminal labels to people and events. It should be emphasized at the outset that some theories of crime defy easy classification because they bridge the conventional distinction between structure and process. This is true of the social disorganization theories advanced by the Chicago School (see Lilly, Cullen, and Ball, 1989:60), and it is also true of conflict theory. In the end, *all* criminological theories are saying something about the behavior of individuals, for it is individuals who make and enforce the criminal law or who behave in ways that violate it. The theories are grouped in different categories to emphasize their similarities and differences, and to show how they build upon each other, and how they compete. Chapters 15 and 17 will also examine some theories of crime that purport to be general theories and/or to integrate structure and process.

Crime and Social Disorganization

Sociological investigations of crime and delinquency have given considerable attention to the so-called "sins of cities" (Moore, 1964:905). The basic argument is that decaying urban environments generate high rates of crime and delinquency. Two monumental nineteenth-century studies of life in London helped draw attention to the relationship between the behavior of individuals and the physical and social space they occupy. Henry Mayhew's *London Labour and the London Poor* and Charles Booth's *Life and Labour of the People of London* were early contributions to what is now called the field of human ecology.

Beginning in the early 1900s, sociologists at the University of Chicago published a series of studies of life in Chicago. Under the guidance of Robert Park and E. W. Burgess, these studies were designed to document the belief that problems such as crime and delinquency resulted from *social disorganization*. Simply put, the idea is that the amount of crime in a community depends on the ability of the community to regulate itself (Bursik, 1988:542). Social organization is maintained by a group's commitment to social rules;

when this commitment breaks down, social control breaks down. Members of the Chicago School believed that this breakdown in social control could occur through ecological changes, as when communities experience rapid population change through social mobility and migration.

By examining voluminous data on the city of Chicago, Clifford Shaw and Henry McKay (1942) were able to confirm that certain areas of Chicago experienced relatively high rates of crime and delinquency and that these areas also showed the telltale signs of social disorganization. They were close to the central business district and, consequently, areas of population transition. These areas of high crime were also characterized by overcrowding, physical deterioration, concentrations of minority and foreign-born residents, concentrated poverty, lack of home ownership, lack of locally supported community organizations, and concentrations of unskilled and unemployed workers. Further analysis showed that these areas also had other problems: high rates of infant mortality, tuberculosis, mental disorder, and juvenile delinquency (Shaw and McKay, 1942; Morris, 1958).

Shaw (1931:387) summarized the links between ecological change, social disorganization, and the development of "delinquency areas" as follows:

> In the process of city growth, the neighborhood organizations, cultural institutions, and social standards in practically all areas adjacent to the central business district and the major industrial centers are subject to rapid change and disorganization. The gradual invasion of these areas by industry and commerce, the continuous movement of the older residents out of the area and the influx of newer groups, the confusion of many divergent cultural standards, the economic insecurity of the families, all combine to render difficult the development of a stable and efficient neighborhood for the education and control of the child and the suppression of lawlessness.

One of Shaw and McKay's most important observations was that the *relative* levels of delinquency and crime in local communities tended to remain stable over many years, despite changing ethnic and racial composition (Bursik, 1988:524). Thus, a city area with high rates of delinquency compared to other areas would tend to remain that way, as would an area with low rates relative to another. They showed this to be true of Chicago over a period spanning several decades. Shaw and McKay argued that delinquent values and traditions were being passed from one generation of residents to another; in other words a form of cultural transmission was taking place. In Shaw and McKay's view, the only way to combat the tendency for areas to become permanently crime-prone was to develop neighborhood organizations that could help promote informal social controls, and encourage residents to look out for each other's welfare (see also Sampson, 1986, 1987; Stark, 1987).

Shaw and McKay and their colleagues at Chicago had a major influence on the development of sociological criminology. They not only showed how social organization and culture unite to influence social behavior, but they drew attention to the processes by which youthful residents adopt the criminal lifestyles of an area and thus reinforce them. Even though their theory is essentially a macrolevel explanation of variations in *group* rates of crime (Bursik, 1988:521), they clearly believed that interactions between parents and children, and between neighborhood youths themselves, helped mediate the influences of structure and culture. Indeed, Shaw spent many years helping youths find alternative solutions to their problems, and he persuaded former delinquents and crooks to help him reverse the spread of delinquent values and lifestyles. The resulting Chicago Area Projects became a model for delinquency prevention efforts.

Social disorganization theory eventually fell out of favor, so that by the 1960s few criminologists identified themselves with the perspective. Various reasons can be advanced for this decline in popularity. For some it was sufficient to point out that many youngsters do not become delinquent despite living in high crime areas. Others wondered whether crime and delinquency are not a *part of* social disorganization rather than a *result of* it. Furthermore, how could one explain the emergence of highly organized, cohesive youth gangs in neighborhoods that are supposedly so disorganized? Finally, there was concern that the social disorganization model diverts attention away from the delinquency and crime of middle-class neighborhoods and from nonstreet crimes such as price-fixing and the sale of unsafe products. On the other hand, Robert Bursik (1988) points to signs of a rebirth of interest in social disorganization theory and describes some important research that once more draws attention to the impact of ecological forces on rates of crime and delinquency. Shaw and McKay would be pleased.

Strain Theories

Strain theories focus explicitly on negative aspects of a person's relationship with other individuals or with the larger society (Agnew, 1992). As a result of experiencing adversity, people are *pressured* into delinquency and crime through anger and related emotions. These negative emotions may result in actions that attack or provide escape from the source of the adversity or that help the individual "manage" adversity, for example, through drug use. Strain theories owe a substantial debt to the work of Emile Durkheim (1964a, 1964b). Durkheim believed that a certain amount of crime was normal rather than pathological or abnormal, and he developed a functional theory to explain it.

Durkheim and Merton

By *normal* Durkheim meant two things: First, crime is present "in all societies of all types." Durkheim (1964b:65–66) goes on: "There is no society that is not confronted with the problem of criminality. Its form changes; the acts thus characterized are not the same everywhere; but, everywhere and always, there have been men who have behaved in such a way as to draw upon themselves penal repression."

But for Durkheim, crime is normal in a second sense: Because it is everywhere it must fulfill a societal need. The function of crime (or any kind of deviance), Durkheim argued, is to provide society with something to punish so that its citizens are reminded of the boundaries between what is acceptable and what is not and are (incidentally) deterred from doing the unacceptable. A certain amount of crime is therefore necessary to help society preserve order. Unfortunately, Durkheim never says how much, though it is clear from his writing that he felt Western industrial societies have more crime than they "needed"—in fact, too much for their own health.

If crime is normal, however, why is it not distributed evenly throughout society? This basic question underlies social structural theories of crime (for another view of the normality of crime, see Machalek and Cohen, 1991).

In a book on suicide, Durkheim ([1897] 1952) used the term *anomie* (sometimes spelled *anomy*) to mean a social condition in which "normlessness" prevails. The structure regulating social relationships is disrupted and as a result solidarity and social cohesion are weakened. Anomie is most likely during periods of rapid social change when traditional rules are less effective in regulating behavior. For example, the rapid industrialization of Western societies promoted anomic conditions for many workers because it forced them into unfamiliar jobs and surroundings, Durkheim believed.

Durkheim's notion of anomie was extended and elaborated on by Robert K. Merton (1938; 1957), who made it a central feature of a *strain* theory of crime. According to Merton, a state of anomie exerts pressure on people to commit crime. While all societies establish institutionalized means, or rules, for the attainment of culturally supported goals, these means and goals are not always in a state of harmony or integration. The way the society or group is organized interferes with the attainment of valued goals by acceptable means for some of its members. A condition of anomie therefore exists.

Looking at America in the 1930s, Merton saw an inordinate emphasis on material success, which was held up as achievable by all Americans. Not all segments of American society, however, could realistically expect to have material success if they followed the rules of the game. Blacks and the lower classes were routinely excluded from access to legitimate means of achievement. The acceptable routes to success—a good education, a good job, the "right" background, promotions, special skills—typically were not the routes open to them. Unfortunately, things are only marginally better today (see Farley, 1988).

Merton believes that various "modes of adaptation" are possible in response to the strain resulting from unrealized expectations. Many people will conform, simply accepting that they will never "make it big"—unless they win the lottery! Perhaps the "bite of conscience" (Wilson and Herrnstein, 1985) holds them back from crime; perhaps they fear punishment; perhaps they have too much to lose, if not materially, then in terms of relationships with family and friends; perhaps they cannot recognize—or take advantage of—illegitimate opportunities. Merton prefers the idea that conformity reflects social acceptance of the rule of law.

Other people may engage in *ritualism*. They give up on the goals but continue to support the socially approved means. They cling "all the more closely to the safe routines and institutional norms" (Merton, 1957:151). Imagine the platoon leader who gives up on the apparently impossible task of taking the enemy position but berates his men for having dirty belt buckles, or the loyal corporate manager who gives up on being promoted himself but punishes his subordinates for not "playing the game."

Still others reject both means and goals. Such *retreatism* is an adaptation to anomic conditions in which people may even withdraw from society altogether. The inner-city heroin addict is most often mentioned in this context. The drug-using, anti-establishment "hippies" of the 1960s and the short-lived commune movement also come to mind. On the other hand, some people substitute new sets of norms and goals, and Merton calls this adaptation *rebellion*. Unfortunately, the logical separation between these two modes of adaptation is unclear. For example, are the anti-establishment hippies retreatists or rebels? Can rebellion occur without retreatism?

The adaptation that Merton identifies most closely with crime is *innovation*. Innovators accept the goals, but they reject the institutional means and substitute illegal alternatives. Merton uses innovation to explain the relatively high rates of property crime among lower-class and minority segments of American society. Their disadvantaged status coupled with the high cultural priority given to material success as a goal for all makes high rates of crime a "normal outcome" for those segments of society.

Merton's theory of anomic strain and crime had a profound influence on subsequent structural theories despite some serious criticisms. In many ways his "theory" is merely a catalog of potential reactions to anomie: It does not tell us when to expect one mode of adaptation rather than another, or whether different segments of the population are likely to select different adaptations.

Another line of criticism repeats that directed at the social disorganization theory of Shaw and McKay: Too much is made of the high rates of crime officially observed among the lower classes. Even if the data are credible, the preoccupation with criminal behavior among the lower classes diverts theory and research from the behavior of other classes and from the power relations that exist between classes.

On the other hand, of course, it can be argued that the disadvantages of being black or lower class include a constant struggle with crime, both as offenders and as victims. If the quality of life is measured by the degree to which a particular group escapes involvement with crime, then the lower classes do poorly, and their predicament needs explaining.

Crime and Unemployment

One of the routine hardships for many lower-class people is being out of a job. Unemployment is commonly considered a leading cause of crime, especially crimes of theft. Sometimes the arguments are typical of strain theories. Unemployed people, it is said, cannot take advantage of legitimate opportunities, and hence cannot compete successfully in the competition for scarce resources. Crime offers an alternative route to material satisfactions. At other times the argument encompasses elements of utilitarian theory (to be discussed in Chapter 16): People who are out of work have less to lose and more to gain by committing crime.

The findings on unemployment and crime have been mixed. It seems that whenever one study shows a positive relationship between unemployment and crime (e.g., Berk, Lenihan, and Rossi, 1980; Calvin, 1981), another shows a negative relationship or no relationship at all (e.g., Orsagh, 1980). Box and Hale (1986) reviewed over 30 studies and found the evidence inconclusive either way. In some studies, it seems that even when economic factors such as unemployment relate to crime, other, noneconomic factors are more important in explaining variations in crime rates (e.g., Patterson, 1991).

Part of the problem is that the various studies do not use the same kinds of measures and/or data. Another difficulty is that unemployment is only one aspect of economic conditions, and other aspects (such as general prosperity, extent of welfare benefits, or job-training opportunities) may exacerbate or reduce the impact of unemployment, thus affecting its relationship with crime.

Crime May Cause Unemployment   A number of authors have recently pointed out that the "unemployment causes crime" hypothesis simplifies a much more complex relationship. Thornberry and Christensen (1984), for example, suggest that the relationship between unemployment and crime is actually *reciprocal* rather than unidirectional. In other words, crime may also cause unemployment. For instance, a person who invests time and energy in crime might suffer in the legitimate job market, or might find that the gains from crime outweigh the expected gains from holding a legitimate job. Either way, the person's criminal activity encourages subsequent unemployment. Thornberry and Christensen point out that the reciprocal view is not incompatible with strain theory or other prominent perspectives; it is merely unexplored.

Using a 10-percent sample of 9945 males born in Philadelphia in 1945 for whom police records have been maintained through age 30, Thornberry and Christensen found strong support for a reciprocal model. In this particular case, unemployment appeared to be an immediate stimulus to criminal activity (as measured by contacts with the police), while criminal activity was a longer-term stimulus to unemployment.

Another largely unexplored model of the unemployment-crime connection has been suggested by Box and Hale (1986). They argue that under periods of high unemployment, a "crisis of legitimacy" leads government officials to spread the idea that street crime has risen dramatically. This "reality" (true or not) is then used as grounds for a law-and-order campaign, which in turn results in more concentrated police activity, leading to more arrests and hence more apparent crime. Thus, unemployment is branded the culprit in a process that unearths more crime even when the true rates of criminal activity may not have increased. This view illustrates an idea that will be explored further when conflict theory is discussed—namely, that those in power create an official picture of crime that supports and reflects their application of criminal definitions which, *inter alia*, is designed to protect their own interests.

Female Criminal Activities   Another way in which the unemployment-causes-crime hypothesis bears the imprint of power relations is the lack of its application to females. Traditionally, the criminal activities of females are not subjected to the same theories as those of men. The theoretical preoccupation in discussions of female crime is with such things as sexuality, family relations, and dependency (see Morris, 1987; Chesney-Lind, 1987). Criminologists are for the most part males, and they are therefore much more in tune with the experiences and preoccupations of males. Unemployment is one such experience and preoccupation. While it is usually acknowledged that women do work "gainfully," such employment is often considered secondary to their primary roles of housewife and mother.

As a result, Christine Alder (1986) argues, the consequences of unemployment for women and older girls have been largely ignored in criminology. Alder's review of the available research coupled with her own interviews with 50 unemployed young women in Melbourne, Australia, produced an interesting finding: While many young women are very much concerned about their employment prospects, it is rare for unemployed females to engage in criminal activity, and when they do it is more often expressive (i.e., marijuana, or alcohol use) than instrumental (i.e., theft). So, even if there is a positive association between unemployment and crime for males, the relationship should not be generalized to females without considerably more research.

Cultural Transmission of Crime and Delinquency

As noted previously, ecological studies of crime and Merton's theory of anomie emphasized the high rates of crime officially observed among the poor. From 1940 to 1960, sociologists seemed preoccupied with explanations of criminal activity among the lower classes. Most of the theories produced in the period emphasized social structure, especially the ways in which the behavior of adolescents and young adults is shaped by the lifestyles and values to which they are exposed.

Delinquent Subcultures

A number of theories focus on what is called the "delinquent subculture." Any heterogeneous society is likely to have a parent, or dominant, culture and a variety of different subcultures. The dominant culture consists of the beliefs, attitudes, symbols, ways of behaving, meanings, ideas, values, and norms shared by those who regularly make up the membership of a society.

Subcultures differ from the dominant culture and consist of the beliefs, values, and lifestyles shared by those members of society who belong to identifiable subgroups. For example, rodeo cowboys, circus performers, residents of a retirement community, homosexuals who have "come out," the hippies of the 1960s, and Polish Americans who belong to clubs and organizations that emphasize their common heritage are identifiable subgroups whose members share a common subculture.

Some subcultures are merely different from the dominant culture, while others are in active opposition to it. *Delinquent subcultures* fit neither characterization exactly. According to Cloward and Ohlin (1960:7), a delinquent subculture "is one in which certain forms of delinquent activity are essential for the performance of the dominant roles supported by the subculture. It is the central position accorded to specifically delinquent activity that distinguishes the delinquent subculture from other deviant subcultures [such as homosexual activists]." However, even in its support of delinquent activities, a delinquent subculture may nevertheless also share aspects of the dominant culture; for example, an emphasis on material possessions, or an acceptance of gender differences in social roles.

Subcultural theories of crime and delinquency begin with the assumption that people are socialized into the norms and values of the immediate groups to which they belong. In a sense, all people are conformists, but the values and norms with which they conform may be different from, or at odds with, those of the dominant culture, and the behaviors that result are sometimes illegal. In other words, some kinds of conformity turn out to be delinquent or criminal. So it is with the activities central to delinquent subcultures.

Albert K. Cohen   One of the first sociologists to propose a subcultural explanation of crime—or, rather, delinquency—was Albert K. Cohen (1955). In *Delinquent Boys*, Cohen suggests that high rates of lower-class delinquency reflect a basic conflict between lower-class youth subculture and the dominant middle-class culture. The delinquent subculture arises as a reaction to the dominant culture, which is seen as discriminating against lower-class people. Told in school and elsewhere to strive for middle-class goals and to behave according to middle-class values (be orderly, clean, responsible, ambitious, and so forth), lower-class youth find that their socialization has not prepared them for the challenge. They become "status frustrated" as a result of their inability to meet middle-class standards and in reaction turn to delinquent activities and form delinquency-centered groups. Cohen describes the delinquency that results as nonutilitarian (for example, stealing "for the hell of it"), malicious (enjoying the discomfort of others), and negativistic (taking pride in doing things *because* they are wrong by middle-class standards).

Cloward and Ohlin   Expanding on Merton and Cohen, sociologists Richard Cloward and Lloyd Ohlin (1960) developed a theory of delinquency and youth crime that incorporates the concept of *opportunity structures*. The authors point out that society provides both legitimate and illegitimate opportunities for behavior, and these opportunities (whether legitimate or not) meet different kinds of needs—some help a person achieve status (and with it, membership in the middle class); others help a person achieve economic success. Not all youths aspire to the same things, and Cloward and Ohlin believe that those youth who aspire to economic success but are denied legitimate opportunities to achieve are at greatest risk of becoming embroiled in gang subcultures.

Cloward and Ohlin's theory is more than a rehash of strain theory because the introduction of opportunity variables enables them to explain why a particular form or type of deviance arises in response to structural strain (see Cullen, 1983:41–45). While anomie theory predicts that strain is a motivating force behind deviance and crime, it does not explain why one form of deviance (say, retreatism) occurs rather than another (such as innovation). Cloward and Ohlin (in Cullen, 1983:44) argue:

> The pressures that lead to deviant patterns do not necessarily determine the particular pattern of deviance that results. . . . Several delinquent adaptations are conceivably available in any given situation; what, then, are the determinants of the process of selection? Among delinquents who participate in subcultures, for example, why do some become apprentice criminals rather than street fighters or drug addicts? These are distinctive subcultural adaptations; an explanation of one may not constitute an explanation of the other.

Applying opportunity theory to the world of business (conventionally thought to be a far cry from delinquency), Braithwaite (1989a:33) shows how a criminal subculture of price fixing might arise:

> Let us imagine, for example, that the government suddenly decides to double sales tax on beer in an effort to discourage consumption. The brewing companies might find as a consequence that legitimate opportunities are blocked for them to achieve their profit or growth targets. They might get together at trade association meetings to curse the government, to begin to suggest to each other that they have no choice but to conspire to fix prices, in other words to fashion a criminal subculture which rationalizes price fixing by blaming the government for it, appealing to the higher loyalty of saving the jobs of their workers, and which evolves new criminal conduct norms for the industry.

Cloward and Ohlin identify three delinquent subcultures to which lower-class youths may belong and that help structure a youngster's response to the absence of legitimate opportunities. These subcultures are criminal, conflict, or retreatist.

Criminal subcultures are characterized by illegal money-making activities and often provide a stepping-stone toward adult criminal careers. They tend to arise in slum areas where relatively well-organized age hierarchies of criminal involvement exist. This condition provides youth with adult criminal role models and encourages their recruitment into money-making crime. Also, the existence of adult roles such as "fixer" and "fence," which bridge the worlds of legitimate enterprise and crime, helps facilitate illegal money-making activities as an alternate route to economic success.

The *conflict subculture* is dominated by gang fighting and other violence. It arises in disorganized slum areas with weak social controls, an absence of institutionalized channels (legal or otherwise) to material goals, and a predominance of personal failure. Violence is a route to status as well as a release for pent-up frustrations.

Finally, the *retreatist subculture* is marked by the prevalence of drug use and addiction. This subculture arises as an adaptation for some lower-class youth who have failed in both the criminal and conflict subcultures, or have not successfully accessed either the legitimate or illegitimate opportunity structures. Like Merton's retreatists, they disengage from the competitive struggle for success goals.

Lower-Class "Focal Concerns"

The works of Cohen and of Cloward and Ohlin focus mainly on youthful gangs, and to that extent they ignore a tremendous amount of delinquency and crime that is not gang-oriented. Their work also focuses on the organization and culture of the American lower classes, and to that extent it may not apply to lower-class behavior in other societies.

The same observations can be made of Walter Miller's (1958) well-known study of youth gangs, a study in which he delineates the special themes or issues prominent in lower-class youth culture. The material and social deprivations that are commonplace among the urban lower class contribute to the development of special themes, or "focal concerns," as Miller calls them. Focal concerns command a high degree of emotional commitment. Among the focal concerns identified by Miller are "trouble" (a concern to avoid entanglements with the law), "toughness" (an ability to handle physical and emotional challenges), "smartness" (being able to con, hustle, or outwit others), "autonomy" (remaining free from domination or control by others), and "excitement" (getting kicks, avoiding the routine and the monotonous).

Some of the activities shaped by these focal concerns are delinquent or criminal, for the law reflects and supports the dominant standards of middle-class society. But even when given a choice *not* to engage in delinquency or crime, youngsters will often find the "deviant" activity more attractive because the norms of groups with whom they identify, as well as peer group pressures, point to it as a means of acquiring prestige, status, and respect.

The social structural theories reviewed thus far purport to explain the relationship between the organization or structure of society and the behavior of its people. The almost exclusive focus on lower-class delinquency obviously limits the scope of the theories, and none of them was initially advanced as a general theory.

Unfortunately, one of the undesirable (and probably unintended) consequences of the lower-class emphasis has been the respectability it has given to the stereotypical view of crime and criminals. This view associates being criminal with being a member of the lower class. Interestingly, the considerable media publicity given to crimes by members of the middle and especially the upper classes sensationalizes their crimes, and by doing so seems only to confirm the idea that "real" crime is committed by the poor, the unemployed, and the disreputable. The misbehaviors of "real" criminals are, by definition, unsensational. We *expect* crime from the "criminal classes." The objection to the criminological emphasis on lower-class crime is essentially that it lends the weight of "expert opinion" to this popular stereotype. If this (i.e., the lower class) is where *criminologists* look to find crime, then it must be where crime really is!

Crime and Inequality

A common thread runs through social structural theories of crime, a thread that explains to a large extent why they have been almost exclusively theories of lower-class crime. These theories see crime as a consequence of *inequality in the distribution of material resources*. Lack of economic opportunities, the social disorganization of inner-city neighborhoods, the subculture of youth gangs, and unrealized expectations of affluence are hallmarks of inequality. They are the products of a social organization that puts some people at a disadvantage in the competition for scarce resources. Crime is therefore an unexceptional consequence of unpleasant circumstances.

This common thread reflects an assumption that is made about human nature: Human beings are basically good people. When they become "bad," it is because they are pushed or pulled into crime by adverse conditions. If the lot of the lower classes was improved, there would be less crime. Since food, clothing, and shelter are material resources, the bettering of conditions must begin with economic change that distributes material resources to segments of society where they are most needed. This is a major policy implication of social structural theories.

This implication poses a rather awkward dilemma: If criminological theory and research follow the traditional focus of social structural theories, criminologists will lend credence to stereotypical views of crime that emphasize its lower-class character. On the other hand, if theory and research do not address the lower-class connection, criminologists will be ignoring the real pains and problems of life at the bottom of a class society. Elliott Currie (1985:160) reminds us that "harsh inequality is not only morally unjust but also enormously destructive of human personality and of social order. Brutal conditions breed brutal behavior. To believe otherwise [is] to [ignore] . . . the genuine social disaster wrought by the extremes of economic inequality . . . tolerated in the United States."

Conflict, Crime, and Criminality

The social and economic inequities to which social structural theories draw attention are central to *conflict theory*. The conflict perspective sees a society shaped by conflicts among people who have competing self-interests.

A common thread in social structural theories of crime is inequality. Some people are at a disadvantage in the competition over scarce resources, and crime is seen as an unexceptional consequence of conditions that both cause and flow from that disadvantage.

Conflict Theory

Even though at any time a society may seem to agree on basic values and goals, the existence of scarce resources and the tendency for them to be allocated unequally means that someone (or some group) is benefiting at the expense of someone else. People on the "losing end" may not recognize or admit that their interests are in conflict with the interests of others, when in fact they are. During the nineteenth century, Karl Marx and Friedrich Engels spent a great deal of energy trying to point out such unrecognized conflicts.

Even though the struggle over scarce resources may be unrecognized or unacknowledged, conflict theorists believe it is historic and ubiquitous. It usually consists of a struggle over three related things: money, power, and influence. Those who have more of them try to keep things the way they are; those who have less of them favor change so that they can obtain a bigger share. The groups with wealth, power, and influence are favored in the conflict precisely because those resources put them in a dominant position. It is the "haves" rather than the "have-nots" who make the rules, control the content and flow of ideas and information, and design (and impose) the penalties for nonconformity. Dominance means people are in a position to promote their self-interest, even at the expense of others.

Sometimes the struggle over scarce resources is blatant and bloody, but more often it is subtle and restrained. Conflict theorists point to various factors as part of the complex reasons for the restraint. For example, by controlling ideas and information, the dominant group is able to promote beliefs and values that support the existing order. In this way, the disadvantaged classes in society may develop what Marx and Engels (1947) called "false consciousness": a belief that prevailing social conditions are in their interest, when in fact they are not. Marx and Engels (1947:39) illustrate how this happens in the case of law. Law is presented to the masses as "the will of the people," and this "juridical illusion" undermines the development of opposition and resistance among the disadvantaged. People are likely to feel uncomfortable challenging a law that they believe reflects public consensus. In reality, law reflects the interests of the ruling class, according to Marx and Engels.

A second way that the struggle over scarce resources is kept in check is through the *institutionalization* of conflict. Special mechanisms such as courts, tribunals, and (in modern times) arbitration and civil rights hearings are set up to settle disputes. Disputes between individuals and groups are often conflicts over the distribution of scarce resources. When institutionalized avenues of settling disputes exist, the underlying struggle tends to be moderated and obscured. Aggrieved parties in the immediate dispute are pacified if not by talk of "justice," then by the emphasis on procedures. Nowhere is this more evident than in the realm of crime, where victims often experience a complete loss of purpose as they face interminable delays and the intricacies of judicial procedure.

The consensus (functionalist/interest) view mentioned in Chapter 1 (p. 23) sees law and other political arrangements as useful for society as a whole, which justifies their existence. Conflict theorists, on the other hand, see them as useful for the dominant group(s), and perhaps even harmful to other groups or to the larger society. Law and politics protect the interests of the powerful, who in turn resist efforts to change them. It might be illustrative to consider how a conflict theorist might view the crime of rape.

Rape Laws: An Illustration of Conflict

In the first place, far from meeting the needs of society as a whole, rape laws have historically served the interests of males, the dominant group, and have actually victimized the women they are ostensibly designed to protect. While there is clearly broad agreement that rape should be a crime (a consensus that has probably existed for centuries), we saw in Chapter 4 that rape laws have been written and enforced in such a way that males benefit. For example, many criminal codes do not recognize rape in marriage, and in most jurisdictions, rape is a narrowly defined offense and successful prosecution depends as much on the victim's behavior as on the attacker's.

Second, conflict theorists are likely to view rape not merely as an unfortunate consequence of otherwise useful arrangements (such as dating), but as a manifestation of unequal power relations among males and females. Indeed, psychologist Nicholas Groth (1979) believes that most rape is an assertion of male control and domination. Other writers (e.g., Russell, 1983), argue that rape extends patriarchy into the most intimate and private realm: Men not only control how women behave in general; they also control how their bodies will be used (see also Messerschmidt, 1986:130–156).

Conflict Theory of Criminality

Austin Turk (1966; 1969) has developed a conflict theory of criminality, and his work illustrates many of the points made above. What makes Turk's work distinctive is his emphasis on authority and power relations rather than on economic inequality.

Turk begins by rejecting the conception of crime as behavior, arguing instead that crime is a *status* acquired when those with authority to create and enforce legal rules (lawmakers, police, prosecuting attorneys, judges) apply those rules to others (the "subjects" in authority relations). He then constructs a theory to explain this process of criminalization. Turk believes that criminology needs a theory "stating the conditions under which cultural and social differences between authorities and subjects will probably result in conflict, the conditions under which criminalization will probably occur in the course of conflict, and the conditions under which the degree of deprivation associated with becoming a criminal will probably be greater or lesser" (1969:53).

Turk hypothesizes that conflict between groups is most likely when authorities and subjects disagree about a particular activity, but the actions of both groups (social norms) correspond with what they each think ought to happen (cultural norms). For example, if the authorities hold that marijuana use is wrong and refrain from using it themselves, but a group of subjects holds that marijuana use is okay and they use it, then conflict is likely because there is no room for compromise. In such a case, Turk argues, the authorities are likely to resort to coercion in order for their view to prevail. Conflict is least likely when neither authorities nor subjects act in accordance with their beliefs: Neither group is sufficiently committed to a value or belief to make an issue out of it. Other factors can affect the probability of conflict, including the degree to which subjects who resist are organized and the level of their sophistication. Conflict is more likely when norm resisters are poorly organized and unsophisticated.

Given the existence of conflict, the probability of criminalization depends on power differentials between authorities and subjects and on the realism of moves (i.e., tactical skills) employed by opposing parties. Criminalization is more likely when the power difference favors authorities and the moves adopted by resisters are unrealistic. Examples of unrealistic moves are those that: (1) increase the visibility of an attribute or behavior perceived by authorities as offensive; (2) draw attention to additional offensive attributes or violate even more significant norms upheld by authorities; and (3) increase the level of consensus among authorities, for example, by turning opposition to a particular rule into an attack on the whole system; or (4) increase the power differences in favor of the enforcers (Turk, 1969:72).

While Turk's theory still awaits careful test and evaluation (after almost 25 years), it represents one of the finest examples of theory construction in criminology, and highlights some critical issues in the explanation of variations in criminality. Foremost among these issues is the nature of the relationship between those who create, interpret, and enforce legal rules and those who are subject to them. Crime has no objective reality apart from the meanings attached to it, and criminality is an expression of those meanings. As Turk makes clear, the structure of authority relations must be included in a comprehensive theory of criminalization.

Radical-Critical Criminology

Turk's theory focuses on authority relations and explains how it is that some people are labeled as criminals. Radical-critical theorists go further, casting conflicts of authority and criminal labeling within a general theory of political economy having roots in the work of Karl Marx.

The Marxian Heritage   Although Karl Marx said little about crime, radical criminologists recognize a substantial debt to him. His ideas about the nature of humanity, the nature of society and social relations under capitalism, and the nature of social change provide a framework for the analysis of crime. His desire to strip away the "false consciousness" created and fostered by those in power has become a major component of the radical perspective (Taylor, Walton, and Young, 1975).

First is Marx's view that the mode of economic production—the manner in which the production of goods and services is organized—determines in large part the organization of social relations, that is, the structure of individual and group interaction. Under a capitalistic mode of production, social relations are structured differently than under the mode of production found in feudal societies. Accordingly, to "know" society one must first understand how the forces of material production are organized.

In addition, Marx believed that those who own and control the means of production are in a position to control the lives of others. They have the power, for they are the ones who control the most basic of socially meaningful human activities: work. Marx also asserted that this ruling class controls the formulation and implementation of moral and legal norms, and even ideas. As he put it in *The German Ideology* (1947:39): "The ideas of the ruling class are

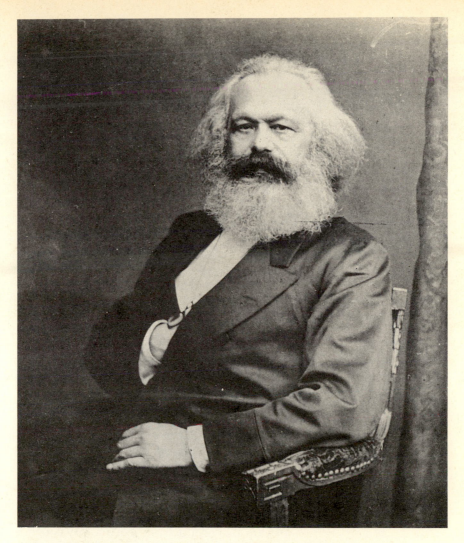

Karl Marx wrote little on crime, but his analysis of capitalist society spurred others to apply his class theories to crime, and the rise of radical criminology in the 1970s brought about a reexamination of the relevance of Marxian theory for structural explanations of crime.

in every epoch the ruling ideas. . . . The class that has the means of material production at its disposal has control at the same time over the means of mental production."

Marx identified two great classes in advanced capitalistic societies—the *bourgeoisie*, owners of the means of production (capital), and the *proletariat*, sellers of their ability to work. Inevitably, the interests of these two classes conflict, for capitalism places them in a relationship of asymmetry and exploitation. For the bourgeoisie, survival and growth depend on success in the competition for scarce resources and the drive for maximization of profits. For the proletariat, survival depends on the ability to sell themselves as workers. But since the ruling class controls production, it also controls work. The worker is thus a pawn in the game of competition and profit maximization that the bourgeoisie inevitably must play. Relations between the two classes are marked by the bourgeoisie's exploitation of the worker, just as the chess player exploits pawns in the effort to beat an opponent.

Some authors point out that Marx's method, more than anything else, helped shape contemporary radical criminology. It is a critical method in the sense that it encourages the attempt not only to know the "real" reality but also to think negatively. As Richard Quinney (1979:17–18) describes it:

> A critical mode of inquiry is a radical philosophy—one that goes to the roots of our lives, to the foundations and the fundamentals, to the essentials of consciousness. In rooting out presuppositions we are able to assess every actual and possible experience. The operation is one of demystification, removing the myths created by the official reality. Conventional experience is revealed as a reification of the social order, exposing the underside of official reality. . . .
>
> A critical philosophy lets us break with the ideology of the age, for built into critical thinking is the ability to think negatively. This *dialectical* form of thought, by being able to entertain an alternative, allows us to question current experience and better understand what exists. Instead of merely looking for an objective reality, we are interested in negating the established order, which will make us better able to understand what we experience. By applying this dialectic in our thought we can comprehend and surpass the present.

Important to Marx's critical thought was his refusal to separate people from society. People are social products and cannot be understood apart from society. But people are also products of history, for society is shaped by the past as well as the present. In the view of Marx and the radical criminologists, social relations must be examined in their historical context.

Willem Bonger on Crime and Economic Conditions   Though Marx said little about crime in particular, Willem Bonger sought to apply various of Marx's arguments to crime in capitalistic societies. In *Criminality and Economic Conditions* (published in English in 1916), Bonger observed that capitalistic societies appear to have considerably more crime than do other societies. Furthermore, while capitalism developed, crime rates increased steadily.

Under capitalism, Bonger argued, the characteristic trait of humans is self-interest (egoism). Given the emphasis on profit maximization and competition, and the fact that social relations are class-structured and geared to economic exchange, capitalistic societies spawn intraclass and interclass conflicts as individuals seek to survive and prosper. Interclass conflict is one-sided, however, since those who own and control the means of production are in a position to coerce and exploit their less fortunate neighbors. Criminal law, as one instrument of coercion, is used by the ruling class to protect its position and interests. Criminal law "is principally constituted according to the will of" the dominant class, and "hardly any act is punished if it does not injure the interests of the dominant class" (1969:379–380). Behavior threatening the interests of the ruling class is designated as criminal.

Since social relations are geared to competition, profit seeking, and the exercise of power, altruism is subordinated to egoistic tendencies. These tendencies lead, in Bonger's view, to a weakening of internal restraint. Both the bourgeoisie and proletariat become prone to crime. The working class is subject to further demoralization, however, because of its inferior exchange position and its exploitation at the hands of the ruling class. "Long working hours and monotonous labor brutalize those who are forced into them; bad housing conditions contribute also to debase the moral sense, as do the uncertainty of existence, and, finally, absolute poverty, the frequent consequence of sickness and unemployment" (1969:195).

In Bonger's view, economic conditions that induce egoism, coupled with a system of law creation and enforcement controlled by the capitalist class, account for (1) higher crime rates in capitalistic societies than in other societies, (2) crime rates increasing with industrialization, and (3) the working class character of official crime.

Radical Criminology in the 1970s   In America, the 1970s saw the first systematic statements on crime from the perspective of radical criminology. The views of David M. Gordon and Richard Quinney illustrate two versions of the perspective.

According to David Gordon (1971; 1973), most crime is a rational response to the structure of institutions found in capitalistic societies. Crime is "a means of survival in a society within which survival is never assured" (1971:59). Gordon finds three types of crime in America as the best examples of this rationality: ghetto crime; organized crime; and corporate, or white-collar, crime. These types offer a chance at survival, status, and respect in a society geared to competitive forms of social interaction and characterized by substantial inequalities in the distribution of social, economic, and political resources.

Involvement in different types of crime is explained by class position. Those in the upper socioeconomic classes have access to jobs in which paper transactions, large amounts of money, and unobtrusive communication are important features. Illegal opportunities are manifest in the many forms of white-collar crime. Those in the lower classes, especially those who are "raised in poverty," do not have easy access to money and nonviolent means to manipulate it. Accordingly, illegal activities tend to involve taking things by force or physical stealth.

Gordon sees duality in American justice in that the state tends to ignore certain kinds of crime—most notably corporate and white-collar crime—and concerns itself "incessantly" with crimes among the poor. According to Gordon, this duality is understandable only if one views the state through the radical perspective. First of all, government in a capitalistic society exists primarily to serve the interests of the capitalist class, and preservation of the system itself is the priority. So long as power and profits are not undermined, the offenses that tend in general to harm members of other classes receive little interest. Second, even though offenses of the poor tend to harm others who are poor, they are collectively viewed as a threat to the stability of the system and the interests of the ruling class. Furthermore, an aggressive lower class is a dangerous class, and the spread of ghetto crime (conveniently identified with African-Americans) to other parts of the nation's cities heightens the fears of the affluent classes who are in a position to influence policy. Gordon's critical approach provides a framework for explaining both the status of criminality and the behavior of the criminal (see also Spitzer, 1975).

Richard Quinney (1975) has written a more detailed radical theory of crime. Dealing with the problem of crime in America, Quinney advocates recognition of the links between the nature of our society, its criminal laws, conceptions of crime, and crime-control practices. Quinney sets down six propositions that make up a critical-Marxian theory, which, he argues, strips away the "official reality" of crime and uncovers the "social reality of crime." The social reality of crime is a reality constructed out of conflict and the exercise of power; it consists of the meanings people attach to events and activities as they interact with others. The theory's propositions are

1. *The Official Definition of Crime.* Crime as a legal definition of human conduct is created by agents of the dominant class in a politically organized society.
2. *Formulating Definitions of Crime.* Definitions of crime are composed of behaviors that conflict with the interests of the dominant class.
3. *Applying Definitions of Crime.* Definitions of crime are applied by the class that has the power to shape the enforcement and administration of criminal law.
4. *How Behavior Patterns Develop in Relation to Definitions of Crime.* Behavior patterns are structured in relation to definitions of crime, and within this context people engage in actions that have relative probabilities of being defined as criminal.
5. *Constructing an Ideology of Crime.* An ideology of crime is constructed and diffused by the dominant class to secure its hegemony.
6. *Constructing the Social Reality of Crime.* The social reality of crime is constructed by the formulation and application of definitions of crime, the development of behavior patterns in relation to these definitions, and the construction of an ideology of crime. (Quinney, 1975:37–41)

Proposition 1 is a definition, and Proposition 6 a composite of the first five propositions; accordingly, Quinney identifies the body of his theory in the four middle propositions.

Quinney calls these propositions a theory, but a careful reading leaves unclear precisely what they explain. Furthermore, the theory offers no specific predictions about variations in either crime or crime control. Such deficiencies are not peculiar to Quinney's work, nor are they found only among those who subscribe to the radical perspective. However, they certainly do not help in formulating a critical theory that will "demystify" crime.

The radical perspective is not a unified approach, nor are its diverse views adequately summarized in this brief discussion of Gordon's and Quinney's works. Vigorous debate has ensued within the radical camp itself. One major point of controversy concerns the perspective's relationship to Marxism. Radicals are not in agreement as to how Marx's theories should be applied to crime, and some have criticized their colleagues for a shallow and selective reading of Marx (Greenberg, 1981:11–13).

Major differences among radical criminologists have been outlined by Robert Bohm (1982; see also Lynch and Groves, 1989). Briefly stated, some of these are as follows:

- Some radicals see the state and its apparatus of law as manipulated by and serving the parochial interests of individual members of the ruling class; others see them as determined by impersonal forces within capitalism; for example, the "market."
- Some radicals believe that the ruling class has intentionally pulled the wool over the eyes of the populace as to the true sources of domination and power; others believe that the mystification of domination results from the ideology of free enterprise that inheres in the capitalistic mode of production itself.
- For some radicals, the solution of the crime problem in capitalist societies lies in the replacement of capitalism with socialism; for others socialism is no answer at all.

Evaluation of Radical Criminology   Radical criminology has stirred up considerable debate, which tells us that the perspective is important; despite predictions of its demise, it has remained viable for the past 20 years. On the other hand, it has not supplanted mainstream liberal criminology, and while its respectability within academe is more secure than within policy and research circles, its long-term imprint on the criminological enterprise is a matter of conjecture. If radical criminologists indeed had a "master plan" to replace existing perspectives with their own grand scheme, as Paul Rock (1973) once suggested, then an account of their failure would acknowledge both the conservatism of tradition and the refusal of the social world to conform to any one theory (Cohen, 1988:232).

A major problem with the radical treatment of the structural sources of crime is its vision of the ruling class itself. Sometimes the image conjured up

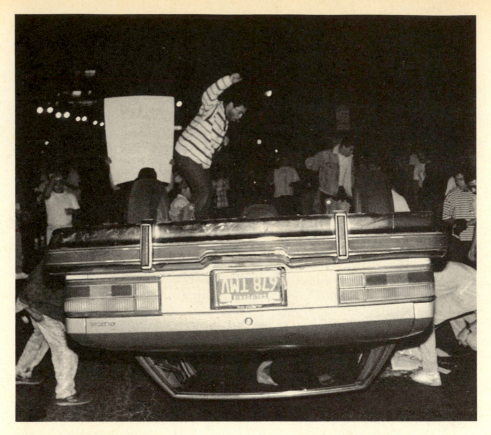

The Los Angeles riot following the Rodney King verdict in May, 1992, brought renewed attention to the plight of the truly disadvantaged in America's inner cities.

is of a small band of powerful individuals in constant touch with one another who determine the destinies of all. At other times the image suggests a category broad enough to include almost anybody. Thus, Young (1986:12) defines the ruling class as "the police, the corporations, and the state agencies." Such ambiguities in the definition of fundamental concepts leave the perspective vulnerable to the criticism that its theories muddy rather than clarify the waters (see also Pfohl, 1985:377).

There are many other criticisms of the perspective. These range from the argument that criminals are portrayed as victimized prisoners of circumstance whose criminal actions are political and therefore not their responsibility, to the argument that some radicals are against short-term reforms of the criminal justice system because such actions would undermine the militant opposition necessary for a socialist revolution. David Greenberg (1981:489) calls the latter a "pernicious model, since it encourages socialists to sit back and do nothing while social conditions deteriorate."

Realist Criminology: A New Twist

Another line of criticism comes from Jock Young and Roger Matthews, British criminologists who were among the earliest proponents of a radical perspective. Young and Matthews propose that the "left idealism" of the radical perspective be replaced by "left realism." According to Young (1986), left idealism has tended to downplay the severity of crime and the fact that it is most often intraclass and intraracial. In addition, Young charges that left idealism has failed to build on past theories of criminal etiology and in consequence has failed in its theoretical mission to explain crime. Young (1986:25) believes that the central tasks of radical criminology still remain: "to create an adequate explanation of crime, victimization, and the reaction of the state."

The alternative—realist criminology—will deal with that agenda while uncovering the reality of crime, "its origins, its nature, and its impact" (Young, 1986:21). Official data and research will not be rejected out of hand, nor will current definitions of crimes and their severity constrain the realist's search for this reality (Matthews, 1986:8). Left realism emphasizes going behind appearances that pass as reality. As Matthews (1986:14) sees it, the "central tension" in left realism will be that of working both "in" and "against" the state. The question is this: How can the victimization and suffering of crime, especially among the lower classes, be reduced without extending the coercive and bureaucratic apparatus of the state?

Like other social structural perspectives, one of the central ideas of realist criminology leads to the lower classes. But rather than looking there only for offenders the realists see the lower class as a victim of crime "from all sides" (Young, 1986:23). The lower class generally, and racial minorities in particular, are doubly vulnerable to crime because they are victims of predatory street crimes as well as white-collar crimes. They are victims of the poor and the powerful.

Realist criminology is in its infancy, and critical evaluations of it are therefore rare. In an address to the American Society of Criminology in 1985, Stanley Cohen (1988:235–276) offers one account of its strengths and weaknesses:

> It responds to the realities of street crime by elevating the victims' demands for protection and justice into a socialist program for reconstructing social democracy. And it seeks to extend the demand for protection and justice by criminalizing the depradations of the powerful. But, however politically expedient and morally sensitive this solution might seem, it is prone to theoretical amnesia. What is gained by giving up the romantic and visionary excesses of the 1960s is lost by forgetting the truisms of the new criminology of that decade: that rules are created in ongoing collective struggles; that "crime" is only one of many possible responses to conflict, rule breaking, and trouble; that the criminal law model (police, courts, prison) has hopelessly failed as a guarantee of protection and social justice for the weak; that crime-control bureaucracies and professionals become self-serving and self-fulfilling. These are truths that have not been refuted.

Gender-Class Theory

As we have seen, social structural theories of crime that focus on class relations and economic inequality owe a heavy debt to Marx and Engels. However, some criminologists believe that an adequate theory of crime requires the incorporation of a second aspect of social structure, what Messerschmidt (1986) calls *relations of reproduction*. "[I]n all societies," Messerschmidt writes, "people need to reproduce, socialize, and maintain the species. Consequently, people organize into relations of reproduction to satisfy these needs" (1986:ix).

In capitalist societies such as the United States, Messerschmidt goes on, "relations of reproduction take the form of *patriarchal gender relations*, in which the male gender appropriates the labor power and controls the sexuality of the female gender" (1986:ix–x). However, the domination of women as a group by men as a group is intertwined with class domination: "Women labor in both the market and the home, and suffer masculine dominance in each. But in addition, their experience in both realms is determined by their class" (1986:xi). In production and in reproduction, behavior is shaped by power relations that cut across both spheres. In the United States, "we do not simply live in a 'capitalist' society, but rather a 'patriarchal capitalist' society" (Messerschmidt, 1986:35). One can therefore distinguish two basic groups: "a *powerless* group, comprising women and the working class, and a *powerful* group, made up of men and the capitalist class" (1986:41).

Messerschmidt endeavors to show how interlocking class and gender relations affect both criminal behavior and its control. For example, the well-documented gap between female rates of serious crime (which are low) and male rates (which are high)—the so-called "gender ratio problem" (Daly and Chesney-Lind, 1988:119; see also Chesney-Lind and Shelden, 1992:7–28)—is explained in terms of the lack of female opportunities for legitimate *and* illegitimate activities that results from the fact that women are subordinate, "and therefore less powerful in economic, religious, political, and military institutions" (Messerschmidt, 1986:43). On the other hand, males have power, which provides them with far more opportunities to commit crime. When class is brought into the picture, the argument is this: Lower-class males have less power, hence commit less crime, than capitalist and middle-class males, but in *all* social classes, males are more powerful than females. "Their powerful position allows some men to engage in crimes specifically *as men* to maintain their dominant position" (Messerschmidt, 1986:45). Rape and wife beating are examples.

Messerschmidt calls his approach a "socialist feminist" criminology. John Hagan and various collaborators have taken a similar approach to youth crime and call it "neo-Marxian" (Hagan, Gillis, and Simpson, 1985). Whatever the label, the approaches are similar in that two fundamental elements in social structure—class and gender—are linked in an explanation of crime and delinquency based on power relations.

While Messerschmidt combines existing research with left-liberal and radical commentary to substantiate his theory, Hagan and colleagues test their version with data from interviews they conducted with 458 adolescents in Toronto, Canada. The results show promise: While the delinquency involvement of higher-class individuals was greater than that of lower-class adolescents, and while male rates were higher than those of females in all social classes, the gender differences were greatest in the highest ("employer") class and least in the lowest ("surplus") class. Thus, this initial study documents both the effect of power differentials on delinquency and the intertwining of gender and class.

The Messerschmidt and Hagan position requires further systematic test with other samples and across a broad range of crimes and delinquencies. Some of this work is now being done (see Hagan, Gillis, and Simpson, 1990; O'Brien, 1991). What makes their work important is its improvement over the traditional Marxist focus on economic inequality, and particularly its specification of how class and gender together affect crime. Perhaps most important is the prediction that more crime will be found among the more powerful—not, as traditional liberal theories insist, among the powerless. Even so, the approach is not without its critics. A foremost feminist criminologist, Meda Chesney-Lind (1987), objects that the work (Hagan's in particular) represents a "not-so-subtle variation" of the now discredited view that "liberated" females commit more crime. This issue will be addressed in more detail in Chapter 16.

Summary of Chapter 14

This chapter has focused on theories of crime that emphasize the relationship between criminality and social structure. Social disorganization theories argue that crime and delinquency result when there is a breakdown in social control. Members of the "Chicago School" believed that such a breakdown could result from ecological changes, as when communities experience rapid population change through social mobility and migration.

Strain theory, on the other hand, argues that when people find they cannot achieve valued goals through socially approved means, they experience stress and frustration, which in turn may lead to crime. Strain theory borrows heavily from the work of Emile Durkheim, who believed that crime rises when social relationships are disrupted and existing social norms are no longer effective in regulating goal-seeking behavior.

Advocates of both social disorganization and strain theories have made much of the relatively high rates of crime found among the lower classes according to police statistics. This preoccupation has diverted attention from the behavior of other classes and from the power relations that exist between classes. It has also perpetuated the popular stereotype that criminals come mainly from the lower classes.

Cultural transmission theories also seem preoccupied with lower-class life. These theories relate the criminal behavior of adolescents and young adults to the values, norms, and lifestyles to which they are exposed. Delinquency and crime are learned through exposure to a crimigenic culture. Delinquent subcultures sometimes form in response to the restricted opportunities that face economically disadvantaged youth. Delinquency and crime become a central activity within these subcultures, according to Cloward and Ohlin.

The almost exclusive emphasis on lower-class criminality reflects a common thread running through social structural theories: that crime is a consequence of inequality in the distribution of material resources. Conflict theory makes that inequality an explicit issue. Crime and criminality result because people in positions of wealth, power, and influence use their dominant status to create and apply criminal laws that protect their own self-interests. Radical-critical theory goes further, placing conflicts of authority and criminal labeling within a general theory of political economy rooted in the work of Karl Marx. This social structural view of crime focuses on class relations and on the consequences of economic and political exploitation.

Finally, new developments in criminological theory have been influenced by the conflict and radical camps. Realist criminologists believe that lower-class people generally, and racial minorities in particular, are the ones most vulnerable to crime, not only as offenders but also as victims who are preyed upon by the powerful as well as by each other. Proponents of gender-class theories of crime link economic inequalities to relations between the sexes, arguing that an adequate social structural explanation of crime must take these interlocking power structures into account.

Recommended Readings

Stanley Cohen (1988). *Against Criminology.* New Brunswick, N.J.: Transaction Books.

Francit T. Cullen (1983). *Rethinking Crime and Deviance Theory: The Emergence of a Structuring Tradition.* Totowa, N.J.: Rowman and Allanheld.

Elliott Currie (1985). *Confronting Crime: An American Challenge.* New York: Pantheon.

Roger Matthews, and Jock Young, eds. (1986). *Confronting Crime.* Beverly Hills, Calif.: Sage.

James W. Messerschmidt (1986). *Capitalism, Patriarchy, and Crime.* Totowa, N.J.: Rowman and Littlefield.

George Vold, and Thomas J. Bernard (1986). *Theoretical Criminology.* New York: Oxford University Press.

Chapter 15

Crime and Social Process

Social process theories recognize that people exposed to the same social structure may not develop the same kinds of behavior, and that people who come from vastly different social environments may still behave in similar ways. Social process theories are microsociological theories concerned with how individuals acquire social attributes through interaction with others. A person's attributes are what identify a person in the eyes of others, distinguishing one person from another. If you are told to look for a "tall" person, you will look for someone whose height (a physical attribute) is greater than that of another. Of course, in a land of pygmies, a tall pygmy would not be tall in any absolute sense, only *relative* to other pygmies. When thinking about attributes, then, it is important to keep in mind that their meaning is always contextual; how one person looks to another is always a matter of how other people in a similar situation look to that person.

Social attributes, such as being reliable or being "forward," convey messages about a person's behavior, status, and ideas. They are part of that person's social identity, and other people use them to determine how they should behave toward that individual and to distinguish that person from others. A person is not born with these attributes, but acquires them through interaction with others. Criminality is a social attribute. People *become* criminals, and that status is confirmed when others treat them like criminals, and confirmed again when people so identified actually engage in criminal behavior.

The Process of Association

In criminology, social process theories attempt to describe and explain the ways in which individuals become criminals. They deal with the links between an individual's interaction with others and that person's motivations, perceptions, self-conceptions, attitudes, behavior, and identity. Although many interactionist theories seem to place greater emphasis on the behavior of others than on the behavior of "self," the goal is the same: to explain the emergence and consequences of behavior. An underlying assumption is that criminal behavior can be explained within the same framework as any other behavior. A common theme in many social process theories is that criminal behavior is learned through interaction with others.

The Theory of Differential Association

In the 1939 edition of *Principles of Criminology*, Edwin H. Sutherland introduced the theory of *differential association*. According to this theory, criminal behavior patterns are acquired through processes of interaction and communication, just as are other behavior patterns. The principle of differential association accounts for the particular behavior pattern acquired through these processes: Individuals acquire criminal behavior patterns because they are exposed to situations in which the learning of crime outweighs the learning of alternative, noncriminal behaviors. Sutherland wanted it clearly understood that criminal behavior was not the result of biological or psychological pathology, but rather was one possible outcome of normal interactive processes. In their daily lives, people are participants in a variety of group situations, in which they are exposed to the behavior and influence of others. What they "pick up" in these situations helps shape their own behavior. When a person is more involved with delinquent or criminal groups, he or she is more likely to become delinquent or criminal as a result. The theory as a whole consists of the following nine propositions (Sutherland and Cressey, 1974:75–77):

1. Criminal behavior is learned.
2. Criminal behavior is learned in interaction with other persons in a process of communication.
3. The principle part of the learning of criminal behavior occurs within intimate personal groups.
4. When criminal behavior is learned, the learning includes (a) techniques of committing the crime, which are sometimes very complicated, sometimes very simple; (b) the specific direction of motives, drives, rationalizations, and attitudes.
5. The specific direction of motives and drives is learned from definitions of the legal codes as favorable or unfavorable.
6. A person becomes delinquent because of an excess of definitions favorable to violation of law [the principle of differential association].
7. Differential association may vary in frequency, duration, priority, and intensity.
8. The process of learning criminal behavior by association with criminal and anticriminal patterns involves all of the mechanisms that are involved in any other learning.
9. While criminal behavior is an expression of general needs and values, it is not explained by those general needs and values, since noncriminal behavior is an expression of the same needs and values.

Two important observations should be made about this theory. First, the theory of differential association purports to explain noncriminal as well as criminal behavior. Noncriminal behavior emerges because of an excess of definitions unfavorable to law violation. Thus, if a child spends a great deal of time interacting intensely with people whose behavior and ideas stress conformity to the law, the child is likely to grow up a conformist (in terms of the law, at least).

Second, the theory can be used to explain variations in group rates of crime as well as individual criminality. Although the theory focuses on how individuals come to engage in criminal behavior, a compatible explanation of variations in rates of crime for whole populations is possible. Thus, relatively high crime rates are predicted for people and places having extensive exposure to definitions favorable to law violation, especially when there is a high probability that such definitions will be learned by a relatively large number of people. Shaw and McKay's delinquency areas, discussed in the preceding chapter, would meet these criteria.

It is fair to say that the theory of differential association has been very influential in criminology. It is, after all, hard to argue with the idea that people learn criminal ways from others. Yet few theories have been subject to more criticism: The language is imprecise; the theory is untestable because major variables such as "definitions favorable or unfavorable to law violations" cannot be measured; the theory deals with the acquisition and performance of behavior and yet leaves out any mention of personality traits or other psychological variables; and the theory does not explain the fact that people often respond differently to the same situation. C. Ray Jeffery (1959) observes that since crime is learned, it must first exist. What accounts for the first criminal act? How does one explain crimes that are committed "out of the blue" or by people with no prior interaction with criminals?

One answer to the last question is suggested by Daniel Glaser (1956), who proposes that *all* forms of interaction between an individual and his or her social environment be incorporated in a modified theory of "differential identification." "A person," writes Glaser (1956:440) "pursues criminal behavior to the extent that he identifies himself with real or imaginary persons from whose perspective his criminal behavior seems acceptable." These people serve as behavior models, and they need not come into direct, personal contact with the individual. Hence Glaser acknowledges something that Sutherland did not: the possibility that portrayal of criminal roles in the mass media is linked with the adoption of criminal behavior patterns.

Another modification of Sutherland's original theory has been proposed by Robert Burgess and Ronald Akers (1966). They argue that Sutherland's formulation does not identify the mechanism by which individuals in fact learn. Taking a *social learning* approach, the authors restate Sutherland's theory in terms of operant conditioning. A certain behavior is learned because past examples have been rewarded. Thus, people engage in crime because it has been more highly rewarded in the past than has other behavior. That some people become criminals and others do not is explained by noting that all people do not go through the same socialization process, nor are they exposed to the same nonsocial situations of reinforcement.

Testing the original formulation of differential association is not easy, and both the methods used and the results have been inconsistent. Usually researchers *infer* support (or nonsupport) of the theory and do not test it directly. This is largely Sutherland's fault because he did not specify how the theory might be tested, and he left major concepts undefined. D. A. Andrews (1980) claims that use of an experimental method is needed for proper tests of the theory. His own efforts in this direction are interesting: A seven-year series of experimental studies in correctional settings shows that highly cohesive groups tend to exert considerable influence on the adoption of definitions favorable or unfavorable to law violation.

In a more recent study, Raymond Paternoster and Ruth Triplett (1988) interviewed 1544 students in nine high schools in the Southeast. They reported strong support for differential association. Friends' definitions of appropriate and inappropriate behavior and friends' actual behavior were

Edwin Sutherland's theory of differential association argues that crime is learned through interaction with others whose attitudes and behaviors support criminal activity. This does not mean that every time a group of teenagers gathers on a street corner they are hatching their next criminal escapade.

significantly related to an individual's own use of marijuana, drinking behavior, petty theft, and vandalism. In another study, Warr and Stafford (1991) used National Youth Survey data (see Chapter 2) to evaluate associational theory. They found that peers' behavior—what they actually do—was a more important predictor of self-reported delinquency than peers' attitudes about behavior.

The social learning reformulation proposed by Burgess and Akers has shown some promise. But in addition, whereas Sutherland was primarily concerned with the acquisition of behavior patterns, Burgess and Akers deal with both acquisition and maintenance. Consider the opiate user. According to their differential association-reinforcement theory, individuals become opiate users because the rewarding effects of the drug itself combine with social reinforcements such as peer group approval. They continue as users for the same reasons; however, if addiction occurs, use is further reinforced because it enables the addict to avoid the distress of withdrawal. When addicts succeed in breaking their physiological dependence on the drug, however, they may still experience a relapse because the rewards gained through association with peers are once again combined with the reinforcing effects—the "jolt," "kick"—of the drug. In this way the cycle continues (Akers et al., 1968).

Peer Groups and Serious Delinquency

The observation that association with friends who are delinquent or criminal is associated with high rates of offending is not new (see Glueck and Glueck, 1950; Knight and West, 1975) but has been reconfirmed by recent data from the National Youth Survey (Elliott, Ageton, and Huizinga, 1985). Recall that the associational argument states when youths are involved with delinquent friends, the association encourages further delinquency. *How* it does it is a matter of debate, but various mechanisms are possible: the group's power to sanction behavior of members; the social rituals that confirm membership and confer status; the role models provided by the group's leader(s); the facilitation of activities that are not easily (or successfully) performed alone. The essential idea is that the delinquency of the group influences its members, and vice versa.

It all sounds simple enough, but the issue of peer influence remains controversial. In the first place, some studies have found that seriously delinquent youths are *weakly* attached to delinquent peers (e.g., Chapman, 1986; also Gottfredson and Hirschi, 1990:154–157). They are loners. Other studies have found quite the opposite, at least for youths involved in illicit drug use (Kandel and Davies, 1991). Youths in drug-using networks display extremely strong interactive ties with peers. Second, a study of incarcerated offenders found that group members who conformed to conventional standards were more popular than less conforming members (Osgood et al., 1986). Third, at least two observational studies, one in the United States (Schwendinger and Schwendinger, 1985) and one in England (Parker, 1974), have shown that occasional and serious delinquents participate side by side in the same streetcorner networks, and the occasionals remain sporadic offenders.

Another issue further complicates what appeared to be a simple matter. Rather than influencing a youth's propensity to commit crimes, it has been suggested that delinquent peer groups merely *facilitate* crime among individuals whose tendencies are already compatible with it (Linden and Hackler, 1973; Gottfredson and Hirschi, 1988). A network of delinquency-prone individuals creates and responds to criminal opportunities in its milieu. The type and frequency of criminal acts will be determined largely by that milieu. A chronic delinquent is most often a lower-class streetcorner male who keeps company with other lower-class streetcorner males. This suggests that, quite apart from the intimate interaction among peers, the social structure of lower-class streetcorner society is conducive to high rates of serious crime (for further discussion of this point, see Barlow and Ferdinand, 1992:60–79).

Self-Concept

The discussion so far has drawn attention to the ways in which youths, in particular, come to adopt patterns of delinquent or criminal offending. Learning, communication, and interaction are the fundamental processes by which individuals acquire their social identities. These processes are also crucial to the development of an individual's personality—motivations, ideas and beliefs, perceptions, feelings, preferences, attitudes, values, self-control, inhibitions, and awareness or sense of self. Some authors have argued that a person's sense of self, or *self-concept*, is a major element among the forces that control behavior.

Self-Concept and Criminality

One of the first to propose a link between self-concept and criminal behavior was Walter Reckless. Reckless (1973) believes that the individual confronted by choices of action feels a variety of "pulls" and "pushes." The pulls are environmental factors—such as adverse living conditions, poverty, lack of legitimate opportunities, abundance of illegitimate opportunities, or family problems—that serve to pull the individual away from the norms and values of the dominant society. The pushes take the form of internal pressures—hostility, biopsychological impairments, aggressiveness, drives, or wishes—that may also divert the individual away from actions supported by dominant values and norms.

But not all people faced with the same pulls and pushes become delinquent or criminal. To explain why some do not, Reckless advances the idea of *containment*. According to Reckless (1973:55–56), there are two kinds of containment, inner and outer.

> Inner containment consists mainly of self components, such as self-control, good self-concept, ego strength, well-developed superego, high frustration tolerance, high resistance to diversions, high sense of responsibility, goal orientation, ability to find substitute satisfactions, tension-reducing rationalizations, and so on. These are the inner regulators.

> Outer containment represents the structural buffer in the person's immediate social world which is able to hold him within bounds. It consists of such items as a presentation of a consistent moral front to the person, institutional reinforcement of his norms, goals, and expectations, the existence of a reasonable set of social expectations, effective supervision and discipline (social controls), provisions for reasonable scope of activity (including limits and responsibilities) as well as for alternatives and safety-valves, opportunity for acceptance, identity, and belongingness. Such structural ingredients help the family and other supportive groups contain the individual.

In Reckless's view, the inner control system, primarily self-concept, provides a person with the strongest defense against delinquency involvement. Commenting on the results of a follow-up study of white schoolboys in high-delinquency areas in Columbus, Ohio, Reckless and Simon Dinitz (1967:517) observe:

> In our quest to discover what insulates a boy against delinquency in a high delinquency area, we believe we have some tangible evidence that a good self-concept, undoubtedly a product of favorable socialization, veers slum boys away from delinquency, while a poor self-concept, a product of unfavorable socialization, gives the slum boy no resistance to deviancy, delinquent companions, or delinquent subculture. We feel that components of the self strength, such as a favorable concept of self, act as an inner buffer or inner containment against deviancy, distraction, lure, and pressures.

The work of Reckless and his associates has not gone without criticism (see Schwartz and Tangri, 1965). Nevertheless, interest in self-concept and its connection with criminality has remained very much alive in some circles. One recent study seems to confirm the importance of favorable family experiences in protecting a child against criminogenic influences, even in slum neighborhoods. Joan McCord (1991) used case records of visits to the homes 232 boys as well as records of their juvenile and adult criminal activity covering a 30-year period. She found that sons of mothers who were self-confident, offered leadership, and were affectionate and consistently non-punitive in discipline tended to escape delinquency involvement. However, McCord also discovered that a different mechanism seemed to relate to whether a child subsequently became an adult criminal: a father's behavior toward wife and children. Apparently, fathers who undermine their wives, who fight with the family, and who are aggressive "teach their sons how to behave when they become adults" (McCord, 1991:412). Thus, juvenile crime may be more susceptible to control mechanisms, including self-concept, whereas adult crime may be more susceptible to the influence of role expectations.

One interesting theoretical contribution bearing on self-concept comes from David Matza and Gresham Sykes. Matza (1964) argues that individuals are rarely committed to or compelled to perform delinquent or criminal behavior. Rather, they drift into and out of it, retaining a commitment neither to convention nor to crime. Braithwaite (1989b) has made a similar observation about corporations.

In Matza's view, delinquents are never totally immune to the demands for conformity made by the dominant social order. At most they are merely flexible in their commitment to them. In a joint publication, Sykes and Matza (1957) argue that if delinquents do form subcultures in opposition to dominant society, they are surprisingly weak in their commitment to them. They show guilt and shame, though one would expect none; they frequently accord respect and admiration to the "really honest" person and to law-abiding people in their immediate social environment; and they often draw a sharp line between appropriate victims and those who are not fair game—all of which suggests that "the virtue of delinquency is far from unquestioned." In terms of the dominant normative order, the delinquent appears to be both conforming and nonconforming.

Sykes and Matza believe that in order to practice nonconformity, delinquents must somehow handle the demands for conformity to which they accord at least some recognition. In the view of these authors, delinquents handle those demands by learning to neutralize them in advance of violating them. That is, they redefine their contemplated action to make it "acceptable" if not "right." The authors identify five "techniques of neutralization" that facilitate the juvenile's drift into delinquency: (1) *denial of responsibility* ("alcohol causes me to do it; I am helpless"); (2) *denial of injury* ("my action won't hurt anyone"); (3) *denial of the victim* ("he 'has it coming' "); (4) *condemnation of the condemners* ("those who condemn me are worse than I am"); and (5) *appeal to higher loyalties* ("my friends, or family, come first, so I must do it"). Yet Sykes and Matza caution us:

> Techniques of neutralization may not be powerful enough to fully shield the individual from the force of his own internalized values and the reactions of conforming others, for as we have pointed out, juvenile delinquents often appear to suffer from feelings of guilt and shame when called into account for their deviant behavior. And some delinquents may be so isolated from the world of conformity that techniques of neutralization need not be called into play. Nonetheless, we would argue that techniques of neutralization are critical in lessening the effectiveness of social controls and that they lie behind a large share of delinquent behavior. (1957:669–670)

Good empirical evaluations of the neutralization hypothesis are scarce. The scarcity is partly explained by the difficulty of establishing what happens cognitively *before* a law violation occurs. Almost all research has looked at rationalizations after the fact, which provides at best only inferential evidence.

In any case, the evidence is not very supportive. The absence of neutralizations, however, does not mean they might not have operated at some time in the mind of an offender. Hirschi (1971:208) suggests that neutralizations might arise *after* earlier transgressions and act as rationalizations for later ones, perhaps contributing to a "hardening" process that leads to a commitment to deviance. Hamlin (1988:432) goes even further and calls the prior sequencing argument "a fallacy." He argues that the motives for doing things are created during the process of legitimizing actions that have been criticized or challenged.

William Minor (1980:103–120) has suggested that neutralization may be necessary only for certain offenders. Neutralization, he writes, "should only be necessary when a potential offender has both a strong desire to commit an offense and a strong belief that to do so would violate his personal morality. . . . If one's morality is *not* constraining, however, then neutralization or rationalization is simply unnecessary."

Control Theory

Like Matza and others, control theorists emphasize the episodic character of much crime and delinquency, but unlike their colleagues they build in no assumptions about what motivates people to commit deviance. In the words of Steven Box (1981:122), "They assume that human beings are born free to break the law and will refrain from doing so only if special circumstances exist."

Hirschi's Theory

The most prominent version of control theory is that of Travis Hirschi (1971:16–34). According to Hirschi, these special circumstances exist when the individual's bond to conventional, or moral, society is strong. As originally conceived, Hirschi's theory posits that this bond is based on four elements: attachment, commitment, belief, and involvement. *Attachment* refers to the individual's affective involvement with conventional others (e.g., parents, teachers, friends), including sensitivity to their thoughts, feelings, and desires. When that attachment is weakened, the individual is free to deviate. *Commitment* is the "rational" component in conformity. It refers to the weighing of the costs and risks of deviance in light of that person's investment, or "stake," in conformity. "When or whenever he considers deviant behavior, he must consider the costs of this deviant behavior, the risks he runs of losing the investment he has made in conventional behavior" (Hirschi, 1971:20). The weaker the commitment to conformity, the lower the costs of deviance; hence the freer one is to deviate. (For more on rationality, see Chapter 16.)

Belief Hirschi defines as "a common value system within the society or group whose norms are being violated." But individuals differ in the strength of their belief in the moral validity of these social rules. If for some reason these beliefs are weakened, the individual will be freer to deviate. By including *involvement*, Hirschi suggests that deviance is in part a matter of opportunities to deviate. He argues that the more one is involved in conventional things, the less one has the opportunity to do deviant things. This is one of the weakest parts of the theory, as Hirschi himself discovered in his research with over 4000 California junior high and high school students. The reason is that opportunities for criminal or delinquent activities *increase* along with opportunities for noncriminal activities (see Chapter 16).

Both the clarity of its exposition and the many research findings supporting it have given Hirschi's control theory a prominent place in criminology. A recent study by Robert Agnew (1985), however, questions its utility as an explanation of youth crime. Agnew studied a national sample of 1886 male youths interviewed first in the tenth grade and again at the end of the eleventh grade. He found delinquency involvement to be remarkably stable over the two-year period, with the delinquency measured in the tenth grade accounting for 65 to 68 percent of the delinquency measured later.

In contrast, Agnew found that the social bond variables of parental attachment, school grades, and commitment explained only 1 to 2 percent of the variance in delinquency. Agnew speculates that as children grow older, the importance of the bonds discussed by Hirschi may diminish, but he does not rule out that they may be important among younger children.

One final comment on this prominent theory is in order. Some criminologists contend that control theory ignores the criminal activity of career offenders, as well as the crimes of people in positions of economic and political power (e.g., Box, 1981; Hagan, 1985). John Hagan, in particular, suggests that the "upperworld" individual is actually freed by conventional society to engage in "indiscretions" because these are not viewed as especially disreputable, much less criminal. Such a person may thus exhibit strong social bonds to conventional society *and* considerable involvement in illegal activities. Hagan (1985:171) argues that "expanding the attention of control theory to upperworld crime and deviance will serve to correct a limitation in its previous application." Indeed, support for control theory has been found in studies of occupational crime (Lasley, 1988), and Makkai and Braithwaite (1991) show support for the importance of attachment and belief in their study of regulatory compliance among Australian nursing home executives.

The Labeling Process and Its Impact

Up to this point, the focus has been on crime and delinquency as behavior and on people who commit crimes and the distinctions between them and those who do not. The questions What causes or influences criminal behavior? and What factors are associated with committing crime or becoming criminals? are underlying concerns in the work reviewed. However, the conception of crime and the criminal that underlies such questions is not the only one that has been recognized. Instead of viewing crime simply as illegal behavior and the criminal as one who engages in it, some criminologists draw attention to the behavior of other people with whom an individual interacts. Crime is a label attached to behavior, and the criminal is one whose behavior has been labeled crime. Crime is thus problematic and a question of social definitions. Nothing intrinsic in behavior makes it a crime.

Labeling theory, or the societal reactions approach, gained immense popularity in the fields of crime and deviance during the 1960s. Sociologists Howard Becker (1963), Kai Erikson (1962), and John Kitsuse (1962) helped develop interest in it. Labeling theory ranks today as a major perspective in sociology. In its applications to the crime scene, labeling theory has been used to explain why individuals continue to engage in activities that others define as criminal, why individuals become career criminals, why the official data on crime and criminals look the way they do, why crime waves occur, why law enforcement is patterned the way it is, why criminal stereotypes emerge and persist, and why some groups in society are more likely to be punished, and punished more severely, than others.

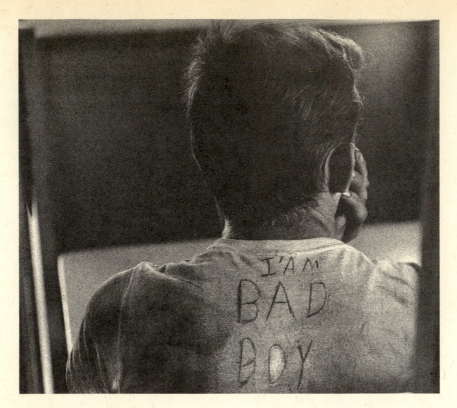

The labeling process begins early in life as significant others—parents, teachers, peers—react to a child's behavior. The labels that contribute to a deviant self-image often remain with the individual throughout his or her life.

Though labeling theory gained popularity during the 1960s, it is based on the much earlier contributions of Frank Tannenbaum (1938) and Edwin Lemert (1951; 1972). Forty years ago, Tannenbaum pointed out that society's efforts at social control may actually help create precisely what those efforts are meant to suppress: crime. By labeling individuals as "delinquents" or "criminals" and by reacting to them in a punitive way, Tannenbaum argued, the community encourages those individuals to redefine themselves in accordance with the community's definition. A change in self-identification (or self-concept) may occur, so that individuals "become" what others say they are. As Tannenbaum (pp. 17–18) described the process:

> From the community's point of view, the individual who used to do bad and mischievous things has now become a bad and unredeemable human being. From the individual's point of view there has taken place a similar change. He has gone slowly from a sense of grievance and injustice, of being unduly mistreated and punished, to recognition that the definition of him as a human

being is different from that of other boys in his neighborhood, his school, street, community. This recognition on his part becomes a process of self-identification and integration with the group which shares his activities. It becomes, in part, a process of rationalization; in part, a simple response to a specialized type of stimulus. The young delinquent becomes bad because he is defined as bad and because he is not believed if he is good. There is a persistent demand for consistency in character. The community cannot deal with people whom it cannot define. Reputation is this sort of public definition.

Even if people act in ways normally defined as good, their goodness will not be believed. Once stigmatized, they find it extremely difficult to be free of the label "delinquent" or "criminal." As Erikson (1966:17) notes in *Wayward Puritans*, "The common feeling that deviant persons never really change . . . may derive from a faulty premise; but the feeling is expressed so frequently and with such conviction that it eventually creates the facts which later 'prove' it to be correct."

Societal reaction to crime and delinquency helps turn offending individuals away from an image of themselves as bascially "straight" and respectable and toward an image of themselves as criminal. Thus, some people who are reacted to as criminals come to think of themselves as criminals, or at least they participate in what becomes a self-fulfilling prophecy. In a study of used car fraud, one of Braithwaite's (1978) informants said, "They think because you're a used car dealer you're a liar. So they treat you like one and lie to you. Can you blame the dealer for lying back?"

Lemert (1951; 1972) uses the term *secondary deviation* to refer to the criminal acts associated with the individual's acquired status as a criminal and his or her ultimate acceptance of it. Lemert thinks secondary deviation emerges from a process of reaction and adjustment to the punishing and stigmatizing actions of significant others, such as schoolteachers, parents, and law enforcement officials. Although initially the individuals engage for a short time in deviant acts that they regard as incompatible with their true selves (suggesting the need for the techniques of neutralization discussed earlier), they eventually come to accept their new identities as deviants and are well advanced toward a career in deviance. Lemert (1951:77) pictures the process this way:

The sequence of interaction leading to secondary deviation is roughly as follows: (1) primary deviation [initial acts of deviance prompted by any number of reasons]; (2) social penalties; (3) further primary deviation; (4) stronger penalties and rejections; (5) further deviation, perhaps with hostilities and resentments beginning to focus upon those doing the penalizing; (6) crisis reached in the tolerance quotient, expressed in formal action by the community stigmatizing of the deviant; (7) strengthening of the deviant conduct as a reaction to the stigmatizing and penalties; (8) ultimate acceptance of deviant social status and efforts at adjustment on the basis of the associated role.

Whether an individual moves from primary to secondary deviation depends greatly on the degree to which others' disapproval finds expression in concrete acts of punishment and stigmatization. In a later paper, Lemert (1974:457) notes: "While communication of invidious definitions of persons or groups and the public expression of disapproval were included [in earlier discussions] as part of the societal reaction, the important point was made that these had to be validated in order to be sociologically meaningful. Validation was conceived as isolation, segregation, penalties, supervision, or some kind of organized treatment." Support for the criminogenic impact of validation comes from Shannon's (1991) famous cohort study in Racine, Wisconsin. Boys who experienced repeated contacts with the police were at much greater risk of chronic delinquency.

In one attack on labeling theory, Charles Wellford (1975:342) argues that many of its key assumptions are not supported by the bulk of available evidence. In addition, he asserts that the supposed connection between punitive reactions, changes in self-concept, and secondary deviation is "a simplistic view of behavior causation, one that stresses the explanation of intellectual as opposed to behavioral characteristics of the subject." According to Wellford, the claim that changes in self-concept produce changes in behavior has yet to be demonstrated. He prefers to view behavior as situationally determined and argues that crime may well occur quite independently of the actor's self-concept.

Uniting Structure and Process: Integrated Theories

Social process theories deal with the dynamic aspects of the relationship between individuals and their immediate social environments. They explain how it is that certain people learn criminal behavior patterns, and how they acquire criminal status. Where social structural theories focus on the relationship of organization and culture to values, norms, resources, and opportunities, social process theories consider how the actions of individuals and groups influence what people do and become.

Even though process has been separated from structure in this review of prominent theories, the two are in reality intimately connected. One way to think of that connection is to visualize structure as setting the stage for process which in turn brings structure to life. When thinking about crime, structure promotes and restrains criminal activity among different segments of the population, while process determines which individuals within those segments will become criminally active (or be singled out for criminal labeling), and which will not.

Two questions are therefore relevant when considering why crime varies from place to place or from group to group: (1) How do social structures compare? and (2) How do the activities and experiences of individuals compare? Often it is not possible to answer both questions at the same time because the kinds of information or methodologies needed are not available or not used. Sometimes the criminologist who engages in research is simply not interested in process questions, for example, but wants to evaluate the relationship between structure and crime, perhaps at a class or societal level.

It is helpful, nevertheless, to illustrate how structure and process can be linked in research. One recent study assesses the criminal behavior of individuals who live in different family and neighborhood environments (structure) and are exposed to different interactional experiences (process). The study is by John Laub and Robert Sampson (1988), and it reanalyses data compiled by Sheldon and Eleanor Glueck some forty years ago.

The Gluecks (1950) collected data on 500 officially defined delinquents and 500 nondelinquents. All subjects were white males growing up in poor, deteriorated neighborhoods close to the industrial and commercial zones of Boston. Their average age was just under 15. Data on all sorts of social, psychological, and biological variables were collected in a multifactor design. Despite a variety of criticisms leveled at the Gluecks' research design (see Laub and Sampson, 1988:357–361), the study remains a classic in the field.

The reanalysis of the Gluecks' data by Laub and Sampson focused primarily on the relationship between family factors and delinquency. The family factors were divided into two categories that reflect the distinction between structure and process. Structural factors included household crowding, economic dependence, residential mobility, and parental criminality. Process variables included parental discipline and supervision of a child, and emotional rejection.

Figure 15.1 shows the model developed by the authors. They hypothesize that parental child-rearing practices and other family management skills

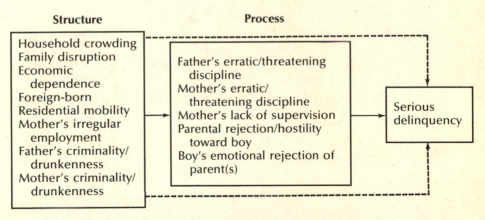

— — — Broken line indicates hypothesized weak or insignificant relationship.
▬▬▬ Solid line indicates hypothesized strong effect.

FIGURE 15.1   Structure and Process United in a Model of Delinquency.
Source: Taken from John H. Laub and Robert J. Sampson (1988). "Unraveling families and delinquency: A reanalysis of the Gluecks' data." *Criminology* 26:366.

would be most directly related to the delinquent behavior of a child since they constitute the emotional atmosphere and control environment to which the child is exposed while growing up. Basing their argument on work by Hirschi (1983) and others, Laub and Sampson predict that good parenting skills and a supportive emotional climate help prevent the emergence of delinquency in a child because they enhance family social control.

The authors also predict, however, that parental discipline and family emotional climate are directly influenced by background factors such as economic dependency, irregular employment, and parental criminality. Thus, the structural variables influence delinquency through their impact on family process. "For instance, it is likely that residential mobility and irregular employment by mothers are related to difficulties in supervising and monitoring children. Similarly, family disruption not only affects supervisory capacity, but also attachment and disciplinary practices" (Laub and Sampson, 1988:367–368).

In this manner, Laub and Sampson show how structure and process can be linked in the explanation of delinquency. When they reanalyzed the Gluecks' data to test this model, they found that the quality of family social control was indeed directly and strongly related to serious and persistent delinquency among boys. Equally important, however, was the finding that the social structural variables helped set the stage by directly influencing the ways in which parents supervise and discipline their children and the quality of the emotional relationship between parent and child.

Summary of Chapter 15

This chapter has considered the social processes by which people acquire the attributes of a criminal. A common theme running through many social process theories is that criminal behavior is learned through association with others who have criminal attributes. Associational theories focus on the ways in which relationships with others provide opportunities and incentives to learn criminal behavior patterns.

Self-concept theories of criminality suggest that a person's sense of self, which is grounded in the reactions of others, is an important element in the internal control of behavior. A strong self-concept is a defense against criminal influence. Neutralization theories suggest that self-respecting individuals will occasionally drift into crime or delinquency, provided they can rationalize their misdeeds so as to protect their self-image as essentially good and honest people.

Control theory, on the other hand, asserts that by nature people will tend to do whatever they want, including crime, so the important theoretical question is What stops them? Hirschi believes that people are less likely to become criminals the more attached they are to the people, values, and activities of conventional (i.e., noncriminal) society.

Labeling theory revolves around the idea that crime is a label attached to behavior and to people; there is nothing intrinsic in behavior that makes it a crime. Labeling theory emphasizes how the stigmatizing reactions of others may turn an individual's infrequent or spontaneous criminal behavior into persistent involvement that matches a criminal identity.

This chapter ended with a model of delinquency causation that unites social structure and social process. The fact that Laub and Sampson discovered a more direct effect on behavior from family process rather than from structural background does not lessen the importance of social structure in the etiology of crime and delinquency. This is particularly true at the macrosociological level, where the structural characteristics and crime rates of whole communities are compared. Even at the level of individual behavior, the impact of social structure is felt *through* its effects on social process. Social structure sets the stage for the interactions and relationships that individuals experience and participate in. Social process theories deal with the interactions between individuals and their immediate social environment and the effect these interactions have on their behavior.

Recommended Readings

Hugh D. Barlow, and Theodore N. Ferdinand (1992). *Understanding Delinquency*. New York: HarperCollins.

Delbert S. Elliott, David Huizinga, and Suzanne S. Ageton (1985). *Explaining Delinquency and Drug Use*. Beverly Hills, Calif.: Sage.

Kai T. Erikson (1966). *Wayward Puritans: A Study in the Sociology of Deviance*. New York: Wiley.

Travis Hirschi (1971). *Causes of Delinquency*. Berkeley, Calif.: University of California Press.

Howard J. Parker (1974). *View From the Boys*. London: David and Charles.

Herman Schwendinger, and Julia Siegel Schwendinger (1985). *Adolescent Subcultures and Delinquency*. New York: Praeger.

Gresham M. Sykes (1972). "The future of criminality." *American Behavioral Scientist* 15:409–419.

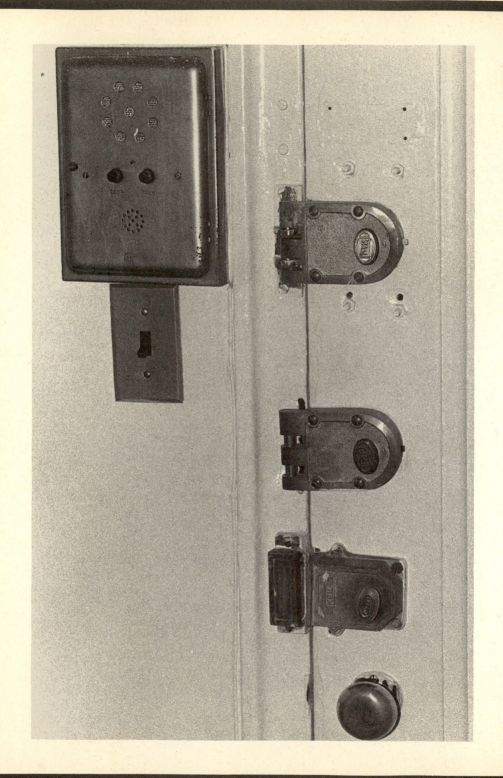

Chapter **16**

Rationality-Opportunity Theories of Crime

During the mid-1960s in the United States, rates of assault, rape, robbery, and other "street" crimes took an alarming upward turn and continued to rise dramatically throughout the 1970s. Crime quickly emerged as the number one problem facing the country, and President Lyndon Johnson created a commission to study the problem and offer solutions. Evaluations of existing theory and research as well as original research were undertaken by the commission. Two years later, the final report of The President's Commission on Law Enforcement and the Administration of Justice included more than twelve volumes.

Crime became a cause célèbre for the President and for Congress, which was quick to enact the Omnibus Crime Control and Safe Streets Act (1968). Among other provisions, this act established the Law Enforcement Assistance Administration (LEAA), through which billions of dollars would eventually be funneled in the effort to combat crime. Scrambling to obtain pieces of this largesse were agencies ranging from universities wanting to fund research and to create academic programs, to police departments and correctional institutions wanting to professionalize, rationalize, and expand.

As the money flowed and the effort grew, so did crime. A sense of failure hung in the air. "Nothing works," was a popular lament. Efforts were redoubled and budgets grew. By 1976 the annual budget of LEAA stood at more than $1 billion. Still crime grew.

Mainstream positivistic theories and the crime-prevention strategies they informed, such as rehabilitation, came under attack from many quarters. Yochelson and Samenow's (1976, 1977) claim that criminals are calculating and hedonistic could not have appeared at a more receptive time. "It is not the environment that turns a man into a criminal . . . but a series of choices he makes. . . ." (Yochelson and Samenow, 1976:247). This conclusion linked their research to an old idea: Criminals control their own actions and believe that the benefits of crime outweigh the risks. In other words: Crime pays. Not surprisingly, *deterrence*, the idea that authorities must make the choice of committing crime less attractive, became one of the hottest crime issues of the 1970s (see Chapter 12).

Arguments in favor of deterrence came from many quarters and were promoted by such highly respected criminologists as James Q. Wilson (1975). Taking a somewhat different tack, some authors proposed an alternative strategy, but one also predicated on the assumption that criminals are rational actors. Why not reduce crime by manipulating the *opportunities* for its occurrence? Steering locks were introduced in automobiles, street lamps were made brighter, private security forces were beefed up, dead-bolt locks and home alarm systems were sold everywhere, new gun-control laws were proposed, and all varieties of environmental modifications were envisioned. Simply put, the idea was that many criminal events can be prevented if opportunities are reduced through "target hardening."

Rationality and Criminal Decision Making

This section presents the criminological theory underlying deterrence and target hardening. First it ventures back in time to "classical criminology," which flourished in the late eighteenth century and is now undergoing a rebirth. The economic model of crime is a modern formulation of this classical view. The rationality model modifies the older approach in many aspects and introduces such interesting concepts as "crime displacement" and "able criminals."

"Classical Criminology"

Italian Cesare Beccaria and Englishman Jeremy Bentham are credited with forming many of the essential ideas of classical criminology. Writing in the late eighteenth century, these authors believed that criminals are free, rational, and hedonistic. Like other people, they choose among a variety of actions according to expected benefits. They avoid behavior that is likely to bring pain unless pain is expected to be outweighed by pleasure.

Although Bentham and Beccaria recognized that individuals are sometimes forced to engage in behavior they would not choose, the decision to act in a certain way is considered to be voluntary, and individuals are therefore responsible for their actions. "For classicism," writes David Garland (1985:120), "it was an article of faith that each individual (except the mad and the infant) possessed the faculties of will, responsibility, and reason."

The Economic Model of Crime

A modern formulation of the classical view has been advanced by economists, among them Gary Becker (1968). Many complicated models have been developed, but they all share certain key ideas. First, the approach "is predicated on the assumption that individuals choose to commit crimes" (Warren, 1978:439). Second, it is assumed that people choose the same course of action when confronted by the same alternatives. This is *rationality* as economists use the term. The choice itself is guided by maximization of satisfactions, or "utility."

Individuals evaluate possible activities according to utility. The utility of a crime is the expected gain weighed against the probability of being caught and convicted, and the monetary costs, real and foregone, if convicted. When the expected utility of a criminal act is greater than the utility of a noncriminal alternative, the economic model predicts that the crime will be selected.

The classical model of criminal behavior assumes that crime follows a calculation in which the perceived rewards, costs, and risks of alternative actions are compared. In itself this is a bold assumption because it not only implies that people are capable of making such calculations but also that they have the information necessary to do so.

Economists who develop models of criminal behavior often ignore non-criminal alternatives, concentrating instead on variations of estimated costs and benefits associated with crimes. The likelihood of a particular crime (robbery, for instance) is then calculated in terms of variations in the probabilities of arrest, conviction, and imprisonment, and in the economic losses (offenders' gains) for robbery, compared with other predatory property crimes. If the gains from robbery are small compared to the risks and costs, but the gains from burglary are greater, then a person acting rationally and voluntarily would choose to commit burglary.

Voluntarism versus Determinism　The classical model is not accepted by those scientists who believe that people are "pushed" or "pulled" into crime by forces beyond their control. From this *deterministic* point of view, all assumptions of the classical model are questionable, especially the notion that choices are freely made. How can one speak of free will, critics assert, when biological, cultural, or economic factors determine not only the choices but who can take advantage of them? In response, the advocates of *voluntarism* claim that it is reasonable to speak of free will, regardless of circumstances, *whenever* a person has a choice. If one can say yes or no to an action, the final choice is the exercise of free will.

These positions represent two poles between which more moderate views exist. One view is expressed in the observation that "offenders are not ineluctably propelled by social conditions. They have individual moral choice within the context of circumstances that beset them. After all, even though crime is distinctly related to poverty, only a tiny proportion of the poor at any given time commit crimes. Crime is a subjective choice in a given objective situation" (Kinsey, Lea, and Young, 1986:75).

The assumption that choice making is a fully rational exercise—a key assumption of the economic model and also implied in the writings of Beccaria and Bentham—is tempered by some authors who believe in a more limited rationality. It is argued, for example, that most people cannot know all the information necessary to evaluate *all* possible actions, but rather they reflexively react to opportunities that arise in ordinary situations (Trasler, 1986:20).

The limited rationality view holds that behavioral choices arise in peoples' lives routinely and some involve decisions to commit crime. These choices are structured by several factors, including the social distribution of opportunities and access to them; the knowledge, past experiences, and capabilities of individuals; the conditions that characterize and are created by the social situations in which individuals find themselves; and the measures taken by victims and authorities to prevent them. Behavioral decisions are made by individuals within the boundaries created by these factors. The chosen actions are rational to the extent that they are *purposive* (conscious and goal-oriented) and *reasonable* (efficient, economical) in light of goals and alternatives. It is not necessary to assume that criminals carefully plan and execute their crimes or use the most sophisticated techniques. Rational choice theories need only assume that some minimal level of planning or foresight occurs (Hirschi, 1985).

Rationality and Crime

The rationality model of decision making predicts that individuals think about the expected rewards, costs, and risks of alternative actions and choose actions best suited to their goals. If the model has merit, it should be revealed not only in the choice to commit crime, but also in the choice to commit one kind of crime rather than another and in the decision to direct crime against one victim rather than another.

Research about these choices is still in its infancy, but some promising work has been done about the decision making of property offenders (see, especially, Tunnell, 1992). This may reflect the prevalent view that property offenders are more likely to act rationally than, for example, drug addicts or rapists, whose crimes are popularly thought to be expressive rather than instrumental. (Despite its popularity, this view has been challenged throughout the text. Suffice it to say, many crimes involve rationality if only to the extent that they hardly ever occur in front of a police officer.)

An example of the research on decisions by property offenders is Thomas Reppetto's (1974) study of residential burglary and robbery. Interviews with offenders confirmed that target preferences existed and were taken into account when they contemplated committing crimes. Burglars looked for unoccupied single-family homes (thus reducing the risk of being seen or heard), with easy access (thus reducing the amount of skill needed to gain entry), which appeared affluent (thus increasing the possible reward), and which were located in neighborhoods where offenders felt they "fit in" (another way to reduce the risk of being noticed). Weighing the risks, robbers tended to select lone victims who were just outside their homes and could be quickly hustled inside. The risk of being seen or interrupted also appeared to be a major factor influencing target selection of burglars in four Chicago-area communities (*The Compiler*, vol. 8, 1987).

The rationality model receives additional support from studies in England. Walsh's (1980) study of Exeter burglars found that although few burglars admitted doing much preplanning or "casing" of targets, most were very concerned about being seen, and avoided entering houses likely to be occupied. Walsh constructed a "decision tree" indicating typical selection considerations of burglars (see Figure 16.1). Both architectural and social factors were weighed when assessing the suitability of a target.

A second study of English burglars is more detailed and lends further support to the rationality model while pointing to the importance of situational cues in decision making. Using videotapes of 36 houses seen from a passing van, Bennett and Wright (1981, 1984) asked 58 convicted burglars to evaluate the houses as potential burglary targets. Most of the burglars were very experienced so there is no indication whether the findings would apply to occasional thieves or beginners.

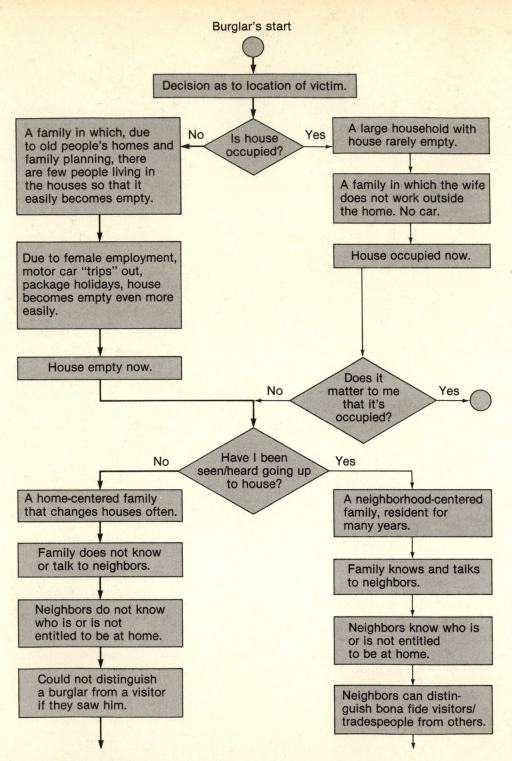

FIGURE 16.1 Decision Making by Burglars. The pathway most commonly used is marked ———. *Source:* From Dermot Walsh (1980). *Break-ins: Burglary from Private Houses.* London: Constable, pp. 144–145. Reprinted with permission of Constable Publishers.

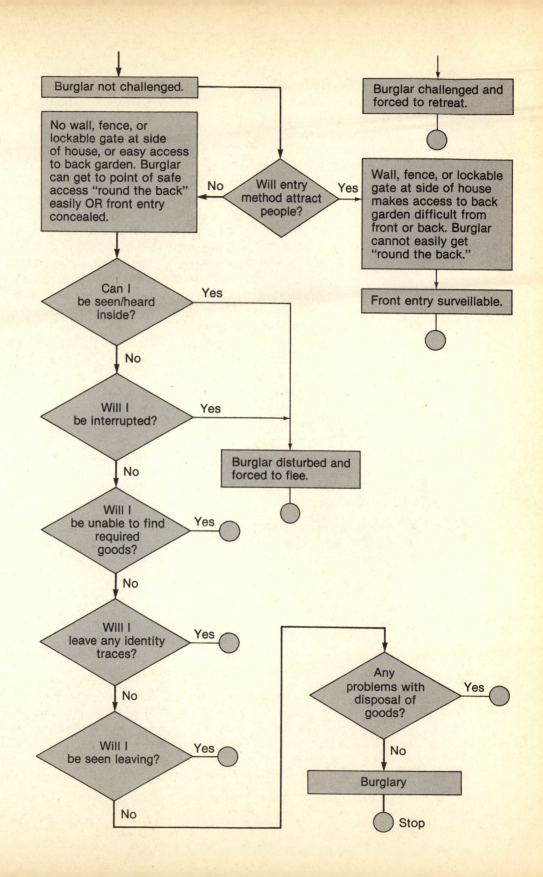

Although there was considerable variation in target choice, the burglars strongly agreed about certain blocks of houses or about one or two specific homes. When the authors grouped evaluations according to risk, reward, or skill factors, the authors found that the burglars most frequently mentioned risk of being seen or heard as the decisive consideration. Reward factors became more important than those connected with skill only when given as reasons to disregard a target. A house may not be worth burglarizing regardless of how easy it is to enter.

These studies did not investigate actual criminal behavior, only what offenders said about it. For that reason they give only inferential support for the rationality model. Bennett and Wright (1981:16) also point out that criminals might not evaluate situational cues about ease of access and neighborhood surveillance all the time, especially when they are "desperate for money, feeling impulsive or bloody-minded, or simply too lazy."

It is important to remember that a full-fledged theory of criminal decision making needs to address not just the crime itself, but also the offender's initial involvement in crime. As Cornish and Clarke (1986a, 1987) point out, such a theory must also account for decisions to continue and to terminate criminal activity. Traditionally, they argue, criminology has been more concerned with background influences such as social structure and prior experience and less with situational and transitory influences, which may influence certain types of criminal activity even more significantly.

Crime Displacement

Whenever criminally motivated persons decide not to commit a crime or avoid certain victims in favor of others, the substitution is commonly referred to as *displacement*. Five types of displacement have been identified (Hakim and Rengert, 1981):

- *Temporal displacement.* Here, an offender substitutes one time of day, week, or even season for another.
- *Spatial displacement.* An offender substitutes one street, neighborhood, area, or region for another.
- *Target displacement.* An offender substitutes an easier, less risky, or more rewarding target in the same location.
- *Tactical displacement.* An offender substitutes one *modus operandi* (method of operation) for another.
- *Type of crime displacement.* One type of crime is substituted for another, usually one that is less risky or more easily performed.

Displacement is important for two reasons. First, its occurrence is predicted by the rationality model. The idea is that criminals generally take advantage of or seek the best criminal opportunities, those with the greatest rewards at the least risk and cost. Second, displacement is important because it is one of the potential costs of crime prevention efforts. For example, when criminal opportunities are reduced by police surveillance or other "target-hardening" measures, the net result may be an increase in crime in another place. Criminally motivated individuals simply move to the "safer" areas to commit crime. Therefore, one community may benefit from crime prevention efforts while another may suffer because of them.

Research on crime displacement is sparse because it is extremely difficult to measure substitution behavior as it occurs. At the least, one would need to show that one criminal event occurred and some other did not because the offender changed his or her mind after evaluating the situation. Criminologists often infer displacement from studies of spatial or temporal changes in the volume of crime or by asking offenders if, when, and why they made substitutions. Most studies are further limited because they focus only on temporal or spatial displacement.

After reviewing American evidence, John McIver (1981:32) suggests that spatial displacement is probably quite limited "because criminals prefer to operate in known territory." This in itself is a sign of rationality, for familiarity reduces an offender's risk of being caught and may contribute to successful completion of the crime. Nevertheless, McIver cites four studies showing that police crime prevention efforts resulted in "spillover" effects: Crime rates increased in neighborhoods adjacent to areas with more concentrated police enforcement. However, displacement occurred with property crimes, not with crimes of violence. The latter may be relatively impervious to displacement pressures because they are more likely to be spur-of-the-moment and tend to occur at the criminals' homes, near local bars, and so forth.

English studies lend tentative support to the displacement argument, at least for some crimes. When steering locks were introduced in British cars as a target-hardening measure, the rates of auto crime did not drop significantly. Apparently many thieves turned their attention to the abundant older cars that did not have steering locks (Riley, 1980). In addition, determined thieves could quickly learn how to overcome the devices. This suggests that displacement brought about by changes in skill factors is probably limited to amateur and opportunistic thieves.

A massive car-locking publicity campaign in 1977 apparently had little effect on car-locking behavior, but it did seem to affect the behavior of car thieves. Daytime thefts dropped appreciably while nighttime thefts rose—a temporal displacement. Thieves probably feared greater public surveillance as a result of the campaign. These English findings may be taken as evidence that criminally motivated individuals are more concerned with the risks of being detected than with a crime's degree of difficulty. If correct, this would complement findings on target selection (Burrows and Heal, 1980).

A third British study surveyed the impact of installing closed-circuit television in some London subway stations (Mayhew et al., 1979). Generally, stations with the greatest volume of traffic experienced more robberies and other property crimes. After authorities installed television cameras in high-traffic stations, the volume of robberies declined there but increased dramatically in stations without TV surveillance. On the other hand, other thefts declined throughout the subway system during the three-year test period.

This sign is a warning to criminals that residents are on the lookout for crime in the area and will report suspicious activity to the police. Based on the assumption that people act rationally, such signs stand little chance of deterring crime unless criminals who read them feel that the risks of being caught are unacceptable. Even then, they may simply commit their crimes elsewhere.

This finding suggests that an offense-specific spatial displacement took place rather than any general displacement. Apparently robbers took the new surveillance into consideration, merely changing location. Other, perhaps less committed or less experienced thieves were apparently more likely to view the TV cameras as evidence of a more concerted law-enforcement effort. Reacting to this perception, offenders reduced their activity, at least for a time.

Displacement is thus not an inevitable result of crime-prevention efforts such as target hardening (see Cornish and Clarke, 1987; also Tunnell, 1992:106). Prostitution is another case in point. A study showed that increased police enforcement in a North London suburb did not cause prostitutes to move elsewhere (Matthews, 1986). Studies by Clarke and Mayhew (1988) of the effects of detoxification of the British gas supply on suicide rates showed marked decreases in suicides and no evidence that suicide-prone individuals were shifting to other means. Finally, the introduction of motor-cycle helmets in various countries has apparently had the unintended consequence of reducing motorcycle thefts (presumably because thieves must carry a helmet with them), but there is no evidence that similar forms of crime, for example auto theft, have increased as a result (Mayhew, Clarke, and Elliott, 1989).

It is unlikely that many offenders substitute new crimes for old when the calculus of risks, costs, and benefits changes. Income tax evaders, shoplifters, and employee thieves will not become burglars, con artists, and robbers. Some professional or habitual criminals may respond to such changes by increasing their skills and directing their energies only toward the most lucrative targets. They may become better criminals in the process, and they may also become more dangerous—willing to take greater risks, combining into more formida-ble groups, or increasing their willingness to use deadly force when con-fronted. Such changes have occurred in the realm of bank heists, as a tactical displacement shifted crime from safe cracking to over-the-counter robbery to robbery of armored cars (Ball, Chester, and Perrott, 1978).

Those criminals most likely to shift from one crime to another, and least likely to continue a given line of crime in the face of increased risks and costs, are the less skilled but more experienced opportunistic offenders. They take advantage of easily accessible opportunities. They are unlikely to increase their efforts and risks in search of less hardened targets with which they may be unfamiliar or which may be too far from home. These are speculations although a new study of decision-making among property offenders lends them credence (see Tunnell, 1992: 149). Cornish and Clarke (1987) are right when they observe that considerably more work must be done in both theory and research to untangle the complexities of displacement. The fact that there are at least twelve distinct techniques of situational prevention makes both tasks all the more difficult. These twelve techniques are described in detail by Clarke (1992:12–21) and are illustrated in Box 16.1.

Able Criminals

Some criminals reduce the risk and increase the likelihood of successfully completing a crime through planning, organization, and skill. This is the reasonable answer to overcoming risks when the anticipated rewards are compelling. It has the added benefit of increasing future rewards by improv-ing the feasibility of undertaking more difficult but more lucrative crimes.

Though relatively few in number, a hard core of offenders is responsible for a large portion of the street crimes that come to police attention, as well as those that do not. For some of these offenders crime is a livelihood and they can make more money at crime than they ever could legally. These are the "able criminals"—experienced, and often skilled, connected, and informed. They seek out opportunities even if that means charting new waters. For many years the bulk of serious property crime in England appeared to have been committed by such offenders (Mack, 1964). Newly emerging evidence sug-

Box 16.1 ■ The Twelve Techniques of Situational Prevention

Increasing the Effort	Increasing the Risks	Reducing the Rewards
Target Hardening	*Entry/Exit Screening*	*Target Removal*
Steering locks	Border searches	Removable car radio
Bandit screens	Baggage screening	Exact change fares
Slug rejector device	Automatic ticket gates	Cash reduction
Vandal-proofing	Merchandise tags	Remove coin meters
Toughened glass	Library tags	Phonecard
Tamper-proof seals	EPoS	Pay by check
Access Control	*Formal Surveillance*	*Identifying Property*
Locked gates	Police patrols	Cattle branding
Fenced yards	Security guards	Property marking
Parking lot barriers	Informant hotlines	Vehicle licensing
Entryphones	Burglar alarms	Vehicle parts marking
ID badges	Red light cameras	PIN for car radios
PIN numbers	Curfew decals	LOJACK
Deflecting Offenders	*Surveillance by Employees*	*Removing Inducements*
Bus stop placement	Bus conductors	"Weapons effect"
Tavern location	Park attendants	Graffiti cleaning
Street closures	Concierges	Rapid repair
Graffiti board	Pay phone location	Plywood road signs
Litter bins	Incentive schemes	Gender-neutral phone lists
Spittoons	CCTV systems	Park Camarro off street
Controlling Facilitators	*Natural Surveillance*	*Rule Setting*
Spray-can sales	Pruning hedges	Drug-free school zone
Gun control	"Eyes on the street"	Public park regulations
Credit card photo	Lighting bank interiors	Customs declaration
Ignition interlock	Street lighting	Income tax returns
Server intervention	Defensible space	Hotel registration
Caller-ID	Neighborhood Watch	Library check-out

Source: Ronald V. Clarke ed. (1992). *Situational Crime Prevention: Successful Case Studies.* New York: Harrow and Heston, page 13. Reprinted by permission.

gests that times have changed and the picture is now similar to that of America (see Kinsey, Lea, and Young, 1986). In the United States, most predatory crimes seem to be committed by a core of relatively young but experienced offenders, many with a history of heavy drug use.

A study using interviews and records of California prison inmates estimated that a typical group of 100 inmates convicted of robbery would have committed 490 armed robberies, 310 assaults, 720 burglaries, 70 auto thefts, 100 forgeries, and 3400 drug sales in one year of street freedom (Peterson, Braiker, and Polich, 1980). Predictably, the most mobile offenders committed the greatest number of crimes.

In this study there is evidence that some offenders face obstacles that limit the amount and range of criminal activity. For example, even though blacks were overrepresented in the California prison population, "they reported committing the least number of different types of crime and reported the lowest rates for the crimes they committed" (Peterson, Braiker, and Polich, 1980:ix). This finding remained the same even after age, prior record, drug use, and various psychological factors were taken into account. It could be that inmates were lying to the interviewers—blacks might have underreported and whites overreported their criminal activity. What is more likely is that the differences reflect the effects of lower resources and restricted mobility. In various respects, blacks are simply less advantaged than whites, and this reduces their ability to pursue criminal (and noncriminal) opportunities and increases the risks and costs when they do so.

These structural impediments to free movement may come into play as "background" forces affecting the decisions of able criminals rather than as proximate variables that affect decision making *in situ*. For example, some individuals take for granted that committing crimes in certain parts of town is out of the question for them, and so decision making as it takes place is affected by other considerations—ease of access, perhaps, or anticipated profits, availability of partners, required skills, and so on.

Able criminals may actually spend little time contemplating the risks of crime. Interviews with 46 persistent property offenders found that the majority gave little or no thought to the possibility of arrest and confinement. Here are some typical comments (Shover and Honaker, Forthcoming:5):

Q. Did you think about getting caught?

A. No.

Q. How did you manage to put that out of your mind?

A. [I]t never did come into it. . . . It didn't bother me.

Another subject said:

A. I wasn't worried about getting caught or anything, you know. I didn't have no negative thoughts about it whatever.

And another said:

A. When I went out to steal, I didn't think about negative things. 'Cause if you think negative, negative things are going to happen. . . . You just, you just put [the thought of arrest] out of your mind, you know.

Retrospective interviews are not without drawbacks, not least among which is the validity of reconstructions of events long past (see also Shover

Target hardening that failed?

and Thompson, 1992). It remains to be seen whether more proximal memories confirm the lack of a negative relationship between perceptions of risk and criminal activity among able offenders.

Opportunity and Crime

Now it is appropriate to consider how the nature and distribution of opportunities for crime influence criminal activity and shape the contours of crime for specific groups of people. It will be necessary to shift gears somewhat. So far the exercise of will and the rationality of decision making in the face of choices have been discussed. Now it is important to think about the factors that shape those choices.

Crime as an Event

It will help to think of crime as an *event*. Crime is not an event until it has occurred, for an event is an occurrence or happening. A criminal event occurs when a situation fortuitously brings together factors that facilitate it. Advocates of a "situational" approach look at crimes that have occurred and ask what things came together to make them happen.

Crimes differ in so many ways that any attempt to identify basic elements that criminal events share would be doomed from the start (but see Gottfredson and Hirschi, 1990; see also Chapter 17). A criminal event need not even have an offender present when it occurs. Some bombings and arson, forms of extortion, and many forms of consumer fraud take place when the criminal is elsewhere, even dead. The point is not as trivial as it may seem; detection, arrest, prosecution, conviction, and punishment all rely on tying a suspect to the event. Strangely enough, some crimes occur *only* in the presence of police officers, as in resisting arrest and police brutality.

An effort is underway to identify the elements in different types of crime. The crimes that the public fears most are predatory crimes, in which the offender "definitely and intentionally takes or damages the person or property of another" (Glaser, 1971:4). Robbery, burglary, rape, auto theft, embezzlement, shoplifting, hijacking, and arson are examples.

According to Lawrence Cohen and Marcus Felson (1979), predatory criminal events contain the following minimal elements: (1) motivated offenders, (2) suitable targets, and (3) the absence of capable guardians. If any one of these elements is lacking, a predatory criminal event will not occur. Notice that no mention is made of "capable" offenders, those able to "pull crimes off" (though they may later be caught). In fact, much crime is unsuccessful, making the distinction between completed and uncompleted crime an important one for theory and research. Indeed, the law has long recognized the distinction, treating attempted crimes less severely than completed ones. From the situational point of view the distinction is interesting because it prompts one to compare attempted and completed crimes in order to establish the differences, and which elements account for the outcomes. This was discussed in Chapter 3 in relation to murder and assault.

If there is a common element in all events, criminal or not, it is opportunity. An opportunity makes an event possible; a criminal opportunity makes a crime possible. One cannot rob a bank without the opportunity to do so—without the existence of banks. Notice, however, that banks provide not only criminal opportunities, but noncriminal ones as well. In fact, the purpose of most things is not crime, but their existence creates criminal opportunities. A functionalist would say that the above principle is a "latent dysfunction" of otherwise useful objects and institutions.

It needs to be said that no event is criminal until those who create and administer the law say it is. This means that two otherwise similar societies may have different criminal opportunities simply because the authorities in one society have labeled more (or different) activities as crimes. In one society, for example, people who take advantage of the opportunity to buy pornographic material may be committing a crime, while in another they would not be. Thus, the amount and kinds of crime committed among different jurisdictions depend on the existence of appropriate criminal labels. If the appropriate labels exist in all jurisdictions, then variations in the amount and kind of crime will reflect variations in criminal opportunities and access to them.

Social Change and Crime

As societies grow increasingly complex and as knowledge grows and technology advances, both noncriminal and criminal opportunities expand. The range of what is possible grows, and so does crime. This is probably what nineteenth-century Italian scholar Francesco Poletti meant when he observed that the more honest activity there is, the more dishonest activity there is. This would be true even if there were no changes in criminal law. Technological change makes new activities possible, and some will be criminal. The United States government is obviously concerned: It is in the process of changing $100 bills now that advanced copying machines have made counterfeiting easier (*St. Louis Post-Dispatch* July 26, 1991 p. 1).

Consider what many people now take for granted: electronic fund transfer. Not long ago this computer-based service was known and used only by banks and large corporations. Now the automatic teller machine (ATM) is familiar to most people. Those with personal computers may also take advantage of home banking services. With the spread of electronic fund transfer has come growth in criminal abuse. The U.S. Justice Department now recognizes four generic types of ATM crime (Bureau of Justice Statistics, 1984a):

- *Unauthorized use.* This is when an access card is stolen and used without the permission of the authorized holder.
- *Fraud by legitimate* holder. For example, a person makes an authorized withdrawal and then denies any knowledge of it, demanding that the bank refund the money.
- *Insider manipulation.* In this instance a bank employee steals directly from the machine, takes a card that should have been mailed to a customer, or creates a fictitious account by manipulating the computer.
- *Physical attack.* Automated teller machines often hold considerable amounts of cash and thus become targets of attempts to break them open. Customers who use machines can become robbery targets after they have withdrawn money.

According to Department of Justice estimates, about $262 billion was processed through 2.7 billion ATM transactions in 1983. Of this, $70 to $100 million was lost through unauthorized use or fraud (Bureau of Justice Statistics, 1987:19).

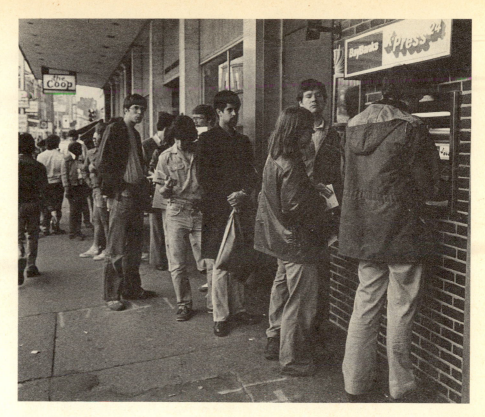

The automatic teller machine (ATM) has made banking easier but has also increased opportunities for crime, from fraud and theft to rape and robbery.

Many criminologists believe that the global increase in crime throughout the past 150 years can be traced to an increase in criminal opportunities (e.g., Shelley, 1980; Sparks, 1980; Mack, 1975). In one American study, Leroy Gould (1969) showed that the significant rise in property crime rates from 1930 to 1967 directly reflected the growing abundance of property. On a different plane, some studies of changes in homicide rates have attributed increases to the growing availability and use of firearms (see Chapter 3).

In an analysis of the relationship between social change and crime, Mary McIntosh (1971) argues that changes in English society not only increased the opportunities for property crime but also changed the nature of those opportunities. A corresponding shift occurred from what she calls "craft crime" to "project crime." Craft crime developed during Elizabethan times as cities grew and more people carried cash and valuables. The thief could steal small amounts from many victims and with practice could master a variety of skills. Pocket picking, shoplifting, gambling cheats, and con games were examples of craft crime.

Project crime emerged as a by-product of industrialization. It is similar to what Werner Einstadter (1969) has called the "planned operation"—a high-risk crime for high stakes. It arises in response to the opportunity to steal large amounts from small numbers of commercial victims such as banks and other businesses that go to greater lengths to protect their property by developing new methods which the criminal must then overcome. Innovations created by potential victims result in counterinnovations made by thieves. One does not hijack a Brinks armored truck alone, on the spur of the moment, or with a pocketknife.

The Routine Activity Approach

Change sooner or later affects all social institutions in addition to the environments in which people live, work, and play. The growth of cities, the smashing of the atom, the conquest of near space, the invention of the assembly line, the discovery of penicillin, the defeat of the Axis powers in World War II, the migration from southern states to northern states, the invention of the personal computer—all have affected our daily lives.

The relationship between change, opportunities, and criminal events has been explored in studies by Cohen and Felson (1979; 1980) who developed a *routine activities* approach. A routine activity is any recurring and prevalent goal-seeking activity. Work is a routine activity, but so are sex, child rearing, eating, going to the movies, and vacationing. Much crime is also routine activity.

Advocates of the approach argue that changes in noncriminal routine activities affect criminal opportunities by affecting the convergence in time and space of the elements necessary for a crime to occur. Cohen and his colleagues focus on such "direct contact" predatory crimes as robbery, murder, and burglary, but the perspective can be applied to other types of criminal events. The basic proposition is as follows: "The probability that a violation will occur at any specific time and place . . . is . . . a function of the convergence of likely offenders and suitable targets in the absence of capable guardians" (Cohen and Felson, 1979:590).

This proposition is examined for both groups and individuals. At the group level, changing rates of predatory crime in America from 1947 to 1974 (and later to 1977) are largely the result of the dispersion of routine activities away from the household. Increased participation in work, play, and family activities outside the home increases the likelihood that suitable unguarded targets will be available to motivated offenders. To explain it another way, when fewer people stay at home, more household property is unguarded, and when more people leave home after dark or are alone, more people are unprotected. Looking at robbery from the standpoint of potential victims, for example, the chances of victimization are greater for people who are alone or away from home. In a study by Cohen, Cantor, and Klugel (1981), the risk of being robbed while alone was ten times greater than when accompanied by others.

"The Guardian Angels" strive to protect subway riders against assault, robbery, and rape. According to routine activity theory, the Guardian Angels will prevent some crimes by providing capable guardianship of potential crime targets. They are controversial, however, because they are not bound by the laws that govern police action, because they are prepared to use force, and because they stir up images of vigilantism.

Another way of looking at routine activities is to think of the locations where crimes are likely to occur. Consider the data in Figure 16.2. Where would you expect handgun crimes to occur most often? Your answer will depend on the routine activities of typical offenders and victims, and on the relationship between the two. Thus, handgun crimes involving relatives are most likely to occur in the home; those involving strangers are most likely to occur on the street.

Dangerous Places

Routine activities are carried out in a wide variety of places, and some are more dangerous than others. Crime risks differ in places that offer varying levels of guardianship to life and property (see Roncek and Maier, 1991, for recent work). A place that offers few opportunities to observe what is going on, where anonymity is characteristic, and where strangers can come and go with

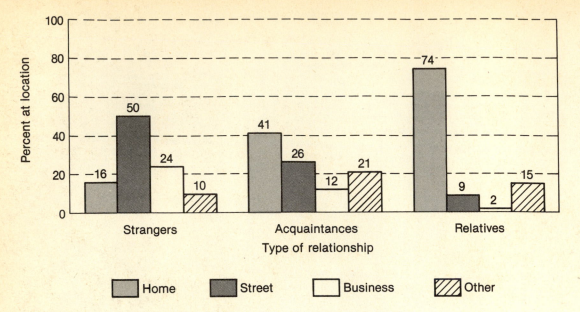

FIGURE 16.2   Location of Handgun Crimes. By victim–offender relationship, 1979–1987 (percent).   *Source:* Compiled from Bureau of Justice Statistics
(1990). *Special Report: Handgun Crime Victims.* Washington, D.C.: U.S. Department
of Justice, p. 5.

ease lacks what Oscar Newman (1972) has called "defensible space." Such
places are crime-prone.

Newman developed the idea of defensible space in a study of public
housing projects in New York. He found that rates of serious crimes such as
robbery increased along with the height of buildings, from 8.3 per 1000 people
in 3-story buildings to 20.2 per 1000 people in buildings 16 stories or higher.
He found also that more than half of the crime in high-rise buildings occurred
in easily accessible corridors and other communal areas that were poorly
monitored. He concluded that building design influences the opportunities
for crime by affecting residents' surveillance and control of semipublic
places.

Despite criticism of Newman's approach (e.g., S. Wilson, 1980; Booth,
1981), the idea of defensible space has continued to draw attention. Other
research (e.g., Pyle, 1976) shows that architectural features of the environment do influence the occurrence of crime, but that influence is mediated by
such factors as age (the more young people, the more crime), household
composition (the more single-parent families, the more crime), and size and
density of both resident and surrounding populations (the more people in a
given space, the more crime). In fact, a growing consensus is that the value of
defensible space in explaining crime rates is lessened by its almost exclusive
emphasis on architectural features of buildings (see Roncek, 1981). What goes
on in and around the buildings is the key. Anonymity and lowered guardian-

ship are especially important in areas where people come together precisely for the purpose of having a good time—more bars and taverns means more risk of crime (Roncek and Maier, 1991).

Access to Opportunities

The routine activity approach is a promising perspective on the relationship between criminal events and the organization of everyday behavior of individuals and groups. In the case of direct-contact, predatory property crimes, the perspective correctly predicts that younger people are more likely to be victims and offenders than older persons, as are the poor more than the rich, the unemployed more than the employed, the active more than the inactive, and urban residents more than rural residents. It also correctly predicts that small but valuable pieces of property—stereos, car radios, VCRs, portable TVs—and property left unguarded are the items most vulnerable to theft.

One factor that proponents of the routine activity approach have not researched is the manner in which the organization of routine activities influences the *range* of crime. This is not just a question of the nature of criminal opportunities, but of access to them.

Structural theories tell us that neither opportunities nor access are distributed evenly in time and space or throughout a population. Obviously, opportunities for auto theft are greater in areas where there are more cars, but getting to them, especially the more valuable ones, is not as easy for some thieves as it is for others. The opportunities for shoplifting are greater in areas where there are more stores, larger stores, and stores with open displays, but these stores may be clustered in certain areas only. The opportunities to pilfer at work increase as more people work and as work places grow larger and more impersonal, but only the employed can pilfer, and some employees can pilfer much more valuable things than others. The opportunities for executive crime—price fixing, bribery and kickbacks, corporate fraud—increase as the economy expands, but relatively few people are able to take advantage of them. Of course, even though restrictions in access may effectively reduce the opportunities for a particular type of crime, they may actually increase the opportunities for other types. For example, higher rates of unemployment may result in lower rates of work-related crime and higher rates of loitering and public intoxication.

Spatial Aspects of Crime The spatial distribution of crime is affected by the constraints that govern behavioral decisions. Geographers have studied the locations where crimes occur and the movement of offenders to and from crime sites. Coupled with studies of target selection, this research offers insight into the links between criminal opportunities, routine activities, and criminal decision making.

According to Brantingham and Brantingham (1981:35): "[O]ne of the striking things about criminals is that most of them behave as ordinary people most of the time." In being "ordinary," people grow familiar with certain parts of the city—their neighborhoods, local shopping centers, entertainment districts, and areas where friends and relatives live. These areas constitute a person's "awareness" or "action" space. They are the familiar environment, the places a person knows well.

Choices are influenced by knowledge. Regardless of where the best criminal opportunities are located, criminals will tend to commit crimes within their action space. Studies of the distance between crime site and an offender's home show that this rarely exceeds two miles (McIver, 1981). There is also evidence that the number of crimes a person commits decreases as the distance increases from home base.

Motivated offenders living in places with few criminal opportunities have a problem. They must either forego some or all crime or move from their action space. Doing the latter increases the risks and costs of crime because: (1) they are more likely to be unfamiliar with the territory, and therefore the targets and guardians; (2) they use more of their resources in travel, in getting their bearings, and in returning home; and (3) they are more likely to be recognized as strangers and therefore are watched more closely by those who "belong" there.

These problems are exacerbated for people who lack the resources to find opportunities in unfamiliar places or who stand out because of some characteristic that cannot be easily hidden, such as race or sex. In a fascinating study of crime in Oklahoma City, Carter and Hill (1979) found that black offenders had to forego areas they designated as having "easy marks" in favor of highly familiar areas. For white offenders, easy marks and familiarity had equal weight in their selection of target areas. Further, it was discovered that black offenders had a much more restricted image of the city than whites, who moved from area to area more freely.

A study of St. Louis crime patterns by a pioneer researcher of opportunity theory substantiates the importance of restricted action space as a factor in black crime. Sarah Boggs (1964) found that black homicides, assaults, and residential burglaries were committed most often in the neighborhoods in which offenders lived, whereas white offenses were more dispersed.

Offenders who commit crimes in areas beyond their action space may be "pulled" to those areas when the opportunities are especially abundant (such as in "red light" districts) or when the anticipated rewards are especially high. The rationality model predicts selection of those areas that maximize utility, and even high-risk areas may be selected when the expected returns significantly outweigh those from safer areas.

Criminal Resources   Access to criminal opportunities is governed by available resources. The greater the resources, the greater the range of accessible criminal activities. Some crimes require special skills (safe cracking, counterfeiting, con games); some crimes require special equipment (computer crime, record pirating, bombing, heroin production); some crimes require special planning (embezzlement, numbers running, prostitution); some crimes require lots of money (heroin importation, large-scale gambling, loan sharking) or lots of muscle (extortion, hijacking, racketeering, terrorism); some crimes require prestige or social position (bribery, corporate crime, police corruption, welfare fraud); and some crimes require "connections" (drug dealing, fencing).

Despite (or perhaps because of) its obviousness, the resources aspect of criminal activity has not been carefully explored in relation to crime theory (Agnew, 1990). This is even more surprising given the long-standing interest in inequality noted in Chapter 14. Still, one can point to a few studies that address the issue of criminal resources.

In an analysis of fraud in economic transactions, Graeme Newman and associates (1981) show that opportunities for fraud vary considerably, and the extent and type of fraud committed depend on access to positions of authority, communications media, technology, and mass markets. They also point out that personal skills involving manipulation of people, use of status, management abilities, and technical expertise facilitate fraud.

Activities most likely to improve access to criminal opportunities are those related to work. Through work people gain access to many resources and skills that can be channeled in either criminal or noncriminal directions. The importance of work is stressed by Gibbs and Short (1974), who argue that there will be a wider range of criminal activities in populations with a wider range of occupations. Their analysis of arrests and occupations for different age groups in the United States confirmed this prediction.

Access to criminal opportunities influences not only which crimes are likely to occur but also the range of possible crimes. Criminal events occur more often if they involve relatively few resources. However, the range of criminal events is narrower when there are fewer available resources. Thus, those who are poor, unemployed, or otherwise disadvantaged in the competition for scarce resources are similarly restricted in access to criminal opportunities. One would therefore predict that there would be less, not more, crime among such people and that the range of offenses they commit will be narrower. The first part of the proposition is predicated on the assumption that wealthier people have the same access to criminal opportunities as poorer people plus what they can access because of their advantaged position. As demonstrated in Chapter 14, Messerschmidt (1986), Hagan (1987), and others have reached a similar conclusion about the distribution of criminal events in the class structure, though from an entirely different perspective.

Resources have been found to facilitate juvenile crime and delinquency. Shannon (1982) found that youths who had an automobile were more likely to report that they had committed crimes. Similarly, Agnew (1990) discovered that youths with cars and other resources showed higher levels of delinquency involvement than other delinquency-prone youths. He concluded that resources confer power and autonomy and help to increase a person's ability to activate their predispositions, whether criminal or otherwise. This, in turn, increases their sense of self-efficacy as well as the potential profits from an activity.

Opportunities and Female Crime

"It is not uncommon," Allison Morris (1987:1) writes, "for criminology textbooks, even critical reviews, to contain nothing at all on women. . . . Criminology, like most academic disciplines, has been concerned with the activities and interests of men." Since women make up over 50 percent of the population, one might ask: Why the neglect?

The answer is obvious, according to Morris and others (e.g., Leonard, 1982; Chesney-Lind and Shelden, 1992:2): The field was founded by men and has been dominated by males ever since. If nothing else, this would tend to focus theory and research on the experiences and activities of men. Such an emphasis is easily justified: Women commit fewer and largely petty crimes compared to men.

Some authors believe this neglect has been detrimental to the study of crime and delinquency. Morris addresses one commonly held concern, that prominent theories about crime are really theories about male crime and may not be valid when applied to women. She goes on (1987:2):

> A theory is weak if it does not apply to half of the potential criminal population; women, after all, experience the same deprivations, family structures, and so on that men do. To study only men or boys to assess whether or not delinquency springs from, for example, poverty makes little sense. Similarly, to refer to the "subcultural style" of working-class boys as a solution to the problems of redevelopment, housing, depopulation, and community solidarity begs an important question: how do working-class girls solve these problems? Theories of crime should be able to take account of both men's and women's behavior and to highlight those factors which operate differently on men and women.

There is ample evidence to suggest that female rates of some crimes and delinquencies have been rising faster than those of males in recent years (see also Chesney-Lind and Shelden, 1992:7–28). This is particularly true of arrests for violent crime other than homicide and rape and weapons offenses (see Figures 16.3 and 16.4). One explanation of the recent growth in female crime is couched in terms of opportunity theory and routine activities. The argument goes as follows.

The greater supervision and control of females, especially girls, restricts their routine participation in activities that are open to males, and hence the experience and opportunities that may lead to crime and delinquency. Furthermore, as long as females remain "housebound" and schooled for mothering, they will not learn how to "make it" in what is essentially a man's world, except in the restricted contexts of marriage and "women's" work. In essence, women become "auxiliaries" in a man's world, and this is true of criminal as well as noncriminal activities. Through the years, researchers of delinquent gangs have documented an auxiliary role for girls—as helpers, girlfriends, lookouts, but rarely as full participants (e.g., Thrasher, 1929; Klein, 1971; Campbell, 1984).

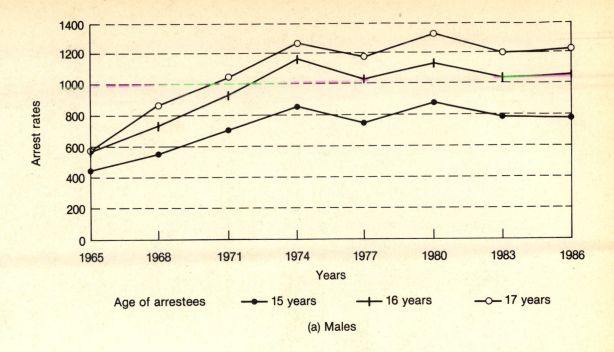

Age of arrestees   ●— 15 years   +— 16 years   ○— 17 years

(a) Males

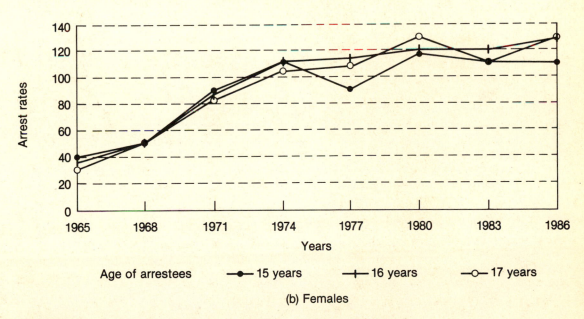

Age of arrestees   ●— 15 years   +— 16 years   ○— 17 years

(b) Females

FIGURE 16.3   Arrests, Violent Crime, 1965–1986. (a) Males 15, 16, and 17 years old. (b) Females 15, 16, and 17 years old.   *Source:* Compiled from Federal Bureau of Investigation (1988). *Age-Specific Arrest Rates and Race-Specific Arrest Rates for Selected Offenses.* Washington, D.C.: U.S. Department of Justice.

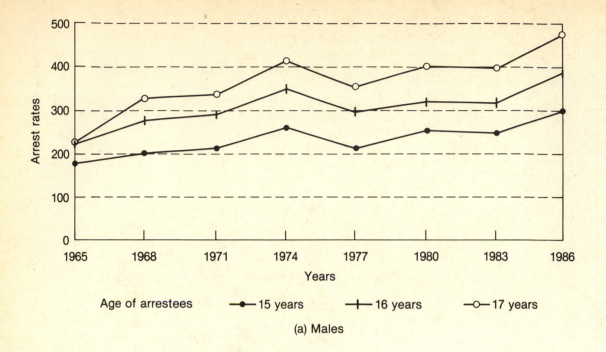

Age of arrestees   ●— 15 years   + 16 years   ○ 17 years

(a) Males

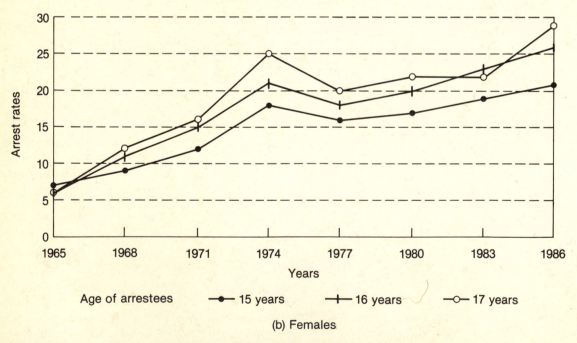

Age of arrestees   ●— 15 years   + 16 years   ○ 17 years

(b) Females

FIGURE 16.4   Arrests, Weapon Offenses, 1965–1986. (a) Males 15, 16, and 17 years old. (b) Females 15, 16, and 17 years old.   *Source:* Compiled from Federal Bureau of Investigation (1988). *Age-Specific Arrest Rates and Race-Specific Arrest Rates for Selected Offenses.* Washington, D.C.: U.S. Department of Justice.

Some authors believe the female criminal role is changing and that the shift reflects changes in the opportunities open to women. The expansion of Western economies has drawn many women into the labor force and out of the home. The women's liberation movement has pushed for equality between the sexes. The result, Adler (1976) and Simon (1976) believe, has been a convergence of gender roles as many of the experiences and opportunities previously reserved for males (and a few "lucky" females) open to more and more females. In Adler's terms, a "virilization" of women is taking place, and the new masculine female will become less distinguishable from her male counterpart in all areas of life, including crime. The changes, because they affect home life and the socialization process, presumably will filter down to young girls. This "liberation/opportunity" theory predicts that the crime rates of women and girls will increase and broaden.

The theory weakens under empirical scrutiny. Tests of the virilization hypothesis have found no support in studies of girls' delinquency (e.g., Cullen, Golden, and Cullen, 1979; Thornton and James, 1979). One study discovered that girls who expressed liberated views tended to be less delinquent than those who conformed to traditional gender roles (Giordano and Cernkovich 1979). A similar finding was reported by James and Thornton (1980) in their study of Nashville youths. Figueira-McDonough (1986), on the other hand, suggests that the impact of liberated views may differ with the kind of school environment girls are exposed to: The more traditional and restrictive the environment, the greater the pressures on liberated females to deviate. Steffensmeier and Allan (1988:69) point out that "the emancipation hypothesis is at odds with the profile of the female offender, who is typically unemployed or has a poor employment history, espouses traditional sex role attitudes, manifests high emotional dependency on males, and has a high incidence of drug use or psychiatric history."

As for the new opportunities around which the theory revolves, most scholars have followed Smart (1979) and Leonard (1982) in arguing that there has been little real change. Females are still more likely to hold low-paying jobs that are often auxiliary to the "more important" and better-paying jobs of men. Morris (1987:72) suggests that many women actually are less free today than they were 40 years ago. They are expected to contribute to family income, and yet child-care facilities are woefully inadequate. This is particularly burdensome on young single mothers, many of whom are teenagers.

Messerschmidt (1986:72–76) reveals another way that modern working women actually have less freedom, especially if they have children. Such women inevitably work longer hours since they are subject to the "double burden" of wage labor plus housework and childcare. Messerschmidt finds no evidence that males (boyfriends, brothers, husbands) are taking up the slack in household chores and childcare created when women go to work. In many families that include working mothers, the daughters (but not the sons) take on added responsibilities. On the other hand, with more mothers working, children are less subject to parental supervision and some observers believe this will increase delinquency, especially among girls.

Hagan's (1987) power-control theory of delinquency, reviewed in Chapter 14, takes this position.

Most recent theory argues that female crime has not changed—it is still largely nonviolent, mostly petty, and linked to conventional female roles. If accessible opportunities have expanded for women, they have done so in relation to mundane activities that do not require special skills and resources. Women who are criminally motivated do what men do: They take advantage of the situations in which they routinely find themselves. What remains unclear is how much of the difference in male and female crime rates can be accounted for by opportunity/situation factors and how much by differences in inclination and motivation. It is also quite possible that sex interacts with other demographic variables (e.g., race) so that generalizations about female rates are misleading (see Hill and Crawford, 1990). Black female crime rates appear closest to white male rates, and it is important that future theory and research on female crime take this into account.

Summary of Chapter 16

The central message of opportunity–rationality theories is, first, that crime cannot be understood apart from the nature and distribution of opportunities for *both* criminal and noncriminal behavior. Criminal opportunities are tied to the noncriminal activities that characterize a population. As these opportunities change, so does crime. Second, when criminals find themselves in situations in which they have opportunities to commit crime, the decision to do so or not to do so is a rational one.

Since neither the availability nor the accessibility of criminal opportunities is distributed evenly throughout society, modern theory generally asserts that behavioral choices are not exercised freely but within constraints resulting from conditions beyond control. Because of the uneven distribution of criminal opportunities, some criminals can participate in a wider range of crimes than others.

Geographers have demonstrated that criminal events cluster where opportunities exist, but sometimes the "best" opportunities must be foregone. Unfamiliar places tend to inhibit potential offenders, and this problem is compounded for criminals who are younger or less experienced or who have traits that would cause them to be noticed. Displacement, one of the potential costs of situational crime prevention, is predicated on the assumption that offenders alter their criminal behavior in response to changing risks and costs, but it has been seen that displacement is not an inevitable result of target hardening.

The routine activity approach brings rationality and opportunities together to explain the distribution of crime in time and space. Advocates of the approach argue that the everyday activities of people influence the convergence of criminally motivated individuals and suitable, unguarded, criminal targets.

The rational view of crime assumes that criminals think about their crimes before doing them, but does this apply to the apparently impulsive, spur-of-the-moment actions typical of many offenders? The best answer is a weak "yes." It is unreasonable to separate present behavior from past actions, and what may appear to be impulsive actions may be linked to previous actions that were preceded by rational thought. Furthermore, behavior that is routine and ordinary often takes place without much thought, but this does not make it any less rational. Finally, the narrow view that reason somehow does not belong in explanations for murder, rape, child molesting, drug abuse and other so-called "expressive" offenses ignores the fact that the manner of execution and the choice of victim are rarely, if ever, mindless.

Recommended Readings

Paul J. Brantingham, and Patricia L. Brantingham (1981). *Environmental Criminology*. Beverly Hills: Sage.

Ronald L. Carter, and Kim Q. Hill (1979). *The Criminal's Image of the City*. New York: Pergamon.

Meda Chesney-Lind, and Randall G. Shelden (1992). *Girls Delinquency and Juvenile Justice*. Pacific Grove, Calif.: Brooks/Cole.

Ronald V. Clarke (1992). *Situational Crime Prevention: Successful Case Studies*. New York: Harrow and Heston.

Lawrence E. Cohen, and Marcus Felson (1979). "Social change and crime rate trends: A routine activity approach," *American Sociological Review* 44:588–608.

Derek B. Cornish, and Ronald V. Clarke (1986b). *The Reasoning Criminal: Rational Choice Perspectives on Offending*. New York: Springer-Verlag.

Kenneth D. Tunnell (1992). *Choosing Crime: The Criminal Calculus of Property Offenders*. Chicago: Nelson-Hall.

Chapter 17

General Theories of Crime

The late 1980s may go down in history as the time criminology finally took stock of its achievements and rediscovered general theory. Five important theories of crime appeared during this period, each purporting to explain a broad range of criminological facts that are not restricted to any one historical or social setting. The five theories are the sociobiological/learning theory of James Q. Wilson and Richard J. Herrnstein (1985), Jack Katz's (1988) theory of moral transcendence, the theory of reintegrative shaming by John Braithwaite (1989a), the evolutionary ecological theory of expropriative crime by Lawrence Cohen and Richard Machalek (1988), and the general theory of crime and criminality by Michael R. Gottfredson and Travis Hirschi (1990). It seems quite appropriate to end this text with a review of these theories. They set the agenda for research in the nineties, and they point to the theoretical challenges that await criminologists in the twenty-first century.

First, a word about general theory. As noted in Chapter 13, general theories explain a broad range of facts and are not restricted to any one time or place. This does not mean that a particular general theory has to explain *all* crime, but if exceptions keep turning up its generality is obviously suspect. By the same token, successful tests of a general theory with a particular crime, say armed robbery, cannot be the basis for inferring that the theory applies equally well to, say, embezzlement or even to other forms of robbery. Only repeated tests of a theory with different people, places, or events will establish its degree of generality. Needless to say, the person who constructed the theory should not be faulted for claiming it to be general in the absence of evidence to the contrary.

A General Theory of What?

As we have seen throughout this text, crime varies in many ways. There are variations from one population, place, and time to another, and from one individual to another; there are variations in the frequency with which people commit crimes (called the "incidence" of crime), and variations in the proportion of people who commit those crimes (the "prevalence" of crime); there are variations in the way crimes are committed, and in the consequences that follow for offenders as well as for victims; there are variations in criminalization, from the declaration that certain activities are crimes all the way to the imposition of penalities.

A general theory that explains all these variations would be impressive indeed. In the first place, it would need to explain variations at the individual level as well as variations at the societal level. The things that account for differences among individuals may not account for differences among societies, and vice versa. "There is some evidence, for example, that while unemployment is a strong predictor of individual criminality, societies with high unemployment rates do not necessarily have high crime rates . . ." (Braithwaite, 1989a:104). In the second place, a theory that accommodates all these variations would have to explain not only the behavior that constitutes crime, but also the propensity of people to engage in that behavior *and* the propensity of others to apply criminal labels to those people and acts.

A third reason such an all-encompassing theory would be impressive related to the conceptualization of crime as an event. One way to think of crime as an event is illustrated by the routine activities approach, discussed in Chapter 16. In this conceptualization, crime occurs when opportunities and motivated offenders fortuitously come together in the absence of capable guardians. From this vantage point, a general theory of crime would have to explain variations in the situational matrix that gives rise to criminal events.

Another way to visualize crime as an event is in the form of a situated transaction that is constructed through the acts and reactions of participants as they occur *in situ*. In Chapter 3 we discussed murder from this perspective, and there have been other applications to particular types of crime as well as to the judicial process (e.g., LaFree, 1989; Matoesian, 1993). Katz (1988) makes a distinction between "background" and "foreground" factors in the explanation of crime, and this is relevant here. Background factors are the traditional focus of positivistic criminology: the biology underlying criminal behavior, the psychological determinants, the socioeconomic and cultural forces that push or pull people into criminal activity. Foreground factors have to do with the quality of the "lived experience" that is crime—in Katz's terms, the compulsions and seductions of crime felt by individuals as they live and breathe. Could a general theory of crime that accommodates background factors also explain the lived experience of crime?

The central concepts of a theory usually reflect the training of its author(s). It comes as no surprise when a sociologist includes social variables in a theory of crime, nor when a psychologist includes personality variables, a biologist constitutional variables, or a geographer spatial variables. Yet some scholars see discipline boundaries as a hindrance to the development of a general theory of crime. Gottfredson and Hirschi (1990:274) make this point, arguing that "much of the research generated by these disciplines is beyond the reach of their own explanations of crime." They "find no adequate positivistic theory that accounts for a range of well-documented facts about crime (e.g., the age curve [crime rates peak at age 20 to 24 and fall off rapidly thereafter], the gender gap, the disproportionate involvement of minorities, the high correlation between crime rates and rates of other 'deviancy'), and the characteristics of crime itself" (Barlow, 1991:231). And so Gottfredson and Hirschi claim to base their theory on a conception of human nature and of crime that escapes the fetters of disciplines.

If the discipline baggage theorists carry around restricts their ability to construct a general theory of crime, the competition among different theoretical perspectives within a discipline is surely more restrictive. This has led some criminologists to seek *integrated* theories that borrow from otherwise competing paradigms. In sociological criminology, for example, attempts have been made to unite control theory with rationality—opportunity theory, associational theory with strain theory, and cultural deviancy theory with control theory. These efforts expose some of the commonalities among ostensibly competing theories (see Barlow and Ferdinand, 1992:201–222), though tests of integrated theories (usually with juveniles) have had mixed success. To the extent that an integrated theory explains a wider range of phenomena, it is more general than the individual theories of which it is constructed, and that makes theoretical integration a worthwhile challenge.

The Five Theories

These observations might well evoke pessimism about the possibility of constructing a general theory of crime. Yet the challenge has now been taken up, although it should be said that Katz (1988) makes no claim that his work constitutes a general theory. In truth, his is as much method as theory, but the two are so intertwined as to be indistinguishable, as we shall see. Here, then, are the five theories. There is space to do only a superficial job, and readers are strongly advised to read the original sources in their entirety. Always remember that the further removed one is from the original author, the more likely it is that arguments and ideas will be misrepresented. Though I have tried to remain faithful to the essential ideas in these important works, I have also left out a tremendous amount. This is another good reason to read the original works.

I begin with two theories that share a common grounding in sociobiology, although one is an evolutionary theory and the other is a behaviorist learning theory.

Wilson and Herrnstein

Wilson and Herrnstein (1985) offer an integrative theory of criminal behavior that combines sociobiological, psychological (behaviorist), and rationality–opportunity perspectives on crime. Their theory is about "the forces that control individual behavior" (p. 42), and it incorporates behaviorial, biological, and environmental factors to explain why some people commit "serious" street crimes and others do not.

An underlying assumption of the theory is that when individuals are faced with choices of action, they evaluate them according to their consequences and will prefer those with the highest anticipated ratio of rewards to costs. To the extent that individuals act on this basis, their behavior is rational. Therefore, both stealing and bestiality can be rational. Wilson and Herrnstein believe that individuals can choose to commit or not commit a crime, and for any given level of internal restraint (the "bite of conscience"), they will select crime over noncrime whenever the reward–cost ratio is greater for the crime than for the noncrime.

What any given individual considers rewarding (or costly) is part human nature (i.e., it satisfies such primary drives as hunger and sex) and part learned. These rewards may be material or nonmaterial, certain or uncertain, and immediate or delayed. The evaluation of any particular action will be influenced by how well a person handles uncertainty and delay, which Wilson and Herrnstein believe is influenced by nature, temperament, and social environment. Aggressive individuals, for example, are inclined to be more impulsive and less able to delay gratification, a trait characteristic also of youth. The rewards of noncrime are often delayed, whereas the rewards of crime generally precede their costs and will therefore be preferred by less mature and more impulsive individuals. Finally, there is the important question of equity: Crime may be preferred to noncrime if it is perceived to correct an imbalance in distributive justice. Such an imbalance occurs when people feel that in comparison to them, others get more than they deserve on the basis of their contribution.

Wilson and Herrnstein's theory is controversial partly because of their claim that the theory is general enough to encompass most sociological theories of criminal behavior (1985:63–66), partly because it is used to justify conservative crime control policies (pp. 528–529), and, perhaps most of all, because it links criminal behavior to constitutional factors, as we noted in Chapter 13. On the other hand, Wilson and Herrnstein have explored some new avenues and some old ones in a way that merits serious study.

A major criticism of their approach is its focus on "serious" street crime—murder, theft, rape—to the exclusion of other forms of criminality. A general theory of crime that explains only a small range of behaviors is not so general, and in any case it is certainly not established that embezzlers, con artists, organized criminals, fences, and pilferers are constitutionally different from noncriminals, or for that matter, from other criminals. It is also curious that despite their declared focus on serious street crime, the voluminous research that Wilson and Herrnstein bring to bear on their theory often does not make that distinction. Finally, Wilson and Herrnstein's approach manifests the ideology of conservative criminology in its thinly veiled search for the criminal type (for additional criticisms, see Gibbs, 1985).

Cohen and Machalek

The evolutionary ecological theory proposed by Cohen and Machalek (1988) is also integrative, and what is remarkable is the simplicity of the result. The theory is heavily influenced by biological developments and is described as a general theory even though the authors apply it to a restricted range of crimes. Even though the theory remains to be fully developed, it unites the perspectives of routine activity, structure, social psychology, and biology.

Cohen and Machalek (1988:467) argue that variation in individual behavior is explained by the "alternative behavioral strategies" that are used as people try to meet their needs. Some of these strategies are "expropriative" because they involve depriving others of valuable things. Many crimes are expropriative, and it is these crimes to which the theory is applied.

Behavioral strategies develop over time as people (like other organisms) strive to meet their needs. The successful strategies tend to become "major" ones. However, the more prevalent a strategy becomes within society, the more vulnerable the population is to "invasion" by alternative strategists, or to "nonconformists" who are willing to be creative. This is one way that new strategies evolve and behavior diversifies.

In addition, individuals differ in their physical and behavioral traits and resources. These differences may result in the selection (intentional or not) of different strategies, just as they may help or hinder a person's successful adoption of a preferred strategy. In this way, "conditional" strategies arise alongside major strategies, and again behavioral diversity grows.

Human beings possess intelligence, meaning they can think; however, people do not always act with conscious purpose. "It is thus unnecessary to assume that criminal acts are perpetrated by rational, calculating individuals who understand fully the strategic implications of their chosen actions" (Cohen and Machalek, 1988:479). Indeed, people may have resource advantages that they do not realize or intend, and yet these advantages explain why they have adopted a strategy. If a strategy works well it will probably be tried again, although the individual may never question or realize *why* it worked.

Cohen and Machalek argue that property crimes, as expropriative strategies, are promoted by various factors, some pertaining to individuals, others to the type and mix of noncriminal strategies that exist in a time and place. Deficiencies in social, cultural, and physical resources may promote criminal strategies (such as burglary) that are employed as alternatives to inaccessible noncriminal strategies. However, criminal alternatives may also be promoted by resource advantages: "[An] individual who is rich in [resources] may be even more predisposed to commit a criminal act precisely because he or she commands the resources required to implement an expropriative strategy successfully" (Cohen and Machalek, 1988:483).

If *both* resource deficiencies and advantages promote crime, it is difficult to see how resource differences can explain individual or group differences in the selection of expropriative crime. Cohen and Machalek get around this problem by taking a conventional and conservative approach: People who are socially and economically disadvantaged are more likely to be exposed to values and experiences that encourage criminal behavior. They do not tell us why this should be so. On the other hand, resource variability can explain the type of crime selected, for as seen repeatedly in Chapter 16, access to criminal opportunities often requires the right combination of resources.

Because expropriative strategies arise as alternatives to legitimate production activities, they are promoted by the expansion and proliferation of noncriminal activities. For example, Cohen and Machalek (1988:480) observe that "large-scale concentrations of producers offer rich and inviting opportunities" to both advantaged and conditional strategists. Once discovered, a particular theft strategy is likely to proliferate through conventional social-psychological processes such as imitation and social learning, and through independent discovery.

This brief sketch does not do justice to Cohen and Machalek's theory, which contains other elements and emphasizes the evolutionary dynamics that underlie the development and acquisition of behavioral strategies (see also Machalek and Cohen, 1991). Nevertheless, it is important to note again that none of the elements described above is new. One can find them in the theories reviewed in the last four chapters. A new idea that does emerge is the notion that crime is shaped by "strategy evolution" in general, and that the characteristics, frequency, and mix of behavioral strategies explain the amount and types of crime that exist in any particular place, time, or group.

Gottfredson and Hirschi*

Crime can be thought of as a form of cheating, where one person or group extracts resources from another without compensating the victim (Machalek and Cohen, 1991:223). What crimes have in common is the fact that they victimize. When crime is conceptualized this way, questions about the ubiquity and evolution of crime follow naturally enough, for how can societies survive in the face of such parasitic conduct? Gottfredson and Hirschi (1990) take a different approach in conceptualizing crime, although they acknowledge that suffering occurs. Much of the account that follows is taken from a critical review of their theory (Barlow, 1991; for another view, see Akers, 1991).

Taking classical (rational choice) theory as a starting point, Gottfredson and Hirschi argue that crime, as any other behavior, turns on the likelihood that it will bring pleasure. Its characteristics must in general be consistent with that result irrespective of the specific motives, interests, or talents of the people doing it. Gottfredson and Hirschi observe that most crimes are in fact *attempts*, and this implies something about the nature of crimes: they are unlikely to be carefully thought out, skillfull acts involving special expertise, technology, or organization. Criminal acts are relatively easy and simple to commit, involve little skill or planning, and tend to be exciting, risky, or thrilling.

What makes crimes distinct from analogous acts is that they entail the use of force and fraud, and this helps make gratification *immediate*. On the other hand, force and fraud also threaten the self-interests of victims and are therefore universally resisted. Like Machalek and Cohen (1991) and Durkheim ([1893] 1964a) before them, Gottfredson and Hirschi see potential retaliation as the inseparable other side of crime. And so we have three other characterisitcs of crimes: they provide immediate gratification but also produce pain and suffering for victims and the risk of long-term costs for offenders.

Beyond the commonalities already noted, crimes will not occur unless an appropriate opportunity exists. That opportunity is defined by the logical structure of the crime itself, and therefore will vary from one specific offense (embezzlement) to another (rape). Gottfredson and Hirschi describe the "typical or standard" characteristics and the logical structures (necessary

---

*Parts of this section are from Barlow (1991). Reprinted with permission.

elements or conditions) of burglary, robbery, homicide, auto theft, rape, embezzlement, and drug use. The characteristics and elements of the offenses are strikingly similar. However, it is also apparent that the likelihood of any particular crime being committed is influenced by the availability of opportunities and a person's access to them, issues the authors do not explore. Presumably, the characteristics of situations and the personal properties of individuals jointly affect the use of force or fraud in pursuit of self-interest.

Gottfredson and Hirschi maintain that crimes are interchangeable not only among themselves but also with analogous acts that do not involve force or fraud. They call this the "versality construct." And so they end up rejecting traditional distinctions among crimes (e.g., petty and serious, personal and property, attempted and completed, street and suite) as "without import" and "a waste of time." They look for what crimes have in common as a basis for inferring what criminals have in common.

Criminality: Low Self-Control   If crimes differ in opportunities for their commission, individuals differ in the extent to which they are vulnerable to the temptations provided by those opportunities. Gottfredson and Hirschi use the notion *self-control* to represent that vulnerability, and criminality is synonymous with low self-control. Criminality refers to the propensity to use force and fraud in the pursuit of self-interest. Its characteristics are inferred from the characteristics of crime. In this way Gottfredson and Hirschi ensure that the conception of criminality is consistent with their conception of crime.

The traits associated with low self-control include: short-time perspective; low diligence, persistence, and tenacity; a tendency to be "adventuresome, active, and physical"; a tendency to be "self-centered, indifferent, or insensitive to the suffering and needs of others"; and a tendency to have "unstable marriages, friendships, and job profiles." Since these traits are also implicated in many noncriminal acts (e.g., alcohol use, accidents, smoking, running away, truancy) "crime is not an automatic or necessary consequence of low self-control" (Gottfredson and Hirschi, 1990:91). In other words, there is no theoretical basis for predicting *which* of many possible crimes and analogous acts will be committed by individuals with low self-control.

Gottfredson and Hirschi identify the major cause of low self-control as "ineffective parenting." However, individual differences among children (and parents) may affect the prospects for good parenting. Thus low intelligence tends to compromise the recognition of low self-control and the willingness or ability to do anything about it. Other factors affecting parental control and the prospects for effective socialization include parental criminality and anything that interferes with the monitoring and supervision of children. Gottfredson and Hirschi acknowledge that schools and other socializing institutions (marriage, work, Boy or Girl Scouts) may have a positive effect on self-control; but the further from early childhood one moves, the harder it is to make up for early deficiencies. Besides, the traits characteristic of low self-control are inconsistent with success at school, work, and interpersonal relationships. This fact explains, in their view, why delinquent

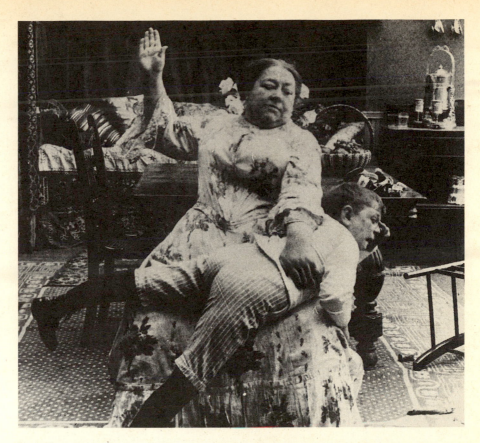

Gottfredson and Hirschi's general theory of crime and Braithwaite's theory of reintegrative shaming both identify parental discipline as an explanatory factor in crime. What would the authors have to say about this picture?

youths end up in the company of each other ("birds of a feather") and why failure in school, marriage, and work correlates strongly with delinquency and crime (they all require diligence, hard work, and willingness to defer gratification).

The Stability Postulate   Central to the theory is the proposition that levels of self-control are relatively stable throughout the life course. Put another way, "differences between people in the likelihood that they will commit criminal acts persist over time" (Gottfredson and Hirschi, 1990:107). This "stability postulate" is predicated on the belief that the early failure of control and socialization cannot readily be overcome later in life any more than effective control and socialization of a child can later be undone. Together with the notion that there are many noncriminal acts that are analogous to crimes, the stability postulate explains why the so-called age-curve of crime is invariant across space and across crimes, as well as why "[m]en are always and everywhere more likely than women to commit criminal acts" (p. 145).

To summarize, the central proposition of Gottfredson and Hirschi's general theory of crime is as follows: Crime rate differences among individuals are explained by the independent effects of variations in the characteristics of crime itself (i.e., the opportunity to pursue self-interest through the use of force or fraud) and variations in self-control (criminality, or the propensity to use force or fraud in the pursuit of self-interest). Criminal opportunities held constant, low self-control predicts relatively high rates of offending, low self-control earlier in life predicts criminality later in life, and criminality earlier in life predicts low self-control later in life.

Scope of The Theory   Despite continued reference to "ordinary" or "common" crimes, Gottfredson and Hirschi call their theory general, going so far as to claim that the theory "is meant to explain all crime, at all times, and, for that matter, many forms of behavior that are not sanctioned by the state" (p. 117). In short, the independent effects of crime opportunities and criminality explain bait-and-switch scams in appliance stores, police brutality, bid-rigging, employee theft, fraudulent advertising, insider trading, tax evasion, smuggling, gang crimes, labor racketeering, prison rape, armed robbery, arson, burglary, murder, rape, and shoplifting; and they also explain drug use, accidents, smoking, and eating between meals. No specialized theories are needed because all crimes and analogous acts "provide relatively quick and relatively certain benefit with minimal effort" (Gottfredson and Hirschi, 1990:190).

Unfortunately, Gottfredson and Hirschi do not develop the opportunity (crime) side of their theory sufficiently well to predict which of all these varied acts individuals are likely to commit (at a high or low rate) at any given time, or when they might switch from one crime to another or from crime to a noncriminal but analogous act. Nor do they provide a basis for deducing what kind of social or cultural setting would experience a high (or low) rate of any particular crime or analogous act. Their treatment of these issues as theoretically irrelevant or inconsequential hardly lessens the theory's vulnerability to attack.

One attack will probably come where the theory is most vulnerable, in its application to occupational crime—the use of force and fraud in the context of a job. Gottfredson and Hirschi present FBI arrest data on embezzlement and fraud to show that correlates of "white collar" crime are similar to those of murder (and therefore other common crimes), and they also refer to "good research" that shows just how mundane, simple, and easy occupational crimes are and that the people who commit them also tend to commit analogous acts (drug and alcohol use, for example).

The evidence is certainly inconclusive on these issues. Indeed, much of it clearly challenges another assertion of their theory—that crime is more prevalent among those outside the occupational structure than among those in it (see Barlow, 1991, for relevant citations). The lack of consistent evidence of a relationship between unemployment and crime is one challenge, but another comes from abundant evidence that employee fraud and theft, though often mundane, are widespread in all sectors of the U.S. economy as well as in those of other countries. Furthermore, evidence of widespread crime in the fields of health, real estate, banking, insurance, defense contracting, and politics hardly supports the contention that high-end occupations are inconsistent with criminality.

Gottfredson and Hirschi do not assert that criminality is *absent* among corporate executives or other high-level employees, merely that it is less prevalent the higher one climbs the occupational ladder. Even if this is true, many of the crimes committed at the high end display characteristics opposite to those indicative of low self-control. Compared to low-end crime, high-end crime is much more likely to involve planning, special expertise, organization, delayed gratification, and persistence—as well as considerably larger potential gains with arguably less long-term cost. Such distinctions are also apparent when comparing the activities of fences with thieves, "good" burglars with "kick-it-in men," pickpockets with purse-snatchers, and confidence artists who work the "big con" with those who do "short con" (see Chapter 6). Gottfredson and Hirschi's theory can accommodate these observations in only one of two ways: Either temptations to commit force and fraud in the pursuit of self-interest overwhelm the resistance associated with self-control, or (many) individuals with low self-control manage somehow to become managers, professionals, and entrepreneurs.

If their stability postulate is wrong, however, it is possible for people with low self-control early in life to develop it later and for individuals with self-control early in life to lose it later. Braithwaite's theory of reintegrative shaming (discussed below) presumes this to be true, while Gottfredson and Hirschi's theory requires that it not be. Recall that low self-control is inconsistent with effective control and socialization, and that includes socialization into as well as out of crime. Hence the groups and organizations to which offenders belong are regarded as facilitating crime among people who *already* lack self-control. Gottfredson and Hirschi thus dismiss as misguided (or poor) research suggesting that the social and cultural milieu of an organization generates criminality among its members. Besides, they argue, there is little social support of white-collar offenders because their offenses usually victimize the organizations in which they work and are detrimental to fellow employees.

My reading of wide-ranging research is different (see Chapter 8; also Barlow, 1991, for citations of specific works). Whether the subject is police corruption, employee pilfering, the ethics of corporate managers, antitrust violations, "underground" trading, or city politics, one finds social support of criminality through subcultures of criminality—accommodating norms and values and networks of cooperation. Gottfredson and Hirschi's view that such support relates to the nature and context of crime itself rather than to the propensity of individuals to commit it would perhaps constitute a fatal counterattack if they could also show that self-control cannot be undermined by external (group) influence.

Minority Crime   Among the facts about crime in America are these: African-Americans constitute roughly 12 percent of the population; yet nearly 50 percent of those arrested for violent crime are black, as are 33 percent of those arrested for property crimes, 40 percent of those serving jail time, and 47 percent of those in state prisons (Bureau of Justice Statistics, 1988a). How would the general theory of Gottfredson and Hirschi explain these facts?

They reject traditional explanations of minority involvement in crime (e.g., inequality and subcultural theories) and resort to an emphasis on the self-control component of their theory. In their view, parental management of children is the key to understanding racial variations in crime; and within the realm of parenting, discipline is considered more important than supervision, which affects access to criminal opportunities. However, Gottfredson and Hirschi cite no evidence, saying only that "[p]artitioning race or ethnic differences into their crime and self-control components is not possible with currently available data" (p. 153).

On Gottfredson and Hirschi's side, the relationship between parenting and delinquency is one of the strongest in the literature, and evidence is piling up that the impact of structural factors (e.g., family composition, socioeconomic status) on delinquency is mediated by parental management (see Barlow and Ferdinand, 1992). Nevertheless, if poverty, community disorganization, large family size, and family instability impact negatively on parental management, rates of crime and delinquency will be affected. Such structural conditions are prevalent in inner-city black communities (Wilson, 1987), where rates of victimization by force and fraud are also high. Gottfredson and Hirschi do not explore the implications of this for their theory.

In rejecting inequality theories of race differences in crime, Gottfredson and Hirschi point out that "[offenders] tend to victimize people who share their unfortunate circumstances" (p. 152). True, but then this question arises: Are there race differences in the tendency for offenders to victimize people who are like themselves? According to their theory, crime is a matter of "proximity, ease, and convenience of rewards"; hence there is no *a priori* basis for predicting such differences. Nevertheless, studies of the urban distribution of crime indicate that black offenders have a more restricted image of the city than white offenders, who can move around more freely and need not concentrate their criminal activities in areas close to home, thereby foregoing "easy marks" (Carter and Hill, 1979; Boggs, 1964). This suggests that while most crime tends to be intraracial, crimes committed by whites are likely to be more dispersed and hence potentially more rewarding—but also more costly and risky—than crimes committed by blacks. If access to profitable criminal opportunities is skewed in favor of whites, Gottfredson and Hirschi are silent on the issue and its implications for their theory.

Braithwaite

Like Gottfredson and Hirschi, Braithwaite (1989a) believes that "there is sufficient in common between different types of crime to render a general explanation possible" (p. 1). However, Braithwaite explicitly rejects the idea that crimes are *inherently* similar, arguing instead that they are qualitatively similar by virtue of the stigma attached to them and by the fact that the offender makes a "defiant choice" in grasping the opportunity to perpetrate a crime:

> The homogeneity presumed between disparate behaviors such as rape and embezzlement in this theory is that they are choices made by the criminal actor in the knowledge that he is defying a criminal proscription which is mutually intelligible to actors in the society as criminal. (Braithwaite, 1989a:3)

Braithwaite excludes acts that are formally crimes but whose criminalization is without support in the society at large, for example, "laws against marijuana use in liberal democracies or laws that create political crimes against the state in communist societies . . ." (p. 3). Braithwaite's theory applies to predatory crimes, acts that involve victimization of one person or group by another.

We encountered the central idea in Braithwaite's theory, reintegrative shaming, in our discussion of criminal punishment in Chapter 12. But the theory is much more than this. Braithwaite offers yet another integrative theory, one that incorporates elements of major sociological theories of crime and delinquency: control theory, labeling theory, subcultural theory, associational theory, strain theory, and social learning theory.

Braithwaite's diagram of his theory is reproduced in Figure 17.1. The arrows indicate the direction or flow of influence between linked variables, and the signs indicate whether the relationship between them is positive (i.e., a plus sign indicates the more of one, the more of the other) or negative (i.e., a minus sign indicates the more of one, the less of the other). On the integrative and original aspects of his theory, Braithwaite (1989a:107) has this to say:

> The top left of [the figure] incorporates the key variables of control theory; the far right—opportunity [strain] theory; the middle and bottom right—subcultural theory; the right side of the middle box—labeling theory. With one crucial exception (reintegrative shaming), there is therefore no originality in the elements of this theory, simply originality of synthesis.

The central proposition of the theory is this: Crime rates of individuals and groups are influenced directly by processes of shaming. High crime rates result from shaming that stigmatizes, because rule-breakers who are shamed but not forgiven are more likely to become "outlaws" and to participate in subcultures of crime. On the other hand, when rule-breakers are shamed but then forgiven and welcomed back to the fold (reintegrated), the unpleasant, punitive experience of being shamed is offset by the pleasant relief of discovering that one is still accepted (loved, wanted, cared about) despite the transgression. The process of shaming and reintegrating confirms the validity of the rules and reestablishes the transgressor's place as a member in good standing. While Braithwaite hypothesizes that either kind of shaming is likely

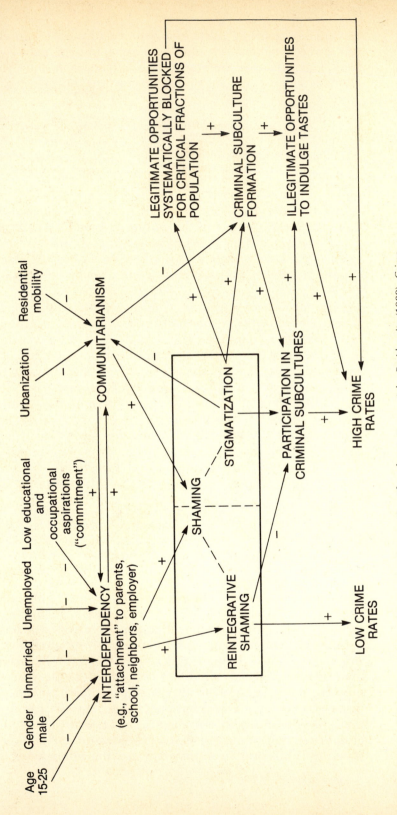

FIGURE 17.1 Summary of the Theory of Reintegrative Shaming. *Source:* John Braithwaite (1989). *Crime, Shame and Reintegration.* Cambridge: Cambridge University Press. Reprinted by permission.

to be more successful at combatting predatory crime than "punishment without associated moralizing and denunciation" (p. 86), systems of punishment that encourage reintegration should experience the lowest crime rates.

> As a mechanism of social control, shaming works best among closely connected people whose fortunes, reputations, and futures are interdependent—as in families, for example, or among workmates, colleagues, and friends. Justice officials in Western industrialized societies are at a decided disadvantage: "Most of us will care less about what a judge (whom we meet only once in our lifetime) thinks of us than we will care about the esteem in which we are held by a neighbor we see regularly" (Braithwaite, 1989a:87). Interdependence among individuals has a societal correlate—"communitarianism"—which has three elements:

> (1) densely enmeshed interdependency, where interdependencies are characterized by (2) mutual obligation and trust, and (3) are interpreted as a matter of group loyalty rather than individual convenience. Communitarianism is therefore the antithesis of individualism. (Braithwaite, 1989:86)

Western industrialized societies, with their high rates of urbanization and residential mobility, are more individualistic than less-developed agrarian societies. The model in Figure 17.1 shows that communitarianism has a positive effect on shaming, but is itself undermined by shaming that is merely stigmatizing. This is because shaming without reintegration makes criminal subcultures more attractive and encourages their formation "by creating populations of outcasts with no stake in conformity" (Braithwaite, 1989a:102). Criminal subcultures are also fostered by blocked legitimate opportunities, and once formed they encourage crime directly by providing illegitimate opportunities and incentives to deviate from the norms of conventional society.

At the individual level, interdependency is associated with age, marital status, gender, employment status, and aspirations within societally approved opportunity systems. More so than other people, older teenagers and young adults—especially if they are male—are freed from the constraints and obligations of interdependency, as are single people, those without work, and those with low commitment to legitimate ways of "getting ahead." Absent the close ties of interdependency, such people are less likely to be exposed to or affected by shaming. They are more susceptible to crime because controls are weak.

Evaluation of the Theory   Braithwaite's work is an important contribution to criminological theory. Not only does he show how "old" competing theories can be integrated into one model, but his addition of the social-psychological variable, shaming, is a major innovation. Along with associational theories, his theory is one of the few that can be applied to upper-echelon occupational crime. Other notable accomplishments are that the theory of reintegrative shaming can be applied at both individual and societal levels of analysis, and that it incorporates background and foreground variables, although discussion of the lived experience of shaming is largely limited to the mechanics of gossip (see Braithwaite, 1989a:75–77). The latter is certainly an area for future research and elaboration and will be considered when we discuss Katz.

Braithwaite suggests ways his theory could be tested and even mentions modifications that could be made to accommodate additional variables. Despite the absence of specific tests, Braithwaite confidently asserts the merits of his theory by claiming that it accounts for the 13 best established findings in criminology, which no other existing theory can do. Among these findings are the high rates of crime among males, people living in large cities, certain categories of young people (e.g., those with low aspirations, poor school performance, weak attachments to school or parents, or strong attachments to delinquent peers), and among disadvantaged people. The theory also accounts for the low rate of crime in Japan—an industrialized nation—when compared with other industrialized nations such as the United States (see Braithwaite, 1989a, especially pages 61–66).

One of the theory's most interesting aspects is its implications for criminal justice policy in highly individualized societies such as our own (see Braithwaite, 1989a: Chapter 10). Given that reintegrative shaming works best in the informal contexts of family, friends, and neighborhood, a justice policy aimed at preventing or reducing crime should be a community-based, largely informal system that uses traditional process and punishment as a last resort. Expanding on this idea, Braithwaite and Pettit (1990; also Braithwaite, 1991) advocate a "republican" approach to criminal justice in which formal interventions are minimized and in which subjective assurances of liberty, equality, fraternity, and dialogue are guaranteed all citizens. In such a setting, the reintegrative prospects of community shaming are enhanced and the likelihood is greater that the offender will recognize his offense and shame himself. In this manner, shaming becomes conscience-building, the essence of crime prevention in Braithwaite's view.

Despite its originality, broad scope, and impressive integration of existing theories, the theory of reintegrative shaming leaves at least one important issue unresolved. For example, Braithwaite (1989a:13) claims his theory accommodates the existence of "multiple moralities" in modern societies whereas some others do not. He argues, "[a] severe limitation of theories that deny this, like Hirschi's control theory, is that they give no account of why some uncontrolled individuals become heroin users, some become hit men, and others price fixing conspirators." This is fair enough, but aside from identifying criminal subcultures as the milieu in which crime is learned and via which tastes may be indulged in illegitimate ways, it is by no means clear how one would derive predictions about variations in the prevalence and incidence of particular types of crime, or about crime selection by predisposed individuals. Braithwaite may wish to reconsider the contributions of the rationality–opportunity perspective we reviewed in Chapter 16.

Katz

I end this discussion of general theory, and the text itself, with a few words about a beautifully written book that has caused quite a stir in criminology and behavioral science generally. The book's title is enough to raise eyebrows in sociological circles: *Seductions of Crime: Moral and Sensual Attractions in Doing Evil.*

In this book, Katz explores the relationship between doing crime and the emotional states of the offender. His focus is the foreground of crime as opposed to the background variables traditionally emphasized in positivistic criminology. It is an analysis of the seductions and compulsions that are felt by people as they engage in criminal activity and that draw them into and through criminal "projects." To understand (and explain) crime *as action*, it is first necessary to reconstruct criminal events as they are experienced by participants. Criminology, Katz argues, should move from the inside of crime outward, rather than the other way around.

For Katz (1988:9), the commonality among such diverse crimes as pilfering, robbery, gang violence, and apparently senseless robbery-murders is the "family of moral emotions" that are subjectively experienced by offenders: "humiliation, righteousness, arrogance, ridicule, cynicism, defilement, and vengeance. In each [crime] the attraction that proves to be most fundamentally compelling is that of overcoming a personal challenge to moral—not material—existence." The following passage illustrates Katz's central argument:

> The closer one looks at crime, at least at the varieties examined here, the more vividly relevant become the moral emotions. Follow vandals and amateur shoplifters as they duck into alleys and dressing rooms and you will be moved by their delight in deviance; observe them under arrest and you may be stunned by their shame. Watch their strutting street display and you will be struck by the awesome fascination that symbols of evil hold for the young men who are linked in the groups we often call gangs. If we specify the opening moves in muggings and stickups, we describe an array of "games" or tricks that turn victims into fools before their pockets are turned out. The careers of persistent robbers show us, not the increasingly precise calculations and hedged risks of "professionals," but men for whom gambling and other vices are a way of life, who are "wise" in the cynical sense of the term, and who take pride in a defiant reputation as "bad." And if we examine the lived sensuality behind events of cold-blooded "senseless" murder, we are compelled to acknowledge the power that may still be created in the modern world through the sensualities of defilement, spiritual chaos, and the apprehension of vengeance.
>
> Running across these experiences of criminality is a process juxtaposed in one manner or another against humiliation. In committing a righteous slaughter, the impassioned assailant takes humiliation and turns it into rage; through laying claim to a moral status of transcendent significance, he tries to burn humiliation up. The badass, with searing purposiveness, tries to scare humiliation off; as one ex-punk explained to me, after years of adolescent anxiety about the ugliness of his complexion and the stupidity of his every word, he found a wonderful calm in making "them" anxious about *his* perceptions and understandings. Young vandals and shoplifters innovate games with the risks of humiliation, running along the edge of shame for its exciting reverberations. . . . Against the historical background of a collective insistence on the moral nonexistence of their people, "bad niggers" exploit

ethically unique possibilities for celebrating assertive conduct as "bad." (Katz, 1988:312–313)

Katz's "empirical" theory is, then, a theory of moral self-transcendence constructed through examination of the doing of crime as experienced and understood by its participants. Crime becomes a "project" through which offenders transcend the self that is caught up in the mundane routines of modern life. Crime embodies a creative exploration of emotional worlds beyond the realm of rational controls—it is spiritual, nonrational, self-fulfilling, and self-proclaiming. The lure of crime is, *inter alia*, its promise of providing "expanded possibilities of the self . . . ways of behaving that previously seemed inaccessible" (Katz, 1988:73).

Katz (1988:9) argues that there are three necessary and sufficient steps through which the construction of crime takes place: "(1) a path of action—distinctive practical requirements for successfully committing the crime; (2) a line of interpretation—unique ways of understanding how one is and will be seen by others; and (3) an emotional process—seductions and compulsions that have special dynamics."

If there is a link between the foreground and background in Katz's theory, the path of action is one obvious place to look. O'Malley and Mugford (1991:16) observe:

> As a consequence of the inequality of resources in society, some of the ways of transcending mundane life are more open to some groups of people than to others. Sky diving, for example, may offer a transcendent experience, but it is unlikely to be available to many young black members of the urban underclass. Crack, on the other hand, may provide a similarly transcending experience . . . but unlike sky diving is available to all, rich and poor. Moreover, the poor, perhaps more than any others in modernity, are faced with lives in which meaninglessness and the destruction of the self are ever present possibilities.

O'Malley and Mugford make this observation in the face of criticism that Katz cannot explain the shape of crime, that is, its distribution among social classes, between cities, or among racial or ethnic groups, because he rejects structural perspectives, particularly strain theory. Yet one strength of Katz's work likes precisely in the fact that it begins with no assumptions about how predispositions to crime might be distributed and concludes that only through examination of the experience of elite (or white-collar) crime can we construct the necessary comparative picture (Katz, 1988:313–324). However, Katz is not confident of criminology's ability to study the foreground of white-collar crime:

> Now, where would we get the data? With white-collar crime, we have a special problem in locating facts to demonstrate the lived experience of deviance. Despite their presumably superior capacity to write books and the healthy markets that await their publication efforts, we have virtually no

"how-I-did-it-and-how-it-felt-doing-it" autobiographies by corrupted politicians, convicted tax frauds, and chief executive officers who have been deposed by scandals over inside trading. (Katz, 1988:319)

Katz goes on to suggest that what will turn out to be distinctive about elite crime is not its motivations or consequences but its emotional quality: Feelings of shame often attend its discovery. In contrast, "[s]tickup men, safecrackers, fences, and drug dealers often wear the criminal label with pride, apparently relishing the opportunity to tell their criminal histories in colorful, intimate detail" (Katz, 1988:319).

Bringing up the issue of shame returns us to the central element in Braithwaite's (1989a) theory of crime. We noted that Braithwaite is largely silent on the emotional process involved in shaming except to say that people find shaming a humiliating experience that provokes fear and anxiety and, consequently, avoidance behavior on the part of the person shamed. The avoidance may come in the form of conformity (most likely if the shamed also experience pangs of conscience), or it may come in the form of withdrawal from the group and participation in deviant subcultures—behavior that provoked shaming now becomes behavior that is rewarded. If the shaming is followed by forgiveness and other reintegrative processes, it becomes a particularly powerful mechanism for reinforcing cultural (group) values and identity.

Katz complements Braithwaite, it seems to me, in his documentation of the emotions moving around the edge of shame. His analysis of the process of transcendence may help criminologists understand more completely the dynamics of shaming, especially when it fails. The humiliating subordination that shaming is (when there is no self-participation or reintegration) represents a moral affront that must be "put right" through a transcendent process of self-reaffirmation, of reconstruction that salvages honor, identity, and worth. The formation and persistence of criminal subcultures, crucial to understanding the forms that deviance takes, and an important criminogenic source in Braithwaite's model (see Figure 17.1), can be explored within the framework of foreground analysis of the kind Katz has demonstrated.

Importantly, Katz's (1988:52–79) analysis of "sneaky thrills"—shoplifting, pilfering, vandalism, joyriding—also shows how shaming can act as a *stimulus* for crime as well as a reaction to be avoided. It is precisely the people who have some emotional investment in the conventional order (especially their standing in it) who are likely to be responsive to shaming—otherwise, who cares if a parent, teacher, police officer, or judge bawls you out? Yet the euphoria or thrill of sneaky theft—the seduction of the crime itself—lies precisely in the risk that one will be shamed if caught:

Thus, the other side of the euphoria felt from being successful is the humiliation from being caught. What the sneak thieves are avoiding, or getting away with by not being caught, is the shame they would feel if they were caught. . . .

The thrills of sneaky thefts are metaphysically complex matters. On the one hand, shoplifters and vandals know what they are doing is illegal; the deviant character of the practice is part of the appeal. On the other hand, they typically register a kind of metaphysical shock when an arrest induces a sense that what they are doing might be treated as *real* crime. . . . Once an arrest occurs, the shoplifting career typically ends in response to an awareness that persistence would now clearly signal a commitment to a deviant identity. (Katz, 1988:64–66)

Summary of Chapter 17

This brief excursion into general theories of crime brings the text to a close. Consistent with the goal of general theory, these works seek to identify the things diverse crimes have in common and to build explanations around them. Most of the theories are heavily indebted to existing ideas about crime, and what is new is more in the packaging than in the substance. On the other hand, Katz shows us a way of thinking about crime that departs significantly from the other approaches even as it complements Braithwaite's.

It is safe to say that criminologists will be examining these theories closely in the years ahead. Do not expect that one will emerge as *the* explanation of crime. For one thing, criminologists disagree on the definition of their subject matter. For another, the data and methodology for adequate tests of all theories do not yet exist. What is likely to happen is continued refinement and reshaping, so that the dominant theories a decade from now will show their indebtedness but will not be the same.

Remember, too, that the criminological enterprise is affected not only by the ideas and values of its participants but also by the ideology underlying public policy. That ideology affects the funding of research. Theories that challenge established paradigms tend in any case to be embraced with great caution, all the more so if they conflict with the funding priorities of governments and universities.

If the measure of criminology is its success at explaining crime, where do you think we stand? We certainly know a lot about the crime scene, and well we should after more than 100 years of research. We can also point to theories that have remained prominent for many, many years—differential association is perhaps the best example. Some of the general theories we have reviewed in this chapter address crime at both micro and macro levels of analysis, and some integrate theories that once appeared incompatible. Some also bring together behaviors that were once thought to be so different as to require different explanations—rape and shoplifting, for example. It is noteworthy, too, that an argument made long ago by French sociologist Emile Durkheim now seems more relevant than ever: that crime and punishment are two parts of an inseparable whole; that one cannot be explained without also explaining the other. So how are we doing?

Recommended Readings

John Braithwaite (1989a). *Crime, Shame and Reintegration.* Cambridge: Cambridge University Press.

Lawrence E. Cohen, and Richard Machalek (1988). "A general theory of expropriative crime: An evolutionary ecological approach." *American Journal of Sociology* 94:465–501.

Michael R. Gottfredson, and Travis Hirschi (1990). *A General Theory of Crime.* Stanford: Stanford University Press.

Jack Katz (1988). *Seductions of Crime: Moral and Sensual Attractions in Doing Evil.* New York: Basic Books.

James Q. Wilson, and Richard J. Herrnstein (1985). *Crime and Human Nature.* New York: Simon and Schuster.

Appendix

Throughout the text are references to various criminal offenses. All the chapters in Part II of this book deal with the historical development of relevant offenses, and an effort is made to acquaint the reader with contemporary criminal law definitions. However, the FBI maintains its own offense classification and definitional system, as does the National Crime Victimization Survey. When data are presented for certain offenses, the conception of that offense may not strictly agree with dominant criminal law definitions, and sometimes the FBI includes in its offense categories a number of discrete criminal law offenses. So that the reader will know exactly how the FBI and NCVS define any particular offense category, the following list is presented.

FBI Part I Offenses

Part I, or Index Offenses, are serious crimes that are considered bellwether offenses.

Criminal Homicide.   (a) Murder and nonnegligent manslaughter: all willful felonious homicide as distinguished from death caused by negligence. *Excludes* attempt to kill, suicide, accidental death, or justifiable homicide. (b) Manslaughter by negligence: any death that police investigation established was primarily attributable to gross negligence of some individual other than the victim.

Forcible Rape.   The carnal knowledge of a female, forcibly and against her will in the categories of rape by force, assault by rape, and attempted rape. *Excludes* statutory offenses (no force used, victim under age of consent).

Robbery.   Stealing or taking of anything of value from the care, custody, or control of a person by force or violence or by putting in fear, such as strong-arm robbery, stickup, armed robbery, assault to rob, and attempt to rob.

Burglary, Breaking or Entering.   Burglary, housebreaking, safecracking, or any breaking or unlawful entry of a structure with the intent to commit a felony or a theft. Includes attempted forcible entry.

Aggravated Assault.   Assault with intent to kill or for the purpose of inflicting severe bodily injury by shooting, cutting, stabbing, maiming, poisoning, scalding, or the use of acids, explosives, or other means. *Excludes* simple assault.

Larceny-Theft (Except Auto Theft).   The unlawful taking, carrying, leading, or riding away of property from the possession or constructive possession of another. *Excludes* embezzlement, con games, forgery, worthless checks, etc.

Auto Theft. Unlawful taking or stealing or attempted theft of a motor vehicle. Specifically excluded from this category are motor boats, construction equipment, airplanes, and farming equipment.

Arson. Willful or malicious burning with or without intent to defraud. Includes attempts.

FBI Part II Offenses

Other Assaults (Simple). Assaults that are not of an aggravated nature.

Forgery and Counterfeiting. Making, altering, uttering, or possessing, with intent to defraud; anything false that is made to appear true. Includes attempts.

Fraud. Fraudulent conversion and obtaining money or property by false pretenses. Includes bad checks except forgeries and counterfeiting. Also includes larceny by bailee.

Embezzlement. Misappropriation or misapplication of money or property entrusted to person's care, custody, or control.

Stolen Property—Buying, Receiving, Possessing. Buying, receiving, and possessing stolen property, and attempts.

Vandalism. Willful or malicious destruction, injury, disfigurement, or defacement of property without consent of owner or person having custody or control.

Weapons—Carrying, Possessing, Etc. All violations of regulations or statutes controlling the carrying, using, possession, furnishing, and manufacturing of deadly weapons or silencers. Includes attempts.

Prostitution and Commercialized Vice. Sex offenses of a commercial nature and attempts, such as prostitution, keeping a bawdy house, procuring, or transporting women for immoral purposes.

Sex Offenses (Except Forcible Rape and Last Category). Statutory rape, offenses against chastity, common decency, morals, and the like. Includes attempts.

Narcotic Drug Laws. Offenses relating to narcotic drugs, such as unlawful possession, sale, use, growing, manufacturing, and making of narcotic drugs.

Gambling. Promoting, permitting, or engaging in gambling.

Offenses Against the Family and Children. Nonsupport, neglect, abuse, etc.

Driving under the Influence. Driving or operating any motor vehicle while drunk or under the influence of alcohol or narcotics.

Liquor Laws. State or local liquor law violations, except drunkenness and driving under the influence.

Drunkenness. Intoxication.

Disorderly Conduct. Breach of the peace.

Vagrancy. Vagabondage, begging, loitering, etc.

Suspicion. Arrest for no specific offense and release without formal charges being placed. [It is interesting that the FBI considers suspicion an offense. See Chapter 10 for a discussion of police views of suspicion.]

Curfew and Loitering Laws (Juveniles). Offenses relating to violation of local curfew or loitering ordinances where such laws exist.

Runaway (Juveniles). Limited to juveniles taken into protective custody as runaways under provisions of local statutes.

Crime Definitions from the National Crime Victimization Survey

Assault. An unlawful physical attack, whether aggravated or simple, upon a person, including attempted or threatened attacks with or without a weapon. Excludes rape and attempted rape, as well as attacks involving theft or attempted theft, which are classified as robbery. Severity of crimes in this category range from threats to attacks that result in life-threatening injuries.

Burglary (Completed). Unlawful or forcible entry of a residence, usually, but not necessarily, attended by theft. The entry may be by force, such as breaking a window or slashing a screen, or it may be through an unlocked door or an open window. As long as the person entering had no legal right to be present in the structure, a burglary has occurred. Furthermore, the structure need not be the house itself for a household burglary to take place. Illegal entry of a garage, shed, or any other structure on the premises also constitutes household burglary. In fact, burglary does not necessarily have to occur on the premises. If the breaking and entering occurred in a hotel or in a vacation residence, it still would be classified as a burglary for the household whose member or members were staying there at the time.

Household Larceny (Completed). Theft of property or cash from a residence or its immediate vicinity. For a household larceny to occur within the home itself, the thief must be someone with a right to be there, such as a maid, a delivery person, or a guest. Forcible entry, attempted forcible entry, or unlawful entry are not involved.

Motor Vehicle Theft (Completed). Stealing or unauthorized taking of a motor vehicle.

Personal Theft. Includes both personal larceny with contact and personal larceny without contact. *Personal larceny with contact* is theft of purse, wallet, or cash by stealth directly from the person of the victim, but without force or the threat of force, including attempted purse snatching. *Personal larceny without contact* is theft or attempted theft, without direct contact between victim and offender, of property or cash from any place other than the victim's home or its immediate vicinity. The property need not be strictly personal in nature; the act is distinguished from household larceny solely by place of occurrence. Examples of personal larceny without contact include the theft of a briefcase or umbrella from a restaurant, a portable radio from the beach, clothing from an automobile parked in a shopping center, a bicycle from a school yard, food from a shopping cart in front of a supermarket, etc. In rare cases, the victim sees the offender during the commission of the act.

Rape. Carnal knowledge through the use of force or the threat of force, including attempts. Statutory rape (without force) is excluded. Both heterosexual and homosexual rape are included.

Robbery. Completed or attempted theft, directly from a person, of property or cash by force or threat of force, with or without a weapon.

Source: Federal Bureau of Investigation (1984). *Uniform Crime Reports, 1983.* Washington, D.C.: U.S. Government Printing Office; Bureau of Justice Statistics (1991). *Criminal Victimization in the United States, 1989,* pp. 140–142.

References

Abadinsky, Howard (1990). *Organized Crime*. 3rd ed. Chicago: Nelson-Hall.

Adler, Freda (1975). *Sisters in Crime: The Rise of the New Female Criminal*. New York: McGraw-Hill.

Adler, Patricia A. (1985). *Wheeling and Dealing: An Ethnography of an Upper-Level Drug Dealing and Smuggling Community*. New York: Columbia University Press.

Agnew, Robert (1985). "Social control theory and delinquency: A longitiudinal test," *Criminology* 23:47–60.

Agnew, Robert (1990). "Adolescent resources and delinquency," *Criminology* 28:535–566.

Agnew, Robert (1992). "Foundation for a general strain theory of crime and delinquency," *Criminology* 30:47–87.

Akers, Ronald L. (1973). *Deviant Behavior: A Social Learning Approach*. Belmont, Calif.: Wadsworth.

Akers, Ronald L. (1991). "Self-control as a general theory of crime," *Journal of Quantitative Criminology* 7:201–211.

Akers, Ronald L., Robert L. Burgess, and Weldon I. Johnson (1968). "Opiate use, addiction and relapse," *Social Problems* 15:459–469.

Alder, Christine (1985). "Self-reported sexual aggression," *Crime and Delinquency* 31:306–331.

Alder, Christine (1986). "Unemployed women have got it heaps worse: Exploring the implications of female youth unemployment," *Australian and New Zealand Journal of Criminology* 19:210–224.

Alix, Ernest K. (1969). "The functional interdependence of crime and community social structure," *Journal of Criminal Law, Criminology, and Police Science* 60:332–339.

Allen, Francis A. (1959). "Criminal justice, legal values, and the rehabilitative ideal," *Journal of Criminal Law, Criminology, and Police Science* 50:226–236.

Allen, Francis A. (1974). *The Crimes of Politics*. Cambridge, Mass.: Harvard University Press.

Allen, John (1977). *Assault with a Deadly Weapon: The Autobiography of a Street Criminal*. New York: Pantheon Books.

Allen-Hagan, Barbara (1991). "Children in custody 1989" *OJJDP Update on Statistics* January:1–10.

Alschuler, Albert W. (1978). "Sentencing reform and prosecutorial power: A critique of recent proposals for 'fixed' and 'presumptive' sentencing," in *Determinate Sentencing: Reform or Regression, Proceedings of the Special Conference on Determinate Sentencing*, University of California, Berkeley, June 2–3, 1977.

Altman, Janet R., and Richard O. Cunningham (1967). "Preventive detention," *George Washington University Law Review* 36:178–189.

American Bar Association (1970). *Standards Relating to Probation*. New York: Institute of Judicial Administration.

Amir, Menachim (1971). *Patterns in Forcible Rape.* Chicago: University of Chicago Press.

Andenaes, Johannes (1966). "The general preventive effects of punishment," *Pennsylvania Law Review* 114:949–983.

Andenaes, Johannes (1974). *Punishment and Deterrence.* Ann Arbor, Mich.: University of Michigan Press.

Andrews, D. A. (1980). "Some experimental investigations of the principles of differential association through deliberate manipulation of the structure of service systems," *American Sociological Review* 45:448–462.

Andrews, D. A., Ivan Zinger, Robert D. Hoge, James Bonta, Paul Gendreau, and Francis T. Cullen (1990). "Does correctional treatment work? A clinically relevant and psychologically informed meta-analysis," *Criminology* 28:369–404.

Andrews, George, ed. (1967). *The Book of Grass: An Anthology of Indian Hemp.* New York: Grove Press.

Angel, Arthur R. (1971). "Preventive detention: An empirical analysis," *Harvard Civil Rights-Civil Liberties Law Review* 6:309–332.

Anglin, Douglas M., and George Speckart (1988). "Narcotics use and crime: A multisample, multimethod analysis," *Criminology* 26:197–233.

Anonymous (1972). "Editorial," *Yale Law Journal* 81:1380.

Archambeault, William G., and Charles R. Fenwick (1983). "A comparative analysis of Japanese and American police organizational models," *Police Studies* Fall: 3–12.

Archer, Dane, and Rosemary Gartner (1984). *Violence and Crime in Cross-National Perspective.* New Haven, Conn.: Yale University Press.

Ashley, Barbara Renchkovsky, and David Ashley (1984). "Sex as violence: The body against intimacy," *International Journal of Women's Studies* 7:352–371.

Attenborough, F. L. (1963). *The Laws of the Earliest English Kings.* New York: Russell and Russell.

Audett, Blackie (1954). *Rap Sheet: My Life Story.* New York: William Sloane.

Austin, William, and Thomas A. Williams III (1977). "A survey of judges' responses to legal cases: Research notes on sentencing disparity," *Journal of Criminal Law and Criminology* 68:306–310.

Babbington, Anthony (1968). *The Power to Silence.* London: Robert Maxwell.

Bacon, Sheldon (1935). *The Early Development of American Municipal Police.* Ph.D. diss., Yale University.

Badillo, Herman, and Milton Haynes (1972). *A Bill of No Rights: Attica and the American Prison System.* New York: Auterbridge and Lazard.

Bailey, Ronald H. (1976). *Violence and Aggression.* New York: Time Life Books.

Baker, Michael A., and Alan F. Westin (1987). *Employer Perceptions of Workplace Crime.* Washington, D.C.: U.S. Department of Justice.

Ball, J., L. Chester, and R. Perrott (1978). *Cops and Robbers: An Investigation into Armed Bank Robbery.* London: Andre Deutsch.

Ball, J. C. (1982). "Lifetime criminality of heroin addicts in the United States," *Journal of Drug Issues* 12:225–239.

Ball, J. C., J. W. Shaffer, and D. N. Nurco (1983). "Day-to-day criminality of heroin addicts in Baltimore—A study of the continuity of offense rates," *Drug and Alcohol Dependence* 12:119–142.

Bandura, Albert (1973). *Aggression: A Social Learning Analysis.* Englewood Cliffs, N.J.: Prentice-Hall.

Banton, Michael (1973). *Police Community Relations.* London: William Collins.

Barak-Glantz, Israel L., and Elmer H. Johnson (1983). *Comparative Criminology*. Beverly Hills, Calif.: Sage.

Barlow, Hugh D. (1983). "Factors affecting the lethality of criminal assaults," presented at the annual meeting of the American Society of Criminology, Denver, Colo.

Barlow, Hugh D. (1985a). "The medical factor in homicide victimization," presented at the Fifth International Symposium on Victimology, Zagreb, Yugoslavia.

Barlow, Hugh D. (1985b). "Victim injuries and the prosecution of violent offenders," presented at the annual meeting of the Academy of Criminal Justice Sciences, Las Vegas, Nev.

Barlow, Hugh D. (1987). "Of secrets and visions: Stanley Cohen on crime control," *Journal of Criminal Law and Criminology* 78:430–441.

Barlow, Hugh D. (1991). "Explaining crimes and analogous acts, or the unrestrained will grab at pleasure whenever they can," *Journal of Criminal Law and Criminology* 82:229–242.

Barlow, Hugh D., and Lynne Schmidt Barlow (1988). "More on the role of weapons in homicidal violence, *Medicine and Law* 7:347–358.

Barlow, Hugh D., and Theodore N. Ferdinand (1992). *Understanding Delinquency*. New York: Harper Collins.

Bastion, Lisa D., and Bruce M. Taylor (1991). *School Crime: A National Crime Survey Report*. Washington, D.C.: U.S. Department of Justice.

Baum, Rudy M. (1985). "New variety of street drug poses growing problem," *Chemical and Engineering News* September 9:7–16.

Baumer, Terry L., and Dennis P. Rosenbaum (1984). *Combatting Retail Theft: Programs and Strategies*. Boston: Butterworths.

Bayley, David H., and Harold Mendelsohn (1968). *Minorities and the Police: Confrontation in America*. New York: Free Press.

Bazelon, David L. (1981). "Foreword, The morality of criminal law: The rights of the accused," *Journal of Criminal Law and Criminology* 72:1143–1170.

Beccaria, Cesare (1963). *Essay on Crimes and Punishments*, trans. by Henry Paolucci. Indianapolis, Ind.: Bobbs–Merrill.

Becker, Gary S. (1968). "Crime and punishment: An economic approach," *Journal of Political Economy* 76:493–517.

Becker, Howard S. (1963). *Outsiders: Studies in the Sociology of Deviance*. New York: Free Press.

Becker, Howard S., ed. (1964). *The Other Side: Perspectives on Deviance*. New York: Free Press.

Beirne, Piers (1983). "Generalization and its discontents: The comparative study of crime," in Israel L. Barak-Glantz and Elmer H. Johnson, eds., *Comparative Criminology*. Beverly Hills, Calif.: Sage.

Bell, Daniel (1965). "Crime as an American way of life: A queer ladder of social mobility," in Daniel Bell, *The End of Ideology*, rev. ed. New York: Free Press.

Bennett, Georgette (1987). *Crimewarps: The Future of Crime in America*. New York: Anchor Books.

Bennett, James (1981). *Oral History and Delinquency*. Chicago: University of Chicago Press.

Bennett, Trevor (1985). "A decision-making approach to opioid addiction," presented at the Home Office Conference on Criminal Decision Making, Cambridge, England.

Bennett, Trevor, and Richard Wright (1981). "Burglars' choice of targets: The use of situational cues in offender decision making," presented at the annual meeting of the American Society of Criminology, Washington, D.C.

Bensing, Robert G., and Oliver Schroeder (1960). *Homicide in an Urban Community*. Springfield, Ill.: Thomas.

Benson, Allen L. (1927). "The propaganda against prohibition," in Lamar T. Beman, ed., *Prohibition: Modification of the Volstead Law*. New York: H. W. Wilson, pp. 133–147.

Benson, Michael L. (1985). "Denying the guilty mind: Accounting for involvement in white-collar crime," *Criminology* 23:583–607.

Benson, Michael L., and Esteban Walker (1988). "Sentencing the white collar offender," *American Sociological Review* 53:294–302.

Bent, Alan Edward (1974). *The Politics of Law Enforcement*. Lexington, Mass.: D. C. Heath.

Bentham, Jeremy (1948). *The Principles of Morals and Legislation*. New York: Hofner Publishing.

Bequai, August (1978). *White-Collar Crime: A Twentieth Century Crisis*. Lexington, Mass.: Lexington Books.

Berk, Richard A., Kenneth J. Lenihan, and Peter H. Rossi (1980). "Crime and poverty: Some experimental evidence from ex-offenders," *American Sociological Review* 45:766–786.

Berkowitz, Leonard (1962). *Aggression: A Social Psychological Analysis*. New York: McGraw Hill.

Beschner, George M., and William Brower (1985). "The scene," in Bill Hanson, George Beschner, James M. Walters, and Elliott Bovelle, eds., *Life With Heroin*. Lexington, Mass.: Lexington Books.

Beyleveld, Deryck (1980). *A Bibliography on General Deterrence*. London: Saxon House.

Bickle, Gayle S., and Ruth D. Peterson (1991). "The impact of gender-based family roles on criminal sentencing," *Social Problems* 38:372–394.

Biderman, Albert (1967). Report on a Pilot Study in the District of Columbia on Victimization and Attitudes Toward Law Enforcement, Field Survey 1. Washington, D.C.: U.S. Government Printing Office.

Binder, Arnold, and Gilbert Geis (1983). *Methods of Research in Criminology and Criminal Justice*. New York: McGraw-Hill.

Bishop, Donna (1984). "Deterrence: A panel analysis," *Justice Quarterly* 1:311–328.

Bittner, Egon, and Anthony M. Platt (1966). "The meaning of punishment," *Issues in Criminology* 2:81–105.

Black, Donald J. (1970). "Production of crime rates," *American Sociological Review* 35:733–748.

Black, Donald (1980). *The Manners and Customs of the Police*. New York: Academic Press.

Blackstone, Sir William (1962). *Commentaries on the Laws of England*, vol. 4. Boston: Beacon Press.

Blanchard, W. H. (1959). "The group process in gang rape," *Journal of Social Psychology* 49:259–266.

Blankenship, Ralph L. (1974). "Toward a sociolinguistic perspective on deviance labeling," *Sociology and Social Research* 58:253–261.

Blau, Judith, and Peter M. Blau (1982). "The cost of inequality: Metropolitan structure and crime," *American Sociological Review* 47:114–129.

Bleich, Jeff (1989). "The politics of prison crowding," *California Law Review* 77:5–35.

Bloch, Herbert A., and Gilbert Geis (1970). *Man, Crime, and Society*. 2nd ed. New York: Random House.

Bloch, Peter B., and Deborah Anderson (1974). *Policewomen on Patrol: Final Report.* Washington, D.C.: The Police Foundation.

Block, Alan A. (1991). *The Business of Crime: A Documentary Study of Organized Crime in the American Economy.* Boulder, Colo.: Westview Press.

Block, Alan A., and Frank Scarpitti (1986). "Casinos and banking: Organized crime in the Bahamas," *Deviant Behavior* 7:301–312.

Block, Anton (1974). *The Mafia of a Sicilian Village.* New York: Harper Torchbooks.

Block, Carolyn Rebecca (1987). *Homicide in Chicago.* Chicago: Loyola University of Chicago Urban Insight Series.

Block, Carolyn Rebecca (1991). "Trends in homicide syndromes and economic cycles in Chicago over 25 years." Presented at the Annual Meeting of the American Society of Criminology, San Francisco, November 18–23.

Block, Richard (1976). "Homicide in Chicago: A nine year study (1965–1973)," *Journal of Criminal Law and Criminology* 66:496–510.

Block, Richard, and Carolyn Rebecca Block (1991). "Beginning with Wolfgang: An agenda for homicide research." Presented at the Annual Meeting of the American Society of Criminology, San Francisco, November 18–23.

Block, Richard, and Franklin E. Zimring (1973). "Homicide in Chicago; 1965–1970," *Journal of Research in Crime and Delinquency* 10:1–12.

Blum, Richard, and Associates (1972). *The Dream Sellers.* San Francisco: Jossey-Bass.

Blumberg, Abraham S. (1967). "The practice of law as a confidence game: Organizational cooptation of a profession," *Law and Society Review* 1:15–39.

Blumenthal, Monica, Robert L. Kahn, Frank M. Andrews, and Kendra B. Head (1972). *Justifying Violence: Attitudes of American Men.* Ann Arbor, Mich.: Institute for Social Research.

Blumstein, Alfred, Jacqueline Cohen, and Daniel Nagin, eds. (1978). *Deterrence and Incapacitation: Estimating the Effects of Criminal Sanctions on Crime Rates.* Washington, D.C.: National Academy of Science.

Blumstein, Alfred, Jacqueline Cohen, and David P. Farrington (1988a). "Criminal career research: Its value for criminology," *Criminology* 26:1–35.

Blumstein, Alfred, Jacqueline Cohen, and David P. Farrington (1988b). "Longitudinal and criminal career research: Further clarifications," *Criminology* 26:57–74.

Blumstein, Alfred, Jacqueline Cohen, Jeffrey Roth, and Christy A. Visher, eds. (1986). *Criminal Careers and Career Criminals,* vol. 1. Washington, D.C.: National Academy Press.

Boggs, Sarah Lee (1964). "The Ecology of Crime Occurrence in St. Louis: A Reconceptualization," Ph.D. diss., Washington University, St. Louis, Mo.

Bohannan, Paul (1960). *African Homicide and Suicide.* Princeton, N.J.: Princeton University Press.

Bohm, Carol (1974). "Judicial attitudes toward rape victims," *Judicature* Spring 303–307.

Bohm, Robert M. (1982). "Radical criminology: An explication," *Criminology* 19:565–589.

Bonger, Willem (1916). *Criminality and Economic Conditions.* Boston: Little, Brown.

Bonger, Willem (1969). *Criminality and Economic Conditions,* abridged version. Bloomington, Ind.: Indiana University Press.

Booth, Alan (1981). "The built environment as a crime deterrent: A reexamination of defensible space," *Criminology* 18:557–570.

Bordua, David J., ed. (1967). *The Police: Six Sociological Essays.* New York: Wiley.

Boris, Steven Barnet (1979). "Stereotypes and dispositions for criminal homicide," *Criminology* 17:139–158.

Boritch, Helen, and John Hagan (1990). "A century of crime in Toronto: Gender, class, and patterns of social control, 1859–1955," *Criminology* 28:567–600.

Bottomley, A. Keith (1970). *Prison Before Trial*. London: G. Bells and Sons.

Bottomley, A. Keith (1973a). *Decisions in the Penal Process*. London: Martin Robinson.

Bottomley, A. Keith (1973b). "Parole decisions in a long-term closed prison," *British Journal of Criminology* 13:26–40.

Bottomley, A. Keith, and C. Coleman (1981). *Understanding Crime Rates*. Farnborough, England: Gower.

Bowers, William J. (1974). *Exeuctions in America*. Lexington, Mass.: D. C. Heath.

Bowker, Lee H. (1977). *Prisoner Subcultures*. Lexington, Mass.: D. C. Heath.

Bowker, Lee H. (1978). "Victimization in correctional institutions: An interdisciplinary analysis." Presented at the annual meeting of the Academy of Criminal Justice Sciences, New Orleans, La., March.

Bowman, Phillip J. (1980). "Toward a dual labor-market approach to black-on-black homicide," *Public Health Reports* 95:555–556.

Box, Steven (1983). *Power, Crime, and Mystification*. London: Tavistock.

Box, Steven, and Chris Hale (1986). "Unemployment, crime and imprisonment, and the enduring problem of prison overcrowding," in Roger Matthews and Jock Young, eds., *Confronting Crime*. Beverly Hills, Calif.: Sage.

Box-Grainger, Jill (1986). "Sentencing rapists," in Roger Matthews and Jock Young, eds., *Confronting Crime*. Beverly Hills, Calif.: Sage.

Bradley, Robert J. (1984). "Trends in state crime-control legislation," in Search Group, Inc., *Information Policy and Crime Control Strategies*. Washington, D.C.: U.S. Department of Justice.

Bradshaw, Tausha L., and Alan E. Marks (1990). "Beyond a reasonable doubt: Factors that influence the legal disposition of child sexual abuse cases," *Crime and Delinquency* 36:276–285.

Braithwaite, John (1978). "An exploratory study of used car fraud," in P. R. Wilson and J. B. Braithwaite, eds. *Two Kinds of Deviance: Crimes of the Powerless and Powerful*. Brisbane: University of Queensland Press.

Braithwaite, John (1982). "Challenging just desserts: Punishing white collar criminals," *Journal of Criminal Law and Criminology* 73:723–763.

Braithwaite, John (1989a). *Crime, Shame and Reintegration*. Cambridge, England: Cambridge University Press.

Braithwaite (1989b). "Organizational theory and organizational shame," *Justice Quarterly* 6:401–426.

Braithwaite, John (1991). "Inequality and Republican Criminology." Presented at the Annual Meeting of the American Society of Criminology, San Francisco, November 18–23.

Braithwaite, John, and Philip Pettit (1990). *Not Just Desserts: A Republican Theory of Criminal Justice*. Oxford, England: Oxford University Press.

Brantingham, Paul J., and Patricia L. Brantingham (1981). *Environmental Criminology*. Beverly Hills, Calif.: Sage.

Brecher, Edwin M. (1972). *Licit and Illicit Drugs*. Boston: Little, Brown.

Bredemeier, Harry C., and Toby Jackson (1961). *Social Problems in America*. New York: Wiley.

Brockway, Zebulon R. ([1912]1969). *Fifty Years of Prison Service: An Autobiography*. Montclair, N.J.: Patterson Smith.

Brodie, H. Keith H. (1973). "The effects of ethyl alcohol in man," in National Commission on Marijuana and Drug Abuse (1973), *Patterns and Consequences of Drug Use*. Washington, D.C.: U.S. Government Printing Office.

Brooks, Laura Weber (1989). "Police discretionary behavior: A study of style," in Roger G. Durham and Geoffrey P. Alpert, eds., in *Critical Issues in Policing*. Prospect Heights, Ill.: Waveland Press.

Brosi, Kathleen B. (1979). *A Cross-City Comparison of Felony Case Processing*. Washington, D.C.: U.S. Government Printing Office.

Brown, Brenda A. (1974). "Crime Against Women Alone," mimeograph. Memphis, Tenn.: Memphis Police Department.

Brown, Michael (1988). *Working the Streets: Police Discretion and Dilemmas of Reform*. New York: Russell Sage.

Brown, Richard Maxwell (1969). "Violence in America," in Donald J. Mulvihill, Melvin Tumin, and Lynn Curtis, eds., *Crimes of Violence*. Washington, D.C.: U.S. Government Printing Office.

Browne, Angela (1987). *When Battered Women Kill*. New York: Macmillan.

Browne, Angela, and Kirk R. Williams (1987). "Gender specific effects on patterns of homicide perpetration." Presented to the American Psychological Association.

Brownmiller, Susan (1975). *Against Our Will*. New York: Simon and Schuster.

Bryan, James H. (1965). "Apprenticeships in prostitution," *Social Problems* 12:287–297.

Bryan, James H. (1966). "Occupational ideologies and individual attitudes of call girls," *Social Problems* 13:441–450.

Bryant, Clifton D., and C. Eddie Palmer (1975). "Massage parlors and 'hand whores': Some sociological observations, *Journal of Sex Research* 11:227–241.

Buckle, Abigail, and David P. Farrington (1984). "An observational study of shoplifting," *British Journal of Criminology* 24:63–72.

Buikhuisen, Wouter (1988). "Chronic juvenile delinquency: A theory," in Wouter Buikhuisen and Sarnoff A. Mednick, eds., *Explaining Criminal Behavior*. Linden, Netherlands: E. J. Brill.

Bullock, Henry Allen (1961). "Significance of the racial factor in length of prison sentences," *Journal of Criminal Law, Criminology and Police Science* 52:411–417.

Burchard, John D., and Sara N. Burchard, eds. (1987). *Prevention of Delinquent Behavior*. Beverly Hills, Calif.: Sage.

Bureau of the Census (1985). *Statistical Abstract of the United States*. Washington, D.C.: U.S. Government Printing Office.

Bureau of the Census (1990). *Statistical Abstract of the United States 1990*. Washington, D.C.: U.S. Department of Commerce.

Bureau of Justice Statistics (1983): *Special Report: Career Patterns in Crime*. Washington, D.C.: U.S. Department of Justice.

Bureau of Justice Statistics (1984a). *Special Report: Electronic Fund Transfer and Crime*. Washington, D.C.: U.S. Department of Justice.

Bureau of Justice Statistics (1984b). *Special Report: Family Violence*. Washington, D.C.: U.S. Department of Justice.

Bureau of Justice Statistics (1984c). *Tracking Offenders: The Child Victim*. Washington, D.C.: U.S. Department of Justice.

Bureau of Justice Statistics (1984d). *Special Report: Time Served in Prison*. Washington, D.C.: U.S. Department of Justice.

Bureau of Justice Statistics (1984e). *Prison Admissions and Releases, 1981*. Washington, D.C.: U.S. Department of Justice.

Bureau of Justice Statistics (1985a). *Special Report: Reporting Crimes to the Police*. Washington, D.C.: U.S. Department of Justice.

Bureau of Justice Statistics (1985b). *The Crime of Rape*. Washington, D.C.: U.S. Department of Justice.

Bureau of Justice Statistics (1985c). *Special Report: Examining Recidivism*. Washington, D.C.: U.S. Department of Justice.

Bureau of Justice Statistics (1985d). *Household Burglary*. Washington, D.C.: U.S. Department of Justice.

Bureau of Justice Statistics (1985e). *The Growth of Appeals*. Washington, D.C.: U.S. Department of Justice.

Bureau of Justice Statistics (1985f). *Pretrial Release and Misconduct*. Washington, D.C.: U.S. Department of Justice.

Bureau of Justice Statistics (1985g). *Capital Punishment, 1984*. Washington, D.C.: U.S. Department of Justice.

Bureau of Justice Statistics (1985h). *Special Report: Felony Sentencing in 18 Local Jurisdictions*. Washington, D.C.: U.S. Department of Justice.

Bureau of Justice Statistics (1985i). *Prisoners in 1984*. Washington, D.C.: U.S. Department of Justice.

Bureau of Justice Statistics (1985j). *Special Report: The Prevalence of Imprisonment*. Washington, D.C.: U.S. Department of Justice.

Bureau of Justice Statistics (1987). *Special Report: Robbery Victims*. Washington, D.C.: U.S. Department of Justice.

Bureau of Justice Statistics (1988a). *Crime and Justice in America*, 2nd ed. Washington, D.C.: U.S. Department of Justice.

Bureau of Justice Statistics (1988b). *BJS Data Report, 1987*. Washington, D.C.: U.S. Department of Justice.

Bureau of Justice Statistics (1988c). *Criminal Victimization in the United States, 1986*. Washington, D.C.: U.S. Department of Justice.

Bureau of Justice Statistics (1988d). *Bulletin: Households Touched by Crime, 1987*. Washington, D.C.: U.S. Department of Justice.

Bureau of Justice Statistics (1988e). *Special Report: International Crime Rates*. Washington, D.C.: U.S. Department of Justice.

Bureau of Justice Statistics (1988f). *Jail Inmates in 1987*. Washington, D.C.: U.S. Department of Justice.

Bureau of Justice Statistics (1990a). *Black Victims*. Washington, D.C.: U.S. Department of Justice.

Bureau of Justice Statistics (1990b). *Criminal Victimization, 1989*. Washington, D.C.: U.S. Department of Justice.

Bureau of Justice Statistics (1990c). *Special Report: Handgun Crime Victims*. Washington, D.C.: U.S. Department of Justice.

Bureau of Justice Statistics (1990d) *Prison Time*. Washington, D.C.: U.S. Department of Justice.

Bureau of Justice Statistics (1991a). *Crime and the Nation's Households, 1990*. Washington, D.C.: U.S. Department of Justice.

Bureau of Justice Statistics (1991b). *Criminal Victimization in the United States: 1973–1988 Trends*. Washington, D.C.: U.S. Department of Justice.

Bureau of Justice Statistics (1991c). *Drug Crime Facts, 1990*. Washington, D.C.: U.S. Department of Justice.

Bureau of Justice Statistics (1991d). *National Update*. Washington, D.C.: U.S. Department of Justice.

Bureau of Justice Statistics (1991e). *Profile of Jail Inmates*. Washington, D.C.: U.S. Department of Justice.

Bureau of Justice Statistics (1991f). *Bulletin: Capital Punishment 1990*. Washington, D.C.: U.S. Department of Justice.

Bureau of Justice Statistics (1991g). *Pretrial Release of Felony Defendants, 1988: National Pretrial Reporting Program*. Washington, D.C.: U.S. Department of Justice.

Bureau of Justice Statistics (1991h). *Jail Inmates, 1990*. Washington, D.C.: U.S. Department of Justice.

Bureau of Justic Statistics (1991i). *Special Report: Women in Prison*. Washington, D.C.: U.S. Department of Justice.

Bureau of Justice Statistics (1991j). *Bulletin: Prisoners in 1990*. Washington, D.C.: U.S. Department of Justice.

Bureau of Justice Statistics (1992). *National Update, Volume 2*. Washington, D.C.: U.S. Department of Justice.

Burgess, Robert L. (1979). "Family violence: Some implications from evolutionary biology." Presented to the annual meeting of the American Society of Criminology, San Francisco.

Burgess, Robert L., and Ronald L. Akers (1966). "A differential association-reinforcement theory of criminal behavior," *Social Problems* 14:128–147.

Burrows, John N., and Kevin Heal (1980). "Police car security campaigns," in Ronald V. Clarke and Pat Mayhew, eds., *Designing Out Crime*. London: H.M.S.O.

Bursik, Robert J., Jr. (1980). "The dynamics of specialization in juvenile offenses," *Social Forces* 59:851–864.

Bursik, Robert J., Jr. (1988). "Social disorganization and theories of crime and delinquency: Problems and prospects," *Criminology* 26:519–551.

Calhoun, George (1927). *The Growth of Criminal Law in Ancient Greece*. Berkeley, Calif.: University of California Press.

Calvert E. Roy (repr. 1971). *Capital Punishment in the Twentieth Century*. New York: Kennikat Press.

Calvin, Allen D. (1981). "Unemployment among black youths, demographics and crime," *Crime and Delinquency* 27:234–244.

Cameron, Mary Owen (1964). *The Booster and the Snitch*. New York: Free Press.

Campbell, Ann (1984). *Girls in the Gang*. Oxford: Basil Blackwell.

Cannavale, Frank J. (1976). *Witness Cooperation*. Lexington, Mass.: D. C. Heath.

Carey, James T. (1968). *The College Drug Scene*. Englewood Cliffs, N.J.: Prentice-Hall.

Caringella-MacDonald, Susan (1991). "An assessment of rape reform: Victim and case treatment under Michigan's model," *International Review of Victimology* 1:347–361.

Carlin, Jerome E. (1968). *Lawyer's Ethics*. New York: Russell Sage.

Carroll, Leo (1974). *Hacks, Blacks, and Cons: Race Relations in a Maximum Security Prison*. Lexington, Mass.: D. C. Heath.

Carter, Robert M. (1965). "The Johnny Cain story: A composite of men executed in California," *Issues in Criminology* 1:66–76.

Carter, Robert M., and Leslie T. Wilkins (1967). "Some factors in sentencing policy," *Journal of Criminal Law, Criminology, and Police Science* 58:503–514.

Carter, Robert M., and Leslie T. Wilkins, eds. (1976). *Probation, Parole, and Community Corrections*, 2nd ed. New York: Wiley.

Carter, Ronald L., and Kim Q. Hill (1979). *The Criminal's Image of the City*. New York: Pergamon.

Casper, Jonathan D. (1971). "Did you have a lawyer when you went to court? No I had a public defender," *Yale Review of Law and Social Action* 1:4–9.

Casper, Jonathan D. (1972). *American Criminal Justice: The Defendant's Perspective*. Englewood Cliffs, N.J.: Prentice-Hall.

Cavan, Sherri (1966). *Liquor License: An Ethnography of Bar Behavior*. Chicago: Aldine.

Center for Research on Criminal Justice (1975). *The Iron Fist and the Velvet Glove*. Berkeley, Calif.: Center for Research on Criminal Justice.

Centers for Disease Control (1985). *Morbidity and Mortality, Weekly Report* October 11:613–618.

Cernkovich, Stephen A., and Peggy C. Giordano (1987). "Family relationships and delinquency," *Criminology* 25:295–319.

Cernkovich, Stephen A., Peggy C. Giordano, and Meredith D. Pugh (1985). "Chronic offenders: The missing cases in self-report delinquency research," *Journal of Criminal Law and Criminology* 76:705–732.

Chaiken, Marcia R., and Jan M. Chaiken (1991). "Priority prosecution of high rate dangerous offenders," *NIJ Research in Action* March 1–8.

Chambers, Carl D. (1971). *An Assessment of Drug Use in the General Population*. New York: Narcotics Addiction Control Commission.

Chambliss, William J. (1967). "Types of deviance and the effectiveness of legal sanctions," *Wisconsin Law Review* Summer:703–719.

Chambliss, William J. (1971). "Vice, corruption, bureaucracy, and power," *Wisconsin Law Review* Fall:1150–1173.

Chambliss, William J. (1973). "The saints and the roughnecks," *Society* 11:24–31.

Chambliss, William J. (1975a). "The political economy of crime: A comparative study of Nigeria and the U.S.A., " in Ian Taylor, Paul Walton, and Jock Young, eds., *Critical Criminology*. London: Routledge and Kegan Paul.

Chambliss, William J. (1975b). *Criminal Law in Action*. Santa Barbara, Calif.: Hamilton.

Chambliss, William J., ed. (1972). *Box Man: A Professional Thief's Journey*. New York: Harper & Row.

Chambliss, William J. (1978). *On the Take: From Petty Crooks to Presidents*. Bloomington, Ind.: Indiana University Press.

Chambliss, William J., and John T. Liell (1966). "The legal process in the community setting," *Crime and Delinquency* 12:310–317.

Chambliss, William J., and Robert B. Siedman (1971). *Law and Order*. Reading, Mass.: Addison-Wesley.

Chancer, Lynn S. (1987). "New Bedford, Massachusetts, March 6, 1983–March 22, 1984: The 'before and after' of a group rape," *Gender and Society* 1:239–260.

Chapman, Dennis (1968). *Sociology and the Stereotype of the Criminal*. London: Tavistock.

Chapman, William R. (1986). "The role of peers in strain models of delinquency." Presented to annual meeting of the American Society of Criminology, Atlanta, Ga.

Chappell, Duncan, Robley Geis, and Gilbert Geis (1977). *Forcible Rape: The Crime, the Victim, and the Offender*. New York: Columbia University Press.

Cheatwood, Darrell (1988). "Is there a season for homicide?" *Criminology* 26:287–306.

Chesney-Lind, Meda (1987a). *Girls' Crime and Women's Place: Toward a Feminist Model of Female Delinquency*. Honolulu, Haw.: University of Hawaii Youth Development and Research Center.

Chesney-Lind, Meda (1987b). "Female status offenders and the double standard of juvenile justice: An international problem." Presented at the Annual Meeting of the American Society of Criminology, Montreal, November 11–14.

Chesney-Lind, Meda (1988). "Girls in jail," *Crime and Delinquency* 34:150–168.

Chesney-Lind, Meda, and Randall G. Shelden (1992). *Girls, Delinquency, and Juvenile Justice.* Pacific Grove, Calif.: Brooks/Cole.

Chimbos, P. D. (1978). *Marital Violence: A Study of Interspouse Homicide.* San Francisco: R and E Research Associates.

Chodorkoff, Bernard, and Seymour Baxter (1969). "Psychiatric and psychoanalytic theories of violence and its origins," in Donald J. Mulvihill, Melvin Tumin, and Lynn Curtis, eds., *Crimes of Violence.* Washington, D.C.: U.S. Government Printing Office.

Christiansen, Harold T., and Christina Gregg (1970). "Changing sex norms in America and Scandinavia," *Journal of Marriage and the Family* 32:625–626.

Christiansen, K. O. (1977a). "A preliminary study of criminality among twins," in Sarnoff A. Mednick and K. O. Christiansen, eds., *Biosocial Basis of Criminal Behavior.* New York: Wiley.

Christiansen, K. O. (1977b). "A review of studies of criminality among twins," in Sarnoff A. Mednick and K. O. Christiansen, eds., *Biosocial Basis of Criminal Behavior.* New York: Wiley.

Cicourel, Aaron V. (1968). *The Social Organization of Juvenile Justice.* New York: Wiley.

Clark, Alexander L., and Jack P. Gibbs (1965). "Social control: A reformulation," *Social Problems* 12:398–415.

Clarke, Ronald V., and Patricia Mayhew, eds. (1980). *Designing Out Crime.* London: H.M.S.O.

Clarke, Ronald V., and Patricia Mayhew (1988). "The British gas suicide story and its criminological implications," in Michael N. Tonry and Norval K. Morris, eds., *Crime and Justice,* vol. 10. Chicago: University of Chicago Press.

Clear, Todd R., John D. Hewitt, and Robert M. Regoli (1978). "Discretion and the determinate sentence: Its distribution, control, and effect on time served," *Crime and Delinquency* 24:428–445.

Clinard, Marshall B. (1983). *Corporate Ethics and Crime: The Role of Middle Management.* Beverly Hills, Calif.: Sage.

Clinard, Marshall B. (1989). "Reflections of a typologic, corporate, comparative criminologist," *The Criminologist* 14:1, 6, 11, 14–15.

Clinard, Marshall B., and Daniel J. Abbot (1973). *Crime in Developing Countries.* New York: Wiley.

Clinard, Marshall B., and Richard Quinney, eds. (1967). *Criminal Behavior Systems: A Typology.* New York: Holt, Rinehart, & Winston.

Clinard, Marshall B., Peter C. Yeager, Jeanne Brissette, David Petrashek, and Elizabeth Hames (1979). *Illegal Corporate Behavior.* Washington, D.C.: LEAA.

Cloward, Richard A., and Lloyd E. Ohlin (1960). *Delinquency and Opportunity: A Theory of Delinquent Gangs.* New York: Free Press.

Cohen, Albert K. (1951). *Juvenile Delinquency and the Social Structure.* Cambridge, Mass.: Harvard University Press.

Cohen, Albert K. (1955). *Delinquent Boys: The Culture of the Gang.* New York: Free Press.

Cohen, Jacqueline (1983). *Incapacitating Criminals: Recent Research Findings, NIJ Reports.* Washington, D.C.: National Institute of Justice.

Cohen, Lawrence E., David Cantor, and James R. Klugel (1981). "Robbery victimization in the U.S.: Analysis of a nonrandom event," *Social Science Quarterly* 62:644–657.

Cohen, Lawrence E., and Marcus Felson (1979). "Social change and crime rate trends: A routine activity approach," *American Sociological Review* 44:588–608.

Cohen, Lawrence E., Marcus Felson, and Kenneth C. Land (1980). "Property crime rates in the United States: A macrodynamic analysis, 1947–1977, with ex-ante forecasts for the mid-1980's," *American Journal of Sociology* 86:90–118.

Cohen, Lawrence E., and Richard Machalek (1988). "A general theory of expropriative crime: An evolutionary ecological approach," *American Journal of Sociology* 94:465–501.

Cohen, Stanley, ed. (1971). *Images of Deviance.* Harmondsworth, England: Penguin Books.

Cohen, Stanley (1985). *Visions of Social Control: Crime, Punishment and Classification.* New York: Polity Press.

Cohen, Stanley (1988). *Against Criminology.* New Brunswick, N.J.: Transaction Books.

Cole, George F. (1970). "The decision to prosecute," *Law and Society Review* 4:331–343.

Cole, George F. (1975). *The American System of Criminal Justice.* North Scituate, Mass.: Duxbury Press.

Cole, George F. (1989). *The American System of Criminal Justice,* 5th ed. Pacific Grove, Calif.: Brooks/Cole.

Coleman, James W. (1989). *The Criminal Elite,* 2nd ed. New York: St. Martin's Press.

Collins, James T., Robert L. Hubbard, and J. Valley Rachel (1985). "Expensive drug use and illegal income: A test of explanatory hypotheses," *Criminology* 23:743–763.

Conklin, John E. (1972). *Robbery and the Criminal Justice System.* Philadelphia: Lippincott.

Conklin, John E., ed. (1973). *The Crime Establishment: Organized Crime and American Society.* Englewood Cliffs, N.J.: Prentice-Hall.

Conklin, John E., and Egon Bittner (1973). "Burglary in a suburb," *Criminology* 11:206–232.

Conrad, John P. (1975). "We should never have promised a hospital," *Federal Probation* 39:1–12.

Cook, Philip J. (1987). "Robbery violence," *Journal of Criminal Law and Criminology* 78:357–376.

Cornish, Derek B., and Ronald V. Clarke (1986a). "Situational prevention, displacement of crime and rational choice theory," in Kevin Heal and Gloria Laycock, eds., *Situational Crime Prevention.* London: H.M.S.O.

Cornish, Derek B., and Ronald V. Clarke (1986b). *The Reasoning Criminal: Rational Choice Perspectives on Offending.* New York: Springer-Verlag.

Cornish, Derek B., and Ronald V. Clarke (1987). "Understanding crime displacement: An application of rational choice theory," *Criminology* 25:933–947.

Cramer, James A., ed. (1978a). *Preventing Crime.* Beverly Hills, Calif.: Sage.

Cressey, Donald R. (1953). *Other People's Money: A Study in the Social Psychology of Embezzlement.* New York: Free Press.

Cressey, Donald R. (1965). "The respectable criminal," *Transaction* 3:12–15.

Cressey, Donald R. (1969). *Theft of the Nation: The Structure and Operations of Organized Crime in America.* New York: Harper & Row.

Critchley, T. A. (1972). *A History of Police in England and Wales,* 2nd ed. Montclair, N.J.: Patterson Smith.

Croall, Hazel (1989). "Who is the white collar criminal?" *British Journal of Criminology* 29:157–174.

Cullen, Francis T. (1983a). "Paradox in policing: A note on perceptions of danger," *Journal of Police Science and Administration* 11:457–462.

Cullen, Francis T. (1983b). *Rethinking Crime and Deviance Theory: The Emergence of a Structuring Tradition.* Totowa, N.J.: Rowman and Allanheld.

Cullen, Francis T., Kathryn M. Golden, and John B. Cullen (1975). "Sex and delinquency: A partial test of the masculinity hypothesis," *Criminology* 17:301–310.

Cullen, Francis T., Gregory A. Clark, John R. Cullen, and Richard A. Matthews (1985a). "Attribution, salience, and attitudes toward criminal sanctioning," *Criminal Justice and Behavior* 12:305–331.

Cullen, Francis T., Bruce G. Link, Lawrence F. Travis III, and John F. Wozniack (1985b). "Consensus of crime seriousness: Empirical reality or methodological artifact?" *Criminology* 23:99–118.

Cullen, Francis T., William J. Maakestad, and Gary Cavender (1987). *Corporate Crime Under Attack: The Ford Pinto Case.* Cincinnati: Anderson.

Cumming, Elaine, Ian Cumming, and Laura Edell (1965). "Policeman as philosopher, guide and friend," *Social Problems* 12:276–286.

Cunningham, William C., John T. Strauchs, and Clifford M. Van Meter (1991). *Private Security: Patterns and Trends.* Washington, D.C.: U.S. Department of Justice.

Cunningham, William C., and Todd Taylor (1985). *The Hallcrest Report: Private Security and Police in America.* Portland, Ore.: Chancellor Press.

Currie, Elliott (1985). *Confronting Crime: An American Challenge.* New York: Pantheon.

Cusson, Maurice, and Pierre Pinsonneault (1986). "The decision to give up crime," in Derek B. Cornish and Ronald V. Clarke, eds., *The Reasoning Criminal.* New York: Springer-Verlag.

Czajkoski, Eugene H. (1973). "Exposing the quasi-judicial role of the prosecutor's office," *Federal Probation* 37:9–13.

Dale, Robert (1974). *Memoirs of a Contemporary Cutpurse.* Cambridge, Mass.: Schenkman.

Daly, Kathleen (1987a). "Structure and practice of familial-based justice in a criminal court," *Law and Society Review* 21:267–290.

Daly, Kathleen (1987b). "Gender and white-collar crime." Revised version of a paper presented to the annual meeting of the American Society of Criminology, Montreal, Canada.

Daly, Kathleen (1988). "The social control of sexuality: A case study of the criminalization of prostitution in the Progressive Era," *Research in Law, Deviance and Social Control* 9:171–206.

Daly, Kathleen (1989). "Neither conflict nor labeling nor paternalism will suffice: Intersections of race, ethnicity, gender, and family in criminal court decisions," *Crime and Delinquency* 35:136–168.

Daly, Kathleen, and Meda Chesney-Lind (1988). "Feminism and criminology," *Justice Quarterly* 5:101–143.

Daly, Martin, and Margo Wilson (1988a). "Evolutionary social psychology and family homicide," *Science* 242:519–524.

Daly, Martin, and Margo Wilson (1988b). *Homicide.* New York: Aldine DeGruyter.

Damaska, Mirjam R. (1968). "Adverse legal consequences of conviction and their removal: A comparative study," *Journal of Criminal Law, Criminology, and Police Science* 59:347–360 and 542–568.

Daniel, A. E., and P. W. Harris (1982). "Female homicide offenders referred for pre-trial psychiatric examination: A descriptive study," *Bulletin of The American Academy of Psychiatry and Law* 10:261–269.

Darrow, W., H. Jaffee, and J. Curran (1983). "Passive anal intercourse as a risk factor for AIDS in homosexual men," *Lancet* 2:309–313.

Datesman, Susan K., and Frank R. Scarpitti (1980). *Women, Crime and Justice*. New York: Oxford University Press.

Davidson, Ralph (1965). "The promiscuous fine," *Criminal Law Quarterly* 8:74–76.

Davis, Alan J. (1968). "Sexual assaults in the Philadelphia prison system and sheriffs' vans," *Transaction* 6:9–16.

Davis, F. James (1962). *Law as a Type of Social Control*. New York: Free Press.

Dawley, David (1992). *A Nation of Lords: The Autobiography of the Vice Lords,* 2nd ed. Prospect Heights, Ill.: Waveland Press.

DeFrancis, Vincent (1969). *Protecting the Child Victims of Sex Crimes Committed by Adults*. Denver, Colo.: American Humane Society.

Denno, Deborah W. (1985). "Sociological and human developmental explanations of crime," *Criminology* 23:711–741.

Denno, Deborah W. (1990). *Biology and Violence from Birth to Adulthood*. Cambridge, England: Cambridge University Press.

Dershowitz, Allen M. (1961). "Increasing control over corporate crime: A problem in the law of sanctions," *Yale Law Journal* 71:291.

Dirks, Raymond L., and Leonard Gross (1974). *The Great Wall Street Scandal*. New York: McGraw-Hill.

Doerner, William G. (1983). "Why does Johnny Reb die when shot? The impact of medical resources upon lethality," *Sociological Inquiry* 53:1–12.

Doleisch, Wolfgang (1960). "Theft in department stores," *Proceedings of Fourth International Criminological Congress, The Hague,* vol. 2, sec. 2:4–7.

Dollard, John, N. Miller, L. Doob, O. H. Mowrer, and R. R. Sears (1939). *Frustration and Aggression*. New Haven, Conn.: Yale University Press.

Dorman, Michael (1972). *Payoff: The Role of Organized Crime*. New York: David McKay.

Douglas, Jack D., ed. (1970). *Observations of Deviance*. New York: Random House.

Downie, Leonard, Jr. (1972). *Justice Denied*. Baltimore, Md.: Penguin Books.

Doyle, James C. (1953). "Unnecessary Hysterectomies," *American Medical Association Journal* 151:360–365.

Dunford, Franklyn W., and Delbert S. Elliott (1984). "Identifying career offenders using self-reported data," *Journal of Research in Crime and Delinquency* 21:57–86.

Dunford, Franklyn W., David Huizinga, and Delbert S. Elliott (1990). "The role of arrest in domestic assault: The Omaha police experiment," *Criminology* 28:183–206.

Dunham, Roger G., and Geoffrey P. Alpert (1989). *Critical Issues in Policing*. Prospect Heights, Ill.: Waveland Press.

Durkheim, Emile (1900). "Deux lois de l'évolution pénale," l'Année Sociologique IV:65–93.

Durkheim, Emile (1952). *Suicide*. London: Routledge and Kegan Paul.

Durkheim, Emile (1964a). *The Division of Labor in Society*. New York: Free Press.

Durkheim, Emile (1964b). *The Rules of Sociological Method*. New York: Free Press.

Dworkin, Andrea (1981). *Pornography: Men Possessing Women*. New York: Putnam.

Earle, Alice M. (1969). *Curious Punishments of By-Gone Days*. Montclair, N.J.: Patterson Smith.

Edelhertz, Herbert (1970). *The Nature, Impact, and Prosecution of White-Collar Crime.* Washington, D.C.: U.S. Government Printing Office.

Edelhertz, Herbert, and Marilyn Walsh (1978). *The White-Collar Challenge to Nuclear Safeguards.* Lexington, Mass.: Lexington Books.

Edwards, John N. (1972). *Sex and Society.* Chicago: Markham.

Edwards, Loren E. (1958). *Shoplifting and Shrinkage Protection for Stores.* Springfield, Ill.: Charles C. Thomas.

Egger, Steve (1990). *Serial Murder: The Elusive Phenomenon.* New York: Praeger.

Einstadter, Werner J. (1969). "The social organization of armed robbery," *Social Problems* 17:64–83.

Ekland-Olson, Sheldon, John Lieb, and Louis Zurcher (1984). "The paradoxical impact of criminal sanctions: Some microstructural findings," *Law and Society Review* 18:159–178.

Elias, Robert (1986). *The Politics of Victimization.* New York: Oxford University Press.

Elliott, Delbert S., David Huizinga, and Suzanne S. Ageton (1985). *Explaining Delinquency and Drug Use.* Beverly Hills, Calif.: Sage.

Ellis, Albert, and Ralph Brancale (1965). *The Psychology of Sex Offenders.* Springfield, Ill.: Thomas.

Ellis, Lee, and Harry Hoffman, eds. (1990). *Crime: Biological, Social, and Moral Contexts.* New York: Praeger.

Empey, LaMar T., and Maynard L. Erickson (1972). *The Provo Experiment: Evaluating Community Control of Delinquency.* Lexington, Mass.: Lexington Books.

Enker, Arnold (1967). "Perspectives on plea bargaining," in President's Commission on Law Enforcement and the Administration of Justice, *Task Force Report: The Courts.* Washington, D.C.: U.S. Government Printing Office.

Erickson, Maynard L., Jack P. Gibbs, and Gary L. Jensen (1977). "The deterrence doctrine and perceived certainty of legal punishments," *American Sociological Review* 42:305–317.

Erickson, Rosemary J., Waymon J. Crow, Louis A. Zurcher, and Archie V. Connett (1973). *Paroled But Not Free.* New York: Behavioral Publications.

Erikson, Kai T. (1962). "Notes on the sociology of deviance," *Social Problems* 9:307–314.

Erikson, Kai T. (1966). *Wayward Puritans: A Study in the Sociology of Deviance.* New York: Wiley.

Erikson, Richard V. (1990). "Review," *Policing and Society* 1:77–89.

Ermann, David M., and Richard J. Lundman (1982). *Corporate Deviance.* New York: Holt, Rinehart and Winston.

Esbensen, Finn, and Scott Menard (1990). "Is longitudinal research worth the price?" *The Criminologist* 15:1, 3, 5, 6.

Eskridge, Chris (1989). "College and the police: A review of issues," in Dennis Jay Kenney, ed., *Police and Policing: Contemporary Issues.* New York: Praeger.

Esselzstyn, C. (1968). "Prostitution in the United States," *The Annals* 376:126–143.

Evans-Pritchard, E. E. (1940). *The Nuer.* Oxford: Clarendon Press.

Fagan, Jeffrey (1990). "Intoxification and aggression," in Michael Tonry and James Q. Wilson, eds., *Drugs and Crime,* vol. 13, *Crime and Justice: A Review of Research.* Chicago: University of Chicago Press.

Farley, John E. (1988). *Majority–Minority Relations,* 2nd ed. Englewood Cliffs, N.J.: Prentice-Hall.

Farley, John E. (1992). *Introduction to Sociology.* Englewood Cliffs, N.J.: Prentice-Hall.

Farley, Reynolds (1980). "Homicide trends in the United States," *Demography* 17:177–188.

Farrington, David P. (1988). "Social, psychological and biological influences on juvenile delinquency and adult crime," in Wouter Buikhuisen and Sarnoff A. Mednick, eds., *Explaining Criminal Behaviour*. Leiden, Netherlands: E. J. Brill.

Farrington, David P., Lloyd Ohlin, and James Q. Wilson (1986). *Understanding and Controlling Crime: Toward a New Research Strategy*. New York: Springer-Verlag.

Faupel, Charles E. (1991). *Shooting Dope: Career Patterns of Hard-Core Heroin Users*. Gainesville: University of Florida Press.

Faupel, Charles E., and Carl B. Klockars (1987). "Drugs-Crime Connections: Elaborations from the Life Histories of Hard-core Heroin Addicts," *Social Problems* 34:54–68.

Federal Bureau of Investigation (1965). "Profile of a robber," *Law Enforcement Bulletin* 34:21.

Federal Bureau of Investigation (1988a). *Crime in the United States, 1987*. Washington, D.C.: U.S. Department of Justice.

Federal Bureau of Investigation (1988b). *Population-at-Risk Rates and Selected Crime Indicators*. Washington, D.C.: U.S. Department of Justice.

Federal Bureau of Investigation (1988c). *Age-Specific Arrest Rates and Race-Specific Arrest Rates for Selected Offenses*. Washington, D.C.: U.S. Department of Justice.

Federal Bureau of Investigation (1991). *Crime in the United States, 1990*. Washington, D.C.: U.S. Department of Justice.

Federal Bureau of Prisons (1986). *1985 Annual Report*. Washington, D.C.: U.S. Department of Justice.

Federal Bureau of Prisons (1991). *State of the Bureau 1990*. Washington, D.C.: U.S. Department of Justice.

Ferdinand, Theodore N. (1968). "Sex behaviors and the American class structure: A mosaic," *The Annals* 376:82–84.

Ferguson, Florence S. (1987). "Sentencing guidelines: Are (black) offenders given just treatment?" Presented at the annual meeting of the American Society of Criminology, Montreal.

Field, Simon (1990). *Trends in Crime and Their Interpretation. Home Office Research Study* No. 119. London: HMSO.

Fields, Allen, and James M. Walters (1985). "Hustling: Supporting a heroin habit," in Bill Hanson et al., *Life with Heroin*. Lexington, Mass.: Lexington Books.

Finkelhor, David, and Kersti Yllo (1985). *License to Rape: Sexual Abuse of Wives*. New York: Free Press.

Figueira-McDonough, Josefina (1986). "School context, gender, and delinquency," *Journal of Youth and Adolescence* 15:79–97.

Fishbein, Diana H. (1990). "Biological perspectives in criminology," *Criminology* 28:27–72.

Fisher, Joseph C. (1976). "Homicides in Detroit: The role of firearms," *Criminology* 14:387–400.

Fisse, Brent (1985). "Sanctions against corporations: The limitations of fines and the enterprise of creating alternatives," in Brent Fisse and Peter A. Finch, eds., *Corrigible Corporations and Unruly Law*. San Antonio: Trinity University Press.

Fisse, Brent, and John Braithwaite (1988). "The allocation of responsibility for corporate crime: Individualism, collectivism and accountability," *Sydney Law Review* 11:468–513.

Fitch, J. H. (1952). "Men convicted of sex offenses against children: A follow-up study," *British Journal of Sociology* 13:18–37.

Flanagan, Timothy J., and Katherine M. Jamieson, eds. (1988). *Sourcebook of Criminal Justice Statistics*. Washington, D.C.: U.S. Department of Justice.

Foldessy, Edward P. (1971). *The Paper Hangers*. Princeton, N.J.: Dow Jones Books.

Foote, Caleb (1958). "A study of the administration of bail in New York City," *University of Pennsylvania Law Review* 106:633–658.

Foote, Caleb (1978). "Deceptive determinate sentencing." In proceedings of the Special Conference on Determinate Sentencing, University of California, Berkeley, June 2–3.

Ford, Daniel, and Amesley K. Schmidt (1985). "Electronically monitored home confinement," *NIJ Reports, November*. Washington, D.C.: U.S. Department of Justice.

Forst, Brian E., and Jolene C. Hernon (1985). "The criminal justice response to victim harm," *NIJ Research in Brief*. Washington, D.C.: U.S. Department of Justice.

Fort, Joel (1973). *Alcohol: Our Biggest Drug Problem*. New York: McGraw-Hill.

Frazier, Charles E., and E. Wilbur Bock (1982). "Effects of court officials on sentence severity," *Criminology* 20:257–272.

Freeman, Kenneth R., and Terry Estrada-Mullaney (1988). "Using dolls to interview child victims: Legal concerns and interview procedures," *NIJ Reports* No. 207:2–6.

Friday, Paul C. (1977). "Changing theory and research in crminology," *International Journal of Criminology and Penology* 5:159–170.

Friedland, Martin (1965). *Detention Before Trial*. Toronto: University of Toronto Press.

Fyfe, James J. (1982). "Blind justice: Police shootings in Memphis," *Journal of Criminal Law and Criminology* 73:707–722.

Fyfe, James J. (1987). *Police Personnel Practices, 1986*. Washington, D.C.: International City Management Association.

Gabor, Thomas, Micheline Baril, Maurice Cusson, Daniel Elie, Marc LeBlanc, and André Normandeau (1988). *Armed Robbery: Cops, Robbers, and Victims*. Springfield, Ill.: Thomas.

Gaes, Gerald G. (1991). "Challenging beliefs about prison crowding," *Federal Prisons Journal* 2:19–23.

Gager, Nancy, and Cathleen Schurr (1976). *Sexual Assault: Confronting Rape in America*. New York: Grosset and Dunlap.

Gallo, Jon J. (1966). "The consenting adult homosexual and the law: An empirical study of enforcement and administration in Los Angeles County," *UCLA Law Review* 13:647–832.

Garfinkel, Harold (1949). "Research note on inter- and intra-racial homicides," *Social Forces* 27:369–381.

Garland, David (1985). *Punishment and Welfare: A History of Penal Strategies*. London: Gower.

Garner, Joel H. (1987). "Delay reduction in the federal courts: Rule 50(b) and the federal Speedy Trial Act of 1974," *Journal of Quantitative Criminology* 3:229–250.

Garner, Joel H., and Elizabeth Clemer (1986). "Danger to police in domestic disturbances—A new look," *NIJ Research in Brief* November:1–18.

Gartner, Michael, ed. (1971). *Crime as Business*. Princeton, N.J.: Dow Jones Books.

Gartner, Rosemary (1990). "The victims of homicide: A temporal and cross-national comparison," *American Sociological Review* 55:92–106.

Gasser, Robert Louis (1963). "The confidence game," *Federal Probation* 27:47–54.

Gastil, Raymond (1971). "Homicide and a regional culture of violence," *American Sociological Review* 36:412–427.

Gebhard, Paul, John H. Gagnon, Wardell B. Pomeroy, and Cornelia V. Christiansen (1965). *Sex Offenders: An Analysis of Types*. New York: Harper & Row.

Geis, Gilbert (1978a). "Rape-in-marriage: Law and law reform in England, the United States, and Sweden," *Adelaide Law Review* 6:284–303.

Geis, Gilbert (1978b). "Lord Hale, witches, and rape," *British Journal of Law and Society* 5:26–44.

Geis, Gilbert (1978c). "Deterring corporate crime," in M. David Ermann and Richard J. Lundman, eds., *Corporate and Governmental Deviance*. New York: Oxford University Press.

Geis, Gilbert (1988). "From Deuteronomy to deniability: A historical perlustration on white-collar crime," *Justice Quarterly* 5:7–32.

Geis, Gilbert, and Robley Geis (1979). "Rape in Stockholm," *Criminology* 17:311–322.

Geis, Gilbert, Paul Jesilow, and Henry N. Pontell (1982). "Policing physicians: Practitioner fraud and abuse in a government Medicaid program," *Social Problems* 30:117–125.

Geis, Gilbert, Paul Jesilow, and Henry N. Pontell (1985). "Fraud and abuse of government Medicaid benefits by psychiatrists," *American Journal of Psychiatry* February:117–125.

Geller, William A., and Kevin J. Karales (1981). "Shooting of and by Chicago police: Uncommon crises, Part I: Shootings by Chicago police," *Journal of Criminal Law and Criminology* 72:1813–1866.

Geller, William A., and Kevin J. Karales (1982). "Shootings of and by Chicago police: Uncommon crises, Part II: Shootings of police, shooting correlates, and control strategies," *Journal of Criminal Law and Criminology* 73:331–378.

Gelles, Richard J. (1978). "Violence toward children in the U.S.," *American Journal of Orthopsychiatry* 48:580–592.

Gelles, Richard J., and Murray A. Straus (1979). "Violence in the American family," *Journal of Social Issues* 35:15–39.

Gibbons, Don C. (1973). *Society, Crime, and Criminal Careers*, 2nd ed. Englewood Cliffs, N.J.: Prentice-Hall.

Gibbons, Don C., and Peter Garabedian (1974). "Conservative, liberal and radical criminology: Some trends and observations," in Charles E. Reasons, *The Criminologist: Crime and the Criminal*. Pacific Palisades, Calif.: Goodyear.

Gibbs, Jack P. (1966). "Crime and the sociology of law," *Sociology and Social Research* 51:23–38.

Gibbs, Jack P. (1975). *Crime, Punishment and Deterrence*. New York: Elsevier.

Gibbs, Jack P. (1985). "Review essay," *Criminology* 23:381–388.

Gibbs, Jack P. (1987). "An incorrigible positivist," *The Criminologist* 12 #4:1, 4.

Gibbs, Jack P. (1988). "Reply to Michalowski," *The Criminologist* 13 #4:4–5.

Gibbs, Jack P., and Glenn Firebaugh (1990). "The artifact issue in deterrence research," *Criminology* 28:347–367.

Gibbs, Jack P., and James F. Short (1974). "Criminal differentiation and occupational differentiation," *Journal of Research in Crime and Delinquency* 11:89–100.

Gigeroff, Alex K. (1968). *Sexual Deviation and the Criminal Law*. Toronto: University of Toronto Press.

Gillespie, Robert W. (1980). "Fines as an alternative to incarceration: The German experience," *Federal Probation* 44:20–26.

Giordano, Peggy C., and Stephen A. Cernkovich (1979). "On complicating the relationship between liberation and delinquency," *Social Problems* 26:467–481.

Gitchoff, Thomas G. (1988). "Privatization and the criminologist: Some first-hand observations," *The Criminologist* 13:14–15, 17.

Glaser, Daniel (1956). "Criminality theories and behavioral images," *American Journal of Sociology* 61:433–444.

Glaser, Daniel (1971). *Social Deviance.* Chicago: Markham.

Glueck, Sheldon, and Eleanor Glueck (1950). *Unraveling Juvenile Delinquency.* New York: Commonwealth Fund.

Goffman, Erving (1952). "On cooling the mark out: Some aspects of adaptation to failure," *Psychiatry* 15:451–463.

Goldcamp, John (1979). *The Classes of Accused: A Study of Bail and Detention in American Justice.* Cambridge, Mass.: Ballinger.

Goldfarb, Ronald L., and Linda R. Singer (1973). *After Conviction.* New York: Simon and Schuster.

Goldstein, Joseph (1960). "Police discretion not to invoke the criminal process: Low visibility decisions in the administration of justice," *Yale Law Journal* 69:543–570.

Goode, Erich (1972). *Drugs in American Society.* New York: Knopf.

Goode, William (1973). *Explorations in Social Theory.* New York: Oxford University Press.

Gordon, Cyrus H. (1957). *The Code of Hammurabi: Quaint or Forward Looking?* New York: Holt, Rinehart & Winston.

Gordon, David M. (1971). "Class and the economics of crime," *Review of Radical Economics* 3:51–75.

Gordon, David M. (1973). "Capitalism, class and crime in America," *Crime and Delinquency* 19:163–186.

Gordon, Judy G. (1991). "The female offender: ACA's look to the future," *Federal Prisons Journal* 2:3–5.

Gordon, Margaret A., and Daniel Glaser (1991). "The use and effects of financial penalties in municipal courts," *Criminology* 29:651–676.

Gordon, Robert A. (1987). "SES versus IQ in the race-IQ-delinquency model," *International Journal of Sociology and Social Policy* 7:30–88.

Gottfredson, Michael R., and Don M. Gottfredson (1988). *Decision-making in Criminal Justice,* 2nd ed. New York: Plenum.

Gottfredson, Michael R., and Travis Hirschi (1987). "The methodological adequacy of longitudinal research on crime," *Criminology* 26:581–614.

Gottfredson, Michael R., and Travis Hirschi (1988). "Science, public policy, and the career paradigm," *Criminology* 26:37–55.

Gottfredson, Michael R., and Travis Hirschi (1990). *A General Theory of Crime.* Stanford, Calif.: Stanford University Press.

Gottman, Jon (1989). "Decriminalizing marijuana," *American Behavioral Scientist* 32:243–248.

Gould, Leroy C. (1969). "The changing structure of property crime in an affluent society," *Social Forces* 48:50–59.

Gove, Walter R., Michael Hughes, and Michael Geerken (1985). "Are uniform crime reports a valid indicator of index crime? An affirmative answer with minor qualifications," *Criminology* 23:451–501.

Grabowski, John (1984). *Cocaine: Pharmacology, Effects and Treatment of Abuse.* Washington, D.C.: National Institute of Drug Abuse.

Green, Gary S. (1990). *Occupational Crime*. Chicago: Nelson-Hall.

Green, Mark J., with Beverly C. Moore and Bruce Wasserstein (1976). "Criminal law and corporate disorder," in Jerome Skolnick and Elliott Currie, eds., *Crisis in American Institutions*, 3rd ed. Boston: Little, Brown.

Greenberg, David F. (1975). "The incapacitative effect of imprisonment: Some estimates," *Law and Society Review* 9:541–580.

Greenberg, David F. (1977). "Crime and deterrence research and social policy," in Stuart S. Nagel, ed., *Modelling the Criminal Justice System*. Beverly Hills, Calif.: Sage.

Greenberg, David F., ed. (1981). *Crime and Capitalism*. Palo Alto, Calif.: Mayfield.

Greenberg, David F. (1985). "Age, crime, and social explanation," *American Journal of Sociology* 91:1–21.

Greenberg, Martin S., Chauncey E. Wilson, and Michael K. Mills (1982). "Victim decision-making: An experimental approach," in Vladimair J. Konecni and Ebbe B. Ebbesen, eds., *The Criminal Justice System and Social Psychological Analysis*. San Francisco: W. H. Freeman.

Greene, Jack R. (1989). "Police and community relations: Where have we been and where are we going?" in Roger G. Dunham and Geoffrey P. Alpert, eds., *Critical Issues in Policing*. Prospect Heights, Ill.: Waveland Press.

Greenfield, Lawrence A., and Stephanie Minor-Harper (1991). *Women in Prison*. BJS Special Report. Washington, D.C.: U.S. Department of Justice.

Greenwood, Peter W. (1984). "Selective incapacitation: A method of using our prisons more effectively," *NIJ Reports*. Washington, D.C.: National Institute of Justice.

Greenwood, Peter W., and Allan Abrahamse (1982). *Selective Incapacitation*. Santa Monica, Calif.: Rand.

Griffin, Susan (1971). "Rape: The all-American crime," *Ramparts* 10:34–35.

Griffiths, John (1970). "Ideology in criminal procedure, or a third 'model' of the criminal process," *Yale Law Journal* 79:359–417.

Grossman, Brian (1974). "The discretionary enforcement of law," in Sawyer F. Sylvester and Edward Sagarin, eds., *Politics and Crime*. New York: Praeger.

Groth, Nicholas (1979). *Men Who Rape: The Psychology of the Offender*. New York: Plenum.

Guenther, Anthony L. (1975). "Compensations in a total institution: The forms and functions of contraband," *Crime and Delinquency* 243–254.

Guerry, André Michel (1833). *Essai sur la Statistique Morale*. Paris.

Hackney, Sheldon (1969). "Southern violence," in Hugh D. Graham and Robert T. Gurr, eds., *Violence in America*. Washington, D.C.: U.S. Government Printing Office.

Hagan, Frank E. (1982). *Research Methods in Criminal Justice and Criminology*. New York: Macmillan.

Hagan, John (1974). "Extra-legal attributes and criminal sentencing: An assessment of a sociological viewpoint," *Law and Society Review* 8:357–383.

Hagan, John (1982a). "Victims before the law: A study of victim involvement in the criminal process," *Journal of Criminal Law and Criminology* 73:317–330.

Hagan, John (1982b). "The corporate advantage: The involvement of individual and organizational victims in the criminal justice process," *Social Forces* 60:993–1022.

Hagan, John, ed. (1982c). *Deterrence Reconsidered: Methodological Innovations*. Beverly Hills, Calif.: Sage.

Hagan, John (1985). *Modern Criminology: Crime, Criminal Behavior and Its Control*. New York: McGraw-Hill.

Hagan, John, A. R. Gillis, and J. Chan (1978). "Explaining official delinquency: A spatial study of class, conflict and control," *Sociological Quarterly* 19:386–398.

Hagan, John, A. R. Gillis, and John Simpson (1985). "The class structure, gender and delinquency: Toward a power-control theory of common delinquent behavior," *American Journal of Sociology* 90:1151–1175.

Hagan, John, and Alberto Palloni (1988). "Crimes as social events in the life course: Reconceiving a criminological controversy," *Criminology* 26:87–100.

Hagan, John, A. R. Gillis, and John Simpson (1990). "Clarifying and extending power-control theory," *American Journal of Sociology* 95:1024–1037.

Hagarth, John (1971). *Sentencing as a Human Process*. Toronto: Toronto University Press.

Hakim, Simon, and George F. Rengert, eds. (1981). *Crime Spillover*. Beverly Hills, Calif.: Sage.

Hall, Jerome (1952). *Theft, Law, and Society*, rev. ed. Indianapolis, Ind.: Bobbs-Merrill.

Hall, Jerome (1960). *General Principles of Criminal Law*. Indianapolis, Ind.: Bobbs-Merrill.

Haller, Mark H. (1976). "Historical roots of police behavior: Chicago, 1890–1925," *Law and Society Review* 10:303–324.

Haller, Mark H. (1990). "Illegal enterprise: A theoretical and historical interpretation," *Criminology* 28:207–235.

Haller, Mark H. (1991). *Life Under Bruno: The Economics of an Organized Crime Family*. Philadelphia: Pennsylvania Crime Commission.

Hamlin, John E. (1988). "The misplaced role of rational choice in neutralization theory," *Criminology* 23:223–240.

Hanson, Bill, George Beschner, James M. Walters, and Elliott Bovelle (1985). *Life with Heroin*. Lexington, Mass.: Lexington Books.

Harland, Alan T. (1981). *Restitution to Victims of Personal and Household Crimes, Analytic Report VAD-9*. Washington, D.C.: U.S. Department of Justice.

Harlow, Caroline Wolf (1991a). *Female Victims of Violent Crime*. Washington, D.C.: U.S. Department of Justice.

Harlow, Caroline Wolf (1991b). *Drugs and Jail Inmates*. Washington, D.C.: U.S. Department of Justice.

Harries, Keith D. (1989). "Homicide and assault: A comparative analysis of attributes in Dallas neighborhoods, 1981–1985," *The Professional Geographer* 41:29–38.

Harris, Richard N. (1973). *The Police Academy: An Inside View*. New York: Wiley.

Hartjen, Clayton (1974). *Crime and Criminalization*. New York: Praeger.

Hartogs, Renatus, and Eric Artzt (1970). *Violence: Causes and Solutions*. New York: Dell.

Hartstone, Eliot, and Karen V. Hansen (1984). "The violent juvenile offender: An empirical portrait," in Robert A. Mathias, Paul DeMuro, and Richard S. Allinson, eds., *Violent Juvenile Offenders: An Anthology*. San Francisco: National Council on Crime and Delinquency.

Hawkins, Gordon (1976). *The Prison: Policy and Practice*. Chicago: University of Chicago Press.

Hay, Douglas (1975). *Albion's Fatal Tree: Crime and Society in Eighteenth Century England*. London: Allen Lowe.

Healy, William (1915). *The Individual Delinquent: A Textbook and Prognosis for All Concerned in Understanding Offenders*. Boston: Little, Brown.

Henry, Stuart (1978). *The Hidden Economy*. Oxford: Martin Robinson.

Hepburn, John R. (1985). "The exercise of power in coercive organizations: A study of prison guards," *Criminology* 23:145–164.

Hickey, Eric W. (1991). *Serial Murderers and Their Victims*. Pacific Grove, Calif.: Brooks/Cole.

Hill, Gary D., and Elizabeth M. Crawford (1990). "Women, race, and crime," *Criminology* 28:601–626.

Hill, Susan, and Bob Edelman (1972). *Gentleman of Leisure*. New York: New American Library.

Hills, Stuart L. (1971). *Crime, Power, and Morality*. Scranton, Penn.: Chandler.

Hills, Stuart L., and Ron Santiago (1992). *Tragic Magic: The Life and Crimes of a Heroin Addict*. Chicago: Nelson-Hall.

Hillsman, Sally T., Barry Mahoney, George F. Cole, and Bernard Auchter (1987). "Fines as criminal sanctions," *Research in Brief*. Washington, D.C.: U.S. Department of Justice.

Hindelang, Michael J. (1974). "Decisions of shoplifting victims to invoke the criminal justice process," *Social Problems* 21:580–593.

Hindelang, Michael J. (1978). "Race and involvement in common law personal crimes," *American Sociological Review* 43:93–109.

Hindelang, Michael J., Travis Hirschi, and Joseph G. Weiss (1979). "Correlates of delinquency: The illusion of discrepancy between self-report and official measures," *American Sociological Review* 44:995–1014.

Hirschi, Travis (1971). *Causes of Delinquency*. Berkeley, Calif.: University of California Press.

Hirschi, Travis (1986). "On the compatibility of rational choice and social control theories of crime," in Derek B. Cornish and Ronald V. Clarke, eds., *The Reasoning Criminal*. New York: Springer-Verlag.

Hirschi, Travis, and Michael R. Gottfredson (1983). "Age and the explanation of crime," *American Journal of Sociology* 89:552–584.

Hirschi, Travis, and Michael R. Gottfredson (1987). "Causes of white-collar crime," *Criminology* 25:949–974.

Hirschi, Travis, and Michael R. Gottfredson (1988). "Toward a general theory of crime," in Walter Buikhuisen and Sarnoff A. Mednick, eds., *Explaining Criminal Behavior: Interdisciplinary Approaches*. Linden, Netherlands: E. J. Brill.

Hirschi, Travis, and Michael J. Hindelang (1977). "Intelligence and delinquency: A revisionist view," *American Sociological Review* 42:572–587.

Hochstedler, Ellen, ed. (1984). *Corporations as Criminals*. Beverly Hills, Calif.: Sage.

Hoebel, E. Adamson (1941). *The Cheyenne Way*. Norman, Okla.: University of Oklahoma Press.

Hoebel, E. Adamson (1954). *The Law of Primitive Man*. Cambridge, Mass.: Harvard University Press.

Hogarth, John (1971). *Sentencing as a Human Process*. Toronto: Toronto University Press.

Hood, Roger (1962). *Sentencing in Magistrates' Courts*. London: Stevens.

Hood, Roger (1972). *Sentencing the Motoring Offender*. London: Heinemann.

Hooton, Earnest A. (1939). *Crime and the Man*. Cambridge, Mass.: Harvard University Press.

Horning, Donald N. M. (1970). "Blue-collar theft: Conceptions of property, attitudes toward pilfering, and work group norms in a modern industrial plant," in Erwin O. Smigel and H. Laurence Ross, eds., *Crimes Against Bureaucracy*. New York: Van Nostrand.

Horowitz, Ruth (1987). "Community tolerance of group violence," *Social Problems* 34:437–449.

Hotchkiss, Susan (1978). "Realities of rape," *Human Behavior* December:18–23.

Hough, J. Michael, Ronald V. Clarke, and Pat Mayhew (1980). "Introduction," in Ronald V. Clarke and Pat Mayhew, eds., *Designing Out Crime*. London: H.M.S.O.

Hough, Michael J., and Pat Mayhew (1983). *The British Crime Survey*. London: H.M.S.O.

Hudson, Joe, and Burt Galoway (1975). *Restitution in Criminal Justice*. Lexington, Mass.: Lexington Press.

Huff-Corzine, Lin, Jay Corzine, and David C. Moore (1986). "Southern exposure: Deciphering the South's influence on homicide rates," *Social Forces* 64:906–924.

Hughes, Everett C. (1964). "Good people and dirty work," in Howard S. Becker, ed., *The Other Side: Perspectives on Deviance*. New York: Free Press.

Hughes, Helen MacGill (1961). *The Fantastic Lodge: The Autobiography of a Girl Drug Addict*. New York: Houghton Mifflin.

Huizinga, David, and Delbert S. Elliott (1987). "Juvenile offenders: Prevalence, incidence, and arrest rates by race," *Crime and Delinquency* 33:206–223.

Humphreys, Laud (1970). *Tearoom Trade*. Chicago: Aldine.

Hunt, Dana F. (1990). "Drugs and Consensual Crime," in Michael Tonry and James Q. Wilson, eds., *Drugs and Crime*. vol. 13, *Crime and Justice: A Review of Research*. Chicago: University of Chicago Press.

Hunt, Jennifer (1991). "Police accounts of normal force," in Henslin, James M. (1991). *Down to Earth Sociology*, 6th ed. New York: Free Press.

Hutchinson, John (1969). "The anatomy of corruption in the trade unions," *Industrial Relations* 8:135–137.

Ianni, Francis A. J. (1974). "New Mafia: Black, Hispanic and Italian styles," *Society* 11:30–36.

Ianni, Francis A. J. (1975). *Black Mafia: Ethnic Succession in Organized Crime*. New York: Pocket Books.

Ianni, Francis A. J., and Elizabeth Reuss-Ianni (1973). *A Family Business: Kinship and Control in Organized Crime*. New York: Russell Sage.

Illinois Criminal Justice Information Authority (1985). *The Compiler*, vol. 6. Chicago: ICJIA.

Imlay, Carl H., and Charles R. Glasheen (1971). "See what conditions your conditions are in," *Federal Probation* 35:3–11.

Inciardi, James A. (1975). *Careers in Crime*. Chicago: Rand McNally.

Inciardi, James A. (1979). "Heroin use and street crime," *Crime and Delinquency* 25:335–346.

Inciardi, James A. (1986). *The War on Drugs*. Palo Alto, Calif.: Mayfield.

Inciardi, James A. (1987). "Beyond cocaine: Basuco, crack and other coca products." Presented to the annual meeting of the Academy of Criminal Justice Sciences, St. Louis, Mo.

Innes, Christopher A. (1988). *Special Report: Drug Use and Crime*. Washington, D.C.: U.S. Department of Justice.

Inwald, Robin, and Dennis Jay Kenney (1989). "Psychological testing of police candidates," in Dennis Jay Kenney, ed., *Police and Policing: Contemporary Issues*. New York: Praeger.

Irwin, John (1970). *The Felon*. Englewood Cliffs, N.J.: Prentice-Hall.

Irwin, John (1980). *Prisons in Turmoil*. Boston: Little, Brown.

Irwin, John, and Donald R. Cressey (1962). "Thieves, convicts and the inmate culture," *Social Problems* 10:142–155.

Jackall, Robert (1988). *Moral Mazes: The World of Corporate Managers.* New York: Oxford University Press.

Jackman, Norman R., Richard O'Toole, and Gilbert Geis (1963). "The self-image of the prostitute," *Sociological Quarterly* 4:150–161.

Jackson, Bruce (1969a). *A Thief's Primer.* New York: Macmillan.

Jackson, Bruce (1969b). "Exile from the American dream: The junkie and the cop," *Atlantic Monthly* 219:44–51.

Jacobs, James B. (1974). "Street gangs behind bars," *Social Problems* 21:395–409.

Jacobs, James B. (1976). "Stratification and conflict among prison inmates," *Journal of Criminal Law and Criminology* 66:476–482.

Jacobs, James B. (1977). *Stateville: The Penitentiary in Mass Society.* Chicago: University of Chicago Press.

Jacobs, James B., and Harold G. Retsky (1975). "Prison guard," *Urban Life and Culture* 4:5–29.

Jaffee, Harold W., William W. Darrow, and Dean F. Echenberg et al. (1985). "The Acquired Immunodeficiency Syndrome in a cohort of homosexual men: A six-year follow-up study," *Annals of Internal Medicine* 103:210–214.

James, Jennifer, and William Thornton (1980). "Women's liberation and the female delinquent," *Journal of Research in Crime and Delinquency* 17:230–244.

James, J. T. (1817). *Journal of a Tour.* London: John Murray.

Jaspan, Norman, and Hillel Black (1960). *The Thief in the White Collar.* New York: Lippincott.

Jefferson, T., and J. Clarke (1973). "Down these mean streets: The meaning of mugging." Stencilled occasional paper, the Centre for Contemporary Cultural Studies, The University of Birmingham, England.

Jefferson, T., and J. Clarke (1975). "Mugging and law 'n order." Stencilled occasional paper, Centre for Contemporary Cultural Studies, University of Birmingham, England.

Jeffery, C. Ray (1957). "The development of crime in early English society," *Journal of Criminal Law, Criminology, and Police Science* 47:533–552.

Jeffery, C. Ray (1959). "An integrated theory of crime and criminal behavior," *Journal of Criminal Law, Criminology, and Police Science* 49:533–552.

Jeffery, C. Ray (1977). *Crime Prevention Through Environmental Design.* Beverly Hills, Calif.: Sage.

Jenkins, P. (1988). "Myth and Murder: The serial killer panic of 1983–85," *Criminal Justice Research Bulletin* 3:1–7.

Jensen, A. R. (1969). "How much can we boost IQ and scholastic achievement?" *Harvard Educational Review* 39:1–123.

Jesilow, Paul, Henry N. Pontell, and Gilbert Geis (1993). *Prescription for Profit.* Los Angeles: University of California Press.

Johnson, B., P. Goldstein, E. Preble, J. Schmeidler, D. Lipton, B. Spunt, and T. Miller (1985). *Taking Care of Business.* Lexington, Mass.: Lexington Books.

Johnson, David R., and Laurie K. Scheuble (1991). "Gender bias in the disposition of juvenile court referrals: The effects of time and location," *Criminology* 29:677–699.

Johnson, Guy B. (1941). "The negro and crime," *The Annals* 277:93–104.

Johnson, Richard E. (1986). "Family structure and delinquency: General patterns and gender differences," *Criminology* 24:65–84.

Johnson, Robert (1990). *Death Work: A Study of the Modern Execution Process.* Pacific Grove, Calif.: Brooks/Cole.

Jones, David P. H., and J. Melbourne McGraw (1987). "Reliable and fictitious accounts of sexual abuse to children," *Journal of Interpersonal Violence* 2:1–6.

Jordon, Philip D. (1970). *Frontier Law and Order.* Lincoln, Neb.: University of Nebraska Press.

Kadish, Mortimer R., and Sanford H. Kadish (1973). *Discretion to Disobey.* Palo Alto, Calif.: Stanford University Press.

Kandel, Denise, and Mark Davies (1991). "Friendship networks, intimacy, and illicit drug use in young adulthood: A comparison of two competing theories." *Criminology* 29:441–469.

Kandel, Elizabeth, and Sarnoff A. Mednick (1991). "Perinatal complications predict violent offending," *Criminology* 29:519–529.

Kanin, Eugene J. (1967). "Reference groups and sex conduct norms violation," *Sociological Quarterly* 8:495–504.

Kantor, Glenda Kaufman, and Murray A. Straus (1987). "The 'drunken bum' theory of wife beating," *Social Problems* 34:214–230.

Katz, Jack (1988). *Seductions of Crime: Moral and Sensual Attractions of Doing Evil.* New York: Basic Books.

Kelling, George L. (1988). *Police and Communities: The Quiet Revolution.* Washington, D.C.: National Institute of Justice.

Kelly, Robert J. (1991). "AIDS and the Societal Reaction," in Robert J. Kelly and Donal E. J. MacNamara, eds., *Perspectives on Deviance: Domination, Degradation and Denigration.* Cincinnati: Anderson.

Kempf, Kimberly L., ed. (1990). *Measurement Issues in Criminology.* New York: Springer-Verlag.

Kennedy, Leslie W., Robert A. Silverman, David R. Forde (1991). "Homicide in urban Canada: Testing the impact of income inequality and social disorganization," *Canadian Journal of Sociology* 16:397–410.

King, Harry (1972). *Boxman: A Professional Thief's Journey,* William Chambliss, ed. New York: Harper & Row.

Kinsey, Richard, John Lea, and Jock Young (1986). *Losing the Flight Against Crime.* Oxford: Basil Blackwell.

Kirkpatrick, Clifford, and Eugene J. Kanin (1957). "Male sex aggression on a university campus," *American Sociological Review* 22:53–62.

Kitsuse, John I. (1962). "Societal reactions to deviant behavior: Problems of theory and method," *Social Problems* 9:247–256.

Kittrie, Nicholas N. (1973). *The Right to Be Different: Deviance and Enforced Therapy.* Baltimore, Md.: Penguin Books.

Klebba, Joan A. (1975). "Homicide trends in the United States, 1900–1974," *Public Health Reports* 90:195–204.

Kleck, Gary (1981). "Racial discrimination in criminal sentencing: A critical evaluation of the evidence with additional evidence on the death penalty," *American Sociological Review* 46:783–805.

Kleiman, Mark A. R., and Kerry D. Smith (1990). "State and local drug enforcement: In search of a strategy," in Michael Tonry and James Q. Wilson, eds., *Drugs and Crime,* vol. 13 of *Crime and Justice: A Review of Research.* Chicago: University of Chicago Press.

Klein, Malcom W. (1971). *Street Gangs and Street Workers.* Englewood Cliffs, N.J.: Prentice-Hall.

Klein, Malcom W. (1989). *Cross National Research in Self-Reported Crime and Delinquency.* Dordrecht: Kluwer.

Klein, Malcom W., Cheryl L. Maxson, and Lea C. Cunningham (1991). " 'Crack,' street gangs, and violence," *Criminology* 29:623–650.

Klockars, Carl B. (1974). *The Professional Fence.* New York: Free Press.

Knapp Commission Report on Police Corruption (1972). New York: George Braziller.

Knight, B. J., and D. J. West (1975). "Temporary and continuing delinquency," *British Journal of Criminology* 15:43–50.

Knoohuizen, Ralph, Richard P. Fahey, and Deborah J. Palmer (1972). *The Police and Their Use of Fatal Force in Chicago.* Evanston, Ill.: Chicago Law Enforcement Study Group.

Kobetz, Richard W. (1978). *Criminal Justice Education Directory, 1978–1980.* Gaithersburg, Md.: International Association of Chiefs of Police.

Kolata, Gina (1982). "When criminals turn to computers, is anything safe?" *Smithsonian,* 13:117–126.

Kramer, John H., and Robin L. Lubitz (1985). "Pennsylvania's sentencing reform: The impact of commission-established guidelines," *Crime and Delinquency* 31:481–500.

Kramer, Ronald C. (1984). "Corporate criminality: The development of an idea," in Ellen Hochstedler, ed., *Corporations as Criminals.* Beverly Hills, Calif.: Sage.

Kuykendall, Jack, and David Burns (1980). "The black police officer: An historical perspective," *Journal of Contemporary Criminal Justice* 4:103–113.

Lab, Steven P., and J. T. Whitehead (1990). "From 'nothing works' to 'the appropriate works': The latest stop on the search for the secular grail," *Criminology* 28:405–417.

LaFree, Gary D. (1989). *Rape and Criminal Justice: The Social Construction of Sexual Assault.* Belmont, Calif.: Wadsworth.

LaFree, Gary D., Reskin, Barbara F., and Christy Visher (1991). "Jurors' responses to victims' behavior and legal issues in sexual assault trials," *Social Problems* 32:389–407.

Lane, Roger (1967). *Policing the City: Boston, 1821–1885.* Cambridge, Mass.: Harvard University Press.

Langan, Patrick A. (1991). *Race of Prisoners Admitted to State and Federal Institutions, 1926–1986.* Washington, D.C.: U.S. Department of Justice.

Lanza-Kaduce, Lonn (1988). "Perceptual deterrence and drinking and driving among college students," *Criminology* 26:321–334.

Lasley, Jim (1988). "Toward a control theory of white-collar offending", *Journal of Quantitative Criminology* 4:347–362.

Laub, John H., and Robert J. Sampson (1988). "Unraveling families and delinquency: A reanalysis of the Gluecks' data," *Criminology* 26:355–380.

Law Enforcement Assistance Administration (1970). *National Jail Census, 1970: A Report on the Nation's Local Jails and Types of Inmates.* Washington, D.C.: U.S. Government Printing Office.

Law Enforcement Assistance Administration (1975a). *Census of State Correctional Facilities, 1974, Advance Report.* Washington, D.C.: U.S. Government Printing Office.

Law Enforcement Assistance Administration (1975b). *The Nation's Jails.* Washington, D.C.: U.S. Government Printing Office.

Law Enforcement Assistance Administration (1977). *Forcible Rape: A National Survey of Response by Prosecutors.* Washington, D.C.: U.S. Department of Justice.

Lederer, Laura, ed. (1980). *Take Back the Night*. New York: Bantam Books.

Leiser, Burton M. (1973). *Liberty, Justice and Morals*. New York: Macmillan.

Lejeune, Robert (1977). "The management of a mugging," *Urban Life* 6:123–148.

Lemert, Edwin M. (1951). *Social Pathology*. New York: McGraw-Hill.

Lemert, Edwin M. (1953). "An isolation and closure theory of naive check forgery," *Journal of Criminal Law, Criminology, and Police Science* 44:297–298.

Lemert, Edwin M. (1958). "The behavior of the systematic check forger," *Social Problems* 6:141–148.

Lemert, Edwin M. (1972). *Human Deviance, Social Problems and Social Control*, 2nd ed. Englewood Cliffs, N.J.: Prentice-Hall.

Lemert, Edwin M. (1974). "Beyond Mead: The societal reaction to deviance," *Social Problems* 21:457–468.

Leonard, Eileen B. (1982). *Women, Crime and Society*. New York: Longman.

Leonard, William N. and Marvin Glenn Weber (1970). "Automakers and dealers: A study of crimogenic market forces," *Law and Society Review* 4:408–422.

Letkemann, Peter (1973). *Crime as Work*. Englewood Cliffs, N.J.: Prentice-Hall.

Levin, Jack, and James Alan Fox (1985). *Mass Murder: America's Growing Menace*. New York: Plenum.

Lichter, Linda S., and S. Robert Lichter (1983). *Prime Time Crime: Criminals and Law Enforcement in TV Entertainment*. Washington, D.C.: Media Institute.

Lilly, J. Robert, Richard A. Ball, and Jennifer Wright (1987). "Home incarceration with electronic monitoring in Kenton County, Kentucky: An evaluation," in Belinda R. McCarthy, ed., *Intermediate Punishments: Intensive Supervision, Home Confinement, and Electronic Monitoring*. Monsey, N.J.: Criminal Justice Press.

Lilly, Robert J., Francis T. Cullen, and Richard A. Ball (1989). *Criminological Theory: Context and Consequences*. Newbury Park, Calif.: Sage.

Lincoln, Alan J., and Murray A. Straus (1985). *Crime and the Family*. Springfield, Ill.: Thomas.

Linden, E., and J. C. Hackler (1973). "Affective ties and delinquency," *Pacific Sociological Review* 16:27–47.

Lindesmith, Alfred R. (1967). *The Addict and the Law*. New York: Random House.

Linsky, Arnold S., Jr., John P. Colby, and Murray Straus (1986). "Drinking norms and alcohol-related problems in the United States," *Journal of Studies on Alcohol* 47:384–393.

Lintott, A. W. (1968). *Violence in Republican Rome*. Oxford: Clarendon Press.

Lippmann, Walter (1931). "The underworld as servant," in Gus Tyler, ed., *Organized Crime in America*. Ann Arbor, Mich.: University of Michigan Press.

Lipsky, Michael, ed. (1970). *Law and Order: Police Encounters*. Chicago: Aldine.

Lizotte, Alan J. (1985). "The uniqueness of rape: Reporting assaultive violence to the police," *Crime and Delinquency* 31:169–190.

Lizotte, Alan J., and David J. Bordua (1980). "Firearms ownership for sport and protection: Two divergent models," *American Sociological Review* 45:229–244.

Lloyd, Charles, and Roy Walmsley (1989). *Changes in Rape Offences and Sentencing*. London: H.M.S.O.

Loeber, Rolph, and Thomas J. Dishion (1983). "Early predictors of male delinquency," *Psychological Bulletin* 94:68–99.

Lofland, John (1977). *The Dramaturgy of State Executions*. Montclair, N.J.: Patterson Smith.

Loftin, Colin, and Robert H. Hill (1974). "Regional subculture and homicide: An examination of the Gastil-Hackney thesis," *American Sociological Review* 39:714–724.

Lombroso, Cesare (1911). *Crime, Its Causes and Remedies.* Boston: Little, Brown.

Lorenz, Konrad (1971). *On Aggression.* New York: Bantam Books.

Lovald, Keith, and Helger R. Stub (1968). "The revolving door: Reactions of chronic drunkenness to court sanctions," *Journal of Criminal Law, Criminology and Police Science* 59:525–530.

Luckenbill, David F. (1977). "Criminal homicide as a situated transaction," *Social Problems* 25:176–186.

Lunde, Donald T. (1970). *Murder and Madness.* San Francisco: San Francisco Book Co.

Lundesgaarde, Henry P. (1977). *Murder in Space City.* New York: Oxford University Press.

Lundman, Richard J. (1980). *Police and Policing.* New York: Holt, Rinehart & Winston.

Lundman, Richard J. (1984). *Prevention and Control of Juvenile Delinquency.* New York: Oxford University Press.

Lundman, Richard J. (1991). "Police and drunk driving: baseline data and DUI arrests, 1960–1989." Presented at the Annual Meeting of the American Sociological Association, Cincinnati, August 22–26.

Lupsha, Peter A. (1981). "Individual choice, material culture, and organized crime," *Criminology* 19:3–24.

Lyman, Stanford M., and Marvin B. Scott (1975). *The Drama of Social Reality.* New York: Oxford University Press.

Lynch, Michael J., and W. Byron Groves (1989). *A Primer in Radical Criminology* 2nd Ed. New York: Harrow and Heston.

Maas, Peter (1968). *The Valachi Papers.* New York: Putnam.

MacDonald, John M. (1971). *Rape: Offenders and Their Victims.* Springfield, Ill.: Thomas.

Machalek, Richard, and Lawrence E. Cohen (1991). "The nature of crime: Is cheating necessary for cooperation?" *Human Nature* 2:215–233.

Mack, J. A. (1964). "The able criminal," *British Journal of Criminology* 12:45–55.

Mack, J. A. (1975). *The Crime Industry.* London: Saxon House.

MacKinnon, C. (1989). *Toward a Feminist Theory of the State.* Cambridge: Harvard University Press.

MacNamara, Donal E. J. (1968). "Sex offenses and sex offenders," *The Annals* 376:153–162.

Maguire, Kathleen, and Timothy Flanagan (1991). *Sourcebook of Criminal Justice Statistics.* Washington, D.C.: U.S. Department of Justice.

Maine, Sir Henry Sumner (1905). *Ancient Law,* 10th ed. London: John Murray.

Mair, George (1991). "What works: Nothing or everything?" *Home Office Research Bulletin No. 30* London: H.M.S.O.

Makkai, Toni, and John Braithwaite (1991). "Criminological theories and regulatory compliance." *Criminology* 29:191–217.

Malinowski, Bronislaw (1926). *Crime and Custom in Savage Society.* New York: Harcourt Brace, Jovanovich.

Mannheim, Hermann (1946). *Criminal Justice and Social Reconstruction.* London: Routledge and Kegan Paul.

Manning, Peter K. (1977). *Police Work: The Social Organization of Policing.* Cambridge, Mass.: MIT Press.

Manning, Peter K. (1988). *Symbolic Communication: Signifying Calls and the Police Response*. Cambridge: MIT Press.

Manning, Peter K. (1989). "Community policing," in Roger G. Dunham and Geoffrey P. Alpert, eds., *Critical Issues in Policing*. Prospect Heights, Ill.: Waveland Press.

Mars, Gerald (1983). *Cheats at Work: An Anthropology of Workplace Crime*. London: Unwin Paperbacks.

Martin, J. B. (1952). *My Life in Crime*. New York: Harper & Row.

Martin, Susan E. (1989). "Female officers on the move? A status report on women in policing," in Roger G. Dunham and Geoffrey P. Alpert, eds., *Critical Issues in Policing*. Prospect Heights, Ill.: Waveland Press.

Martinson, Robert (1974). "What works? Questions and answers about prison reform," *The Public Interest* 35:22–54.

Marx, Karl, and Frederick Engels ([1846] 1947). *The German Ideology*. New York: International Publishers.

Marx, Karl ([1862] 1969). *Theories of Surplus Value*, vol 1. Moscow: Foreign Languages Publishing House.

Marx, Karl ([1859] 1971). *A Contribution to the Critique of Political Economy*. London: Lawrence and Wishart.

Matoesian, Gregory (1993). *Reproducing Rape: Domination Through Talk in the Courtroom*. London: Polity Press.

Matthews, Roger (1986). "Policing prostitution," in Roger Matthews and Jock Young, eds., *Confronting Crime*. Beverly Hills, Calif.: Sage.

Matthews, Roger (1987). "Taking realist criminology seriously." Presented to the annual meeting of the American Society of Criminology, November, Montreal.

Matthews, Roger, and Jock Young, eds. (1986). *Confronting Crime*. Beverly Hills, Calif.: Sage.

Matza, David (1964). *Delinquency and Drift*. New York: Wiley.

Maurer, D. W. (1940). *The Big Con*. Indianapolis, Ind.: Bobbs-Merrill.

Maurer, D. W. (1964). *Whiz Mob*. New Haven, Conn.: College and University Press.

Maxfield, Michael A., Dan A. Lewis, and Ron Szoc (1980). "Producing official crimes: Verified crime reports as measures of police output," *Social Science Quarterly* 61:221–236.

Mayhew, P., R. V. G. Clark, J. N. Burrows, J. M. Hough, and S. W. Winchester (1979). "Crime in Public Places," *Home Office Research Study No. 49*, London: H.M.S.O.

Mayhew, Patricia, Ronald V. Clarke, and David Elliott (1989). "Motorcycle theft, helmet legislation and displacement," *The Howard Journal* 28:1–8.

Maynard, Douglas W. (1982). "Defendant attributes in plea bargaining: Notes on the modeling of sentencing decisions," *Social Problems* 29:347–360.

Maynard, Douglas W. (1984). *Inside Plea Bargaining*. New York: Plenum Press.

Mayor of New York's Committee on Marijuana (1944). *The Marijuana Problem in the City of New York*. New York: Cattell.

McCaghy, Charles H. (1967). "Child molesters: A study of their careers as deviants," in Marshall B. Clinard and Richard Quinney, eds., *Criminal Behavior Systems: A Typology*. New York: Holt, Rinehart & Winston.

McCaghy, Charles H. (1976). *Deviant Behavior: Crime, Conflict and Interest Groups*. New York: Macmillan.

McCarthy, Belinda Rodgers, and Charles A. Lindquist (1988). "The impact of guilty pleas on the sentencing process: A crime-specific analysis of prosecutorial, defendant, and judicial behavior." Presented to the annual meeting of the Academy of Criminal Justice Sciences, Chicago.

McCartt, John M., and Thomas J. Mangogna (1976a). "The history of halfway houses in the U.S.," in Robert M. Carter and Leslie T. Wilkins, eds., *Probation, Parole, and Community Corrections,* 2nd ed. New York: Wiley.

McCartt, John M., and Thomas J. Mangogna (1976b). "Overview of issues relating to halfway houses and community treatment centers," in Robert M. Carter and Leslie T. Wilkins, eds., *Probation, Parole, and Community Corrections.* New York: Wiley.

McCord, Joan (1978). "A thirty-year follow-up of treatment effects," *American Psychologist* 33:284–289.

McCord, Joan (1980). "The treatment that did not help," *Social Action and Law* 5:85–87.

McCord, Joan (1986). "Instigation and insulation: How families affect antisocial behavior," in D. Olweus, J. Block, and M. Radke-Yarrow, eds., *Development of Antisocial and Prosocial Behavior.* Orlando, Fla.: Academic Press.

McCord, Joan (1991). "Family relationships, juvenile delinquency, and adult criminality," *Criminology* 29:397–417.

McCord, William, and Joan McCord (1959). *Origins of Crime: A New Evaluation of the Cambridge-Somerville Youth Study.* New York: Columbia University Press.

McDermott, M. Joan (1979). *Rape Victimization in 26 American Cities.* Washington, D.C.: U.S. Department of Justice.

McDonald, William F., ed. (1976). *Criminal Justice and the Victim.* Beverly Hills, Calif.: Sage.

McDonald, William F. (1985). *Plea Bargaining: Critical Issues and Common Practices.* Washington, D.C.: U.S. Department of Justice.

McEwen, J. Thomas (1989). *Dedicated Computer Crime Units.* Washington, D.C.: U.S. Department of Justice.

McGarrell, Edmund F., and Timothy J. Flanagan, eds., (1985). *Sourcebook of Criminal Justice Statistics.* Washington, D.C.: U.S. Government Printing Office.

McIntosh, Mary (1971). "Changes in the organization of thievery," in Stanley Cohen, ed., *Images of Deviance.* Hammondsworth, England: Penguin Books.

McIntyre, Donald M., and David Lippman (1970). "Prosecutors and early disposition of felony cases," *American Bar Association Law Journal* 56:1154–1159.

McIntyre, Jennie J., and Thelma Myint (1979). "Sexual assault outcomes: Completed and attempted rapes." Presented at the annual meeting of the American Sociological Association, August, Boston.

McIver, John P. (1981). "Criminal mobility: A review of empirical studies," in Simon Hakim and George F. Rengert, eds., *Crime Spillover.* Beverly Hills, Calif.: Sage.

McKusick, Leon, William Horstman, and Thomas J. Coates (1985). "AIDS and sexual behavior reported by gay men in San Francisco," *American Journal of Public Health* 75:493–496.

McNamara, John H. (1967). "Uncertainties of police work: Recruits' background and training," in David Bordua, ed., *The Police: Six Sociological Essays.* New York: Wiley.

Mednick, Sarnoff A. Jr., and K. O. Christiansen (1977). *Biosocial Basis of Criminal Behavior.* New York: Wiley.

Mednick, Sarnoff A., Jr., W. F. Garbrielli, and B. Huthings (1984). "Genetic influences in criminal convictions: Evidence from an adoption cohort," *Science* 224:891–895.

Mendelsohn, Alan J. (1956). "The influence of defendants' plea on judicial determination of sentence," *Yale Law Journal* 66:204–222.

Merry, Sally Engle (1981). *Urban Danger: Life in a Neighborhood of Strangers.* Philadelphia: Temple University Press.

Merton, Robert K. (1938). "Social structure and anomie," *American Sociological Review* 3:672–682.

Merton, Robert K. (1957). *Social Theory and Social Structure.* New York: Free Press.

Messerschmidt, James W. (1986). *Capitalism, Patriarchy, and Crime.* Totowa, N.J.: Rowman and Littlefield.

Messner, Steven F. (1983). "Regional and racial effects on the urban homicide rate: The subculture of violence revisited," *American Journal of Sociology* 88:997–1007.

Messner, Steven F. (1989). "Economic discrimination and homicide rates: Further evidence on the cost of inequality," *American Sociological Review* 54:597–611.

Metz, Tim (1971). "Hot Stocks," in Michael Gartner, ed., *Crime as Business.* New York: Dow Jones Books.

Meyers, Martha A. (1988). "Social background and the sentencing behavior of judges," *Criminology* 26:649–675.

Michalowski, Raymond J. (1985). *Order, Law, and Crime.* New York: Random House.

Michalowski, Raymond J. (1987). "Reply to Gibbs" *The Criminologist* 12 #6:12, 18.

Michalowski, Raymond J. (1988). "Response to Nettler," *The Criminologist* 13 #4:4.

Michalowski, Raymond J., and Ronald C. Kramer (1987). "The space between the laws: The problem of corporate crime in a transnational context," *Social Problems* 34:34–53.

Miethe, Terance D. (1982). "Public consensus on crime seriousness: Normative structure or methodological artifact?" *Criminology* 20:513–526.

Miller, Walter B. (1958). "Lower class culture as a generating milieu of gang delinquency," *Journal of Social Issues* 14:5–19.

Miller, Walter B. (1966). "Violent crimes in city gangs," *The Annals* 364:109–112.

Miller, Walter B. (1973). "Ideological and criminal justice policy: Some current issues," *Journal of Criminal Law and Criminology* 64:141–162.

Mills, C. Wright (1956). *White Collar.* New York: Galaxie Books.

Millspaugh, Arthur G. ([1937] 1972). *Crime Control by the National Government.* New York: Da Capo Press.

Milner, Christina, and Richard Milner (1972). *Black Players: The Secret World of Black Pimps.* Boston: Little, Brown.

Milton, C. (1972). *Women in Policing.* Washington, D.C.: Police Foundation.

Minor, W. William (1975). "Political crime, political justice, and political prisoners," *Criminology* 12:385–397.

Minor, W. William (1978). "Deterrence research: Problems of theory and method," in James A. Cramer, *Preventing Crime.* Beverly Hills, Calif.: Sage.

Minor, W. William (1980). "The neutralization of criminal offense," *Criminology* 18:103–120.

Mintz, Morton (1965). *The Therapeutic Nightmare: A Report on Prescription Drugs, the Men Who Take Them, and the Agency That Controls Them.* Boston: Houghton Mifflin.

Monahan, John (1981). *Predicting Violent Behavior: An Assessment of Clinical Techniques.* Beverly Hills, Calif.: Sage.

Monahan, John, and Henry J. Steadman (1983). "Crime and mental disorder: An epidemiological approach," in Michael Tonry and Norval K. Morris, eds., *Crime and Justice: An Annual Review.* Chicago: University of Chicago Press.

Moore, Mark A. and Robert C. Trojanowicz (1988). *Policing and the Fear of Crime.* Washington, D.C.: National Institute of Justice.

Moore, Mark A., Robert C. Trojanowicz, and George Kelling (1988). *Crime and Policing.* Washington, D.C.: National Institute of Justice.

Moore, Mark H. (1986). "Organized crime as a business enterprise." Presented to the annual meeting of the American Society of Criminology, Atlanta, November.

Moore, Mark H. (1990). "Supply reduction and drug law enforcement," in Michael Tonry and James Q. Wilson, eds., *Drugs and Crime*, vol. 13, *Crime and Justice: A Review of Research*. Chicago: University of Chicago Press.

Moore, Wilbert E. (1964). *Social Aspects of Economic Development*. Chicago: Rand McNally.

Morash, Merry (1986). "Understanding the contribution of women to police work," in Louis A. Radalet, ed., *The Police and the Community*, 4th ed. New York: Macmillan.

Morash, Merry, and Jack R. Greene (1986). "Evaluating women on patrol: A critique of contemporary wisdom," *Evaluation Review* 10:230–255.

Morris, Allison (1987). *Women, Crime and Criminal Justice*. Oxford: Basil Blackwell.

Morris, Norval (1991). "The case for intermediate punishments," *Federal Prison Journal* 2:11–14.

Morris, Terrence (1958). *The Criminal Area*. New York: Humanities Press.

Mulvihill, Donald J., Melvin Tumin, and Lynn Curtis (1969). *Crimes of Violence*. Washington, D.C.: U.S. Government Printing Office.

Munford, Robert S., Ross J. Kazer, Roger A. Feldman, and Robert R. Strivers (1976). "Homicide trends in Atlanta," *Criminology* 14:213–232.

Murphy, J. E. (1984). "Date abuse and forced intercourse among college students." Presented to the National Conference for Family Violence Researchers, University of New Hampshire.

Nader, Ralph (1967). "We're still in the jungle," *The New Republic* 161:11–12.

Nader, Ralph, and Mark Green (1972). "Coddling the corporations: Crime in the suites," *The New Republic* 166:18–24.

Nagel, Stuart S. (1967). "Disparities in criminal procedures," *UCLA Law Review* 14:1296.

Nagel, Stuart S., ed. (1977). *Modelling the Criminal Justice System*. Beverly Hills, Calif.: Sage.

Nagel, William G. (1973). *The New Red Barn: A Critical Look at the Modern American Prison*. New York: Walker.

Nagin, Daniel S., and Raymond Paternoster (1991). "The preventive effects of the perceived risk of arrest: Testing an expanded conception of deterrence," *Criminology* 29:561–587.

Nathan, Robert Stuart (1980). "Corporate criminals who kept their jobs," *Business and Social Review* 33:19–20.

National Commission on Marijuana and Drug Abuse (1973). *Patterns and Consequences of Drug Use*. Washington, D.C.: U.S. Government Printing Office.

National Institute on Drug Abuse (1985). *Highlights from Drugs and American High School Students, 1975–1983*. Washington, D.C.: U.S. Government Printing Office.

National Institute of Justice (1991a). *Drug Use Forecasting*. Washington, D.C.: U.S. Department of Justice.

National Institute of Justice (1991b). *Research in Brief*. Washington, D.C.: U.S. Department of Justice.

Nelson, Stephen (1988). "To catch a thief," *INC* January:89–90.

Nettler, Gwynne (1974). "Embezzlement without problems," *British Journal of Criminology* 14:70–77.

Nettler, Gwynne (1988). "Christian Science vs. social science: Michalowski vs. Gibbs," *The Criminologist* 13 #2:4–5.

Newman, Donald J. (1958). "White collar crime," *Law and Contemporary Problems* 283:735–753.

Newman, Graeme R. (1978). *The Punishment Response*. Philadelphia: Lippincott.

Newman, Graeme R. (1979). *Understanding Violence*. Philadelphia: Lippincott.

Newman, Graeme R., Jean C. Jester, and Donald J. Articolo (1981). "A structural analysis of fraud," in Edith Flynn and John P. Conrad, eds., *The New and the Old Criminology*. New York: Praeger.

Newman, Graeme R., and Pietro Marongiu (1990). "Penological reform and the myth of Beccaria," *Criminology* 28:325–346.

Newman, Oscar (1972). *Defensible Space: Crime Prevention Through Urban Design*. New York: Macmillan.

Newton, George, D., and Franklin E. Zimring (1969). *Firearms and Violence in America*. Washington, D.C.: U.S. Government Printing Office.

Niederhoffer, Arthur J. (1967). *Behind the Shield: The Police in Urban Society*. New York: Anchor.

Nobile, Philip, and Eric Nadler (1986). *United States of America vs. Sex*. New York: Minotaur Press.

Normandeau, Andre (1968). *Trends and Patterns in Crimes of Robbery*. Ph.D. diss., University of Pennsylvania.

Nurco, David N., Thomas E. Hanlon, Timothy W. Kinlock, and Karen R. Duszynski (1988). "Differential crime patterns of narcotic addicts over an addictive career," *Criminology* 26:407–423.

O'Brien, Robert M. (1991). "Sex ratios and rape rates: A power control theory," *Criminology* 29:99–114.

O'Leary, Vincent, and Kathleen Hanrahan (1977). "Law and practice in parole proceedings: A national survery," *Criminal Law Bulletin* 13:205–211.

O'Malley, Pat, and Stephen Mugford (1991). "Crime, excitement and modernity." Presented at the annual meeting of the American Society of Criminology, San Francisco, November 18–23.

Orsagh, Thomas (1980). "Unemployment and crime," *Journal of Criminal Law and Criminology* 71:181–183.

Pace, Denny F., and Jimmie Y. Styles (1983). *Organized Crime: Concepts and Control*. Englewood Cliffs, N.J.: Prentice-Hall.

Packer, Herbert L. (1964). "The crime tariff," *American Scholar* 33:551–557.

Packer, Herbert L. (1968). *The Limits of the Criminal Sanction*. Stanford, Calif.: Stanford University Press.

Palley, Howard A., and Dana A. Robinson (1988). "Black on black crime," *Society* 25:59–62.

Palmer, Stuart (1968). "Murder and suicide in forty non-literate societies," *Journal of Criminal Law, Criminology, and Police Science* 56:320–324.

Parker, Howard J. (1974). *View from the Boys*. London: David and Charles.

Paternoster, Raymond (1983). "The decision to seek the death penalty in South Carolina," *Journal of Criminal Law and Criminology* 74:754–787.

Paternoster, Raymond (1987). "The deterrent effect of the perceived certainty and severity of punishment: A review of the evidence and issues," *Justice Quarterly* 4:173–217.

Patterson, E. Britt (1991). "Poverty, income inequality and community crime rates," *Criminology* 29:755–773.

Pearl, Michael (1974). *The Confessions of a Master Fence*. Cambridge, Mass.: Schenkman.

Petersilia, Joan (1985a). "Racial disparities in the criminal justice system: A summary," *Crime and Delinquency* 31:15–34.

Petersilia, Joan (1985b). *Granting Felons Probation: Public Risks and Alternatives.* Santa Monica, Calif.: Rand Corp.

Petersilia, Joan (1985c). *Probation and felony offenders, NIJ Reports.* Washington, D.C.: National Institute of Justice.

Petersilia, Joan (1987). *Expanding Options for Criminal Sentencing.* Santa Monica, Calif.: Rand Corp.

Petersilia, Joan, Allan Abrahamse, and James Q. Wilson (1990). "The relationship between police practice, community characteristics, and case attrition" *Policing and Society* 1:23–38.

Petersilia, Joan, and S. Turner (1985). *Guidelines-Based Justice: The Implications for Racial Minorities.* Santa Monica, Calif.: Rand Corp.

Peterson, David M., and Paul C. Friday (1975). "Early release from incarceration: Race as a factor in the use of 'shock probation'," *Journal of Criminal Law and Criminology* 66:79–87.

Peterson, Mark A., Harriett B. Braiker, and Suzanne M. Polich (1980). *Doing Crime: A Survey of California Prison Inmates.* Santa Monica, Calif.: Rand Corp.

Peterson, Ruth D., and William C. Bailey (1991). "Felony murder and capital punishment: An examination of the deterrence question," *Criminology* 29:367–395.

Pfohl, Stephen J. (1985). *Images of Deviance and Social Control.* New York: McGraw-Hill.

Phillips, David P. (1983). "The impact of mass media violence on homicide," *American Sociological Review* 48:560–568.

Pike, Luke Owen (1968). *A History of Crime in England,* vol. 2. Montclair, N.J.: Patterson Smith.

Pileggi, Nicholas (1968). "1968 has been the year of the burglar," *New York Times Magazine,* November 17.

Piliavin, Irving, and Scott Briar (1964). "Police encounters with juveniles," *American Journal of Sociology* 70:206–214.

Piliavin, Irving, Rosemary Gartner, Craig Thornton, and Ross L. Matsueda (1986). "Crime, deterrence, and rational choice," *American Sociological Review* 51:101–119.

Pittman, David J., and William Handy (1964). "Patterns in criminal aggravated assault," *Journal of Criminal Law, Criminology, and Police Science* 55:462–470.

Platt, Anthony M. (1971). *The Politics of Riot Commissions.* New York: Macmillan.

Platt, Anthony M. (1974). "Prospects for a radical criminology in the United States," *Crime and Social Justice* 1:3–10.

Ploscowe, Morris (1951). *Sex and the Law.* Englewood Cliffs, N.J.: Prentice-Hall.

Plucknett, Theodore F. T. (1948). *A Concise History of Common Law.* London: Butterworth.

Polk, Kenneth (1991). "Male-to-male homicides: Scenarios of masculine violence." Presented at annual meeting of the American Society of Criminology, San Francisco, November 18–23.

Pollock, Sir Frederick, and Frederick William Maitland (1968). *The History of English Law,* vol. 2, 2nd ed. Cambridge, England: Cambridge University Press.

Pollock-Byrne, Joycelyn M. (1990). *Women, Prison and Crime.* Pacific Grove, Calif.: Brooks/Cole.

Polsky, Howard W. (1962). *Cottage Six.* New York: Wiley.

Polsky, Ned (1967). *Hustlers, Beats, and Others.* Chicago: Aldine.

Pontell, Henry N. (1984). *A Capacity to Punish.* Bloomington, Ind.: Indiana University Press.

Porkorny, Alex D. (1965). "Human violence: A comparison of homicide, aggravated assault, and attempted suicide," *Journal of Criminal Law, Criminology, and Police Science* 56:488–497.

Post, James E., and Edwin Baer (1978). "Demarketing infant formula: Consumer products for the developing world," *Journal of Contemporary Business* 7: 17–37.

Pound, Roscoe (1923). *Intepretations of Legal History.* New York: Macmillan.

Pound, Roscoe (1943). "A survey of social interests," *Harvard Law Review.* 57:1–39.

Powers, Edwin, and Helen L. Witmer (1951). *An Experiment in the Prevention of Delinquency: The Cambridge-Somerville Study.* New York: Columbia University Press.

Pratt, Michael (1980). *Mugging as a Social Problem.* London: Routledge and Kegan Paul.

Preble, Edward A., and John J. Casey (1969). "Taking care of business—The heroin user's life on the street," *International Journal of the Addictions* 4:8–12.

President's Commission on Law Enforcement and the Administration of Justice (1967a). *Task Force Report: Organized Crime.* Washington, D.C.: U.S. Government Printing Office.

President's Commission on Law Enforcement and the Administration of Justice (1967b). *Task Force Report: The Courts.* Washington, D.C.: U.S Government Printing Office.

President's Commission on Law Enforcement and the Administration of Justice (1969). *Task Force Report: Crime and Its Impact.* Washington, D.C.: U.S. Government Printing Office.

Pringle, Patrick (n.d.). *Stand and Deliver: The Story of the Highwayman.* New York: Norton.

Pyle, Gerald F. (1976). "Spatial and temporal aspects of crime in Cleveland, Ohio," *American Behavioral Scientist* 20:175–178.

Quetelet, Adolphe (1835). *Sur l'Homme et le Dévélopment de Ses Facultés; un Essai de Physique Sociale.* Paris.

Quinney, Richard (1963). "Occupational structure and criminal behavior: Prescription violations by retail pharmacists," *Social Problems* II:179–183.

Quinney, Richard (1970). *The Problem of Crime.* New York: Dodd, Mead.

Quinney, Richard (1974). *Critique of Legal Order: Crime Control in Capitalistic Society.* Boston: Little, Brown.

Quinney, Richard (1975). *Criminology: Analysis and Critique of Crime in America.* Boston: Little, Brown.

Quinney, Richard (1979). *Criminology,* 2nd ed. Boston: Little, Brown.

Rada, Richard (1975). "Alcohol and rape," *Medical Aspects of Human Sexuality* 9:48–65.

Rada, Richard (1976). "Testosterone levels in the rapist," *Psychosomatic Medicine* 38:257–268.

Radcliffe-Brown, A. R. (1948). *The Andaman Islanders.* New York: Free Press.

Radzinowicz, Leon (1966). *Ideology and Crime.* New York: Columbia University Press.

Rand, Michael (1990). *Handgun Crime Victims.* Washington, D.C.: U.S. Department of Justice.

Rankin, Joseph (1979). "Changing attitudes toward capital punishment," *Social Forces* 58:194–211.

Rau, Richard M. (1991). "Forensic science and criminal justice technology: High tech tools for the 90s," *NIJ Research in Action* June:1–10.

Reasons, Charles E. (1974). *The Criminologist: Crime and the Criminal*. Pacific Palisades, Calif.: Goodyear Publishing.

Reasons, Charles E., and Russell L. Kaplan (1975). "Tear down the walls?—Some functions of prisons," *Crime and Delinquency* 21:360–372.

Reckless, Walter (1973). *The Crime Problem*. 5th ed. Englewood Cliffs, N.J.: Prentice-Hall.

Reckless, Walter C., and Simon Dinitz (1967). "Pioneering with self concept as a vulnerability factor in delinquency," *Journal of Criminal Law, Criminology, and Police Science* 58:515–523.

Reed, John Shelton (1971). "To live . . . and die . . . in Dixie: A contribution to the study of Southern violence," *Political Science Quarterly* 86:424–443.

Reed, John Shelton (1977). "Below the Smith and Wesson line: Reflections on Southern violence." Lecture to the second annual Hugo Black Symposium, Birmingham, Alabama.

Reid, Sue Titus (1989). *Criminal Law*. New York: Macmillan.

Reiman, Jeffrey H. (1984). *The Rich Get Richer and the Poor Get Prison*. 2nd ed. New York: Wiley.

Reiss, Albert J., Jr. (1970). "Police brutality: Answers to key questions," in Michael Lipsky, ed., *Law and Order: Police Encounters*. Chicago: Aldine.

Reiss, Albert J., Jr. (1971). *The Police and The Public*. New Haven, Conn.: Yale University Press.

Reiss, Albert J., Jr. (1988). "Private employment of public police," *NIJ Research in Brief*. December:1–6.

Reiss, Albert J., Jr., and Michael Tonry, eds. (1986). *Communities and Crime*. Chicago: University of Chicago Press.

Remington, Frank J., Donald J. Newman, Edward L. Kimball, Marygold Melli, and Herman Goldstein (1969). *Criminal Justice Administration*. Indianapolis, Ind.: Bobbs-Merrill.

Reppetto, Thomas A. (1974). *Residential Crime*. Cambridge, Mass.: Ballinger.

Reuter, Peter (1983). *Disorganized Crime: Illegal Markets and the Mafia*. Cambridge, Mass.: MIT Press.

Reuter, Peter, and Mark Kleiman (1986). "Risks and prices: An economic analysis of drug enforcement," in Michael Tonry and Norval Morris, eds., *Crime and Justice: An Annual Review of Research*, vol. 7 Chicago: University of Chicago Press.

Riedel, Marc, and Margaret A. Zahn (1985). *The Nature and Patterns of American Homicide*. Washington, D.C.: National Institute of Justice.

Riis, Roger, and John Patric (1942). *The Repairman Will Get You If You Don't Watch Out*. New York: Doubleday.

Riley, D. (1980). "An evaluation of a campaign to reduce vandalism," in Ronald V. Clarke, and Pat Mayhew, eds., *Designing Out Crime*. London: H.M.S.O.

Robin, Gerald D. (1967). "The corporate and judicial disposition of employee thieves," *Wisconsin Law Review* Summer:635–702.

Robin, Gerald D. (1987). *Introduction to the Criminal Justice System*. 3rd ed. New York: Harper & Row.

Robin, Gerald D. (1991). *Violent Crime and Gun Control*. Cincinnati: Anderson.

Rock, Paul (1973). "Feature review symposium," *Sociological Quarterly* 14:595.

Rockwell, Robin (1990). "The Advent of Computer Related Crimes," *Secured Lender* July/August: 40–42.

Roebuck, Julian B., and Thomas Barker (1974). "A typology of police corruption," in Ronald L. Akers and Edward Sagarin, eds., *Crime Prevention and Social Control*. New York: Praeger.

Roebuck, Julian B., and Ronald C. Johnson (1964). "The 'short con' man," *Crime and Delinquency* 10:235–248.

Rolph, C. H. (1955). *Women of the Streets*. London: Secker and Warburg.

Roncek, Dennis W. (1981). "Dangerous places: Crime and residential environment," *Social Forces* 60:74–96.

Roncek, Dennis W., and Pamela A. Maier (1991). "Bars, blocks, and crimes revisited: Linking the theory of routine activities to the empiricism of 'hot spots', " *Criminology* 29:725–753.

Rose, Harold M., and Paula McClain (1981). *Black homicide and the Urban Environment*. Rockville, Md.: National Institute of Mental Health.

Rosefsky, Robert S. (1973). *Frauds, Swindles, and Rackets*. Chicago: Follett.

Rosett, Arthur, and Donald R. Cressey (1976). *Justice by Consent*. Philadelphia: Lippincott.

Ross, H. Laurence (1982). "Interrupted time series studies of deterrence of drinking and driving," in John Hagan, ed., *Deterrence Reconsidered: Methodological Innovations*. Beverly Hills, Calif.: Sage.

Rossi, Peter H., Emily Waite, Christine E. Bose, and Richard E. Berk (1974). "The seriousness of crimes: Normative structure and individual differences," *American Sociological Review* 39:224–237.

Rowe, David C. (1986). "Genetic and environmental components of antisocial behavior: A study of 265 twin pairs," *Criminology* 23:223–40.

Rowe, David C., and W. D. Osgood (1984). "Heredity and sociological theories of delinquency: A reconsideration," *American Sociological Review* 49:526–40.

Rowe, David C., Wayne D. Osgood, and Alan D. Nicewander (1990). "A latent trait approach to unifying criminal careers," *Criminology* 28:237–230.

Rowe, David C., and Joseph L. Rodgers (1988). "The etiology of deviance: Sibling mutual influence, heredity, and 'd'." Presented to the Society for Research on Adolescence, March.

Rubin, Sol (1965). "Cops, guns, and homicides," *The Nation* December 27, 1965:527–531.

Rubinstein, Jonathan (1973). *City Police*. New York: Farrar, Straus & Giroux.

Rubinstein, Michael L., Stevens H. Clarke, and Teresa J. White (1980). *Alaska Bans Plea Bargaining*. Washington, D.C.: U.S. Department of Justice.

Runkle, Gerald (1976). "Is violence always wrong?" *Journal of Politics* 38:367–389.

Russell, Diana E. H. (1983). *Rape in Marriage*. New York: Collier.

Sagalyn, Arnold (1971). *The Crime of Robbery in the U.S.* Washington, D.C.: National Institute of Law Enforcement and Administration Justice.

Sagarin, Edward (1974). "Sexual criminality," in Abraham S. Blumberg, ed., *Current Perspectives on Criminal Behavior*. New York: Knopf.

Sagarin, Edward (1979). *Criminology: New Concerns*. Beverly Hills, Calif.: Sage.

Salerno, Ralph, and John S. Tompkins (1969). *The Crime Confederation*. Garden City, N.Y.: Doubleday.

Sampson, Robert J. (1985). "Race and criminal violence: A demographically disaggregated analysis of urban homicide," *Crime and Delinquency* 31:47–82.

Sampson, Robert J. (1986). "Crime in cities: The effects of formal and informal social control," in Albert J. Reiss and Michael Tonry, eds., *Communities and Crime*. Chicago: University of Chicago Press.

Sampson, Robert J. (1987a). "Communities and crime," in Michael R. Gottfredson and Travis Hirschi, eds., *Positive Criminology*. Beverly Hills, Calif.: Sage.

Sampson, Robert J. (1987b). "Urban Black Violence: The effect of male joblessness and family disruption," *American Journal of Sociology* 93:348–382.

Sampson, Robert J., and Jacqueline Cohen (1988). "Deterrent effects of the police on crime: A replication and theoretical extension," *Law and Society Review* 22:163–189.

Sampson, Robert J., and William Julius Wilson (1991). "Toward a theory of race, crime, and urban inequality." Paper presented to the Annual Meeting of the American Society of Criminology, San Francisco, November 21.

Sanders, William (1983). *Criminology*. Reading, Mass.: Addison-Wesley.

San Marco, Louise R. (1979). "Differential sentencing patterns among criminal homicide offenders in Harris County, Texas." Ph.D. diss., Sam Houston State University.

Saunders, Edward J. (1986). "Judicial attitudes toward child sexual abuse: A preliminary examination," *Judicature* 70:95–98.

Schafer, Stephen (1969). *Theories in Criminology*. New York: Random House.

Schafer, Stephen (1971). "The concept of the political criminal," *Journal of Criminal Law, Criminology, and Police Science* 62:380–387.

Schelling, Thomas D. (1967). "Economic analysis of organized crime." In President's Commission on Law Enforcement and the Administration of Justice, *Task Force Report: Organized Crime*. Washington, D.C.: U.S. Government Printing Office.

Schmidt, Amesley K. (1985). "Deaths in the line of duty," *NIJ Reports* January:6.

Schneider, Anne L. (1977). *The Portland Forward Check of Crime Victims: Final Report*. Eugene, Ore.: Oregon Research Institute.

Schuessler, Karl (1954). "Review," *American Journal of Sociology* 49:604–610.

Schwartz, Michael, and Sandra S. Tangri (1965). "A note on self-concept as an insulator against delinquency," *American Sociological Review* 30:922–926.

Schwendinger, Herman, and Julia Siegel Schwendinger (1985). *Adolescent Subcultures and Delinquency*. New York: Praeger.

Schwendinger, Julia Siegel, and Herman Schwendinger (1983). *Rape and Inequality*. Newbury Park: Sage Publications.

Scull, Andrew T. (1977). *Decarceration: Community Treatment and the Deviant—A Radical View*. Englewood Cliffs, N.J.: Prentice-Hall.

Scully, Diana, and Joseph Marolla (1985). "Riding the bull at Gilley's: Convicted rapists describe the rewards of rape," *Social Problems* 32:251–263.

Sellin, Thorsten (1935). "Race prejudice in the administration of justice," *American Journal of Sociology* 41:212–217.

Sellin, Thorsten (1937). "The Lombrosian myth in criminology," *American Journal of Sociology* 42:898–899.

Sellin, Thorsten (1938). *Culture Conflict and Crime*. New York: Social Science Research Council.

Sellin, Thorsten, and Marvin E. Wolfgang (1964). *The Measurement of Delinquency*. New York: Wiley.

Shaffer, Howard J., and Stephanie B. Jones (1989). *Quitting Cocaine*. Lexington, Mass.: Lexington Books.

Shannon, Lyle W. (1982). *Assessing the Relationship of Adult Criminal Careers to Juvenile Careers: A Summary*. Washington, D.C.: U.S. Department of Justice.

Shannon, Lyle W. (1991). *Changing Patterns of Delinquency and Crime*. Boulder, Colo.: Westview Press.

Shapiro, Susan P. (1990). "Collaring the crime, not the criminal: 'Liberating' the concept of white-collar crime." Presented at the Edwin Sutherland Conference on White-Collar Crime: 50 Years of Research and Beyond. Indiana University, May 12–15.

Shaw, Clifford R. (1930). *The Jack-Roller: A Delinquent Boy's Own Story*. Chicago: University of Chicago Press.

Shaw, Clifford R. (1931a). *Delinquency Areas*. Chicago: University of Chicago Press.

Shaw, Clifford R. (1931b). *The Natural History of a Delinquent Career*. Chicago: University of Chicago Press.

Shaw, Clifford R., Henry D. McKay, and James F. McDonald (1938). *Brothers in Crime*. Chicago: University of Chicago Press.

Shaw, Clifford R., and Henry D. McKay (1942). *Juvenile Delinquency and Urban Areas*. Chicago: University of Chicago Press.

Shearing, Clifford D. (1979). "Subterranean processes, the maintenance of power: An examination of the mechanisms coordinating police action." Presented to the annual meeting of the American Sociological Association, August 17–21.

Sheehy, Gail (1973). *Hustling: Prostitution in Our Wide-Open Society*. New York: Delacorte.

Shelley, Louise (1980). *Crime and Modernization*. Edwardsville, Ill.: Southern Illinois University Press.

Sherman, Lawrence, and Richard Berk (1984). "Specific deterrent effects of arrest for domestic assault." *American Sociological Review* 49:261–272.

Sherman, Lawrence W., Janell D. Schmidt, Dennis P. Rogan, Patrick R. Gartin, Ellen G. Cohn, Dean J. Collins, and Anthony R. Bacich (1991). "From initial deterrence to long-term escalation: Short-custody arrest for poverty ghetto domestic violence," *Criminology* 29:821–850.

Shover, Neal (1973). "The social organization of burglary," *Social Problems* 20:499–514.

Shover, Neal (1983). "The later stages of ordinary property offender careers," *Social Problems* 31:208–218.

Shover, Neal (1985). *Aging Criminals*. Beverly Hills, Calif.: Sage.

Shover, Neal (1991). "Burglary," in Michael Tonry and James Q. Wilson, eds., *Crime and Justice: A Review of Research*, vol. 14. Chicago: University of Chicago Press.

Shover, Neal, and David Honaker (Forthcoming). "The socially bounded decision making of persistent property offenders." *The Howard Journal of Criminal Justice*.

Shover, Neal, Greer Littonfox, and Michael Mills (1991). "Victimization by white collar crime and institutional delegitimation." Unpublished paper, University of Tennessee, Knoxville.

Shover, Neal, and Carol Y. Thompson (1992). "Age, differential expectations, and crime desistance," *Criminology* 30:601–616.

Silver, Allan (1967). "The demand for order in civil society," in David Bordua, ed., *The Police: Six Sociological Essays*. New York: Wiley.

Silverman, Robert A., and Leslie W. Kennedy (1987). "The female perpetrator of homicide in Canada," *Discussion Paper II*, Center for Criminological Research, University of Alberta.

Silverman, Robert A., and Leslie W. Kennedy (1988). "Women who kill their children," *Violence and Victims* 3:113–127.

Silverstein, Lee (1966). "Bail in the state courts—A field study and report," *Minnesota Law Review* 50:621–631.

Simon, David R., and D. Stanley Eitzen (1990). *Elite Deviance.* 3rd ed. Boston: Allyn and Bacon.

Simon, Rita J. (1975). *Women and Crime.* Lexington, Mass.: Lexington Books.

Simpson, Sally (1990). "Corporate crime deterrence and corporate control policies: Views from the inside." Presented at the Edwin Sutherland Conference on White-Collar Crime: 50 Years of Research and Beyond. Indiana University, May 12–15.

Sinclair, Andrew (1964). *Era of Excess: A Social History of the Prohibition Movement.* New York: Harper & Row.

Singer, Neil M. (1973). *The Value of Inmate Manpower.* Washington, D.C.: American Bar Association.

Skogan, Wesley G. (1977). "Dimensions of the dark figure of unreported crime," *Crime and Delinquency* 23:41–50.

Skogan, Wesley G. (1986). "Fear of crime and neighborhood change," in Albert J. Reiss, Jr. and Michael Tonry, eds., *Crime and Justice: A Review of Research, vol. 8: Communities and Crime.* Chicago: University of Chicago Press.

Skogan, Wesley G., and Michael G. Maxfield (1981). *Coping with Crime: Individual and Neighborhood Reactions.* Beverly Hills, Calif.: Sage.

Skolnick, Jerome H. (1966). *Justice Without Trial: Law Enforcement in a Democratic Society.* New York: Wiley.

Skolnick, Jerome H. (1975). *Justice Without Trial,* 2nd ed. New York: Wiley.

Skolnick, Jerome H., and Elliott P. Currie (1976). *Crisis in American Institutions,* 3rd ed. Boston: Little, Brown.

Sloan, John Henry, Arthur L. Kellerman, and Donald T. Reay (1988). "Handgun regulations, crime, assaults, and homicide," *New England Journal of Medicine* 319:1256–1262.

Smart, Carol (1979). "The new female criminal: Reality or myth?" *British Journal of Criminology* 19:50–59.

Smigel, Erwin O. (1956). "Public attitudes toward stealing as related to the size of the victim organization," *American Sociological Review* 21:320–327.

Smigel, Erwin O., and Ross H. Lawrence, eds. (1970). *Crimes Against Bureaucracy.* New York: Van Nostrand.

Smith, Alexander B., and Harriett Pollack (1975). *Some Sins Are Not Crimes.* New York: Franklin Watts.

Smith, Douglas A. (1986). "The neighborhood context of police behavior," in Albert J. Reiss, Jr., and Michael Tonry, eds, *Communities and Crime.* Chicago: University of Chicago Press.

Smith, Lorna J. F. (1989). *Concerns About Rape.* London: H.M.S.O.

Snodgrass, Jon (1982). *The Jack-Roller at Seventy.* Lexington, Mass.: Lexington Books.

Snyder, Howard N. (1990). "Growth in minority detentions attributed to drug law violators," *Juvenile Justice Bulletin.*

Snyder, Howard N., and Terrence A. Finnegan (1987). *Delinquency in the United States, 1983.* Washington, D.C.: U.S. Department of Justice.

Sowle, Claude R., ed. (1962). *Police Power and Individual Freedom.* Chicago: Aldine.

Sparks, Richard F. (1980). "Criminal opportunities and crime rates," in Stephen F. Feinberg and Albert J. Reiss, eds., *Indicators of Crime and Criminal Justice: Quantitative Studies.* Washington, D.C.: U.S. Government Printing Office.

Speiglman, Richard (1976). "Building the walls inside medicine, corrections and the state apparatus for repression," Ph.D. diss., University of California, Berkeley.

Spergel, Irving (1964). *Racketville, Slumtown, Haulberg: An Exploratory Study of Delinquent Subcultures.* Chicago: University of Chicago Press.

Spitzer, Steven (1975). "Toward a Marxian theory of deviance," *Social Problems* 22:638–651.

Stanko, Elizabeth (1990). *Everyday Violence.* London: Pandora.

Stark, Rodney (1987). "Deviant places: A theory of the ecology of crime," *Criminology* 25:893–909.

Steffensmeier, Darrell J. (1986). *The Fence: In the Shadow of Two Worlds.* Totowa, N.J.: Rowman and Littlefield.

Steffensmeier, Darrell J., and Emilie Anderson Allan (1988). "Sex disparities in arrests by residence, job and age: An assessment of the gender convergence hypothesis," *Justice Quarterly* 5:53–80.

Steffensmeier, Darrell J., and Robert M. Terry (1986). "Institutional sexism in the underworld: A view from the inside," *Sociological Inquiry* 56:305–323.

Stellwagen, Lindsey P. (1985). *Use of Forfeiture Sanctions in Drug Cases.* Washington, D.C.: National Institute of Justice.

Stewart, J. (1987). *The Prosecutors.* New York: Touchstone.

Stoddard, Ellwyn R. (1968). "The informal 'code' of police deviancy: A group approach to 'Blue Coat Crime'," *Journal of Criminal Law, Criminology, and Police Science* 59:201–213.

Straus, Murray A. (1986). "Domestic violence and homicide antecedents," *Bulletin of New York Academy of Medicine* 62:446–465.

Straus, Murray A., and Richard J. Gelles (1986). "Societal change and change in family violence from 1975 to 1985 as revealed by two national surveys," *Journal of Marriage and the Family* 48:465–479.

Straus, Murray A., Richard T. Gelles, and Suzanne K. Steinmetz (1980). *Behind Closed Doors: Violence in the American Family.* New York: Anchor Books.

Sullivan, Peggy S. (1989). "Minority officers: Current issues," in Roger G. Dunham and Geoffrey P. Alpert, eds., *Critical Issues in Policing.* Prospect Heights, Ill.: Waveland Press.

Sutherland, Edwin H. (1937a). *Criminology.* New York: Lippincott.

Sutherland, Edwin H. (1937b). *The Professional Thief.* Chicago: University of Chicago Press.

Sutherland, Edwin H. (1949). *White Collar Crime.* New York: Dryden Press.

Sutherland, Edwin H., and Donald R. Cressey (1974). *Criminology,* 9th ed. Philadelphia: Lippincott.

Sykes, Gresham M. (1958). *The Society of Captives.* Princeton, N.J.: Princeton University Press.

Sykes, Gresham M. (1972). "The future of criminality," *American Behavioral Scientist* 15:409–419.

Sykes, Gresham M. (1978). *Criminology.* New York: Harcourt Brace Jovanovich.

Sykes, Gresham M., and David Matza (1957). "Techniques of neutralization: A theory of delinquency," *American Sociological Review* 22:664–670.

Sylvester, Sawyer F., and Edward Sagarin, eds. (1974). *Politics and Crime*. New York: Praeger.

Takagi, Paul (1979). "Death by 'police intervention'," in U.S. Department of Justice, *A Community Concern: Police Use of Deadly Force*. Washington, D.C.: U.S. Government Printing Office.

Tangri, Sandra S., and Michael Schwartz (1967). "Delinquency research and the self-concept variable," *Journal of Criminal Law, Criminology, and Police Science* 58:182–190.

Tannenbaum, Frank (1938). *Crime and the Community*. New York: Columbia University.

Tappan, Paul W. (1947). "Who is the criminal?" *American Sociological Review* 12:96–102.

Taylor, Bruce M. (1989). *New Directions for the National Crime Survey*. Washington, D.C.: U.S. Department of Justice.

Taylor, G. Rattray (1965). *Sex in History*. London: Panther.

Taylor, Ian, Paul Walton, and Jock Young, eds. (1975). *Critical Criminology*. London: Routledge and Kegan Paul.

Temple, Mark, and Patricia Ladoucer (1986). "The alcohol-crime relationship as an age-specific phenomenon: A longitudinal study," *Contemporary Drug Problems* 86:89–115.

Terry, C. E., and Mildred Pellens ([1928], 1970). *The Opium Problem*. Montclair, N.J.: Patterson Smith.

Thomas, D. A. (1967). "Sentencing: The basic principles," *Criminal Law Review* 514–520.

Thornberry, Terence P. (1973). "Race, socioeconomic status, and sentencing in the juvenile justice system," *Journal of Criminal Law and Criminology* 64: 90–98.

Thornberry, Terence P., and R. L. Christenson (1984). "Unemployment and criminal involvement: An investigation of reciprocal causal structures," *American Sociological Review* 49:398–411.

Thornton, William E., and Jennifer James (1980). "Masculinity and delinquency revisited," *British Journal of Criminology* 19:225–241.

Thrasher, Frederick M. (1929). *The Gang*. Chicago: University of Chicago Press.

Tittle, Charles R. (1980). *Sanctions and Deterrence*. New York: Praeger.

Tittle, Charles R. (1988). "Two empirical regularities (maybe) in search of an explanation: Commentary on the age/crime debate," *Criminology* 26:75–85.

Toch, Hans (1977). *Police, Prisons, and the Problem of Violence*. Rockville, Md.: National Institute of Mental Health.

Tonry, Michael N., and Norval K. Morris, eds. (1983). *Crime and Justice: An Annual Review of Research*, vol. 4. Chicago: University of Chicago Press.

Tonry, Michael N., and Norval K. Morris, eds. (1988). *Crime and Justice*, vol. 10. Chicago: University of Chicago Press.

Toro-Calder, Jaime (1950). "Personal crimes in Puerto Rico," Master's thesis, University of Wisconsin.

Trasler, Gordon (1986). "Situational crime control and rational choice," in Kevin Heal and Gloria Laycock, eds., *Situational Crime Prevention: From Theory into Practice*. London: H.M.S.O.

Trotter, R. T. (1972). "Clockwork orange in a California prison," *Science News* 101:174–175.

Tunnell, Kenneth D. (1992). *Choosing Crime: The Criminal Calculus of Property Offenders*. Chicago: Nelson-Hall.

Turk, Austin T. (1966). "Conflict and criminality," *American Sociological Review* 31:338–352.

Turk, Austin T. (1969). *Criminality and Legal Order*. Chicago: Rand McNally.

Turner, J. W. Cecil, ed. (1966). *Kenney's Outlines of Criminal Law*, 19th ed. Cambridge, England: Cambridge University Press.

Tyler, Gus, ed. (1962). *Organized Crime in America*. Ann Arbor, Mich.: University of Michigan Press.

U.S. Center for Women Policy Studies (1979). *Violence in the Home Is a Crime Against the Whole Family*. Washington, D.C.: U.S. Government Printing Office.

U.S. Department of Justice (1976). *The LEAA: A Partnership for Crime Control*. Washington, D.C.: U.S. Government Printing Office.

U. S. Department of Justice (1979). *A Community Concern: Police Use of Deadly Force*. Washington, D.C.: U.S. Government Printing Office.

Valentine, Alan (1956). *Vigilante Justice*. New York: Reynal.

van den Berghe, Pierre L. (1974). "Bringing beasts back in: Toward a biosocial theory of aggression," *American Sociological Review* 39:777–778.

Vander-May, Brenda J., and Donald L. Neff (1984). "Adult–child incest: A sample of substantiated cases," *Family Relations* 33:549–557.

Vander Zanden, James W. (1970). *Sociology: A Systematic Approach*, 2nd ed. New York: Ronald Press.

Velarde, Albert J., and Mark Warlick (1973). "Massage parlors: The sensuality business," *Society* 11:63–74.

Vetri, Dominick R. (1964). "Guilty-plea bargaining: Compromise by prosecutors to secure guilty pleas," *University of Pennsylvania Law Review* 112:896–908.

Vold, George B. (1958). *Theoretical Criminology*. New York: Oxford University Press.

Vold, George B. (1979). *Theoretical Criminology*, 2nd ed., prepared by Thomas J. Bernard. New York: Oxford University Press.

Vold, George B., and Thomas J. Bernard (1986). *Theoretical Criminology*. New York: Oxford University Press.

von Hentig, Hans (1948). *The Criminal and His Victim*. New Haven, Conn.: Yale University Press.

von Hirsch, Andrew (1976). *Doing Justice: The Choice of Punishments*. New York: Hill and Wang.

von Hirsch, Andrew (1984). "Selective incapacitation: A critique," *NIJ Reports*. Washington, D.C.: National Institute of Justice.

Voss, Harwin L, and John R. Hepburn (1968). "Patterns in criminal homicide in Chicago," *Journal of Criminal Law, Criminology, and Police Science* 59:499–508.

Waegel, William B. (1989). "The use of lethal force by police: The effect of statutory change," *Crime and Delinquency* 30:121–140.

Wagstaff, Alan, and Alan Maynard (1988). *Economic Aspects of the Illicit Drug Market and Drug Enforcement Policies in the United Kingdom*. London: H.M.S.O.

Walker, Samuel (1985). *Sense and Nonsense about Crime: A Policy Guide*. Monterey, Calif.: Brooks/Cole.

Walker, Samuel (1989). "Broken windows and fractured history: The use and misuse of history in recent police patrol analysis," in Roger G. Dunham and Geoffrey P. Alpert, eds., *Critical Issues in Policing*. Prospect Heights, Ill.: Waveland Press.

Walsh, Dermot (1980). *Break-ins: Burglary from Private Houses*. London: Constable.

Walsh, Marilyn (1977). *The Fence*. Westport, Conn.: Greenwood Press.

Walters, James M. (1985). " 'Taking care of business' updated: A fresh look at the daily routine of the heroin user," in Bill Hanson, George Beschner, James M. Walters, and Elliott Bovelle, eds., *Life with Heroin*. Lexington, Mass.: Lexington Books.

Walton, Robert P. (1938). *America's New Drug Problem*. Philadelphia: Lippincott.

Waltz, Jon R. (1953). "Shoplifting and the law of arrest," *Yale Law Journal* 62:788–805.

Ward, David A., Maurice Jackson, and Renee E. Ward (1969). "Crimes of violence by women," in Donald J. Mulvihill, Melvin Tumin, and Lynn Curtis, eds., *Crimes of Violence*. Washington, D.C.: U.S. Government Printing Office.

Warr, Mark, and Mark Stafford (1991). "The influences of delinquent peers: What they think or what they do?" *Criminology* 29:851–866.

Warren, E. H., Jr. (1978). "The economic approach to crime," *Canadian Journal of Criminology* 10:437–449.

Warshaw, R. (1989). *I Never Called it Rape*. New York: Harper & Row.

Weber, Max (1954). *Law in Economy and Society*. Cambridge, Mass.: Harvard University Press.

Weinberg, Martin S., and Colin J. Williams (1975). *Male Homosexuals: Their Problems and Adaptations*. Baltimore, Md.: Penguin Books.

Weiner, Norman (1974). "The effect of education on police attitudes," *Journal of Criminal Justice* 2:323–330.

Weis, Kurt, and Sandra S. Borges (1973). "Victimology and rape: The case of the legitimate victim," *Issues in Criminology* 8:85–89.

Wellford, Charles (1975). "Labeling theory and criminology: An assessment," *Social Problems* 22:332–345.

Werner, Emmy E. (1987). "Vulnerability and resiliency in children at risk for delinquency: A longitudinal study from birth to young adulthood," in John D. Buchard and Sara N. Buchard, eds., *Prevention of Delinquent Behavior*. Beverly Hills, Calif.: Sage.

Werner, E. E., J. M. Bierman, and F. E. French (1971). *The Children of Kauai: A Longitudinal Study from the Prenatal Period to Age Ten*. Honolulu: University of Hawaii Press.

Werner, E. E., and R. S. Smith (1977). *Kauai's Children Come of Age*. Honolulu: University of Hawaii Press.

Werthman, Carl (1967). "The function of social definitions in the development of delinquent careers," in *Task Force Report: A Report of the President's Commission on Law Enforcement and the Administration of Justice*. Washington, D.C.: U.S. Government Printing Office.

Werthman, Carl, and Irving Piliavin (1967). "Gang members and the police," in David Bordua, ed., *The Police: Six Sociological Essays*. New York: Wiley.

West, Donald J. (1967). *The Young Offender*. Harmondsworth, England: Penguin Books.

West, Donald J. (1982). *Delinquency: Its Roots, Careers, and Prospects*. London: Heinemann.

West, Donald J., and David P. Farrington (1973). *Who Becomes Delinquent?* London: Heinemann.

West, Donald J., and David P. Farrington (1977). *The Delinquent Way of Life*. London: Heinemann.

Westerman, Ted D., and James W. Burfeind (1991). *Crime and Justice in Two Societies: Japan and the United States*. Pacific Grove, Calif.: Brooks/Cole.

Westley, William A. (1970). *Violence and the Police: A Sociological Study of Law, Custom and Morality*. Cambridge, Mass.: MIT Press.

Weston, Paul B., and Kenneth M. Wells (1972). *Law Enforcement and Criminal Justice*. Pacific Palisades, Calif.: Goodyear.

Whitaker, Catherine J. (1989). *The Redesigned National Crime Survey: Selected New Data*. Washington, D.C.: U.S. Department of Justice.

Whitaker, Catherine J., and Lisa D. Bastian (1991). *Teenage Victims: A National Crime Survey Report*. Washington, D.C.: U.S. Department of Justice.

Whitcomb, Debra (1985). "Prevention of child sexual abuse: Innovations in practice," *NIJ Research in Brief* November:1–7.

White, Leslie T. (1972). "The definitions and prohibitions of incest," in John N. Edwards, ed., *Sex and Society*. Chicago: Markham.

Whitehead, J. T., and Steven P. Lab (1989). "A meta-analysis of juvenile correctional treatment," *Journal of Research in Crime and Delinquency* 26:276–295.

Whitman, Howard (1951). *Terror in the Streets*. New York: Dial Press.

Whyte, William Foote (1943). *Streetcorner Society*. Chicago: University of Chicago Press.

Wilbanks, William (1984). *Murder in Miami*. New York: University of America Press.

Wilbanks, William (1985). "Is violent crime intraracial?," *Crime and Delinquency* 31:117–128.

Wilkins, Leslie T., Jack M. Kress, Don M. Gottfredson, Joseph C. Calpin, and Arthur M. Gelman (1978). *Sentencing Guidelines: Structuring Judicial Discretion*. Washington, D.C.: U.S. Government Printing Office.

Williams, Frank P. III, and Marilyn D. McShane (1988). *Criminological Theory*. Englewood Cliffs, N.J.: Prentice-Hall.

Williams, Hubert, and Patrick V. Murphy (1990). "The evolving strategy of police: A minority view," *Perspectives on Policing*, vol. 13, Washington, D.C.: National Institute of Justice.

Williams, Joyce E., and Karen Holmes (1981). *The Second Assault: Rape and Public Attitudes*. Westport, Conn.: Greenwood Press.

Williams, Kirk R. (1984). "Economic sources of homicide: Re-estimating the effects of poverty and inequality," *American Sociological Review* 49:283–289.

Williams, Kirk R., and Robert L. Flewelling (1988). "The social production of criminal homicide: A comparative study of disaggregated rates in American cities," *American Sociological Review* 53:421–431.

Williams, Kristen M. (1976). "The effects of victim characteristics on the disposition of violent crimes," in William McDonald, ed., *Criminal Justice and the Victim*. Beverly Hills, Calif.: Sage.

Williams, Kristen M. (1978). *The Role of Victims in the Prosecution of Violent Crime*. Washington, D.C.: Institute for Law and Social Policy.

Williams, Linda (1984). "Sex, race, and rape: An analysis of interracial sexual violence." Presented to the annual meeting of the American Society of Criminology, Cincinnati, Ohio.

Wilson, James Q. (1975). *Thinking about Crime*. New York: Basic Books.

Wilson, James Q. (1984). "Problems in the creation of adequate criminal justice information systems," in Search Group, Inc., *Information Policy and Crime Control Strategies*. Washington, D.C.: U.S. Department of Justice.

Wilson, James Q. (1988). "Entering criminology through the back door," *The Criminologist* 13:6, 4, 7–8.

Wilson, James Q., and Barbara Boland (1978). "The effect of the police on crime," *Law and Society Review* 12:367–390.

Wilson, James Q., and Richard J. Herrnstein (1985). *Crime and Human Nature*. New York: Simon and Schuster.

Wilson, Sheena (1980). "Vandalism and defensible space in London housing estates," in R. V. G. Clarke and P. Mayhew, eds., *Designing Out Crime*. London: H.M.S.O.

Wilson, William Julius (1987). *The Truly Disadvantaged: The Inner City, the Underclass, and Public Policy*. Chicago: University of Chicago Press.

Winick, Charles (1962). "Maturing out of narcotic addiction," *Bulletin on Narcotics* 14:1–7.

Winick, Charles, and Paul M. Kinsie (1971). The Lively Commerce: Prostitution in the United States. Chicago: Quadrangle Books.

Wiseman, Jacqueline P. (1970). *Stations of the Lost: The Treatment of Skid Row Alcoholics*. Englewood Cliffs, N.J.: Prentice-Hall.

Wolfgang, Marvin E. (1958). *Patterns in Criminal Homicide*. Philadelphia: University of Pennsylvania Press.

Wolfgang, Marvin E. (1961). "Pioneers in criminology: Cesare Lombroso (1835–1909)," *Journal of Criminal Law, Criminology, and Police Science* 52:361–391.

Wolfgang, Marvin E. (1967). *Crimes of Violence: A Report to the President's Commission on Law Enforcement and the Administration of Justice*. Washington, D.C.: U.S. Government Printing Office.

Wolfgang, Marvin E., and Bernard Cohen (1970). *Crime and Race*. New York: Institute of Human Relations Press.

Wolfgang, Marvin E., and Franco Ferracuti (1967). *The Subculture of Violence*. London: Tavistock.

Wolfgang, Marvin E., and Marc Riedel (1973). "Law, judicial discretion, and the death penalty," *The Annals* 407:119–133.

Wolfgang, Marvin E., Robert M. Figlio, Paul E. Tracy, and Simon I. Singer (1985). *The National Survey of Crime Severity*. Washington, D.C.: U.S. Department of Justice.

Wolin, Sheldon S. (1970). "Violence and the western political tradition," in Renatus Hartogs and Eric Artzt, *Violence: Causes and Solutions*. New York: Dell.

Wright, Helena (1968). *Sex and Society*. London: Allen and Unwin.

Wright, James D., and Peter H. Rossi (1981). *Weapons, Crime, and Violence in America*. Washington, D.C.: National Institute of Justice.

Wright, James D., and Peter H. Rossi (1986). *Armed and Considered Dangerous: A Survey of Felons and Their Firearms*. New York: Aldine de Gruyter.

Wright, Richard A., and David O. Friedrichs (1991). "White collar crime in the criminal justice curriculum," *Journal of Criminal Justice Education* 2:97–98.

Yablonsky, Lewis (1966). *The Violent Gang*. New York: Penguin Books.

Yochelson, Samuel, and Stanton E. Samenow (1976, 1977). *The Criminal Personality*, vols. 1 and 2. New York: Jason Aronson.

Young, James H. (1967). *The Medical Messiahs*. Princeton, N.J.: Princeton University Press.

Young, Jock (1986). "The failure of criminology: The need of radical realism," in Roger Matthews and Jock Young, eds., *Confronting Crime*. Beverly Hills, Calif.: Sage.

Zahn, Margaret A., and Philip C. Sagi (1987). "Stranger homicide in nine American cities," *Journal of Criminal Law and Criminology* 78:377–397.

Zeitz, Dorothy (1981). *Women Who Embezzle or Defraud: A Study of Convicted Felons.* New York: Praeger.

Zimbardo, Philip G. (1972). "The pathology of imprisonment," *Society* 9:4–8.

Zimring, Franklin E. (1972). "The medium is the message: Firearm caliber as a determinant of death from assault," *Journal of Legal Studies* 15:97–123.

Zimring, Franklin E., and Gordon J. Hawkins (1973). *Deterrence: The Legal Threat in Crime Control.* Chicago: University of Chicago Press.

Photo Acknowledgments

Author Index

Milner, Christina, 307, 308
Milner, Richard, 307, 308
Milton, C., 352
Minor, W. William, 458, 459, 529
Mintz, Morton, 223
Monahan, John, 402, 486
Moore, Beverly, C., 260
Moore, Mark A., 5–7, 366, 367
Moore, Mark H., 117, 272, 290, 336
Moore, Wilbert E., 494
Morash, Merry, 353
Morris, Allison, 428, 500, 562, 565
Morris, Desmond, 106
Morris, Norval, 17, 426
Morris, Terrence, 495
Mugford, Stephen, 586
Mulvihill, Donald J., 92, 107, 108, 116, 162
Munford, Robert S., 94
Murphy, J. E., 136, 368
Myint, Thelma, 132

Nader, Ralph, 256
Nadler, Eric, 141
Nagel, Stuart S., 420
Nagel, William G., 462
Nagin, Daniel S., 458, 459
Neff, Donald L., 146
Nettler, Gwynne R., 229, 480
Newman, Donald J., 220, 406
Newman, Graeme, 434, 471, 561
Newman, Oscar, 558
Newton, George D., 102
Nicewander, Alan D., 487
Niederhoffer, Arthur J., 351, 356
Nobile, Philip, 141
Normandeau, Andre, 161
Nurco, David, 337

O'Brien, Robert M., 517
Ohlin, Lloyd, 501–503
O'Malley, Pat, 586
Orsagh, Thomas, 499
Osgood, D. W., 487, 526

Packer, Herbert L., 27, 28, 40, 292
Palley, Howard A., 109
Palloni, Alberto, 75
Palmer, C. Eddie, 307
Palmer, Deborah J., 371
Palmer, Stuart, 95
Parker, Howard J., 75, 76, 83, 526, 537
Paternoster, Raymond, 73, 418, 459, 524
Patric, John, 249
Patterson, E. Britt, 499
Pearl, Michael, 204

Pellens, Mildred, 316
Perrott, R., 549
Petersilia, Joan, 50, 403, 419, 422, 427, 428, 447, 465
Peterson, David M., 417
Peterson, Mark A., 338, 551
Peterson, Ruth D., 417, 458
Pfohl, Stephen J., 491, 514
Pileggi, Nicholas, 193, 211
Piliavin, Irving, 77, 358, 359
Pinsonneault, Pierre, 214
Pittman, David J., 96
Platt, Anthony M., 433, 478
Ploscowe, Morris, 302
Polich, Suzanne M., 338, 551
Polk, Kenneth, 97, 110
Pollack, Harriett, 21
Pollock, Sir Frederick, 157
Polsky, Ned, 321
Pontell, Henry N., 29, 253, 407, 426, 428
Porkorny, Alex D., 94
Post, James E., 23
Pound, Roscoe, 11, 22
Preble, Edward A., 330
Pringle, Patrick, 158
Pugh, Meredith D., 61
Pyle, Gerald F., 558

Quetelet, Adolphe, 479
Quinney, Richard, 23, 223, 253, 510, 512, 513

Rachel, J. Valley, 338
Rada, Richard, 143
Radcliffe–Brown, A. R., 20
Radzinowicz, Leon, 479
Rand, Michael, 100
Rankin, Joseph, 442
Reckless, Walter, 305, 309, 527
Reed, John Shelton, 116, 117
Regoli, Robert M., 424
Reid, Sue Titus, 18, 134
Reiman, Jeffrey H., 34, 35
Reiss, Albert J., Jr., 33, 48, 77, 382, 383, 389
Rengert, George F., 546
Reppetto, Thomas A., 543
Reskin, Gary D., 151
Retsky, Harold G., 469
Reuss–Ianni, Elizabeth, 76, 275, 279, 280, 296
Reuter, Peter, 269–272, 283–285, 295, 296
Riedel, Marc, 93, 94, 100, 437
Rieman, Jeffrey, 8
Riis, Roger, 249
Riley, D., 547
Robin, Gerald D., 101, 102, 121, 257, 411, 412
Robinson, Dana A., 109

Rock, Paul, 513
Rockwell, Robin, 229
Rodgers, Joseph L., 487
Roebuck, Julian B., 199, 200, 211, 380–382
Rolph, C. H., 305
Roncek, Dennis W., 557–559
Rose, Harold M., 94, 102
Rosefsky, Robert S., 250
Rosenbaum, Dennis P., 188, 189
Rosett, Arthur, 407
Rossi, Peter H., 12, 101, 163, 178
Rowe, David C., 487
Rubin, Sol, 376
Rubinstein, Jonathan, 381, 383, 391
Rubinstein, Michael L., 411
Runkle, Gerald, 91
Russell, Diana E. H., 124, 126, 134, 135, 138, 139, 144, 153, 507
Sagalyn, Arnold, 161
Sagarin, Edward, 145
Salerno, Ralph, 275, 288, 294
Samenow, Stanton E., 486, 540
Sampson, Robert J., 109, 116, 366, 478, 479, 495, 534–536
Sanders, William, 140
San Marco, Louise R., 118
Santiago, Ron, 64
Saunders, Edward J., 151
Scarpitti, Frank, 255
Schafer, Stephen, 21
Schelling, Thomas D., 292
Scheuble, Laurie K., 417
Schmidt, Amesley K., 375, 454
Schneider, Anne L., 47
Schroeder, Oliver, 94
Schuessler, Karl, 229
Schurr, Cathleen, 140
Schwartz, Michael, 528
Schwendinger, Herman, 255, 326, 526, 537
Schwendinger, Julia Siegel, 255, 326, 526, 537
Scott, Marvin B., 158, 160
Scully, Diana, 141–143
Sellin, Thorsten, 8, 12
Shaffer, J. W., 337
Shannon, Lyle W., 533, 561
Shapiro, Susan P., 257
Shaw, Clifford R., 64, 75, 78–80, 495
Sheehy, Gail, 305
Shelden, Randall G., 516, 562
Shelley, Louise, 555

Subject Index

f indicates figure or illustration
t indicates table

Outcome of felony arrests, 404t
Outcome variable, 70
Outlaws, frontier, 158–160
Overpolicing, 52

Panel study, 72, 73
Parole, 451
Participant observation, 76, 77
Partnership in robbery, 171, 172
Paternalism, 417
Pathology of imprisonment, 462, 463
Pawn shops, 202
Payne v. Tennessee, 18
Peel, Robert, 348
Peer groups and serious delinquency, 526
Penal code; see Model Penal Code
Penalties, 435–454
    financial, 452–454
Personal gain, occupational crimes for, 227–241
Personal theft, NCVS definition of, 592
Personality in violence, 107, 108
Petty theft, 183, 184
Philadelphia, organized crime in, 269, 270
Phone phreaking, 233
Pigeon drop, 199
Pimping, 307, 308
Piracy, 158
Pizza connection, 286
Plea bargaining, 405–412
    future of, 411, 412
    judges and, 410, 411
    supreme court decisions supporting, 410
Plea concessions, 406f
Poletti, Francesco, 554
Police; see also Policing
    and criminal drug use, 332–341
    origin and growth of modern, 347, 348
    in production of crime data, 46–48
    recruitment and training of, 350–352
    shooting of, 375, 376
Police authority, corruption and abuses of, 379–389
Police commissions, 349
Police corruption, 389
Police departments, types of, 362, 363t
Police perspectives, training and acquisition of, 355–361
Police/citizen encounters, 48, 49
Policing

in America, 348, 349
corruption and abuses of police authority, 379–389
history of, 316–349
police at work in, 350–368
police exercise of discretion in, 368–379
proactive, 365–368
shooting of police in, 375, 376
styles of, 361–364
training and acquisition of police perspective, 355–361
use of deadly force in, 371–374
Policy, 283, 284; see also Public policy
Political corruption
    ABSCAM, 239
    forms of, 235–237
    and fraud in defense industry, 238, 239
    for money, 237, 238
    in organized crime, 272
    for power, 239, 240
Politicization of law enforcement, 349
Pollution, 226
Population, crime rates and, 56, 57
Pornography, 311, 312
    commission on, 141
    rape and, 141, 142
Pornography Victim Compensation Act, 312
Positivism, 479, 460
Power
    political corruption for, 239, 240
    and prison guard, 469
Pragmatic induction, 359
Precipitation, victim, 104
Predatory crime, 45
Preliminary hearing, 396
Prescription violations, 253
Presentence investigation, 413–415
Presentence reports, impact of, 415, 416
President's Commission on Law Enforcement and the Administration of Justice, 267, 268, 540
Presser, Jackie, 288
Prestige in professional theft, 208–210
Pretrial detention, 399
Prevalence of criminality, 60, 61
Prevention
    punishment and, 434, 435
    situational, 550
Price-fixing, 242, 243

Primitive law, decline of, 20, 21
Principles of moral criminal process, 37–39
Prison admissions, 448f
Prison guard, power and, 469
Prison population, 446f
Prisoners, victimization of, 467–469
Prisons, 445–449
    development of in America, 443–445
    private, 33
    and rehabilitation, 462–464
    tomorrow, 470
    women in, 449
Private jails, 33
Private prisons, 33
Private wrongs, 20, 21
Privatization, 31–33
Proactive policing, 365–368
    new initiatives in, 367, 368
Probabilities of being imprisoned, 447t
Probation, 451
Procedural rules, 24
Process
    of association, 522–526
    structure and, 535f
Professional robber, 167–170
Professional style patrol officers, 364
Professional theft, 206–215
    aging property offenders in, 213, 214
    consensus and professional ethics in, 211, 212
    fix in, 214, 215
    getting into, 207, 208
    self images and world view in, 210, 211
    status and prestige in, 208–210
Professionalism, 356, 357
Prohibition, 317
    impact of, 280–282
    repeal of, 318
Proletariat, 510
Property, defense of, 16
Prosecution, 402–405
    decision not to prosecute and, 404, 405
    and guilty pleas, 407, 408
Prosecutor perspective, 146
Prostitute at work, 305, 306
Prostitution, 304–311
    bars and massage parlors as places of, 306, 307
    entering, 308–311
    FBI definition of, 591
    pimp in, 307, 308
Protection of illegal activities, 381